Longman Annotated Anthologies of English Verse

English Verse 1830–1890

Longman Annotated Anthologies of English Verse
General Editor: Alastair Fowler

English Verse 1830–1890

Edited by Bernard Richards

Longman   London and New York

Addison Wesley Longman Limited
Edinburgh Gate, Harlow
Essex CM 20 2JE, England
and Associated Companies throughout the world.

*Published in the United States of America
by Addison Wesley Longman Inc., New York*

This edition © Longman Group Limited 1980

First published 1980
Seventh impression 1997

British Library Cataloguing in Publication Data

English verse, 1830–1890.—(Longman annotated
anthologies of English verse; vol. 6).
1. English poetry—19th century

I. Richards, Bernard

821'.8'08   PR1221   79-40455

ISBN 0-582-48388-3

Set in Times New Roman
Produced through Longman Malaysia, VP

Contents

Note by the General Editor

This series is meant to provide period anthologies of representative English and Scottish poems, with full annotation of the kind that any serious reading will require. Most period anthologies offer little or no annotation, apparently on the assumption that only the learned will wish to read a variety of authors. Yet it is very often the beginner who samples a period through an anthology. Course readers designed for beginners, on the other hand, mostly treat their users as a species of idiot, to be written down to. The present series addresses itself to intelligent readers, who may nevertheless not know what needs to be known in order to make sense of poems. It attempts to provide a reading instrument that will ease immediate difficulties and, by reference to fuller treatments elsewhere, open ways to deeper understanding for those who care to take them. Where the anthologies are used in teaching they should make for a quicker advance, beyond exchange of information, to critical discussion. More generally, they may serve to introduce the non-specialist to some of the best critical thought about an unfamiliar period of literature.

Incidentally, several anonymous or minor classics here receive for the first time explanatory and critical commentary – an attention previously confined to a comparatively small number of poets. In this way the series forms a natural extension of the Longman Annotated English Poets. Indeed, the two series overlap (though without coinciding), in that a few poems already edited have been allowed to reappear in their period context, with different annotation. A similar redundancy is tolerated in divisions of material between periods. Here, overlaps help to avoid specious discontinuities of periodization; and they may have positive interest in offering different editors' views of the same poet or poem.

In textual presentation the series tries to acknowledge the distinct needs of different periods and different kinds of writing. In general, unless there is indication to the contrary, spelling is modernized or normalized but old punctuation kept. Old spelling hardly repays keeping, except in a textual edition, since orthographic structures mainly signal a vocabulary selection – take this word, not that. Such signals, where they are unambiguous, can be replaced with modern signals without loss: and where they are ambiguous they need a note anyway. With punctuation, no such direct translation can be performed satisfactorily, because there are no entities so publicly and clearly recognized as words. Elizabethan comma does not equal modern full stop. Or not always. Nevertheless, punctuation has far too important a role in grammatical structure, and hence in the communication of meaning, for us to set light to it by modernizing casually, at our convenience. This (the usual practice) would be to impose an editor's reconstruction of meaning so secretly that the reader would be in no position to disagree. Thus, the series aims at combining maximum ease in reading with as much as possible of the textual evidence on which sound interpretation must ultimately be based.

This general policy cannot be imposed uniformly. In medieval texts much old spelling has to be retained, for a variety of reasons. Intervening sound changes, for example, are so great that the metrical and assonantal patterns would otherwise be lost. Again, MS. texts in all periods may have little or no punctuation; and then an editor is reasonably expected to supply it – and to say that he has done so. Further problems are presented by Scots and by dialectal spellings. When the poet aimed to write in 'standard Scots', the editors aim at a regionally neutral regularization that designates words without specifying any particular variants of them. But where regional flavour matters (as with Barnes and sometimes with Burns), this policy would obviously lose more than it gained. Each editor explains his own practice in textual matters, and draws attention to local exceptions. In this way we hope always to keep the evidential status of the text as clear as possible.

Acknowledgements

My principal debt is to the general editor of the series, Professor Fowler. He helped to solve many problems, in addition to alerting me to problems, interpretations and readings that had completely escaped my attention. There is evidence of his scholarly sensitivity and vigilance on virtually every page. I am also grateful for the encouragement and active support given by my wife Sandra, who gave practical help with all aspects of the work, including the typing.

It will be apparent throughout the work that any reader of Victorian poetry must be indebted to the tradition of criticism which began at the time of the first publication of the poems and has been continued honourably and efficiently by countless modern scholars. Their contributions are recorded in the headnotes and footnotes, but I should like to put on record here my special indebtedness to K. Allott, W.C. De Vane, F.E. Faverty, W. Fredeman, W.H. Gardner, P. Honan, E.D.H. Johnson, N.H. Mackenzie, F.L. Mulhauser, C. Ricks and P. Turner.

I am grateful to the following libraries for allowing me to consult and quote from their manuscripts: the Bodleian Library, the British Library, the Humanities Research Centre, Texas and Trinity College Library, Cambridge.

Abbreviations

Periodicals

BJRL	Bulletin of the John Rylands Library
EC	Essays in Criticism
ELH	Journal of English Literary History
ELN	English Language Notes
ES	English Studies
JHI	Journal of the History of Ideas
MLN	Modern Language Notes
MLQ	Modern Language Quarterly
MLR	Modern Language Review
MP	Modern Philology
N & Q	Notes and Queries (volume numbers refer to New Series)
PBA	Proceedings of the British Academy
PMLA	Publications of the Modern Language of America
PQ	Philological Quarterly
RES	Review of English Studies (n.s. = new series)
SP	Studies in Philology
TLS	The Times Literary Supplement
UTQ	University of Toronto Quarterly
VP	Victorian Poetry
VS	Victorian Studies

Other Abbreviations

Armstrong	The Major Victorian Poets: Reconsiderations (1969) I. Armstrong, ed.
B.L.	British Library (formerly British Museum)
EDD	The English Dialect Dictionary (1896–1905) J. Wright, ed.
Faverty	The Victorian Poets: A Guide to Research (2nd ed. Cambridge, Mass. 1968) F.E. Faverty, ed.
Johnson	The Alien Vision of Victorian Poetry (Princeton, N.J. 1952) E.D.H. Johnson
MS.	manuscript
NCBEL	New Cambridge Bibliography of English Literature
N.T.	New Testament
OED	Oxford English Dictionary
O.T.	Old Testament
Ruskin Works	The Works of John Ruskin (1903–1912) E.T. Cook and A. Wedderburn, eds.
Tervarent	Attributs et symboles dans l'art profane 1450–1600 (Geneva 1958) Guy de Tervarent

Abbreviations relating to individual poets are given following the relevant headnotes.

Chronological Table

	Literary events		Other events
1830	Tennyson's *Poems, chiefly Lyrical.*	1830	Accession of William IV. Lyell's *Principles of Geology.*
1832	Tennyson's *Poems* (dated 1833).	1832	Great Reform Bill.
1833	Browning's *Pauline.*	1833	Oxford Movement commences.
1834	William Morris born.		
1835	Clare's *The Rural Muse.*		
		1837	Accession of Queen Victoria.
1840	Browning's *Sordello.*	1840	Marriage of Queen Victoria and Prince Albert.
1841	Browning's *Pippa Passes.*		
1842	Tennyson's *Poems.*		
1844	Barnes's *Poems of Rural Life;* G.M. Hopkins born; R. Bridges born.	1844	Chambers's *Vestiges of Creation.*
1845	Browning's *Dramatic Romances and Lyrics.*		
1846	Charlotte, Emily and Anne Brontë's *Poems.*	1846	Repeal of the Corn Laws.
1847	Tennyson's *The Princess.*		
1848	Clough's *The Bothie of Tober-Na-Vuolich;* Emily Brontë dies.	1848	Formation of Pre-Raphaelite Brotherhood.
1849	Arnold's *Strayed Reveller;* Clough and Burbidge's *Ambarvalia.*		
1850	E.B. Browning's *Poems;* Rossetti and others *The Germ;* Tennyson's *In Memoriam;* Wordsworth's *The Prelude,* Wordsworth dies; Tennyson Poet Laureate.		
1851	Meredith's *Poems.*	1851	The Great Exhibition.
1852	Arnold's *Empedocles on Etna and other Poems.*		
1853	Arnold's *Poems;* Patmore's *Tamerton Church Tower.*	1853	Outbreak of Crimean War.
1854	Patmore's *Angel in the House,* pt 1.		
1855	Arnold's *Poems, second series;* Browning's *Men and Women;* Tennyson's *Maud and Other Poems.*		

1877	Patmore's *The Unknown Eros.*	1877	Grosvenor Gallery exhibitions begin.
1878	Swinburne's *Poems and Ballads*, 2nd series.	1878	Whistler *vs.* Ruskin.
1879	Barnes's *Poems of Rural Life.*		
1880	Swinburne's *Heptalogia.*		
1881	Rossetti's *Ballads and Sonnets;* Wilde's *Poems.*	1881	Disraeli dies. Social Democratic Federation founded.
1882	Rossetti dies; James Thomson dies.		
1883	Meredith's *Poems and Lyrics of the Joy of Earth;* FitzGerald dies.	1883	Fabian Society founded.
1884	Browning's *Ferishtah's Fancies.*	1884	Third Reform Bill.
1885	Tennyson's *Tiresias and Other Poems.*		
1886	Kipling's *Departmental Ditties.* Tennyson's *Locksley Hall, sixty years after.*	1886	Gladstone's defeat on Home Rule for Ireland.
1887	Browning's *Parleyings with Certain People;* Meredith's *Ballads and Poems of Tragic Life.*		
1888	Meredith's *A Reading of Earth.* Arnold dies. T.S. Eliot born.		
1889	Browning's *Asolando;* Swinburne's *Poems and Ballads,* 3rd series; Tennyson's *Demeter and Other Poems:* Yeats's *The Wanderings of Oisin.* Browning dies; Hopkins dies.		
1890	J.H. Newman dies.		
1892	Tennyson's *Death of Œnone.* Tennyson dies.		
1893	Thompson's *The Hound of Heaven.*		
		1895	Trials of Wilde.
1896	Morris dies; Patmore dies.		
1898	Hardy's *Wessex Poems;* Wilde's *Ballad of Reading Gaol.*	1898	Gladstone dies.
		1899	Outbreak of Boer War.
1900	Wilde dies.		
1901	Yeats's *Poems.*	1901	Queen Victoria dies.
		1902	End of Boer War.

Introduction

Since this volume covers the period between 1830 and 1890 it is not, strictly speaking, an anthology of 'Victorian poetry'; the Queen came to the throne in 1837 and died in 1901. However, there is a sense in which we are dealing with a recognizable literary period. Eighteen-thirty marks the end of the Romantic Movement – unless one considers, as some do, that Carlyle is also a quintessentially Romantic figure. Byron, Keats and Shelley were all dead; Wordsworth was in a state (as younger poets saw it) of living death; and Scott died in 1832. Many contemporaries regarded 1830 as a particularly bad time for poetry. Bentham, who died in 1832, adumbrated the middle-class philistine position, *vis-à-vis* the arts, when he allowed them as a source of pleasure with measurable standards of efficiency, but denied those claims for significance and visionary insight that the serious Romantics had been anxious to accord. He writes, in 'The Rationale of Reward', that the utility of the arts 'is exactly in proportion to the pleasure they yield. Every other species of the pre-eminence which may be attempted to be established among them is altogether fanciful. Prejudice apart, the game of push-pin is of equal value with the arts and sciences of music and poetry'. Thomas Love Peacock playfully thought that since mankind had grown up it was time to put away childish things and speak as a man, in prose rather than verse (*The Four Ages of Poetry* 1819). This occasioned Shelley's famous riposte *The Defence of Poetry* (1820). One witnesses in the 1820s a much more serious continuation of the onslaught on the value of poetry. Macaulay's Milton essay of 1825 expresses typical misgivings: he follows ideas similar to Peacock's, observing that progress is an impediment in the history of poetry, in that civilized societies, though they may provide good language for the purposes of science and philosophy, fail to do so for poetry. The poet, used as he is to dealing with individual reflections rather than universal analysis, requires 'a degree of credulity which almost amounts to a partial and temporary derangement of the intellect. Hence of all people children are the most imaginative'. Macaulay, like Peacock, thought it was time to stop looking through the glass darkly, to see truths face to face and in clear light: 'As the magic lantern acts best in a dark room, poetry effects its purpose most completely in a dark age. As the light of knowledge breaks upon its exhibitions, as the outlines of certainty become more and more definite and the shades of probability more and more distinct, the hues and lineaments of the phantoms which the poet calls up grow fainter and fainter'. He believes that feelings of rapture in the readers of poetry are 'very rare in a civilised community, and most rare among those who participate most in its improvements'. To some degree Wordsworth himself concurred with this view by going to the peasantry for the sources of his vision. During the rest of the century there was a great body of people who would have agreed with Macaulay that one could not 'unite the incompatible advantages of reality and deception, the clear discernment of truth and the exquisite enjoyment of fiction'.

Even among thinkers who believed that there was still a viable form of life for poetry, the view was in 1830 that it would have to be sought afresh. An important document for the new movement is Sir Henry Taylor's preface to *Philip Van Artevelde* (1834). He too criticized the Romantic Movement and the poetry produced under the influence of 'impassioned sentiment', which was far from the realms of wisdom and reason. He wanted a return to poetry of which sense was the basis; the grave offenders against his concept of a rational and lucid poetry were Shelley and the earlier Byron. In his eyes, 'Poetry is Reason's self sublimed'. What he stood for, in effect, was a new classicism, and his position was very similar to that adopted by Matthew Arnold in the 1853 preface to *Poems*. Although severe classicism remained very much a minority taste, what Taylor espoused was symptomatic of a more general wish for poetry to be closer to life as lived by ordinary people than it had been in the Romantic Movement.

Something had to be done to make poetry attractive and market-able; since in 1830, in addition to the low critical esteem in which it was held, the market for poetry was slack. And it remained slack in the thirties though this was the decade that witnessed the emergence of the new generation of poets led by Tennyson and Browning.

The terminal date 1890 is a little more open to question; since the consensus opinion has always been that the big watershed in poetry was around 1917 with *Prufrock*, with developments of any signifi-cance only beginning after the First World War, when the tempera-ment of the audience had been changed sufficiently to make modern poetry a serious going concern. As Eliot, Pound and the young iconoclasts of *Blast* (1914) saw it, the sins of Victorian poetry continued even when the presiding goddess Victoria was in her grave. Yet many of the foundations of modern poetry were being laid in the 1890s, though it may require the wisdom of hindsight to recognize them. New rhythms, new diction, new themes were being tentatively sought then, especially by poets such as Hardy, Davidson, Dowson and Housman. If it is true, as Holbrook Jackson observed, that the decade represented the tired end of an era, it could also be said to represent the beginning, with new movements, the New Woman, and a fresh group of young poets, some of whom died young and made up what Yeats called the Tragic Generation. The

Introduction

Victorian poetic voices continued in the nineties, but with an increasing lack of conviction and inventiveness that often rings hollow. In social history High Victorianism came to an end in the eighties, and it is probably true that the corresponding High Victorianism of poetry ended at the same time. Certainly some major figures died at this time – one thinks of Rossetti (1882), Hopkins (1889), Browning (1889) and Tennyson (1892). Of the old guard, Meredith and Swinburne went on living and even writing, but their really significant poetic work was over.

In poetic endeavour the years 1830 to 1890 present a far from homogeneous or undynamic unity. We witness significant events, such as the publication of *Sordello* in 1840, of *Maud* and *Men and Women* in 1855 and the composition of *The Wreck of the Deutschland* in 1875-6, but we fail to detect a uniform development of poetic style, poetic themes or even poetic theory. This was not entirely unprecedented in the history of English poetry, but we notice a new feature: a lot of the *major* poetry within the period was based on widely differing theories and principles, and may be identified as belonging to widely divergent traditions. In previous periods very different kinds of poetry were produced simultaneously, but usually what has survived and what is in the main line of the great tradition comes from one sphere of creation, with alien products remaining as objects of historical curiosity, sometimes given an artificial resuscitation by the activity of literary history. The Romantic Movement poets are well known; we tend to forget that other poets, such as Wolcot, Moore and Campbell, were at work at the same time. However, these were minor poets, however popular they may have been in their own time. In the Victorian period a quite different phenomenon is encountered, in which we find, side by side, major poets as diverse as Tennyson and Browning, Arnold and Clough, Swinburne and Hopkins. This rich and chaotic eclecticism arose in the wake of the decline of both the classical and romantic visions: so comprehensive a disillusion provided no firm basis for orderly progression. In addition, there was no literary establishment powerful enough to dictate the direction poetry should take, and no one public to which the poetry was addressed. The multiplication of literary publics (not only for poetry) is another noteworthy pheno-menon of the period. In economic and social thinking a *laissez faire* philosophy encouraged individual and small groups to produce a workable way of life, and it could be said that the poetic scene developed an analogous pattern. There were increased opportunities for individual initiative – increased literacy too – but all operating in a social setting that progressively came to lack homogeneity.

Given this diversity, given a house of poetry that resembles the Tower of Babel more than the Tower of Ivory, one wonders if there are any common features uniting the disparate elements. One pervasive feature stands out immediately: that, on the whole, the poets all made a bid to be serious and respected, despite the threats to their status from the utilitarian and mechanized society. They thought that poetry had prime importance in life and could not be dispensed with, but they took very different views on how poetry should administer to life. Some followed the Tennysonian view (which bore a close affinity to the Romanticism of Keats) that poetry should strike deep wells in the poet's own psyche and tap the sources of dream, reverie and even madness; they believed that the poet should be distracted from the mundane world, and should hope to distract his readers, not to provide them with empty and self-gratifying dreams, but with ultimately informative and consoling visions of the universe. Swinburne took a similar view, but pushed the madness and deviancy further, and the delight in sound that was an integral part of the Tennysonian poetic. Tennyson himself, despite his instinctive feelings of isolation, chose not to turn his back on the assumptions of the public, but rather to maintain a discreet deference to them. These poets found their audience, but it was not always functioning on the same wavelength as themselves: at any given time some people were reading Tennyson for quasi-religious reassurance (this was the spirit in which Queen Victoria read *In Memoriam* after the death of Albert), others for a detached and aesthetic delight. By a paradox, Tennysonian poetry was appreciated by the great philistine audience because it gave respite and release after a hard day with the mechanized society.

When one starts reading poetry in this tradition, the most striking features are the mellifluous language and the musical rhythms. These, as much as the dreamlike subject matter, removed the poetry from the diurnal world. A good deal of this poetry was descended from the Romantic Movement, and it lasted long enough as a lively tradition for the young Yeats to be able to draw on it at the outset of his career. But it also drew sustenance from the classical tradition, which regarded poetry as something that was *made* rather than *expressed*. Tennyson used to say that he *made* his poems. A good deal of this 'objective poetry', as it was sometimes called, was men singing for men rather than men speaking to men.

Opening the following selection at random, one will almost certainly be struck not only by the quality of the craftsmanship, which is likely to be high, but by the fact that (with certain exceptions) the poetry resolutely occupies a position in which the poetic transaction is emphatically at variance with the mundane transactions of everyday prose: every factor establishes this, the syntax, the rhythms, the diction, the poetic forms.

The poetic forms are various. No one form dominated; they were all tackled by poets keen to do a professional job. In a century in which poets often cultivated the image of the alienated artist, the

Introduction

employment of distinct verse forms was one way of keeping this distance and drawing attention to their distinctiveness. A great range of stanzaic forms was available – the sonnet, the Spenserian stanza – in addition to the ones invented, such as the stanza for *The Scholar Gipsy* and *Thyrsis*, which carried on a tradition of Keatsian inventiveness. Blank verse continued, with its complex line of descent through Shakespeare, Milton, Wordsworth and Keats. Fashions came and went for such forms as the ballade, the rondeau and the villanelle. There was considerable metrical variety and experimentation, a typical example being the conscientious assault on the hexameter by Clough and Kingsley. Clough has the reputation of being a 'controversial poet', and with justification, but when one reads *Dipsychus* one is pleasantly struck by its rich variety of poetic texture, by the sensitive and constantly changing interplay of subject and expression.

The standard work on prosody is still G. Saintsbury's *English Prosody* (1906); in the Victorian period itself there were technical guides, typical examples being Thomas Smibert's *Rhyming Dictionary for the use of Young Poets: with an Essay on English Versification* (1852), and Tom Hood's *The Rules of Rhyme* (1869). The traditions of Victorian poetic diction and poetic syntax go back for centuries. An excellent introductory study is Bernard Groom's *The Diction of Poetry from Spenser to Bridges* (1955). Poetic diction had always been distinct from everyday speech, but in Spenser's time there was always a chance that some of the highly coloured vocabulary would eventually find its way into common speech. However, by the nineteenth century there was an iron curtain between the different sections of the language, with no prospect of interpenetration. And this is the situation today: very few words ever manage, in the conditions of lexical apartheid, to cross the colour line, one way or the other. If one takes a representative piece of Victorian poetry, the situation will become immediately apparent.

The Morte d'Arthur (1842)

185   ... His own thought drove him, like a goad.
       Dry clashed his harness in the icy caves
       And barren chasms, and all to left and right
       The bare cliff clanged round him, as he based
       His feet on juts of slippery crag that rang
190   Sharp-smitten with the dint of armèd heels –

186 dry in association with clashing it is synaesthetic, and it is in the adverbial form without the 'ly' which Milton much favoured; other examples are **sharp** (line 190), **loud** (line 210), **loose** (line 219).
188 based poetic form of 'placed'.
190 armèd allowed in poetry as metrical make-weight, and for its archaic flavour.

And on a sudden, lo! the level lake,
And the long glories of the winter moon.
Then saw they how there hove a dusky barge,
Dark as a funeral scarf from stem to stern,
195 Beneath them; and descending they were ware
That all the decks were dense with stately forms
Black-stoled, black-hooded, like a dream – by these
Three Queens with crowns of gold – and from them
    rose
A cry that shivered to the tingling stars,
200 And, as it were one voice, an agony
Of lamentation, like a wind, that shrills
All night in a waste land, where no one comes,
Or hath come, since the making of the world.
Then murmured Arthur, 'Place me in the barge,'
205 And to the barge they came. There those three
    Queens
Put forth their hands, and took the King, and wept.
But she, that rose the tallest of them all
And fairest, laid his head upon her lap,
And loosed the shattered casque, and chafed his hands,
210 And called him by his name, complaining loud,
And dropping bitter tears against his brow
Striped with dark blood: for all his face was white
And colourless, and like the withered moon
Smote by the fresh beam of the springing east;
215 And all his greaves and cuisses dashed with drops
Of onset; and the light and lustrous curls –

192 long glories an elliptical way of saying moonbeams, or long reflection of the moon on the ripples.
193 hove archaic form.
195 beneath them a prepositional phrase separated from its subject by a considerable gap – a Miltonic form of syntax.   **ware** archaic form of aware.
199 shivered *OED* v² 2 'to give forth with a trembling motion' (a C19 usage).   **tingling stars** thrilling (*OED* 1), but the only example cited of an inanimate object performing the action.
201 shrill (intr.) to sound shrilly: poetic, used by Spenser.
203 hath obsolete form.
206 Put forth archaic.
208 And fairest adjective tacked on almost as an afterthought – a Miltonic device.
209 casque specialized term for helmet: part of medieval flavour.
214 springing east periphrasis for dawn.
215 greaves and cuisses armour for shin and thigh: specialized terms conveying flavour of authenticity.
216 onset assault.   **lustrous** mostly found in poetry.

Introduction

their forms of speech, but for the rural classes and other uneducated people. On the whole the experience of the latter was not voiced by themselves but by educated sympathetic persons such as William Barnes, Hardy, James Thomson B.V., Hood and Meredith. Poems in this category form an appealing and important part of the output, whether they render the dialect faithfully (as in Tennyson's *Northern Farmer* poems), or adapt and transform it (as in Hopkins's *Felix Randal*).

The picture sketched of 'schools' and 'traditions' is only applicable in a broad sense. The poets themselves would have been wary of talking of 'schools' because there was little or no cohesion in the poetic establishment. There is one remarkable poet in the period who is almost impossible to place in the categories just outlined, uniting as he does virtually all the strands. By working at tremendous inspirational pressure Hopkins was able to fuse the various traditions of bardic song and expressive colloquial utterance, though ordinary speech in his work is intensified to such a degree as to be fully transformed into a highly idiosyncratic medium. He is the only poet in English who reminds one simultaneously of both Milton and Donne. He was committed enough as a poet to persist in writing even though he had a vague suspicion that it was not quite virtuous, and even though the coterie who saw his work only partially understood it. One way or another, Hopkins seems to be the answer to the prayer of those looking for a great Victorian poet. There is no doubt that his reputation is very high at the moment. His poetry has a life that leaps out from the page rather than one that is unearthed by patient digging. There are almost none of the dead poeticisms that mar other poetry: they were anathema to him, as was anything connected with mere decorative art. But faced with the task of casting Hopkins in the role of the great Victorian poet one has misgivings. There are times when his diction and syntax leave the language of men so far behind that one is reminded of what Ben Jonson said of Spenser, that he 'writ no language'. Here is individuality pushed to the point of eccentricity. And there is also the question of his slightness (see Hopkins headnote).

Hopkins was a poet who managed to exist without a public; but generally when one considers poetry of the period the public has to be borne in mind as an influential factor. Some consumers of poetry regarded it as a distraction and an anodyne, others as a source of moral truth. Either of these views, existing singly, would have guaranteed the continuation of poetry: in conjunction they made its survival a certainty. But the survival was bought at a cost, in that the anodyne view encouraged an evasion of significance and the 'moral teacher' view endangered response to technique. One only has to look at criticism before about 1914 to see the concentration of moral content: there were titles such as Henry Jones's *Browning as a*

the accessibility that such a combination would have given and wished instead for the mystery and intransigence that poets had traditionally enjoyed.

An interesting poet, who bridges the gap between the two main movements and reminds us of the perilousness of inventing exclusive categories, is Arnold. He was deeply concerned, especially in his inaugural lecture as Professor of Poetry at Oxford in 1857, with the problem of how poetry was to address the new age. What he yearned for, both for himself and for his fellow practitioners, was the adequacy he thought poetry had achieved in the age of Sophocles; though considering the names of predecessors who had failed to measure up to these high demands of relevance and poetic power (Aristophanes, Lucretius, Wordsworth, Byron, and so on) he could not have been very sanguine of success. When he himself tried to scale these heights he produced rather chilly and inert poetry: *Sohrab and Rustum* is an example. What is included of Arnold here tends to be examples of poetry that he may have regarded as 'inadequate', in that it was more critical than consolatory. Our century has appreciated it more because it is the product of a sentient being rather than a *vates* with his singing robes wrapped round about him. The poetry of, say, *The Scholar Gipsy* has the note of elegiac reverie rather than of magisterial didacticism: in spite of the poeticisms one hears a speaking rather than an intoning voice. And in other poems Arnold comes even closer to the colloquial voice, especially if one considers his rhythms rather than his diction. Yet he regretted the tendency of modern poetry to veer away from what Coleridge would have called 'the sense of musical delight' in the direction of flat rhythms and mundane diction. The poet he was most wary of, perhaps because his own poetry could easily have gone to similar excesses, was that of his friend Clough. In their correspondence we trace the details of Arnold's disquiet, his 'growing sense of the deficiency of the *beautiful*' in Clough's poems. Clough articulated the state of mind of the earnest, troubled, middle-class Victorian better than any other poet, and rules pre-eminent in his specialized domain.

Of course, a more distant ancestor than Wordsworth and Byron presides over the colloquiality and toughness of mind of poets such as Clough and Browning: namely, Donne. Donne was very much a minority taste in the period: he was not represented, for instance, in Palgrave's *Golden Treasury* (1861); but for poets of discernment (notably Browning, who quotes him a good deal in his letters) he was an influence. The best C19 poetry in the colloquial tradition comes reasonably close to the intensity and appeal of Donne; however, it would be true to say that none poses a serious rival – with the exception, perhaps, of Hopkins.

There was a colloquial tradition not only for the middle classes and

That made his forehead like a rising sun
High from the daïs-throne – were parched with dust;
Or, clotted into points and hanging loose,
220 Mixed with the knightly growth that fringed his lips.
So like a shattered column lay the king;
Not like that Arthur who, with lance in rest,
From spur to plume a star of tournament,
Shot through the lists at Camelot, and charged
225 Before the eyes of ladies and of kings.

220 the knightly growth one of the most notorious examples of poetic periphrasis.
223 from spur to plume a poetic adaptation of the colloquial 'from top to toe'.

The notes above are the distinctive points to notice about the passage. Since its subject matter is remote it is not be wondered that its poetic character is highly wrought, but many of the following features occur in Victorian poetry ostensibly dealing with familiar subjects. There are four inversions, nine lines with alliteration. Much more prominent are the unusual words, and the unusual forms of words.

Although most of the features indicated here do not seem extreme taken one by one, the aggregate is a poetic style that is highly coloured, and quite distinct from the world of everyday speech. When the average Victorian reader thought of Poetry with a capital P, he thought of something like the passage just analysed.

But contemporaneous with poetry of the Tennysonian kind there flourished a wholly alien type, which was nearer to colloquial speech than song. Browning is pre-eminently a poet of this other school. Swinburne was not far wrong when he said that 'in the huge bulk of Browning's lyrical baggage there is not one good song'. However, to say that Browning is in a colloquial tradition is not to say that he reproduces the authentic speech of the man in the street. By the time colloquial speech appears in his poetry it has been significantly alchemized and bears little resemblance to the point of departure. Here too the Romantic Movement was a source, though not the exclusive one, of one of the diverse traditions of Victorian poetry: proximity of poetry to ordinary speech is to be heard in Wordsworth and Byron. One might expect that poetry of this kind was suitable for the head-on encounter with the problems and new conditions of Victorian life, but usually it did not make the direct assault, preferring instead to come round obliquely and cope with life by way of some distant time or remote place. Poetry often failed to rise to the challenge of the age. Perhaps the case for Browning may be made to speak for all: it seems possible that he did not want

Philosophical and Religious Teacher (1891) and J. Oates's *The Teaching of Tennyson* (1895). Earnest institutions such as the Browning Society encouraged such approaches. Many readers, without having Arnold's sensitive and profound literary consciousness, took too much to heart the Arnoldian recommendation that, with the decline of religious belief, poetry should step into the gap as the *magister vitae*. It is a depressing thought for those who espouse poetry as the repository of moral truth that the prophet of this doctrine should himself have abandoned poetry as a vehicle of thought and taken up criticism instead: Arnold was perfectly well aware that thought that is going to lead directly to behaviour is best conducted in the medium of analytical prose.

But there was a literary mode that posed greater threats to poetry than prose. This was the novel. Dramatic prose represented a much weaker threat since the theatre during the period was in such a shaky state. The novel competes for our attention as the dominant literary form to such a degree that there are times when one wonders if it is not a better reflection of the age and a greater literary achievement than the poetry. It was able to provide the Victorians with most of what they needed by way of distraction and instruction. Into its loose and baggy form anything could be dropped, with almost no intermediary transformation. Observations on the strength of sea shells appearing in poetry could be converted into symbolic imagery (as they are in *Maud*), whereas in a novel such as Kingsley's *Two Years Ago* learned disquisitions on marine biology could be dropped in next to those on sanitary reform with no intervention of imaginative coalescing energy. In addition, the novel had the appeal of story and characterization. During the century it was slowly making its bid for respectable status against various kinds of prejudice, ranging from True Blue Tory to Evangelical, and though no one quite said that it could replace the Bible and the Thirty-nine Articles as the *magister vitae*, many recognized that it stood a better chance than poetry of being the unacknowledged legislator of mankind. The prestige of the novel and the novel-reading habits of the public (and even of the poets) had an identifiable effect on the poetry. Many of the poets tried, with varying degrees of success, to satisfy their readers with the features they had come to expect from the novels – plot, settings, characterization, low pitch of language and, alas, length. Often the poetry competed on grounds unfavourable to its potential; but occasionally, as in *Maud*, the poet came up with an amalgam of novelistic and poetic features that was not imitable by the novel proper.

Considered as a whole, Victorian poetry is a remarkable and impressive achievement. The days are gone when its merit has to be asserted against a chorus of derision and amused contempt. It should be remembered that the serious detractors early in the

Introduction

century could only make their own headway as creative artists by turning their immediate predecessors into figures of scorn. This is a pattern not unfamiliar in cultural history. Poets and critics now are under less compulsion of this kind, and hence are able to appreciate its merits with more objectivity. However, it has to be recognized that many of the poems in this collection were less regarded, in the poets' own time, than some of the poems left out. We are not impressed by some of the large-scale achievements such as *Angel in the House, Aurora Leigh, Idylls of the King*. They speak to their own age more surely and effectively than they do to ours, and some of them survive as little more than curios. The output in the century was so enormous, and so disparate, that it would almost be possible to turn the occupation of the anthologizer into one of creativity, so that one quarried out a book of twentieth-century poetry, or even a book of one's own poetic predilections. To some degree this is what George Macbeth did in his *Penguin Book of Victorian Verse*. One encounters a splendid collection of off-beat, even kinky, verse. Such extremes are avoided here; the acclaimed poems are represented, and the less well-known are here because they claim one's attention by being striking, intense and strange. Features of this kind are common in Victorian poetry and they probably constitute its most salient, differentiating characteristic. Eighteen poets are represented, and no poet of any importance is left out, with the exception of Robert Bridges, who was born in 1844, and did publish before 1890, but the bulk of whose important work really belongs to post-1890. One should remember that in addition to the well-known names there were hundreds of forgotten or barely known poets: the *NCBEL* lists 193 poets from 1835 to 1900, and Arthur Miles's *Poets of the Century* in eight volumes (first edition 1895) has about 190 Victorian poets, 42 of them women. Many of those poets wrote worthy and striking poetry. In an anthology of a different kind it could be presented, but the effect would be more of a trial sampling than a presentation of a large enough body of work to enable one to come to worthwhile conclusions on the character of the poet concerned. Although these poets are not here, they should not be forgotten altogether, and though some of them wrote execrable poetry, the sheer volume and ubiquity of poetry in the century makes one pause in one's tracks before one asserts that it was an unpoetic age.

John Clare

John Clare is something of an anomaly in this collection: he was born in 1793, two years before Keats, and by 1830 his publishing career was almost over. The only collection published in our period was *The Rural Muse* (1835). Clare satisfied the late eighteenth-century taste for unsophisticated rural poetry: *Poems Descriptive of Rural Life and Scenery* (1820), *The Village Minstrel* (1821) and *The Shepherd's Calender* (1827) are collections that have much in common with Cowper and the early Wordsworth. They brought him a degree of fame, and friendship with men such as Tom Hood, Allan Cunningham, Charles Wentworth Dilke, William Hone and John Taylor (Keats's publisher). His literary roots were older still, in Thomson, Milton, Bunyan and Shakespeare, and he wrote pastiches of Marvell and Sir John Harington without effort because he was spiritually still attached to their world. He may well have been the last English poet to read Donne without any sense of being engaged in a revival or a rediscovery. It is in character that he thought the Hilton portrait of him as a Romantic poet (1820) slightly absurd. His situation was not unlike Crabbe's and Robert Bloomfield's (1766–1823), except that he was less prosperous and well-educated than Crabbe – indeed, he had scarcely any formal education at all – and he was less in contact with urban life than Bloomfield. He was brought up in the remote Northamptonshire village of Helpston, on the edge of the Lincolnshire fens; however, he was a lover of books to the point of bookishness, so that the directness of his poetry is actually a more calculated and admirable artistic triumph than one might suppose. His poetry before the 1830s was largely descriptive: the work of a close observer rather than of a speculative and wide-ranging thinker. Keats, who admired it, nevertheless thought that 'the description overlaid and stifled that which ought to be the prevailing idea'. *The Progress of Rhyme* is a poetic account of his career and personality.

Then in the 1830s and 1840s a change came over his poetic character; his work began to represent more of the inner man; it gave signs of a greater forthrightness and purposeful commitment. He was reaching for a kind of self-centredness which is necessary for great poetry – but alas, in his case the movement was a sign of incipient madness rather than an artistic sense of direction. He spent the last two decades of his life in asylums: at Matthew Allen's establishment in High Beech, Epping Forest (where he met Tennyson who was a visitor), and in Northampton asylum (where he died in 1864). He absconded from High Beech in 1841 and walked the eighty miles home, celebrating the pilgrimage in moving prose and poetry. As in the case of the painter Richard Dadd, who was an inmate of Broadmoor at about the same time, the authorities encouraged Clare to be creative. He continued to exhibit that prolixity of output which is frequently associated with un-balanced minds. Clare then was writing in the Victorian period. The late poems were not collected together until his death, and then with makeshift editing and drastic selection. His poetry has extraordinary power, perhaps because it was written by such an isolated figure. Hopkins, who is often held

John Clare

up as *the* example of the isolated artist in the period, was positively sociable and genial by comparison.

In the following selection there are poems that continue in the directions of Clare's earlier career: they deal with nature seen directly; he reciprocated Keats's criticism by recognizing in the mythological appendages of *Endymion* and the like 'the stigma of Cockneyism' and the town-bred vision of the countryside. Clare's view of the countryside was extremely detailed; not surprisingly it led to his having a minor reputation as a naturalist. His country, Northamptonshire, has none of the sublime and remarkable grandeur of the Lake District; it is entirely unremarkable, and its charms and secrets are only revealed to a patient and habitual denizen such as Clare. To be uprooted and moved even four miles was a major trauma for such a sensitive soul. In addition to the poems, there have survived prose passages on natural phenomena which bear a relation to the poetry similar to that between Hopkins's *Journals* and poems. Clare wrote: 'To look on Nature with a poetic eye magnifies the pleasure, she herself being the essence and soul of poesy.' In addition to the figurative use of the word 'magnify' one could envisage an almost physical sense, since his poetic eye, by being so scrupulous, did in fact function as an instrument of magnification when confronted with the neglected minutiae of nature. Clare could not have known the works of Traherne, whose poetry was buried in the Burney collection in the British Museum, but there is an affinity between the two: both saw the possibility of a kind of paradise on earth; but both realized (when they could no longer keep adult awareness from their predominantly childlike consciousness) that to reach Eden would mean travelling back into the past. Henry Vaughan expressed a similar view. For Clare a particular source of heartbreak was that much of the natural scene he had known as a child had been despoiled by land enclosures: for a poet as sensitive as he was, this revolution in rural scenery was as devastating as the coming of the railways to the next generation of nature lovers. A poem castigating the spoliation is *The Moors* (no. 2). The usual tone employed by Clare when he regrets the passing of beauty and of wholesome rural life is elegiac, but like Blake, he could effect an unusual combination of visionary and satirical perception. There is a documentary element in his work, and Clare was cited in the Hammonds' *The Village Labourer 1760–1832* (1911).

In addition to the nature poems there are poems on the state of his mind and his soul, and these are undeniably powerful. Many women are celebrated in them, usually as shadowy attendant spirits of the landscape; one gets an impression of their abundance in *A Health to all Pretty Girls:* 'To forty nine young happy girls I drink love peace and joy.' Mary Joyce, who he imagined had been his first wife, is the chief inmate of his imaginary rural harem; only a few poems celebrate his real wife, Martha Turner (Patty). In some instances these poems are the outcrop of an obsession with sex, which is another facet of madness; but one has the predominant impression that they add up to a search for happiness and wholeness. The search for psychic health through love necessarily displaced the search for intellectual sanity and conditions favourable to the vigorous life of the mind. By a tragic irony, he once described the healthy mental life as 'the son of earth – it lives on when the clouds and paraphernalia of pretension are forgotten', and as 'the most lasting and least liable to change'. Some of the poetry from the years of madness was part and parcel of delusion –

especially that dominated by his obsession with Byron (he wrote a *Child Harold* and a *Don Juan*), but most of it is a lifeline to a form of sanity and continuity. At times, the lack of balance led to a vision as highly charged and vivid as Van Gogh's: 'Corn poppies burnt me through | Blue caps intensely blue | Seemed flowers among the weeds.'

The text Clare poses a serious problem for any editor. He was an original and even stubborn man, and went much further than Cobbett in attacking pedantic grammarians: he came to the conclusion that since there was no agreement on punctuation it was better not to punctuate at all, and the manuscripts of his poetry and prose are virtually free of punctuation. In addition, by the standards of the time, he was an indifferent speller. Even for purists such as Eric Robinson and Geoffrey Summerfield this is too much; in *Selected Poems and Prose* (1967) they leave gaps to indicate the beginnings of sentences. Ideally, perhaps, there is a case for printing exact transcripts of manuscripts, but that is not the task of the present edition. At the same time, it is obvious that the Tibble 1935 edition was often over-punctuated. Similarly with the spelling: there is a case for reproducing Clare's solecisms, but there is an equally strong case for normalizing so long as this does not impede authentic oral presentation. Direct transcripts give an immediate impression that we are dealing with an imperfectly educated man, and someone with a freshness of approach, but these surface features may have the effect of distracting attention from the real originality of the man – which is in the non-accidental features. Clare's original publishers were not content to let their alterations stop at accidentals; they attempted to normalize rhythms and diction. Where manuscripts survive they are often a better guide to Clare's original intentions than the published work, so that some readings from manuscripts have been incorporated. The production of a satisfactory complete edition of Clare is still in progress. For the tribulations that Clare suffered at the hands of his publishers see Eric Robinson and Geoffrey Summerfield, 'John Taylor's editing of Clare's *The Shepherd's Calendar' RES* n.s. 14 (1963) 359–69.

Manuscripts in Clare's own hand survive, from his asylum years and before. Most of them are in Northampton Public Library and Peterborough Museum; some are in the Bodleian, the British Library and collections in the United States. In addition, there are transcripts made by the superintendent of the Northampton asylum, W.F. Knight, though these have to be treated with caution, since he emended Clare to make him a more accessible and conventional poet. Robinson and Summerfield's introduction to *1964* provides the fullest recent statement of the textual difficulties, and this selection is heavily dependent on their readings.

There are compromises in this edition of Clare, as in all previous ones. At the back of one's mind when one changes the poems one remembers Clare's complaint to Taylor of 30 April 1825: 'Editors are troubled with nice amendings, and if doctors were as fond of amputation as they are of altering and correcting the world would have nothing but cripples.'

Criticism The best recent works are J. Barrell *The Idea of Landscape and the Sense of Place 1730–1840* (Cambridge 1972) and G. M. Storey *The Poetry of John Clare* (1974).

[1] John Clare

Abbreviations

1835	*The Rural Muse* (1835)
1865	*The Life of John Clare* (1865) Frederick Martin
1873	*Life and Remains of John Clare* (1873) J. L. Cherry
1920	*John Clare Poems Chiefly from Manuscript* (1920) R. Cobden Sanderson, ed.
1935	*The Poems of John Clare* (1935) J. W. Tibble, ed.
1949	*Poems of John Clare's Madness* (1949) G. Grigson, ed.
1964	*Later Poems of John Clare* (1964) E. Robinson and G. Summerfield, eds.
1965	*John Clare Selected Poems* (1965) J. W. and A. Tibble, eds.
1967	*Selected Poems and Prose of John Clare* (1967) E. Robinson and G. Summerfield, eds.
Barrell	J. Barrell *The Idea of Landscape and the Sense of Place 1730–1840* (Cambridge 1972).
Storey	G. M. Storey *The Poetry of John Clare* (1974)

1 Ballad: The sun had grown on lessening day

Date 1821–4. Written at Helpston. The dairy idyll is reminiscent of Hardy's *Tess of the d'Urbervilles*.
Publication *1835*, *1935*, *1967*.

> The sun had grown on lessening day
>   A table large and round,
> And in the distant vapours grey
>   Seemed leaning on the ground;
> 5 When Mary, like a lingering flower,
>   Did tenderly agree
> To stay beyond her milking hour,
>   And talk awhile with me.
>
> We wandered till the distant town
> 10 Was silenced nearly dumb,
> And lessened on the quiet ear,
>   Small as a beetle's hum.
> She turned her buckets upside down,
>   And made us each a seat,
> 15 And there we talked the evening brown,
>   Beneath the rustling wheat.

Title *The Milking Hour 1835–1935.*
13 buckets] milk pails *1835–1935.*

4

And while she milked her breathing cows
    I sat beside the streams,
In musing o'er our evening joys,
20   Like one in pleasant dreams:
The bats and owls, to meet the night,
    From hollow trees had gone,
And e'en the flowers had shut for sleep,
    And still she lingered on.

25 We mused in rapture side by side,
    Our wishes seemed as one;
We talked of time's retreating tide,
    And sighed to find it gone.
And we had sighed more deeply still
30   O'er all our pleasures past,
If we had known what now we know,
    That we had met the last.

24 And] Yet *1835–1935*.
26 wishes] wishing *1835–1935*.

2 The Moors

Date 1821–4. Written at Helpston. An example of C.'s critical consciousness when faced with what he took to be an abuse: see Barnes's enclosure poem of the 1830s (no. 27). Helpston was enclosed in 1809: this meant not only a restriction in the availability of the common land for grazing, but also a visual change in its openness; see Barrell 189–215.
Text *1967* (the Carl and Lily Pforzheimer manuscript).
Publication *1935, 1965, 1967*.

Far spread the moory ground, a level scene
Bespread with rush and one eternal green,
That never felt the rage of blundering plough,
Though centuries wreathed spring blossoms on its brow,
5   Still meeting plains that stretched them far away
In unchecked shadows of green, brown, and grey.
Unbounded freedom ruled the wandering scene;
No fence of ownership crept in between
To hide the prospect of the following eye;
10 Its only bondage was the circling sky.
One mighty flat, undwarfed by bush and tree,
Spread its faint shadow of immensity
And lost itself, which seemed to eke its bounds
In the blue mist the horizon's edge surrounds.

Title *Enclosure 1935, 1965; The Moors* MS. and *1967*.
1–14 By the Statute of Merton, lords of the manor could claim the right to fence land previously available to those with common rights.

15   Now this sweet vision of my boyish hours,
     Free as spring clouds and wild as summer flowers,
     Is faded all – a hope that blossomed free,
     And hath been once no more shall ever be.
     Enclosure came, and trampled on the grave
20   Of labour's rights, and left the poor a slave;
     And memory's pride, ere want to wealth did bow,
     Is both the shadow and the substance now.
     The sheep and cows were free to range as then
     Where change might prompt, nor felt the bonds of men;
25   Cows went and came with evening morn and night
     To the wild pasture as their common right;
     And sheep, unfolded with the rising sun,
     Heard the swains shout and felt their freedom won,
     Tracked the red fallow field and heath and plain,
30   Then met the brook and drank, and roamed again;
     The brook that dribbled on as clear as glass,
     Beneath the roots they hid among the grass,
     While the glad shepherd traced their tracks along,
     Free as the lark and happy as her song.
35   But now all's fled, and flats of many a dye
     That seemed to lengthen with the following eye,
     Moors losing from the sight, far, smooth, and blea,
     Where swopt the plover in its pleasure free,
     Are vanished now with commons wild and gay
40   As poet's visions of life's early day.
     Mulberry bushes where the boy would run,
     To fill his hands with fruit, are grubbed and done;
     And hedgerow briars – flower lovers overjoyed
     Came and got flower pots – these are all destroyed,
45   And sky-bound moors in mangled garbs are left
     Like mighty giants of their limbs bereft.
     Fence now meets fence in owners' little bounds
     Of field and meadow, large as garden-grounds,
     In little parcels little minds to please,
50   With men and flocks imprisoned, ill at ease.
     Each little path that led its pleasant way,
     As sweet as morning leading night astray,
     Where little flowers bloomed round a varied host,
     That travel felt delighted to be lost

31–2 Omitted *1935, 1965*.
37 **blea** bleak.
41–4 Omitted *1935, 1965*.
42 **grubbed** dug up.
51–74 Omitted *1935, 1965*.

55   Nor grudged the steps that he had ta'en as vain,
     When right roads traced his journeys, and again
     Nay on a broken tree he'd sit awhile,
     To see the moors and fields and meadows smile
     Sometimes with cowslaps smothered – then all white
60   With daisies – then the summer's splendid sight
     Of cornfields crimson o'er the 'headache' bloomed,
     Like splendid armies for the battle plumed.
     He gazed upon them with wild fancy's eye,
     As fallen landscapes from an evening sky.
65   These paths are stopped – the rude philistine's thrall
     Is laid upon them and destroyed them all:
     Each little tyrant with his little sign
     Shows where man claims earth glows no more divine,
     But paths to freedom and to childhood dear
70   A board sticks up to notice 'no road here';
     And on the tree with ivy overhung,
     The hated sign by vulgar taste is hung,
     As though the very birds should learn to know
     When they go there they must no further go.
75   This with the poor scared freedom bade goodbye,
     And much they feel it in the smothered sigh,
     And birds and trees and flowers without a name
     All sighed when lawless law's enclosure came;
     And dreams of plunder in such rebel schemes
80   Have found too truly that they were but dreams.

59 cowslaps cowslips.
61 'headache' scarlet corn poppy.
65 philistine's the oppressive enemy (*OED* 2) rather than the Arnoldian sense
(*OED* 4).

3 The Shepherd's Calendar: August extract

Date C.'s publisher John Taylor suggested in a letter of 1 Aug. 1823 that he
should write the poem. It was mutilated in publication, and C. had to write
a completely new 'July'. The polite world was still not ready for C.'s fresh
and individual vision: for the sorry saga of its emergence see E. Robinson
and G. Summerfield *RES* n.s. 14 (1963) 359–69.
Background The poetic calender of the rustic year is a very ancient tradition,
stretching back to Hesiod, and in English including Tusser's *A hundreth
good pointes of husbandrie* (1557) and Spenser's *Shepherd's Calendar*. In
addition C. draws on a wealth of English rural poetry, which even in the
C17 could exhibit realistic detail at times. The octosyllabic couplet in which
seven of the months are described reminds one of Milton's *Il Pensoroso* and
L'Allegro. In addition to literary antecedents C. draws on his own intensely

[3] John Clare

detailed knowledge and love of the country, which he knew not as a source of picturesque scenery (usually the urban picture of the country), but as the haunt of country people; one often has the impression that his locales are densely populated. Taylor wanted a philosophic poem; C. gave him a minutely and lovingly observed piece of rural England. The full work is over 3,000 lines, and amongst the most readable long poems in the language.

Text The text below is a modernized version of Robinson and Summerfield's 1964 edition (based on the Peterborough MSS). Their introduction remains one of the best criticisms of the work; see also Storey 50–113.

The scene with the child is one of many in the poem; it is not there as a sentimental genre scene, but as a reminder that the deep impressions made upon the memory in childhood isolate what is quintessential and important in an environment.

Publication (in shortened form) *1827.*

Harvest approaches with its bustling day,
The wheat tans brown and barley bleaches grey;
In yellow garb the oat-land intervenes
And tawny glooms the valley thronged with beans.
5   Silent the village grows, wood-wandering dreams
Seem not so lovely as its quiet seems.
Doors are shut up as on a winter's day,
And not a child about them lies at play.
The dust that winnows 'neath the breeze's feet
10   Is all that stirs about the silent street.
Fancy might think that desert-spreading fear
Had whispered terrors into quiet's ear,
Or plundering armies past the place had come,
And drove the lost inhabitants from home.
15   The fields now claim them where a motley crew
Of old and young their daily tasks pursue.
The barley's beard is grey and wheat is brown,
And wakens toil betimes to leave the town.
The reapers leave their beds before the sun
20   And gleaners follow when home toils are done,
To pick the littered ear the reaper leaves,
And glean in open fields among the sheaves.
The ruddy child, nursed in the lap of care,
In toil's rude ways to do its little share,
25   Beside its mother poddles o'er the land,

6 **lovely**] lonely *1827–1935.*
13–14 Memories of the Napoleonic wars were still fresh.
17–18 Not in *1827–1935.*
19 **beds**] rest *1827–1935.*
24 **ways**] strife *1827–1935.*
25 **poddles** toddles.

Sun-burnt and stooping with a weary hand,
Picking its tiny glean of corn or wheat
While crackling stubbles wound its legs and feet.
Full glad it often is to sit awhile
30 Upon a smooth green baulk to ease its toil,
And fain would spend an idle hour to play
With insects, strangers to the moiling day,
Creeping about each rush and grassy stem,
And often wishes it was one of them,
35 In weariness of heart that it might lie
Hid in the grass from the day's burning eye
That raises tender blisters on his skin
Through holes or openings that have lost a pin,
Free from the crackling stubs to toil and glean,
40 And smiles to think how happy it had been,
Whilst its expecting mother stops to tie
Her handful up, and waiting his supply,
Misses the resting younker from her side;
And shouts of rods and morts of threats beside
45 Pointing to the grey willows while she tells
His fears shall fetch one if he still rebels,
Picturing harsh truths in its unpractised eye
How they who idle in the harvest lie
Shall well deserving in the winter pine,
50 Or hunt the hedges with the birds and swine.
In vain he wishes that the rushes' height
Were tall as trees to hide him from her sight.
Leaving his pleasant seat he sighs and rubs
His legs and shows scratched wounds from piercing stubs,
55 To make excuse for play; but she disdains
His little wounds and smiles while he complains;
And as he stoops adown in troubles sore,

28 legs and] little *1827–1935*.
30 baulk] (a strip of ground left unploughed) bank *1827*.
32 moiling toiling.
34–6 Perhaps related to C17 microscopic poetry, e.g. Marvell and Lovelace.
35–40 Not in *1827–1935*.
36 Cf. 'day's garish eye' Milton *Il Pensoroso* line 141.
43 resting] idle *1827*.   **yonder** child *OED* 3.
44 morts lots (corruption of mortal used as an intensive).
45–6 Not in *1927–1935*.
47 eye] breast *1827–1935*.
48 lie] rest *1827–1935*.
49 The mother warns the child, who has been looking at playful insects such as grasshoppers, of the fable of the ant and the grasshopper.

[4] John Clare

	She sees his grief and bids him sob no more,
	As by and by, on the next sabbath-day,
60	She'll give him well-earned pence as well as play,
	When he may buy almost without a stint
	Sweet candied horehound, cakes, and peppermint,
	Or streaking sticks of luscious lollipop,
	Whate'er he chooses from the tempting shop
65	Wi' in whose diamond winder shining lie
	Things of all sorts to tempt his eager eye:
	Rich sugar-plums in phials shining bright,
	In every hue, young fancies to delight,
	Coaches and ladies of gilt gingerbread,
70	And downy plums and apples streaked with red.
	Such promises all sorrows soon displace,
	And smiles are instant kindled in his face;
	Scorning all troubles which he felt before,
	He picks the trailing ears, and mourns no more.

58 sob] mourn *1827–1935*.

62 horehound extract from *marrubium vulgare*, used mainly as a cough medicine.

63 Not in *1827–1935*. Taylor may have decided that the confectionery was beginning to cloy.

4 Decay

Date 1824–32, written at Helpston.
Text based on *1967*.
Publication *1835, 1920, 1935, 1967*.

	Oh poesy is on the wane,
	For fancy's visions all unfitting;
	I hardly know her face again,
	Nature herself seems on the flitting.
5	The fields grow old and common things,
	The grass, the sky, the winds a-blowing,
	And spots where still a beauty clings
	Are sighing, 'Going! all a-going!'
	Oh poesy is on the wane,
10	I hardly know her face again.
	The bank with brambles overspread,
	And little mole-hills round about it,
	Was more to me than laurel shades,

4 flitting a familiar term for moving house: a word that struck terror into C.: see his poem *The Flitting* of 1832–5.

With paths of gravel finely clouted;
15 And streaking here and streaking there
Through shaven grass and many a border,
With rutty lanes had no compare,
And heaths were in a richer order.
But poesy is in its wane,
20 I hardly know her face again.

I sat with love by pasture stream,
Aye beauty's self was sitting by,
Till fields did more than Edens seem,
Nor could I tell the reason why.
25 I often drank when not adry
To pledge her health in draught divine;
Smiles made it nectar from the sky,
Love turned e'en water into wine.
Oh poesy is on the wane,
30 I cannot find her face again.

The sun those mornings used to find
Its clouds were other-country-mountains,
And heaven looked upon the mind,
With groves and rocks and mottled fountains.
35 Those heavens are gone, the mountains grey
Turned mist – the sun, a homeless ranger,
Pursues a naked weary way,
Unnoticed like a very stranger.
Oh poesy is on its wane,
40 Nor love nor joy is mine again.

Love's sun went down without a frown;
For every joy it used to grieve us,
I often think the West is gone;
Ah, cruel Time, to undeceive us!
45 The stream it is a naked stream,
Where we on Sundays used to ramble,
The sky hangs o'er a broken dream,
The bramble's dwindled to a bramble!
Oh poesy is on the wane,
50 I cannot find her haunts again.

Mere withered stalks and fading trees,
And pastures spread with hills and rushes,

14 **clouted** clothed.
17 **rutty lanes** a favourite source of visual pleasure for C.: see *We Passed by Green Closes* No. 16.
21 **with love by**] beside the *1835*.

Are all my fading vision sees;
Gone, gone is rapture's flooding gushes!
55 When mushrooms they were fairy bowers,
Their marble pillars overswelling,
And Danger paused to pluck the flowers
That in their swarthy rings were dwelling.
But poesy's spells are on the wane,
60 Nor joy nor fear is mine again.

Aye, poesy hath passed away,
And fancy's visions undeceive us;
The night hath ta'en the place of day,
And why should passing shadows grieve us?
65 I thought the flowers upon the hills
Were flowers from Adam's open gardens;
And I have had my summer thrills,
And I have had my heart's rewardings.
So poesy is on the wane,
70 I hardly know her face again.

And friendship it hath burned away,
Just like a very ember cooling,
A make-believe in April day
That sent the simple heart a-fooling;
75 Mere jesting in an earnest way
Deceiving on and still deceiving;
And hope is but a fancy play,
And joy the art of true believing;
For poesy is on the wane,
80 Oh, could I feel her faith again!

59 But...spells are] Yes, Poesy is *1835, 1935.*
72 Just like a] Like to a *1835, 1935.*

5 Winter in the Fens

Date 1832–5; written at Northborough.
A poem evocative of the *recherché* charms of fenland.
Publication *1935.*

So moping flat and low our valleys lie,
So dull and muggy is our winter sky,
Drizzling from day to day with threats of rain,
And when that falls still threatening on again;
5 From one wet week so great an ocean flows
That every village to an island grows,

And every road for even weeks to come
Is stopped, and none but horsemen go from home;
And one wet night leaves travel's best in doubt,
10   And horseback travellers ask if floods are out
Of every passer-by, and with their horse
The meadow's ocean try in vain to cross;
The horse's footings with a sucking sound
Fill up with water on the firmest ground,
15   And ruts that dribble into brooks elsewhere,
Can find no fall or flat to dribble here;
But filled with wet they brim and overflow
Till hollows in the road to river grow;
Then wind with sudden rage, abrupt and blea,
20   Twirls every lingering leaf from off each tree.
Such is our lowland scene that winter gives,
And strangers wonder where our comfort lives;
      Yet in a little close, however keen
The winter comes, I find a patch of green,
25   Where robins, by the miser winter made
Domestic, flirt and perch upon the spade;
And in a little garden-close at home
I watch for spring – and there's the crocus come!

19 blea bleak.
26 flirt flutter.

6 Ploughman Singing

Date 1832–5; written at Northborough.
    Typical of those charming poems of the 1830s in which the landscape is animated by a living being.
Publication *1920, 1935*.

Here morning in the ploughman's songs is met
    Ere yet one footstep shows in all the sky,
And twilight in the east, a doubt as yet,
    Shows not her sleeve of grey to know her by.
5   Woke early, I arose and thought that first
    In winter-time of all the world was I.
The old owls might have hallooed if they durst,
    But joy just then was up and whistled by

8–12 C.: '...I am pleasantly disappointed by the whistle of the ploughboy past the window, making himself merry and trying to make the dull weather dance to a very pleasant tune which I know well, and yet cannot recollect the song; but there are hundreds of these pleasant tunes familiar to the plough and the splashing team...' (*1967* 152).

A merry tune which I had known full long,
10   But could not to my memory wake it back,
Until the ploughman changed it to the song.
O happiness, how simple is thy track!
Tinged like the willow shoots, the east's young brow
Glows red and finds thee singing at the plough.

7 The Lout

Date 1832–5; written at Northborough.
  One of the three poems on this subject.
Publication *1920, 1935.*

For Sunday's play he never makes excuse,
But plays at taw, and buys his Spanish juice.
Hard as his toil, and ever slow to speak,
Yet he gives maidens many a burning cheek;
5   For none can pass him but his witless grace
Of bawdry brings the blushes in her face.
As vulgar as the dirt he treads upon,
He calls his cows or drives his horses on;
He knows the tamest cow and strokes her side
10   And often tries to mount her back and ride,
And takes her tail at night in idle play,
And makes her drag him homeward all the way.
He knows of nothing but the football match,
And where hens lay, and when the duck will hatch.

2 taw marbles.   **Spanish juice** liquorice.

8 The Mole-Catcher

Date 1832–5; written at Northborough.
  One of the superb group of rural studies in the ancient 'character' tradition. This, and its companions, are all very much less explicit at a didactic level than Wordsworth's poems.
Publication *1935, 1965.*

Tattered and ragg'd, with greatcoat tied in strings,
    And collared up to keep his chin from cold,
The old mole-catcher on his journey sings,
    Followed by shaggy dog infirm and old,
5   Who potters on and keeps his steady pace;
    He is so lame he scarce can get abroad,

But hopples on and growls at anything;
Yet silly sheep will scarcely leave the road.
With stick and spud he tries the new-made hills
10   And bears his cheating traps from place to place;
Full many are the miners that he kills.
His trotting dog oft looks him in the face;
And when his toils are done he tries to play
And finds a quicker pace and barks him on his way.

7 **hopples** creeps along.
9 **spud** pronged instrument for digging.   **tries**] tried *1935*.

9 Winter Fields

Date 1832–5; written at Northborough.
Publication *1935, 1967*.

Oh for a pleasant book to cheat the sway
Of winter – where rich mirth with hearty laugh
Listens and rubs his legs on corner seat;
For fields are mire and sludge – and badly off
5   Are those who on their pudgy paths delay;
There striding shepherd, seeking driest way,
Fearing night's wetshod feet and hacking cough
That keeps him waken till the peep of day,
Goes shouldering onward and with ready book
10   Progs oft to ford the sloughs that nearly meet
Across the lands; croodling and thin to view,
His loath dog follows – stops and quakes and looks
For better roads, till whistled to pursue;
Then on with frequent jump he hirkles through.

5 **pudgy** muddy.
10 **progs** prods.
11 **croodling** contracting the body from cold, shrinking.
14 **hirkles** crouches.

10 Grasshoppers

Date 1832–5; written at Northborough.
    A piece of almost microscopic observation that resembles some of C.'s
prose notes. C. might also be remembering older traditions of poetry about
insects: e.g. Marvell's *Appleton House.*
Publication *1935.*

[11] John Clare

Grasshoppers go in many a thrumming spring
And now to stalks of tasselled sour-grass cling,
That shakes and swees awhile, but still keeps straight;
While arching oxeye doubles with his weight.
5   Next on the cat-tail grass with farther bound
He springs, that bends until they touch the ground.

2 sour-grass a species of *carex* (*EDD*).
3 swees sways.
4 oxeye *Buphthalmus*, a plant with yellow flowers.
5 cat-tail grass; *SOD* s.v. Cat's tail = Phleum; esp. Timothy grass.

11 Country Letter

Date 1832–5; written at Northborough.
Publication *1920, 1935, 1965.*

Dear brother Robin, this comes from us all
With our kind love, and could Gip write and all
Though but a dog he'd have his love to spare,
For still he knows, and by your corner chair
5   The moment he comes in he lies him down
And seems to fancy you are in the town.
This leaves us well in health, thank God for that!
For old acquaintance Sue has kept your hat
Which mother brushes ere she lays it by
10   And every Sunday goes upstairs to cry.
Jane still is yours till you come back agen
And ne'er so much as dances with the men;
And Ned the woodman every week comes in
And asks about you kindly as our kin;
15   And he with this and goody Thompson sends
Remembrances with those of all our friends.
Father with us sends love until he hears
And mother she has nothing but her tears,
Yet wishes you like us in health the same
20   And longs to see a letter with your name,
So, loving brother, don't forget to write.
Old Gip lies on the hearth stone every night;
Mother can't bear to turn him out of doors
And never noises now of dirty floors;
25   Father will laugh but lets her have her way,
And Gip for kindness gets a double pay.

24 noises complains.

So Robin write and let us quickly see
You don't forget old friends no more than we,
Nor let my mother have so much to blame
30   To go three journeys ere your letter came.

12 The Farmyard

Date 1835–7; written at Northborough.
   A poem that almost seems to transmit the scene without any form of mediation.
Publication *1935*.

    Confusion's plenty lies in every way,
    And hogs and calves are noising all the day;
    The maiden serves them all with merry looks
    And often leaves the pattens in the mucks;
5   Though Hodge is sent to keep the causeys clean,
    His idle toil scarce shows her where he's been;
    With surly speed he sings an idle song,
    And like a walking may-tree lobs along.
    The rattling bucket calls the hogs away;
10   Calves toze the maidens' garments in their play
    The hogs lie rooting underneath the straw,
    The ducks go waddling with a loaded craw;
    The ploughman loads the straw with chubby face,
    And carts and waggons stand in every place.

1 Confusion's plenty one of the not infrequent instances in C. where eighteenth-century phraseology survives.
2 noising making a disturbance.
4 pattens raised wooden overshoes.
5 causeys causeways.
10 toze tug or shake.
12 craw crop.

13 The Frightened Ploughman

Date 1837–41.
Publication *1920, 1935*.

    I went in the fields with the leisure I got;
    The stranger might smile but I heeded him not;
    The hovel was ready to screen from a shower,
    And the book in my pocket was read in an hour.

[14] John Clare

5 The bird came for shelter, but soon flew away;
 The horse came to look, and seemed happy to stay;
 He stood up in quiet, and hung down his head,
 And seemed to be hearing the poem I read.

 The ploughman would turn from his plough in the day
10 And wonder what being had come in his way,
 To lie on a mole-hill and read the day long
 And laugh out aloud when he'd finished his song.

 The pewit turned over and stooped o'er my head
 Where the raven croaked loud like the ploughman ill-bred,
15 But the lark high above charmed me all the day long,
 So I sat down and joined in the chorus of song.

 The foolhardy ploughman I well could endure;
 His praise was worth nothing, his censure was poor;
 Fame bade me go on, and I toiled the day long,
20 Till the fields where he lived should be known in my song.

13 stooped descended.

14 Written in a Thunder Storm July 15th 1841

Date As in title; written a few days before C. absconded from High Beech.
Publication *1935, 1949, 1964.*

 The heavens are wrath – the thunder's rattling peal
  Rolls like a vast volcano in the sky;
 Yet nothing starts the apathy I feel,
  Nor chills with fear eternal destiny.

5 My soul is apathy – a ruin vast;
  Time cannot clear the ruined mass away;
 My life is hell – the hopeless die is cast;
  And manhood's prime is premature decay.

 Roll on ye wrath of thunders – peal on peal,
10 Till worlds are ruins and myself alone;
 Melt heart and soul cased in obdurate steel,
  Till I can feel that nature is my throne.

 I live in love, sun of undying light,
  And fathom my own heart for ways of good;
15 In its pure atmosphere, day without night
  Smiles on the plains, the forest and the flood.

18

Smile on, ye elements of earth and sky,
 Or frown in thunders as ye frown on me;
Bid earth and its delusions pass away,
20 But leave the mind, as its creator, free.

20 Cf. *1967* 100: 'Pleasures are of two kinds: One arises from cultivation of the mind, and are enjoyed only by the few, and these are the most lasting and least liable to change...'

15 'Tis Martinmass from rig to rig'

Date 1841. MS in Bodleian.
Publication *1935*, *1964*.

'Tis Martinmass, from rig to rig
 Ploughed fields and meadow lands are blea;
In hedge and field each restless twig
 Is dancing on the naked tree;
5 Flags in the dykes are bleached and brown,
 Docks by its sides are dry and dead,
All but the ivy boughs are brown
 Upon each leaning dotterel's head.

Crimsoned with awes the awthorns bend
10 O'er meadow dykes and rising floods,
The wild geese seek the reedy fen,
 And dark the storm comes o'er the woods.
The crowds of lapwings load the air
 With buzzes of a thousand wings;
15 There flocks of sturnels too repair
 When morning o'er the valley springs.

1 Martinmass The feast of St Martin: 11 Nov. **rig** ridge.
2 blea bleak.
5 flags irises.
8 dotterel pollarded tree.
9 awes hawthorn berries.
15 sturnels starlings.

16 We Passed by Green Closes

Date A Northampton asylum poem.
 A characteristic description of a close affinity between a woman and her surroundings. Knight transcript.
Publication *1949*, *1964*.

[17] John Clare

The path crossed green closes and went down the lane
Where the black snail reposes and the slime marks remain;
The hook prickle bramble arches over the grass,
And tears in her ramble the gown o' the lass.

5   The wind in her ribbons green wantoned and played,
And danced round as they'd been i' love wi' the maid;
Fine straw was her bonnet, her cheek was the rose,
Passing bees settled on it, by mistake I suppose.

Blue skippers in sunny hours open and shut
10   Where wormwood and grunsel flowers by the cart ruts,
Where bees while birds whistle sung all the lane down,
And passes the thistle for the flowers on her gown.

The footpath all noonday we paced i' the lane,
The day it was Sunday, the bells rung again;
15   The bare mare was snorting beside of her foal –
Love from that day's courting burns my heart to a coal.

9 skippers butterflies of the *Hesperiidae* family.
10 grunsel groundsel.
15 bare] bay *1949.*

17 Song – Last Day

Date After 1845 – the date of the notebook in which the poem appears (*MS 110* Northampton). This is the second of the two versions of the poem.
Publication *1964.*

There is a day, a dreadful day,
   Still following the past,
When sun and moon are past away
   And mingle with the blast.
5   There is a vision in my eye
     A vacuum o'er my mind,
Sometimes as on the sea I lie
     Mid roaring waves and wind.

When valleys rise to mountain waves,
10   And mountains sink to seas,
When towns and cities, temples, graves,
     All vanish like a breeze,
The skies that was are past and o'er,
     That almanac of days.
15   Year chronicles are kept no more
     Oblivion's ruin pays:

Pays in destruction shades and hell.
Sin goes in darkness down
And therein sulphur's shadows dwell;
20 Worth wins and wears the crown,
The very shore, if shore I see,
All shrivelled to a scroll.
The heavens rend away from me
And thunder's sulphurs roll,

25 Black as the deadly thunder cloud,
The stars shall turn to dun,
And heaven by that darkness bowed,
Shall make day's light be done.
When stars and skies shall all decay
30 And earth no more shall be,
When heaven itself shall pass away,
Then thou'lt remember me.

21-4 Printed as a fragment in *1949*.

18 I Am

Date Composed some time between 1844 and 1848.
 One of the most famous of the poems of madness.
Text Knight transcript.
Publication *Bedford Times* Jan. 1848, *1865, 1873, 1920, 1949, 1965, 1967.*

I am: yet what I am none cares or knows;
 My friends forsake me like a memory lost;
I am the self-consumer of my woes –
 They rise and vanish in oblivion's host,
5 Like shadows in love's frenzied, stifled throes:–
 And yet I am, and live – like vapours tossed

Into the nothingness of scorn and noise,
 Into the living sea of waking dreams,
Where there is neither sense of life or joys,
10 But the vast shipwreck of my life's esteems;
Even the dearest, that I love the best,
 Are strange – nay, rather stranger than the rest.

I long for scenes where man hath never trod,
 A place where woman never smiled or wept –

4 **oblivion's**] oblivious *1848–1949.*
5 Like shades in love and death's oblivion lost; *1848–1935.*
6 **vapours**] shadows *1848–1935.*
11 **Even**] And e'en *1848–1935.* **love**] loved *1848–1935.*

15   There to abide with my Creator, God,
        And sleep as I in childhood sweetly slept,
        Untroubling and untroubled where I lie,
        The grass below, above, the vaulted sky.

17 Full of high thoughts, unborn. So let me lie, *1865*.

19 Autumn

Date A Northampton asylum poem.
Publication *1920, 1935, 1949, 1965.*

        The thistledown's flying
        Though the winds are all still,
        On the green grass now lying,
        Now mounting the hill,
5   The spring from the fountain
        Now boils like a pot,
        Through stones past the counting
        It bubbles red hot.

        The ground parched and cracked is
10   Like overbaked bread,
        The greensward all wracked is
        Bents dried up and dead.
        The fallow fields glitter
        Like water indeed,
15   And gossamers twitter,
        Flung from weed unto weed.

        Hill-tops like hot iron
        Glitter hot i' the sun,
        And the rivers we're eyeing
20   Burn to gold as they run;
        Burning hot is the ground,
        Liquid gold is the air;
        Whoever looks round
        Sees Eternity there.

12 Bents clumps of reedy grass.

20 'Oh sweet is the sound'

Date A Northampton asylum poem.
   This poem is very similar, in theme and form, to *Rachel Cooks* (*1949* 200); both celebrate the fusion of a love of nature with the love of a woman whose attributes are essentially natural.
Text Knight transcript.
Publication *1964.*

Oh sweet is the sound o' the dove's clapping wings,
    And the sound o' the wood gate thrown open that clasps;
Oh sweet is the song of the thrush where it sings,
    And sweet the old oak where the woodpecker taps,
5   Where primrose and blue-bell bloom littered around,
    And the ever green ivy feathered round the green tree.
Here spoke my sweet Susan; there was love i' the sound
    O' her voice as she stood calmly talking to me.

Her hand held fine blue-bells and primroses too,
10   Ribbed leaves of the hazels were beautifully green;
Anemones too that were weeping in dew
    In the white hand o' Susan that morning were seen.
How sweet was her inky hair sweetened wi' dew,
    How sweet was her bosom more white than the snow;
15   Her gown it was green speckled over wi' blue,
    O' her hair was jet black like the back of a crow.

Sweet looked the grey lichen upon the green oak;
    The violets looked rich by each root mossy green,
And the raven croaked loud as a rustic had spoke.
20   Here Susan all day wi' her lover would lean
Agen the white bark o' the oak to admire;
    Green mosses and wild flowers spread round at her feet,
    Her eyes were as bright as the sun's liquid fire,
    And the greenwoodlands still in her absence seems sweet.

19 The croaking raven traditionally associated with doom (e.g. *Hamlet*
3.2.264); Clare completely divests it of these associations, to present it as one
more sensuous item.

21 'When I was young'

Date A Northampton asylum poem.
Text Knight transcript.
Publication *1935, 1964, 1965*.

When I was young I fell in love and got but little good on't:
    When she passed I turned away,
At first she would then wouldn't.
    I wished to speak and then the sigh
5   Came first and always stopped it.
    Come silence tell my wishes then,
I thought so and then dropped it
    And never tried to speak agen.

The path that o'er the cornfield lay,
10   I met her one day early;

[23] John Clare

> She turned her face another way,
>> And I walked in the barley.
> A lark that moment sought the sky
>> Close to her gown or nearly;
> Her bright eye looked to see him fly,
>> And then I loved her dearly.
>
> And turns the rosy cheek to clay?
>> 'Tis beauty's face in woman's form
> That steals the senses all away,
>> That rends the bosom like a storm;
> Though mild as evening's sober ray,
>> The winds they sigh, the dews they weep.
> And on the violet's bosom fall:
>> First love and truth unriddles all.

15 (line 15)
20 (line 20)

22 'The thunder mutters louder and more loud'

Date A Northampton asylum poem.
Publication 1964.

> The thunder mutters louder and more loud;
>> With quicker motion hay-folks ply the rake;
> Ready to burst slow sails the pitch black cloud,
>> And all the gang a bigger haycock make
> To sit beneath: the woodlands winds awake.
>> The drops so large wet all through in an hour,
> A tiny flood runs down the leaning rake.
> In the sweet hay yet dry the hay-folks cower
> And some beneath the waggon shun the shower.

5 (line 5)

23 Song — Molly Magee

Date After 1845 – the date of the notebook in which the poem appear (*MS 110* Northampton).
Publication 1964.

> My thoughts are of thee love though thou thinkest not of me,
> Yet dearly I love thee sweet Molly Magee.
> Today i' the morning 'twas nine o' the clock,
> Thy arm went behind thee to button thy frock,
> And in pulling it back wi' sich sweetness and ease
> My heart broke in two love as short as you please.
> So now I'm a cripple as well you may see,
> And all through the beauty of Molly Magee.

5 (line 5)

T'other day she stooped natty to tie up her shoe,
10   It wanted five minutes of a quarter to two,
And lauk sich a foot and a ankle war there
I lost both my eyes as I turned me to stare;
They left me as blind as an owl before day,
And stone heaps and blunders are all in the way.
15   I maun be a blindman and believe I can't see,
And it's all for the beauty of Molly Magee.

She tied up her shoe string, she buttoned her frock,
And my heart was shut up like the bolt i' the lock,
Like the bolt i' the lock, like the chit i' the pea
20   Sich power had the beauty of Molly Magee;
Her back was so white and leg was so round,
The sight o't war worth half the coin in a pound.
But bother the sight, it has stolen my e'e,
I'm blind wi' the beauty o' Molly Magee.

25   I tumble o'er stone heaps and miss the high way,
And am lost i' the dark i' the middle o' day;
If ain opes his mouth I'm as deaf as a tree
They a' seem as talkin o' Molly Magee;
If they mutter agen her and I knew it not
30   My heart leaves my breast like a bird that is shot.
I shall ne'er mak' an old man I plain enough see,
I'm kilt through the beauty of Molly Magee.

14 **blunders** 'obstacles' and 'confusion' *OED* 1.
19 **chit** corruption of chich: lentil.

24 'I hid my love'

Date A Northampton asylum poem.
Publication *1920* etc.

I hid my love when young while I
Couldn't bear the buzzing of a fly;
I hid my love to my despite
Till I could not bear to look at light:
5   I dare not gaze upon her face
But left her memory in each place;
Where'er I saw a wild flower lie
I kissed and bade my love good-bye.

1 **while**] till *1920, 1935, 1949.*

[25] John Clare

I met her in the greenest dells,
Where dewdrops pearl the wood bluebells;
The lost breeze kissed her bright blue eye,
The bee kissed and went singing by,
A sunbeam found a passage there,
A gold chain round her neck so fair;
15   As secret as the wild bee's song
She lay there all the summer long.

I hid my love in field and town
Till e'en the breeze would knock me down;
The bees seemed singing ballads o'er,
20   The fly's buzz turned a lion's roar;
And even silence found a tongue
To haunt me all the summer long;
The riddle nature could not prove
Was nothing else but secret love.

20 buzz] bass *1920, 1935, 1949.* Knight has buss; cf. George Eliot's *Middlemarch:* 'If we had a keen vision and feeling of all ordinary human life, it would be like hearing the grass grow and the squirrel's heart beat, and we should die of that roar which lies on the other side of silence. As it is, the quickest of us walk about well wadded with stupidity' (Ch. 20).

25 Clock-a-clay

Date A Northampton asylum poem.
Publication *1873* etc.

In the cowslip's peeps I lie,
Hidden from the buzzing fly,
While green grass beneath me lies,
Pearled wi' dew like fishes' eyes,
5   Here I lie, a clock-a-clay,
Waiting for the time o' day.

While grassy forests quake surprise,
And the wild wind sobs and sighs,
My gold home rocks as like to fall,
10   On its pillar green and tall;
When the pattering rain drives by
Clock-a-clay keeps warm and dry.

1 cowslip's peep single blossom in a cluster *OED* 2.3.
5 clock-a-clay ladybird.

26

Day by day and night by night,
All the week I hide from sight;
15 In the cowslip's peeps I lie,
In rain and dew still warm and dry;
Day and night, and night and day,
Red, black-spotted clock-a-clay.

My home it shakes in wind and showers,
20 Pale green pillar topped wi' flowers,
Bending at the wild wind's breath,
Till I touch the grass beneath;
Here still I live, lone clock-a-clay,
Watching for the time of day.

26 Written in Prison

Date A Northampton asylum poem.
Publication *1935, 1949, 1965.*

I envy e'en the fly its gleams of joy
In the green woods; from being but a boy
Among the vulgar and the lowly bred,
I envied e'en the hare her grassy bed.
5 Inured to strife and hardship from a child,
I traced with lonely step the desert wild,
Sighed o'er bird pleasures, but no nest destroyed,
With pleasure felt the singing they enjoyed,
Saw nature smile on all and shed no tears,
10 A slave through ages, though a child in years;
The mockery and scorn of those more old,
An Aesop in the world's extended fold.
The fly I envy settling in the sun
On the green leaf, and wish my goal was won.

12 **Aesop** Greek writer of animal fables of the sixth century B.C. Since the stories contained wisdom beneath a surface of light narrative the comparison is appropriate for C.

William Barnes

Life and writings William Barnes was born in 1801 in the parish of Sturminster-Newton, Dorset. This part of the country was later to receive famous treatment as 'The Valley of the Great Dairies' in Hardy's novel *Tess of the d'Urbervilles*. He was educated in Dorchester, and there he married Julia Miles, the central motive of his poetry. He had been planning to be an artist, but meeting with discouragement took to school-teaching, first at Mere in Wiltshire, then in Dorchester. In 1844 he produced *Poems of Rural Life, in the Dorset Dialect*, and thereafter three more collections of dialect poetry, as well as poems in what he called 'National English'. His life was retired and uneventful; he cultivated a very varied range of interests, and was among the best informed of all English poets on matters of language. Palgrave, not unjustly, compared his learning to that of Virgil, Tasso, Spenser and Milton; his first collection of poems was prefaced by a 35-page dissertation on the Dorset dialect, expanded to 50 pages in the second edition. Yet he remained remote from the metropolitan literary scene, and almost the only literary figure he knew was Lady Caroline Norton. He was ordained in 1847. His wife died on 21 June 1852; he was given a Civil List pension of £70 p.a. in 1861 and presented with the living of Winterbourne Came in 1862. He died on 7 October 1886, still not a household name, but cherished and admired by Allingham, Patmore, Tennyson, Hopkins and Hardy.

At first glance it seems perverse to include a backwater dialect poet in this collection; he is not thought worthy of a chapter, for instance, in Faverty. Further investigation will show him to be a more central poet. The best Victorian poetry is fresh and distinct, relying on direct experience. Twentieth-century taste, re-aligned by the focus on Hopkins, is now more attuned to some of the principles that Barnes stood for: the power of idiom and colloquialism in poetry and the strength of the Anglo-Saxon linguistic inheritance. There are affinities among Crabbe, Clare and Barnes (he even shares their acute political vision at times), but those between Barnes and Hopkins are more important: both were interested in forging a new poetic idiom that would be clearly based on folk origins, but would also be in a long and eclectic tradition of poetic artifice. The footnotes indicate the technical expertise of Barnes. He was a man to appreciate the virtues of the ordered and proportioned worlds of nature and art alike, as one observes in his essay for *Macmillan's Magazine*: 'Thoughts on Beauty and Art' (1861). A statement often quoted from the preface of *1862* gives the impression that Barnes is a spontaneous and artless poet: 'To write in what some may deem a fast out-wearing speech-form may seem as writing one's name in the snow of a spring day. I cannot help it. It is my mother tongue, and is to my mind the only true speech of the life that I draw.' Against this should be set the mass of evidence indicating that he was a deliberate and highly intelligent writer. He himself says: 'Without *judgement*, fancy is but mad.'

The other element influencing our taste is that Hardy and Auden are coming more into prominence as important poets, so that one is forced to consider their antecedents. Hardy chose and prefaced a collection of

Barnes's poetry in 1908, recognizing its central features in words that also speak for his own work: 'we find him warbling his native wood-notes with a watchful eye on the predetermined score.'
His popularity is gradually extending; one endorses E. M. Forster's remark in *Two Cheers for Democracy* (1951); 'He should have been a popular poet, for he writes of matters which move everyone and in a way which everyone can understand.'
Criticism Recent critical biographies are G. Dugdale *W. B. of Dorset* (1953) and W. T. Levy *W. B.: the man and the poems* (1960). See also G. Grigson's introduction to *Selected Poems of W. B.* (1950), and R. A. Forsyth, 'The Conserving Myth of W. B.' in *Romantic Mythologies*, ed. I. Fletcher (1967).
The standard edition of the poetry is *Poems of Rural Life, in the Dorset Dialect* (1879), but since B. in this edition was trying to reach a wider audience, there is some toning down of dialect elements.

Abbreviations

1844	*Poems of Rural Life, in the Dorset Dialect* (1844).
1859	*Hwomely Rhymes; a second collection of poems in the Dorset dialect* (1859).
1862	*Poems of Rural Life, in the Dorset Dialect. Third collection* (1862).
1906	*Poems in the Dorset Dialect by the late Rev. W. Barnes* (Dorchester, 1906).
1962	*The Poems of William Barnes* (1962) B. Jones ed.
Baxter	Lucy Baxter [B.'s daughter] *The Life of William Barnes* (1887).

27 The Common a-Took In

Date Perhaps late 1830s.
   One of the two poems B. wrote about enclosure, the other being *Eclogue: The Common a-Took In*. He is probably referring to the enclosure of Bagber Common. Cf. Clare's *The Moors* no. 2.
Publication *1844*.

> Oh! no, Poll, no! Since they've a-took
> The common in, our lew wold nook
> Don't seem a-bit as used to look
>   When we had runnèn room;
> 5 Girt banks do shut up ev'ry drong,
> An' stratch wi thorny backs along

Title See B.'s 'Dissertation...' *1844*. 14: he compares 'The common is inclosed' with the 'English expression' 'The common is a-took in.'
2 lew sheltered.   **wold** old.
4 runnèn] rinnen *1844*.
5 Girt great.   **drong** narrow way.
6 Enclosure introduced the hedges and ditches that are now so familiar a part of English landscape. Making them gave a temporary boost to rural employment.   **thorny**] tharny *1844*.

[27] William Barnes

Where we did use to run among
The vuzzen an' the broom.

Ees; while the ragged colts did crop
10   The nibbled grass, I used to hop
The emmet-buts, vrom top to top,
    So proud o my spry jumps:
Wi thee behind or at my zide,
A-skippèn on so light an' wide
15 'S thy little frock would let thee stride,
    Among the vuzzy humps.

Ah while the lark up over head
Did twitter, I did search the red
Thick bunch o broom, or yollow bed
20   O vuzzen vor a nest;
An' thou di'st hunt about, to meet
Wi strawberries so red an' sweet,
Or clogs or shoes off hosses' veet,
    Or wild thyme vor thy breast;

25 Or when the cows did run about
A-stung, in zummer, by the stout,
Or when they plaÿ'd, or when they foüght,
    Di'st stand a-lookèn on:
An' where white geese, wi long red bills,
30 Did veed among the emmet-hills,
Then we did goo to vind their quills
    Alongzide o the pon'.

What fun there wer among us, when
The haÿward come, wi all his men,
35 To drève the common, an' to pen
    Strange cattle in the pound;
The cows did bleäre, the men did shout
An' toss their eärms an' sticks about,
An' vo'ks, to own their stock, come out
40   Vrom all the housen round.

8 vuzzen furze or gorse.
11 emmet-buts anthills.
14–15 wide | 'S a poetic device that Hopkins used.
17 over] anver *1844*.
19 yollow] yoller *1844*.
26 An' kick an' hold ther taiels out, *1844*.   **stout** gadfly.
27 Or ... plaÿ'd] A-stung by vlees *1844*.
34 haÿward guardian of the fences (both segments O.E.). His activity described in *The Dreven o the Common*.
37 bleäre blare or bellow.
40 housen houses (a dialect plural).

28 Grammer's Shoes

Date Unknown.
   Baxter 10–11 recalls: 'After his mother's death the boy remembered seeing in the house a pair of embroidered shoes which had belonged to her, and which lingering in his memory gave rise to one of his most charming poems.' He tried to obtain the shoes, but without success. Dancing, as one also discovers from Hardy, was a central activity in rural communities.
Publication *1844*.

> I do seem to zee Grammer as she did use
> Vor to show us, at Chris'mas, her wedden shoes,
> An' her flat spreadèn bonnet so big an' roun'
> As a girt pewter dish a-turned upside down;
> 5   When we all did draw near
>   In a cluster to hear
> O the merry wold soul how she did use
> To walk an' to dance wi her high-heel shoes.
>
> She'd a gown wi' girt flowers lik' hollyhocks,
> 10   An' zome stockèns o gramfer's a-knit wi clocks,
> An' a token she kept under lock an' key, –
> A small lock ov his heäir off avore 't wer grey.
>   An' her eyes wer red,
>   An' she shook her head,
> 15 When we'd all a-looked at it, an' she did use
> To lock it away wi her weddèn shoes.
>
> She could tell us such teäles about heavy snows,
> An' o raîns an' o floods when the waters rose
> All up into the housen, an' carr'd awoy
> 20 All the bridge wi a man an' his little bwoy;
>   An' o vog an' vrost,
>   An' o vo'k a-lost,
> An' o peärties at Chris'mas, when she did use
> Vor to walk hwome wi gramfer in high-heel shoes.
>
> 25 Ev'ry Chris'mas she liked vor the bells to ring,
> An' to have in the zingers to heär em zing
> The wold carols she heärd many years a-gone,
> While she warmed em zome cider avore the bron';

4 girt great.
5–6 (and all fifth and sixth lines in subsequent stanzas) Examples of 'adorning', described by Barnes as a device, modelled on Eastern poetry, 'in which every word of a line is answered by another of the same measure and rhyme in the other line of the distich'.
10 clocks ornamental patterns (origin obscure).
28 bron' brand.

    An' she'd look an' smile
30   At our dancèn, while
    She did tell how her friends now a-gone did use
    To reely wi her in their high-heel shoes.

    Ah! an' how she did like vor to deck wi red
    Holly-berries the window an' wold clock's head,
35   An' the clavy wi boughs o some bright green leaves,
    An' to meäke twoast an' eäle upon Chris'mas eves;
        But she's now, drough greäce,
        In a better pleäce,
    Though we'll never vorget her, poor soul, nor lose
40   Gramfer's token ov heäir, nor her weddèn shoes.

32 reely dance reels.
35 clavy mantel.
37 drough through.

29 The Railroad: extract

Date Probably late 1850s. One of the best of the early poems celebrating the
novel delights of rail-travel: cf. Rossetti *London to Folkestone* (no. 114).
Publication *1859*. 2.

    An' while I went 'ithin a traïn,
    A-ridèn on athirt the plaïn,
    A-cleärèn swifter than a hound,
    On twin-laid rails, the zwimmèn ground;
5   I cast my eyes 'ithin a park,
    Upon a woak wi grey-white bark,
    An' while I kept his head my mark,
    The rest did wheel around en.

    An' when in life our love do cling
10   The clwosest round zome single thing,
    We then do vind that all the rest
    Do wheel roun' that, vor vu'st an' best;
    Zoo while our life do last, mid nought,
    But what is good an' feäir be sought,
15   In word or deed, or heart or thought,
    An' all the rest wheel round it.

4 zwimmèn ground he moves so fast the ground seems to swim beneath him.
6 woak oak.
8 did wheel] seemed wheelen *1859*.
12 vu'st first.

30 Leeburn Mill

Date Before 1859.
Publication *1859.*

Ov all the meäds wi shoals an' pools,
Where streams did sheäke the limber zedge,
An' milkèn vo'k did teäke their stools,
In evenèn zun-light under hedge:
5   Ov all the wears the brook did vill,
Or all the hatches where a sheet
O foam did leäp below woone's veet,
The pleäce vor me wer Leeburn Mill.

An' while below the mossy wheel
10   All day the foamèn stream did roar,
An' up in mill the floatèn meal
Did pitch upon the sheäkèn vloor.
We then could vind but vew han's still,
Or veet a-restèn off the ground,
15   An' seldom hear the merry sound
O geämes a-plaÿed at Leeburn Mill.

But when they let the stream goo free,
Bezide the drippèn wheel at rest,
An' leaves upon the poplar-tree
20   Wer dark avore the glowèn west;
An' when the clock, a-ringèn sh'ill,
Did slowly beät zome evenèn hour,
Oh! then 'ithin the leafy bow'r
Our tongues did run at Leeburn Mill.

25   An' when November's win' did blow,
Wi hufflèn storms along the plaîn,
An' blackened leaves did lie below
The neäked tree, a zoaked wi raïn,
I werden at a loss to vill
30   The darkest hour o raïny skies,
If I did vind avore my eyes
The feäces down at Leeburn Mill.

5 wears weirs.
11 floatèn floating.
21 sh'ill shrilly.
26 hufflèn blustering.
29 werden was not.   **vill** feel.

31 The Wife a-Lost

Date Composed probably after the death of his wife in 1852.
The dialect at once distances the experience (he wrote a moving poem on
her death in 'National English') and expresses a depth of feeling.
Publication *1859.*

Since I noo mwore do zee your feäce,
    Up steäirs or down below,
I'll zit me in the lwonesome pleäce,
    Where flat-boughed beech do grow:
5 Below the beeches' bough, my love,
    Where you did never come,
An' I don't look to meet ye now,
    As I do look at hwome.

Since you noo mwore be at my zide,
10   In walks in zummer het,
I'll goo alwone where mist do ride,
    Drough trees a-drippèn wet:
Below the raïn-wet bough, my love,
    Where you did never come,
15 An' I don't grieve to miss ye now,
    As I do grieve at home.

Since now bezide my dinner-bwoard
    Your vaïce do never sound,
I'll eat the bit I can avword,
20   A-vield upon the ground;
Below the darksome bough, my love,
    Where you did never dine,
An' I don't grieve to miss ye now,
    As I at hwome do pine.

25 Since I do miss your vaïce an' feäce
    In praÿer at eventide,
I'll praÿ wi woone sad vaïce vor greäce
    To goo where you do bide;
Above the tree an' bough, my love,
30   Where you be gone avore,
An' be a-waïtèn vor me now,
    To come vor evermwore.

1–8 Cf. Hardy's *Wessex Heights* for a similar avoidance of haunted territory.

32 The Zilver-Weed

Date Some time before 1862.
Publication *1862*.

    The zilver-weed upon the green,
      Out where my sons an' daughters plaÿed,
    Had never time to bloom between
      The litty steps o bwoy an' maïd.
5   But rwose-trees down along the wall,
      That then were'all the maïden's ceäre,
    An' all a-trimmed an' traïned, did bear
      Their bloomèn buds vrom spring to fall.

    But now the zilver leaves do show
10   To zummer day their goolden crown,
    Wi noo swift shoe-zoles' litty blow,
      In merry plaÿ to beät em down.
    An' where vor years zome busy hand
      Did traîn the rwoses wide an' high;
15   Now woone by woone the trees do die,
      An' vew of all the row do stand.

1 zilver-weed genus *Potentilla:* goose-grass.
4 litty light and brisk.
10 goolden a pronunciation widespread in C18: W. H. Dunn *James Anthony Froude* (1961) 1.13: '*goold* she [F.'s grandmother] called it'.
12 em] en *1862*.

33 Woak Hill

Date Some time before 1862.
    Francis Palgrave (*NR* Feb. 1887 833) compares the assonances without rhyme to W. Collins's *Ode to Evening*. The poetic form is the Persian 'pearl': all the second words in the last line of the stanza rhyme. B. experimented with several Persian forms.
Publication *1862*.

    When sycamore leaves were a-spreadèn,
      Green-ruddy, in hedges,
    Bezide the red doust o the ridges,
      A-dried at Woak Hill;
5   I packed up my goods all a-sheenèn
      Wi long years o handlen,
    On dousty red wheels ov a waggon,
      To ride at Woak Hill.

The brown thatchen ruf o the dwellèn,
10   I then were a-leävèn,
Had sheltered the sleek head o Meäry,
     My bride at Woak Hill.

But now vor zome years, her light voot-vall
     'S a-lost vrom the vloorèn,
15   Too soon vor my jaÿ an' my children,
     She died at Woak Hill.

But still I do think that, in soul,
     She do hover about us;
To ho vor her motherless children,
20   Her pride at Woak Hill.

Zoo – lest she should tell me hereafter
     I stole off 'ithout her,
An' left her, uncalled at house-riddèn,
     To bide at Woak Hill –

25   I called her so fondly, wi lippèns
     All soundless to others,
An' took her wi aïr-reachèn hand
     To my zide at Woak Hill.

On the road I did look round, a talkèn
30   To light at my shoulder,
An' then led her in at the door-way,
     Miles wide vrom Woak Hill.

An' that's why vo'k thought, vor a season,
     My mind were a-wandrèn
35   Wi sorrow, when I were so sorely
     A-tried at Woak Hill.

But no; that my Meäry mid never
     Behold herzelf slighted,
I wanted to think that I guided
40   My guide vrom Woak Hill.

11 Had] Vu'st *1862.*
13 zome] o leate *1862.*
19 ho be anxious.
21 Zoo So.
23 house-riddèn leaving the house.
25 lippèns speeches: cf. Hardy (No. 139 p. 487 below).
27 air-reachèn ever reaching.

34 The Wind at the Door

Date 1867.
Publication *Dorset County Chronicle 1867, 1906.*

As day did darken on the dewless grass
  There still wi nwone a-come by me,
  To staÿ a-while at hwome by me;
  Within the house, all dumb by me,
5 I zot me sad as the eventide did pass.

An' there a win'-blast shook the rattlèn door.
  An' seemed, as win' did mwone without,
  As if my Jeäne, alwone without,
  A-stannèn on the stone without,
10 Wer there a-come wi happiness oonce mwore.

I went to door; an' out vrom trees above
  My head, upon the blast by me,
  Sweet blossoms wer a-cast by me,
  As if my love, a-past by me,
15 Did fling em down – a token ov her love.

'Sweet blossoms o the tree where I do murn,'
  I thought, 'if you did blow vor her,
  Vor apples that should grow vor her,
  A-vallèn down below vor her,
20 O then how happy I should zee you kern.'

But no. Too soon I voun my charm abroke.
  Noo comely sould in white like her –
  Noo soul a-steppèn light like her –
  An' nwone o comely height like her –
25 Went by; but all my grief ageän awoke.

5 *1962* omits 'the', following B.'s fair copies, thus making the line metrically regular.
20 kern grow into fruit.

35 The Geate A-Vallen to

Date 13 Oct. 1885. B.'s daughter Lucy recalls him dictating his last poem: 'It was a cold evening, and he was sitting in his easy chair by the fire with his fur-lined cloak and red cap and his feet in a fur foot muff. The firelight fell warm on his face, and even dimly brought out the figures in the ancient tapestry behind his bed' (Baxter 316).
The text follows *1962*, which brought this poem into line with B.'s spelling of the 1850s.
Publication Baxter, *1906.*

[35] William Barnes

    In the zunsheen ov our zummers
        Wi the haytime now a-come,
    How busy were we out a-vield
        Wi vew a-left at hwome,
5   When waggons rumbled out ov yard
        Red wheeled, wi body blue,
    And back behind em loudly slammed
        The geäte a-vallèn to.

    Drough day sheen ov how many years
10   The geäte ha' now a-swung,
    Behind the veet of vull-grown men
        And vootsteps of the young.
    Drough years o days it swung to us
        Behind each little shoe,
15   As we tripped lightly on avore
        The geäte a-vallèn to.

    In evenèn time o starry night
        How mother zot at hwome
    And kept her bleäzen vire bright
20   Till father should ha' come,
    An' how she quickened up an' smiled,
        And stirred her vire anew,
    To hear the trampèn ho'ses' steps
        And geäte a-vallèn to.

25   There's moon-sheen now in nights o fall
        When leaves be brown vrom green,
    When to the slammen o the geäte
        Our Jenny's ears be keen,
    When the wold dog do wag his taîl,
30   And Jeän could tell to who,
    As he do come in drough the geäte,
        The geäte a-vallèn to.

    An' oft do come a saddened hour
        When there must goo away
35   One well-beloved to our heart's core,
        Vor long, perhaps for aye:

8 'When finished he said, "Observe that word 'geäte', that is how King Alfred would have pronounced it, and how it was called in the *Saxon Chronicle*, which tells us of King Edward, who was slain at Corfe's geäte... Ah! if the court had not been moved to London, then the speech of King Alfred – of which our Dorset is the remnant – would have been the Court language of to-day, and it would have been more like Anglo-Saxon than it is now"' (Baxter 317).
18 zot sat.

An' oh! it is a touchèn thing
The lovèn heart must rue,
To hear behind his last farewell
40   The geäte a-vallèn to.

Elizabeth Barrett Browning

Life and writings Elizabeth Barrett was born at Burn Hall, Durham in 1806, but her childhood upbringing was in the beautiful setting of Hope End, near Ledbury in Herefordshire. She was a precocious child, who read Homer in Greek at eight and completed an epic, *The Battle of Marathon*, at twelve. When E.B. was about twenty-two her mother died. Her father ran into financial difficulties, which necessitated leaving Hope End and moving first to Sidmouth then to London. During her teens E.B. became an invalid, suffering possibly from tuberculosis. Living in 50 Wimpole Street she remained locked away from the world from 1838 to 1846, interrupted only by a tragic interval in Torquay when her favourite brother was drowned at sea. Her father was tyrannical, and irrationally opposed to the marriages of her numerous brothers and sisters. In this close, even claustrophobic, atmosphere, E.B.'s literary development continued. *Prometheus Bound* (a translation from Aeschylus) was published in 1833, *The Seraphim* and other poems in 1838, and *The Cry of the Children* in *Blackwood's Magazine*, Aug. 1834. She contributed to R. H. Horne's *A New Spirit of the Age* in 1844. The *Quarterly Review* of 1840 placed her second among the literary women of the time.

In 1845 the relationship with Robert Browning began. His interest was aroused, principally, by the fact that his poetry was mentioned, in company with Wordsworth's, Tennyson's and Howitt's, in *Lady Geraldine's Courtship*. He opened a correspondence with her, then a friendship, which began with the first meeting on 20 May 1845 and led in turn to courtship and marriage. At the time of her wedding, on 12 Sept. 1846, E.B. was almost twenty years past the age of majority, but biographers have always treated the marriage as an elopement. Considering the romance and secretiveness of the affair that is more or less what it was. The couple went to live in Italy, first to Pisa then to Florence; and except for occasional visits to England they spent the rest of their married lives there. In 1849 their son Pen was born. Their house, Casa Guidi, was immortalized in E.B.B.'s *Casa Guidi Windows* (1851). Her other major poetic productions are *Sonnets from the Portuguese* (1850), *Aurora Leigh* (1857) and *Poems before Congress* (1860). She died in Florence on 30 June 1861.

Criticism The state of recent scholarship is reviewed by M. Timko in Faverty (122–36). It has been dominated by her correspondence, which, as one might expect from a literary invalid, is extensive. The standard biography is G. B. Taplin's *The Life of E.B.B.* (1957). The life has always been of interest, and

far more has been written on it so far than on the poetry. One important
critical study is A. Hayter's *Mrs Browning: a poet's work and its setting*
(1963). There seems at the moment no scholarly consensus on her reputation. Her life intruded into her poetry at almost every stage, so that
critical judgement invariably involves itself with the complicated tangle of
strengths and weaknesses in the life – the impetuosity, idealism, ingenuity,
enthusiasm, and independence. Her life and her poetry exhibit many of the
vices and virtues of her husband's, but in the absence of a first-class
disinterested artistic consciousness her poetic status lags a considerable way
behind his. Since her major work is the long novel-poem *Aurora Leigh*,
short anthology extracts fail to do justice to her most characteristically
individual mode.

Editions The standard edition is C. Porter and H. A. Clarke's *Complete
Works of E.B.B.* (1900).

Abbreviations

1850	*Poems* (1850).
1853	*Poems* (1853).
1856	*Poems* (1856).
1857	*Aurora Leigh* (1857).
Letters	*The Letters of E.B.B.* (1897), F. G. Kenyon, ed.

36 Sonnets from the Portuguese: extracts

Date 1845–6; in the MS. '1846, Sept.' is written after the last sonnet. Robert
Browning got wind of the cycle's existence 19 July 1846: 'I wish, dearest, you
would tell me precisely what you have written – all my affectionate pride in
you rises at once when I think of your poetry' (Kintner *Letters* 2.886–7).
Elizabeth, alluding to *Eccles.* 3.1–8, replied: 'You shall see some day at Pisa
what I will not show you now. Does not Solomon say that "there is a time
to read what is written" (*ibid.* 2.892–3). In fact Robert first saw the
sonnets, which celebrated E.B.B.'s love for him, at Bagni di Lucca in the
summer of 1849: 'Yes, that was a strange, heavy crown, that wreath of
Sonnets, put on me one morning unawares, three years after it had been
twined, – all this delay, because I happened early to say something against
putting one's loves into verse: then again, I said something else on the other
side, one evening at Lucca, – and next morning she said hesitatingly "Do
you know I once wrote some poems about *you*?" – and then – "There they
are if you care to see them," – and there was the little Book I have here –
with the last Sonnet dated two days before our marriage.' (R. Curle (ed.)
*Robert Browning and Julia Wedgwood: a broken friendship as revealed in
their letters* (1937) 114).

Title The title is purposely ambiguous, suggesting that the poems are
translated from Portuguese and that they are from the poet Camoëns, who
was left the riband from Catarina's hair (see E.B.B.'s *Poems* (1844) *Catarina
to Camoëns*). In broad terms the theme of the 44 poems is the same as that
of Shakespeare's sonnets 1–126: a self-abasing poet celebrates love for a
superior being, but E.B.B., sometimes self-pitying, without the self-assurance
that Shakespeare demonstrates in his art, and without the touch of pique at

the careless beloved, has less of the complexity and tautness of structure that makes her predecessor far superior. There is a privacy and a confessional authenticity about the cycle that conditions our response in a very particular way. At her best she thinks by images rather in the manner of the great C16 and C17 love poets.

Manuscripts There are three manuscripts: *B.L.* (in the British Library; given by Elizabeth to Robert); *H.* (Houghton Library, the copy from which the first printing was set up); *P.M.* (Pierpont Morgan Library; the earliest, but stopping at no. 29 and without 17 and 18).

Publication *1850, 1853, 1856.* In 1894 E. Gosse brought out an edition, claiming it to be a reprint of a private edition published in Reading in 1847; J. Carter and G. Pollard demonstrated in *An Enquiry into the Nature of Certain Nineteenth Century Pamphlets* (1934) that this was a forgery.

The best edition is that of F. Ratchford and D. Fulton (New York, 1950).

1

    I thought once how Theocritus had sung
      Of the sweet years, the dear and wished for years,
      Who each one in a gracious hand appears
    To bear a gift for mortals, old and young:
5   And, as I mused it in his antique tongue,
      I saw, in gradual vision through my tears,
      The sweet, sad years, the melancholy years,
    Those of my own life, who by turns had flung
    A shadow across me. Straightway I was 'ware,
10   So weeping, how a mystic shape did move
    Behind me, and drew me backward by the hair;
      And a voice said in mastery, while I strove,
    'Guess now who holds thee?' – 'Death!' I said, but, there,
    The silver answer rang, – 'Not death, but Love.'

Title *Death or Love* MSS.
1 Theocritus first Greek pastoral poet, *c.* 310–*c.* 250 B.C.
2 the sweet years perhaps referring to *Idylls* 15 lines 104–5: 'The Seasons, the Seasons, full slow they go and come, | But some sweet things for all they bring.'
12 And a voice cried aloud, the while I strove, *P.M.*

3

    Unlike are we, unlike, O princely heart!
      Unlike our uses and our destinies.
      Our ministering two angels look surprise
    On one another, as they strike athwart
5   Their wings in passing. Thou, bethink thee, art
      A guest for queens to social pageantries,

Title *King's Courting B.L.*
6 A guest for queens to masques and pageantries, – *P.M.*

[36] Elizabeth Barrett Browning

  With gages from a hundred brighter eyes
  Than tears even can make mine, to ply thy part
  Of chief musician. What hast *thou* to do
10 With looking from the lattice-lights at me,
  A poor, tired, wandering singer, singing through
  The dark, and leaning up a cypress tree?
  The chrism is on thine head, – on mine, the dew, –
  And Death must dig the level where these agree.

7 hundred] thousand *P.M.*
13 chrism consecrated oil.
14 'the lover will be equal with the beloved only in death.'

13

  And wilt thou have me fashion into speech
   The love I bear thee, finding words enough,
   And hold the torch out, while the winds are rough,
  Between our faces, to cast light on each? –
5 I drop it at thy feet. I cannot teach
   My hand to hold my spirit so far off
   From myself – me – that I should bring thee proof
  In words, of love hid in me out of reach.
  Nay, let the silence of my womanhood
10 Commend my woman-love to the belief, –
  Seeing that I stand unwon, however wooed,
   And rend the garments of my life, in brief,
  By a most dauntless, voiceless fortitude,
  Lest one touch of this heart convey its grief.

Title *Love's Expression P.M.*
2 words the 'speech' of line 1 suggests spoken words, but there is the implication (line 6) of the written word and the poem, and hence of the traditional subject in love poetry that the unexpressed word may be the best token of love (Shakespeare, Sonnet 73, for instance).
11 And that I stand unwon though not unwooed – *P.M.*

22

  When our two souls stand up erect and strong,
   Face to face, silent, drawing nigh and nigher,
   Until the lengthening wings break into fire
  At either curvèd point, – what bitter wrong

Title *Love's Refuge P.M.*
1–4 *The Explicator* 1 (1942) 24 suggests cherubim on ark of the covenant facing each other. See *Exod.* 25 and *Isa.* 6.1–7.
3 lengthening] widening *P.M.*

42

5   Can the earth do to us, that we should not long
      Be here contented ? Think. In mounting higher,
    The angels would press on us and aspire
    To drop some golden orb of perfect song
    Into our deep, dear silence. Let us stay
    Rather on earth, Belovèd, – where the unfit
    Contrarious moods of men recoil away
    And isolate pure spirits, and permit
    A place to stand and love in for a day,
    With darkness and the death-hour rounding it.

14 rounding encircling.

32

    The first time that the sun rose on thine oath
      To love me, I looked forward to the moon
      To slacken all those bonds which seemed too soon
    And quickly tied to make a lasting troth.
5   Quick-loving hearts, I thought, may quickly loathe;
      And, looking on myself, I seemed not one
      For such man's love! – more like an out-of-tune
    Worn viol, a good singer would be wroth
    To spoil his song with, and which, snatched in haste,
10   Is laid down at the first ill-sounding note.
    I did not wrong myself so, but I placed
      A wrong on *thee*. For perfect strains may float
    'Neath master-hands, from instruments defaced,
    And great souls, at one stroke, may do and doat.

39

    Because thou hast the power and own'st the grace
      To look through and behind this mask of me
      (Against which years have beat thus blanchingly
    With their rains), and behold my soul's true face,
5   The dim and weary witness of life's race, –
      Because thou hast the faith and love to see,
      Through that same soul's distracting lethargy,
    The patient angel waiting for a place
    In the new Heavens! – because nor sin nor woe,
10   Nor God's infliction, nor death's neighbourhood,
    Nor all which others viewing, turn to go,
      Nor all which makes me tired of all, self-viewed –
    Nothing repels thee,... Dearest, teach me so
    To pour out gratitude, as thou dost, good!

11 Grammar unclear. What E.B. meant to say, perhaps, was: 'Nor all those qualities which, when seen by other people, make them turn from me and go away.'

[36] Elizabeth Barrett Browning

42

Publication omitted from *Sonnets from the Portuguese* in *1850* and *1853* since the first line (from *Poems*, 1844) would have disclosed the author. Restored in *1856*.

'My future will not copy fair my past' –
  I wrote that once; and thinking at my side
  My ministering life-angel justified
The word by his appealing look upcast
5 To the white throne of God, I turned at last,
  And there, instead, saw thee, not unallied
  To angels in thy soul! Then I, long tried
By natural ills, received the comfort fast,
  While budding, at thy sight, my pilgrim's staff
10   Gave out green leaves with morning dews impearled.
I seek no copy now of life's first half:
  Leave here the pages with long musing curled,
  And write me new my future's epigraph,
New angel mine, unhoped for in the world!

Title *Future and Past 1850, 1853.*
8 By natural ills... My heart beat wild and fast – *B.L.* canc.
12 The blots will be there on the pages curled! *B.L.* canc.

43

How do I love thee? Let me count the ways.
  I love thee to the depth and breadth and height
  My soul can reach, when feeling out of sight
For the ends of being and ideal grace.
5 'I love thee to the level of everyday's
  Most quiet need, by sun and candle-light.
  I love thee freely, as men strive for right;
I love thee purely, as they turn from praise.
  I love thee with the passion put to use
10   In my old griefs, and with my childhood's faith.
I love thee with a love I seemed to lose
  With my lost saints, – I love thee with the breath,
  Smiles, tears, of all my life! and, if God choose,
I shall but love thee better after death.

Title *A Confession H.* canc.
12 lost saints dead brothers and sisters.

44

44

Belovèd, thou hast brought me many flowers
Plucked in the garden, all the summer through
And winter, and it seemed as if they grew
In this close room, nor missed the sun and showers.
5   So, in the like name of that love of ours,
Take back these thoughts which here unfolded too,
And which on warm and cold days I withdrew
From my heart's ground. Indeed, those beds and bowers
Be overgrown with bitter weeds and rue,
10   And wait thy weeding; yet here's eglantine,
Here's ivy! – take them, as I used to do
Thy flowers, and keep them where they shall not pine.
Instruct thine eyes to keep their colours true,
And tell thy soul, their roots are left in mine.

4 this close room in the Barrett house in Wimpole Street.
9 rue traditionally associated with repentance: *R II* 3.4.105 'the sour herb of Grace'. However in Shakespeare's next line the gardener extends it to pity, 'rue, even for ruth', and E.B. develops it further to 'self-pity'.
10 eglantine an emblem of poetry in Mrs L. Burke *The Illustrated Language of Flowers* (1856).
11 ivy an emblem of fidelity in Mrs Burke; for Rossetti associated with memory: letter to Leyland 4 Oct. 1873, quoted by Val Prinsep in *Art Journal* 54 (1892) 252.

37 Aurora Leigh: extract

Date 12 Apr. 1853 E.B.B. informed Mrs Jameson that she was at work on 'the novel or romance I have been hankering after so long, written in blank verse, in the autobiographical form'; she continues: 'It is intensely modern, crammed from the times...as far as my strength will allow.' (*Letters* 2.112). The poem is the story of Aurora Leigh's tortured love-affair with her cousin Romney Leigh, and the complicated tangle they are caught in with Lady Waldemar and the daughter of the people Marian Erle. There are similarities to Madame de Staël's *Corinne* (1817), Eugène Sue's *Mystères de Paris* (1842–3) and Elizabeth Gaskell's *Ruth* (1853). When finished it was longer than the *Aeneid* and *Paradise Lost*.

Some contemporary readers were highly impressed: Ruskin called it 'the greatest *poem* in the English language, unsurpassed by anything but Shakespeare', adding that he was not making the judgement in a state of excitement (*Works* 36.247); Landor and Swinburne were also very enthusiastic. But reviews in magazines were less favourable. Taplin (310–47) is frequently critical of the work. V. Woolf expresses grave reservations in 'Aurora Leigh', *The Common Reader* (1933) 208: 'Ordinary daylight, current gossip, the usual traffic of human beings left her exhausted, ecstatic, and dazzled into a state where she saw so much and felt so much that she did

[37] Elizabeth Barrett Browning

not altogether know what she felt or what she saw.' This was E.B.B.'s last major work.

Publication *1857*; this extract describes the early education of Aurora Leigh.

FIRST BOOK

I learnt the collects and the catechism,
The creeds, from Athanasius back to Nice,
The Articles, the Tracts *against* the times
395 (By no means Buonaventure's *Prick of Love*),
And various popular synopses of
Inhuman doctrines never taught by John.
Because she liked instructed piety.
I learnt my complement of Classic French
400 (Kept pure of Balzac and neologism)
And German also, since she liked a range
Of liberal education, – tongues, not books.
I learnt a little algebra, a little
Of the mathematics, – brushed with extreme flounce
405 The circle of the sciences, because
She misliked women who are frivolous.
I learnt the royal genealogies
Of Oviedo, the internal laws
Of the Burmese empire, – by how many feet
410 Mount Chimborazo outsoars Teneriffe,
What navigable river joins itself
To Lara, and what census of the year five
Was taken at Klagenfurt, – because she liked
A general insight into useful facts.

392 collects in the Anglican Book of Common Prayer.
393 The Athanasian Creed was a Christian confession of faith; probably not composed by Athanasius (d. 373). The Nicene Creed was a statement of Christian belief based on the formulation of the first Council of Nicaea in 325.
394 The Articles the thirty-nine Articles: summaries of the dogmatic tenets of the Anglican Church.   **the Tracts** probably the ninety tracts, written by the members of the High Church Oxford Movement (1833–41); titled *Tracts for the Times*: they challenged liberal theology.
395 St Bonaventure (1217–74), no longer regarded as the author of *Stimulus divini amoris*, Englished by Walter Hilton (d. 1396) as *The Goad of Love*, and B. Lewis A. as *The Goade of Divine Love* (Douai, 1642), but never as *The Prick of Love*.
408 Oviedo Province in N. Spain.
410 Mount Chimborazo in Ecuador (20,561 feet).   **Teneriffe** the Pico de Teide is 12,198 feet; cf. Milton *Paradise Lost* 4.987–8: 'Like Teneriff or Atlas unremoved; | His [Satan's] stature reached the sky'. See P. Heylin *Cosmographie* (1652) 4.88 and 5.758–9.
412 Lara Province of N.W. Venezuela; the River Tocuyo flows from it.

415 I learnt much music, – such as would have been
     As quite impossible in Johnson's day
     As still it might be wished – fine sleights of hand
     And unimagined fingering, shuffling off
     The hearer's soul through hurricanes of notes
420 To a noisy Tophet; and I drew...costumes
     From French engravings, nereids neatly draped
     (With smirks of simmering godship): I washed in
     Landscapes from nature (rather say, washed out).
     I danced the polka and Cellarius,
425 Spun glass, stuffed birds, and modelled flowers in wax,
     Because she liked accomplishments in girls.
     I read a score of books on womanhood
     To prove, if women do not think at all,
     They may teach thinking (to a maiden aunt
430 Or else the author), – books that boldly assert
     Their right of comprehending husband's talk
     When not too deep, and even of answering
     With pretty 'may it please you,' or 'so it is,' –
     Their rapid insight and fine aptitude,
435 Particular worth and general missionariness,
     As long as they keep quiet by the fire
     And never say 'no' when the world says 'ay,'
     For that is fatal, – their angelic reach
     Of virtue, chiefly used to sit and darn
440 And fatten household sinners, – their, in brief,
     Potential faculty in everything
     Of abdicating power in it: she owned
     She liked a woman to be womanly,
     And English women, she thanked God and sighed
445 (Some people always sigh in thanking God),
     Were models to the universe. And last
     I learnt cross-stitch, because she did not like
     To see me wear the night with empty hands
     A-doing nothing. So, my shepherdess
450 Was something after all (the pastoral saints
     Be praised for't), leaning lovelorn with pink eyes
     To match her shoes, when I mistook the silks;
     Her head uncrushed by that round weight of hat
     So strangely similar to the tortoise-shell
455 Which slew the tragic poet.
                              By the way,
     The works of women are symbolical.

420 Tophet hell *OED* 3b.
455 the tragic poet Aeschylus killed by a tortoise dropped by an eagle.

[37] Elizabeth Barrett Browning

We sew, sew, prick our fingers, dull our sight,
Producing what? A pair of slippers, sir,
To put on when you're weary – or a stool
460 To stumble over and vex you … 'curse that stool!'
Or else at best, a cushion, where you lean
And sleep, and dream of something we are not
But would be for your sake. Alas, alas!
This hurts most, this — that, after all, we are paid
465 The worth of our work, perhaps.
                       In looking down
Those years of education (to return)
I wonder if Brinvilliers suffered more
In the water-torture … flood succeeding flood
To drench the incapable throat and split the veins …
470 Than I did. Certain of your feebler souls
Go out in such a process; many pine
To a sick, inodorous light; my own endured:
I had relations in the Unseen, and drew
The elemental nutriment and heat
475 From nature, as earth feels the sun at nights,
Or as a babe sucks surely in the dark.
I kept the life thrust on me, on the outside
Of the inner life with all its ample room
For heart and lungs, for will and intellect
480 Inviolable by conventions. God,
I thank thee for that grace of thine!
                           At first
I felt no life which was not patience, – did
The thing she bade me, without heed to a thing
Beyond it, sat in just the chair she placed,
485 With back against the window, to exclude
The sight of the great lime-tree on the lawn,
Which seemed to have come on purpose from the woods
To bring the house a message, – ay, and walked
Demurely in her carpeted low rooms,
490 As if I should not, hearkening my own steps,
Misdoubt I was alive.

467 **Brinvilliers** See notes for no. 62.

48

Alfred Tennyson

Life and Writings Alfred Tennyson was born in the small and remote village of Somersby in the Lincolnshire Wolds on 6 Aug. 1809. His early environment was bleak and lonely, with the rarely calm North Sea only seven miles away. T.'s mother Elizabeth was a gentle and pious lady, who had twelve children in all; his father George, the rector of the parish, was a cultivated man, with a large library, but his proneness to manic-depressive states and to alcoholism cast a gloomy shadow over the family. T.'s grandfather, the owner of Bayons Manor near Tealby, disinherited his father (the eldest son) in favour of the second son Charles, who subsequently became a staunch establishment man, took the name d'Eyncourt, and rebuilt Bayons in the latest neogothic style. T.'s side of the family became the poor relations. But time has its revenges: Bayons is now a ruin and T.'s work lives on.

The society in which the child moved was the immediate family; he was especially close to his elder brother Charles. There were four unsatisfactory years at Louth Grammar School; but most of the tuition took place at home. T. was a precocious child who covered 'two sides of a slate with Thomsonian blank verse in praise of flowers' when he was about eight. At twelve he wrote an epic, in the style of Scott, of 6,000 lines, and at fourteen a blank verse drama *The Devil and the Lady* (first published in 1930), followed a year or two later by *The Coach of Death*. In April 1827 Charles and Alfred published *Poems by Two Brothers* (though there were also contributions from Frederick (b. 1807)). T.'s upbringing and literary taste were characterized by a great breadth of culture: the classics, Augustan and Romantic English literature, and a good deal of miscellaneous, cultivated learning; but the local vigour of the ordinary Lincolnshire people also left its mark, as one sees in the lively poems below: Nos. 54 and 55.

In February 1828 Charles and Alfred matriculated at Trinity College, Cambridge. Like Wordsworth before him, he was far from happy with the university, and wrote to an aunt: 'The country is so disgustingly level, the revelry of the place so monotonous, the studies of the University so uninteresting, so much matter of fact'. Nevertheless, he owed much to Cambridge, where he met Arthur Hallam and became a member of 'the Apostles', a group of advanced thinkers concerned with philosophical idealism, social reform, science and the arts, which had begun as a debating club in St John's, but assumed a place of importance in 1824 when John Sterling and F. D. Maurice became its guiding lights. When T. and Arthur Hallam joined the circle in January 1830 it helped them to focus their ideas. The friendship with Hallam was of central importance. He was the son of the distinguished historian Henry Hallam (1777–1859). At Eton he had been a close friend of Gladstone, and he came up to Trinity in June 1828 as the most promising youth of his generation – although there was disagreement as to how the promise was to be realized, especially since his *Remains* of 1834 ran to only 363 pages.

Alfred Tennyson

In 1831 T. left Cambridge without a degree. His only University honour was to win the Chancellor's Gold Medal with the poem *Timbuctoo* (1829). He was well on the way to being known as a poet after *Poems, Chiefly Lyrical* of 1830. Like poets of a much later time, he also had an experience of Spanish politics, going with Hallam to the Pyrenees to bring military instructions to northern insurrectionaries.

In 1831 T.'s father died. In 1832 he published another volume of poems – reviewed very harshly by J. W. Croker in the *Quarterly*. In 1833, Hallam became engaged to T.'s sister Emily (b. 1811), but by the end of September he was dead, struck down by a haemorrhage in Vienna. For the immediate impact of this on T. see headnote to No. 49. Over the next seventeen years he worked away at the poetic dramatization of his grief that became *In Memoriam*. In 1834 he fell in love with Rosa Baring, of the prosperous banking family, but became disillusioned with her in a year or so. His brother Charles married Louisa Sellwood in 1836. T.'s love for her sister Emily began at about this time. The courtship was almost as protracted as the writing of *In Memoriam*, since both the marriage and the publication of the poem took place in 1850. Meanwhile, throughout the 1830s, he was working away in silence (the period is known as 'the ten years' silence'), losing his fortune in a speculative investment in 1840–3, republishing his 1830 and 1832 poems (heavily revised), and publishing new poems in 1842. In 1847 *The Princess* made an interesting contribution to the women's rights debate.

T. was not, in the 1830s and 40s, a misanthropic, mystical recluse: he was developing friendships with Monckton Milnes, Edward Fitzgerald and Carlyle. The latter thought of him 'carrying a bit of Chaos about him...which he is manufacturing into Cosmos'.

The year 1850 was T.'s *annus mirabilis*: he married, published *In Memoriam* (anonymously, but it was widely known who had written it) and succeeded Wordsworth as Poet Laureate. In 1853 the family moved to Farringdon on the Isle of Wight, where he was virtually an institution for twenty years, visited by pilgrims of varying complexions, from Prince Albert to Swinburne, Jowett, Lewis Carroll, the Longfellows, Garibaldi, The Queen of the Sandwich Islands, and Clough's old tutor W. G. Ward. *The Charge of the Light Brigade* gave T. a currency far beyond the usual poetic circles. *Maud* (1855) is perhaps his last unquestionably great work, yet there were almost forty years of prolific poetic activity before him. T. and Browning were often held up as antipodal: they met rarely, and T. did not like or read Browning's work – though there was a memorable evening in 1855 when T. read *Maud*, and Browning read parts of *Men and Women* and D. G. Rossetti sketched T. T. and Browning, for different reasons, were both highly regarded by the Pre-Raphaelites who contributed thirty of the fifty-four illustrations to the famous Moxon edition of T.'s poems (1857).

In 1859 the *Idylls of the King* began to be published (*Enid, Vivien, Elaine* and *Guinevere*); by 1872 they were virtually complete. In 1862, his first audience with Queen Victoria placed the seal on his respectability and centrality in English cultural life. Fame brought drawbacks: when privacy became almost impossible on the tourist-haunted Isle of Wight, he fled (1868) to Aldworth, near Haslemere in Surrey.

An interesting late development was his venture into play-writing, with *Queen Mary* (1875), *Harold* (1876) and *The Cup* (1881). Like Browning's, his

Alfred Tennyson

plays were produced by the foremost actors of the day (Irving and Ellen Terry), but this has not guaranteed the immortality of either.

T. had two sons: Hallam (1852–1928) (the editor of the *Memoir*) and Lionel (1854–86).

Even in old age he continued to write. His career tends to give a static impression; beyond a certain point it is difficult to date works on internal evidence; he often dipped deep into his memory for a phrase that had been lurking there for years. On his deathbed, the proofs of *The Death of Oenone* were placed in his hand. He died on 6 October 1892, and was buried in Westminster Abbey.

Criticism However disregarded T. may have been in his early years he was after 1850 the best selling poet in the country, and in our century only John Betjeman and Dylan Thomas have rivalled his sales. He made different appeals to different sections of his audience: his poetry provided something for the aesthetes and proto-symbolists, something for the lovers of good stories (*Enoch Arden* (1864) was extremely popular), something for people who liked strong feeling, something for the votaries of profitable and improving meaning. Like Browning, before the First World War he was subjected to the 'Thought of Tennyson' type of criticism. His popularity suffered from the general decline that overtook much Victorian literature in the 1930s and 40s, but he has never been entirely eclipsed or forgotten, even though the grounds for his popularity have shifted. A book that marked something of a turning point in Tennyson criticism was Harold Nicolson's *Tennyson* of 1923, which debunked the characteristically Victorian and bardic features, and pointed to the darker, tormented, alienated aspect of his make-up. Nicolson may have overstated the case for the perturbed outcast, but most modern justifications of T. (when they are not recommending him as an ideal representative phenomenon for the scholar who wishes to get a feel for the age) are versions of that image: one names E. D. H. Johnson's *The Alien Vision* (Princeton U.P. 1952) and Christopher Ricks's *Tennyson* (1972).

The poems in the selection are all intense and powerful works; there is 'bad' Tennyson, but it is usually 'bad' not because of technical incompetence or slackness but because it is produced in the spirit of artifice, and has little or no discernible informing life. In all his poetry one observes great technical accomplishment and efficiency of execution. G. M. Hopkins, one of his severest detractors, summed it up thus in a letter to Alexander Baillie of 10 Sept. 1864: 'Great men, poets I mean, have each their own dialect as it were of Parnassian, formed generally as they go on writing, and at last...they see things in this Parnassian way and describe them in this Parnassian tongue, without further effort of inspiration.' Still, Hopkins was enough of a practising poet to realize how highly accomplished T.'s style was. There is much justice in Hopkin's criticism: the aura of artifice is intensified in T.'s poetry by the abundance of literary allusions in his work – some deliberate and integral to the final meaning, some half-echoes, half-reminiscences. For the world of the past, of dream, of reverie, which is so frequently T.'s chief haunt, the timbre of the verse is appropriate; but sometimes, when he is dealing with material that is, or should be, more familiar, the method operates as a smoke-screen. Often the sensitivity to sound, to rhythm, to imagery, drew him further and further into realms of artifice; but on other occasions, notably in *Maud*, and in certain powerful parts of *In Memoriam*,

Alfred Tennyson

that same sensitivity was deployed to produce effects so strong that we fail to notice, or fail to castigate, the skills of artifice.

T. gives an unexpected turn to the conventional image of the escapist artist by attempting to make use of scientific discoveries and hypotheses, not as subjects in themselves (as they had been in Erasmus Darwin's *Loves of the Plants* (1789)), but as correlatives and metaphors for his vision of mankind and of the ethical and religious spheres. In some ways the employment of scientific data is part of the Victorian endeavour to assemble a complete body of knowledge for oneself, if not to find God thereby, at least to find a workable substitute. T. is one of the last in that line, beginning with Renaissance poets, who wished to be in control of a wide range of general knowledge. Some aspects of his learning led him to the precision and detailed observation that one associates with the various realist movements of the C19, but others, curiously, have that distancing effect on his poetry which is equivalent to T.'s misty medievalism. It is a paradox that a body of knowledge which might at first glance seem to take one to the heart of vivid and definite facts is often, as employed by T., yet another agent of his dreamlike and evanescent world.

Tennyson scholarship is now very extensive. It is surveyed by E. D. H. Johnson in Faverty 34–80. Johnson's own *The Alien Vision* is an important work in establishing the place of alienation and reverie; other significant recent studies include J. Buckley *T.: The Growth of a Poet* (Boston 1960); D. J. Palmer ed. *T.* (1973); and J. Killham ed. *Critical Essays on the Poetry of T.* (1960). The language of T. is now rightly attracting renewed interest: see F. E. L. Priestly *Language and Structure in T.'s Poetry* (1973) and A. Sinfield *The Language of T.'s 'In Memoriam'* (1973).

Manuscripts and editions T.'s manuscripts are important for studying the processes of creation, but since T. lived so long, and saw his poetry into print so often he had time to get the best texts established, and the manuscripts tend not to help in arriving at a text. Of equal interest in gaining insights into methods of composition are the trial editions – privately printed volumes in which T. was able to see what his works would look like in type. A full discussion of the MSS. is in *1969* xviii–xx.

The standard edition is the Eversley (9 vols. 1907–8) ed. Hallam Lord Tennyson, but any serious scholar will find C. Ricks's edition in the Longmans Annotated Poets indispensable.

Abbreviations

1830	*Poems, Chiefly Lyrical* (1830).
1833	*Poems* (1833) (published Dec. 1832).
1842	*Poems* (1842).
1850	*In Memoriam* (1850).
1855	*Maud, and Other Poems* (1855).
1864	*Enoch Arden and Other Poems* (1864).
1870	*The Holy Grail and Other Poems* (1870).
1872	*Works* (1872–3).
1889	*Demeter and Other Poems* (1889).
1969	*The Poems of T.* ed. C. B. Ricks (1969).
Memoir	Hallam Lord Tennyson *Alfred Lord Tennyson: A Memoir* (1897).
Critical Heritage	*T.: The Critical Heritage* (1967), ed. J. D. Jump.

Buckley	J. H. Buckley *Tennyson: The Growth of a Poet* (1960).
Killham	J. Killham *Tennyson and 'the Princess'* (1958).
Palmer	*Tennyson* (1973) ed. D. J. Palmer.
Rader	R. W. Rader *Tennyson's 'Maud': the biographical genesis* (1963).
Ricks	C. Ricks *Tennyson* (1972).
Sir Charles Tennyson	Sir Charles Tennyson *Alfred Tennyson* (1949).

The main MSS. cited are:

H. Lpr	Harvard Loosepaper
H. MS.	Harvard Manuscript
H. Nbk.	Harvard Notebook
Hn. MS.	Huntington Library Manuscript
Fitzw. MS.	Fitzwilliam Museum Manuscript
L. MS.	Lincoln Manuscript
T. MS.	Trinity College Cambridge Manuscript
T. Nbk.	Trinity College Cambridge Manuscript
Y. MS.	Yale Manuscript.

38 Mariana

Date *c*. 1830.
Source The ostensible source and subject is Shakespeare's *Measure for Measure*, but there is a strong overlay of Keatsian sentiment and mood, especially from *Isabella*. Shakespeare's subject interpreted by way of T.'s atmosphere appealed to the Pre-Raphaelites, and possibly influenced Millais's painting of 1851. T. probably invented the stanza form.
Publication *1830*.

> *Mariana in the moated grange*
> *(Measure for Measure)*
> With blackest moss the flower-plots
>   Were thickly crusted, one and all:
> The rusted nails fell from the knots
>   That held the pear to the gable-wall.
> 5   The broken sheds looked sad and strange:
>   Unlifted was the clinking latch;
>   Weeded and worn the ancient thatch
> Upon the lonely moated grange.
>   She only said, 'My life is dreary,
> 10   He cometh not,' she said;
>   She said, 'I am aweary, aweary,
>   I would that I were dead!'

Epigraph T. writes: 'The *moated grange* was no particular grange, but one which rose to the music of Shakespeare's words [in 3.1. 212ff]'.
4 pear] peach *1830–1860*. T. writes: '"peach" spoils the desolation of the picture. It is not a characteristic of the scenery I had in mind.'

Her tears fell with the dews at even;
    Her tears fell ere the dews were dried;
15 She could not look on the sweet heaven,
    Either at morn or eventide.
After the flitting of the bats,
    When thickest dark did trance the sky,
    She drew her casement-curtain by,
20 And glanced athwart the glooming flats.
      She only said, 'The night is dreary,
        He cometh not,' she said;
      She said, 'I am aweary, aweary,
        I would that I were dead!'

25 Upon the middle of the night,
    Waking she heard the night-fowl crow:
The cock sung out an hour ere light:
    From the dark fen the oxen's low
Came to her: without hope of change,
30 In sleep she seemed to walk forlorn,
    Till cold winds woke the gray-eyed morn
About the lonely moated grange.
      She only said, 'The day is dreary,
        He cometh not,' she said;
35   She said, 'I am aweary, aweary,
        I would that I were dead!'

About a stone-cast from the wall
    A sluice with blackened waters slept,
And o'er it many, round and small,
40 The clustered marish-mosses crept.
Hard by a poplar shook alway,
    All silver-green with gnarlèd bark:
    For leagues no other tree did mark
The level waste, the rounding gray.
45   She only said, 'My life is dreary,

---

18 trance throw into a trance. T.'s is the earliest figurative use in *OED*.
25 *Meas.* 4.1.35: 'Upon the heavy middle of the night'; and Keats's *Eve of St. Agnes* line 49: 'Upon the honey'd middle of the night'.
31 gray-eyed morn cf. *Rom.* 2.3.1.
36–44 Kingsley *Alton Locke* (1850) Ch. 9 cites the impact of this new type of beauty on the common man: '"I always knew there was something beautiful, wonderful, sublime in those flowery dykes of Battersea-field; in the long gravelly sweeps of that lone tidal shore; and here was a man who had put them into words for me!"'
40 marish-mosses 'the little marsh-moss lumps that float on the surface of water' (T.'s note).

He cometh not,' she said;
She said, 'I am aweary, aweary,
I would that I were dead!'

And even when the moon was low,
50   And the shrill winds were up and away,
In the white curtain, to and fro,
        She saw the gusty shadow sway.
But when the moon was very low,
        And wild winds bound within their cell,
55   The shadow of the poplar fell
Upon her bed, across her brow.
            She only said, 'The night is dreary,
            He cometh not,' she said;
            She said, 'I am aweary, aweary,
60   I would that I were dead!'

All day within the dreamy house,
        The doors upon their hinges creaked;
The blue fly sung in the pane; the mouse
        Behind the mouldering wainscot shrieked,
65   Or from the crevice peered about.
        Old faces glimmered through the doors,
        Old footsteps trod the upper floors,
Old voices called her from without.
            She only said, 'My life is dreary,
70   He cometh not,' she said;
            She said, 'I am aweary, aweary,
            I would that I were dead!'

The sparrow's chirrup on the roof,
        The slow clock ticking, and the sound
75   Which to the wooing wind aloof
        The poplar made, did all confound
Her sense, but most she loathed the hour
        When the thick-moted sunbeam lay
        Athwart the chambers, and the day

---

54 their cell the cave of Aeolus; Virgil *Aen.* 1.52–63 describes his freeing the winds.
55 Many recent critics interpret the shadow as phallic; e.g. J. Wordsworth *EC* 24 (1974) 357.
63–4 Cf. the empty house in *Maud* 257–60 (p. 143), with its 'shrieking rush of the wainscot mouse'; and T. S. Eliot *East Coker* 1.12 and *Little Gidding* 2.6.
75 wooing possibly a pun on whooing.
78 thick-moted densely filled with specks.

80   Was sloping toward his western bower.
        Then, said she, 'I am very dreary,
            He will not come,' she said;
        She wept, 'I am aweary, aweary,
            Oh God, that I were dead!'

80 Downsloped was westering his bower. *1830*. Cf. Milton *Lycidas* line 31:
'has sloped his westering wheel'.

39 Dualisms

Date An early experimental poem.
T. had second thoughts about the use of unhyphenated compound words,
and this led to the suppression of the poem (*Memoir* I. 50). It is unlikely that
Hopkins knew this poem, yet some of the effects in it are reminiscent of his,
and provide a further illustration of H.'s relation to the experimental line of
Victorian poetry.
Publication *1830*; (not reprinted during Tennyson's lifetime).

        Two bees within a chrystal flowerbell rockèd
            Hum a lovelay to the westwind at noontide.
            Both alike, they buzz together,
            Both alike, they hum together
5   Through and through the flowered heather.
        Where in a creeping cove the wave unshockèd
            Lays itself calm and wide,
            Over a stream two birds of glancing feather
            Do woo each other, carolling together.
10   Both alike, they glide together,
                Side by side;
            Both alike, they sing together,
        Arching blueglossed necks beneath the purple weather.

        Two children lovelier than love adown the lea are singing,
15   As they gambol, lilygarlands ever stringing:
            Both in blosmwhite silk are frockèd:
            Like, unlike, they roam together
            Under a summervault of golden weather;
            Like, unlike, they sing together
20   Side by side,
            Mid-May's darling goldenlockèd,
            Summer's tanling diamondeyed.

13 purple weather bright skies. Cf. Shelley's *Stanzas Written in Dejection,
Near Naples* line 4 for a similar use: 'The purple noon's transparent might'.
A. Johnston *RES* n.s. 14 (1963) 389–93 traces C16–C18 uses.
22 tanling someone tanned by the sun's rays. A Shakespeareanism.

40 The Kraken

Date T. comments: 'See the account which Erik Pontoppidan, the Norwegian bishop, born 1698, gives of the fabulous sea-monster – the Kraken (*Biographic Universelle*).' The kraken also appears in Scott's *Minstrelsy* (1802–3) and T. C. Croker's *Fairy Legends* (1828) 2.64, hence composition probably circa 1829. W. D. Paden *T. in Egypt.* (1942) 155 argues that T. was influenced by G. S. Faber's typological interpretations, reading the serpent as the principle of evil.
Publication *1830*; (not reprinted until *1872*).

Below the thunders of the upper deep.
   Far, far beneath in the abysmal sea,
His ancient, dreamless, uninvaded sleep
   The Kraken sleepeth: faintest sunlights flee
5   About his shadowy sides: above him swell
   Huge sponges of millennial growth and height;
   And far away into the sickly light,
From many a wondrous grot and secret cell
Unnumbered and enormous polypi
10   Winnow with giant arms the slumbering green.
There hath he lain for ages and will lie
   Battening upon huge seaworms in his sleep,
   Until the latter fire shall heat the deep;
Then once by man and angels to be seen,
15 In roaring he shall rise and on the surface die.

10 Winnow cf. Milton *Paradise Lost* 5.269–70, where Raphael 'winnows' the air in his flight to earth.   **arms**] fins *1830*.
13–15 Cf. *Rev.* 8.8–9: 'And the second angel sounded, and as it were a great mountain burning with fire was cast into the sea; and the third part of the sea became blood; And the third part of the creatures which were in the sea, and had life, died'.

41 The Palace of Art

Date *c*. 1831/2.
   The poem grew out of a remark made by one of the Cambridge Apostles, Richard Chenevix Trench: 'Tennyson, we cannot live in Art'. T. addressed to him the following poem, preceding *The Palace of Art* in *1833* and *1842*:

I send you here a sort of allegory,
(For you will understand it) of a soul,
A sinful soul possessed of many gifts,
A spacious garden full of flowering weeds,
A glorious Devil, large in heart and brain,
That did love Beauty only, (Beauty seen
In all varieties of mould and mind)

And Knowledge for its beauty; or if Good,
Good only for its beauty, seeing not
That Beauty, Good, and Knowledge, are three sisters
That dote upon each other, friends to man,
Living together under the same roof,
And never can be sundered without tears.
And he that shuts Love out, in turn shall be
Shut out from Love, and on her threshold lie
Howling in outer darkness. Not for this
Was common clay ta'en from the common earth
Moulded by God, and tempered with the tears
Of angels to the perfect shape of man.

For biblical scorning delight of worldly vanities see *Eccles.* 2.1–17 and Luke 12.19–20. Herbert's *The World* and Shelley's *Queen Mab* 2.56–64 have been cited as analogues. The text was very heavily revised for *1842*; see *1969* 401–18. The disapproval of aestheticism is in accord with the tone of the Apostles. Behind the poem are medieval and renaissance descriptions conveying moral messages through palaces, e.g. Chaucer's *House of Fame* and Spenser's 'House of Pride'. Stanzaic form same as that of Vaughan's *They are all gone into the world of light.*
Publication *1833.*

    I built my soul a lordly pleasure-house,
        Wherein at ease for aye to dwell.
    I said, 'O Soul, make merry and carouse,
        Dear soul, for all is well.'

5   A huge crag-platform, smooth as burnished brass
        I chose. The rangèd ramparts bright
    From level meadow-bases of deep grass
        Suddenly scaled the light.

    Thereupon I built it firm. Of ledge or shelf
10   The rock rose clear, or winding stair.
    My soul would live alone unto herself
        In her high palace there.

    And 'while the world runs round and round,' I said,
        'Reign thou apart, a quiet king,
15   Still as, while Saturn whirls, his steadfast shade
        Sleeps on his luminous ring.'

3 Cf. *Luke* 12.19: 'And I will say to my soul, Soul, thou hast much goods laid up for many years; take thine ease, eat, drink, *and* be merry.'
15–16 Although Saturn revolves, the shadow falling across the rings appears to be motionless.

To which my soul made answer readily:
'Trust me, in bliss I shall abide
In this great mansion, that is built for me,
20   So royal-rich and wide.'

Four courts I made, East, West, and South, and North,
In each a squarèd lawn, wherefrom
The golden gorge of dragons spouted forth
A flood of fountain-foam.

25 And round the cool green courts there ran a row
Of cloisters, branched like mighty woods,
Echoing all night to that sonorous flow
Of spouted fountain-floods.

And round the roofs a gilded gallery
30   That lent broad verge to distant lands,
Far as the wild swan wings, to where the sky
Dipped down to sea and sands.

From those four jets four currents in one swell
Across the mountain streamed below
35 In misty folds, that floating as they fell
Lit up a torrent-bow.

And high on every peak a statue seemed
To hang on tiptoe, tossing up
A cloud of incense of all odour steamed
40   From out a golden cup.

So that she thought, 'And who shall gaze upon
My palace with unblinded eyes,
While this great bow will waver in the sun,
And that sweet incense rise?'

45 For that sweet incense rose and never failed,
And, while day sank or mounted higher,
The light aërial gallery, golden-railed,
Burnt like a fringe of fire.

21–2 Ancient royal cities and courts were often divided into four quarters: see H. P. L'Orange *Studies on the Iconography of Cosmic Kingship* (Oslo 1953).
23–4 Ricks *1969* cites D. Bush *MLR* 54 (1959) 423, who compares H. J. Weber's *Tales of the East* (1812) 1.115: 'Four large gilded dragons adorned the angles of the bason, which was of a square form; and these dragons spouted out water clearer than rock crystal.'
30 broad verge 'a broad horizon' (T.'s note).
31–2 Tall towns and mounds, and close beneath the skies | Long lines of amber sands. *1833*.

Likewise the deep-set windows, stained and traced,
50   Would seem slow-flaming crimson fires
From shadowed grots of arches interlaced,
    And tipped with frost-like spires.

Full of long-sounding corridors it was,
    That over-vaulted grateful gloom,
55 Through which the livelong day my soul did pass,
    Well-pleased, from room to room.

Full of great rooms and small the palace stood,
    All various, each a perfect whole
From living Nature, fit for every mood
60   And change of my still soul.

For some were hung with arras green and blue,
    Showing a gaudy summer-morn,
Where with puffed cheek the belted hunter blew
    His wreathèd bugle-horn.

65 One seemed all dark and red – a tract of sand,
    And some one pacing there alone,
Who paced for ever in a glimmering land,
    Lit with a low large moon.

One showed an iron coast and angry waves,
70   You seemed to hear them climb and fall
And roar rock-thwarted under bellowing caves,
    Beneath the windy wall.

And one, a full-fed river winding slow
    By herds upon an endless plain,
75 The ragged rims of thunder brooding low,
    With shadow-streaks of rain.

And one, the reapers at their sultry toil.
    In front they bound the sheaves. Behind
Were realms of upland, prodigal in oil,
80   And hoary to the wind.

54–6 glooms | Roofed with thick plates of green and orange glass | Ending
in stately rooms. *1833.*
69–80 Some showed far-off thick woods mounted with towers, | Nearer, a
flood of mild sunshine | Poured on long walks and lawns and beds and
bowers | Trellised with bunchy vine. *1833.*
77–80 Scenes related to traditional 'Labours of the Months'.
80 'the underside of the olive leaf is white' (T.'s note).

And one, a foreground black with stones and slags,
    Beyond, a line of heights, and higher
All barred with long white cloud the scornful crags,
    And highest, snow and fire.

85   And one, an English home – gray twilight poured
      On dewy pastures, dewy trees,
    Softer than sleep – all things in order stored,
      A haunt of ancient Peace.

Nor these alone, but every landscape fair,
90   As fit for every mood of mind,
Or gay, or grave, or sweet, or stern, was there,
      Not less than truth designed.

Or the maid-mother by a crucifix,
      In tracts of pasture sunny-warm,
95   Beneath branch-work of costly sardonyx
      Sat smiling, babe in arm.

Or in a clear-walled city on the sea,
      Near gilded organ-pipes, her hair
Wound with white roses, slept St. Cecily;
100   An angel looked at her.

Or thronging all one porch of Paradise,
      A group of Houris bowed to see
The dying Islamite, with hands and eyes
      That said, We wait for thee.

105   Or mythic Uther's deeply-wounded son
      In some fair space of sloping greens
Lay, dozing in the vale of Avalon,
      And watched by weeping queens.

Or hollowing one hand against his ear,
110   To list a footfall, ere he saw
The wood-nymph, stayed the Ausonian king to hear
      Of wisdom and of law.

84 Deeptrenched with thunderfires. *1833*.
89–92 Landscapes suggests Georgic, calendrical art.
96 ∧ 7 Or Venus in a snowy shell alone, | Deepshadowed in the glassy brine, |
Moonlike glowed double on the blue, and shone | A naked shape divine.
1833.
99 St. Cecily Cecilia patron saint of music.
105–8 mythic Uther's . . . son cf. Malory 585.
109–16 Or blue eyed Kriemhilt from a craggy hold, | Athwart the lightgreen
rows of vine, | Poured blazing hoards of Nibelungen gold, | Down to the
gulfy Rhine. *1833*.
111 Ausonian king Numa Pompilius, who received laws from the nymph
Egeria; see Plutarch *Lives* (Loeb 1.316–8).   **Ausonian**] Tuscan 1842–8.

    Or over hills with peaky tops engrailed,
      And many a tract of palm and rice,
115 The throne of Indian Cama slowly sailed
      A summer fanned with spice.

    Or sweet Europa's mantle blew unclasped,
      From off her shoulder backward borne;
    From one hand drooped a crocus; one hand grasped
120   The mild bull's golden horn.

    Or else flushed Ganymede, his rosy thigh
      Half-buried in the Eagle's down,
    Sole as a flying star shot through the sky
      Above the pillared town.

125 Nor these alone: but every legend fair
      Which the supreme Caucasian mind
    Carved out of Nature for itself, was there,
      Not less than life, designed.

    Then in the towers I placed great bells that swung.
130   Moved of themselves, with silver sound;
    And with choice paintings of wise men I hung
      The royal dais round.

    For there was Milton like a seraph strong,
      Beside him Shakespeare bland and mild;
135 And there the world-worn Dante grasped his song,
      And somewhat grimly smiled.

    And there the Ionian father of the rest;
      A million wrinkles carved his skin;
    A hundred winters snowed upon his breast,
140   From cheek and throat and chin.

---

113 peaky first recorded use in *OED*.   **engrailed** heraldic term for serrated.
115 Cama 'The Hindu God of young love, son of Brahma' (T.'s note).
117 Europa's scarf blew in an arch unclasped, *1833*.
119–20 Zeus fell in love with Europa, daughter of Agenor King of Tyre; he took the form of a bull and carried her away.
120 ∧ 21 He through the streaming crystal swam, and rolled | Ambrosial breaths that seemed to float | In lightwreathed curls. She from the ripple cold | Updrew her sandalled foot. *1833*.
121–4 Ganymede, son of Tros, was carried off by an eagle of Zeus to be his cup-bearer in heaven.
128 ∧ 9 *1833* had six stanzas on the progress of the soul to higher and more complex states.
133–6 There deephaired Milton like an angel tall | Stood limnèd, Shakespeare bland and mild, | Grim Dante pressed his lips, and from the wall | The bald blind Homer smiled. *1833*.
137 Ionian father Homer.

Above, the fair hall-ceiling stately-set
    Many an arch high up did lift,
And angels rising and descending met
    With interchange of gift.

145 Below was all mosaic choicely planned
    With cycles of the human tale
Of this wide world, the times of every land
    So wrought, they will not fail.

The people here, a beast of burden slow,
150   Toiled onward, pricked with goads and stings;
Here played a tiger, rolling to and fro
    The heads and crowns of kings;

Here rose an athlete, strong to break or bind
    All force in bonds that might endure,
155 And here once more like some sick man declined,
    And trusted any cure.

But over these she trod: and those great bells
    Began to chime. She took her throne:
She sat betwixt the shining oriels,
160   To sing her songs alone.

And through the topmost oriels' coloured flame
    Two godlike faces gazed below;
Plato the wise, and large-browed Verulam,
    The first of those who know.

165 And all those names, that in their motion were
    Full-welling fountain-heads of change,
Betwixt the slender shafts were blazoned fair
    In diverse raiment strange:

Through which the lights, rose, amber, emerald, blue,
170   Flushed in her temples and her eyes,
And from her lips, as morn from Memnon, drew
    Rivers of melodies.

No nightingale delighteth to prolong
    Her low preamble all alone,
175 More than my soul to hear her echoed song
    Throb through the ribbèd stone;

159 oriels large bay windows, usually richly traceried, often with stained glass.
163 large-browed Verulam Francis Bacon, Lord Verulam.
171 Memnon mythical king of Ethiopia; the stones of the colossi of Memnon were said to sing at dawn.

[41] Alfred Tennyson

Singing and murmuring in her feastful mirth,
    Joying to feel herself alive,
Lord over Nature, Lord of the visible earth,
180   Lord of the senses five;

Communing with herself: 'All these are mine,
    And let the world have peace or wars,
'Tis one to me.' She – when young night divine
    Crowned dying day with stars,

185 Making sweet close of his delicious toils –
    Lit light in wreaths and anadems,
And pure quintessences of precious oils
    In hollowed moons of gems,

To mimic heaven; and clapped her hands and cried,
190   'I marvel if my still delight'
In this great house so royal-rich, and wide,
    Be flattered to the height.

'O all things fair to sate my various eyes!
    O shapes and hues that please me well!
195 O silent faces of the Great and Wise,
    My Gods, with whom I dwell!

'O God-like isolation which art mine,
    I can but count thee perfect gain,
What time I watch the darkening droves of swine
200   That range on yonder plain.

'In filthy sloughs they roll a prurient skin,
    They graze and wallow, breed and sleep;
And oft some brainless devil enters in,
    And drives them to the deep.'

205 Then of the moral instinct would she prate,
    And of the rising from the dead,
As hers by right of full-accomplished Fate;
    And at the last she said:

180–4 5 different stanzas in *1833*.
186 anadems crowns; cf. Shelley *Adonais* line 94; 'the wreath upon him, like an anadem.'
186–92 2 different stanzas in *1833*.
203–4 See *Mark* 5.1–14 for the story of the Gadarene swine.
205–12 not in *1833*.

'I take possession of man's mind and deed.
210   I care not what the sects may brawl.
I sit as God holding no form of creed,
    But contemplating all.'

Full oft the riddle of the painful earth
    Flashed through her as she sat alone,
215 Yet not the less held she her solemn mirth,
    And intellectual throne.

And so she throve and prospered: so three years
    She prospered: on the fourth she fell,
Like Herod, when the shout was in his ears,
220   Struck through with pangs of hell.

Lest she should fail and perish utterly,
    God, before whom ever lie bare
The abysmal deeps of Personality,
    Plagued her with sore despair.

225 When she would think, where'er she turned her sight,
    The airy hand confusion wrought,
Wrote 'Mene, mene,' and divided quite
    The kingdom of her thought.

Deep dread and loathing of her solitude
230   Fell on her, from which mood was born
Scorn of herself; again, from out that mood
    Laughter at her self-scorn.

'What! is not this my place of stength,' she said,
    'My spacious mansion built for me,
235 Whereof the strong foundation-stones were laid
    Since my first memory?'

209–12 not in *1833*; I take possession of men's minds and deeds. | I live in all things great and small. | I sit apart, holding no forms of creeds, | But contemplating all. *1842–1848*.
216 Cf. Arnold *The Scholar Gipsy* line 184 (see below p. 362).
219–20 *Acts* 12.21–3 describes the death of Herod when 'he gave not God the glory'.
227 See *Dan.* 5.23–7: at Belshazzar's feast a hand wrote 'Mene, Mene, Tekel, Upharsin'; Daniel interpreted 'Mene' as 'God hath numbered thy Kingdom, and finished it.'
232 ∧ 3 'Who hath drawn dry the fountains of delight, | That from my deep heart everywhere | Moved in my blood and dwelt, as power and might | Abode in Sampson's hair? *1833*.

[41] Alfred Tennyson

But in dark corners of her palace stood
Uncertain shapes; and unawares
On white-eyed phantasms weeping tears of blood,
240   And horrible nightmares,

And hollow shades enclosing hearts of flame,
And, with dim fretted foreheads all,
On corpses three-months-old at noon she came,
That stood against the wall.

245 A spot of dull stagnation, without light
Or power of movement, seemed my soul,
'Mid onward-sloping motions infinite
Making for one sure goal.

A still salt pool, locked in with bars of sand,
250   Left on the shore; that hears all night
The plunging seas draw backward from the land
Their moon-led waters white.

A star that with the choral starry dance
Joined not, but stood, and standing saw
255 The hollow orb of moving Circumstance
Rolled round by one fixed law.

Back on herself her serpent pride had curled.
'No voice,' she shrieked in that lone hall,
'No voice breaks through the stillness of this world:
260   One deep, deep silence all!'

She, mouldering with the dull earth's mouldering sod,
Inwrapped tenfold in slothful shame,
Lay there exilèd from eternal God,
Lost to her place and name;

265 And death and life she hated equally,
And nothing saw, for her despair,
But dreadful time, dreadful eternity,
No comfort anywhere;

Remaining utterly confused with fears,
270   And ever worse with growing time,
And ever unrelieved by dismal tears,
And all alone in crime:

242 fretted 'worm-fretted' (T.'s note).
255 The hollow orb cf. Milton *Paradise Lost* 7.257.   **Circumstance** the totality of surrounding things; *OED* 1.1. This ex. is regarded by *OED* as a nonce use of an obsolete term. T. comments: 'Some old writer calls the Heavens "the Circumstance"...Here it is more or less a play on the word.'

Shut up as in a crumbling tomb, girt round
    With blackness as a solid wall,
275 Far off she seemed to hear the dully sound
    Of human footsteps fall.

As in strange lands a traveller walking slow,
    In doubt and great perplexity,
A little before moon-rise hears the low
280   Moan of an unknown sea;

And knows not if it be thunder, or a sound
    Of rocks thrown down, or one deep cry
Of great wild beasts; then thinketh, 'I have found
    A new land, but I die.'

285 She howled aloud, 'I am on fire within.
    There comes no murmur of reply.
What is it that will take away my sin,
    And save me lest I die?'

So when four years were wholly finishèd,
290   She threw her royal robes away.
'Make me a cottage in the vale,' she said,
    'Where I may mourn and pray.

'Yet pull not down my palace towers, that are
    So lightly, beautifully built:
295 Perchance I may return with others there
    When I have purged my guilt.'

42 The Lotos Eaters

Date Written 1830–32. (*Memoir* 1.86).
Sources Principal source Homer *Od.* 9.82–104: 'We set foot on the land of
the Lotus-eaters, who eat a flowery food ... So they went straightway and
mingled with the Lotus-eaters, and the Lotus-eaters did not plan death for
my comrades, but gave them of the lotus to taste. And whosoever of them
ate of the honey-sweet fruit of the lotus, had no longer any wish to bring
word or to return, but there they were fain to abide among the Lotus-eaters,
feeding on the lotus, and forgetful of their homeward way. These men,
therefore, I brought back perforce to the ships, weeping.' T. was also
influenced by Washington Irving's *Columbus* (1828) which describes the
idyllic life on Haiti, and by the mood of Spenser's *Faerie Queene* in 1.1. 41
(the cave of Morpheus); 1.9.40 (the spell of Despair) and 2.6.10 (the Idle
lake). There is also perhaps a debt to James Thomson's *The Castle of
Indolence* (1748).
Publication *1833*; heavily revised for *1842* (for study of revisions see A. Grob
MP 62 (1964) 118–29).

'Courage!' he said, and pointed toward the land,
'This mounting wave will roll us shoreward soon.'
In the afternoon they came unto a land
In which it seemèd always afternoon.
5   All round the coast the languid air did swoon,
Breathing like one that hath a weary dream,
Full-faced above the valley stood the moon;
And like a downward smoke, the slender stream
Along the cliff to fall and pause and fall did seem.

10   A land of streams! some, like a downward smoke,
Slow-dropping veils of thinnest lawn, did go;
And some through wavering lights and shadows broke,
Rolling a slumbrous sheet of foam below.
They saw the gleaming river seaward flow
15   From the inner land; far off, three mountain-tops,
Three silent pinnacles of agèd snow,
Stood sunset flushed; and, dewed with showery drops,
Up-clomb the shadowy pine above the woven copse.

The charmed sunset lingered low adown
20   In the red West; through mountain clefts the dale
Was seen far inland, and the yellow down
Bordered with palm, and many a winding vale
And meadow, set with slender galingale;
A land where all things always seemed the same!
25   And round about the keel with faces pale,
Dark faces pale against that rosy flame,
The mild-eyed melancholy Lotos-eaters came.

Branches they bore of that enchanted stem,
Laden with flower and fruit, whereof they gave
30   To each, but whoso did receive of them
And taste, to him the gushing of the wave
Far far away did seem to mourn and rave
On alien shores; and if his fellow spake,
His voice was thin, as voices from the grave;
35   And deep-asleep he seemed, yet all awake,
And music in his ears his beating heart did make.

1–45 In Spenserian stanzas; appropriate since the alexandrine has the effect of slowing down movement.
7 Above the valley burned the golden moon; *1833.*
8–11 'Taken from the waterfall at Gavarnie, in the Pyrenees, when I was 20 or 21' (T.'s note). T. and Hallam visited Spain, in the rebel cause, in July–Sept. 1830.
16 Three thundercloven thrones of oldest snow, *1833.*
23 galingale *Cyperus longus* a variety of sedge.
26 Pale in the steady sunset's rosy flame, *MS.*

They sat them down upon the yellow sand,
Between the sun and moon upon the shore;
And sweet it was to dream of Fatherland,
40   Of child, and wife, and slave; but evermore
Most weary seemed the sea, weary the oar,
Weary the wandering fields of barren foam.
Then some one said, 'We will return no more';
And all at once they sang, 'Our island home
45   Is far beyond the wave; we will no longer roam.'

CHORIC SONG

1

There is sweet music here that softer falls
Than petals from blown roses on the grass,
Or night-dews on still waters between walls
Of shadowy granite, in a gleaming pass;
50   Music that gentlier on the spirit lies,
Than tired eyelids upon tired eyes;
Music that brings sweet sleep down from the blissful skies.
Here are cool mosses deep,
And through the moss the ivies creep,
55   And in the stream the long-leaved flowers weep,
And from the craggy ledge the poppy hangs in sleep.

2

Why are we weighed upon with heaviness,
And utterly consumed with sharp distress,
While all things else have rest from weariness?
60   All things have rest: why should we toil alone,
We only toil, who are the first of things,
And make perpetual moan,
Still from one sorrow to another thrown:
Nor even fold our wings,
65   And cease from wanderings,
Nor steep our brows in slumber's holy balm;
Nor harken what the inner spirit sings,
'There is no joy but calm' –
Why should we only toil, the roof and crown of things?

3

70   Lo! in the middle of the wood,
The folded leaf is wooed from out the bud
With winds upon the branch, and there
Grows green and broad, and takes no care,

42 'Made by me on a voyage from Bordeaux to Dublin (1830)' (T.'s note).

Sun-steeped at noon, and in the moon
75 Nightly dew-fed; and turning yellow
Falls, and floats adown the air.
Lo! sweetened with the summer light,
The full-juiced apple, waxing over-mellow,
Drops in a silent autumn night.
80 All its allotted length of days,
The flower ripens in its place,
Ripens and fades, and falls, and hath no toil,
Fast-rooted in the fruitful soil.

4

Hateful is the dark-blue sky,
85 Vaulted o'er the dark-blue sea.
Death is the end of life; ah, why
Should life all labour be?
Let us alone. Time driveth onward fast,
And in a little while our lips are dumb.
90 Let us alone. What is it that will last?
All things are taken from us, and become
Portions and parcels of the dreadful past.
Let us alone. What pleasure can we have
To war with evil? Is there any peace
95 In ever climbing up the climbing wave?
All things have rest, and ripen toward the grave
In silence; – ripen, fall and cease:
Give us long rest or death, dark death, or dreamful ease.

5

How sweet it were, hearing the downward stream,
100 With half-shut eyes ever to seem
Falling asleep in a half-dream!
To dream and dream, like yonder amber light,
Which will not leave the myrrh-bush on the height;
To hear each other's whispered speech;
105 Eating the Lotos day by day,
To watch the crisping ripples on the beach,
And tender curving lines of creamy spray;
To lend our hearts and spirits wholly
To the influence of mild-minded melancholy;
110 To muse and brood and live again in memory,
With those old faces of our infancy

82 *1969* cites Spenser *Faerie Queene:* 'Yet no man for them taketh pains or care,' (Phaedria's Island 2.6.15).
94 In warring with mischances, or what peace *MS*.
100–1 Cf. Thomson *Castle of Indolence* 1.6. 'A pleasing land of drowsyhed it was: | Of dreams that wave before the half-shut eye'.

Heaped over with a mound of grass,
Two handfuls of white dust, shut in an urn of brass!
6
Dear is the memory of our wedded lives,
115 And dear the last embraces of our wives
And their warm tears; but all hath suffered change:
For surely now our household hearths are cold:
Our sons inherit us: our looks are strange:
And we should come like ghosts to trouble joy.
120 Or else the island princes over-bold
Have eat our substance, and the minstrel sings
Before them of the ten years' war in Troy,
And our great deeds, as half-forgotten things.
Is there confusion in the little isle?
125 Let what is broken so remain.
The Gods are hard to reconcile:
'Tis hard to settle order once again.
There *is* confusion worse than death,
Trouble on trouble, pain on pain,
130 Long labour unto agèd breath,
Sore task to hearts worn out by many wars
And eyes grown dim with gazing on the pilot-stars.

7
But, propped on beds of amaranth and moly,
How sweet (while warm airs lull us blowing lowly)
135 With half-dropped eyelid still,
Beneath a heaven dark and holy,
To watch the long bright river drawing slowly
His waters from the purple hill –
To hear the dewy echoes calling
140 From cave to cave through the thick-twinèd vine –
To watch the emerald coloured water falling
Through many a woven acanthus-wreath divine!
Only to hear and see the far-off sparkling brine,
Only to hear were sweet, stretched out beneath the pine.

8
145 The Lotos blooms below the barren peak:
The Lotos blows by every winding creek:

120 The princes wooing Penelope in Ithaca.
133 amaranth an immortal flower.   **moly** the herb used by Ulysses to charm Circe. Cf. Milton *Comus* lines 636–7.
141 watch] hear *1833–50*.
142 acanthus *Acanthus spinosus*, the plant familiar as the decorative device on Corinthian capitals.
145 barren] flowery *1833–50*.

All day the wind breathes low with mellower tone:
Through every hollow cave and alley lone
Round and round the spicy downs the yellow Lotos-dust is blown.
150 We have had enough of action, and of motion we,
Rolled to starboard, rolled to larboard, when the surge was
    seething free,
Where the wallowing monster spouted his foam-fountains in
    the sea.
Let us swear an oath, and keep it with an equal mind,
In the hollow Lotos-land to live and lie reclined
155 On the hills like Gods together, careless of mankind.
For they lie beside their nectar, and the bolts are hurled
Far below them in the valleys, and the clouds are lightly curled
Round their golden houses, girdled with the gleaming world:
Where they smile in secret, looking over wasted lands,
160 Blight and famine, plague and earthquake, roaring deeps and
    fiery sands,
Clanging fights, and flaming towns, and sinking ships, and
    praying hands.
But they smile, they find a music centred in a doleful song
Steaming up, a lamentation and an ancient tale of wrong,
Like a tale of little meaning though the words are strong;
165 Chanted from an ill-used race of men that cleave the soil,
Sow the seed, and reap the harvest with enduring toil,
Storing yearly little dues of wheat, and wine and oil;
Till they perish and they suffer – some, 'tis whispered – down
    in hell
Suffer endless anguish, others in Elysian valleys dwell,
170 Resting weary limbs at last on beds of asphodel.
Surely, surely, slumber is more sweet than toil, the shore
Than labour in the deep mid-ocean, wind and wave and oar;
Oh rest ye, brother mariners, we will not wander more.

150–73 entirely rewritten for *1842*. For text of *1833* see *1969* 435–36.
155–70 Cf. *Lucretius* lines 109–10, and notes (below p. 180).
162–65 Cf. Wordsworth *Tintern Abbey* 'hearing often-times | The still, sad music of humanity, | Nor harsh nor grating, though of ample power | To chasten and subdue', lines 90–3. T. makes the lotos-eaters question the optimism that sees the music of suffering harmonized and made coherent.
170 asphodel the immortal flower said to cover Elysian Fields; *Odyssey* 11.539.
172 Cf. *Ulysses* lines 69–70 for the antipodal view that labour is dignified and worthy (below p. 77).
173 Croker: 'How they got home you must read in Homer: – Mr Tennyson – himself, we presume, a dreamy lotos-eater, a delicious lotos-eater – leaves them in full song' *Critical Heritage* 78.

43 'Hark! the dogs howl!'

Date The poem is one of the first poetic reactions to the death of Arthur Hallam in 1833: 'On the evening of one of these sad winter days my father had already noted down in his scrap-book some fragmentary lines, which proved to be the germ of *In Memoriam*.' At this point in his grief it is the sense of loss that is uppermost: the philosophic and religious structures of *In Mem.* are not yet built. MS. in *H.Nbk* 16.
Publication Odd lines in *Memoir* 1.107; *1969*.

Hark! the dogs howl! the sleetwinds blow,
The church-clocks knoll: the hours haste,
I leave the dreaming world below.
Blown o'er frore heads of hills I go,

5   Long narrowing friths and stripes of snow –
Time bears my soul into the waste.
I seek the voice I loved – ah where
Is that dear hand that I should press,
Those honoured brows that I would kiss?

10   Lo! the broad Heavens cold and bare,
The stars that know not my distress.
My sighs are wasted in the air,
My tears are dropped into the abyss.
Now riseth up a little cloud –

15   Divideth like a broken wave –
Shows Death a drooping youth pale-browed
And crowned with daisies of the grave.
The vapour labours up the sky,
Uncertain forms are darkly moved,

20   Larger than human passes by
The shadow of the man I loved.
I wind my arms for one embrace –

4 frore frozen. Dialect word, also in poetic diction. Cf. Milton: 'the parching air | Burns frore, and cold performs th'effect of fire' *Paradise Lost* 2.595.
5 friths narrow strips of snow.
20 Cf. *In Mem.* 103. 41–3: 'The man we loved was there on deck, | But thrice as large as man he bent | To greet us.' For another presentation of ghosts as large presences see T.'s projected essay on Ghosts for the Cambridge Apostles: 'Forth issue from the inmost gloom the colossal Presences of the Past *majores humano*, some as they lived, seemingly pale with exhaustion and faintly smiling; some as they died in a still agony' (quoted Buckley 33).
22 wind enfold *OED* 16: cf. Beaumont and Fletcher *Maid's Tragedy* 2.1.158: 'Let me wind thee in these arms'.

Can this be he? is that his face?
In my strait throat expires the cry.
25 He bends his eyes reproachfully
And clasps his hands, as one that prays.

25 bends directs; cf. Shakespeare *Ham.* 3.4.115–6: 'Alas, how ist with you, |
That you do bend your eye on vacancy?'

44 Ulysses

Date Written 20 Oct. 1833 (dated, *Heath MS.*). T.'s note in *Eversley:* 'The
poem was written soon after Arthur Hallam's death, and it gives the feeling
about the need of going forward and braving the struggle of life perhaps
more simply than anything in *In Memoriam.*' See also letter to James
Knowles: 'There is more about myself in *Ulysses*, which was written under
sense of loss and that all had gone by, but that still life must be fought out
to the end. It was more written with the feeling of his loss upon me than
many poems in *In Memoriam*' (*Nineteenth Century* 33 (1893) 182).
   This poem is related to *Tithonus* (see headnote p. 173 below) and *Tiresias.*
Sources The main sources are *Odyssey* 11.100–37 and Dante's *Inferno* 26.90
ff. There is the problem that in Homer Ulysses returned without a crew.
Tiresias prophesied that Ulysses would meet death on a 'mysterious voyage'
after his return to Ithaca. For the medieval mind Ulysses was a tainted
figure. Dante placed him in the circle of false counsellors. Discussion varies
between, for instance, J. Pettigrew *VP* 1 (1963) 27–45, who regards it as an
expression of escapism and lassitude, and T. Robbins *VP* 11 (1973) 177–93,
who accepts T.'s own view.
Publication *1842.*

It little profits that an idle king,
By this still hearth, among these barren crags,
Matched with an agèd wife, I mete and dole
Unequal laws unto a savage race,
5 That hoard, and sleep, and feed, and know not me.

I cannot rest from travel: I will drink
Life to the lees: all times I have enjoyed

3 mete cf. *Matt.* 7.2: 'with what measure ye mete, it shall be measured to
you again.'
4 Unequal not affecting everyone in the same manner; paradoxical in view of
'mete'.
5 sleep, and feed Ricks *1969* cites *Ham.* 4.4.33–9: 'What is a man, | If his chief
good and market of his time | Be but to sleep and feed?' etc.; applicable, in
general terms, to the whole poem.
6–9 Much have I suffered both on shore and when *H.MS.*
7 lees dregs; cf. Shakespeare *Mac.* 2.3.94–5: 'The wine of life is drawn, and
the mere lees | Is left this vault to brag of.'

Greatly, have suffered greatly, both with those
That loved me, and alone; on shore, and when
10 Through scudding drifts the rainy Hyades
Vexed the dim sea: I am become a name;
For always roaming with a hungry heart
Much have I seen and known; cities of men
And manners, climates, councils, governments,
15 Myself not least, but honoured of them all;
And drunk delight of battle with my peers,
Far on the ringing plains of windy Troy.
I am a part of all that I have met;
Yet all experience is an arch wherethrough
20 Gleams that untravelled world, whose margin fades
For ever and for ever when I move.
How dull it is to pause, to make an end,
To rust unburnished, not to shine in use!
As though to breathe were life. Life piled on life
25 Were all too little, and of one to me
Little remains: but every hour is saved
From that eternal silence, something more,
A bringer of new things; and vile it were
For some three suns to store and hoard myself,
30 And this gray spirit yearning in desire

10 Hyades a constellation near the Pleiades; associated with rain. T. quotes Virgil: '*pluviasque Hyades*' (*Aen.* 1.744).
13–14 Cf. *Odyssey* 1.3–5: 'Many were the men whose cities he saw'.
14 manners *OED* 4c rather than the currently commoner sense.
16–17 Arnold quotes these lines (*Last Words on Translating Homer* (1862) *Works* 1.205) as too elaborate for the Homeric spirit, adding: 'Perfect simplicity can be obtained only by a genius of which perfect simplicity is an essential characteristic.'
18 T. cites Virgil *Aen.* 2.5–6: '*quaeque ipse miserrima vidi | et quorum pars magna fui*' (sorrowful things I saw myself | wherein I had my share and more). *1969* compares Byron *Childe Harold* 3.70–5.
19–21 Arnold says of these lines (slightly misquoted in *On Translating Homer* (1861) *Works* 1.147): 'It is no blame to their rhythm, which belongs to another order of movement than Homer's, but it is true that these three lines by themselves take up nearly as much time as a whole book of the *Iliad*.'
30 'The accusative after *store* etc.' (T.)
30–2 Cf. Dante *Inferno* 26.94–9: (the central *donnée* for T.): '*nè dolcezza di figlio, nè la pièta | del vecchio padre,...vincer poter dentro da me l'ardore | ch'i' ebbi a divenir del mondo esperto, | e delli vizi umani e del valore*' (Nor fondness for my son, nor reverence | Of my old father...Could overcome in me the zeal I had | T'explore the world, and search the ways of life, | Man's evil and his virtue' (tr. Cary, 1805).

To follow knowledge like a sinking star,
Beyond the utmost bound of human thought.

This is my son, mine own Telemachus,
To whom I leave the sceptre and the isle –
35   Well-loved of me, discerning to fulfil
This labour, by slow prudence to make mild
A rugged people, and through soft degrees
Subdue them to the useful and the good.
Most blameless is he, centred in the sphere
40   Of common duties, decent not to fail
In offices of tenderness, and pay
Meet adoration to my household gods,
When I am gone. He works his work, I mine.

There lies the port; the vessel puffs her sail:
45   There gloom the dark broad seas. My mariners,
Souls that have toiled, and wrought, and thought with me –
That ever with a frolic welcome took
Thy thunder and the sunshine, and opposed
Free hearts, free foreheads – you and I are old;
50   Old age hath yet his honour and his toil;
Death closes all: but something ere the end,
Some work of noble note, may yet be done,
Not unbecoming men that strove with Gods.
The lights begin to twinkle from the rocks:
55   The long day wanes: the slow moon climbs: the deep
Moans round with many voices. Come, my friends,
'Tis not too late to seek a newer world.
Push off, and sitting well in order smite
The sounding furrows; for my purpose holds
60   To sail beyond the sunset, and the baths
Of all the western stars, until I die.
It may be that the gulfs will wash us down:
It may be we shall touch the Happy Isles,

31–2 To be found verbatim in a draft (1833) of *Tiresias* where they formed part of the opening lines (*T. Nbk* 15).
40 decent having a sense of what is fitting (*OED* 1).
45 There gloom] Beyond *H. MS.*
51–2 Not all unworthy of heroic souls added as *H. MS.* 1st reading.
58–9 T. notes that this is a Homeric commonplace: ἑξῆςδεζό μενοι πολιὴν ἅλα τύπτον ερετμοῖς (*Odyssey* 4.580 etc.).
60–1 the baths...stars see *Odyssey* 5.270–5; all constellations except the Bear vanish below the horizon.
63 the Happy Isles beyond the Pillars of Hercules, described by Dante *Inferno* 26.108: 'li suoi riguradi, | acciò che l'uom più oltre non si metta' (the boundaries not to be o'erstepped by man).

And see the great Achilles, whom we knew.
65 Though much is taken, much abides; and though
We are not now that strength which in old days
Moved earth and heaven; that which we are, we are;
One equal temper of heroic hearts,
Made weak by time and fate, but strong in will
70 To strive, to seek, to find, and not to yield.

67 Moved . . . heaven] Swathed Troy with flame *H. MS., Heath MS.*
70 Perhaps an echo of St Ignatius Loyola's prayer: '. . . to give and not to count the cost; to fight and not to heed the wounds; . . . to labour and not to ask for any reward save that of knowing we do thy will.'

45 'Break, break, break'

Date Written in Lincolnshire one spring (*Memoir* 1. 190), so presumably before early 1837, when the Tennysons left Somersby, and after Sept. 1833, since it is on the death of Arthur Hallam.
Publication *1842.*

Break, break, break,
    On thy cold gray stones, O sea!
And I would that my tongue could utter
    The thoughts that arise in me.

5 O well for the fisherman's boy,
    That he shouts with his sister at play!
O well for the sailor lad,
    That he sings in his boat on the bay!

And the stately ships go on
10   To their haven under the hill;
But O for the touch of a vanished hand,
    And the sound of a voice that is still!

Break, break, break,
    At the foot of thy crags, O sea!
15 But the tender grace of a day that is dead
    Will never come back to me.

11–12 Cf. the lines in *Memoir* 1. 107 given by H.T. as the germ of *In Memoriam*: 'Where is the voice I love? ah where | Is that dear hand that I would press?'; appearing with variations in *Hark! the dogs howl* lines 7–8 (above p. 73). The sense of touch is of great importance in *In Memoriam*, e.g. 10.19; 119.12.

46 [Morte d'Arthur]

Date *Morte d'Arthur* written 1833–4: yet another poem in response to Hallam's death (*Memoir* 1.129, 138 and *Heath MS*).

The 'frame', both prologue and epilogue, written 1835–8, was probably intended to forestall criticism, but it did not deter Leigh Hunt (*Critical Heritage* 127–8, 132) nor John Sterling (*Critical Heritage* 119–20) from passing harsh judgements. The 1842 trial edition did not include 'the frame'.

Source The *Morte* (adapted for the *Idylls of the King* as *The Passing of Arthur* (1869)) is of interest and importance as the genesis of a prime motive in T.'s output. His main source was Malory's *Morte d'Arthur* Ch. 21 (in the three-volume 1816 edition), but he also used Geoffrey of Monmouth and Walter Map. Of Arthur T. said: 'How much of history we have in the story of Arthur is doubtful. Let not my readers press too hardly on details, whether for history or for allegory. Some think that King Arthur may be taken to typify conscience. He is anyhow meant to be a man who spent himself in the cause of honour, duty and self-sacrifice, who felt and aspired with his nobler knights, though with a stronger and a clearer conscience than any of them, "reverencing his conscience as a king." "There was no such perfect man since Adam" as an old writer says' (*Memoir* 1.194).

Criticism Critics have usually concentrated on T.'s personal and topical allusiveness in his use of Arthurian material (see Buckley 171–94; C. de L. Ryals *From the Great Deep...* (1967); J. R. Reed *Perception and Design in T.'s Idylls of the King* (1970), and P. J. Eggers *King Arthur's Laureate* (1971). But W. D. Paden (*Tennyson in Egypt* (1924) 80–8) offers an ingenious anthropological reading in the spirit of early C19 mythogony, especially of G. S. Faber *Origin of Pagan Idolatry* (1816). Arthur's death is interpreted as a veiled Helio-Arkite myth of the transmigrating Great Father.

Publication *1842.*

46.1 The Epic

At Francis Allen's on the Christmas-eve, –
The game of forfeits done – the girls all kissed
Beneath the sacred bush and past away –
The parson Holmes, the poet Everard Hall,
5   The host, and I sat round the wassail-bowl,
Then half-way ebbed: and there we held a talk,
How all the old honour had from Christmas gone,

3 sacred bush mistletoe. Gay *Trivia* II.41 refers to 'sacred mistletoe'. The mistletoe of the oak was often called *lignum sanctae crucis* (wood of the Holy Cross). See W. Irving *Sketch Book* (1820) 'Christmas Eve' for a description of the tradition.

5 wassail-bowl a loving-cup for drinking healths (from O.E. *wes hal* – 'be of good health'). See W. Irving 'The Christmas Dinner'.

7–9 W. Irving's Squire Bracebridge regrets the decline of '"Our old games and local customs"'.

Or gone, or dwindled down to some odd games
In some odd nooks like this; till I, tired out
10   With cutting eights that day upon the pond,
Where, three times slipping from the outer edge,
I bumped the ice into three several stars,
Fell in a doze; and half-awake I heard
The parson taking wide and wider sweeps,
15   Now harping on the church-commissioners,
Now hawking at geology and schism;
Until I woke, and found him settled down
Upon the general decay of faith
Right through the world, 'at home was little left,
20   And none abroad: there was no anchor, none,
To hold by.' Francis, laughing, clapped his hand
On Everard's shoulder, with 'I hold by him.'
'And I,' quoth Everard, 'by the wassail-bowl.'
'Why yes,' I said, 'we knew your gift that way
25   At college: but another which you had,
I mean of verse (for we held it then),
What came of that?' 'You know,' said Frank, 'he burnt
His epic, his King Arthur, some twelve books' –
And then to me demanding why? 'Oh, sir,
30   He thought that nothing new was said, or else
Something so said 'twas nothing – that a truth
Looks freshest in the fashion of the day:
God knows: he has a mint of reasons: ask.
It pleased *me* well enough.' 'Nay, nay,' said Hall,
35   'Why take the style of those heroic times?
For nature brings not back the mastodon,
Nor we those times; and why should any man
Remodel models? these twelve books of mine
Were faint Homeric echoes, nothing-worth,
40   Mere chaff and draff, much better burnt.' 'But I,'
Said Francis, 'picked the eleventh from this hearth
And have it: keep a thing, its use will come.

15 An inquiry was set up 1835; the Ecclesiastical Commissioners Act was passed in 1836, and revised in 1840–1.
16 hawking at flying at (*OED* 1.3).   **geology** a perennial source of disquiet for the orthodox in the 1830s. The T. library contained C. Babbage's 9th Bridgewater Treatise (1837).   **schism** adherents of the Oxford Movement (led by Newman and Pusey) were regarded by some churchmen as schismatic.
18 decay of faith regretted in such works as Kenelm Digby *The Broadstone of Honour* (1822 etc.) and Carlyle *Past and Present* (1843).
36 mastodon extinct mammal resembling the elephant. First described by Cuvier 1806.

I hoard it as a sugar-plum for Holmes.'
He laughed, and I, though sleepy, like a horse
45   That hears the corn-bin open, pricked my ears;
For I remembered Everard's college fame
When we were Freshmen: then at my request
He brought it; and the poet little urged,
But with some prelude of disparagement,
50   Read, mouthing out his hollow oes and aes,
Deep-chested music, and to this result.

46.2 Morte d'Arthur

So all day long the noise of battle rolled
Among the mountains by the winter sea;
Until King Arthur's table, man by man,
Had fallen in Lyonnesse about their Lord,
5   King Arthur: then, because his wound was deep,
The bold Sir Bedivere uplifted him,
Sir Bedivere, the last of all his knights,
And bore him to a chapel nigh the field,
A broken chancel with a broken cross,
10   That stood on a dark strait of barren land.
On one side lay the ocean, and on one
Lay a great water, and the moon was full.

      Then spake King Arthur to Sir Bedivere:
'The sequel of today unsolders all
15   The goodliest fellowship of famous knights
Whereof this world holds record. Such a sleep
They sleep – the men I loved. I think that we
Shall never more, at any future time,
Delight our souls with talk of knightly deeds,
20   Walking about the gardens and the halls
Of Camelot, as in the days that were.
I perish by this people which I made, –
Though Merlin sware that I should come again
To rule once more – but let what will be, be,
25   I am so deeply smitten through the helm
That without help I cannot last till morn.

4 Lyonnesse 'the country of legend that lay between Cornwall and the Scilly Islands' (T.'s note).
5–12 See E. Vinaver ed. *The Works of Sir Thomas Malory* (1954) 868.
13–14 *1969* gives 13 lines from *Heath MS.* and *Fitzw. MS.*
23 Malory 873 'Yet som men say in many partys of Inglonde that kynge Arthur ys nat dede, but had by the wyll of oure Lorde Jesu into another place; and men say that he shall com agayne'.

Thou therefore take my brand Excalibur,
Which was my pride: for thou rememberest how
In those old days, one summer noon, an arm
30   Rose up from out the bosom of the lake,
Clothed in white samite, mystic, wonderful,
Holding the sword – and how I rowed across
And took it, and have worn it, like a king:
And, wheresoever I am sung or told
35   In aftertime, this also shall be known:
But now delay not: take Excalibur,
And fling him far into the middle mere:
Watch what thou seëst, and lightly bring me word.'

    To him replied the bold Sir Bedivere:
40   'It is not meet, Sir King, to leave thee thus,
Aidless, alone, and smitten through the helm.
A little thing may harm a wounded man.
Yet I thy hest will all perform at full,
Watch what I see, and lightly bring thee word.'

45   So saying, from the ruined shrine he stepped
And in the moon athwart the place of tombs,
Where lay the mighty bones of ancient men,
Old knights, and over them the sea-wind sang
Shrill, chill, with flakes of foam. He, stepping down
50   By zig-zag paths, and juts of pointed rock,
Came on the shining levels of the lake.

    There drew he forth the brand Excalibur,
And o'er him, drawing it, the winter moon,
Brightening the skirts of a long cloud, ran forth
55   And sparkled keen with frost against the hilt:
For all the haft twinkled with diamond sparks,
Myriads of topaz-lights, and jacinth-work
Of subtlest jewellery. He gazed so long
That both his eyes were dazzled, as he stood,
60   This way and that dividing the swift mind,
In act to throw: but at the last it seemed

27 Excalibur the name of King Arthur's sword; first occurs in this form circa
1300. Perhaps related to the Irish legendary sword Caladbolg: 'voracious'.
29–33 Described Malory 41–2: 'an arme clothed in whyght samyte'.
36–44 Malory 869–70.
45–65 Malory 870.
57 jacinth-work set of garnets, though in C16 the colour was said to range
from sapphire to yellow.
60 T. compares Virgil *Aen.* 4.285: '*atque animum nunc huc celerem, nunc
dividit illuc*' ('And now hither, now thither, he swiftly throws his mind').
61 Cf. Pope *Iliad* 4.570: 'In act to throw; but cautious, looked around.'

Better to leave Excalibur concealed
There in the many-knotted waterflags
That whistled stiff and dry about the marge.
65 So strode he back slow to the wounded King.

Then spake King Arthur to Sir Bedivere:
'Hast thou performed my mission which I gave?
What is it thou hast seen? or what hast heard?'

And answer made the bold Sir Bedivere:
70 'I heard the ripple washing in the reeds,
And the wild water lapping on the crag.'

To whom replied King Arthur, faint and pale:
'Thou hast betrayed thy nature and thy name,
Not rendering true answer, as beseemed
75 Thy fëalty, nor like a noble knight:
For surer sign had followed, either hand,
Or voice, or else a motion of the mere.
This is a shameful thing for men to lie.
Yet now, I charge thee, quickly go again
80 As thou art lief and dear, and do the thing
I bad thee, watch, and lightly bring me word.'

Then went Sir Bedivere the second time
Across the ridge, and paced beside the mere,
Counting the dewy pebbles, fixed in thought;
85 But when he saw the wonder of the hilt,
How curiously and strangely chased, he smote
His palms together, and he cried aloud,

'And if indeed I cast the brand away,
Surely a precious thing, one worthy note,
90 Should thus be lost for ever from the earth,
Which might have pleased the eyes of many men.
What good should follow this, if this were done?
What harm, undone? deep harm to disobey,
Seeing obedience is the bond of rule.
95 Were it well to obey then, if a king demand
An act unprofitable, against himself?
The King is sick, and knows not what he does.
What record, or what relic of my lord

66–81 Malory 870.
71 lapping] wapping *Heath MS;* an archaic word from Malory.
82–112 Malory 870.
83 Not in *1842–1851.*
92–4 With a distinctly Miltonic ring. Cf. *Paradise Lost* 4.42–8.

Should be to aftertime, but empty breath
100 And rumours of a doubt? but were this kept,
Stored in some treasure-house of mighty kings,
Some one might show it at a joust of arms,
Saying, "King Arthur's sword, Excalibur,
Wrought by the lonely maiden of the Lake.
105 Nine years she wrought it, sitting in the deeps
Upon the hidden bases of the hills."
So might some old man speak in the aftertime
To all the people, winning reverence.
But now much honour and much fame were lost.'

110 So spake he, clouded with his own conceit,
And hid Excalibur the second time,
And so strode back slow to the wounded King.

Then spoke King Arthur, breathing heavily:
'What is it thou hast seen? or what hast heard?'

115 And answer made the bold Sir Bedivere:
'I heard the water lapping on the crag,
And the long ripple washing in the reeds.'

To whom replied King Arthur, much in wrath:
'Ah, miserable and unkind, untrue,
120 Unknightly, traitor-hearted! Woe is me!
Authority forgets a dying king,
Laid widowed of the power in his eye
That bowed the will. I see thee what thou art,
For thou, the latest-left of all my knights,
125 In whom should meet the offices of all,
Thou wouldst betray me for the precious hilt;
Either from lust of gold, or like a girl
Valuing the giddy pleasure of the eyes.
Yet, for a man may fail in duty twice,
130 And the third time may prosper, get thee hence:
But, if thou spare to fling Excalibur,
I will arise and slay thee with my hands.'

105 Nine years a traditional length of time for the creation of finished works of art; see Horace *Ars Poetica* 388: '*Nonumque prematur in anum*' (Let your piece be kept until the ninth year).
110 conceit fancy.
113–32 Malory 870.
116 lapping] wapping *Heath MS*.
120 Unknightly not having the qualities of a knight; a Spenserianism; see e.g. *Faerie Queene* 6.3.35.

Then quickly rose Sir Bedivere, and ran,
And, leaping down the ridges lightly, plunged
135 Among the bulrush-beds, and clutched the sword,
And strongly wheeled and threw it. The great brand
Made lightnings in the splendour of the moon,
And flashing round and round, and whirled in an arch,
Shot like a streamer of the northern morn,
140 Seen where the moving isles of winter shock
By night, with noises of the northern sea.
So flashed and fell the brand Excalibur:
But ere he dipped the surface, rose an arm
Clothed in white samite, mystic, wonderful,
145 And caught him by the hilt, and brandished him
Three times, and drew him under in the mere.
And lightly went the other to the King.

Then spoke King Arthur, drawing thicker breath:
'Now see I by thine eyes that this is done.
150 Speak out: what is it thou hast heard, or seen?'

And answer made the bold Sir Bedivere:
'Sir King, I closed mine eyelids, lest the gems
Should blind my purpose, for I never saw,
Nor shall see, here or elsewhere, till I die,
155 Not though I live three lives of mortal men,
So great a miracle as yonder hilt.
Then with both hands I flung him, wheeling him;
But when I looked again, behold an arm,
Clothed in white samite, mystic, wonderful,
160 That caught him by the hilt, and brandished him
Three times, and drew him under in the mere.'

And answer made King Arthur, breathing hard.
'My end draws nigh; 'tis time that I were gone.
Make broad thy shoulders to receive my weight,
165 And bear me to the margin; yet I fear
My wound hath taken cold, and I shall die.'

So saying, from the pavement he half rose,
Slowly, with pain, reclining on his arm,

133–66 Malory 870–1.
139 streamer *Northern Lights.*
140 moving isles icebergs.   **shock** collide with each other (*OED* v² 1); a favourite T. word.
155 T. compares *Odyssey* 3. 245: ʹτρὶς γὰρ δή μίν φασιν ἀνάξασθαι γένεʹ ἀνδρῶνʹ ('For thrice, men say, has he been King for a generation of men').
167–203 Malory 871.

And looking wistfully with wide blue eyes
170 As in a picture. Him Sir Bedivere
Remorsefully regarded through his tears,
And would have spoken, but he found not words,
Then took with care, and kneeling on one knee,
O'er both his shoulders drew the languid hands,
175 And rising bore him through the place of tombs.

But, as he walked, King Arthur panted hard,
Like one that feels a nightmare on his bed
When all the house is mute. So sighed the King,
Muttering and murmuring at his ear, 'Quick, quick!
180 I fear it is too late, and I shall die.'
But the other swiftly strode from ridge to ridge,
Clothed with his breath, and looking, as he walked,
Larger than human on the frozen hills.
He heard the deep behind him, and a cry
185 Before. His own thought drove him, like a goad.
Dry clashed his harness in the icy caves
And barren chasms, and all to left and right
The bare black cliff clanged round him, as he based
His feet on juts of slippery crag that rang
190 Sharp-smitten with the dint of armèd heels –
And on a sudden, lo! the level lake,
And the long glories of the winter moon.

Then saw they how there hove a dusky barge,
Dark as a funeral scarf from stem to stern,
195 Beneath them; and descending they were ware
That all the decks were dense with stately forms
Black-stoled, black-hooded, like a dream – by these
Three Queens with crowns of gold – and from them rose
A cry that shivered to the tingling stars,
200 And, as it were one voice, an agony
Of lamentation, like a wind, that shrills
All night in a waste land, where no one comes,
Or hath come, since the making of the world.

177 Like one on whom a dusky nightmare leaps *Fitzw. MS.*
183 Larger than human '*humano maior*', like the ghost of Romulus in Ovid
Fasti 2. 503.
204–25 Malory 871.
198 Three Queens King Arthur's sister Morgan le Fay, the Queen of
Northgalis and the Queen of the Waste Lands. T. commented: 'Some say
that the three Queens are Faith, Hope, and Charity…They are three of the
noblest of women. They are also those three Graces, but they are much
more.'

Then murmured Arthur, 'Place me in the barge,'
205 And to the barge they came. There those three Queens
Put forth their hands, and took the King, and wept.
But she, that rose the tallest of them all
And fairest, laid his head upon her lap,
And loosed the shattered casque, and chafed his hands,
210 And called him by his name, complaining loud,
And dropping bitter tears against his brow
Striped with dark blood: for all his face was white
And colourless, and like the withered moon
Smote by the fresh beam of the springing east;
215 And all his greaves and cuisses dashed with drops
Of onset; and the light and lustrous curls –
That made his forehead like a rising sun
High from the daïs-throne – were parched with dust;
Or, clotted into points and hanging loose,
220 Mixed with the knightly growth that fringed his lips.
So like a shattered column lay the King;
Not like that Arthur who, with lance in rest,
From spur to plume a star of tournament,
Shot through the lists at Camelot, and charged
225 Before the eyes of ladies and of kings.

Then loudly cried the bold Sir Bedivere,
'Ah! my Lord Arthur, whither shall I go?
Where shall I hide my forehead and my eyes?
For now I see the true old times are dead,
230 When every morning brought a noble chance,
And every chance brought out a noble knight.
Such times have been not since the light that led
The holy Elders with the gift of myrrh.
But now the whole ROUND TABLE is dissolved
235 Which was an image of the mighty world;
And I, the last, go forth companionless,
And the days darken round me, and the years,
Among new men, strange faces, other minds.'

221 shattered column It was traditional to refer to monarchs as columns, e.g.
the pattern-poems on Queen Elizabeth I as a pillar of state (in M. Church
PMLA 61 (1946) 649). For the notion of the broken column and the great
man see Petrarch: '*Rotta e l'alta Colonna e'l verde lauro*'.
225 Before the eyes of ladies thrice as far | As those that win the love of
modern men. *Fitzw. MS.*
226–64 Malory 871.
233–4 The Magi who brought the gifts to Christ.

And slowly answered Arthur from the barge:
240 'The old order changeth, yielding place to new,
And God fulfils Himself in many ways,
Lest one good custom should corrupt the world.
Comfort thyself: what comfort is in me?
I have lived my life, and that which I have done
245 May He within Himself make pure! but thou,
If thou shouldst never see my face again,
Pray for my soul. More things are wrought by prayer
Than this world dreams of. Wherefore, let thy voice
Rise like a fountain for me night and day.
250 For what are men better than sheep or goats
That nourish a blind life within the brain,
If, knowing God, they lift not hands of prayer
Both for themselves and those who call them friend?
For so the whole round earth is every way
255 Bound by gold chains about the feet of God.
But now farewell. I am going a long way
With these thou seëst – if indeed I go –
(For all my mind is clouded with a doubt)
To the island-valley of Avilion;
260 Where falls not hail, or rain, or any snow,
Nor ever wind blows loudly; but it lies
Deep-meadowed, happy, fair with orchard-lawns
And bowery hollows crowned with summer sea,
Where I will heal me of my grievous wound.'

265   So said he, and the barge with oar and sail
Moved from the brink, like some full-breasted swan
That, fluting a wild carol ere her death,
Ruffles her pure cold plume, and takes the flood
With swarthy webs. Long stood Sir Bedivere
270 Revolving many memories, till the hull
Looked one black dot against the verge of dawn,
And on the mere the wailing died away.

242 'e.g. chivalry, by formalism of habit or by any other means' (T.'s note).
255 A beautiful and subtle adaption by T. of the traditional image of the golden chain connecting the world to God.
259 Avilion the form Malory uses: Avalon is an alternative. 'From which he will some day return – the Isle of the Blest' (T.'s note).
260-3 T. compares *Odyssey* 4.566 ff and Lucretius *De Rerum Natura* 3.18 ff (adapted again in *Lucretius* Lines 104–10 (p. 180 below).
265-72 Malory 871.
270 Revolving Miltonic, cf. 'much revolving', *Paradise Lost* 4.31; perhaps also an echo of Virgil *Aen.* 1.305: '*per noctem volvens*'.

[47] Alfred Tennyson

[THE EPIC]

    Here ended Hall, and our last light, that long
    Had winked and threatened darkness, flared and fell:
275 At which the Parson, sent to sleep with sound,
    And waked with silence, grunted 'Good!' but we
    Sat rapt: it was the tone with which he read –
    Perhaps some modern touches here and there
    Redeemed it from the charge of nothingness –
280 Or else we loved the man, and prized his work;
    I know not: but we sitting, as I said,
    The cock crew loud; as at that time of year
    The lusty bird takes every hour for dawn:
    Then Francis, muttering, like a man ill-used,
285 'There now – that's nothing!' drew a little back,
    And drove his heel into the smouldered log,
    That sent a blast of sparkles up the flue:
    And so to bed: where yet in sleep I seemed
    To sail with Arthur under looming shores,
290 Point after point; till on to dawn, when dreams
    Begin to feel the truth and stir of day,
    To me, methought, who waited with a crowd,
    There came a bark that, blowing forward, bore
    King Arthur, like a modern gentleman
295 Of stateliest port; and all the people cried,
    'Arthur is come again: he cannot die.'
    Then those that stood upon the hills behind
    Repeated – 'Come again, and thrice as fair;'
    And, further inland, voices echoed – 'Come
300 With all good things, and war shall be no more.'
    At this a hundred bells began to peal,
    That with the sound I woke, and heard indeed
    The clear church-bells ring in the Christmas-morn.

278 modern touches a principle that T. kept in his mind when he composed the *Idylls*.
282–3 See Shakespeare *Ham.* 1.1. 158–60: 'Some say that ever 'gainst that season comes | Wherein our Saviour's birth is celebrated | This bird of dawning singeth all night long.

47 Locksley Hall

Date Written *c.* 1837–8 (Rader 41–2), but W. D. Templeman (*Booker Memorial Studies* (1950)) and Buckley 271 place it 1840–1, when T. broke his engagement with Emily Sellwood. It is more likely that the work grows from T.'s unhappy love-affair with Rosa Baring (see headnote to *Maud* p. 131 below). Sir Charles Tennyson suggests that much of the poem may be traced back to the Tennyson family feud (194). T. asserted that the work contained 'an imaginary place and imaginary hero'.

Source The main literary source is Sir William Jones's prose translation of the *Moâllakát*: Amriolais broods over a place associated with his lost mistress, and a storm breaks out at the end of his reveries. E. F. Shannon, *N & Q* 204 (1959) 216–17, suggests the influence of Scott's *Ivanhoe*, in which Locksley is the pseudonym of the alienated Robin Hood. As with *Maud*, *Hamlet* is a pervasive influence.

The metre is trochaic: 'Mr (Henry) Hallam said to me that the English people liked verse in trochaics, so I wrote the poem in this metre' (T.). See the *1842* ending of *The Lotos Eaters* for the same 8-stress trochaic line.

The sequel was *Locksley Hall Sixty Years After*, written and published 1886, and reappraising the hero in the light of subsequent Victorian experience.

Publication *1842*.

> Comrades, leave me here a little, while as yet 'tis
>   early morn:
> Leave me here, and when you want me, sound upon the
>   bugle-horn.
>
> 'Tis the place, and all around it, as of old, the
>   curlews call,
> Dreary gleams about the moorland flying over Locksley
>   Hall;
>
> 5   Locksley Hall, that in the distance overlooks the sandy
>   tracts,
> And the hollow ocean-ridges roaring into cataracts.
>
> Many a night from yonder ivied casement, ere I went
>   to rest,
> Did I look on great Orion sloping slowly to the west.
>
> Many a night I saw the Pleiads, rising through the
>   mellow shade,
> 10   Glitter like a swarm of fire-flies tangled in a silver braid.
>
> Here about the beach I wandered, nourishing a youth
>   sublime
> With the fairy tales of science, and the long result of time;
>
> When the centuries behind me like a fruitful land reposed;
> When I clung to all the present for the promise that it
>   closed:

3 'Tis ... it] Round the gable, round the turret *MS*.
3–4 'This means "*while* dreary gleams", not in apposition to "curlews"' (T.'s note).
9–10 From the *Moâllakát* (see headnote): 'It was the hour, when the Pleiads appeared in the firmament, like the folds of a silken sash variously decked with gems.'
14 closed enclosed included; the last occurrence cited, *OED* I. 3d.

[47] Alfred Tennyson

15 　When I dipped into the future far as human eye could see;
　　Saw the vision of the world, and all the wonder that
　　　　would be. –

　　In the spring a fuller crimson comes upon the robin's
　　　　breast;
　　In the spring the wanton lapwing gets himself another
　　　　crest;
　　In the spring a livelier iris changes on the burnished
　　　　dove;
20 　In the spring a young man's fancy lightly turns to
　　　　thoughts of love.

　　Then her cheek was pale and thinner than should be for
　　　　one so young,
　　And her eyes on all my motions with a mute observance
　　　　hung.

　　And I said, 'My cousin Amy, speak, and speak the truth
　　　　to me,
　　Trust me, cousin, all the current of my being sets to thee.'

25 　On her pallid cheek and forehead came a colour and a
　　　　light,
　　As I have seen the rosy red flushing in the northern
　　　　night.

　　And she turned – her bosom shaken with a sudden storm
　　　　of sighs –
　　All the spirit deeply dawning in the dark of hazel eyes –

　　Saying, 'I have hid my feelings, fearing they should do
　　　　me wrong;'
30 　Saying, 'Dost thou love me, cousin?' weeping, 'I have
　　　　loved thee long.'

　　Love took up the glass of time, and turned it in his
　　　　glowing hands;
　　Every moment, lightly shaken, ran itself in golden sands.

　　Love took up the harp of life, and smote on all the
　　　　chords with might;
　　Smote the chord of self, that, trembling, passed in
　　　　music out of sight.

19 iris a rainbow-like or iridescent patch of colour (*OED* 2b quotes this).
24 sets to aims in your direction.
31 glowing hands Ricks *1969* cites Keats *Eve of St. Agnes* lines 271–2 to
indicate that it is a traditional way of demonstrating the largesse of love:
'These delicates he heaped with glowing hand | On golden dishes.'

35 Many a morning on the moorland did we hear the
  copses ring.
  And her whisper thronged my pulses with the fulness of
  the spring.

Many an evening by the waters did we watch the stately
  ships,
And our spirits rushed together at the touching of the
  lips.

O my cousin, shallow-hearted! O my Amy, mine no
  more!
40 O the dreary, dreary moorland! O the barren, barren
  shore!

Falser than all fancy fathoms, falser than all songs have
  sung,
Puppet to a father's threat, and servile to a shrewish
  tongue!

Is it well to wish thee happy? – having known me – to decline
On a range of lower feelings and a narrower heart than
  mine!

45 Yet it shall be: thou shalt lower to his level day by day,
What is fine within thee growing coarse to sympathise
  with clay.

As the husband is, the wife is: thou art mated with a
  clown,
And the grossness of his nature will have weight to drag
  thee down.

He will hold thee, when his passion shall have spent its
  novel force,
50 Something better than his dog, a little dearer than his
  horse.

<hr>

38 ∧ 9 In the hall there hangs a painting, Amy's arms are round my neck, |
Happy children in a sunbeam, sitting on the ribs of wreck. | In my life there
is a picture: she that clasped my neck is flown. | I am left within the shadow,
sitting on the wreck alone. *HnMS*. T. deleted these lines from the proofs of
1842 (*Lincoln*); they became the nucleus of *Locksley Hall Sixty Years After*
(1886).
43–4 Cf. *Ham.* 1.5. 50–2: 'To decline | Upon a wretch whose natural gifts
were poor | To those of mine'.
47 clown a man without refinement or culture (*OED* 2). Cf. *In Memoriam*
111.4: 'By blood a king, at heart a clown.'

What is this? his eyes are heavy: think not they are
    glazed with wine.
Go to him: it is thy duty: kiss him: take his hand in
    thine.

It may be my lord is weary, that his brain is
    overwrought:
Soothe him with thy finer fancies, touch him with thy
    lighter thought.

55 He will answer to the purpose, easy things to understand –
Better thou wert dead before me, though I slew thee
    with my hand!

Better thou and I were lying, hidden from the heart's
    disgrace,
Rolled in one another's arms, and silent in a last embrace.

Cursèd be the social wants that sin against the strength
    of youth!
60 Cursèd be the social lies that warp us from the living
    truth!

Cursèd be the sickly forms that err from honest Nature's
    rule!
Cursèd be the gold that gilds the straitened forehead of
    the fool!

Well – 'tis well that I should bluster! – Hadst thou less
    unworthy proved –
Would to God – for I had loved thee more than ever
    wife was loved.

65 Am I mad, that I should cherish that which bears but
    bitter fruit!
I will pluck it from my bosom, though my heart be at
    the root.

Never, though my mortal summers to such length of
    years should come
As the many-wintered crow that leads the clanging
    rookery home.

Where is comfort? in division of the records of the mind?
70 Can I part her from herself, and love her, as I knew her,
    kind?

62 straitened insufficiently spacious (*OED* 1 quotes this line).
63 Well...bluster!] Cursèd – No I curse not thee. O *MS* 1st reading.
68 crow 'Rooks are called crows in the Northern counties' (T.'s note).

I remember one that perished: sweetly did she speak and
move:
Such a one do I remember, whom to look at was to love.

Can I think of her as dead, and love her for the love she
bore?
No – she never loved me truly: love is love for evermore.

75 Comfort? comfort scorned of devils! this is truth the poet
sings,
That a sorrow's crown of sorrow is remembering happier
things.

Drug thy memories, lest thou learn it, lest thy heart be
put to proof,
In the dead unhappy night, and when the rain is on the
roof.

Like a dog, he hunts in dreams, and thou art staring at
the wall,
80 Where the dying night-lamp flickers, and the shadows
rise and fall.

Then a hand shall pass before thee, pointing to his
drunken sleep,
To thy widowed marriage-pillows, to the tears that thou
wilt weep.

Thou shalt hear the 'Never, never,' whispered by the
phantom years,
And a song from out the distance in the ringing of thine
ears;

85 And an eye shall vex thee, looking ancient kindness on
thy pain.
Turn thee, turn thee on thy pillow: get thee to thy rest
again.

Nay, but Nature brings thee solace; for a tender voice
will cry.
'Tis a purer life than thine; a lip to drain thy trouble dry.

---

75 Comfort...devils] Hollow, hollow, hollow comfort MS. 1st
reading. **the poet** Dante. See *Inferno* 5.121–3: '*Nessun maggior dolore,* |
Che ricordarsi del tempo felice | *Nella miseria.*' (No greater grief than to
remember days | Of joy, when misery is at hand). Said by Francesca da
Rimini. Familiar to T. via Byron's *Corsair* since he was twelve (*Memoir* I.8).
Ricks *1969* suggests T. is countering the consolation of pleasure recollected
in tranquillity in the *Moâllakát*.

Baby lips will laugh me down: my latest rival brings
    thee rest.

90   Baby fingers, waxen touches, press me from the mother's
    breast.

O, the child too clothes the father with a dearness not
    his due.
Half is thine and half is his: it will be worthy of the two.

O, I see thee old and formal, fitted to thy petty part,
With a little hoard of maxims preaching down a
    daughter's heart.

95   'They were dangerous guides the feelings – she herself
    was not exempt –
Truly, she herself had suffered' – Perish in thy
    self-contempt!

Overlive it – lower yet – be happy! wherefore should I
    care?
I myself must mix with action, lest I wither by despair.

What is that which I should turn to, lighting upon days
    like these?
100   Every door is barred with gold, and opens but to golden
    keys.

Every gate is thronged with suitors, all the markets
    overflow.
I have but an angry fancy: what is that which I should
    do?

I had been content to perish, falling on the foreman's
    ground,
When the ranks are rolled in vapour, and the winds are
    laid with sound.

105   But the jingling of the guinea helps the hurt that honour
    feels,
And the nations do but murmur, snarling at each other's
    heels.

92 it will be] God send it MS. 1st reading.
93 fitted ... part] versed in many a vulgar art MS. 1st reading.
98 The panacea advocated in the final section of *Maud*. Clough tends to be a little more sceptical about the efficacy of engaging in action to counteract ennervating mental states.
104 winds are laid i.e. caused to subside. Cf. *Paradise Regained* 4. 429. T. alludes to a belief that gunfire had a stilling effect on the air.
105 jingling ... hurt] tightness of the purse-string salves the sore MS.

Can I but relive in sadness! I will turn that earlier page.
Hide me from my deep emotion, O thou wondrous
    mother-age!

Make me feel the wild pulsation that I felt before the
    strife,
110   When I heard my days before me, and the tumult of
    my life;

Yearning for the large excitement that the coming years
    would yield,
Eager-hearted as a boy when first he leaves his father's
    field,

And at night along the dusky highway near and nearer
    drawn,
Sees in heaven the light of London flaring like a dreary
    dawn;

115   And his spirit leaps within him to be gone before him
    then,
Underneath the light he looks at, in among the throngs
    of men:

Men, my brothers, men the workers, ever reaping
    something new:
That which they have done but earnest of the things
    that they shall do:

For I dipped into the future, far as human eye could see,
120   Saw the vision of the world, and all the wonder that
    would be;

Saw the heavens fill with commerce, argosies of magic
    sails,
Pilots of the purple twilight, dropping down with costly
    bales;

Heard the heavens fill with shouting, and there rained
    a ghastly dew
From the nations' airy navies grappling in the central
    blue;

118 earnest of *OED* sb 2: a pledge of things to come. Cf. Shakespeare *Cymb.*
1.5.65: 'It is an earnest of a farther good.'
122 purple the colour of the imagination in this poem: see line 164 below.
123–4 The aeronaut in Johnson's *Rasselas* Ch. 6 foresaw war in the air: '"If
men were all virtuous..I should with great alacrity teach them all to fly.
But what would be the security of the good, if the bad could invade them
from the sky at pleasure?"' E. F. Shannon *PQ* 31 (1952) 441–5 argues that
T., thinking of Charles Green the balloonist, is more probably referring to
lighter-than-air machines than ornithopters.

125 Far along the world-wide whisper of the south-wind
    rushing warm,
With the standards of the peoples plunging through the
    thunder-storm;

Till the war-drum throbbed no longer, and the
    battle-flags were furled
In the Parliament of man, the Federation of the world.

There the common sense of most shall hold a fretful
    realm in awe,
130 And the kindly earth shall slumber, lapped in universal law.

So I triumphed ere my passion sweeping through me
    left me dry,
Left me with the palsied heart, and left me with the
    jaundiced eye;

Eye, to which all order festers, all things here are out
    of joint:
Science moves, but slowly slowly, creeping on from
    point to point:

135 Slowly comes a hungry people, as a lion creeping nigher,
Glares at one that nods and winks behind a slowly-dying
    fire.

Yet I doubt not through the ages one increasing purpose
    runs,
And the thoughts of men are widened with the process
    of the suns,

What is that to him that reaps not harvest of his
    youthful joys,
140 Though the deep heart of existence beat for ever like a
    boy's?

Knowledge comes, but wisdom lingers, and I linger on ·
    the shore,
And the individual withers, and the world is more and
    more.

127 Saw the peoples brother-minded laying battle-standards furled MS.
133 Cf. Shakespeare *Ham.* 1.5.188–9: 'The time is out of joint, O cursed spite, | That ever I was born to set it right.'
135–6 Or the crowd that stumbling forward in their hunger drawing near, | With a lingering will divided by their famine and their fear, MS.
136∧7 Yet I doubt not that a glory waits upon some later morn – Every moment dies a man and every moment one is born. MS. 1st reading.
142 Paradoxically, growth of interest in the status of the individual developed in the 1830s and 40s, just as it was coming under increasing threat.

Knowledge comes, but wisdom lingers, and he bears a
    laden breast,
Full of sad experience, moving toward the stillness of
    his rest.

145   Hark, my merry comrades call me, sounding on the
    bugle-horn,
They to whom my foolish passion were a target for
    their scorn:

Shall it not be scorn to me to harp on such a mouldered
    string?
I am shamed through all my nature to have loved so
    slight a thing.

Weakness to be wroth with weakness! woman's pleasure,
    woman's pain –
150   Nature made them blinder motions bounded in a
    shallower brain:

Woman is the lesser man, and all thy passions,
    matched with mine,
Are as moonlight unto sunlight, and as water unto wine –

Here at least, where nature sickens, nothing. Ah, for
    some retreat
Deep in yonder shining Orient, where my life began
    to beat;

155   Where in wild Mahratta-battle fell my father
    evil-starred; –
I was left a trampled orphan, and a selfish uncle's ward.

Or to burst all links of habit – there to wander far away,
On from island unto island at the gateways of the day.

Larger constellations burning, mellow moons and happy
    skies,
160   Breadths of tropic shade and palms in cluster, knots of
    Paradise.

Never comes the trader, never floats an European flag,
Slides the bird o'er lustrous woodland, swings the
    trailer from the crag;

155 Mahratta for an account of the Indian campaign 1817–19 see James
Grant Duff *History of the Mahrattas* (1878).
160 ∧ 1 All about a summer ocean, leagues on leagues of golden calm, | And
within melodious waters rolling round the knolls of palm. 'In the first
unpublished edition…omitted lest the description should be too long'
(*Memoir* I.195).   **knots** probably *OED* 7: intricate flower-bed designs.
162 trailer trailing plant.

[47] Alfred Tennyson

Droops the heavy-blossomed bower, hangs the
    heavy-fruited tree –
Summer isles of Eden lying in dark-purple spheres of sea.

165 There methinks would be enjoyment more than in this
    march of mind,
In the steamship, in the railway, in the thoughts that
    shake mankind.

There the passions cramped no longer shall have scope
    and breathing space;
I will take some savage woman, she shall rear my dusky
    race.

Iron jointed, supple-sinewed, they shall dive, and they
    shall run,
170 Catch the wild goat by the hair, and hurl their lances
    in the sun;

Whistle back the parrot's call, and leap the rainbows
    of the brooks,
Not with blinded eyesight poring over miserable books –

Fool, again the dream, the fancy! but I *know* my words
    are wild,
But I count the gray barbarian lower than the
    Christian child.

175 I, to herd with narrow foreheads, vacant of our
    glorious gains.
Like a beast with lower pleasures, like a beast with
    lower pains!

Mated with a squalid savage – what to me were sun or
    clime?
I the heir of all the ages, in the foremost files of time –

I that rather held it better men should perish one by
    one,
180 Than that earth should stand at gaze like Joshua's
    moon in Ajalon!

180 *Joshua* 10.12: the sun and moon stood still whilst the Israelites avenged
themselves upon their enemies.

Not in vain the distance beacons. Forward, forward let
    us range,
Let the great world spin for ever down the ringing
    grooves of change,

Through the shadow of the globe we sweep into the
    younger day:
Better fifty years of Europe than a cycle of Cathay.

185   Mother-age (for mine I knew not) help me as when
    life begun;
Rift the hills, and roll the waters, flash the lightnings,
    weigh the Sun.

O, I see the crescent promise of my spirit hath not set.
Ancient founts of inspiration well through all my fancy
    yet.

Howsoever these things be, a long farewell to Locksley
    Hall!
190   Now for me the woods may wither, now for me the
    roof-tree fall.

Comes a vapour from the margin, blackening over
    heath and holt,
Cramming all the blast before it, in its breast a
    thunderbolt.

Let it fall on Locksley Hall, with rain or hail, or fire
    or snow;
For, the mighty wind arises, roaring seaward, and I go.

---

182 T. notes: 'When I went by the first train from Liverpool to Manchester
(1830) I thought that the wheels ran in a groove. It was a black night, and
there was such a vast crowd round the train at the station that we could not
see the wheels.' Cf. lines 121–4, where T. also employs the new technology.
184 Cathay China.
187 crescent in its root sense: growing (*OED* I.1).
186 ∧ 7 Life is battle, let me fight it: win or lose it? lose it, nay! | Block my
paths with toil and danger, I will find or force a way! Added to J. Knowles's
copy (*Nineteenth Century* 33 (1893) 168).
190 roof-tree the main beam of a house.

48 'Tears, idle tears'

Date Written perhaps in the early 1840s. It is the best of the interpolated songs in *The Princess* (1847), and need not date from the time of composition of the bulk of the poem (*c*. 1845).
Associations and style T. says: 'This song came to me on the yellowing autumn-tide at Tintern Abbey, full for me of its bygone memories. It is the sense of the abiding in the transient.' *Memoir* 2.73 corroborates the details. The 'bygone memories' probably include memories of Wordsworth's *Tintern Abbey* and various associations with Hallam, buried twenty-one miles south-west (*In Memoriam* 19 uses the image of the tidal Wye). T. wrote to J. Knowles: 'It is in a way like St. Paul's "groanings which cannot be uttered." ... It is what I have always felt even from a boy, and what as a boy I called "the passion of the past". And it is so always with me now; it is the distance that charms me in the landscape, the picture and the past, and now the immediate to-day in which I move'. (*Nineteenth Century* 33 (1893) 170). T. comments: 'Few know that it is a blank verse lyric' (*Memoir* 1.253). T. J. Assad studies the scansion in *Tulane Studies in English* 13 (1963) 71–83. J. Sparrow *RES* n.s. 14 (1963) 59 compares Gray's Alcaic fragment *O lachrymarum fons*. C. Brooks in *The Well-Wrought Urn* (New York, 1947) explores the complex paradoxes of the song.
Publication in *The Princess* (1847).

> 'Tears, idle tears, I know not what they mean,
> Tears from the depth of some divine despair
> Rise in the heart, and gather to the eyes,
> In looking on the happy Autumn-fields,
> 5   And thinking of the days that are no more.

> 'Fresh as the first beam glittering on a sail,
> That brings our friends up from the underworld,
> Sad as the last which reddens over one
> That sinks with all we love below the verge;
> 10   So sad, so fresh, the days that are no more.

> 'Ah, sad and strange as in dark summer dawns
> The earliest pipe of half-awakened birds
> To dying ears, when unto dying eyes
> The casement slowly grows a glimmering square;
> 15   So sad, so strange, the days that are no more.

6–10 For the association of ships with love, death and memory see *In Memoriam* 10 and 14.
14 Cf. Leigh Hunt *Hero and Leander* lines 284–5: 'And when the casement, at dawn of light, | Began to show a square of ghastly white'.

'Dear as remembered kisses after death,
And sweet as those by hopeless fancy feigned
On lips that are for others; deep as love,
Deep as first love, and wild with all regret;
20   O Death in Life, the days that are no more.'

49 In Memoriam A.H.H.:

OBIIT MDCCCXXXIII: extracts

Date Written Oct. 1833–1850. The poem is an elegy for T.'s friend Arthur
Hallam, who died in Vienna 15 Sept. 1833. T. received the news on 1 Oct.
from Hallam's uncle Henry Elton (*Memoir* 1.105); see Ricks 114–5 for text.
The shock to T., and to his sister Emily, who had been engaged to Hallam,
was shattering. For an immediate poetic reaction to the event see *Hark! the
dogs howl!* (no. 43). **Associations** Hallam's father set about collecting
Arthur's literary works (published 1834 as *The Remains...*), to which he
wanted T. to contribute, but T. wrote (14 Feb. 1834): 'I attempted to draw
up a memoir of his life and character, but I failed to do him justice.'
However, he began writing elegiac poems on Hallam, usually referred to as
'The Elegies', and many friends saw them in the 1840s. See *1969* 856. The
earliest sections, probably composed as early as 1833, are 9, 30, 17, 18, 30–32,
and 85. For details of the manuscripts see *1969* 857–8. The trial edition of
March 1850 was revised to tone down optimism. The title was suggested by
Emily Sellwood, whom T. married in June 1850.

In Memoriam was published anonymously. T. said of it: 'It must be
remembered that this is a poem, *not* an actual biography...The poem
concludes with the marriage of my youngest sister Cecilia (to his Cambridge
friend Edmund Lushington, 14 Oct. 1842). It was meant to be a kind of
Divina Commedia, ending with happiness. The sections were written at many
different places, and as the phases of our intercourse came to my memory
and suggested them. I did not write them with any view of weaving them into
a whole, or for publication, until I found that I had written so many. The different
moods of sorrow as in a drama are dramatically given, and my conviction
that fear, doubts, and suffering will find answer and relief only through faith
in a God of love. "I" is not always the author speaking of himself, but the
voice of the human race speaking through him. After the death of A.H.H.,
the divisions of the poem are made by first Xmas Eve (Section 28), second
Xmas (Section 78), third Xmas Eve (104 and 105 etc.).' (*Memoir* 1.304–5).
To James Knowles T. said: 'It is rather the cry of the whole human race
than mine. In the poem altogether private grief swells out into thought of,
and hope for, the whole world. It begins with a funeral and ends with a
marriage – begins with death and ends in promise of a new life' (*Nineteenth
Century* 33 (1893) 182).

The spell of Shakespeare's sonnets is over the whole poem, but *1969* 860
demonstrates that Hallam Tennyson was wary of the association.
Criticism The first significant study of the work was A. C. Bradley *A*

[49] Alfred Tennyson

Commentary on 'In Memoriam' (3rd edn. 1910). Others include E. B. Mattes *'In Memoriam': the way of a soul* (1951), K. W. Gransden *T.: 'In Memoriam'* (1964) and J. D. Hunt ed. *T. 'In Memoriam', a casebook* (1970). E. D. H. Johnson *VS* 2 (1958) 139–48 explores T.'s search for an aesthetic creed in the poem. A. Sinfield *The Language of 'In Memoriam'* (1971) concludes that T.'s expression is 'superficially unremarkable', and that we must expect 'not violent shocks, but delicate shades of meaning which gently modify our response' Discussion also in Ricks 211–30. T. S. Eliot has a famous critique in *Essays Ancient and Modern* (1936), in which he recognizes that T. was 'the most instinctive rebel against the society in which he was the most perfect conformist'.

There is an extensive literature relating T. to scientific thought, including L. Stevenson *Darwin Among the Poets* (1932), G. R. Potter *PQ* 16 (1937) 321–43, W. R. Rutland *E & S* 26 (1940) 7–29 and G. Hough *RES* 33 (1974) 244 56. See also D. Bush *Science and English Poetry* (1950) and G. Roppen *Evolution and Poetic Belief* (1956).

The stanza form discussed Bradley 67–70. Lord Herbert of Cherbury used it, but T. said he 'had no notion...that such a poem existed' until 1880, when J. C. Collins pointed it out in *The Cornhill* (Jan. 1880).

Publication *1850*; with section 59 added *1851* and section 39 *1869*.

[Prologue]

Strong Son of God, immortal Love,
 Whom we, that have not seen thy face,
 By faith, and faith alone, embrace,
Believing where we cannot prove;

5 Thine are these orbs of light and shade;
 Thou madest life in man and brute;
 Thou madest death; and lo, thy foot
Is on the skull which thou hast made.

Thou wilt not leave us in the dust:
10 Thou madest man, he knows not why,
 He thinks he was not made to die;
And thou hast made him: thou art just.

Thou seemest human and divine,
 The highest, holiest manhood, thou.
15 Our wills are ours, we know not how;
Our wills are ours, to make them thine.

Prol. Title given by Bradley.
Prol. 2–3 *Pet.* 1.8: 'Whom having not seen, ye love; in whom, though now ye see him not, yet believing.'

Our little systems have their day;
   They have their day and cease to be;
   They are but broken lights of thee,
20 And thou, O Lord, art more than they.

We have but faith: we cannot know,
   For knowledge is of things we see;
   And yet we trust it comes from thee.
A beam in darkness: let it grow.

25 Let knowledge grow from more to more,
   But more of reverence in us dwell;
   That mind and soul, according well,
May make one music as before,

But vaster. We are fools and slight;
30   We mock thee when we do not fear:
   But help thy foolish ones to bear;
Help thy vain worlds to bear thy light.

Forgive what seemed my sin in me,
   What seemed my worth since I began;
35   For merit lives from man to man,
And not from man, O Lord, to thee.

Forgive my grief for one removed,
   Thy creature, whom I found so fair.
   I trust he lives in thee, and there
40 I find him worthier to be loved.

Forgive these wild and wandering cries,
   Confusions of a wasted youth;
   Forgive them where they fail in truth,
And in thy wisdom make me wise.

1

I held it truth, with him who sings
   To one clear harp in divers tones,
   That men may rise on stepping-stones
Of their dead selves to higher things.

Prol. 19 broken lights figurative use of a painting term (*OED* 12): systems give an imperfect view of God.
Prol. 35 merit T. is thinking exclusively of merit earned in human relationships, as opposed to some of the theological senses of the word.
Prol. 44 Make me cognizant of thy wisdom.
1.1–4 'I alluded to Goethe's creed. Among his last words were..."from changes to higher changes"' (T.'s note).

5   But who shall so forecast the years
        And find in loss a gain to match?
        Or reach a hand through time to catch
      The far-off interest of tears?

      Let love clasp grief lest both be drowned,   .
10   Let darkness keep her raven gloss:
        Ah, sweeter to be drunk with loss,
      To dance with death, to beat the ground,

      Than that the victor Hours should scorn
        The long result of love, and boast,
15   'Behold the man that loved and lost,
      But all he was is overworn.'

2

      Old yew, which graspest at the stones
        That name the underlying dead,
        Thy fibres net the dreamless head,
      Thy roots are wrapped about the bones.

5   The seasons bring the flower again,
        And bring the firstling to the flock;
        And in the dusk of thee the clock
      Beats out the little lives of men.

      O not for thee the glow, the bloom,
10   Who changest not in any gale,
        Nor branding summer suns avail
      To touch thy thousand years of gloom;

      And gazing on thee, sullen tree,
        Sick for thy stubborn hardihood,
15   I seem to fail from out my blood
      And grow incorporate into thee.

3

      O sorrow, cruel fellowship,
        O priestess in the vaults of death,
        O sweet and bitter in a breath,
      What whispers from thy lying lip?

1.6 J. H. Newman's novel (1844) was called *Loss and Gain*.
1.8 interest *OED* 7: 'the feeling of one who is concerned'.
1.12 Perhaps a reminiscence of Holbein's Dance of Death.
2.3–4 An image of metaphysical intensity and ingenuity.
2.7 the clock the growth of the yew provides a measurement of time.
2.8 beats out at once 'strikes the hours' and 'flattens'.

5   'The stars,' she whispers, 'blindly run;
       A web is woven across the sky;
       From out waste places comes a cry,
       And murmurs from the dying sun;

       'And all the phantom, Nature, stands –
10   With all the music in her tone,
       A hollow echo of my own, –
       A hollow form with empty hands.'

       And shall I take a thing so blind,
       Embrace her as my natural good;
15   Or crush her, like a vice of blood,
       Upon the threshold of the mind?

4

       To sleep I give my powers away;
       My will is bondsman to the dark;
       I sit within a helmless bark,
       And with my heart I muse and say:

5   O heart, how fares it with thee now,
       That thou shouldst fail from thy desire,
       Who scarcely darest to inquire,
       'What is it makes me beat so low?'

       Something it is which thou hast lost,
10   Some pleasure from thine early years.
       Break, thou deep vase of chilling tears,
       That grief hath shaken into frost!

       Such clouds of nameless trouble cross
       All night below the darkened eyes;
15   With morning wakes the will, and cries,
       'Thou shalt not be the fool of loss.'

3.8 dying sun astronomers were coming to recognize that the sun was slowly being consumed.
3.14–15 Ricks *1969* compares Shelley *Queen Mab* 4.115–20.
3.16 Followed in *H. Lpr* by these lines: But Sorrow cares not for my frown, | And sorrow says, 'We must not part, | For if I die upon thy heart, | Then my dead weight will draw thee down.'
4.3 helmless bark rudderless boat; cf. Chaucer *Troil.* 1.415.
4.11–12 'Water can be brought below freezing-point and not turn into ice – if it be kept still; but if it be moved suddenly it turns into ice and may break the vase' (T.'s note).

5

I sometimes hold it half a sin
  To put in words the grief I feel:
  For words, like Nature, half reveal
And half conceal the Soul within.

5   But, for the unquiet heart and brain,
  A use in measured language lies;
  The sad mechanic exercise,
Like dull narcotics, numbing pain.

In words, like weeds, I'll wrap me o'er,
10   Like coarsest clothes against the cold;
  But that large grief which these enfold
Is given in outline and no more.

6

One writes, that 'other friends remain,'
  That 'loss is common to the race' –
  And common is the commonplace,
And vacant chaff well meant for grain.

5   That loss is common would not make
  My own less bitter, rather more.
  Too common! Never morning wore
To evening, but some heart did break.

O father, wheresoe'er thou be,
10   Who pledgest now thy gallant son,
  A shot, ere half thy draught be done,
Hath stilled the life that beat from thee.

O mother, praying God will save
  Thy sailor, – while thy head is bowed,
15   His heavy-shotted hammock-shroud
Drops in his vast and wandering grave.

5.1–2 Guilt at capitalising on emotional experience is a traditional poetic theme.

5.5–8 Cf. Donne *The Triple Fool* line 10: 'Grief brought to numbers cannot be so fierce'.

5.9 weeds garments.

6.7–8 T. compares Lucretius *De Rerum Natura* 2. 578–80: 'No night ever followed day, or dawn followed night, but has heard mingled with their sickly wailings the lamentations that attend upon death and the black funeral.'

Ye know no more than I who wrought
At that last hour to please him well;
Who mused on all I had to tell,
20   And something written, something thought;

Expecting still his advent home;
And ever met him on his way
With wishes, thinking, 'here to-day,'
Or 'here to-morrow will he come.'

25   O, somewhere, meek, unconscious dove,
That sittest ranging golden hair;
And glad to find thyself so fair,
Poor child, that waitest for thy love!

For now her father's chimney glows
30   In expectation of a guest;
And thinking 'this will please him best,'
She takes a riband or a rose;

For he will see them on tonight;
And with the thought her colour burns;
35   And, having left the glass, she turns
Once more to set a ringlet right;

And, even when she turned, the curse
Had fallen, and her future lord
Was drowned in passing through the ford,
40   Or killed in falling from his horse.

O, what to her shall be the end?
And what to me remains of good?
To her, perpetual maidenhood,
And unto me no second friend.

7

Dark house, by which once more I stand
Here in the long unlovely street,
Doors, where my heart was used to beat
So quickly, waiting for a hand,

6.26 ranging arranging.
6.37–40 curse and **horse** perhaps a perfect rhyme for T., since it is a
Lincolnshire pronunciation.
7.1 Dark house 67 Wimpole Street, Henry Hallam's house. Cf. section 119
below, where T. is in a more optimistic frame of mind.

5   A hand that can be clasped no more –
       Behold me, for I cannot sleep,
       And like a guilty thing I creep
    At earliest morning to the door.

    He is not here; but far away
10   The noise of life begins again,
       And ghastly through the drizzling rain
    On the bald street breaks the blank day.

8

    A happy lover who has come
       To look on her that loves him well,
       Who 'lights and rings the gateway bell,
    And learns her gone and far from home;

5   He saddens, all the magic light
       Dies off at once from bower and hall,
       And all the place is dark, and all
    The chambers emptied of delight:

    So find I every pleasant spot
10   In which we two were wont to meet,
       The field, the chamber, and the street,
    For all is dark where thou art not.

    Yet as that other, wandering there
       In those deserted walks, may find
15   A flower beat with rain and wind,
    Which once she fostered up with care;

    So seems it in my deep regret,
       O my forsaken heart, with thee
       And this poor flower of poesy
20   Which, little cared for, fades not yet.

    But since it pleased a vanished eye,
       I go to plant it on his tomb,
       That if it can it there may bloom,
    Or, dying, there at least may die.

7.7 Cf. Shakespeare *Ham.* 1.1.148: 'And then it (the ghost in the dawn) started like a guilty thing.' Also Wordsworth *Immortality Ode* 148–51: 'Blank misgivings of a creature | Moving about in worlds not realised, | High instincts before which our mortal nature | Did tremble like a guilty thing surprised.'
7.9 Cf. *Luke* 24.6: 'He is not here, but is risen.'
8.1–8 Cf. Chaucer *Troilus and Criseyde* 5.543–5: 'O paleys empty and disconsolate, | O thow lanterne of which queynt is the light | O paleys, whilom day, that now art nyght...'

9

Fair ship, that from the Italian shore
Sailest the placid ocean-plains
With my lost Arthur's loved remains,
Spread thy full wings, and waft him o'er.

So draw him home to those that mourn
In vain; a favourable speed
Ruffle thy mirrored mast, and lead
Through prosperous floods his holy urn.

All night no ruder air perplex
10   Thy sliding keel, till Phosphor, bright
As our pure love, through early light
Shall glimmer on the dewy decks.

Sphere all your lights around, above;
Sleep, gentle heavens, before the prow;
15   Sleep, gentle winds, as he sleeps now,
My friend, the brother of my love;

My Arthur, whom I shall not see
Till all my widowed race be run;
Dear as the mother to the son,
20   More than my brothers are to me.

10

I hear the noise about thy keel:
I hear the bell struck in the night;
I see the cabin-window bright;
I see the sailor at the wheel.

5   Thou bring'st the sailor to his wife,
And travelled men from foreign lands;
And letters unto trembling hands;
And, thy dark freight, a vanished life.

9. *H. Nbk* 16 (1833) has an early draft, dating from the month of Hallam's
death. There are classical precedents for the prayer for safe sea journeys
(Horace *Odes* 1.3), but more usually for the living than the dead. The ship
with Hallam's corpse sailed from Trieste.
9.10 Phosphor the morning star; in Medieval and Renaissance traditions
associated with the risen Christ.
10 For the situation of love and death associated with the ship at sea cf.
'*Tears, idle tears*' (above p. 100).

So bring him: we have idle dreams:
10   This look of quiet flatters thus
Our home-bred fancies: O to us,
The fools of habit, sweeter seems

To rest beneath the clover sod,
That takes the sunshine and the rains,
15   Or where the kneeling hamlet drains
The chalice of the grapes of God;

Than if with thee the roaring wells
Should gulf him fathom-deep in brine;
And hands so often clasped in mine,
20   Should toss with tangle and with shells.

11

Calm is the morn without a sound,
Calm as to suit a calmer grief,
And only through the faded leaf
The chestnut pattering to the ground:

5   Calm and deep peace on this high wold,
And on these dews that drench the furze,
And all the silvery gossamers
That twinkle into green and gold:

Calm and still light on yon great plain
10   That sweeps with all its autumn bowers,
And crowded farms and lessening towers,
To mingle with the bounding main:

Calm and deep peace in this wide air,
These leaves that redden to the fall;
15   And in my heart, if calm at all,
If any calm, a calm despair:

10.11 home-bred fancies 'the wish to rest in the churchyard or in the chancel' (H.T.).

10.12–20 Ricks *1969* cites Ovid *Tristia* 1.2.53–4: '*est aliquid, fatove suo ferrove cadentem | in solida moriens ponere corpus humo*' ('Tis something worth if falling by fate or by the steel one rests in death upon the solid ground').

10.15–16 T. thinks it would be pleasanter to be buried in a village set in a valley of vines shaped like a wine-cup, and hence a perpetual emblem of communion with God.

10.17 roaring wells the ocean.

10.20 tangle oar-weed (T.'s note).

Calm on the seas, and silver sleep,
　　And waves that sway themselves in rest,
　　And dead calm in that noble breast
20　Which heaves but with the heaving deep.

*

14

If one should bring me this report,
　　That thou hadst touched the land today,
　　And I went down unto the quay,
And found thee lying in the port;

5　And standing, muffled round with woe,
　　Should see thy passengers in rank
　　Come stepping lightly down the plank,
And beckoning unto those they know;

And if along with these should come
10　The man I held as half-divine;
　　Should strike a sudden hand in mine,
And ask a thousand things of home;

And I should tell him all my pain,
　　And how my life had drooped of late,
15　And he should sorrow o'er my state
And marvel what possessed my brain;

And I perceived no touch of change,
　　No hint of death in all his frame,
　　But found him all in all the same,
20　I should not feel it to be strange.

*

19

The Danube to the Severn gave
　　The darkened heart that beat no more;
　　They laid him by the pleasant shore,
And in the hearing of the wave.

11.20 Ricks *1969* cites Byron *Bride of Abydos* line 1088: 'His head heaves with the heaving billow.'
14.2–3 Probably a true rhyme as T. pronounced the words.
19.3–4 Hallam was buried at Clevedon (on the east bank of the Severn estuary 12 miles west of Bristol) 3 Jan. 1834.

5   There twice a day the Severn fills;
      The salt sea-water passes by,
      And hushes half the babbling Wye,
And makes a silence in the hills.

The Wye is hushed nor moved along,
10   And hushed my deepest grief of all,
      When filled with tears that cannot fall,
I brim with sorrow drowning song.

The tide flows down, the wave again
      Is vocal in its wooded walls;
15   My deeper anguish also falls,
And I speak a little then.

*

34

My own dim life should teach me this,
      That life shall live for evermore,
      Else earth is darkness at the core,
And dust and ashes all that is;

5   This round of green, this orb of flame,
      Fantastic beauty; such as lurks
      In some wild Poet, when he works
Without a conscience or an aim.

What then were God to such as I?
10   'Twere hardly worth my while to choose
      Of things all mortal, or to use
A little patience ere I die;

'Twere best at once to sink to peace,
      Like birds the charming serpent draws,
15   To drop head-foremost in the jaws
Of vacant darkness and to cease.

*

19.5–8 'Taken from my own observation – the rapids of the Wye are stilled by the incoming sea' (T.'s note). Another poem of grief associated with the Wye is 'Tears, idle tears' (p. 100). The valley was celebrated by Wordsworth in *Lines Composed a Few Miles Above Tintern Abbey* (1978).
19.14 wooded walls the valley is steep-sided; Wordsworth refers to 'steep woods and lofty cliffs' (line 157).
34.1 dim life] dark heart *H. Lpr* 101; *T. MS.* canc.   **should**] can *T. MS.*, trial edition.
34.6 Fantastic fabulous (*OED* 1) rather than the main current sense: very good or amazingly good (not represented in *OED*).
34.8 conscience an inner thought (closer to *OED* I than II).
34.14 charming exercising magical power (*OED* 1).

50

Be near me when my light is low,
      When the blood creeps, and the nerves prick
      And tingle; and the heart is sick,
And all the wheels of being slow.

5   Be near me when the sensuous frame
      Is racked with pangs that conquer trust;
      And Time, a maniac scattering dust,
And Life, a Fury slinging flame.

Be near me when my faith is dry,
10   And men the flies of latter spring,
      That lay their eggs, and sting and sing
And weave their petty cells and die.

Be near me when I fade away,
      To point the term of human strife,
15   And on the low dark verge of life
The twilight of eternal day.

51

Do we indeed desire the dead
      Should still be near us at our side?
      Is there no baseness we would hide?
No inner vileness that we dread?

5   Shall he for whose applause I strove,
      I had such reverence for his blame,
      See with clear eye some hidden shame
And I be lessened in his love?

50.1. my light] the pulse *MS.* 1st reading.
50.2–3 Cf. Shelley *The Cenci* 4.1.163–5: 'My blood is running up and down my veins; | A fearful pleasure makes it prick and tingle; | I feel a giddy sickness of strange awe.'
50.8 The Furies in classical mythology carried torches and were sent from Tartarus to avenge wrong. In later mythology there were three: Tisiphone, Megaera and Alecto.
50.10–11 Cf. Pope *Epistle to Dr. Arbuthnot* lines 309–10: 'Yet let me flap this bug with gilded wings, | This painted child of dirt that stinks and stings.'
51 Edmund Lushington recalls 'On one other occasion (Christmas 1841) he came and showed me a poem he had just composed, saying he liked it better than most he had done lately, this was No. 51' (*Memoir* 1.202–3).
51.7 eye ... hidden] sight my secret *H. Lpr, T. MS.* canc.

I wrong the grave with fears untrue.
10   Shall love be blamed for want of faith?
     There must be wisdom with great Death;
The dead shall look me through and through.

Be near us when we climb or fall;
     Ye watch, like God, the rolling hours
15   With larger other eyes than ours,
To make allowance for us all.

52

I cannot love thee as I ought,
     For love reflects the thing beloved;
     My words are only words, and moved
Upon the topmost froth of thought.

5   'Yet blame not thou thy plaintive song,'
     The Spirit of true love replied;
     'Thou canst not move me from thy side,
Nor human frailty do me wrong.

'What keeps a spirit wholly true
10   To that ideal which he bears?
     What record? not the sinless years
That breathed beneath the Syrian blue;

'So fret not, like an idle girl,
     That life is dashed with flecks of sin.
15   Abide: thy wealth is gathered in,
When Time hath sundered shell from pearl.'

53

How many a father have I seen,
     A sober man, among his boys,
     Whose youth was full of foolish noise,
Who wears his manhood hale and green:

52.3 My words are words and lightly moved *T. MS.*
52.8 human] casual *T. MS.* canc.
52.11 No – not the thirty sinless years *T. MS.*; it is easier to recognise in this version that T. refers to Christ.
52.15 Abide' wait without wearying' (T.'s note).
52.16 Time hath sundered] years have rotted *trial edition*. T. perhaps thinking of the extensive Pearl of Faith tradition, e.g. the medieval poem *The Pearl*, in which the faithful soul is purified after death.
53.5 fancy] doctrine *1850* (1st-2nd).

5   And dare we to this fancy give,
       That had the wild oat not been sown,
       The soil, left barren, scarce had grown
    The grain by which a man may live?

    Or, if we held the doctrine sound
10   For life outliving heats of youth,
       Yet who would preach it as a truth
    To those that eddy round and round?

    Hold thou the good, define it well:
       For fear divine Philosophy
15   Should push beyond her mark, and be
    Procuress to the Lords of Hell.

54

    O, yet we trust that somehow good
      Will be the final goal of ill,
      To pangs of nature, sins of will,
    Defects of doubt, and taints of blood;

5   That nothing walks with aimless feet;
      That not one life shall be destroyed,
      Or cast as rubbish to the void,
    When God hath made the pile complete;

    That not a worm is cloven in vain;
10   That not a moth with vain desire
      Is shrivelled in a fruitless fire,
    Or but subserves another's gain.

    Behold, we know not anything;
      I can but trust that good shall fall
15   At last – far off – at last, to all,
    And every winter change to spring.

    So runs my dream; but what am I?
      An infant crying in the night:
      An infant crying for the light,
20   And with no language but a cry.

53.8 the grain reminiscent both of 'Man shall not live by bread alone' (*Matt.* 4.4) and the parable of the wheat and the tares.
53.14 divine Philosophy cf. Milton *Comus* line 476.
53.16 Procuress] A pandar *T. MS., L. MS.*
54.12 ∧ 13 For hope at awful distance set | Oft whispers of a kindlier plan | Though never prophet came to man | Of such a revelation yet. *T. MS.* canc.
54.18 infant T. plays on the etymology: *infans:* unable to speak.

[49] Alfred Tennyson

55

The wish, that of the living whole
　No life may fail beyond the grave,
　Derives it not from what we have
The likest God within the soul?

5　　Are God and Nature then at strife,
　That Nature lends such evil dreams?
　So careful of the type she seems,
So careless of the single life;

That I, considering everywhere
10　Her secret meaning in her deeds,
　And finding that of fifty seeds
She often brings but one to bear,

I falter where I firmly trod,
　And falling with my weight of cares
15　Upon the great world's altar-stairs
That slope through darkness up to God,

I stretch lame hands of faith, and grope,
　And gather dust and chaff, and call
　To what I feel is Lord of all,
20　And faintly trust the larger hope.

56

'So careful of the type?' but no.
　From scarped cliff and quarried stone
　She cries, 'A thousand types are gone;
I care for nothing, all shall go.

55 The sections on evolution were written 'some years' before the publication of Robert Chambers's *Vestiges of Creation* (1844) (*Memoir* 1.223). T. may have been influenced by Charles Lyell's *Principles of Geology* (1830), which he read in 1837 (*Memoir* 1.162).
55.7–8 Cf. Voltaire *L'A.B.C.* (*Onzième entretien*): 'La Nature conserve les espèces, et se soucie très peu des individus.'
55.11 '"Fifty" should be "myriad"' (T.'s note).
55.13–16 Perhaps a reminiscence of the stairs of Dante's *Purgatorio*. For a full treatment of stairs in poetry see *Silent Poetry* ed. Alastair Fowler (1970) 206 ff.
56.1–4 Cf. Lyell: 'Species cannot be immortal, but must perish, one after the other, like the individuals which compose them' (*Principles of Geology* 4th edn, 1835 3.155).　**type** *OED* 8: a certain general plan of structure characterizing a group of animals, plants, etc. 1st ex. 1850.

5   'Thou makest thine appeal to me:
     I bring to life, I bring to death:
     The spirit does but mean the breath:
     I know no more.' And he, shall he,

     Man, her last work, who seemed so fair,
10   Such splendid purpose in his eyes,
     Who rolled the psalm to wintry skies,
     Who built him fanes of fruitless prayer,

     Who trusted God was love indeed
     And love Creation's final law –
15   Though Nature, red in tooth and claw
     With ravine, shrieked against his creed –

     Who loved, who suffered countless ills,
     Who battled for the True, the Just,
     Be blown about the desert dust,
20   Or sealed within the iron hills?

     No more? A monster then, a dream,
     A discord. Dragons of the prime,
     That tare each other in their slime,
     Were mellow music matched with him.

25   O life as futile, then, as frail!
     O for thy voice to soothe and bless!
     What hope of answer, or redress?
     Behind the veil, behind the veil.

                    57
     Peace; come away: the song of woe
     Is after all an earthly song.
     Peace; come away: we do him wrong
     To sing so wildly: let us go.

56.11 wintry] Sabbath *L. MS.*
56.12 fruitless] praise and *L. MS.*
56.18 Who yearned for True and Good and Just *L. MS.*
56.22 Dragons dinosaurs.   **the prime** the first age of the world (*OED* 6b).
56.28 Mattes 62–3 suggests that T. probably 'had in mind the myth of the veiled statue of Truth at Sais, which one might unveil only at the cost of one's life'; his source may have been William Heckford's *Succinct Account of All the Religions* (1791). In the Hebraic temple the veil separated the inner sanctuary from the body of the tabernacle; in figurative usage, following *Heb.* 6.19 it came to symbolise the barrier separating this world from the next (these lines cited by *OED*).
57 *L. MS.* introduces this with *O Sorrower for the faded leaf* (Ricks *1969* 1773).

[49] Alfred Tennyson

5   Come; let us go: your cheeks are pale;
      But half my life I leave behind.
      Methinks my friend is richly shrined;
    But I shall pass, my work will fail.

    Yet in these ears, till hearing dies,
10   One set slow bell will seem to toll
      The passing of the sweetest soul
    That ever looked with human eyes.

    I hear it now, and o'er and o'er,
      Eternal greetings to the dead;
15   And 'Ave, Ave, Ave,' said,
    'Adieu, adieu,' for evermore.

58

    In those sad words I took farewell.
      Like echoes in sepulchral halls,
      As drop by drop the water falls
    In vaults and catacombs, they fell;

5   And, falling, idly broke the peace
      Of hearts that beat from day to day,
      Half-conscious of their dying clay,
    And those cold crypts where they shall cease.

    The high Muse answered: 'Wherefore grieve
10   Thy brethren with a fruitless tear?
      Abide a little longer here,
    And thou shalt take a nobler leave.'

*

57.8 'The poet speaks of these poems. Methinks I have built a rich shrine to my friend, but it will not last' (T.'s note). *T. MS.* has a stanza questioning the value of his poetry.

57.15–16 T. compares his lines with those in Catullus' *Multas per gentes et multa per aequora vectus: 'Accipe fraterno multum manantia fletu, | atque in perpetuum, frater, ave atque vale.'* ('Take them, wet with many tears of a brother, and for ever, O my brother, hail and farewell!') T. added: 'Nor can any modern elegy, so long as men retain the least hope in the after-life of those whom they loved, equal in pathos the desolation of that everlasting farewell.'

58.9–12 different in *L. MS* 1st reading, which also adds an extra stanza (see *1969* 913).

58.9 T. follows Milton *Paradise Lost* 7.1–20 (and countless others) in making Urania the muse of heavenly poetry.

77

What hope is here for modern rhyme
　　To him, who turns a musing eye
　　On songs, and deeds, and lives, that lie
Foreshortened in the tract of time?

5　These mortal lullabies of pain
　　May bind a book, may line a box,
　　May serve to curl a maiden's locks;
Or when a thousand moons shall wane

A man upon a stall may find,
10　And, passing, turn the page that tells
　　A grief, then changed to something else,
Sung by a long-forgotten mind.

But what of that? My darkened ways
　　Shall ring with music all the same;
15　To breathe my loss is more than fame,
To utter love more sweet than praise.

*

95

By night we lingered on the lawn,
　　For underfoot the herb was dry;
　　And genial warmth; and o'er the sky
The silvery haze of summer drawn;

5　And calm that let the tapers burn
　　Unwavering: not a cricket chirred;
　　The brook alone far-off was heard,
And on the board the fluttering urn:

77.4 Events viewed retrospectively seem compressed together.
77.5 mortal transient, subject to death (*OED* 1).
77.6 May be the lining of a box *T. MS.* canc. The traditional fate awaiting
ephemeral literature: see Pope *Epistle to Augustus* lines 415–19: 'let my dirty
leaves...line trunks'.
77.9 stall book stall.
77.13 darkened] mortal *T. MS.* canc. ·
95 Possibly written 1841–2, when T. described to Dean Stanley 'one
singularly still starlit evening' when 'he and his friends had once sat out far
into the night having tea at a table on the lawn beneath the stars, and that
the candles had burned with steady upright flame, disturbed from time to
time by the inrush of a moth or cockchafer, as though in a closed room'. He
continues: 'I do not know whether he had already written, or was perhaps
even then shaping, the lines in *In Memoriam*, which so many years
afterwards brought back to me the incident' (*Memoir* 1. 205).
95.8 fluttering urn the tea urn shakes slightly as it boils.

And bats went round in fragrant skies,
10   And wheeled or lit the filmy shapes
    That haunt the dusk, with ermine capes
And woolly breasts and beaded eyes;

While now we sang old songs that pealed
    From knoll to knoll, where, couched at ease,
15   The white kine glimmered, and the trees
Laid their dark arms about the field.

But when those others, one by one,
    Withdrew themselves from me and night,
    And in the house light after light
20 Went out, and I was all alone,

A hunger seized my heart; I read
    Of that glad year which once had been,
    In those fallen leaves which kept their green,
The noble letters of the dead.

25 And strangely on the silence broke
    The silent-speaking words, and strange
    Was love's dumb cry defying change
To test his worth; and strangely spoke

The faith, the vigour, bold to dwell
30   On doubts that drive the coward back,
    And keen through wordy snares to track
Suggestion to her inmost cell.

So word by word, and line by line,
    The dead man touched me from the past,
35   And all at once it seemed at last
The living soul was flashed on mine,

95.10 filmy shapes moths (T.'s note).
95.23 fallen leaves leaves of paper (by suggestion also leaves from the trees) and hence Sibylline leaves which have prophetic power.
95.33 *Isa.* 28.13: 'But the word of the Lord was unto them precept upon precept, precept upon precept; line upon line, line upon line.'
95.36 The] His *1850–1870*. T. comments: 'The Deity, maybe. The first reading... troubled me, as perhaps giving a wrong impression.' Hallam Tennyson quotes T., 'The greater Soul may include the less', and 'I have often had that feeling of being whirled up and rapt into the Great Soul.' See also T. *Memoir* I. 320: 'A kind of waking trance I have frequently had... This has generally come upon me thro' repeating my own name two or three times to myself silently, till all at once, as it were out of the intensity of the consciousness of individuality, the individuality itself seemed to dissolve and fade away into boundless being.'

And mine in this was wound, and whirled
   About empyreal heights of thought,
   And came on that which is, and caught
40   The deep pulsations of the world,

Aeonian music measuring out
   The steps of Time – the shocks of Chance –
   The blows of Death. At length my trance
Was cancelled, stricken through with doubt.

45   Vague words! but ah, how hard to frame
   In matter-moulded forms of speech,
   Or even for intellect to reach
Through memory that which I became:

Till now the doubtful dusk revealed
50   The knolls once more where, couched at ease,
   The white kine glimmered, and the trees
Laid their dark arms about the field:

And sucked from out the distant gloom
   A breeze began to tremble o'er
55   The large leaves of the sycamore,
And fluctuate all the still perfume,

And gathering freshlier overhead,
   Rocked the full-foliaged elms, and swung
   The heavy-folded rose, and flung
60   The lilies to and fro, and said

'The dawn, the dawn,' and died away;
   And East and West, without a breath,
   Mixed their dim lights, like life and death,
To broaden into boundless day.

*

108
I will not shut me from my kind,
   And, lest I stiffen into stone,
   I will not eat my heart alone,
Nor feed with sighs a passing wind:

95.37 this] his *1850–70*.
95.41 Aeonian eternal.
95.46 matter ... speech language limited to the material world.
95.54–5 Adapted from *In deep and solemn dreams* (*c.* 1825–6) lines 47–8:
'And the sweet winds tremble o'er | The large leaves of the sycamore.'
108.3 eat my heart suffer from silent grief or vexation.

[49] Alfred Tennyson

5   What profit lies in barren faith,
      And vacant yearning, though with might
      To scale the heaven's highest height,
    Or dive below the wells of Death?

    What find I in the highest place,
10   But mine own phantom chanting hymns?
      And on the depths of death there swims
    The reflex of a human face.

    I'll rather take what fruit may be
      Or sorrow under human skies:
15   'Tis held that sorrow makes us wise,
    Whatever wisdom sleep with thee.

*

118

    Contemplate all this work of Time,
      The giant labouring in his youth;
      Nor dream of human love and truth,
    As dying Nature's earth and lime;

5   But trust that those we call the dead
      Are breathers of an ampler day
      For ever nobler ends. They say,
    The solid earth whereon we tread

    In tracts of fluent heat began,
10   And grew to seeming-random forms,
      The seeming prey of cyclic storms,
    Till at the last arose the man;

108.5–8 Cf. *Rom.* 10.6–7: 'But the righteousness which is of faith speaketh on this wise, Say not in thine heart, Who shall ascend into heaven?...or, Who shall descend into the deep?'
108.12 reflex reflection.
108.16 Whatever] Yet how much *T. MS.* canc.
118.1 Contemplate accented on second syllable.
118.3–4 Do not imagine that the human spirit dies after the fashion of matter.
118.9–11 W. R. Rutland *E & S* 26 (1940) 13 shows that this refers to Cuvier's cataclysmic theory. Killham 246 demonstrates that the theory of a series of fresh creations following on successions of disasters is incompatible with others held by T.
118.12–17 G. R. Potter *PQ* 16 (1937) 337 shows that though this is close to a theory of mutability of species the concept is till of 'an evolving Nature'.

Who throve and branched from clime to clime,
    The herald of a higher race,
15   And of himself in higher place,
If so he type this work of time,

Within himself, from more to more;
    Or, crowned with attributes of woe
    Like glories, move his course, and show
20   That life is not as idle ore,

But iron dug from central gloom,
    And heated hot with burning fears,
    And dipped in baths of hissing tears,
And battered with the shocks of doom

25   To shape and use. Arise and fly
    The reeling Faun, the sensual feast;
    Move upward, working out the beast,
And let the ape and tiger die.

119

Doors, where my heart was used to beat
    So quickly, not as one that weeps
    I come once more; the city sleeps;
I smell the meadow in the street;

5   I hear a chirp of birds; I see
    Betwixt the black fronts long-withdrawn
    A light-blue lane of early dawn,
And think of early days and thee,

And bless thee, for thy lips are bland,
10   And bright the friendship of thine eye;
    And in my thoughts with scarce a sigh
I take the pressure of thine hand.

118.13 Branched divided into different races, but still as man.
118.20–5 A traditional conceit (see anvil 2 in *OED*).
118.25–8 Cf. *Lucretius* lines 21–2 (below p. 177). T. believed that the evolutionary model applied to the psychology of man in a metaphorical sense; see J. Killham *T. and 'The Princess'* (1958) 234–40. The idea continued in the *Epilogue* lines 125–36 (below pp. 127–8).
118.26 sensual feast cf. Shakespeare *Sonnets* 141.
119 An optimistic pendant to 7. Based on an unpublished section from *L. MS.* (1969 1775) '*Let Death and Memory Keep the Face*'.
119.9 bland soft and kindly.
119.12 Cf. 14.11 for the importance to T. of the touch of Hallam's hand.

[49] Alfred Tennyson

120

I trust I have not wasted breath:
   I think we are not wholly brain,
   Magnetic mockeries; not in vain,
Like Paul with beasts, I fought with Death;

5   Not only cunning casts in clay:
   Let Science prove we are, and then
   What matters Science unto men,
At least to me? I would not stay.

Let him, the wiser man who springs
10   Hereafter, up from childhood shape
   His action like the greater ape,
But I was *born* to other things.

121

Sad Hesper o'er the buried sun
   And ready, thou, to die with him,
   Thou watchest all things ever dim
And dimmer, and a glory done.

120.1 The immediate meaning is the colloquial 'I hope I haven't wasted time' (writing the poem), but the more profound suggestion is 'I hope there is more to life than mortality'.

120.3 Magnetic mockeries Of the various mechanistic hypotheses of the animal organism, the magnetic was one of the most popular in the early C19. Bentham identified the 'magnetico-spastic' in 1816. Many of the mechanistic views stemmed from Alessandro Volta (1745–1827), who experimented with electrical stimuli.

120.4 T. compares 1 *Cor.* 15.32: 'If after the manner of men I have fought with beasts at Ephesus, what advantageth it me?'

120.9–11 'Spoken ironically against mere materialism, not against evolution.' (T.'s note).

121 In H. D. Rawnsley *Memories of the Tennysons* (1900) W. F. Rawnsley recalls T. 'visiting my parents at Shiplake, before 1850' and writing 'the "Hesper Phosphor" canto'. Cf. Shelley's translation of an epigram attributed to Plato: 'Thou wert the morning star among the living, | Ere thy fair light had fled; – | Now, having died, thou art as Hesperus, giving | New splendour to the dead.' Also Horace, *Odes* 2.9. 10–12: '*nec tibi Vespero | surgent decedunt amores | nec rapidum fugiente solem*' ('Nor do thy words of love cease either when Vesper comes out at evening, or when he flies before the swiftly coursing sun'). Venus (the planet of love) sets as Hesper (signifying here the past) and rises as Phosphor, the morning star (signifying the present). Hopkins said of this section: 'Surely your maturest judgement will never be fooled out of saying that this is divine, terribly beautiful' (10 Sept. 1864; *Further Letters* 219).

5   The team is loosened from the wain,
      The boat is drawn upon the shore;
      Thou listenest to the closing door,
And life is darkened in the brain.

Bright Phosphor, fresher for the night,
10   By thee the world's great work is heard
      Beginning, and the wakeful bird;
Behind thee comes the greater light.

The market boat is on the stream,
      And voices hail it from the brink;
15   Thou hear'st the village hammer clink,
And see'st the moving of the team.

Sweet Hesper-Phosphor, double name
      For what is one, the first, the last,
      Thou, like my present and my past
20 Thy place is changed; thou art the same.

[EPILOGUE]
65 O happy hour, and happier hours
      Await them. Many a merry face
      Salutes them – maidens of the place,
That pelt us in the porch with flowers.

O happy hour, behold the bride
70   With him to whom her hand I gave.
      They leave the porch, they pass the grave
That has to-day its sunny side.

To-day the grave is bright for me,
      For them the light of life increased,
70   Who stay to share the morning feast,
Who rest to-night beside the sea.

121.11 the wakeful bird cf. *Paradise Lost* 3.38.
121.12 cf. *Gen.* 1.16: 'the greater light to rule the day'.
121.18 the first, the last a ref. to Christ, the Alpha and the Omega.
[Epilogue] first so called by A. C. Bradley. It describes the marriage (10 Oct. 1842) of T.'s sister Cecilia to his friend Edmund Lushington, who recalls that by the summer of 1845 T. had 'completed many of the cantos in *In Memoriam*...He said to me, "I have brought in your marriage at the end of *In Memoriam*," and then showed me those poems of *In Memoriam* which were finished and which were a perfectly novel surprise to me' (*Memoir* 1.203). The poem moves towards a reconciliation of the meaning of public festivities (which in the earlier parts of the work were at odds with private grief) with inner states of mind. See D. H. Lawrence *The Rainbow* Ch. 11 for a similar balance between the individual and the wider social experience.
Epil. 71 Step lightly by the sunny grave *MS*. 1st reading.

Let all my genial spirits advance
    To meet and greet a whiter sun;
    My drooping memory will not shun
80   The foaming grape of eastern France.

It circles round, and fancy plays,
    And hearts are warmed and faces bloom,
    As drinking health to bride and groom
We wish them store of happy days.

85   Nor count me all to blame if I
    Conjecture of a stiller guest,
    Perchance, perchance, among the rest,
And, though in silence, wishing joy.

But they must go, the time draws on,
90   And those white-favoured horses wait;
    They rise, but linger; it is late;
Farewell, we kiss, and they are gone.

A shade falls on us like the dark
    From little cloudlets on the grass,
95   But sweeps away as out we pass
To range the woods, to roam the park,

Discussing how their courtship grew,
    And talk of others that are wed,
    And how she looked, and what he said,
100 And back we come at fall of dew.

Again the feast, the speech, the glee,
    The shade of passing thought, the wealth
    Of words and wit, the double health,
The crowning cup, the three-times-three,

105 And last the dance; – till I retire.
    Dumb is that tower which spake so loud,
    And high in heaven the streaming cloud,
And on the downs a rising fire:

Epil. 80 The foaming grape ... France Champagne.
Epil. 90 white-favoured horses pulling the bridal coach and wearing white cockades.
Epil 97.7 We pace the stubble bare of sheaves, | We watch the brimming river steal | And half the golden woodland reel | Athwart the smoke of burning leaves. *MS.* deleted. The stubble would have been 'bare of sheaves' in October.
Epil 104 three-times-three hip-hip-hooray!

And rise, O moon, from yonder down,
110   Till over down and over dale
All night the shining vapour sail
And pass the silent-lighted town,

The white-faced halls, the glancing rills,
And catch at every mountain head,
115   And o'er the friths that branch and spread
Their sleeping silver through the hills;

And touch with shade the bridal doors,
With tender gloom the roof, the wall;
And breaking let the splendour fall
120   To spangle all the happy shores

By which they rest, and ocean sounds,
And, star and system rolling past,
A soul shall draw from out the vast
And strike his being into bounds,

125   And, moved through life of lower phase,
Result in man, be born and think,
And act and love, a closer link
Betwixt us and the crowning race

Of those that, eye to eye, shall look
130   On knowledge; under whose command
Is Earth and Earth's, and in their hand
Is Nature like an open book;

Epil. 110 and over tower and grove and vale *MS.* 1st reading.
Epil. 114–5 Cf. the visonary flight in the 'germ' of *In Memoriam: 'Hark! the dogs howl'* (above p. 73).
Epil. 125 See note to 118.25–28. Killham 257 suggests that 'in marriage we come closest to participating in the cosmic purpose, though we must continually seek to "type" the qualities we desire to make permanent in man'. *1969* 987 indicated parallels with R. Chambers's *Vestiges of Creation* (1844) 71 and 202.
Epil. 128–30 Cf. Chambers 6: 'A time may come when we shall be much more in the thick of the stars and our astral system than we are now, and have of course much more brilliant nocturnal skies; but it may be countless ages before the eyes which are to see this added resplendence shall exist.'
Epil. 132 The traditional image of Nature as a book was given a new emphasis by geology.

No longer half-akin to brute,
   For all we thought and loved and did,
135   And hoped, and suffered, is but seed
   Of what in them is flower and fruit;

Whereof the man, that with me trod
   This planet, was a noble type
   Appearing ere the times were ripe,
140   That friend of mine who lives in God,

That God, which ever lives and loves,
   One God, one law, one element,
   And one far-off divine event,
To which the whole creation moves.

Epil. 133 T. is probably thinking of the 1662 form for the solemnization of matrimony in the Anglican Church: 'It is not by any to be enterprised, nor taken in hand, unadvisedly, lightly, or wantonly, to satisfy men's carnal lusts and appetites, like brute beasts that have no understanding; etc.'
Epil. 143 divine event the Last Judgement, or perhaps some less orthodox view of a regenerated and perfected Universe.

50 The Charge of the Light Brigade

Date The charge occurred 25 Oct. 1854. T. read the report in *The Times* of 13 Nov. 1854 containing the phrase 'some hideous blunder'. T. described the phrase 'some one had blundered' as 'the origin of the metre of his poem' (*Memoir* 1.381). For discussion and extracts see L. Chambers *MLN* 18 (1903) 228–9. T. was not especially proud of the poem (*Memoir* 1.409–10), but he did record it onto a wax cylinder.

    T. denied the connection with Drayton's *Ballad of Agincourt*. *1969* 1034 notes similarities to Chatterton's *Song of Aella*. For further historical background see Cecil Woodham Smith *The Reason Why* (1953).
Publication *The Examiner* (9 Dec. 1854); *1855*.

Half a league, half a league,
   Half a league onward,
All in the valley of Death
   Rode the six hundred.

3 the valley of Death as the soldiers called it (*The Times*).

5   'Forward, the Light Brigade!
    Charge for the guns!' he said:
    Into the valley of Death
      Rode the six hundred.

2
    'Forward, the Light Brigade!'
10   Was there a man dismayed?
    Not though the soldier knew
      Some one had blundered:
    Their's not to make reply,
    Their's not to reason why,
15   Their's but to do and die:
    Into the valley of Death
      Rode the six hundred.

3
    Cannon to right of them,
    Cannon to left of them,
20   Cannon in front of them
      Volleyed and thundered;
    Stormed at with shot and shell,
    Boldly they rode and well,
    Into the jaws of Death,
25   Into the mouth of Hell
      Rode the six hundred.

4
    Flashed all their sabres bare,
    Flashed as they turned in air
    Sabring the gunners there,
30   Charging an army, while
      All the world wondered:
    Plunged in the battery-smoke

5–12 Omitted *1855*.
5–8 Into the valley of Death
    Rode the six hundred,
For up came an order which
    Some one had blundered.
'Forward, the Light Brigade!
Take the guns,' Nolan said:
Into the valley of Death
    Rode the six hundred. (*The Examiner*).
9–12 No man was there dismayed, *The Examiner*.
13–14 Transposed *1855*.
17 hundred pronounced 'hundered' in Lincolnshire, according to T.'s friend W. F. Rawnsley.
27–32 'Through the clouds of smoke we could see their sabres flashing' (*The Times*).

Right through the line they broke;
Cossack and Russian
35   Reeled from the sabre-stroke
Shattered and sundered.
Then they rode back, but not
Not the six hundred.

5

Cannon to right of them,
40   Cannon to left of them,
Cannon behind them
Volleyed and thundered;
Stormed at with shot and shell,
While horse and hero fell,
45   They that had fought so well
Came through the jaws of Death,
Back from the mouth of Hell,
All that was left of them,
Left of six hundred.

6

50   When can their glory fade?
O the wild charge they made!
All the world wondered.
Honour the charge they made!
Honour the Light Brigade,
55   Noble six hundred!

33 With many a desperate stroke *The Examiner;* Fiercely the line... *1855.*
34 The Russian line they broke; *The Examiner;* Strong was the sabre-stroke; *1855.*
35–6 Not in *The Examiner;* Making an army reel | Shaken and sundered. *1855.*
44 Not in *The Examiner.*
46 ∧ 7 Half a league back again, *1855.*
49 'Only 195 returned' (T.'s note).
50–55 Honour the brave and bold! | Long shall the tale be told, | Yea, when our babes are old – | How they rode onward. *1855.*

51 Maud: A Monodrama

Date Written mostly in 1854–5, but Part II 141–238 composed 1833–4, when T. was working on *In Memoriam,* and published in *The Tribute* (1837) as '*Oh! that 'twere possible*'. Other early composition 2.49–131 ('See what a lovely shell') and 1.571–98 ('Go not happy day'). Textual changes made for *1856;* division into Parts I and II *1859,* into I, II and III *1865.*
Criticism The critical reception was mixed according to E. Shannon *PMLA*

68 (1953) 397–417. Many reviewers did not distinguish between T. and the protagonist. George Eliot's reaction was adverse *Westminster Review* 64 (1855) 597–601. *Critical Heritage* prints reviews by Goldwin Smith, G. Brimley and R. J. Mann. Unfortunately, the poem was implicated in the Spasmodic Movement. Although there are elements reminiscent of Alexander Smith and Sydney Dobell, especially the hero's megalomania, its literary antecedents also include *Romeo and Juliet* and Scott's *Bride of Lammermoor*. G. O. Marshall *Georgia Review* 16 (1962) 463–4 suggests as an influence an anonymous ballad *The Wicked Nephew* which included a *Lady Maud*. The social satire owes something to Charles Kingsley, F. D. Maurice and T. Carlyle. R. W. Rader traces biographical background, with elements of T.'s mother, father, grandfather, Rosa Baring, Sophy Rawnsley and Emily Sellwood present. Hallam Tennyson records: 'My father said, "This poem of *Maud or the Madness* is a little *Hamlet*, the history of the morbid, poetic soul, under the blighting influence of a recklessly speculative age. He is the heir of madness, an egoist with the makings of a cynic, raised to a pure and holy love which elevates his whole nature, passing from the height of triumph to the lowest depth of misery, driven into madness by the loss of her whom he has loved, and, when he has at length passed through the fiery furnace, and has recovered his reason, giving himself up to work for the good of mankind through the unselfishness born of a great passion. The peculiarity of this poem is that different phases of passion in one person take the place of different characters."' Discussion by P. Drew (Palmer 115–46); E. Stokes *VP* 2 (1964) 97–110 (the metrics) and A. S. Byatt (Armstrong 69–92). T. liked reciting the poem; a drawing by D. G. Rossetti of a reading on 27 Sept. 1855 reproduced in *Burlington Mag.* 105 (1963) 118.

Publication 1855.

Title T. originally intended it to be *Maud or the Madness* (*Memoir* 1. 402). 'A Monodrama' added *1875*.

PART I

I

1

I hate the dreadful hollow behind the little wood,
   Its lips in the field above are dabbled with blood-red
      heath,
The red-ribbed ledges drip with silent horror of blood,
And Echo there, whatever is asked her, answers 'Death.'

2

5   For there in the ghastly pit long since a body was found,
   His who had given me life – O father! O God! was it well? –
   Mangled, and flattened, and crushed, and dinted into the
      ground:
There yet lies the rock that fell with him when he fell.

[51] Alfred Tennyson

3

Did he fling himself down? who knows? for a vast
    speculation had failed,
10 And ever he muttered and maddened, and ever wanned with
    despair,
And out he walked when the wind like a broken worldling
    wailed,
And the flying gold of the ruined woodlands drove
    through the air.

4

I remember the time, for the roots of my hair were stirred
By a shuffled step, by a dead weight trailed, by a
    whispered fright,
15 And my pulses closed their gates with a shock on my
    heart as I heard
The shrill-edged shriek of a mother divide the shuddering
    night.

5

Villainy somewhere! whose? One says, we are villains all.
Not he: his honest fame should at least by me be maintained:
But that old man, now lord of the broad estate and the Hall,
Dropped off gorged from a scheme that had left us
20   flaccid and drained.

6

Why do they prate of the blessings of Peace? we have
    made them a curse,
Pickpockets, each hand lusting for all that is not its
    own;
And lust of gain, in the spirit of Cain, is it better
    or worse
Than the heart of the citizen hissing in war on his own
    hearthstone?

7

25 But these are the days of advance, the works of the men
    of mind,
When who but a fool would have faith in a tradesman's
    ware or his word?
Is it peace or war? Civil war, as I think, and that of a
    kind
The viler, as underhand, not openly bearing the sword.

1.27–8 Cf. Carlyle *Sartor Resartus* Bk. 3 Ch. 5: '"Call ye that a
society...where each, isolated, regardless of his neighbour, turned against
his neighbour, clutches what he can get, and cries 'Mine!' and calls it peace,
because in the cut-purse and cut-throat scramble, no steel knives, but only a
far cunninger sort, can be employed?"'

8

Sooner or later I too may passively take the print
30   Of the golden age – why not? I have neither hope nor
       trust;
May make my heart as a millstone, set my face as a flint,
Cheat and 'be cheated, and die: who knows? we are ashes
       and dust.

9

Peace sitting under her olive, and slurring the
       days gone by,
When the poor are hovelled and hustled together,
       each sex, like swine,
35   When only the ledger lives, and when only not
       all men lie;
Peace in her vineyard – yes! – but a company
       forges the wine.

10

And the vitriol madness flushes up in the
       ruffian's head
Till the filthy by-lane rings to the yell of the
       trampled wife,
And chalk and alum and plaster are sold to the
       poor for bread,
40   And the spirit of murder works in the very
       means of life,

11

And Sleep must lie down armed, for the villainous
       centre-bits
Grind on the wakeful ear in the hush of the
       moonless nights,
While another is cheating the sick of a few last
       gasps, as he sits
To pestle a poisoned poison behind his crimson
       lights.

12

45   When a Mammonite mother kills her babe for
       a burial fee,

1.39 Cf. C. Kingsley *Alton Locke* (1850) Ch. 6: '"It was a poison in London.
Bread full o' alum and bones, and sic filth."'
1.41 centre-bits burglars' tools for cutting cylindrical holes.
1.45 Cf. Carlyle *Past and Present* 1.1 describing parents in Stockport who
poisoned 'three of their children, to defraud a "burial society" of some £3.3s
due on the death of each child'.

And Timour-Mammon grins on a pile of children's
    bones,
Is it peace or war? better, war! loud war by
    land and by sea,
War with a thousand battles, and shaking a
    hundred thrones!

13

For I trust if an enemy's fleet came yonder
    round by the hill,
50   And the rushing battle-bolt sang from the three-
    decker out of the foam,
That the smooth-faced, snub-nosed rogue
    would leap from his counter and till,
And strike, if he could, were it but with his
    cheating yardwand, home. –

14

What! am I raging alone as my father raged in
    his mood?
Must *I* too creep to the hollow and dash myself
    down and die
55   Rather than hold by the law that I made,
    nevermore to brood
On a horror of shattered limbs and a wretched
    swindler's lie?

15

Would there be sorrow for *me?* there was *love*
    in the passionate shriek,
Love for the silent thing that had made false
    haste to the grave –
Wrapped in a cloak, as I saw him, and thought
    he would rise and speak
60   And rave at the lie and the liar, ah God, as he
    used to rave.

16

I am sick of the Hall and the hill, I am sick of
    the moor and the main.
Why should I stay? can a sweeter chance ever
    come to me here?
O having the nerves of motion as well as the
    nerves of pain,
Were it not wise if I fled from the place and
    the pit and the fear?

1.46 Timour Tamerlane or Tamberlane. Cf. *Locksley Hall Sixty Years After*
line 82: 'Timur built his ghastly tower of eighty thousand human skulls.'

17

65   Workmen up at the Hall! – they are coming
       back from abroad;
  The dark old place will be gilt by the touch of
       a millionaire:
  I have heard, I know not whence, of the singular
       beauty of Maud;
  I played with the girl when a child; she promised
       then to be fair.

18

  Maud with her venturous climbings and tumbles
       and childish escapes,
70   Maud the delight of the village, the ringing
       joy of the Hall,
  Maud with her sweet purse-mouth when my
       father dangled the grapes,
  Maud the beloved of my mother, the moonfaced
       darling of all, –

19

  What is she now? My dreams are bad. She
       may bring me a curse.
  No, there is fatter game on the moor; she will
       let me alone.
75   Thanks, for the fiend best knows whether
       woman or man be the worse.
  I will bury myself in myself, and the Devil may
       pipe to his own.

II

  Long have I sighed for a calm; God grant I may
       find it at last!
  It will never be broken by Maud, she has
       neither savour nor salt,
  But a cold and clear-cut face, as I found when
       her carriage passed,
80   Perfectly beautiful: let it be granted her: where
       is the fault?
  All that I saw (for her eyes were downcast,
       not to be seen)

1.73–6 Ricks *1969* 1046 cites manuscript drafts of a stronger tone, growing
possibly from exasperation with Rosa Baring.
1.79–87 Reminiscent of the verbal portraits of Rosa Baring in earlier poems,
such as '*I lingered yet awhile*'.

[51] Alfred Tennyson

Faultily faultless, icily regular, splendidly null,
Dead perfection, no more; nothing more, if it
    had not been
For a chance of travel, a paleness, an hour's
    defect of the rose,
85 Or an underlip, you may call it a little too ripe,
    too full,
Or the least little delicate aquiline curve in a
    sensitive nose,
From which I escaped heart-free, with the least
    little touch of spleen.

III

Cold and clear-cut face, why come you so
    cruelly meek,
Breaking a slumber in which all spleenful folly
    was drowned?
90 Pale with the golden beam of an eyelash dead
    on the cheek,
Passionless, pale, cold face, star-sweet on a
    gloom profound;
Womanlike, taking revenge too deep for a
    transient wrong
Done but in thought to your beauty, and ever
    as pale as before
Growing and fading and growing upon me
    without a sound,
95 Luminous, gemlike, ghostlike, deathlike, half
    the night long
Growing and fading and growing, till I could
    bear it no more,
But arose, and all be myself in my own dark
    garden ground,
Listening now to the tide in its broad-flung
    shipwrecking roar,
Now to the scream of a maddened beach
    dragged down by the wave,
100 Walked in a wintry wind by a ghastly glimmer,
    and found
The shining daffodil dead, and Orion low in
    his grave.

1.99 **scream** Cf. T. on the South Coast: 'It seems to shriek as it recoils with
the pebbles along the shore' (*Memoir* 1.196).
1.101 The constellation Orion sinks low in the sky in the spring. The hero's
eye is caught, in the season of growth, by images of death.

IV

1

A million emeralds break from the ruby-budded
    lime
In the little grove where I sit – ah, wherefore
    cannot I be
Like things of the season gay, like the bountiful
    season bland,
105 When the far-off sail is blown by the breeze of
    a softer clime,
Half-lost in the liquid azure bloom of a crescent
    of sea,
The silent sapphire-spangled marriage ring of
    the land?

2

Below me, there, is the village, and looks how
    quiet and small!
And yet bubbles o'er like a city, with gossip,
    scandal, and spite;
110 And Jack on his ale-house bench has as many
    lies as a Czar;
And here on the landward side, by a red rock,
    glimmers the Hall;
And up in the high Hall-garden I see her pass
    like a light;
But sorrow seize me if ever that light be my
    leading star!

3

When have I bowed to her father, the wrinkled
    head of the race?
115 I met her to-day with her brother, but not to
    her brother I bowed:
I bowed to his lady-sister as she rode by on the
    moor;
But the fire of a foolish pride flashed over her
    beautiful face.
O child, you wrong your beauty, believe it, in
    being so proud;
Your father has wealth well-gotten, and I am
    nameless and poor.

4

120 I keep but a man and a maid, ever ready to
    slander and steal;

1.110 Czar Nicholas I of Russia.

I know it, and smile a hard-set smile, like a
    stoic, or like
A wiser epicurean, and let the world have its
    way:
For nature is one with rapine, a harm no
    preacher can heal;
The mayfly is torn by the swallow, the sparrow
    speared by the shrike,
125 And the whole little wood where I sit is a world
    of plunder and prey.

5

We are puppets, Man in his pride, and Beauty
    fair in her flower;
Do we move ourselves, or are moved by an
    unseen hand at a game
That pushes us off from the board, and others
    ever succeed?
Ah yet, we cannot be kind to each other here
    for an hour;
130 We whisper, and hint, and chuckle, and grin at
    a brother's shame;
However we brave it out, we men are a little
    breed.

6

A monstrous eft was of old the lord and
    master of earth,
For him did his high sun flame, and his river
    billowing ran,
And he felt himself in his force to be Nature's
    crowning race.
135 As nine months go to the shaping an infant ripe
    for his birth,
So many a million of ages have gone to the
    making of man:
He now is first, but is he the last? is he not too
    base?

1.132 eft 'The great old lizards of geology' (T.'s note).
1.135–6 See Chambers *Vestiges of Creation* (1844): 'The gestation of a single organism is the work of but a few days, weeks or months; but the gestation, so to speak, of a whole creation is a matter probably involving enormous spaces of time.'
1.137 See Chambers: 'Are there yet to be species superior to us in organization, purer in feeling, more powerful in device and act, and who shall take a rule over us?'

7

The man of science himself is fonder of glory,
    and vain,
An eye well-practised in nature, a spirit
    bounded and poor;
140 The passionate heart of the poet is whirled into
    folly and vice.
I would not marvel at either, but keep a temperate
    brain;
For not to desire or admire, if a man could learn
    it, were more
Than to walk all day like the sultan of old in a
    garden of spice.

8

For the drift of the Maker is dark, an Isis hid
    by the veil.
145 Who knows the ways of the world, how God
    will bring them about?
Our planet is one, the suns are many, the world
    is wide.
Shall I weep if a Poland fall? shall I shriek if a
    Hungary fail?
Or an infant civilization be ruled with rod or
    with knout?
I have not made the world, and He that made
    it will guide.

9

150 Be mine a philosopher's life in the quiet woodland
    ways,
Where if I cannot be gay let a passionless peace
    be my lot,
Far-off from the clamour of liars belied in the
    hubbub of lies;
From the long-necked geese of the world that
    are ever hissing dispraise
Because their natures are little, and, whether he
    heed it or not,
155 Where each man walks with his head in a cloud
    of poisonous flies.

1.143 Cf. *Song of Solomon* 4.16.
1.144 Isis 'The great Goddess of the Egyptians' (T.'s note).
1.147 Poland occupied by Russians and Austrians in 1846; **Hungary**
defeated 1849.

[51] Alfred Tennyson

10

And most of all would I flee from the cruel
    madness of love,
The honey of poison-flowers and all the measureless
    ill.
Ah Maud, you milk-white fawn, you are all
    unmeet for a wife.
Your mother is mute in her grave as her image
    in marble above;
160   Your father is ever in London, you wander
    about at your will;
You have but fed on the roses and lain in the
    lilies of life.

V

1

A voice by the cedar tree
In the meadow under the Hall!
She is singing an air that is known to me,
165   A passionate ballad gallant and gay,
A martial song like a trumpet's call!
Singing alone in the morning of life,
In the happy morning of life and of May,
Singing of men that in battle array,
170   Ready in heart and ready in hand,
March with banner and bugle and fife
To the death, for their native land.

2

Maud with her exquisite face,
And wild voice pealing up to the sunny sky,
175   And feet like sunny gems on an English green,
Maud in the light of her youth and her grace,
Singing of death, and of honour that cannot
    die,
Till I well could weep for a time so sordid and
    mean,
And myself so languid and base.

1.162–72 As the narrator's inclination to Maud is growing, an old battle-song sets the tone – prophetic in the poem, since redemption is sought through solidarity with military vigour. Cf. Wordsworth *The Solitary Reaper*, where a girl sings of 'old unhappy, far-off things, | And battles long ago.'

3

180 Silence, beautiful voice!
Be still, for you only trouble the mind
With a joy in which I cannot rejoice,
A glory I shall not find.
Still I will hear you no more,
185 For your sweetness hardly leaves me a choice
But to move to the meadow and fall before
Her feet on the meadow grass, and adore,
Not her, who is neither courtly nor kind,
Not her, not her, but a voice.

VI

1

190 Morning arises stormy and pale,
No sun, but a wannish glare
In fold upon fold of hueless cloud
And the budded peaks of the wood are
  bowed,
Caught and cuffed by the gale:
195 I had fancied it would be fair.

2

Whom but Maud should I meet
Last night, when the sunset burned
On the blossomed gable-ends
At the head of the village street,
200 Whom but Maud should I meet?
And she touched my hand with a smile so
  sweet,
She made me divine amends
For a courtesy not returned.

3

And thus a delicate spark
205 Of glowing and growing light
Through the livelong hours of the dark
Kept itself warm in the heart of my dreams,
Ready to burst in a coloured flame;
Till at last when the morning came
210 In a cloud, it faded, and seems
But an ashen-gray delight.

4

What if with her sunny hair,
And smile as sunny as cold,
She meant to weave me a snare
215 Of some coquettish deceit,

Cleopatra-like as of old
To entangle me when we met,
To have her lion roll in a silken net
And fawn at a victor's feet.

5

220 Ah, what shall I be at fifty
Should Nature keep me alive,
If I find the world so bitter
When I am but twenty-five?
Yet, if she were not a cheat,
225 If Maud were all that she seemed,
And her smile were all that I dreamed,
Then the world were not so bitter
But a smile could make it sweet.

6

What if though her eye seemed full
230 Of a kind intent to me,
What if that dandy-despot, he,
That jewelled mass of millinery,
That oiled and curled Assyrian bull
Smelling of musk and of insolence,
235 Her brother, from whom I keep aloof,
Who wants the finer politic sense
To mask, though but in his own behoof,
With a glassy smile his brutal scorn –
What if he had told her yestermorn
240 How prettily for his own sweet sake
A face of tenderness might be feigned,
And a moist mirage in desert eyes,
That so, when the rotten hustings shake
In another month to his brazen lies,
245 A wretched vote may be gained?

7

For a raven ever croaks, at my side,
Keep watch and ward, keep watch and ward,
Or thou wilt prove their tool.
Yea, too, myself from myself I guard,
250 For often a man's own angry pride
Is cap and bells for a fool.

1.233 Assyrian bull Layard was bringing Assyrian civilization before the
public eye in the 1850s.
1.243 hustings used in both figurative and concrete sense: the process of
election and the platform from which election speeches are made.

8

Perhaps the smile and tender tone
Came out of her pitying womanhood,
For am I not, am I not, here alone
255 So many a summer since she died,
My mother, who was so gentle and good?
Living alone in an empty house,
Here half-hid in the gleaming wood,
Where I hear the dead at midday moan,
260 And the shrieking rush of the wainscot mouse,
And my own sad name in corners cried,
When the shiver of dancing leaves is thrown
About its echoing chambers wide,
Till a morbid hate and horror have grown
265 Of a world in which I have hardly mixed,
And a morbid eating lichen fixed
On a heart half-turned to stone.

9

O heart of stone, are you flesh, and caught
By that you swore to withstand?
270 For what was it else within me wrought
But, I fear, the new strong wine of love,
That made my tongue so stammer and trip
When I saw the treasured splendour, her hand,
Come sliding out of her sacred glove,
275 And the sunlight broke from her lip?

10

I have played with her when a child;
She remembers it now we meet.
Ah, well, well, well, I *may* be beguiled
By some coquettish deceit.
280 Yet, if she were not a cheat,
If Maud were all that she seemed,
And her smile had all that I dreamed,
Then the world were not so bitter
But a smile could make it sweet.

VII

1

285 Did I hear it half in a doze
    Long since, I know not where?
Did I dream it an hour ago,
    When asleep in this arm-chair?

1.260 Cf. *Mariana* lines 63–4: 'the mouse | Behind the mouldering wainscot shrieked' (above p. 55).

143

2

Men were drinking together,
290   Drinking and talking of me;
'Well, if it prove a girl, the boy
Will have plenty; so let it be.'

3

Is it an echo of something
Read with a boy's delight,
295   Viziers nodding together
In some Arabian night?

4

Strange, that I hear two men,
Somewhere, talking of me;
'Well, if it prove a girl, the boy
300   Will have plenty; so let it be.'

VIII

She came to the village church,
And sat by a pillar alone;
An angel watching an urn
Wept over her, carved in stone;
305   And once, but once, she lifted her eyes,
And suddenly, sweetly, strangely blushed
To find they were met by my own;
And suddenly, sweetly, my heart beat stronger
And thicker, until I heard no longer
310   The snowy-banded, dilettante,
Delicate-handed priest intone;
And thought, is it pride? and mused and sighed,
'No surely, now it cannot be pride.'

IX

I was walking a mile,
315   More than a mile from the shore,
The sun looked out with a smile
Betwixt the cloud and the moor;
And riding at set of day
Over the dark moor land,
320   Rapidly riding far away,
She waved to me with her hand.

1.295–6 See *The Story of Nourredin Ali and Bedreddin Hassan* in Galland's
translation of the Arabian Nights. Brothers promise to pair their children.
1.313 'It cannot be pride that she did not return his bow' (T.'s note): see
lines 116–17.

There were two at her side,
Something flashed in the sun,
Down by the hill I saw them ride,
325   In a moment they were gone:
Like a sudden spark
Struck vainly in the night,
Then returns the dark
With no more hope of light.

X

1

330   Sick, am I sick of a jealous dread?
Was not one of the two at her side
This new-made lord, whose splendour plucks
The slavish hat from the villager's head?
Whose old grandfather has lately died,
335   Gone to a blacker pit, for whom
Grimy nakedness dragging his trucks
And laying his trams in a poisoned gloom
Wrought, till he crept from a gutted mine
Master of half a servile shire,
340   And left his coal all turned into gold
To a grandson, first of his noble line,
Rich in the grace all women desire,
Strong in the power that all men adore,
And simper and set their voices lower,
345   And soften as if to a girl, and hold
Awe-stricken breaths at a work divine,
Seeing his gewgaw castle shine,
New as his title, built last year,
There amid perky larches and pine,
350   And over the sullen-purple moor
(Look at it) pricking a cockney ear.

2

What, has he found my jewel out?
For one of the two that rode at her side
Bound for the Hall, I am sure was he:
355   Bound for the Hall, and I think for a bride.
Blithe would her brother's acceptance be.
Maud could be gracious too, no doubt,
To a lord, a captain, a padded shape,
A bought commission, a waxen face,
360   A rabbit mouth that is ever agape –
Bought? what is it he cannot buy?

And therefore splenetic, personal, base,
A wounded thing with a rancorous cry,
At war with myself and a wretched race,
365   Sick, sick to the heart of life, am I.

3

Last week came one to the county town,
To preach our poor little army down,
And play the game of the despot kings,
Though the state has done it and thrice as well,
370   This broad-brimmed hawker of holy things,
Whose ear is crammed with his cotton, and rings
Even in dreams to the chink of his pence,
This huckster put down war! can he tell
Whether war be a cause or a consequence?
375   Put down the passions that make Earth Hell!
Down with ambition, avarice, pride,
Jealousy, down! cut off from the mind
The bitter springs of anger and fear;
Down too, down at your own fireside,
380   With the evil tongue and the evil ear,
For each is at war with mankind.

4

I wish I could hear again
The chivalrous battle-song
That she warbled alone in her joy!
385   I might persuade myself then
She would not do herself this great wrong,
To take a wanton dissolute boy
For a man and leader of men.

5

Ah God, for a man with heart, head, hand,
390   Like some of the simple great ones gone
For ever and ever by,
One still strong man in a blatant land,
Whatever they call him – what care I? –
Aristocrat, democrat, autocrat – one
395   Who can rule and dare not lie.

1.365 ∧ 6 25 extra lines of a vituperative nature in trial edition; see *1969* 1058–9.
1.366–73 George Eliot objected to what she thought was an attack on John Bright in her *Westminster Review* article on *Maud*. T. retorted: 'I did not even know at the time that he was a Quaker.'
1.382–8 Not in *1855*.

6

And ah for a man to arise in me,
That the man I am may cease to be!

XI

1

O let the solid ground
  Not fail beneath my feet
400 Before my life has found
  What some have found so sweet;
Then let come what come may,
What matter if I go mad,
I shall have had my day.

2

405 Let the sweet heavens endure,
  Not close and darken above me
Before I am quite quite sure
  That there is one to love me;
Then let come what come may
410 To a life that has been so sad,
I shall have had my day.

XII

1

Birds in the high Hall-garden
  When twilight was falling,
Maud, Maud, Maud, Maud,
415   They were crying and calling.

2

Where was Maud? in our wood;
  And I, who else?, was with her,
Gathering woodland lilies,
  Myriads blow together.

3

420 Birds in our wood sang
  Ringing through the valleys,
Maud is here, here, here
  In among the lilies.

4

I kissed her slender hand,
425   She took the kiss sedately;
Maud is not seventeen,
  But she is tall and stately.

1.396–7 Not in *1855*.

5

I to cry out on pride
Who have won her favour!
430 O Maud were sure of heaven
If lowliness could save her.

6

I know the way she went
Home with her maiden posy,
For her feet have touched the meadows
435 And left the daisies rosy.

7

Birds in the high Hall-garden
Were crying and calling to her,
Where is Maud, Maud, Maud?
One is come to woo her.

8

440 Look, a horse at the door,
And little King Charley snarling,
Go back, my lord, across the moor,
You are not her darling.

XIII

1

Scorned, to be scorned by one that I scorn,
445 Is that a matter to make me fret?
That a calamity hard to be borne?
Well, he may live to hate me yet.
Fool that I am to be vexed with his pride!
I passed him, I was crossing his lands;
450 He stood on the path a little aside;
His face, as I grant, in spite of spite,
Has a broad-blown comeliness, red and white,
And six feet two, as I think, he stands;
But his essences turned the live air sick,
455 And barbarous opulence jewel-thick
Sunned itself on his breast and his hands.

1.435 'Because if you tread on the daisy, it turns up a rosy underside' (T.'s note).
1.441 **little King Charley** a lap-dog spaniel.
1.455–6 And those fat fingers foolishly thick | With jewels, stunted obstinate hands. *B. MS.*

2

Who shall call me ungentle, unfair?
I longed so heartily then and there
To give him the grasp of fellowship;
460 But while I passed he was humming an air,
Stopped, and then with a riding-whip
Leisurely tapping a glossy boot,
And curving a contumelious lip,
Gorgonized me from head to foot
465 With a stony British stare.

3

Why sits he here in his father's chair?
That old man never comes to his place:
Shall I believe him ashamed to be seen?
For only once, in the village street,
470 Last year, I caught a glimpse of his face,
A gray old wolf and a lean,
Scarcely, now, would I call him a cheat;
For then, perhaps, as a child of deceit,
She might by a true descent be untrue;
475 And Maud is as true as Maud is sweet:
Though I fancy her sweetness only due
To the sweeter blood by the other side;
Her mother has been a thing complete,
However she came to be so allied.
480 And fair without, faithful within,
Maud to him is nothing akin:
Some peculiar mystic grace
Made her only the child of her mother,
And heaped the whole inherited sin
485 On that huge scapegoat of the race,
All, all upon the brother.

4

Peace, angry spirit, and let him be!
Has not his sister smiled on me?

XIV

1

Maud has a garden of roses
490 And lilies fair on a lawn;
There she walks in her state
And tends upon bed and bower,

1.463 **contumelious** superciliously insolent.
1.464 **Gorgonized** petrified – as by the head of Gorgon.

And thither I climbed at dawn
And stood by her garden-gate.
495 A lion ramps at the top,
He is clasped by a passion-flower.

2

Maud's own little oak-room
(Which Maud, like a precious stone
Set in the heart of the carven gloom,
500 Lights with herself, when alone
She sits by her music and books
And her brother lingers late
With a roistering company) looks
Upon Maud's own garden-gate:
505 And I thought as I stood, if a hand, as white
As ocean-foam in the moon, were laid
On the hasp of the window, and my Delight
Had a sudden desire, like a glorious ghost, to glide,
Like a beam of the seventh heaven, down to my side,
510 There were but a step to be made.

3

The fancy flattered my mind,
And again seemed overbold;
Now I thought that she cared for me,
Now I thought she was kind
515 Only because she was cold.

4

I heard no sound where I stood
But the rivulet on from the lawn
Running down to my own dark wood,
Or the voice of the long sea-wave as it swelled
520 Now and then in the dim-gray dawn;
But I looked, and round, all round the house I beheld
The death-white curtain drawn,
Felt a horror over me creep,
Prickle my skin and catch my breath,
525 Knew that the death-white curtain meant but sleep
Yet I shuddered and thought like a fool of the
sleep of death.

1.495 ramps is rampant (heraldic term).
1.523–4 Cf. *In Mem.* 50.2–3 (p. 113 above).

XV

So dark a mind within me dwells,
   And I make myself such evil cheer,
That if *I* be dear to someone else,
530   Then some one else may have much to fear;
But if *I* be dear to some one else,
   Then I should be to myself more dear.
Shall I not take care of all that I think,
Yea, even of wretched meat and drink,
535 If I be dear,
If I be dear to some one else?

XVI

1

This lump of earth has left his estate
The lighter by the loss of his weight;
And so that he find what he went to seek,
540 And fulsome pleasure clog him, and drown
His heart in the gross mud-honey of town,
He may stay for a year who has gone for a week:
But this is the day when I must speak,
And I see my Oread coming down,
545 O this is the day!
O beautiful creature, what am I
That I dare to look her way
Think that I may hold dominion sweet,
Lord of the pulse that is lord of her breast,
550 And dream of her beauty with tender dread,
From the delicate Arab arch of her feet
To the grace that, bright and light as the crest
Of a peacock, sits on her shining head,
And she knows it not; O, if she knew it,
555 To know her beauty might half undo it
I know it the one bright thing to save
My yet young life in the wilds of time,
Perhaps from madness, perhaps from crime,
Perhaps from a selfish grave.

2

560 What, if she be fastened to this fool lord,
Dare I bid her abide by her word?
Should I love her so well if she
Had given her word to a thing so low?
Shall I love her as well if she
565 Can break her word were it even for me?
I trust that it is not so.

3

Catch not my breath, O clamorous heart,
Let not my tongue be a thrall to my eye,
For I must tell her before we part,
570   I must tell her, or die.

XVII

Go not, happy day,
   From the shining fields,
Go not, happy day,
   Till the maiden yields.
575 Rosy is the west,
   Rosy is the south,
Roses are her cheeks,
   And a rose her mouth.
When the happy Yes
580   Falters from her lips,
Pass and blush the news
   Over glowing ships;
Over blowing seas,
   Over seas at rest,
585 Pass the happy news,
   Blush it through the west;
Till the red man dance
   By his red cedar-tree,
And the red man's babe
590   Leap, beyond the sea.
Blush from west to east,
   Blush from east to west,
Till the west is east,
   Blush it through the west,
595 Rosy is the west,
   Rosy is the south,
Roses are her cheeks,
   And a rose her mouth.

XVIII
1

I have led her home, my love, my only friend.
600 There is none like her, none.
And never yet so warmly ran my blood
And sweetly, on and on
Calming itself to the long-wished-for end,
Full to the banks, close on the promised good.

1.571–98 Included among the songs written in 1849 for the third edn of *The
Princess* (1850) in the MS. in Cambridge Univ. Lib.

2

605 None like her, none.
Just now the dry-tongued laurels' pattering talk
Seemed her light foot along the garden walk,
And shook my heart to think she comes once more;
But even then I heard her close the door
610 The gates of Heaven are closed, and she is gone.

3

There is none like her, none,
Nor will be when our summers have deceased.
O, art thou sighing for Lebanon
In the long breeze that streams to thy delicious east,
615 Sighing for Lebanon,
Dark cedar, though thy limbs have here increased,
Upon a pastoral slope as fair,
And looking to the south and fed
With honeyed rain and delicate air,
620 And haunted by the starry head
Of her whose gentle will has changed my fate,
And made my life a perfumed altar-flame;
And over whom thy darkness must have spread
With such delight as theirs of old, thy great
625 Forefathers of the thornless garden, there
Shadowing the snow-limbed Eve from whom she came?

4

Here will I lie, while these long branches sway,
And you fair stars that crown a happy day
Go in and out as if at merry play,
630 Who am no more so all forlorn
As when it seemed far better to be born
To labour and the mattock-hardened hand
Than nursed at ease and brought to understand
A sad astrology, the boundless plan
635 That makes you tyrants in your iron skies,
Innumerable, pitiless, passionless eyes,
Cold fires, yet with power to burn and brand
His nothingness into man.

l.615 Cf. *Ps.* 104.16: 'The trees of the Lord are full of sap; the cedars of Lebanon, which he hath planted.'
l.634 'The *sad astrology* is modern astronomy, for of old astrology was thought to sympathise with and rule man's fate. The stars are "cold fires", for though they emit light of the highest intensity, no perceptible warmth reaches us' (T.'s note).

5

But now shine on, and what care I,
640 Who in this stormy gulf have found a pearl
The countercharm of space and hollow sky,
And do accept my madness, and would die
To save from some slight shame one simple girl.

6

Would die; for sullen-seeming Death may give
645 More life to Love than is or ever was
In our low world, where yet 'tis sweet to live.
Let no one ask me how it came to pass;
It seems that I am happy, that to me
A livelier emerald twinkles in the grass,
650 A purer sapphire melts into the sea.

7

Not die; but live a life of truest breath,
And teach true life to fight with mortal wrongs.
O, why should Love, like men in drinking-songs,
Spice his fair banquet with the dust of death?
655 Make answer, Maud my bliss,
Maud made my Maud by that long loving kiss,
Life of my life, wilt thou not answer this?
'The dusky strand of Death inwoven here
With dear Love's tie, makes Love himself more dear.'

8

660 Is that enchanted moan only the swell
Of the long waves that roll in yonder bay?
And hark the clock within, the silver knell
Of twelve sweet hours that past in bridal white,
And died to live, long as my pulses play;
665 But now by this my love has closed her sight
And given false death her hand, and stolen away
To dreamful wastes where footless fancies dwell
Among the fragments of the golden day.
May nothing there her maiden grace affright!
670 Dear heart, I feel with thee the drowsy spell.
My bride to be, my evermore delight,
My own heart's heart, my ownest own, farewell;
It is but for a little space I go:
And ye meanwhile far over moor and fell
675 Beat to the noiseless music of the night!
Has our whole earth gone nearer to the glow

1.664 And yet I scarce have heart to break the spell *H. MS.*

Of your soft splendours that you look so bright?
I have climbed nearer out of lonely Hell.
Beat, happy stars, timing with things below,
680 Beat with my heart more blest than heart can tell,
Blest, but for some dark undercurrent woe
That seems to draw – but it shall not be so:
Let all be well, be well.

XIX

1

Her brother is coming back tonight,
685 Breaking up my dream of delight.

2

My dream? do I dream of bliss?
I have walked awake with truth.
O when did a morning shine
So rich in atonement as this
690 For my dark-dawning youth,
Darkened watching a mother decline
And that dead man at her heart and mine:
For who was left to watch her but I?
Yet so did I let my freshness die.

3

695 I trust that I did not talk
To gentle Maud in our walk
(For often in lonely wanderings
I have cursed him even in lifeless things)
But I trust that I did not talk,
700 Not touch on her father's sin:
I am sure I did but speak
Of my mother's faded cheek
When it slowly grew so thin
That I felt she was slowly dying
705 Vexed with lawyers and harassed with debt:
For how often I caught her with eyes all wet,
Shaking her head at her son and sighing
A world of trouble within!

4

And Maud too, Maud was moved
710 To speak of the mother she loved
As one scarce less forlorn,
Dying abroad and it seems apart

1.684–786 Not in *1855*.

From him who had ceased to share her heart,
And ever mourning over the feud,
715 The household Fury sprinkled with blood
By which our houses are torn:
How strange was what she said,
When only Maud and her brother
Hung over her dying bed –
720 That Maud's dark father and mine
Had bound us one to the other,
Betrothed us over their wine,
On the day when Maud was born;
Sealed her mine from her first sweet breath.
725 Mine, mine by a right, from birth till death.
Mine, mine – our fathers have sworn.

5

But the true blood spilt had in it a heat
To dissolve the precious seal on a bond,
That, if left uncancelled, had been so sweet;
730 And none of us thought of a something beyond,
A desire that awoke in the heart of the child,
As it were a duty done to the tomb,
To be friends for her sake, to be reconciled;
And I was cursing them and my doom,
735 And letting a dangerous thought run wild
While often abroad in the fragrant gloom
Of foreign churches – I see her there,
Bright English lily, breathing a prayer
To be friends, to be reconciled!

6

740 But then what a flint is he!
Abroad, at Florence, at Rome,
I find whenever she touched on me
This brother had laughed her down,
And at last, when each came home,
745 He had darkened into a frown,
Chid her, and forbid her to speak
To me, her friend of the years before;
And this was what had reddened her cheek
When I bowed to her on the moor.

7

750 Yet Maud, although not blind
To the faults of his heart and mind,
I see she cannot but love him,
And says he is rough but kind,

And wishes me to approve him,
755 And tells me, when she lay
Sick once, with a fear of worse,
That he left his wine and horses and play,
Sat with her, read to her, night and day,
And tended her like a nurse.

8

760 Kind? but the death-bed desire
Spurned by this heir of the liar —
Rough but kind? yet I know
He has plotted against me in this,
That he plots against me still.
765 Kind to Maud? that were not amiss.
Well, rough but kind; why, let it be so:
For shall not Maud have her will?

9

For, Maud, so tender and true,
As long as my life endures
770 I feel I shall owe you a debt,
That I never can hope to pay;
And if ever I should forget
That I owe this debt to you
And for your sweet sake to yours;
775 O, then, what then shall I say? —
If ever I *should* forget,
May God make me more wretched
Than ever I have been yet!

10

So now I have sworn to bury
780 All this dead body of hate,
I feel so free and so clear
By the loss of that dead weight,
That I should grow light-headed, I fear,
Fantastically merry;
785 But that her brother comes, like a blight
On my fresh hope, to the Hall to-night.

XX

1

Strange, that I felt so gay,
Strange, that *I* tried to-day
To beguile her melancholy;

790   The Sultan, as we name him –
     She did not wish to blame him –
     But he vexed her and perplexed her
     With his worldly talk and folly:
     Was it gentle to reprove her
795   For stealing out of view
     From a little lazy lover
     Who but claims her as his due?
     Or for chilling his caresses
     By the coldness of her manners,
800   Nay, the plainness of her dresses?
     Now I know her but in two,
     Nor can pronounce upon it
     If one should ask me whether
     The habit, hat, and feather,
805   Or the frock and gipsy bonnet
     Be the neater and completer;
     For nothing can be sweeter
     Than maiden Maud in either.

2

     But to-morrow, if we live,
800   Our ponderous squire will give
     A grand political dinner
     To half the squirelings near;
     And Maud will wear her jewels,
     And the bird of prey will hover,
815   And the titmouse hope to win her
     With his chirrup at her ear.

3

     A grand political dinner
     To the men of many acres,
     A gathering of the Tory,
820   A dinner and then a dance
     For the maids and marriage-makers,
     And every eye but mine will glance
     At Maud in all her glory.

4

     For I am not invited,
825   But, with the Sultan's pardon,
     I am all as well delighted,
     For I know her own rose-garden,

1.790–1 Because the lubber dandy *H. MS.*
1.792 **But he**] Had *H. MS.*
1.794 **Was it gentle**] Ah booby *H. MS.*

And mean to linger in it
Till the dancing will be over;
830 And then, oh, then, come out to me
For a minute, but for a minute,
Come out to your own true lover,
That your true lover may see
Your glory also, and render
835 All homage to his own darling,
Queen Maud in all her splendour.

XXI

Rivulet crossing my ground,
And bringing me down from the Hall
This garden-rose that I found,
840 Forgetful of Maud and me,
And lost in trouble and moving round
Here at the head of a tinkling fall,
And trying to pass to the sea;
O rivulet, born at the Hall,
845 My Maud has sent it by thee
(If I read her sweet will right)
On a blushing mission to me,
Saying in odour and colour, 'Ah, be
Among the roses tonight.'

XXII

1

850 Come into the garden, Maud,
For the black bat, night, has flown,
Come into the garden, Maud,
I am here at the gate alone;
And the woodbine spices are wafted abroad,
855 And the musk of the rose is blown.

2

For a breeze of morning moves,
And the planet of Love is on high,
Beginning to faint in the light that she loves
On the bed of daffodil sky,
860 To faint in the light of the sun she loves,
To faint in his light, and to die.

1.850–923 Cf. Dryden *The Pilgrim:* 'Song of a Scholar and his Mistress, who being Crossed by their Friends, fell Mad for one another; and now first meet in Bedlam'. The rhythm and to some extent the situation are similar to *Maud:* 'Shall I marry the man I love? | And shall I conclude my pains? | Now blest be the powers above, | I feel the blood bound in my veins...'

3

All night have the roses heard
    The flute, violin, bassoon;
All night has the casement jessamine stirred
865   To the dancers dancing in tune;
Till a silence fell with the waking bird,
    And a hush with the setting moon.

4

I said to the lily, 'There is but one
    With whom she has heart to be gay.
870 When will the dancers leave her alone?
    She is weary of dance and play.'
Now half to the setting moon are gone,
    And half to the rising day;
Low on the sand and loud on the stone
875   The last wheel echoes away.

5

I said to the rose, 'The brief night goes
    In babble and revel and wine.
O young lord-lover, what sighs are those,
    For one that will never be thine?
880 But mine, but mine,' so I sware to the rose,
    'For ever and ever, mine.'

6

And the soul of the rose went into my blood,
    As the music clashed in the hall;
And long by the garden lake I stood,
885   For I heard your rivulet fall
From the lake to the meadow and on to the wood,
    Our wood, that is dearer than all;

7

From the meadow your walks have left so sweet
    That whenever a March-wind sighs
890 He sets the jewel-print of your feet
    In violets blue as your eyes,
To the woody hollows in which we meet
    And the valleys of Paradise.

8

The slender acacia would not shake
895   One long milk-bloom on the tree;
The white lake-blossom fell into the lake
    As the pimpernel dozed on the lea;

But the rose was awake all night for your sake,
    Knowing your promise to me;
900 The lilies and roses were all awake,
    They sighed for the dawn and thee.

9

Queen rose of the rosebud garden of girls,
    Come hither, the dances are done,
In gloss of satin and glimmer of pearls,
905   Queen lily and rose in one;
Shine out, little head, sunning over with curls,
    To the flowers, and be their sun.

10

There has fallen a splendid tear
    From the passion-flower at the gate.
910 She is coming, my dove, my dear;
    She is coming, my life, my fate;
The red rose cries, 'She is near, she is near';
    And the white rose weeps, 'She is late';
The larkspur listens, 'I hear, I hear';
915   And the lily whispers, 'I wait.'

11

She is coming, my own, my sweet;
    Were it ever so airy a tread,
My heart would hear her and beat,
    Were it earth in an earthy bed;
920 My dust would hear her and beat,
    Had I lain for a century dead;
Would start and tremble under her feet,
    And blossom in purple and red.

PART II

I

1

'The fault was mine, the fault was mine' –
Why am I sitting here so stunned and still,
Plucking the harmless wild-flower on the hill? –
It is this guilty hand! –
5 And there rises ever a passionate cry
From underneath in the darkening land –

1.916–23 These lines survive on a wax cylinder recording made by T.
2.3 J. Wordsworth *EC* 24 (1974) 356–62 discusses the Freudian implications
of this and other images in the section.

[51] Alfred Tennyson

What is it, that has been done?
O dawn of Eden bright over earth and sky,
The fires of Hell brake out of thy rising sun,
10 The fires of Hell and of hate;
For she, sweet soul, had hardly spoken a word,
When her brother ran in his rage to the gate,
He came with the babe-faced lord,
Heaped on her terms of disgrace;
15 And while she wept, and I strove to be cool,
He fiercely gave me the lie,
Till I with as fierce an anger spoke,
And he struck me, madman, over the face,
Struck me before the languid fool,
20 Who was gaping and grinning by:
Struck for himself an evil stroke,
Wrought for his house an irredeemable woe.
For front to front in an hour we stood,
And a million horrible bellowing echoes broke
25 From the red-ribbed hollow behind the wood,
And thundered up into Heaven the Christless code,
That must have life for a blow.
Ever and ever afresh they seemed to grow.
Was it he lay there with a fading eye?
30 'The fault was mine,' he whispered, 'fly!'
Then glided out of the joyous wood
The ghastly wraith of one that I know;
And there rang on a sudden a passionate cry,
A cry for a brother's blood:
35 It will ring in my heart and my ears, till I die, till I die.

2

Is it gone? my pulses beat –
What was it? a lying trick of the brain?
Yet I thought I saw her stand,
A shadow there at my feet,
40 High over the shadowy land.
It is gone; and the heavens fall in a gentle rain,
When they should burst and drown with deluging storms
The feeble vassals of wine and anger and lust,
The little hearts that know not how to forgive.
45 Arise, my God, and strike, for we hold Thee just,
Strike dead the whole weak race of venomous worms,
That sting each other here in the dust;
We are not worthy to live.

2.9 brake past tense of break.

II

1

See what a lovely shell,
50   Small and pure as a pearl,
Lying close to my foot,
Frail, but a work divine,
Made so fairily well
With delicate spire and whorl,
55   How exquisitely minute,
A miracle of design!

2

What is it? a learned man
Could give it a clumsy name.
Let him name it who can,
60   The beauty would be the same.

3

The tiny cell is forlorn,
Void of the little living will
That made it stir on the shore.
Did he stand at the diamond door
65   Of his house in a rainbow frill?
Did he push, when he was uncurled,
A golden foot or a fairy horn
Through his dim water-world?

4

Slight, to be crushed with a tap
70   Of my finger-nail on the sand,
Small, but a work divine,
Frail, but of force to withstand,
Year upon year, the shock
Of cataract seas that snap
75   The three-decker's oaken spine
Athwart the ledges of rock,
Here on the Breton strand!

5

Breton, not Briton; here
Like a shipwrecked man on a coast
80   Of ancient fable and fear –
Plagued with a flitting to and fro,

2.49 'In Brittany. The shell undestroyed amid the storm perhaps symbolises to him his own first and highest nature preserved amid the storms of passion' (T.'s note).
2.49–56 Written in 1830s.

[51] Alfred Tennyson

A disease, a hard mechanic ghost
That never came from on high
Nor ever rose from below,
85 But only moves with the moving eye,
Flying along the land and the main –
Why should it look like Maud?
Am I to be overawed
By what I cannot but know
90 Is a juggle born of the brain?

6

Back from the Breton coast,
Sick of nameless fear,
Back to the dark sea-line
Looking, thinking of all I have lost;
95 An old song vexes my ear,
But that of Lamech is mine.

7

For years, a measureless ill,
For years, for ever, to part –
But she, she would love me still;
100 And as long, O God, as she
Have a grain of love for me,
So long, no doubt, no doubt,
Shall I nurse in my dark heart,
However weary, a spark of will
105 Not to be trampled out.

8

Strange, that the mind, when fraught
With a passion so intense
One would think that it well
Might drown all life in the eye, –
110 That it should, by being so overwrought,
Suddenly strike on a sharper sense
For a shell, or a flower, little things
Which else would have been passed by!
And now I remember, I,
115 When he lay dying there,
I noticed one of his many rings
(For he had many, poor worm) and thought
It is his mother's hair.

2.96 **Lamech** *Gen.* 4.23: 'I have slain a man to my wounding, and a young man to my hurt.'

164

9

Who knows if he be dead?
120   Whether I need have fled?
Am I guilty of blood?
However this may be,
Comfort her, comfort her, all things good,
While I am over the sea!
125   Let me and my passionate love go by,
But speak to her all things holy and high,
Whatever happen to me!
Me and my harmful love go by;
But come to her waking, find her asleep,
130   Powers of the height, Powers of the deep,
And comfort her though I die!

III

Courage, poor heart of stone!
I will not ask thee why
Thou canst not understand
135   That thou art left for ever alone:
Courage, poor stupid heart of stone! –
Or if I ask thee why,
Care not thou to reply:
She is but dead, and the time is at hand
140   When thou shalt more than die.

IV

1

O that 'twere possible
After long grief and pain
To find the arms of my true love
Round me once again!

2

145   When I was wont to meet her
In the silent woody places
By the home that gave me birth,
We stood tranced in long embraces
Mixed with kisses sweeter sweeter
150   Than anything on earth.

2.132–40 Not in *1855*. Cf. *Ezek.* 9.19.
2.141–238 Written 1833–4; published in *The Tribute* (1837). Cf. C16 lyric:
'Western wind, when wilt thou blow, | The small rain down can rain? |
Christ if my love were in my arms, | And I in my bed again' (A very early draft in *T.
Nbks*).

3

A shadow flits before me,
Not thou, but like to thee.
Ah, Christ, that it were possible
For one short hour to see
155 The souls we loved, that they might tell us
What and where they be.

4

It leads me forth at evening,
It lightly winds and steals
In a cold white robe before me,
160 When all my spirit reels
At the shouts, the leagues of lights,
And the roaring of the wheels.

5

Half the night I waste in sighs,
Half in dreams I sorrow after
165 The delight of early skies;
In a wakeful doze I sorrow
For the hand, the lips, the eyes,
For the meeting of the morrow,
The delight of happy laughter,
170 The delight of low replies.

6

'Tis a morning pure and sweet,
And a dewy splendour falls
On the little flower that clings
To the turrets and the walls;
175 'Tis a morning pure and sweet,
And the light and shadow fleet;
She is walking in the meadow,
And the woodland echo rings;
In a moment we shall meet;
180 She is singing in the meadow
And the rivulet at her feet
Ripples on in light and shadow
To the ballad that she sings.

7

Do I hear her sing as of old,
185 My bird with the shining head,
My own dove with the tender eye?
But there rings on a sudden a passionate cry,
There is some one dying or dead
And a sullen thunder is rolled;

190   For a tumult shakes the city,
      And I wake, my dream is fled;
      In the shuddering dawn, behold,
      Without knowledge, without pity,
      By the curtains of my bed
195   That abiding phantom cold.

8

      Get thee hence, nor come again,
      Mix not memory with doubt,
      Pass, thou deathlike type of pain,
      Pass and cease to move about!
200   'Tis the blot upon the brain
      That *will* show itself without.

9

      Then I rise, the eave-drops fall,
      And the yellow vapours choke
      The great city sounding wide;
205   The day comes, a dull red ball
      Wrapped in drifts of lurid smoke
      On the misty river-tide.

10

      Through the hubbub of the market
      I steal, a wasted frame;
210   It crosses here, it crosses there,
      Through all that crowd confused and loud,
      The shadow still the same;
      And on my heavy eyelids
      My anguish hangs like shame.

11

215   Alas for her that met me,
      That heard me softly call,
      Came glimmering through the laurels
      At the quiet evenfall,
      In the garden by the turrets
220   Of the old manorial hall.

12

      Would the happy spirit descend
      From the realms of light and song,
      In the chamber or the street,
      As she looks among the blest,
225   Should I fear to greet my friend
      Or to say 'Forgive the wrong,'
      Or to ask her, 'Take me, sweet,
      To the regions of thy rest'?

[51] Alfred Tennyson

13

But the broad light glares and beats,
230 And the shadow flits and fleets
And will not let me be;
And I loathe the squares and streets,
And the faces that one meets,
Hearts with no love for me:
235 Always I long to creep
Into some still cavern deep,
There to weep, and weep, and weep
My whole soul out to thee.

V

1

Dead, long dead,
240 Long dead!
And my heart is a handful of dust,
And the wheels go over my head,
And my bones are shaken with pain,
For into a shallow grave they are thrust,
245 Only a yard beneath the street,
And the hoofs of the horses beat, beat,
The hoofs of the horses beat,
Beat into my scalp and my brain,
With never an end to the stream of passing feet,
250 Driving, hurrying, marrying, burying,
Clamour and rumble, and ringing and clatter;
And here beneath it is all as bad,
For I thought the dead had peace, but it is not so;
To have no peace in the grave, is that not sad?
255 But up and down and to and fro,
Ever about me the dead men go;
And then to hear a dead man chatter
Is enough to drive one mad.

2.239–58 Cf. 1.916–923 where there is a similar idea of a dead man revived and disturbed by sounds from the land of the living, but in the former instance the idea is evoked in the context of hyperbolic love conceits, whereas here it is the product of dementia, and a death-in-life state. In both passages there are beat/feet rhymes.

2.255–6 T. S. Eliot may have recalled these lines in *The Love Song of J. Alfred Prufrock* lines 13–14 'In the room the women come and go | Talking of Michelangelo.' T. had experience of lunatic asylums: see Charles Tennyson 185–8 for an account of his friendship with Dr Allen of High Beech.

2

Wretchedest age, since time began,
200 They cannot even bury a man;
And though we paid our tithes in the days that are gone,
Not a bell was rung, not a prayer was read;
It is that which makes us loud in the world of the dead;
There is none that does his work, not one;
265 A touch of their office might have sufficed,
But the churchmen fain would kill their church,
As the churches have killed their Christ.

3

See, there is one of us sobbing,
No limit to his distress;
270 And another, a lord of all things, praying
To his own great self, as I guess;
And another, a statesman there, betraying
His party-secret, fool, to the press;
And yonder a vile physician, blabbing
275 The case of his patient – all for what?
To tickle the maggot born in an empty head,
And wheedle a world that loves him not,
For it is but a world of the dead.

4

Nothing but idiot gabble!
280 For the prophecy given of old
And then not understood,
Has come to pass as foretold;
Not let any man think for the public good,
But babble, merely for babble.
285 For I never whispered a private affair
Within the hearing of cat or mouse,
No, not to myself in the closet alone,
But I heard it shouted at once from the top of the house;
Everything came to be known.
290 Who told *him* we were there?

5

Not that gray old wolf, for he came not back
From the wilderness, full of wolves, where he used to lie,
He has gathered the bones for his o'ergrown whelp to crack –
Crack them now for yourself, and howl, and die.

2.287–8 *Luke* 12.3: 'Therefore whatsoever ye have spoken in darkness shall be heard in the light; and that which ye have spoken in the ear in closets shall be proclaimed upon the house-tops.'
2.291 See 1.471.
2.294 'For his son is, he thinks, dead' (T.'s note).

6

295   Prophet, curse me the blabbing lip,
      And curse me the British vermin, the rat;
      I know not whether he came in the Hanover ship,
      But I know that he lies and listens mute
      In an ancient mansion's crannies and holes:
300   Arsenic, arsenic, sure, would do it,
      Except that now we poison our babes, poor souls!
      It is all used up for that.

7

      Tell him now: she is standing here at my head;
      Not beautiful now, not even kind;
305   He may take her now; for she never speaks her mind,
      But is ever the one thing silent here.
      She is not *of* us, as I divine;
      She comes from another stiller world of the dead,
      Stiller, not fairer than mine.

8

310   But I know where a garden grows,
      Fairer than aught in the world beside,
      All made up of the lily and rose
      That blow by night, when the season is good,
      To the sound of dancing music and flutes:
315   It is only flowers, they had no fruits,
      And I almost fear they are not roses, but blood,
      For the keeper was one, so full of pride,
      He linked a dead man there to a spectral bride;
      For he, if he had not been a Sultan of brutes,
320   Would he have that hole in his side?

9

      But what will the old man say?
      He laid a cruel snare in a pit
      To catch a friend of mine one stormy day;
      Yet now I could even weep to think of it;
325   For what will the old man say
      When he comes to the second corpse in the pit?

2.296–7 The brown Norwegian rat is supposed to have come to England with the House of Hanover in 1714.
2.318 **dead man** 'himself in his fancy' (T.'s note).
2.319 **a Sultan** Maud's brother.
2.325 **the old man** Maud's father.

10

Friend, to be struck by the public foe,
Then to strike him and lay him low,
That were a public merit, far,
330   Whatever the Quaker holds, from sin;
But the red life spilt for a private blow
I swear to you, lawful and lawless war
Are scarcely even akin.

11

O me, why have they not buried me deep enough?
335   Is it kind to have made me a grave so rough,
Me, that was never a quiet sleeper?
Maybe still I am but half-dead;
Then I cannot be wholly dumb.
I will cry to the steps above my head
340   And somebody, surely, some kind heart will come
To bury me, bury me
Deeper, ever so little deeper.

PART III
1

My life has crept so long on a broken wing
Through cells of madness, haunts of horror and fear,
That I come to be grateful at last for a little thing.
My mood is changed, for it fell at a time of year
5   When the face of night is fair on the dewy downs,
And the shining daffodil dies, and the Charioteer
And starry Gemini hang like glorious crowns
Over Orion's grave low down in the west,
That like a silent lightning under the stars
10   She seemed to divide in a dream from a band
      of the blest,
And spoke of a hope for the world in the coming wars –
'And in that hope, dear soul, let trouble have rest,
Knowing I tarry for thee,' and pointed to Mars
As he glowed like a ruddy shield on the Lion's breast.

2.330 the Quaker Cf. I. 370 for an earlier objection to the Quaker's point of view.
Part III divided in *1865*, but 'section VI' not renumbered. Ricks *1969* suggests it may be an oversight. Of Part III T. writes: 'Sane, but shattered. Written when the cannon was heard booming from the battleships in the Solent before the Crimean War.'
3.6–14 The position of the constellations indicates late Spring. Mars is in Leo, and Auriga and Gemini are above the declining Orion. The Lion is also a symbol of Britain.
3.6 shining daffodil dies indicates late spring.

2

15 And it was but a dream, yet is yielded a dear delight
To have looked though but in a dream, upon eyes so fair,
That had been in a weary world my one thing bright;
And it was but a dream, yet it lightened my despair
When I thought that a war would arise in defence
of the right,
20 That an iron tyranny now should bend or cease,
The glory of manhood stand on his ancient height,
Nor Britain's one sole God be the millionaire:
No more shall commerce be all in all, and Peace
Pipe on her pastoral hillock a languid note,
25 And watch her harvest ripen, her herd increase,
Nor the cannon-bullet rust on a slothful shore,
And the cobweb woven across the cannon's throat
Shall shake its threaded tears in the wind no more.

3

And as months ran on and rumour of battle grew
30 'It is time, it is time, O passionate heart,' said I
(For I cleaved to a cause that I felt to be pure
and true),
'It is time, O passionate heart and morbid eye,
That old hysterical mock-disease should die.'
And I stood on a giant deck and mixed my breath
35 With a loyal people shouting a battle cry,
Till I saw the dreary phantom arise and fly
Far into the north, and battle, and seas of death.

4

Let it go or stay, so I wake to the higher aims
Of a land that has lost for a little her lust of gold,
40 And love of a peace that was full of wrongs and shames,
Horrible, hateful, monstrous, not to be told;
And hail once more to the banner of battle unrolled!
Though many a light shall darken, and many shall weep
For those that are crushed in the clash of jarring claims,
45 Yet God's just wrath shall be wreaked on a giant liar;
And many a darkness into the light shall leap,
And shine in the sudden making of splendid names,
And noble though be freër under the sun,
And the heart of a people beat with one desire;

3.23–8 For a representation in Victorian painting of the image of peace,
similarly portrayed, see Edwin Landseer's *Time of Peace* (1846), reproduced
in Allen Staley *The Pre-Raphaelite Landscape* (Oxford 1973) plate 29b.
3.45 wrath] doom *1855*.

50 For the peace, that I deemed no peace, is over and done,
And now by the side of the Black and the Baltic deep,
And deathful-grinning mouths of the fortress, flames
The blood-red blossom of war with a heart of fire.

5

Let it flame or fade, and the war roll down like a wind,
55 We have proved we have hearts in a cause, we are noble still,
And myself have awaked, as it seems, to the better mind;
It is better to fight for the good than to rail at the ill;
I have felt with my native land, I am one with my kind,
I embrace the purpose of God, and the doom assigned.

3.50 peace, that I deemed no peace] long, long, canker of peace *1855*.

52 Tithonus

Date A shorter form, *Tithon*, written 1833, was prompted, like *Ulysses*, by the death of Hallam (published by M. J. Donahue from *Heath MS. PMLA* 64 (1949) 401–2 and *1969* 566–8). Drafts in *T. Nbks*.

Associations When Hallam died his betrothed, Emily Tennyson, wrote to T.: (12 July 1834) 'What is life to me! If I die (which the Tennysons never do)...' (*Memoir* I.135), and T. might have thought his situation analogous to Tithonus', who was given eternal life by Aurora, but not eternal youth (see the Homeric *Hymn to Aphrodite* and Horace *Odes*. I.28 and 2.16). In this identification Hallam's situation is Aurora's (*1969* 1113 quotes a letter to T. of 10 Apr. 1859 from Jowett, who had just visited Arthur Hallam's grave: 'It is a strange feeling about those who are taken young that while we are getting old and dusty they are as they were'), but it is also possible that Hallam might be Tithonus, growing older in the after-life.

In 1859 Thackeray asked T. for a poem for his new magazine the *Cornhill*. T. contributed his work, wishing that the circumstances of composition might be appended, but the proprietor thought 'it would lower the value of the contribution in the public eye' (*Memoir* I.459). T. revised the original before publication.

Publication *Cornhill Magazine* (Feb. 1860) 'at the tail of a flashy modern novel' (Trollope's *Framley Parsonage*) (T.) (*Memoir* I.459); *1864*.

The woods decay, the woods decay and fall,
The vapours weep their burthen to the ground,
Man comes and tills the field and lies beneath,
And after many a summer dies the swan.

1. The woods decay] Ay me! ay me! *Cornhill*.
1–2 The stars blaze out and never rise again. *T. Nbk*. canc.
3 field] earth *Cornhill*.
4 the swan a symbol of white-haired age. An improvement on 'the rose' of *Tithon* line 4.

5   Me only cruel immortality
Consumes: I wither slowly in thine arms,
Here at the quiet limit of the world,
A white-haired shadow roaming like a dream
The ever-silent spaces of the East,
10   Far-folded mists, and gleaming halls of morn.

      Alas! for this gray shadow, once a man –
So glorious in his beauty and thy choice
Who madest him thy chosen, that he seemed
To his great heart none other than a God!
15   I asked thee, 'Give me immortality.'
Then didst thou grant mine asking with a smile,
Like wealthy men who care not how they give.
But thy strong Hours indignant worked their wills,
And beat me down and marred and wasted me,
20   And though they could not end me, left me maimed
To dwell in presence of immortal youth,
Immortal age beside immortal youth,
And all I was, in ashes. Can thy love,
Thy beauty, make amends, though even now,
25   Close over us, the silver star, thy guide,
Shines in those tremulous eyes that fill with tears
To hear me? Let me go: take back thy gift:
Why should a man desire in any way
To vary from the kindly race of men,
30   Or pass beyond the goal of ordinance
Where all should pause, as is most meet for all?

      A soft air fans the cloud apart; there comes
A glimpse of that dark world where I was born.
Once more the old mysterious glimmer steals
35   From thy pure brows, and from thy shoulders pure,
And bosom beating with a heart renewed.
Thy cheek begins to redden through the gloom,
Thy sweet eyes brighten slowly close to mine,

---

18 Hours female divinities (Lat. *Horae*) presiding over the changes of the seasons. Used by Milton in *Comus* line 986.
25 star 'Venus' (T.'s note).
26 tremulous eyes Cf. Keats *I stood tip-toe* lines 146–7: 'And how they kissed each other's tremulous eyes'.
29 kindly possibly sense 1.1. *OED* (natural) in addition to the familiar 2.5 and 6, genial etc.
30 goal of ordinance 'appointed limit' (T.'s note).

Ere yet they blind the stars, and the wild team
40 Which love thee, yearning for thy yoke, arise,
And shake the darkness from their loosened manes,
And beat the twilight into flakes of fire.

Lo! ever thus thou growest beautiful
In silence, then before thine answer given
45 Departest, and thy tears are on my cheek.

Why wilt thou ever scare me with thy tears,
And make me tremble lest a saying learnt,
In days far-off, on that dark earth, be true?
'The Gods themselves cannot recall their gifts.'

50   Ay me! ay me! with what another heart
In days far-off, and with what other eyes
I used to watch – if I be he that watched –
The lucid outline forming round thee; saw
The dim curls kindle into sunny rings;
55 Changed with thy mystic change, and felt my blood
Glow with the glow that slowly crimsoned all
Thy presence and thy portals, while I lay,
Mouth, forehead, eyelids, growing dewy-warm
With kisses balmier than half-opening buds
60 Of April, and could hear the lips that kissed
Whispering I knew not what of wild and sweet,
Like that strange song I heard Apollo sing,
While Ilion like a mist rose into towers.

Yet hold me not for ever in thine East:
65 How can my nature longer mix with thine?
Coldly thy rosy shadows bathe me, cold

39–42 Meanwhile thy dappled coursers without noise | Sealing the twilight to the morning star | Will draw thee and with dewy breast divide | The rosy shadows flowing either way; | Thou wilt renew thy beauty with the morn | I earth in earth abide with baleful night. *Trinity Nbk.* first draft of *Tithon.* Each version recalls phrases from Marston's *Antonio's Revenge*: 'dapple grey coursers of the morn' I.1.107; 'flakes of fire' I.2.120.
46–76 For a fuller account of the complex textual variants in *T. Nbk.* and *Heath MS.* see *1969* 1116–18.
63 Troy was built by the music of Apollo; T.'s *Ilion, Ilion* of circa 1830 (*1969* 258–9) refers to the city as 'melody born'. Cf. Milton's Pandaemonium, *Paradise Lost* I.711–2: 'Rose like an exhalation, with the sound | Of dulcet symphonies and voices sweet.' The mythologist Jacob Bryant wrote of 'towers' in *New System of Ancient Mythology* (1807 edn 2. 127–8): 'Tithonus, whose longevity is so much celebrated, was nothing more than one of these structures, a Pharos, sacred to the sun, as the name plainly shews.'

Are all thy lights, and cold my wrinkled feet
Upon thy glimmering thresholds, when the steam
Floats up from those dim fields about the homes
70   Of happy men that have the power to die,
And grassy barrows of the happier dead.
Release me, and restore me to the ground;
Thou seëst all things, thou wilt see my grave:
Thou wilt renew thy beauty morn by morn;
75   I earth in earth forget these empty courts,
And thee returning on thy silver wheels.

75 earth in earth *1969* 1118 cites T.'s admission that this is influened by
Dante *Paradiso* 25.124: 'In terra terra e'l mio corpo' ('My body is earth in
the earth').

53 Lucretius

Date Oct. 1865–Jan. 1868 (*Memoir* II.28).

Background Lucretius (*c*. 98–55 B.C.) had an appeal to thoughtful Victorians,
perhaps because they regarded him as out of step with his age, and an early
student of the physical basis of life: see F.M. Turner *VS* 16 (1973) 329–48.
Arnold was planning to write a tragedy on L.'s life as early as 1845, but
only finished about sixty lines. He discussed his lack of 'adequacy' in the
inaugural lecture at Oxford as Professor of Poetry (1857). T. was able to
draw on H. A. J. Munro's edition of L. (1864), in which he would have
found reference to the legend of the poet's death in St Jerome's addition to the
Eusebian Chronicle: 'Titus Lucretius poeta nascitur qui postea amatorio
poculo in furorem versus, cum aliquot libros per intervalla insaniae con-
scripsisset, quos postea Cicero emendavit, propria se manu interfecit anno
aetatis XLIV.' (Titus Lucretius the poet was born, who having been thrown
into a fury by a love potion and having written some books in the intervals
of sanity, which Cicero later emended, took his own life, aged 44.) The
vision of L.'s *De Rerum Natura* haunts the demented imagination of the
philosopher, and the rational man falls under the spell of a pathological
condition. Modern scholars tend to be sceptical about the account: see K.
Ziegler *Hermes* 71 (1936) 429 and C. Bailey in his edition of the *De Rerum*
(Oxford U.P. 1947 8–18).

    For discussion of classical background see R. C. Jebb *Macmillan's*
Magazine 18 (1868) 97–103; K. Allen *Poet-Lore* 11 (1899) 529–48; W. P.
Mustard *Classical Echoes in T.* (1904); and O. L. Wilner *Classical Journal*
25 (1930) 347–66.

Text Textual study in W. D. Paden *The Library* 8 (1953) 269–73, with
corrections by C. Ricks *The Library* 20 (1965) 63–4. Johnson 34 thinks
Lucretius' madness is 'a metaphor for the mood of introspective depression
which throughout his life harried T.'s attempts to fix his faith'; Buckley 168
thinks it demonstrates 'the inadequacy of even the highest naturalistic
philosophy to provide an incentive for either the humane life or the arts that
embody humanity's aspiration'; and Ricks 290–1 states that it 'compacts

three of T.'s horrors: at erotic madness, at a Godless world, and at a juggernaut universe.' Other discussion, W. D. Shaw *MLQ* 33 (1972) 130–9.

MS. draft in *Trinity Nbks.*

Publication *Macmillan's Magazine* (May 1868); *Every Saturday* (2 May 1868); *1870.*

> Lucilia, wedded to Lucretius, found
> Her master cold; for when the morning flush
> Of passion and the first embrace had died
> Between them, though he loved her none the less,
> 5 Yet often when the woman heard his foot
> Return from pacings in the field, and ran
> To greet him with a kiss, the master took
> Small notice, or austerely, for – his mind
> Half buried in some weightier argument,
> 10 Or fancy-borne perhaps upon the rise
> And long roll of the hexameter – he passed
> To turn and ponder those three hundred scrolls
> Left by the Teacher, whom he held divine.
> She brooked it not, but wrathful, petulant,
> 15 Dreaming some rival, sought and found a witch
> Who brewed the philtre which had power, they said,
> To lead an errant passion home again.
> And this, at times, she mingled with his drink,
> And this destroyed him; for the wicked broth,
> 20 Confused the chemic labor of the blood,
> And tickling the brute brain within the man's
> Made havoc among those tender cells, and checked
> His power to shape. He loathed himself, and once
> After a tempest woke upon a morn
> 25 That mocked him with returning calm, and cried:
>
> 'Storm in the night! for thrice I heard the rain
> Rushing; and once the flash of a thunderbolt –
> Methought I never saw so fierce a fork –
> Struck out the streaming mountain-side, and showed

11 The *De Rerum Natura* is written in hexameters.

13 the Teacher Epicurus (341–270 B.C.) was an important influence on Lucretius in recommending a philosophy that would give free range for the mind: *De rer. nat.* 5.8–10: 'he was a god...who first discovered that reasoned plan of life which is now called Wisdom...'

21–2 The 1833 edition of *The Palace of Art* discussed the evolution of the brain: "'So through all phases of all thought I come | Into perfect man'" lines 103–4. The implication is that one could regress. For similar ideas see *In Memoriam* Epilogue lines 125–44 and notes (above pp. 127–8).

26–32 Cf. *De rer. nat.* 6.281–92.

[53] Alfred Tennyson

30   A riotous confluence of watercourses
     Blanching and billowing in a hollow of it,
     Where all but yester-eve was dusty-dry.

       'Storm, and what dreams, ye holy Gods, what dreams!
     For thrice I wakened after dreams. Perchance
35   We do but recollect the dreams that come
     Just ere the waking: terrible! for it seemed
     A void was made in Nature; all her bonds
     Cracked; and I saw the flaring atom-streams
     And torrents of her myriad universe,
40   Ruining along the illimitable inane,
     Fly on to clash together again, and make
     Another and another frame of things
     For ever. That was mine, my dream, I knew it –
     Of and belonging to me, as the dog
45   With inward yelp and restless forefoot plies
     His function of the woodland; but the next!
     I thought that all the blood by Sylla shed
     Came driving rainlike down again on earth,
     And where it dashed the reddening meadow, sprang
50   No dragon warriors from Cadmean teeth,
     For these I thought my dream would show to me,
     But girls, hetairai, curious in their art,
     Hired animalisms, vile as those that made
     The mulberry-faced dictator's orgies worse
55   Than aught they fable of the quiet Gods.
     And hands they mixed and yelled and round me drove
     In narrowing circles till I yelled again
     Half-suffocated, and sprang up, and saw –
     Was it the first beam of my latest day?

60   'Then, then, from utter gloom stood out the breasts,
     The breasts of Helen, and hoveringly a sword
     Now over and now under, now direct,

---

47 Sylla Emperor 82–79 B.C. Described by Plutarch in *Life of Sulla* as 'mulberry-faced' (*Lives*, Loeb edn 4. 327).
50 Cadmean teeth Cadmus killed a serpent guarding the Spring of Ares. Athene told him to sow the teeth in the soil, where upon armed men sprang up and began to brawl amongst each other. Hyginus *Fabula* 178.
52 hetairai 'courtesans' (T.'s note).
55 *De rer. nat.* 3.42: 'nothing at any time impairs their peace of mind.'
60–6 *De rer. nat.* 1.473–5 is adapted, the source of warlike fire being transferred from Alexander to Helen: 'no love's fire fanned to flame by the beauty of Tyndaris, and glowing beneath the breast of Phrygian Alexander, would ever have set alight blazing battles of savage war.'

Pointed itself to pierce, but sank down shamed
At all that beauty; and as I stared, a fire
65   The fire that left a roofless Ilion,
Shot out of them, and scorched me that I woke.

    'Is this thy vengeance, holy Venus, thine,
Because I would not one of thine own doves,
Not even a rose, were offered to thee? thine,
70   Forgetful how my rich pro-oemion makes
Thy glory fly along the Italian field,
In lays that will outlast thy deity?

    'Deity? nay, thy worshippers. My tongue
Trips, or I speak profanely. Which of these
75   Angers thee most, or angers thee at all?
Not if thou be'st of those who, far aloof
From envy, hate and pity, and spite and scorn,
Live the great life which all our greatest fain.
Would follow, centred in eternal calm.

80   'Nay, if thou canst, O Goddess, like ourselves
Touch, and be touched, then would I cry to thee
To kiss thy Mavors, roll thy tender arms
Round him, and keep him from the lust of blood
That makes a steaming slaughter-house of Rome.

85   'Ay, but I meant not thee; I meant not her
Whom all the pines of Ida shook to see
Slide from that quiet heaven of hers, and tempt
The Trojan, while his neatherds were abroad:
Nor her that o'er her wounded hunter wept
90   Her deity false in human-amorous tears;

70 **rich pro-oemion** the opening lines of *De rer. nat.* The tenor of the work is to deride the power of the gods, and suggest they are as subject as mortals to atomic law, though some of the poetry praising Venus is beautiful, and should excuse suffering: 'Mother of Aeneas and his race, darling of men and gods, nurturing Venus, who beneath the smooth-moving heavenly signs fillest with thyself the sea full-laden with ships, the earth with her kindly fruits' (lines 1–14).

80–4 Wilner (1930) compares 1.37–40: 'There as [Mars] reclines, goddess, upon thy sacred body do thou, illustrious one, bending around him from above, pour from thy lips sweet coaxings, and for thy Romans crave quiet peace.'

87 Slide from her quiet seat, and clasp *T. Nbk.*

88 **The Trojan** Ricks *1969* says Endymion, but he was not a Trojan, and his relationship was with Diana not Venus. Anchises (Aeneas' father) is meant here, and in *T. Nbk.* (canc.) T. names Anchises.

89 **her wounded hunter** Adonis.

Nor whom her beardless apple-arbiter
Decided fairest. Rather, O ye Gods,
Poet-like as the great Sicilian called
Calliope to grace his golden verse –
95   Ay, and this Kypris also – did I take
That popular name of thine to shadow forth
The all-generating powers and genial heat
Of Nature, when she strikes through the thick blood
Of cattle, and light is large, and lambs are glad
100 Nosing the mother's udder, and the bird
Makes his heart voice amid the blaze of flowers
Which things appear the work of mighty Gods

'The Gods! and if I go *my* work is left
Unfinished – *if* I go. The Gods, who haunt
105 The lucid interspace of world and world
Where never creeps a cloud, or moves a wind,
Nor ever falls the least white star of snow,
Nor ever lowest roll of thunder moans,
Nor sound of human sorrow mounts to mar
110 Their sacred everlasting calm! and such,
Not all so fine, nor so divine a calm,
Not such, nor all unlike it, man may gain
Letting his own life go. The Gods, the Gods!
If all be atoms, how then should the Gods
115 Being atomic not be dissoluble,
Not follow the great law? My master held
That Gods there are, for all men so believe.
I pressed my footsteps into his, and meant
Surely to lead my Memmius in a train
120 Of flowery clauses onward to the proof
That Gods there are, and deathless. Meant? I meant?
I have forgotten what I meant; my mind
Stumbles, and all my faculties are lamed.

91 beardless apple-arbiter Paris, deciding in the contest for beauty between Venus, Juno and Minerva.
92 Decided fairest Pronounced the prettiest *T. Nbk.* canc.
93 the great Sicilian Empedocles. Praised by Lucretius *De rer. nat.* 1.729: '[Sicily] seems to have in it nothing more illustrious than this man.'
94 Calliope Muse of epic poetry. There is a fragmentary invocation to her by Empedocles.
95 Kypris Venus as the Goddess of Cyprus (Hesiod claims that is where she came to land).
97–101 Cf. *De rer. nat.* 1.7 ff.; 2.367–70.
104–10 Cf. *De rer. nat.* 3.18–24.
119 Caius Memmius was the dedicatee of the *De rer. nat.*

'Look where another of our Gods, the Sun,
125 Apollo, Delius, or of older use
All-seeing Hyperion – what you will –
Has mounted yonder; since he never sware,
Except his wrath were wreaked on wretched man,
That he would only shine among the dead
130 Hereafter – tales! for never yet on earth
Could dead flesh creep, or bits of roasting ox
Moan round the spit – nor knows he what he sees;
King of the East although he seem, and girt
With song and flame and fragrance, slowly lifts
135 His golden feet on those empurpled stairs
That climb into the windy halls of heaven.
And here he glances on an eye new-born,
And gets for greeting but a wail of pain;
And here he stays upon a freezing orb
140 That fain would gaze upon him to the last:
And here upon a yellow eyelid fallen
And closed by those who mourn a friend in vain
Not thankful that his troubles are no more.
And me, although his fire is on my face
145 Blinding, he sees not, nor at all can tell
Whether I mean this day to end myself,
Or lend an ear to Plato where he says,
That men like soldiers may not quit the post
Allotted by the Gods. But he that holds
150 The Gods are careless, wherefore need he care
Greatly for them, nor rather plunge at once,
Being troubled, wholly out of sight, and sink
Past earthquake – ay, and gout and stone, that break
Body toward death, and palsy, death-in-life,
155 And wretched age – and worst disease of all,
These prodigies of myriad nakednesses,
And twisted shapes of lust, unspeakable,
Abominable, strangers at my hearth
Not welcome, harpies miring every dish,
160 The phantom husks of something foully done,
And fleeting through the boundless universe,
And blasting the long quiet of my breast
With animal heat and dire insanity?

129–32 Cf. *Odyssey* 12.374–96: 'the Sun was angry that Odysseus's companions killed his oxen, and the flesh moaned.'
147–9 *Phaedo* 6 (T.'s note).
149–52 Wilner (1930) cites *De rer. nat.* 3. 940–3.

'How should the mind, except it loved them, clasp
165   These idols to herself? or do they fly
Now thinner, and now thicker, like the flakes
In a fall of snow, and so press in, perforce
Of multitude, as crowds that in an hour
Of civic tumult jam the doors, and bear
170   The keepers down, and throng, their rags and they
The basest, far into that council-hall
Where sit the best and stateliest of the land?

'Can I not fling this horror off me again,
Seeing with how great ease Nature can smile,
175   Balmier and nobler from her bath of storm,
At random ravage? and how easily
The mountain there has cast his cloudy slough,
Now towering o'er him in serenest air,
A mountain o'er a mountain, – ay, and within
180   All hollow as the hopes and fears of men?

'But who was he that in the garden snared
Picus and Faunus, rustic Gods? a tale
To laugh at – more to laugh at in myself –
For look! what is it? yon arbutus
185   Totters; a noiseless riot underneath
Strikes through the wood, sets all the tops quivering –
The mountain quickens into Nymph and Faun;
And here an Oread – how the sun delights
To glance and shift about her slippery sides,
190   And rosy knees and supple roundedness,
And budded bosom-peaks – who this way runs
Before the rest! – A satyr, a satyr, see,

165 idols nearer to our meaning of images. See *De rer. nat.* 4.30–2: 'images, which, like films drawn from the outermost surface of things, flit about hither and thither through the air.'
168–72 Cf. *In Memoriam* 21.13–16: 'an hour... | When more and more the people throng | The chairs and thrones of civil power.'
176–80 Cf. *De rer. nat.* 6. 189–98.
181–2 Numa caught Picus and Faunus, and learned from them the secret of averting Jove's lightning (Ovid *Fasti* 3. 285 ff).
186 Stirs all the summits of the copse, and now *T. Nbk.* canc.
189–91 And here an Oread, and this way she runs *Macmillan's Magazine.* Dropped from the magazine version to avoid disturbing the squeamish public, though W. E. Buckler (*RES* n.s. 5 (1954) 269–71) quotes a letter from David Masson suggesting that there were also aesthetic reasons, the lines 'not good enough, not near enough, not poetical enough for Tennyson.' Wilner compares *De rer. nat.* 4. 580 ff.

Follows; but him I proved impossible;
Twy-natured is no nature: yet he draws
195 Nearer and nearer, and I scan him now
Beastlier than any phantom of his kind
That ever butted his rough brother-brute
For lust or lusty blood or provender:
I hate, abhor, spit, sicken at him; and she
200 Loathes him as well; such a precipitate heel.
Fledged as it were with Mercury's ankle-wing,
Whirls her to me – but will she fling herself
Shameless upon me? Catch her, goat-foot! nay,
Hide, hide them, million-myrtled wilderness,
205 And cavern-shadowing laurels, hide! do I wish –
What? – that the bush were leafless? or to whelm
All of them in one massacre? O ye Gods,
I know you careless, yet, behold, to you
From childly wont and ancient use I call –
210 I thought I lived securely as yourselves –
No lewdness, narrowing envy, monkey-spite,
No madness of ambition, avarice, none;
No larger feast than under plane or pine
With neighbours laid along the grass, to take
215 Only such cups as left us friendly-warm,
Affirming each his own philosophy –
Nothing to mar the sober majesties
Of settled, sweet, Epicurean life.
But now it seems some unseen monster lays
220 His vast and filthy hands upon my will,
Wrenching it backward into his, and spoils
My bliss in being; and it was not great;
For save when shutting reasons up in rhythm,
Or Heliconian honey in living words,
225 To make a truth less harsh, I often grew
Tired of so much within our little life,
Or of so little in our little life –
Poor little life that toddles half an hour
Crowned with a flower or two, and there an end –
230 And since the nobler pleasure seems to fade,
Why should I, beastlike as I find myself,
Not manlike end myself? – our privilege –
What beast has heart to do it? And what man,
What Roman would be dragged in triumph thus?

---

224 Heliconian honey Helicon the mountain from which rose the poetic
springs of Aganippe and Hippocrene.

[53] Alfred Tennyson

235 Not I; not he, who bears one name with her
Whose death-blow struck the dateless doom of kings,
When, brooking not the Tarquin in her veins,
She made her blood in sight of Collatine
And all his peers, flushing the guiltless air,
240 Spout from the maiden fountain in her heart
And from it sprang the Commonwealth, which breaks
As I am breaking now!
      'And therefore now
Let her, that is the womb and tomb of all,
Great Nature, take, and forcing far apart
245 Those blind beginnings that have made me man,
Dash them anew together at her will
Through all her cycles – into man once more,
Or beast or bird or fish, or opulent flower:
But till this cosmic order everywhere
250 Shattered into one earthquake in one day
Cracks all to pieces, – and that hour perhaps
Is not so far when momentary man
Shall seem no more a something to himself,
But he, his hopes and hates, his homes and fanes,
255 And even his bones long laid within the grave,
The very sides of the grave itself shall pass,
Vanishing, atom and void, atom and void,
Into the unseen for ever, – till that hour,
My golden work in which I told a truth
260 That stays the rolling Ixionian wheel,
And numbs the Fury's ringlet-snake, and plucks
The mortal soul from out immortal hell,
Shall stand: ay, surely: then it fails at last
And perishes as I must; for O Thou,
265 Passionless bride, divine Tranquillity,
Yearned after by the wisest of the wise,
Who fail to find thee, being as thou art
Without one pleasure and without one pain,
Howbeit I know thou surely must be mine
270 Or soon or late, yet out of season, thus

235–40 Lucretius' name is similar to Lucretia's, the wife of Collatinus, who was raped by Sextus son of the Roman King Tarquin. This led to a rebellion in which the Tarquins were expelled and a republic established (see Ovid *Fasti* and Livy *Historia*).

243 womb and tomb of all Hopkins probably recalls these lines in *Spelt from Sibyl's Leaves* line 2: 'womb-of-all, home-of-all'. The sense of macrocosmic dissolution is similar (p. 515 below).

260 Ixionian wheel a wheel in the underworld on which Ixion was bound as punishment for seducing Hera.

I woo thee roughly, for thou carest not
How roughly men may woo thee so they win –
Thus – thus: – the soul flies out and dies in the air.'
    With that he drove the knife into his side:
275 She heard him raging, heard him fall: ran in,
Beat breast, tore hair, cried out upon herself
As having failed in duty to him, shrieked
That she but meant to win him back, fell on him,
Clasped, kissed him, wailed: he answered, 'Care not thou!
280 Thy duty? What is duty? Fare thee well!'

279–80 'It is done | What matters? What is duty? fare thee well.' *T. Nbk.*
and other mss.
280 Thy...duty?] What matters? All is over: *Macmillan's Magazine.*

54 Northern Farmer: Old Style

Date Written Feb. 1861 (*Memoir* I.471) to Oct. 1861 (F. T. Palgrave *Journals* (1899) 64).
Source T. says it was based 'on the dying words of a farm-bailiff, as reported...by my old great-uncle..."God A'mighty little knows what He's about a-taking me. An' Squire will be so mad an' all".' A very different kind of farmer appears in the following poem (though equally set in his ways). The dialect reproduced is broad Lincolnshire, but P. M. Tilling shows in M. F. Wakelin ed. *Patterns in the Folk Speech of the British Isles* (1972) 88–108 that T. does not give an accurate transcript.
Criticism Generally the dialect poems have been neglected in Tennyson criticism, but C. Wilson *Durham Univ. Journ.* 52 (1959) 22–8 claims, with some justification, that 'save for Chaucer, no one has portrayed bucolic life with technique so consummate or knowledge so intimate'.
Publication *1864.*

1
Wheer 'asta beän saw long and meä liggin' 'ere aloän?
Noorse? thourt nowt o' a noorse: whoy, Doctor's abeän an'
    agoän:
Says that I moänt 'a naw moor aäle: but I beänt a fool:
Git ma my aäle, fur I beänt a-gawin' to breäk my rule.

2
5 Doctors, they knaws nowt, fur a says what's nawways true:
Naw soort o' koind o' use to saäy the things that a do.
I've 'ed my point o' aäle ivry noight sin' I beän 'ere,
An' I've 'ed my quart ivry market-noight for foorty year.

7 **point** pint.

3

Parson's a beän loikewoise, an' a sittin' 'ere o' my bed.
10   'The amoighty's a taäkin o' you to 'issén, my friend,' a said,
An' a towd ma my sins, an's toithe were due, an' I gied it
      in hond;
I done moy duty boy 'um, as I 'a done boy the lond.

4

Larned a ma' beä. I reckons I 'annot sa mooch to larn.
But a cast oop, thot a did, 'bout Bessy Marris's barne.
15   Thaw a knaws I hallus voäted wi' Squoire an' choorch an'
      staäte,
An' i' the woost o' toimes I wur niver agin the raäte.

5

An' I hallus coomed to 's chooch afoor moy Sally wur deäd,
An' 'eard 'um a bummin' awaäy loike a buzzard-clock ower
      my 'eäd,
An' I niver knawed whot a meäned but I thowt a 'ad
      summat to saäy,
20   An' I thowt a said whot a owt to 'a said an' I coomed awaäy.

6

Bessy Marris's barne! tha knaws she laäid it to meä.
Mowt a beän, mayhap, for she wur a bad un, sheä.
'Siver, I kep 'um, I kep 'um, my lass, tha mun understond;
I done moy duty boy 'um as I 'a done boy the lond.

7

25   But Parson a cooms an' a goäs, an' a says it eäsy an' freeä
'The amoighty's a taäkin o' you to 'issén, my friend,' says 'eä.
I weänt saäy men be loiars, thaw summun said it in 'aäste:
But 'e reäds wonn sarmin a weeäk, an' I 'a stubbed
      Thurnaby waäste.

10 you 'pronounced ou as in hour' (T.'s note).
14 a cast oop he brought it up.   **barne** child.
15 hallus always.
18 buzzard-clock 'cockchafer' (T.'s note).
23 'Siver howsoever.
25-8 Although faithful, primarily at a social level, to 'Church and State' the
farmer has a mild hostility to parsons comparable to the 'new style'
Northern Farmer of no. 55.
27 *Ps* 116.11: 'I said in my haste, All men are liars.'
28 stubbed cleared of trees and furze.

8

D'ya moind the waäste, my lass? naw, naw, tha was not
   born then;
30 Theer wur a boggle in it, I often 'eärd 'um mysen;
Moäst loike a butter-bump, fur I 'eärd 'um about an' about,
But I stubbed 'um oop wi' the lot, an' raäved an' rembled
   'um out.

9

Keäper's it wur; fo' they fun 'um theer a-laäid of 'is faäce
Down i' the woild 'enemies afoor I coomed to the plaäce,
35 Noäks or Thimbleby – toäner 'ed shot 'um as deäd as a naäil.
Noäks wur 'anged for it oop at 'soize – but git ma my aäle.

10

Dubbut looök at the waäste: theer warn't not feeäd for a
   cow;
Nowt at all but bracken an' fuzz, an' looök at it now –
Warnt worth nowt a haäcre, an' now theer's lots o' feeäd,
40 Fourscoor yows upon it an' some on it down i' seeäd.

11

Nobbut a bit on it's left, an' I meäned to 'a stubbed it at
   fall,
Done it ta-year I meäned, an' runned plow thruff it an' all,
If godamoighty an' parson 'ud nobbut let ma aloän,
Meä, wi' haäte hoonderd haäcre o' Squoire's, an' lond o'
   my oän.

12

45 Do godamoighty knaw what a's doing a-taäkin' o' meä?
I beänt wonn as saws 'ere a beän an' yonder a peä;
An' Squoire 'ull be sa mad an' all – a' dear a' dear!
And I 'a managed for Squoire coom Michaelmas thutty year.

13

A mowt 'a taäen owd Joänes, as 'ant not a 'aäpoth o' sense,
50 Or a mowt 'a taäen young Robins – a niver mended a fence:
But godamoighty a moost taäke meä an' taäke ma now
Wi' aäf the cows to cauve an' Thurnaby hoälms to plow!

30 **boggle** goblin.
31 **butter-bump** bittern: a marsh bird that makes a booming sound.
32 **raäved** tore (rave *OED* 3).   **rembled** moved (last example in *OED*).
34 **'enemies** anemones.
35 **toäner** one or other.
36 **oop at 'soize** up at the assize.
49 **'aäpoth** half pence.
52 **hoälms** meadows.

[55] Alfred Tennyson

14

Loook 'ow quoloty smoiles when they seeäs ma a passin' boy,
Says to thessén naw doubt 'what a man a beä sewer-loy!'
55   Fur they knaws what I beän to Squoire sin fust a coomed
     to the 'All;
I done moy duty by Squoire an' I done moy duty boy hall.

15

Squoire's i' Lunnon, an' summun I reckons 'ull 'a to wroite,
For whoä's to howd the lond ater meä thot muddles ma quoit;
Sartin-sewer I beä, thot a weänt niver give it to Joänes,
60   Naw, nor a moänt to Robins – a niver rembles the stoäns.

16

But summun 'ull come ater meä mayhap wi' 'is kittle o'
   steäm
Huzzin' an' maäzin' the blessèd feälds wi' the Divil's
   oän teäm.
Sin' I mun doy I mun doy, thaw loife they says is sweet,
But sin' I mun doy I mun doy, for I couldn' abeär to
   see it.

17

65   What atta stannin' theer fur, an' doesn' bring ma the
     aäle?
Doctor's a 'toättler lass, an a's hallus i' the owd taäle;
I weänt breäk rules fur Doctor, a knaws naw moor nor a
   floy;
Git ma my aäle I tell tha, an' if I mun doy I mun doy.

54 sewer-loy surely.
57 Lunnon London.   **summun** someone.
58 howd hold.
60 Naw, nor] Noither *1864–9*.
61 kittle o' steam steam plough.
62 Huzzin' buzzing.   **maäzin'** bewildering.
63 thaw though.
66 'toättler tee-totaller.
67 naw moor nor a floy no more than a fly.

55 Northern Farmer: New Style

Date *Circa* 1865: *1969* 1189 quotes letter from the Duke of Argyll to T., 18
Feb. 1865: 'I hear you have got something new to match the *Lincolnshire
Farmer*'. T. says it was 'founded on a single sentence: "When I canters my
'erse along the ramper (highway) I 'ears 'proputty, proputty, proputty"'.' Cf.
Northern Farmer, Old Style (No. 54).
Publication *1870.*

1

Dosn't thou 'ear me 'erse's legs, as they canters awaäy?
Proputty, proputty, proputty – that's what I 'ears 'em saäy.
Proputty, proputty, proputty – Sam thou's an ass for thy
    paaïns:
Theer's moor sense i' one o' 'is legs nor in all thy braaïns.

2

5   Woä – theer's a craw to pluck wi' tha, Sam: yon's parson's
    'ouse –
Dosn't thou knaw that a man mun be eäther a man or a
    mouse?
Time to think on it then; for thou'll be twenty to weeäk.
Proputty, proputty – woä then woä – let ma 'ear mysén speäk.

3

Me an' thy muther, Sammy, 'as beän a-talkin' o' thee;
10   Thou's beän talkin' to muther, an' she beän a tellin' it me.
Thou'll not marry for munny – thou's sweet upo' parson's lass –
Noä – thou'll marry for luvv – an' we boäth on us thinks
    tha an ass.

4

Seeä'd her todaäy goä by – Saäint's-daäy – they was ringing
    the bells.
She's a beauty thou thinks – an' soä is scoors o' gells,
15   Them as 'as munny an' all – wot's a beauty? – the flower as
    blaws.
But proputty, proputty sticks, an' proputty, proputty graws.

5

Do'ant be stunt: taäke time: I knaws what maäkes tha sa
    mad.
Warn't I craäzed fur the lasses mysén when I wur a lad?
But I knawed a Quaäker feller as often 'as towd ma this:
20   'Doänt thou marry for munny, but goä wheer munny is!'

6

An' I went wheer munny war: an' thy muther coom to 'and,
Wi' lots o' munny laäid by, an' a nicetish bit o' land.
Maäybe she warn't a beauty: – I niver giv it a thowt –
But warn't she as good to cuddle an' kiss as a lass as 'ant nowt?

5 **theer's a craw to pluck wi' tha** there's a difference to settle with you.
7 **to weeäk‛** this week' (T.'s note).
17 **stunt** 'obstinate' (T.'s note).
19 **Quaäker feller** typical of T.'s hostility to the sect: cf. *Maud* I.366–74.

7

25 Parson's lass 'ant nowt, an' she weänt 'a nowt when 'e's deäd,
    Mun be a guvness, lad, or summut, and addle her breäd:
    Why? fur 'e's nobbut a curate, an' weänt niver git hissen clear,
    An' 'e maäde the bed as 'e ligs an afoor e' coomed to the shere.

8

    An' thin 'e coomed to the parish wi' lots o' Varsity debt,
30 Stook to his taaïl they did, an' 'e 'ant got shut on 'em yet.
    An' 'e ligs on 'is back i' the grip, wi' noän to lend 'im a shuvv,
    Woorse nor a far-weltered yowe: fur, Sammy, 'e married
        fur luvv.

9

    Luvv? what's luvv? thou can luvv thy lass an' 'er munny too,
    Maakin' 'em goä togither as they've good right to do.
35 Could'n I luvv thy muther by cause o' 'er munny laaïd by?
    Naäy – fur I luvved 'er a vast sight moor fur it: reäson why.

10

    Ay an' thy muther says thou wants to marry the lass,
    Cooms of a gentleman burn: an' we boäth on us think tha
        an ass.
    Woä then, proputty, wiltha? – an ass as near as mays nowt –
40 Woä then, wiltha? dangtha! – the bees is as fell as owt.

11

    Breäk me a bit o' the esh for his 'eäd lad, out o' the fence!
    Gentleman burn! what's gentleman burn? is it shillins an'
        pence?
    Proputty, proputty's ivrything 'ere, an', Sammy, I'm blest
    If it isn't the saäme oop yonder, fur them as 'as it's the best.

12

45 Tis'n them as 'as munny as breäks into 'ouses an' steäls,
    Them as 'as coäts to their backs an' taäkes their regular meäls.
    Noa, but it's them as niver knaws wheer a meäl's to be 'ad.
    Taäke my word for it, Sammy, the poor in a loomp is bad.

26 addle 'earn' (T.'s note).
27 hissen clear] naw 'igher *1869–86*.
29 Varsity debt debts contracted at the University.
32 far-weltered 'or fow-weltered, – said of a sheep lying on its back' (T.'s note).
39 mays nowt 'makes nothing' (T.'s note).
40 the bees is as fell as owt 'the flies are as fierce as anything' (T.'s note).
44 oop yonder probably in heaven.

13

Them or thir feythers, tha sees, mun 'a beän a laäzy lot,
50   Fur work mun 'a gone to the gittin' whiniver munny was got.
Feyther 'ad ammost nowt; leästways 'is munny was 'id.
But 'e tued an' moiled 'issén deäd, an 'e died a good un, 'e did.

14

Look thou theer wheer Wrigglesby beck cooms out by the 'ill!
Feyther run oop to the farm, an' I runs oop to the mill;
55   An' I'll run oop to the brig, an' that thou'll live to see;
And if thou marries a good un I'll leäve the land to thee.

15

Thim's my noätions, Sammy, wheerby I means to stick;
But if thou marries a bad un, I'll leäve the land to Dick. –
Coom oop, proputty, proputty – that's what I 'ears 'im saäy –
60   Proputty, proputty, proputty – canter an' canter awaäy.

52 tued worked.
53 beck stream.
55 brig bridge.

56 The Higher Pantheism

Date Written Dec. 1867 (*Memoir* II.28). It was read at the first formal
meeting of the Metaphysical Society in June 1869.
    For an account of T. and the Society see *Memoir* II.166–72. There is a
Christian pantheistic tradition, based on texts such as *Romans* 1.20: 'For the
invisible things of him from the creation of the world are clearly seen, being
understood by the things that are made, even his eternal Power and
Godhead.'
Publication *1870*.

The sun, the moon, the stars, the seas, the hills and
    the plains –
Are not these, O soul, the vision of Him who reigns?

Is not the vision He? though He be not that which He
    seems?
Dreams are true while they last, and do we not live in
    dreams?

5   Earth, these solid stars, this weight of body and limb,
Are they not sign and symbol of thy division from Him?

Dark is the world to thee: thyself are the reason why;
For is He not all but that which has power to feel 'I
    am I'?

Glory about thee, without thee; and thou fulfillest
    thy doom,

10   Making Him broken gleams, and a stifled splendour and
          gloom.

      Speak to Him thou for He hears, and Spirit with Spirit
          can meet –
      Closer is He than breathing, and nearer than hands and
          feet.

      God is law, say the wise; O soul, and let us rejoice,
      For if He thunder by law the thunder is yet His voice.

15   Law is God, say some: no God at all, says the fool;
      For all we have power to see is a straight staff bent in a pool;

      And the ear of man cannot hear, and the eye of man
          cannot see;
      But if we could see and hear, this vision – were it not
          He?

12 Cf. *Memoir* II.90: '...depend on it the spiritual is the real – it belongs to
one more than his hand or foot.'
15 Cf. *Ps.* 14.1: 'The fool hath said in his heart, There is no God.'
17 Cf. 1 *Cor.* 2.9: 'But as it is written, Eye hath not seen, nor ear heard,
neither have entered into the heart of man, the things which God hath
prepared for them that love him.'

57 The Higher Pantheism in a Nutshell
(A. C. Swinburne)

Date 1880. One of Swinburne's parodies in *Heptalogia*. Parody at its most
destructive: it is virtually impossible to take the Tennyson poem (which is
little more than versified ideology) seriously after reading this. In addition to
glancing at the absurdity of trying to sum up a metaphysical system in 18
lines, S. probably has in mind Hamlet's 'I could be bounded in a nutshell'
(2.2.260), i.e. metaphysical thought can accomplish much.
Publication *1880*.

      One who is not, we see: but one, whom we see not, is:
      Surely this is not that: but that is assuredly this.
      What, and wherefore, and whence? for under is over
          and under:
      If thunder could be without lightning, lightning could
          be without thunder.

5   Doubt is faith in the main: but faith, on the whole,
          is doubt:
      We cannot believe by proof: but could we believe
          without?

Why, and whither, and how? for barley and rye are
    not clover:
Neither are straight lines curves: yet over is under
    and over.

Two and two may be four: but four and four are not
    eight:
10   Fate and God may be twain: but God is the same thing as
    fate.

Ask a man what he thinks, and get from a man what
    he feels:
God, once caught in the fact, shows you a fair pair
    of heels.

Body and spirit are twins: God only knows which is
    which:
The soul squats down in the flesh, like a tinker drunk
    in a ditch.

15   More is the whole than a part: but half is more than
    the whole:
Clearly, the soul is the body: but is not the body the
    soul?

One and two are not one: but one and nothing is
    two:
Truth can hardly be false, if falsehood cannot be
    true.

Once the mastodon was: pterodactyls were common
    as cocks:
20   Then the mammoth was God: now is He a prize ox.

Parallels all things are: yet many of these are askew:
You are certainly I: but certainly I am not you.

Springs the rock from the plain, shoots the stream
    from the rock:
Cocks exist for the hen: but hens exist for the cock.

25   God, whom we see not, is: and God, who is not, we
    see:
Fiddle, we know, is diddle: and diddle, we take it,
    is dee.

---

20 A superbly ambivalent line, suggesting (i) that images of God are more
sophisticated in modern times, (ii) that God is as stupid as an ox.

58 Crossing the Bar

Date Written Oct. 1889 while crossing the Solent: 'When he repeated it to me in the evening, I said, "That is the crown of your life's work." He answered, "It came in a moment"' (Hallam Tennyson). J. Tennyson says it had been in T.'s mind since April or May 1889, when his nurse suggested he write a hymn after his recovery from a serious illness (*The Times* 5 Nov. 1936).
Publication *1889*.

Sunset and evening star,
    And one clear call for me!
And may there be no moaning of the bar,
    When I put out to sea,

5   But such a tide as moving seems asleep,
      Too full for sound and foam,
When that which drew from out the boundless deep
    Turns again home.

Twilight and evening bell,
10   And after that the dark!
And may there be no sadness of farewell,
    When I embark;

For though from out our bourne of time and place
    The flood may bear me far,
15   I hope to see my Pilot face to face
    When I have crossed the bar.

2 call nautical term, a summons to duty; in this context suggesting the call of God, to duty and to death.
3 bar the sandbank across the harbour-mouth. *1969* cites C. Kingsley's *The Three Fishers* (1858) as a possible source for the connection of the bar and death. When the bar is 'moaning' it is perilous.
7 Cf. *In Memoriam:* Epil. 123–4: 'A soul shall draw from out the vast | And strike his being into bounds.'
13 Cf. Shakespeare *Ham.* 3.1.79–80: 'from whose bourne | No traveller returns.'
15 Cf. 1 *Cor.* 13.12: 'For now we see through a glass darkly; but then face to face.' The allegory is not applicable in all senses, since one sees a pilot in harbour and drops him once the open sea is reached; however it is the case that one would not see a pilot face to face while the harbour entrance is negotiated. 'T. explained the Pilot as "that Divine and Unseen Who is always guiding us"' (Hallam Tennyson). T. J. Assad *Tulane Studies in English* 8 (1958) 153–63 notes the possible objections to the images, but defends them.

Edward FitzGerald

FitzGerald is now almost exclusively remembered for the one work from which the following extracts are taken: *The Rubáiyát of Omar Khayyám*. His life was largely uneventful: one observes parallels with William Barnes's: both poets remaining in obscure parts of the country and cultivating tastes in the literature of other countries and the local dialect and folk-lore. FitzGerald's part of the world was Suffolk, the county also associated with Crabbe. He was born at Bredfield Hall in March 1809 and his early education was partly in France. In 1826 he went up to Trinity College, Cambridge, where he was familiar with the Speddings and Thackeray, and on nodding terms with Tennyson, the latter eventually becoming a close friend. Most of his life was spent in or near Woodbridge, Suffolk. His marriage was shortlived: he found the company of stalwart East Coast sailors more congenial. His tastes were not in line with the main current of Victorian culture, harking back as they do to the patrician self-indulgences and rationality of the Hanoverian era.

After the publication of *The Rubáiyát* FitzGerald did very little more writing. He had no need to write for money; he was careless enough and prosperous enough to use banknotes as bookmarkers. He died in 1883.

The most complete edition is the *Variorum...*, ed. G. Bentham (1902–3); the standard biography is by A. McKinley Terhune (1947).

59 The Rubáiyát of Omar Khayyám of Naishápúr: extracts

Date and origins In July 1856 E. B. Cowell introduced F. to the Bodleian copy of Omar Khayyám (the *Ouseley MSS.* containing 158 stanzas), 'curious infidel and epicurean tetrastichs' F. describes them in a letter to Tennyson. He later sent from Calcutta a copy of the manuscript in the Asiatic Society's Library (with 516 *Rubáiyát*). These were the sources of the first edition; other manuscripts and information came F.'s way for subsequent ones. F. collected a good deal of his local colour from R. B. Binning *A Journal of Two Years' Travel in Persia, Ceylon, etc.* (1857).

Omar Khayyám was a Persian astronomer and poet who died *c.* 1123. His poetic name signifies a tent-maker. The epicurean philosophy in the poetry has affinities with Lucretius – a poet F. was often reading in the 1850s. His beliefs were much more sceptical than the later Sufi poet Hafiz; he preferred to dwell on the certitudes offered by the world of the senses rather than on speculations of the after-life.

Form *Rubáiyát* is the plural of the Persian *rubai*, an irregular four-line poem. F.'s quatrain form was new to English, and subsequently imitated (with some variations) by Swinburne in *Laus Veneris*. In the original, the quatrains are strung together with no particular regard to theme. F. made his own arrangement and choice, but E. Heron-Allen, *E. F.'s Rubáiyát of Omar Khayyám* (1899), discovered that 49 of the 101 'are faithful and beautiful paraphrases of single quatrains.'

An edition of FitzGerald's translation, with a commentary by H. M. Batson and a biographical introduction by E. D. Ross (1900), is helpful. **Content and influence** F. comments on the tone of the work: 'Either way, the result is sad enough: saddest perhaps when most ostentatiously merry: more apt to move sorrow than anger toward the old tent-maker, who, after vainly endeavouring to unshackle his steps from destiny, and to catch some authentic glimpse of *Tomorrow*, fell back upon Today (which has outlasted so many Tomorrows!) as the only ground he'd stand upon, however momentarily slipping from under his Feet.'

F. wrote to Cowell 27 Apr. 1859: 'I suppose very few people have ever taken such pains in translation as I have: though certainly not to be literal. But at all cost, a thing must *live*: with a transfusion of one's own worse Life if one can't retain the original's better. Better a live sparrow than a stuffed eagle' (*Letters of E.F.* (1907) 2.5). The notion of 'transfusion' becomes clear when one considers the date, and remembers the mustering of forces in England of free-thinking and aestheticism. The poem could be smuggled into earnest middle-class households as a piece of antiquarianism, but below the surface was an up-to-date sensuousness and free-thinking.

Its earliest circulation was in advanced and aesthetic circles: Rossetti waxes excited about it to Swinburne and Meredith, and a public initiated into hedonism in the 1870s and 80s by Pater and others found it a central poem. Tennyson said the *Rubáiyát* was 'A planet equal to the Sun | That cast it'. There have been many translations of the *Rubáiyát* since F., but none equal in beauty and literary quality to his. For a study of the original see A. J. Arberry *Omar Khayyám: A New Version Based upon Recent Discoveries* (1952); see also his *Omar Khayyám and FitzGerald* (1959). F. offered the work to *Fraser's Magazine*, who refused it, Quaritch published the first edition, which sold so poorly that of the 250 copies 200 were remaindered at a penny each. The revised editions sold better, and the work became one of the show pieces of Victorian poetry.

Publication *1859; 1868; 1872; 1879* (the text followed here).

1

Wake! for the Sun, who scattered into flight
The stars before him from the field of night,
   Drives night along with them from Heaven, and strikes
The Sultan's turret with a shaft of light.

1–4 Awake! for morning in the bowl of night | Has flung the stone that puts the stars to flight: | And lo! the hunter of the east has caught | The Sultan's turret in a noose of light. *1859*. (Flinging a stone into a cup was the signal for 'To horse' in the desert.) Wake! For the sun behind yon Eastern height | Has chased the session of the stars from night; | And, to the field of heaven ascending, strikes | The Sultan's turret with a shaft of light. *1868*.

2

5   Before the phantom of false morning died,
    Methought a voice within the tavern cried,
      'When all the temple is prepared within,
    Why nods the drowsy worshipper outside?'

3

    And, as the cock crew, those who stood before
10   The tavern shouted, 'Open then the door!
    You know how little while we have to stay,
    And, once departed, may return no more.'

4

    Now the New Year reviving old desires,
    The thoughtful soul to solitude retires,
15   Where the white hand of Moses on the bough
    Puts out, and Jesus from the ground suspires.

5

    Iram indeed is gone with all his rose,
    And Jamshyd's seven-ringed cup where no one knows;
     But still a ruby kindles in the vine,
20   And many a garden by the water blows.

6

    And David's lips are locked; but in divine
    High-piping Pehlevi, with 'Wine! Wine! Wine!
     Red Wine!' – the nightingale cries to the rose
    That sallow cheek of hers to incarnadine.

5 phantom ... morning 'a transient light on the horizon about an hour before the ... true dawn.' (F.'s note).

7–8 'Awake, my little ones, and fill the cup | Before life's liquor in its cup be dry.' *1859.*

10 Omar's 'worldly pleasures are what they profess to be without any pretence at divine allegory: his wine is the veritable juice of the grape: his tavern where it was to be had' (F.).

15 the white hand of Moses a spring plant in Persia; see *Exod.* 4.6: the prophet's hand became 'leprous as snow' when he put it in his bosom.

16 Jesus ... suspires Christ's breath has healing powers; the Muslims call Christ 'the Breath of God'.

17 Iram planted by King Shaddad and lost in the sands of Arabia.

18 Jamshyd's ... cup Jamshid, fifth king of the Pishadian dynasty. The cup invented by Kay Khosru (Cyrus, king of the Medes and Persians) showed the past, present and future of the whole world.

21 David the type of musician in Islamic literature; see Tabari in C9: 'God sent David the Psalms, and gave him a goodly voice.'

22 Pehlevi the ancient pre-Islamic language of Persia. Cf. Keats *Ode to a Nightingale* lines 61–4 for the notion of continuity of the bird's song.

24 incarnadine make red. Cf. Shakespeare, *Mac.* 2.2.61–3.

7

25 Come, fill the cup, and in the fire of spring
    Your winter-garment of repentance fling:
        The bird of time has but a little way
    To flutter – and the bird is on the wing.

8

    Whether at Naishápúr or Babylon,
30 Whether the cup with sweet or bitter run,
        The wine of life keeps oozing drop by drop,
    The leaves of life keep falling one by one.

*

11

    With me along the strip of herbage strown
    That just divides the desert from the sown,
        Where name of slave and Sultan is forgot –
    And peace to Mahmud on his golden throne!

12

45 A book of verses underneath the bough,
    A jug of wine, a loaf of bread – and thou
        Beside me singing in the wilderness –
    Oh, wilderness were paradise enow!

*

17

65 Think, in this battered caravanserai
    Whose portals are alternate night and day,
        How Sultan after Sultan with his pomp
    Abode his destined hour, and went his way.

28 To...and] To fly – and Lo! *1859.*
29–32 Not in *1859.*
29 Naishápúr Omar's birthplace.
31 The wine of life Cf. *Mac.* 2.4.100.
32 The leaves of life Cf. *Mac.* 5.3.22–3: 'my way of life │ Is fall'n into the sear, the yellow leaf'.
43–4 Where name of slave and Sultan scarce is known, │ And pity Sultan Mahmud on his throne. *1859.*
65 caravanserai inn; Binning 1.171 describes such an establishment.
66 portals] doorways *1859.*
68 destined hour] hour or two *1859.*

18

They say the lion and the lizard keep
70   The courts where Jamshyd gloried and drank deep:
    And Bahrám, that great hunter – the wild ass
    Stamps o'er his head, but cannot break his sleep.

19

I sometimes think that never blows so red
    The rose as where some buried Caesar bled;
75   That every hyacinth the garden wears
    Dropped in her lap from some once lovely head.

20

And this reviving herb whose tender green
    Fledges the river-lip on which we lean –
    Ah, lean upon it lightly! for who knows
80   From what once lovely lip it springs unseen!

21

Ah, my beloved, fill the cup that clears
    Today of past regret and future fears:
    To-morrow! – why, to-morrow I may be
    Myself with yesterday's seven thousand years.

*

25

Alike for those who for to-day prepare,
    And those that after some to-morrow stare,
    A muezzin from the tower of darkness cries,
100   'Fools! your reward is neither here nor there.'

*

70 The courts Persepolis, founded by the Jamshyd of line 18; described by
Binning Ch. 22.
71 Bahrám the Sassanian king, buried in the quicksands of the plains of
Veramin. His full name Bahrám Gur, Bahrám of the wild ass.
72 but ... sleep] and he lies fast asleep. *1859.*
73–6 The palace that to Heaven his pillars threw, | And Kings the forehead
on his threshold drew – | I saw the solitary ringdove there, | And 'Coo, coo,
coo,' she cried; and 'Coo, coo, coo.' *1868. Ku* Persian for 'where?' F.'s source
Binning 2.20.
75 hyacinth violet in Omar.
77 reviving] delightful *1859.*
84 seven thousand years the age of the earth as Omar's contemporaries
believed it to be.
97–100 Batson 168 compares with Tennyson's *Confessions of a Second-rate
Sensitive Mind* lines 172–7.
99 muezzin one who calls Muslims to prayer from the tower of the mosque.

31

Up from Earth's centre through the seventh gate
I rose, and on the throne of Saturn sate,
    And many a knot unravelled by the road;
But not the master-knot of human fate.

32

125 There was the door to which I found no key;
There was the veil through which I might not see:
    Some little talk awhile of me and thee
There was – and then no more of thee and me.

33

Earth could not answer; nor the seas that mourn
130 In flowing purple, of their Lord forlorn;
    Nor rolling Heaven, with all his signs revealed
And hidden by the sleeve of night and morn.

34

Then of the thee in me who works behind
The veil, I lifted up my hands to find
135   A lamp amid the darkness; and I heard,
As from without – 'The me within thee blind!'

35

Then to the lip of this poor earthen urn
I leaned, the secret of my life to learn:
    And lip to lip it murmured – 'While you live,
140 Drink ! for, once dead, you never shall return.'

121 the throne of Saturn The sphere of Saturn was the seventh of these surrounding the earth, and the limit of man's understanding of the universe.
124 But not the knot of human death and fate *1859*.
136 Cf. Tennyson *In Memoriam* 56. 25–8.
127–36 Heron-Allen quotes from Ferid-ud din 'Attar: 'The Creator of the world spake thus to David from behind the Curtain of the Secret; "Everything in the world...is mere substitute unless it be Me,... Since long ago, really, I am Thee and Thou art Me – We two are but one.' This is the Sufi account of the unity with God, but Omar is sceptical about it as a sustained exercise.
129–32 Then to the rolling Heaven itself I cried, | Asking, 'What lamp had destiny to guide | Her little children stumbling in the dark?' | And – 'A blind understanding!' Heaven replied. *1859*.
137–8 Then to this earthen bowl did I adjourn | My lip the secret well of life to learn: *1859*.
138 I leaned, the secret well of life to learn; *1868*.

36

I think the vessel, that with fugitive
Articulation answered, once did live,
    And drink; and Ah! the passive lip I kissed,
How many kisses might it take – and give!

37

145 For I remember stopping by the way
To watch a potter thumping his wet clay:
    And with its all-obliterated tongue
It murmured – 'Gently, brother, gently, pray!'

38

And has not such a story from of old
150 Down man's successive generations rolled
    Of such a clod of saturated earth
Cast by the Maker into human mould?

39

And not a drop that from our cups we throw
For earth to drink of, but may steal below
155   To quench the fire of anguish in some eye
There hidden – far beneath, and long ago.

40

As then the tulip for her morning sup,
Of heavenly vintage from the soil looks up
    Do you devoutly do the like, till heaven
160 To earth invert you – like an empty cup.

*

66

I sent my soul through the invisible,
Some letter of that after-life to spell:
    And by and by my soul returned to me,
And answered, 'I myself am heaven and hell':

143 And merry-make; and the cold lip I kissed, *1859*. And drink; and that impassive lip I kissed, *1868*. It is generally true of this poem that the sexual identity of the beloved is ambiguous, and nowhere more so than in this stanza.
145–8 Cf. F.'s translation of Attar's *Mantik-ut-tair* (Bird Parliament); also biblical, eg. *Isa.* 30.14.
149–52 A reference to the Promethean creation of man, see Pausanias *Description of Greece* 10.4.4.
153–6 Not in *1859*.
154 For . . . of] On the parched herbage *1868*.
261–4 Not in *1859*.
264 Cf. Milton *Paradise Lost* 4.75: 'Which way I fly is hell; my self am hell'.

67

265 Heaven but the vision of fulfilled desire,
And hell the shadow from a soul on fire,
    Cast on the darkness into which ourselves,
So late emerged from, shall so soon expire.

68

We are no other than a moving row
270 Of magic shadow-shapes that come and go
    Round with the sun-illumined lantern held
In midnight by the master of the show;

69

But helpless pieces of the game He plays
Upon this chequer-board of nights and days;
275   Hither and thither moves, and checks, and slays,
And one by one back in the closet lays.

70

The ball no question makes of ayes and noes,
But here or there as strikes the player goes;
    And He that tossed you down into the field,
280 *He* knows about it all – He knows – He knows!

71

The moving finger writes; and, having writ,
Moves on: nor all your piety nor wit
    Shall lure it back to cancel half a line,
Nor all your tears wash out a word of it.

72

285 And that inverted bowl they call the sky,
Whereunder crawling cooped we live and die,
    Lift not your hands to *It* for help – for it
As impotently moves as you or I.

*

265–8 Not in *1859*.
269–72 Not in *1859*. F. refers to the figures on revolving cylinders, lit by a light, and appearing to move when rotated.
270 Of...shapes] Of visionary shapes *1868*.
273–4 'Tis all a chequer-board of nights and days | Where destiny with men for pieces plays: *1859*.
281–4 The book of life is pre-written. Also a memory of the writing on the wall in *Dan. 5*.
288 Rolls impotently on as Thou or I. *1859*.

80

O Thou, who didst with pitfall and with gin
Beset the road I was to wander in,
   Thou wilt not with predestined evil round
320 Enmesh, and then impute my fall to sin!

81

O Thou, who man of baser earth didst make,
And even with paradise devise the snake:
   For all the sin wherewith the face of man
Is blackened – man's forgiveness give – and take!

*

96

Yet Ah, that Spring should vanish with the rose!
That youth's sweet-scented manuscript should close!
   The nightingale that in the branches sang,
Ah whence, and whither flown again, who knows!

97

385 Would but the desert of the fountain yield
One glimpse – if dimly, yet indeed, revealed,
   To which the fainting traveller might spring,
As springs the trampled herbage of the field!

98

Would but some wingèd angel ere too late
390 Arrest the yet unfolded roll of fate,
   And make the stern recorder otherwise
Enregister, or quite obliterate!

99

Ah, love! could you and I with Him conspire
To grasp this sorry scheme of things entire,
395   Would not we shatter it to bits – and then
Re-mould it nearer to the heart's desire!

319 predestined evil] predestination *1859.*
322 And ... paradise] And who with Eden didst *1859.*
324 Omar offering God forgiveness is totally foreign to the original, which reads in R. Cowell's version: 'O Thou who givest repentance and acceptest the excuses of everyone.'
389–92 Not in *1859.*
393 Ah love! could thou and I with fate conspire *1859.* Ah love! could you etc. *1868.*

Robert Browning

100

Yon rising moon that looks for us again –
How oft hereafter will she wax and wane;
How oft hereafter rising look for us
400   Through this same garden – and for *one* in vain!

101

And when like her, oh Sáki, you shall pass
Among the guests star-scattered on the grass,
And in your joyous errand reach the spot
Where I made one – turn down an empty glass!

Tamám

397–8 Ah, moon of my delight, who know'st no wane, | The moon of heaven is rising once again; *1859*; But see! The rising moon of heaven again | Looks for us, sweet-heart, through the quivering plane: *1868*.
401 And when thyself with shining foot shall pass *1859*; And when yourself with silver foot shall pass *1868*.
404 Where I made one where I am buried.
Tamám it is ended.

Robert Browning

Early life Robert Browning was born in 1812 in Camberwell, a suburb of London, and was brought up in a middle-class urban environment. Events in the family history demonstrate that his background was markedly unlike that of the typical bourgeois philistine. His father, revolted by the slave system on the family estates on St Kitt's, came home, planning to devote himself to some form of artistic pursuit, but found it necessary to work as a clerk in the Bank of England. He devoted his spare time to collecting books on many topics – ancient and modern history, scholasticism, politics, and lives of poets and painters. He had a library of 6,000 volumes, which constituted much the most important element in his son's education. He did not forgo the creative arts entirely: according to Rossetti he had 'a real genius for drawing': and he wrote poetry, including a *Pied Piper of Hamelin*. Understandably therefore, he took great vicarious pleasure in his son's artistic achievements. B.'s mother was Sarah Anna Wiedemann, of Scottish and German background. She was a subdued but powerful personality, very religious and quite musical. The home environment was secure, relaxed and well protected for B. and his younger sister Sarianna.

Another source of B.'s informal education was the local Dulwich Gallery. B. had contacts with sensitive and educated people who lived nearby: Eliza and Sarah Flower (the latter now best known as the author of *Nearer, my God, to Thee*), Alfred Domett (the original of Waring and later Prime

Minister of New Zealand), and Joseph Arnould. A good deal in his training unfitted him for the rough and tumble of disciplined, competitive life: an early failure to relate to the conventional world was his inability to pursue formal education at London University. Indeed, one detects in adolescence signs of the strengths and weaknesses of B.'s poetic personality: the strengths residing in his capacity to draw on deeply felt, private and even eccentric resources, the weaknesses springing from a half-grasped notion of the conventions and interests of society at large. Typical of his unconventionality was his worship of Shelley, who was generally regarded in the 1820s as poetically interesting but ideologically dangerous. B. did not retain the atheistic beliefs imbibed from Shelley for very long, but he retained the Shelleyan image of the poet, as one sees both in *Pauline* (1833) and in the essay on Shelley of 1852. The plan (not executed) for *Pauline* was to produce a series of poems emanating from a group of invented characters, and the 'world was never to guess that [they]...were no other than one and the same invidual'. The presentation of poetic material through personae was thus laid down as a method at an early stage in his career. B. was further impelled to pursue the self-protective device of drama after seeing John Stuart Mill's comment in a copy of the poem: 'With considerable poetic powers, the writer seems to me possessed with a more intense and morbid self-consciousness than I ever knew in any sane human being.' The annotated copy is now in the Forster-Dyce Collection in the Victoria and Albert Museum.

In the spring of 1834 B. accompanied the Russian consul-general on a mission to Russia. There is a vivid reminiscence of the journey in *Ivan Ivanovitch* (1878). He wrote *Porphyria's Lover* in St Petersburg. On his return he applied for a place on a mission to Persia, but without success. B. probably regarded activities of this kind as opportunities for widening his knowledge of life and gaining stores of poetic material. The most important journeys, however, were the ones to Italy in 1838 and 1844.

Two important early poems are *Paracelsus* (1835) and *Sordello* (1840). The latter has been hailed as one of the key works in the Victorian era, but one hesitates to assign an important place to a work so manifestly lacking in clarity and accessibility. The ten years from 1837 to 1847 were mainly taken up with playwriting. On 27 November 1835 B. had met the actor Macready, who hoped that work from the young poet would somehow revivify his flagging career. The first play B. wrote (*Strafford*, finished Autumn 1836) impressed him – except for 'the meanness of plot, and occasional obscurity.' These initial misgivings were to grow in the association. Posterity has agreed with Macready that B.'s theatrical gifts were limited, despite the dramatic sensitivity of his poetic make-up. After reading through *The Return of the Druses* in 1840 Macready said: 'I yield to the belief that he will never write again – to any purpose. I fear his intellect is not quite clear.' The next play to be submitted was *A Blot in the 'Scutcheon*, which was acted without acclaim in Februrary 1843 and terminated B.'s connection and friendship with Macready.

Colombe's Birthday was submitted to Kean in 1844, but not acted until 1853, when Samuel Phelps produced it at the Haymarket. B. also published plays that were not acted: *King Victor and King Charles* (1842), *A Soul's Tragedy* (1846), *Luria* (1846) and, most interesting of the dramatic experiments, *Pippa Passes* (1841).

Robert Browning

The dramatic years had come to little in establishing B.'s fame, but they had helped him to develop his most characteristic poetic feature: the dramatic monologue. Many of the poems that appeared in the series of eight pamphlets called *Bells and Pomegranates* (1841–6) took this form. The title is taken from *Exodus* 28.33–4; the verses suggested to B. 'something like an alternation, or mixture, of music with discoursing, sound with sense, poetry with thought'. At this point in his career one begins to notice the strong, vigorous influence of Shakespeare and Donne. B., untypically for his age, responded less to the sensuous beauty of C16 and C17 poetry than to its vigour and emotional vividness, conveyed in colloquial speech. The dramatic method adopted by B. was so employed that his own ethical views – always assuming he had any – appeared only in the most oblique way. Elizabeth Barrett regretted this, urging him to speak for himself 'out of that personality which God made, and with the voice which he turned.' B. did not heed the advice: even in *One Word More* (no. 75) there is more than a trace of the poetic mask.

Marriage and after In January 1845 Elizabeth and Robert had begun a correspondence that led to a meeting, to several hundred more letters, and to love and marriage. The word 'elopement' is sometimes used to describe Elizabeth's escape from the suffocating atmosphere of Wimpole Street, although Elizabeth was forty at the time of her marriage in September 1846, and it was only the hysterical opposition of her father that gave it such an atmosphere. The honeymoon was spent in Italy, partly in the company of the art historian Mrs Jameson. Mrs Browning was a considerable poet at the time of the marriage – more famous and more commercially successful than her husband: her *Poems of 1844* were a success, her *Sonnets from the Portuguese* of 1850 were highly popular, and *Aurora Leigh* of 1856 was a sensational best-seller. For reasons of Elizabeth's health the Brownings set up home in Italy, making periodic visits to England. B. only took up permanent residence in England after her death on 29 June 1861. Some of his most important work was influenced by Italy, which continued to dominate it even after he left.

The marriage was happy on the whole, the only serious differences arising over politics, spiritualism, the upbringing of Pen and the lurid Roman murder story of the C17 which Elizabeth thought unsuitable material for poetry. When she died Browning wrought the material into *The Ring and the Book* (1868), one of the most compelling long poems in the language. After Elizabeth's death B. was emotionally entangled with Frances Julia Wedgwood (a cousin and niece of Charles Darwin) and with Lady Ashburton – to whom he proposed, probably in 1869. His deportment with these ladies seems to have been as awkward and strained as his relations with his public and with the English language. There were mental blocks in B.'s make-up, suggestively analysed in S. W. Holmes's 'Browning: semantic stutterer,' *PMLA* 60 (1945) 231–55, from the psychological point of view.

In the 1860s the process whereby B. became something of an institution began, with Oxford University conferring an M.A. by diploma and the University of St Andrews offering him the Lord Rectorship. He dined out frequently, managing to conceal the poetic side of his personality so effectively that he gave Henry James the donnée for an allegorical short story of the split artistic personality (*The Private Life* 1892). The adulation accorded to B. in the latter decades of his life (typified most fully by

206

Robert Browning

The Browning Society) was based on a respect not so much for his poetry as for the message and the instruction. The general air of optimism and humanistic confidence and the imprecise but deeply felt religion of love were welcome anodynes in an age that was losing its religious faith. Many of the books and articles on B. from this period have titles such as *Browning as a Religious Teacher*. Edward Dowden regarded his poetry as a galvanic battery for spiritual paralytics. In the last two decades of his life B. composed prolifically, but with a few exceptions little has emerged from this period that is worth reading as poetry, however interesting it may be as a comment on the man and the age that produced it. Some of the exceptions are in this selection.

Appropriately, B. died in Venice on 12 Dec. 1889, on the same day that *Asolando* was published in London. He had spent the last Autumn of his life revisiting the small Italian hill town of Asolo, associated with the *Sordello* and *Pippa Passes* of years before. The scene of his last burst of creativity brought the wheel of his career full-circle. His body was taken back to England for burial in Westminster Abbey.

Reputation B.'s reputation has never fallen into a severe decline, though there has been an adjustment since the cult worship of the Browningites. The love, the optimism, the detailed interest in nature may have fallen out of favour in our century, but he adumbrated some of the most significant features of twentieth-century poetry. His method of presenting morality was not to import a ready-made solution but to reveal the process of judgement and experience in the poetry itself. This is curiously modern. He believed in the relativity of truth – at the level of the individual percipient – but unlike modern upholders of relativity he was temperamentally reluctant to espouse amorality: rather like Fra Lippo Lippi he believed that the world 'means intensely, and means good'. The greatest gift man could receive and give was love; the value to which his poetry insistently returns is the salvation of those who love and the damnation of those who do not.

Themes Much of his poetry is exotic: it deals with romantic characters in spatially and temporally remote settings, at moments of distinct and unusual crisis. B.'s eccentric education partly explains this. The themes of the poetry reflect evasion and escape from the present – though it is frequently true that one detects oblique connections with modern issues in the most unlikely circumstances (see no. 63 for instance). These connections should not be pushed too far: there is a lot to recommend the simple observation that B. found the past intrinsically fascinating, since it provided him with what he thought the present was inclined to lack: vivid characters involved in vivid action. The Italian Renaissance was a particularly fruitful source for such types. B.'s tastes are glimpsed in a revealing letter of 20 August 1861, in which he makes plans for Pen now that he is free from the baneful influence of Elizabeth: 'I distrust all hybrid and ambiguous natures and nationalities and want to make something decided of the poor little fellow.' This could stand for his attitude to creations of his own mind.

B.'s poetic output was considerable; so that the selection can give no impression of the prodigious amount of bad poetry he wrote. The main source of both his poetic disasters and poetic successes was his curious language (which gives the impression of having been specially made rather than received) embodying his original and out-of-the-way experiences. When all the elements are mustered and under taut control the poetry can be

Robert Browning

marvellous, but too often the effect is of confusion and dissipation. B.'s friend Landor wrote, apropos of *Sordello*: 'I only wish he would atticize a little. Few of the Athenians had such a quarry on their property, but they constructed better roads for the conveyance of the material.' The Victorian age was the great age of parody, and B. received his fair share of merciless parodies. In his own life time the critics of his work were often insensitive and extreme. This meant that he did not enjoy an easy commerce with an audience such as has been the lot of more fortunate poets. At the height of his career he wrote revealingly to W. G. Kinglands: 'I can have but little doubt but that my writing has been, in the main, too hard for the many I should have been pleased to communicate with; but I never designedly tried to puzzle people, as some of my critics have supposed. On the other hand, I never pretended to offer such literature as should be a substitute for a cigar, or a game of dominoes, to an idle man. So perhaps, on the whole, I get my deserts and something over – not a crowd, but a few I value more.' (27 Nov. 1868).

Criticism The best survey of Browning studies is by P. Honan, in F. E. Faverty 82–120. The best biographies are by Maisie Ward (1967–9) and W. Irvine and P. Honan (1975). In addition to the critical works in the list of abbreviations, the following are useful: H. H. Hatcher *The Versification of R. B.* (1928); W. O. Raymond *The Infinite Moment* (1950), W. D. Shaw *The Dialectical Temper: the Rhetorical Art of R. B.* (1968) and R. E. Gridley *Browning* (1972). There are collections of essays in *The B. Critics* (1965), ed. B. Litzinger and K. L. Knickerbocker, *R. B.: A Collection of Critical Essays* (1966), ed. P. Drew, and *B.'s Mind and Art* (1968), ed. C. Tracy. Modern studies tend to concentrate on themes and techniques, but the Victorian approach – of trying to place B.'s philosophy and religion – continues in works such as Hillis Miller *The Disappearance of God* (1963), N. B. Crowell *The Triple Soul: B.'s Theory of Knowledge* (Albuquerque 1963) and H. Martin *The Faith of R. B.* (1963).

The standard edition is *Poetical Works* (1888–94).

Abbreviations

Poetical Works

1842	*Dramatic Lyrics*
1845	*Dramatic Romances and Lyrics*
1849	*Poems* (2 vols.)
1855	*Men and Women* (2 vols.).
1863	*Poetical Works* (3 vols.)
1889	*Asolando: Fancies and Facts*
1970	*Browning: Poetical Works 1835–1864* ed. I. R. J. Jack
Critical Heritage	*The Critical Heritage* (1970). B. Litzinger and D. Smalley, eds.
Crowell	N. B. Crowell, *A Reader's Guide to Robert Browning* (Albuquerque: New Mexico, 1972).
De Vane	W. C. De Vane, *A Browning Handbook* (2nd edn, New York, 1955).
De Vane and Knickerbocker *Letters*	W. C. De Vane and K. L. Knickerbocker, *New Letters of Robert Browning* (1951).

Griffin and Minchin	W. H. Griffin and H. C. Minchin, *The Life of Robert Browning*. (1910).
Honan	Park Honan, *Browning's Characters* (1962).
Hood *Letters*	T. L. Hood, *Letters of Robert Browning* collected by T. J. Wise (1933).
Irvine and Honan	W. Irvine and P. Honan, *The Book, the Ring and the Poet: a Biography of Robert Browning* (1975).
King	Roma King, *The Bow and the Lyre* (1957).
Kintner *Letters*	E. Kintner, *The Letters of Robert Browning and Elizabeth Barrett Browning 1845–1846* (Cambridge: Mass., 1969).
Miller	Betty Miller, *Robert Browning: A Portrait* (1952).
Orr	Mrs S. Orr, *A Handbook to the Works of Robert Browning* (1885).

60 Porphyria's Lover

Date Griffin and Minchin 73 suggest Apr. or May 1834, when B. was in St Petersburg. This is at once one of B.'s earliest studies of mental aberration and one of his earliest dramatic monologues.

Publication *Monthly Repository* (Jan. 1836) signed 'Z'; *1842* (as No. 2 of *Madhouse Cells*); *1863* (as an independent poem in *Dramatic Romances*).

    The rain set early in to-night,
      The sullen wind was soon awake,
    It tore the elm-tops down for spite,
      And did its worst to vex the lake:
5   I listened with heart fit to break.
    When glided in Porphyria; straight
      She shut the cold out and the storm,
    And kneeled and made the cheerless grate
      Blaze up, and all the cottage warm;
10   Which done, she rose, and from her form
    Withdrew the dripping cloak and shawl,
      And laid her soiled gloves by, untied
    Her hat and let the damp hair fall,
      And, last, she sat down by my side
15   And called me. When no voice replied,
      She put my arm about her waist,
    And made her smooth white shoulder bare,
      And all her yellow hair displaced,
      And, stooping, made my cheek lie there,
20   And spread, o'er all, her yellow hair,
    Murmuring how she loved me – she
      Too weak, for all her heart's endeavour,
    To set its struggling passion free

Title *Porphyria 1836; Porphyria's Lover 1842.*

From pride, and vainer ties dissever,
25   And give herself for me for ever.
But passion sometimes would prevail,
    Nor could to-night's gay feast restrain
A sudden thought of one so pale
    For love of her, and all in vain:
30   So, she was come through wind and rain.
Be sure I looked up at her eyes
    Happy and proud; at last I knew
Porphyria worshipped me; surprise
    Made my heart swell, and still it grew
35   While I debated what to do.
That moment she was mine, mine, fair,
    Perfectly pure and good: I found
A thing to do, and all her hair
    In one long yellow string I wound
40   Three times her little throat around,
And strangled her. No pain felt she;
    I am quite sure she felt no pain.
As a shut bud that holds a bee,
    I warily oped her lids: again
45   Laughed the blue eyes without a stain.
And I untightened next the tress
    About her neck; her cheek once more
Blushed bright beneath my burning kiss:
    I propped her head up as before
50   Only, this time my shoulder bore
Her head, which droops upon it still:
    The smiling rosy little head,
So glad it has its utmost will
    That all it scorned at once is fled,
55   And I, its love, am gained instead!
Porphyria's love: she guessed not how
    Her darling one wish would be heard.
And thus we sit together now,
    And all night long we have not stirred,
60   And yet God has not said a word!

61 My Last Duchess: Ferrara

Date De Vane 107 suggests Summer 1842. B. read about Ferrara, when preparing to write *Sordello* (1840), in Muratori's *Rerum Italicarum Scriptores* (1723–51), but a more immediate impetus came when he reviewed R. H. Wilde's *Conjectures and Researches concerning the Love Madness and Imprisonment in Torquato Tasso* for the *Foreign Quarterly Review* 29 (1842). (See D. Smalley's edn of the essay, Cambridge, Mass. 1948.)

Sources In these works, and the *Biographie universelle* (1822). B. would have encountered Alfonso II, fifth Duke of Ferrara, whom L. S. Friedland was the first to identify as the most plausible original for B.'s Duke, *SP* 33 (1936) 656–84. The weak and unsubstantiated suggestion by J. D. Rea in *SP* 29 (1932) 120–2 that B. had in mind Vespasiano Gonzago, Duke of Sabbioneta (1531–91) was accepted in the 1935 edn. of De Vane's handbook, but rejected by 1955. The original for the Duchess was probably Alfonso's first wife, Lucrezia, daughter of Cosimo I de Medici (Fra Lippo Lippi's patron), whom he married in 1558. When she died in 1561 there was a suspicion that she had been poisoned. No portrait of the Duchess exists in Ferrara. After Lucrezia's death he began negotiations to marry Barbara, daughter of Ferdinand I, and ward of her uncle, the Count of Tyrol, after her father died. The negotiator was Nikolaus Madruz of Innsbruck. For a vivid picture of the ruthlessness and connoisseurship of the Este family of Ferrara, and other Renaissance dukes of that ilk, see J. A. Symonds *Renaissance in Italy* (1913) 1. 77–150.
Criticism Interpretations of the Duke's behaviour vary; on the one hand there is B. R. Jerman (see *PMLA* 72 (1957) 488–93), who thinks him 'witless', and on the other hand L. Perrine (*PMLA* 74 (1959) 157–9 and G. Monteiro (*VP* I (1963) 234–7), who think him shrewd. The most comprehensive study is R. J. Berman *Browning's Duke* (N.Y. 1972).
Publication *1842* (as I. *Italy* of *Italy and France*); *1849* (with present title); *1863* (in *Dramatic Romances*).

That's my last Duchess painted on the wall,
Looking as if she were alive. I call
That piece a wonder, now: Frà Pandolf's hands
Worked busily a day, and there she stands.
5   Will't please you sit and look at her? I said
'Frà Pandolf' by design, for never read
Strangers like you that pictured countenance,
The depth and passion of its earnest glance,
But to myself they turned (since none puts by
10   The curtain I have drawn for you, but I)
And seemed as they would ask me, if they durst,
How such a glance came there; so, not the first
Are you to turn and ask thus. Sir, 't was not
Her husband's presence only, called that spot
15   Of joy into the Duchess' cheek: perhaps
Frà Pandolf chanced to say 'Her mantle laps
Over my lady's wrist too much,' or 'Paint
Must never hope to reproduce the faint
Half-flush that dies along her throat:' such stuff

1 **painted on the wall** seems to suggest a fresco, but B. almost certainly had an easel painting in mind.
3 **Frà Pandolf** an imaginary artist.

20   Was courtesy, she thought, and cause enough
      For calling up that spot of joy. She had
      A heart – how shall I say? – too soon made glad,
      Too easily impressed; she liked whate'er
      She looked on, and her looks went everywhere.
25   Sir, 't was all one! My favour at her breast,
      The dropping of the daylight in the West,
      The bough of cherries some officious fool
      Broke in the orchard for her, the white mule
      She rode with round the terrace – all and each
30   Would draw from her alike the approving speech,
      Or blush, at least. She thanked men, – good! but thanked
      Somehow – I know not how – as if she ranked
      My gift of a nine-hundred-years-old name
      With anybody's gift. Who'd stoop to blame
35   This sort of trifling? Even had you skill
      In speech – (which I have not) – to make your will
      Quite clear to such an one, and say, 'Just this
      Or that in you disgusts me; here you miss,
      Or there exceed the mark' – and if she let
40   Herself be lessoned so, nor plainly set
      Her wits to yours, forsooth, and made excuse,
      – E'en then would be some stooping; and I choose
      Never to stoop. Oh sir, she smiled, no doubt,
      Whene'er I passed her; but who passed without
45   Much the same smile? This grew; I gave commands;
      Then all smiles stopped together. There she stands
      As if alive. Will 't please you rise? We'll meet
      The company below, then. I repeat,
      The Count your master's known munificence
50   Is ample warrant that no just pretence
      Of mine for dowry will be disallowed;
      Though his fair daughter's self, as I avowed

20 courtesy perhaps nearer the *curteisie* of Chaucer, including the graceful arts of courtly compliment, than the modern sense of polite and deferential bearing.

32–4 The old aristocrat rankling at marriage with an upstart is also the situation of *The Ring and the Book*. From the perspective of the Estes, the Medici were wealthy *nouveaux*.

45–6 H. Corson questioned B. on these lines, and he replied, 'the commands were that she should be put to death...or he might have had her shut up in a convent' (*An Introduction to the Study of Robert Browning's Poetry* (Boston, 1886) pp. vii–viii).

52 In the source the wife-to-be is the niece of the Count.

At starting, is my object. Nay, we'll go
Together down, sir. Notice Neptune, though,
55   Taming a sea-horse, thought a rarity,
Which Claus of Innsbruck cast in bronze for me!

54–5 A symbolic comment on the Duke's relationship to his wives, who are brought under control by an imperious master.
56 **Claus of Innsbruck** an imaginary artist.

62 The Laboratory
Ancien Régime

Date Unknown.
Source B. modelled his portrait on Marie Madeleine Marguerite D'Aubray Brinvillers (*c.* 1630–76), who poisoned her father and her two brothers, and was planning to poison her husband. Her motive was not sexual jealousy. B.'s source was either the *Biographie Universelle* or Dumas's *Crimes Célèbres* (Paris 1841), which he knew either at first hand or in a review in *FQR* 30 (1842) 36–60 (anonymous: too clearly written to be B.). B. was familiar with *FQR* (see headnote to no. 61). The poem is an interesting contribution to B.'s cult of ugliness (see Irvine and Honan 195); E.B. did not like it (Kintner *Letters* 131). Rossetti did a spirited drawing based on the incident in 1849 (reproduced Surtees pl. 25).
Publication *Hood's Magazine* 1 (June 1844) 513–14; *1845* (coupled with *The Confessional* as *France and Spain*). Separately in *1849*; *1863* (in *Dramatic Lyrics*).

1
Now that I, tying thy glass mask tightly,
May gaze through these faint smokes curling whitely,
As thou pliest thy trade in this devil's-smithy –
Which is the poison to poison her, prithee?

2
5   He is with her, and they know that I know
Where they are, what they do: they believe my tears flow
While they laugh, laugh at me, at me fled to the drear
Empty church, to pray God in, for them! – I am here.

1 Now I have tied thy glass mask on tightly, *1844*; B. changed this line, and others that were rhythmically awkward, for *1845*, in deference to E. Barrett: 'I object a little to your tendency...which is almost a habit...and is very observable in this poem I think...of making lines difficult for the reader to read...see the opening lines of this poem. Not that...music is required everywhere, not in *them* certainly, but that the uncertainty of rhythm throws the reader's mind off the *rail*...' (Kintner *Letters* 131; 21 July 1845). Other lines altered are 13, 15–26 (for *1849*), 34, 37. B. could have learnt of the masks used in the manufacture of poison either in the *Biographie Universelle* or *FQR* 30 (1842) 51.

3

Grind away, moisten and mash up thy paste,
10   Pound at thy powder, – I am not in haste!
Better sit thus, and observe thy strange things,
Than go where men wait me and dance at the King's.

4

That in the mortar – you call it a gum?
Ah, the brave tree whence such gold oozings come!
15   And yonder soft phial, the exquisite blue,
Sure to taste sweetly, – is that poison too?

5

Had I but all of them, thee and thy treasures,
What a wild crowd of invisible pleasures!
To carry pure death in an earring, a casket,
20   A signet, a fan-mount, a filigree basket!

6

Soon, at the King's, a mere lozenge to give,
And Pauline should have just thirty minutes to live!
But to light a pastile, and Elise, with her head
And her breast and her arms and her hands, should drop
    dead!

7

25   Quick – is it finished? The colour's too grim!
Why not soft like the phial's, enticing and dim?
Let it brighten her drink, let her turn it and stir,
And try it and taste, ere she fix and prefer!

8

What a drop! She's not little, no minion like me!
30   That's why she ensnared him: this never will free
The soul from those masculine eyes, – say, 'no!'
To that pulse's magnificent come-and-go.

9

For only last night, as they whispered, I brought
My own eyes to bear on her so, that I thought
35   Could I keep them one half minute fixed, she would fall
Shrivelled; she fell not; yet this does it all!

12 the King's at the court of Louis XIV.
13 mortar ... gum?] mortar – call you a gum? *1844*.
15 yonder] yon *1844*.
17–20 Cf. Lodovico in Webster *The White Devil* for a C17 character who also considers murder as one of the fine arts.
26 not ... phial's] not like the phial's *1844, 1845*.
29 *FQR* 52 quotes from Dumas: 'the figure was small, but perfectly formed.'
31 those masculine eyes] those strong great eyes *1844*.

10

Not that I bid you spare her the pain;
Let death be felt and the proof remain:
Brand, burn up, bite into its grace –
40   He is sure to remember her dying face!

11

Is it done? Take my mask off! Nay,
    be not morose;
It kills her, and this prevents seeing it close:
The delicate droplet, my whole fortune's fee!
If it hurts her, beside, can it ever hurt me?

12

45   Now, take all my jewels, gorge gold to your fill,
You may kiss me, old man, on my mouth if you will!
But brush this dust off, lest horror it brings
Ere I know it – next moment I dance at the King's!

37 her the pain] her pain *1844.*

63 The Bishop Orders his Tomb at Saint Praxed's Church, Rome, 15 –

Date Composed Oct. 1844–Feb. 1845.
Associations B. visited the church of Santa Prassede in Rome. Ironically the saint used her wealth to assist poor Christians. B. Melchiori asserts *REL* 5 (1964) 7–26 that the church has no dome and there is no tomb corresponding to the Bishop's (he is an imaginary character), though there are worldly Renaissance tombs – including Bernini's early tomb of Bishop Santori (*c.* 1615) – reproduced in Howard Hibbard *Bernini* (1965) 31. J. D. Rea *SP* 29 (1932) 120–2 suggested Ireneo Affo's *Vita de Vespasio Gonzaga* (1780) 111–28 as a source, but this was challenged by L. S. Friedland, *SP* 53 (1936), 656–84. L. Stevenson, *UTQ* 21 (1952) 240–1, argues, more plausibly, that B.'s source was Cardinal Ippolito d'Este. Melchiori traces the influence of Gerard de Lairesse's *Art of Painting* (1778 edn.) on the details of the art work.
    Surprisingly, the poem has a contemporary relevance; B. wrote to F. O. Ward (sub-editor of *Hood's Magazine*) (18 Feb. 1845) 'I pick it out as being a pet of mine, and just the thing for the time – what with the Oxford business…' (De Vane and Knickerbocker *New Letters* 35–6).
Discussion For a full explication of the background see R. A. Greenberg *PMLA* 84 (1969) 1588–94. The 1830s and 40s saw an attack on the neo-Paganism of the Renaissance, especially in Pugin's *Contrasts* (1836). Although medieval piety was being revived a reaction was visible: on 13 Feb. 1845 W. G. Ward (see Clough introduction below p. 288) was deprived of his Oxford degrees, and Newman's Tract 90 was a live issue. B. may not have been inviting his readers to take sides, but to reflect on the persistence of religious controversy concerning opulence and restraint in ecclesiastical

decoration. The highest praise for B.'s evocation of the decadent spirit of the High Renaissance church is in Ruskin's *Modern Painters* 4 (1856): 'I know of no other piece of modern English, prose or poetry, in which there is so much told... of the Renaissance spirit, – its worldliness, inconsistency, pride, hypocrisy, ignorance of itself, love of art, of luxury, and of good Latin' (*Works* 6.449).

See also, R. King 52–75, G. Monteiro *VP* 8 (1970) 209–18; C. T. Phipps *ibid.* 199–208; De Vane 166–8.

Publication *Hood's Magazine* (March 1845); 1845, 1849 (in *Dramatic Romances and Lyrics*); 1863 (in *Men and Women*).

> Vanity, saith the preacher, vanity!
> Draw round my bed: is Anselm keeping back?
> Nephews – sons mine... ah, God, I know not! Well –
> She, men would have to be your mother once,
> 5 Old Gandolf envied me, so fair she was!
> What's done is done, and she is dead beside,
> Dead long ago, and I am Bishop since,
> And as she died so must we die ourselves,
> And thence ye may perceive the world's a dream.
> 10 Life, how and what is it? As here I lie
> In this state-chamber, dying by degrees,
> Hours and long hours in the dead night, I ask
> 'Do I live, am I dead?' Peace, peace seems all.
> Saint Praxed's ever was the church for peace;
> 15 And so, about this tomb of mine. I fought
> With tooth and nail to save my niche, ye know:
> – Old Gandolf cozened me, despite my care;
> Shrewd was that snatch from out the corner South
> He graced his carrion with, God curse the same!
> 20 Yet still my niche is not so cramped but thence
> One sees the pulpit o' the epistle-side,
> And somewhat of the choir, those silent seats,
> And up into the aery dome where live
> The angels, and a sunbeam's sure to lurk:
> 25 And I shall fill my slab of basalt there,
> And 'neath my tabernacle take my rest,

Title *The Tomb at St. Praxed's Hood's; 1845.*
1 Cf. *Eccles.* 1.2: the Bishop relishes the words, but pays insufficient regard to their tenor.
3 Nephews euphemism for illegitimate sons.
5 Gandolf an imaginary character.
17 Old Gandolf came me in, despite my care *Hood's*.
18 South the most coveted place.
21 the epistle-side the south side.
23 Santa Prassede's church has no dome.
26 tabernacle canopy.

With those nine columns round me, two and two,
The odd one at my feet where Anselm stands:
Peach-blossom marble all, the rare, the ripe
30   As fresh-poured red wine of a mighty pulse.
– Old Gandolf with his paltry onion-stone,
Put me where I may look at him! True peach,
Rosy and flawless: how I earned the prize!
Draw close: that conflagration of my church
35   – What then? So much was saved if aught were missed!
My sons, ye would not be my death? Go dig
The white-grape vineyard where the oil-press stood,
Drop water gently till the surface sink.
And if ye find...Ah God, I know not, I!...
40   Bedded in store of rotten fig-leaves soft,
And corded up in a tight olive-frail,
Some lump, ah God, of *lapis lazuli*,
Big as a Jew's head cut off at the nape,
Blue as a vein o'er the Madonna's breast...
45   Sons, all have I bequeathed you, villas, all,
That brave Frascati villa with its bath,
So, let the blue lump poise between my knees,
Like God the Father's globe on both his hands
Ye worship in the Jesu Church so gay,
50   For Gandolf shall not choose but see and burst!
Swift as a weaver's shuttle fleet our years:
Man goeth to the grave, and where is he?
Did I say basalt for my slab, sons? Black –
'T was ever antique-black I meant! How else
55   Shall ye contrast my frieze to come beneath?

30 pulse fig. power, vitality.
31 onion-stone a poor stone that peels away in layers. See Ruskin – Browning correspondence, ed. D. DeLaura *BJRL* 54 (1972) 329: asked by R. for meaning B. replied: 'onion-stone is the grey *cipollino* – good for pillars and the like, bad for finer work, through its being laid coat upon coat, onion-wise...' (1 Feb. 1856).
41 olive-frail rush basket for holding olives.
42 lapis lazuli Melchiori 255 quotes Lairesse: 'It was an ancient tomb or sepulchre of light red marble, intermixed with dark grey, and white eyes and veins, with a lid a cover of lapis lazuli.'
46 Frascati a resort ten miles S.E. of Rome.
49 Jesu Church Il Gesù in Rome. Designed by Barozzi da Vignola for the Jesuits, begun 1568. One of the most influential buildings in the development of the Baroque. See Nikolaus Pevsner 'The Architecture of Mannerism' *The Mint* (1946) 131–2.
51 Cf. *Job* 7.6 'My days are swifter than a weaver's shuttle, and are spent without hope.'
54 antique-black black marble.

[63] Robert Browning

The bas-relief in bronze ye promised me,

Those Pans and Nymphs ye wot of, and perchance

Some tripod, thyrsus, with a vase or so,

The Saviour at his sermon on the mount,
60   Saint Praxed in a glory, and one Pan

Ready to twitch the Nymph's last garment off,

And Moses with the tables... but I know

Ye mark me not! What do they whisper thee,

Child of my bowels, Anselm? Ah, ye hope
65   To revel down my villas while I gasp

Bricked o'er with beggar's mouldy travertine

Which Gandolf from his tomb-top chuckles at!

Nay, boys, ye love me – all of jasper, then!

'T is jasper ye stand pledged to, lest I grieve
70   My bath must needs be left behind, alas!

One block, pure green as a pistachio-nut,

There's plenty jasper somewhere in the world –

And have I not Saint Praxed's ear to pray

Horses for ye, and brown Greek manuscripts,
75   And mistresses with great smooth marbly limbs?

– That's if ye carve my epitaph aright,

Choice Latin, picked phrase, Tully's every word,

No gaudy ware like Gandolf's second line –

Tully, my masters? Ulpian serves his need!
80   And then how I shall lie through centuries,

And hear the blessed mutter of the mass,

And see God made and eaten all day long,

And feel the steady candle-flame, and taste

Good strong thick stupefying incense-smoke!
85   For as I lie here, hours of the dead night,

Dying in state and by such slow degrees,

I fold my arms as if they clasped a crook

And stretch my feet forth straight as stone can point,

And let the bedclothes, for a mortcloth, drop

---

58 tripod three-legged stool on which the Delphic oracles sat. In the Renaissance pagan mythology was used as a form of auxiliary typology for Christianity.   **thyrsus** staff carried in Dionysian ceremonies.
60 in a glory in a halo.
62 the tables the tablets with the Ten Commandments.
64 Child of my bowels biblical, e.g. *Sam.* 10.11: 'my son which came out of my bowels.'
66 travertine limestone.
77 Tully Cicero: a writer of a Latin the Bishop hopes will survive as long as the most durable stone monument. Some ecclesiastics in the Renaissance were reluctant to say mass for fear of spoiling their Ciceronian Latin.
79 Ulpian Domitius Ulpianus, a Latin jurist of the C3 A.D.
89 mortcloth funeral pall.

90 Into great laps and folds of sculptor's-work:
And as yon tapers dwindle, and strange thoughts
Grow, with a certain humming in my ears,
About the life before I lived this life,
And this life too, popes, cardinals and priests,
95 Saint Praxed at his sermon on the mount,
Your tall pale mother with her talking eyes,
And new-found agate urns as fresh as day,
And marble's language, Latin pure, discreet,
– Aha, ELUSCESCEBAT quoth our friend?
100 No Tully, said I, Ulpian at the best!
Evil and brief hath been my pilgrimage.
All *lapis*, all, sons! Else I give the Pope
My villas! Will ye ever eat my heart?
Ever your eyes were as a lizard's quick,
105 They glitter like your mother's for my soul,
Or ye would heighten my impoverished frieze,
Piece out its starved design, and fill my vase
With grapes, and add a vizor and a Term,
And to the tripod ye would tie a lynx
110 That in his struggle throws the thyrsus down,
To comfort me on my entablature
Whereon I am to lie till I must ask
'Do I live, am I dead?' There, leave me, there!
For ye have stabbed me with ingratitude
115 To death – ye wish it – God, ye wish it! Stone –
Gritstone, a-crumble! Clammy squares which sweat
As if the corpse they keep were oozing through –
And no more *lapis* to delight the world!
Well go! I bless ye. Fewer tapers there,
120 But in a row: and, going, turn your backs
– Ay, like departing altar-ministrants,

95 Saints were allowed to appear, anachronistically, at Christ's sermon on the mount in religious paintings.
99 ELUCESCEBAT 'He was illustrious': the second-rate Latin on Gandolf's tomb. The Ciceronian form would have been ELUCEBAT.
106–8 Not in *Hood's*.
108 vizor front piece of a helmet.   **Term** statue growing out of a pillar or pedestal.
111 entablature the platform supported by columns on which his effigy will lie.
116 Gritstone coarse sandstone, usually used for making grindstones and mill-stones.
121 altar-ministrants the phrase completing the pervasive impression that the Bishop has made his body, rather than Christ's, into the dominant object of worship in the church.

And leave me in my church, the church for peace,
That I may watch at leisure if he leers –
Old Gandolf, at me, from his onion-stone,
125 As still he envied me, so fair she was!

64 The Lost Leader

Date Between Apr. 1843 and Nov. 1845.
Subject Wordsworth was probably in B.'s mind. W. Thornbury recorded in 1874 that 'two years ago *Mr Browning himself*, in reply to a correct guess of mine, told me that Wordsworth was the "Lost Leader"' (*N & Q* 5th ser. 1 (1874) 213). Orr's *Life* (1908) 123 quotes a letter to Miss Lee of 7 Sept. 1875: 'I have been asked the question you put to me...I suppose a score of times: and I can only answer, with something of shame and contrition, that I undoubtedly had Wordsworth in my mind – but simply as "a model"..., I thought of the great Poet's abandonment of liberalism, at an unlucky juncture, and no repaying consequence that I could ever see. But – once call my fancy-portrait *Wordsworth* – and how much more ought one to say, – how much more would not I have attempted to say!' See also B. to A. B. Grosart 24 Feb. 1875 (Wise *Letters* 1.28). B. regrets Wordsworth's gradual abandonment of radical, even moderate, political views, but the immediate occasion was Wordsworth's acceptance in Apr. 1843 of the Poet Laureateship on the death of Southey (see Mary Moorman *William Wordsworth: The Later Years* (1965) 558–60). B. shared Haydon's 'righteous indignation at the "great fact" and gross impropriety of any man who has "thoughts too deep for tears" agreeing to wear a "bagwig"' (Kintner *Letters* 82), and wrote to E. Barrett that Wordsworth at court 'fell down upon both knees in the superfluity of etiquette, and had to be picked up by two lords in waiting' (*ibid.* 84). On 22 Aug. 1846 he wrote: 'I am sure...that I could not get up enthusiasm enough to cross the room if at the other end of it all Wordsworth, Coleridge and Southey were condensed into the little china bottle yonder, after the Rosicrucian fashion...they seem to "have their reward" and want nobody's love or faith' (*ibid.* 986).
Discussion See A. V. Dicey *Statesmanship of Wordsworth* (1917) 105–15; H. C. Minchin 'Browning and Wordsworth' *FR* 97 (1912) 813–24; De Vane 159–62.
Publication *1845*.

1
Just for a handful of silver he left us,
    Just for a riband to stick in his coat –
Found the one gift of which fortune bereft us,
    Lost all the others she lets us devote;
5   They, with the gold to give, doled him out silver,

1–5 In addition to the metals of payment, there may be a suggestion of artistic alchemy: a letter to E.B. of 22 Aug. 1846 discusses Wordsworth in such terms (Kintner *Letters* 986).
2 riband possibly of the Laureateship.

So much was theirs who so little allowed:
How all our copper had gone for his service!
Rags – were they purple, his heart had been proud!
We that loved him so, followed him, honoured him,
10   Lived in his mild and magnificent eye,
Learned his great language, caught his clear accents,
Made him our pattern to live and to die!
Shakespeare was of us, Milton was for us,
    Burns, Shelley, were with us – they watch from their graves!
15 He alone breaks from the van and the freemen,
    – He alone sinks to the rear and the slaves!

2

We shall march prospering, – not through his presence;
Songs may inspirit us, – not from his lyre;
Deeds will be done, – while he boasts his quiescence,
20   Still bidding crouch whom the rest bade aspire:
Blot out his name, then, record one lost soul more,
    One task more declined, one more footpath untrod,
One more devils'-triumph and sorrow for angels,
    One wrong more to man, one more insult to God!
25 Life's night begins: let him never come back to us!
    There would be doubt, hesitation and pain,
Forced praise on our part – the glimmer of twilight,
    Never glad confident morning again!
Best fight on well, for we taught him – strike gallantly,
30   Menace our heart ere we master his own;
Then let him receive the new knowledge and wait us,
    Pardoned in heaven, the first by the throne!

14 Shelley a significant name in the catalogue. He detected Wordsworth's betrayal as early as 1816 in *To Wordsworth*, noting the riches-poverty contrast: 'In honoured poverty thy voice did weave | Songs consecrate to truth and liberty.' His most sustained onslaught was *Peter Bell the Third* (1819), of which lines 298–9 are incorrectly quoted by B. in a letter to E. B.: 'He had no more *imagination* than a pint pot' (Kintner *Letters* 986).
15 van vanguard: foremost division of an army.
29 for we taught him obscure: B. seems to be saying that the radical poets taught Wordsworth enlightened principles.
30 Menace our heart elliptical: he would endanger us if we were not careful; or let him menace our heart (rather than attempt a false reconciliation).
31–2 There will be an opportunity for Wordsworth purged of his mistakes to be God's poet laureate. De Vane 161 suggests an echo of *Stafford* 5.2.268–303, in which Pym pardons the visionary Stafford, 'purged from error, gloriously renewed'. The names Wentworth and Wordsworth are not dissimilar.

65 Meeting at Night

Date Unknown. This poem and the following constitute a linked pair.
Publication *1845*.

1

The grey sea and the long black land;
And the yellow half-moon large and low;
And the startled little waves that leap
In fiery ringlets from their sleep,
5   As I gain the cove with pushing prow,
And quench its speed i' the slushy sand.

2

Then a mile of warm sea-scented beach;
Three fields to cross till a farm appears;
A tap at the pane, the quick sharp scratch
10   And the blue spurt of a lighted match,
And a voice less loud, through its joys and fears,
Than the two hearts beating each to each!

Title *I.– Night* (in *Night and Morning*) *1845*.
10 lighted match matches were first in common use in the 1830s; this is
OED's only poetic example of the word in this sense.

66 Parting at Morning

See headnote to *Meeting at Night*.
Publication *1845*.

Round the cape of a sudden came the sea,
And the sun looked over the mountain's rim:
And straight was a path of gold for him,
And the need of a world of men for me.

Title *II.– Morning* (in *Night and Morning*) *1845*.
3 him the sun.
4 In answer to a query about the poem, B. wrote (22 Feb. 1889): 'it is *his*
confession of how fleeting is the belief (implied in the first part) that such
raptures are self-sufficient and enduring – as for the time they appear' (*1914*
1350–1).

67 Love Among the Ruins

Date Griffin and Minchin 189 say 1 Jan, 1852; De Vane 212 prefers 3 Jan. 1852. B. resolved to write a poem a day, and composed this one, *Childe Roland* (see headnote) and *Women and Roses* in the first three days of the New Year. However, J. Parr, *PQ* 32 (1953) 443–6, working on B.'s letter to Forster of 5 June 1854 (De Vane and K. *New Letters* 77) argues for 1853. See J. Huebenthal *VP* 4 (1966) 51–4.

Location B. seems to have had an Italian location in mind: he was able to draw on Roman experiences of 1844, reinforced by writings about ancient cities in the 1840s. J. Parr, *PMLA* 68 (1953) 128–37, describes the vogue for excavations and the impact made by Layard's *Nineveh and its Remains* (1849). C. R. Tracy *PMLA* 61 (1946) 600–1 compares Goldsmith's *Citizen of the World* (1760–1) Letter 117, in which a future London as a desert is imagined.

Style The form was invented by B.: couplets of six-stress lines alternating with two-stress lines. The stanzas break in the middle to move from present to past. In *1855* the stanzas were 6 lines.

Publication *1855*; *1863* (*Dramatic Lyrics*).

1

> Where the quiet-coloured end of evening smiles,
>   Miles and miles
> On the solitary pastures where our sheep
>   Half-asleep
> Tinkle homeward through the twilight, stray or stop
>   As they crop –
> Was the site once of a city great and gay,
>   (So they say)
> Of our country's very capital, its prince
>   Ages since
> Held his court in, gathered councils, wielding far
>   Peace or war.

2

> Now, – the country does not even boast a tree,
>   As you see,
> To distinguish slopes of verdure, certain rills
>   From the hills
> Intersect and give a name to, (else they run
>   Into one)
> Where the domed and daring palace shot its spires
>   Up like fires

Line numbers: 5, 10, 15, 20

Title *Sicilian Pastoral* in MS. draft (Lowell Collec., Harvard). B. never visited Sicily.

[67] Robert Browning

O'er the hundred-gated circuit of a wall
   Bounding all,
Made of marble, men might march on nor be pressed,
   Twelve abreast.

3

25   And such plenty and perfection, see, of grass
      Never was!
Such a carpet as, this summer time, o'erspreads
   And embeds
Every vestige of the city, guessed alone,
30   Stock or stone –
Where a multitude of men breathed joy and woe
   Long ago;
Lust of glory pricked their hearts up, dread of shame
   Struck them tame;
35   And that glory and that shame alike, the gold
     Bought and sold.

4

Now, – the single little turret that remains
   On the plains,
By the caper overrooted, by the gourd
40   Overscored,
While the patching houseleek's head of blossom winks
   Through the chinks –
Marks the basement whence a tower in ancient time
   Sprang sublime,
45   And a burning ring, all round, the chariots traced
     As they raced,
And the monarch and his minions and his dames
   Viewed the games.

5

And I know, while thus the quiet-coloured eve
50   Smiles to leave
To their folding, all our many-tinkling fleece
   In such peace,
And the slopes and rills in undistinguished grey
   Melt away –
55   That a girl with eager eyes and yellow hair
     Waits me there

33 pricked urged arch. *OED* II.10 (as in Chaucer *Prol.* line 11: 'priketh hem nature in hir corages').
39 overrooted covered with roots; only ex. in *OED*.

In the turret whence the charioteers caught soul
　For the goal,
When the king looked, where she looks now, breathless, dumb
60　　Till I come.

6

But he looked upon the city, every side,
　Far and wide,
All the mountains topped with temples, all the glades'
　Colonnades,
65　All the causeys, bridges, aqueducts, – and then,
　All the men!
When I do come, she will speak not, she will stand,
　Either hand
On my shoulder, give her eyes the first embrace
70　　Of my face,
Ere we rush, ere we extinguish sight and speech
　Each on each.

7

In one year they sent a million fighters forth
　South and North,
75　And they built their gods a brazen pillar high
　As the sky,
Yet reserved a thousand chariots in full force –
　Gold, of course.
Oh heart! oh blood that freezes, blood that burns!
80　　Earth's returns
For whole centuries of folly, noise and sin!
　Shut them in,
With their triumphs and their glories and the rest!
　Love is best!

68 'Childe Roland to the Dark Tower Came'
(see Edgar's Song in *Lear*)

Date and Theme Griffin and Minchin 189 report that it was composed on 3 Jan. 1852. Date discussed by J. Huebenthal, *VP* 4 (1966) 51–4. B. seems to have made a New Year Resolution to write a poem a day (see headnote to no. 67): ''Twas like this: one year in Florence, I had been very lazy; I resolved that I would write something every day. Well, the first day I wrote about some roses, suggested by a magnificent basket that some one had sent my wife (*Women and Roses*). The next day *Childe Roland* came upon me as a kind of dream. I had to write it, then and there, and I finished it the same day, I believe' (Lilian Whiting *The Brownings* (Boston 1917) 261).
　The Brownings were in Paris at the time, and had recently witnessed the

triumphal entry of Louis Napoleon into the city. B. and his wife were at serious political loggerheads (Miller 176–7; Irvine and Honan 287–91). Since B. had just finished an essay on Shelley, the archetypal advocator of freedom, the sense of betrayal was probably in the forefront of his mind.
Sources The immediate source is the snatch of song uttered by Edgar in *Lear* 3.4.186–8. It is a line quoting from a lost ballad, 'His word was still: *Fie, foh, and fum*, I smell the blood of a British man' (the Giant's speech from *Jack the Giant-Killer*). In a letter to A. W. Hunt (who painted a watercolour of the tower, based on Dolbadarn Castle in N. Wales) B. wrote: 'My own "marsh" was only made out of my head, – with some recollection of a strange solitary little tower I have come upon more than once in Massa-Carrara, in the midst of low hills...' (De Vane and K. *Letters* 172–3; 29 Apr. 1866). Orr 266 thought 'the figure of a horse in the tapestry in his own drawing-room suggested elements in the work' (reproduced *Browning Collections* 158–9). As De Vane shows in *PMLA* 40 (1925) 426–32, the most significant literary source (other than the folk tales discussed by H. Golder in *PMLA* 39 (1924) 963–78) is Gerard de Lairesse's *The Art of Painting in All its Branches* (trans. 1778), which provided much of the grotesque landscape: Bk. 6 Ch. 17 is called 'Of Things Deformed and Broken, Falsely called Painter-like'. B. Melchiori *English Miscellany* 14 (1963) 185–93 traces connections between the horse of lines 76–84 and E. A. Poe's Count Berlifitzing, diabolically reincarnated as a horse.
Interpretations B. was reluctant to invite allegorical readings: L. Whiting asked if he agreed with one, and B. replied: 'Oh no, not at all. Understand, I don't repudiate it, either. I only mean I was conscious of no allegorical intention in writing it... it was simply that I had to do it. I did not know what I meant beyond that, and I'm sure I don't know now.' J. W. Chadwick asked if the poem argued that 'He that endureth to the end shall be saved', to which B. replied, 'Yes, just about that' – probably to get rid of the questioner (*The Christian Register* 19 Jan. 1888). Allegorical and symbolical interpretations continue: D. V. Erdmann, *PQ* 36 (1957) 417–35, sees the work as a protest against the industrial age; V. Hoar, *VN* no. 27 (1965) 26–8, as a version of archetypal myth, and R. E. Hughes, *Literature and Psychology* 9 (1959) 18–19, as an oblique expression of B.'s subconscious. Irvine and Honan 298 hear 'an echo of the obsessions with disharmony and dark frustration'.
Discussion De Vane 228–32.
Publication *1855; 1863* (*Dramatic Romances*).

1

<blockquote>

My first thought was, he lied in every word,
  That hoary cripple, with malicious eye
  Askance to watch the working of his lie
On mine, and mouth scarce able to afford
5   Suppression of the glee, that pursed and scored
  Its edge, at one more victim gained thereby.

</blockquote>

Title Childe a candidate for knighthood.

2

What else should he be set for, with his staff?
What, save to waylay with his lies, ensnare
All travellers who might find him posted there,
10   And ask the road? I guessed what skull-like laugh
Would break, what crutch 'gin write my epitaph
For pastime in the dusty thoroughfare,

3

If at his counsel I should turn aside
Into that ominous tract which, all agree,
15   Hides the Dark Tower. Yet acquiescingly
I did turn as he pointed: neither pride
Nor hope rekindling at the end descried,
So much as gladness that some end might be.

4

For, what with my whole world-wide wandering,
20   What with my search drawn out through years, my hope
Dwindled into a ghost not fit to cope
With that obstreperous joy success would bring, –
I hardly tried now to rebuke the spring
My heart made, finding failure in its scope.

5

25   As when a sick man very near to death
Seems dead indeed, and feels begin and end
The tears and takes the farewell of each friend,
And hears one bid the other go, draw breath
Freelier outside, ('since all is o'er,' he saith,
30   'And the blow fallen no grieving can amend;')

6

While some discuss if near the other graves
Be room enough for this, and when a day
Suits best for carrying the corpse away,
With care about the banners, scarves and staves:
35   And still the man hears all, and only craves
He may not shame such tender love and stay.

7

Thus, I had so long suffered in this quest,
Heard failure prophesied so oft, been writ
So many times among 'The Band' – to wit,

18 might] should *1855*.
25–36 R. L. Lowe *N & Q* 198 (1953) 491, suggests a parallel with Donne's *A Valediction Forbidding Mourning*.

40 The knights who to the Dark Tower's search addressed
Their steps – that just to fail as they, seemed best,
And all the doubt was now – should I be fit?

8

So, quiet as despair, I turned from him,
That hateful cripple, out of his highway
45 Into the path he pointed. All the day
Had been a dreary one at best, and dim
Was settling to its close, yet shot one grim
Red leer to see the plain catch its estray.

9

For mark! no sooner was I fairly found
50 Pledged to the plain, after a pace or two,
Than, pausing to throw backward a last view
O'er the safe road, 't was gone; grey plain all round:
Nothing but plain to the horizon's bound.
I might go on; nought else remained to do.

10

55 So, on I went. I think I never saw
Such starved ignoble nature; nothing throve:
For flowers – as well expect a cedar grove!
But cockle, spurge, according to their law
Might propagate their kind, with none to awe,
60 You'd think; a burr had been a treasure-trove.

11

No! penury, inertness and grimace,
In some strange sort, were the land's portion. 'See
Or shut your eyes,' said Nature peevishly,
'It nothing skills: I cannot help my case:
65 'T is the Last Judgment's fire must cure this place,
Calcine its clods and set my prisoners free.'

12

If there pushed any ragged thistle-stalk
Above its mates, the head was chopped; the bents
Were jealous else. What made those holes and rents
70 In the dock's harsh swarth leaves, bruised as to baulk
All hope of greenness? 't is a brute must walk
Pashing their life out, with a brute's intents.

48 estray stray animal.
57 a cedar grove biblically a symbol of nobility and prosperity: *Ps.* 92.12
'The righteous shall grow like a cedar.'
58 cockle wheat gall.   **spurge** shrubby plant, genus *Euphorbia*.
64 It nothing skills it avails nothing.

13

As for the grass, it grew as scant as hair
    In leprosy; thin dry blades pricked the mud
75   Which underneath looked kneaded up with blood.
One stiff blind horse, his every bone a-stare,
Stood stupefied, however he came there:
    Thrust out past service from the devil's stud!

14

Alive? he might be dead for aught I know,
80   With that red gaunt and colloped neck a-strain,
    And shut eyes underneath the rusty mane;
Seldom went such grotesqueness with such woe;
I never saw a brute I hated so;
    He must be wicked to deserve such pain.

15

85   I shut my eyes and turned them on my heart.
    As a man calls for wine before he fights,
    I asked one draught of earlier, happier sights,
Ere fitly I could hope to play my part.
Think first, fight afterwards – the soldier's art:
90   One taste of the old time sets all to rights.

16

Not it! I fancied Cuthbert's reddening face
    Beneath its garniture of curly gold,
    Dear fellow, till I almost felt him fold
An arm in mine to fix me to the place,
95   That way he used. Alas, one night's disgrace!
    Out went my heart's new fire and left it cold.

17

Giles then, the soul of honour – there he stands
    Frank as ten years ago when knighted first.
    What honest men should dare (he said) he durst.
100   Good – but the scene shifts – faugh! what hangman-hands
Pin to his breast a parchment? his own bands
    Read it. Poor traitor, spit upon and curst!

18

Better this present than a past like that;
    Back therefore to my darkening path again!
105   No sound, no sight as far as eye could strain.

76–84 See headnote.
80 colloped 'with thick folds of fat' is the usual sense. B. seems to have in
mind creased scrawny flesh.

Will the night send a howlet or a bat?
I asked: when something on the dismal flat
Came to arrest my thoughts and change their train.

19

A sudden little river crossed my path
110 As unexpected as a serpent comes.
No sluggish tide congenial to the glooms;
This, as it frothed by, might have been a bath
For the fiend's glowing hoof – to see the wrath
Of its black eddy bespate with flakes and spumes.

20

115 So petty yet so spiteful! All along,
Low scrubby alders kneeled down over it;
Drenched willows flung them headlong in a fit
Of mute despair, a suicidal throng:
The river which had done them all the wrong,
120 Whate'er that was, rolled by, deterred no whit.

21

Which, while I forded, – good saints, how I feared
To set my foot upon a dead man's cheek,
Each step, or feel the spear I thrust to seek
For hollows, tangled in his hair or beard!
125 – It may have been a water-rat I speared,
But, ugh! it sounded like a baby's shriek.

22

Glad was I when I reached the other bank.
Now for a better country. Vain presage!
Who were the strugglers, what war did they wage,
130 Whose savage trample thus could pad the dank
Soil to a plash? Toads in a poisoned tank,
Or wild cats in a red-hot iron cage –

23

The fight must so have seemed in that fell cirque.
What penned them there, with all the plain to choose?

106 howlet owl.
114 bespate bespattered.
133 cirque circular arena. Cf. Keats *Hyperion* 2.34–5: 'a dismal cirque | Of Druid stones upon a forlorn moor.' B. may have had the Keats passage in mind, describing the despairing inertia of the Titans. *Hyperion* 2.45 has 'plashy' – used by B. line 131.

135   No foot-print leading to that horrid mews,
      None out of it. Mad brewage set to work
      Their brains, no doubt, like galley-slaves the Turk
      Pits for his pastime, Christians against Jews.

24

      And more than that – a furlong on – why, there!
140   What bad use was that engine for, that wheel,
      Or brake, not wheel – that harrow fit to reel
      Men's bodies out like silk? with all the air
      Of Tophet's tool, on earth left unaware,
      Or brought to sharpen its rusty teeth of steel.

25

145   Then came a bit of stubbed ground, once a wood,
      Next a marsh, it would seem, and now mere earth
      Desperate and done with; (so a fool finds mirth,
      Makes a thing and then mars it, till his mood
      Changes and off he goes!) within a rood –
150   Bog, clay and rubble, sand and stark black dearth.

26

      Now blotches rankling, coloured gay and grim,
      Now patches where some leanness of the soil's
      Broke into moss or substances like boils;
      Then came some palsied oak, a cleft in him
155   Like a distorted mouth that splits its rim
      Gaping at death, and dies while it recoils.

27

      And just as far as ever from the end!
      Nought in the distance but the evening, nought
      To point my footstep further! At the thought,
160   A great black bird, Apollyon's bosom-friend,
      Sailed past, nor beat his wide wing dragon-penned
      That brushed my cap – perchance the guide I sought.

135 mews coop or cage. Originally a falconry term: birds were shut up when moulting. It came to be used for stables when the Royal Mews was built on the site where hawks were formerly kept.
141 brake implement for breaking or crushing.
143 Tophet Valley near Gehenna, S. of Jerusalem, a place of sacrifice for the Jews (*Jer.* 29.4), and type of Hell.
149 rood a piece of land containing 40 square poles.
160 Apollyon's bosom-friend a bird like Apollyon: *Rev.* 9.11: 'And they had a king over them which is the angel of the bottomless pit, whose name in the Hebrew tongue is Abaddon, but in the Greek tongue hath his name Apollyon.'
161 dragon-penned feathered like a dragon.

28

For, looking up, aware I somehow grew,
    'Spite of the dusk, the plain had given place
165   All round to mountains – with such name to grace
    Mere ugly heights and heaps now stolen in view.
    How thus they had surprised me, – solve it, you!
    How to get from them was no clearer case.

29

    Yet half I seemed to recognize some trick
170   Of mischief happened to me, God knows when –
    In a bad dream perhaps. Here ended, then,
    Progress this way. When, in the very nick
    Of giving up, one time more, came a click
    As when a trap shuts – you're inside the den!

30

175   Burningly it came on me all at once,
    This was the place! those two hills on the right,
    Crouched like two bulls locked horn in horn in fight;
    While to the left, a tall scalped mountain ... Dunce,
    Dotard, a-dozing at the very nonce,
180   After a life spent training for the sight!

31

    What in the midst lay but the Tower itself?
    The round squat turret, blind as the fool's heart,
    Built of brown stone, without a counterpart
    In the whole world. The Tempest's mocking elf
185   Points to the shipman thus the unseen shelf
    He strikes on, only when the timbers start.

32

    Not see? because of night perhaps? – why, day
    Came back again for that! before it left,
    The dying sunset kindled through a cleft:
190   The hills, like giants at a hunting, lay,
    Chin upon hand, to see the game at bay –
    'Now stab and end the creature – to the heft!'

33

    Not hear? when noise was everywhere! it tolled
    Increasing like a bell. Names in my ears
195   Of all the lost adventurers my peers, –

179 Dotard, a-dozing] Fool, to be dozing *1855–1863*.   **nonce** specific
occasion.
192 heft hilt.

How such a one was strong, and such was bold,
And such was fortunate, yet eacʰ of old
Lost, lost! one moment knelled the woe of years.

34

      There they stood, ranged along the hill-sides, met
200   To view the last of me, a living frame
      For one more picture! in a sheet of flame
I saw them and I knew them all. And yet
Dauntless the slug-horn to my lips I set.
And blew. 'Childe Roland to the Dark Tower came.'

203 slug-horn B. follows Chatterton in mistaking an earlier form of slogan (battle-cry) for horn. Challenges were issued by trumpets: 'If any man of quality or degree within the lists of the army will maintain upon Edmund, supposed Earl of Gloucester, that he is a manifold traitor, let him appear by the third sound of the Trumpet' *Lear* 5.3.110–3. The trumpet is answered by Edgar – the reciter (in disguise) of 'Childe Roland...'

69 Fra Lippo Lippi

Date Probably composed at the same time as *Andrea del Sarto* (see headnote p. 245). B. wrote to Milsland 24 Feb. 1853: 'I am writing – a first step towards popularity for me – lyrics with more music and painting than before, so as to get people to hear and see...' (Griffin and Minchin 189).

Sources B. was reading Vasari's *Lives.. of the Most Eminent Painters* in the Milanesi edn. (Florence, 1846–57). B. also may have confirmed details in Filippo Baldinucci's *Delle Notizie de' Professori del Disegno da Cimabue...*(1767–74) 3. 212–20; see Hood *Letters* 104. It is likely that B. remembered Landor's use of Lippi in 'Fra Filippo Lippi and Pope Eugenius the Fourth' *Imaginary Conversations* (1846). Lippi's paintings themselves (see notes below) were also a useful suggestive source.

    Fra Filippo Lippi (1406–69) was one of the artists associated with the development in the Quattrocento of a kind of verisimilitude in painting. Others were Uccello, Masaccio, Castagno and Veneziano. Berenson *The Italian Painters of the Renaissance* (1952) 56 says that his impulse was 'toward the expression of the pleasant, genial, spiritually comfortable feelings of ordinary life'. B. does not place Lippi with great precision, and a certain amount of his feeling was conditioned by the realistic movements in art in England and France of the 1850s, and beliefs about his own medium but in general terms the evaluation is adequate.

Discussion For a fuller account see J. Parr, *ELN* 3 (1966) 197–201 and *ELN* 5 (1968) 277–83, who argues that B. derived the view of Andrea and realism partly from Mrs Jameson's article on Lippi in *Knight's Penny Magazine* (1843), reprinted in *Memoirs of the Early Italian Painters* (1845). Recent studies of Fra Lippo Lippi include Robert Oertel *Fra Filippo Lippi* (Vienna, 1942) and Mary Pittaluga *Filippo Lippi* (Florence, 1949).

    At the time B.'s poem was seen as relevant to current discussion on

[69] Robert Browning

realism: George Eliot said she 'would rather have *Fra Lippo Lippi* than an essay on Realism in Art,...' (*Critical Heritage* 177). Recent studies include De Vane 216–219, Crowell 108–124, Omans *VP* 7 (1969) 129–45. This poem was recited by B. at 13 Dorset Street London on 27 Sept. 1855. Tennyson read *Maud* the same evening.

Publication *1855.*

I am poor brother Lippo, by your leave!
You need not clap your torches to my face.
Zooks, what's to blame? you think you see a monk!
What, 't is past midnight, and you go the rounds,
5   And here you catch me at an alley's end
Where sportive ladies leave their doors ajar?
The Carmine's my cloister: hunt it up.
Do, – harry out, if you must show your zeal,
Whatever rat, there, haps on his wrong hole,
10   And nip each softling of a wee white mouse,
Weke, weke, that's crept to keep him company!
Aha, you know your betters? Then, you'll take
Your hand away that's fiddling on my throat,
And please to know me likewise. Who am I?
15   Why, one, sir, who is lodging with a friend
Three streets off – he's a certain...how d'ye call?
Master – a...Cosimo of the Medici,
I' the house that caps the corner. Boh! you were best!
Remember and tell me, the day you're hanged,
20   How you affected such a gullet's-gripe!
But you, sir, it concerns you that your knaves
Pick up a manner nor discredit you:
Zooks, are we pilchards, that they sweep the streets
And count fair prize what comes into their net?
25   He's Judas to a tittle, that man is!
Just such a face! Why, sir, you make amends,
Lord, I'm not angry! Bid your hangdogs go
Drink out this quarter-florin to the health
Of the munificent House that harbours me
30   (And many more beside, lads! more beside!)
And all's come square again. I'd like his face –
His, elbowing on his comrade in the door

3 **Zooks** gadzooks (God's hooks, i.e. God's nails); early C17.
7 **Carmine** Carmelite monastery on the south bank of the Arno.
17 **Cosimo of the Medici** (1389–1464) ruler of Florence and patron of many artists. His palace (designed by Michelozzi) was on the corner of Via dei Gori and Via Cavour.

Robert Browning [69]

With the pike and lantern, – for the slave that holds
John Baptist's head a-dangle by the hair
35   With one hand ('Look you, now,' as who should say)
And his weapon in the other, yet unwiped!
It's not your chance to have a bit of chalk,
A wood-coal or the like? or you should see!
Yes, I'm the painter, since you style me so.
40   What, brother Lippo's doings, up and down,
You know them and they take you? like enough!
I saw the proper twinkle in your eye –
'Tell you, I liked your looks at very first.
Let's sit and set things straight now, hip to haunch.
45   Here's spring come, and the nights one makes up bands
To roam the town and sing out carnival,
And I've been three weeks shut within my mew,
A-painting for the great man, saints and saints
And saints again. I could not paint all night –
50   Ouf! I leaned out of window for fresh air.
There came a hurry of feet and little feet,
A sweep of lute-strings, laughs, and whifts of song, –
Flower o' the broom,
Take away love, and our earth is a tomb!
55   *Flower o' the quince,*
I let Lisa go, and what good in life since?
Flower o' the thyme – and so on. Round they went.
Scarce had they turned the corner when a titter
Like the skipping of rabbits by moonlight, – three slim shapes,
60   And a face that looked up...zooks, sir, flesh and blood,
That's all I'm made of! Into shreds it went,
Curtain and counterpane and coverlet,
All the bed furniture – a dozen knots,
There was a ladder! Down I let myself,
65   Hands and feet, scrambling somehow, and so dropped,
And after them. I came up with the fun

34 There is a fresco of John the Baptist's head on a dish in Prato Cathedral,
see lines 323–4 (reproduced Eve Borsook *The Mural Painters of Tuscany*
(1960) p. 64).
53–7 imitations of *stornelli* – three-line Tuscan songs based on the names of
flowers.
61–6 Vasari 2. 3 (Everyman edn 1963): 'Cosimo...shut him up in the house,
so that he might not go out and waste time. He remained so for two days,
but overcome by his amorous and bestial desires, he cut up his sheet with a
pair of scissors, and, letting himself down out of the window, devoted many
days to his pleasures.'

Hard by St Laurence, hail fellow, well met. –
Flower o' the rose,
If I've been merry, what matter who knows?
70 And so as I was stealing back again
To get to bed and have a bit of sleep
Ere I rise up to-morrow and go work
On Jerome knocking at his poor old breast
With his great round stone to subdue the flesh.
75 You snap me of the sudden. Ah, I see!
Though your eye twinkles still, you shake your head –
Mine's shaved, – a monk, you say – the sting's in that!
If Master Cosimo announced himself,
Mum's the word naturally; but a monk!
80 Come, what am I a beast for? tell us, now!
I was a baby when my mother died
And father died and left me in the street.
I starved there, God knows how, a year or two
On fig-skins, melon-parings, rinds and shucks,
85 Refuse and rubbish. One fine frosty day,
My stomach being empty as your hat,
The wind doubled me up and down I went.
Old Aunt Lapaccia trussed me with one hand,
(Its fellow was a stinger as I knew)
90 And so along the wall, over the bridge,
By the straight cut to the convent. Six words there,
While I stood munching my first bread that month:
'So, boy, you're minded,' quoth the good fat father
Wiping his own mouth, 'twas refection-time, –
95 'To quit this very miserable world?
Will you renounce'...'the mouthful of bread?' thought I;
By no means! Brief, they made a monk of me;
I did renounce the world, its pride and greed,
Palace, farm, villa, shop and banking-house,
100 Trash, such as these poor devils of Medici
Have given their hearts to – all at eight years old.
Well, sir, I found in time, you may be sure,
'Twas not for nothing – the good bellyful,
The warm serge and the rope that goes all round,
105 And day-long blessed idleness beside!
'Let's see what the urchin's fit for' – that came next.
Not overmuch their way, I must confess.

---

67 St. Laurence San Lorenzo – a few yards from the Medici Palace.
73 Jerome St Jerome, pre-eminently the saint of asceticism and celibacy.
88 Aunt Lapaccia Andrea's father's sister; the name in Vasari.

Such a to-do! they tried me with their books:
Lord, they'd have taught me Latin in pure waste!
110 *Flower o' the clove,*
All the Latin I construe is, 'amo' I love!
But, mind you, when a boy starves in the streets
Eight years together, as my fortune was,
Watching folk's faces to know who will fling
115 The bit of half-stripped grape-bunch he desires,
And who will curse or kick him for his pains, –
Which gentleman processional and fine,
Holding a candle to the Sacrament,
Will wink and let him lift a plate and catch
120 The droppings of the wax to sell again,
Or holla for the Eight and have him whipped, –
How say I? – nay, which dog bites, which lets drop
His bone from the heap of offal in the street, –
Why, soul and sense of him grow sharp alike,
125 He learns the look of things, and none the less
For admonition from the hunger-pinch.
I had a store of such remarks, be sure,
Which, after I found leisure, turned to use.
I drew men's faces on my copy-books,
130 Scrawled them within the antiphonary's marge,
Joined legs and arms to the long music-notes,
Found eyes and nose and chin for A's and B's,
And made a string of pictures of the world
Betwixt the ins and outs of verb and noun,
135 On the wall, the bench, the door. The monks looked black.
'Nay,' quoth the Prior, 'turn him out, d' ye say?
In no wise. Loose a crow and catch a lark.
What if at last we get our man of parts,
We Carmelites, like those Camaldolese
And Preaching Friars, to do our church up fine
And put the front on it that ought to be!'
And hereupon he bade me daub away.
Thank you! my head being crammed, the walls a blank,
Never was such prompt disemburdening.
145 First, every sort of monk, the black and white,
I drew them, fat and lean: then, folk at church,
From good old gossips waiting to confess
Their cribs of barrel-droppings, candle-ends, –

121 the Eight the magistrates of Florence.
129–35 Vasari 2. 1: '…instead of studying [he] did nothing but cover his books and those of the others with caricatures.'
139 Camaldolese a strict semi-eremetical order founded by St Romualdo.

To the breathless fellow at the altar-foot,
150 Fresh from his murder, safe and sitting there
With the little children round him in a row
Of admiration, half for his beard and half
For that white anger of his victim's son
Shaking a fist at him with one fierce arm,
155 Signing himself with the other because of Christ
(Whose sad face on the cross sees only this
After the passion of a thousand years)
Till some poor girl, her apron o'er her head,
(Which the intense eyes looked through) came at eve
160 On tiptoe, said a word, dropped in a loaf,
Her pair of earrings and a bunch of flowers
(The brute took growling), prayed, and so was gone.
I painted all, then cried, "'T is ask and have;
Choose, for more's ready!' – laid the ladder flat,
165 And showed my covered bit of cloister-wall.
The monks closed in a circle and praised loud
Till checked, taught what to see and not to see,
Being simple bodies, – 'That's the very man!
Look at the boy who stoops to pat the dog!
170 That woman's like the Prior's niece who comes
To care about his asthma: it's the life!'
But there my triumph's straw-fire flared and funked;
Their betters took their turn to see and say:
The Prior and the learned pulled a face
175 And stopped all that in no time. 'How? what's here?
Quite from the mark of painting, bless us all!
Faces, arms, legs and bodies like the true
As much as pea and pea! it's devil's-game!
Your business is not to catch men with show,
180 With homage to the perishable clay,
But lift them over it, ignore it all,
Make them forget there's such a thing as flesh.
Your business is to paint the souls of men –
Man's soul, and it's a fire, smoke...no, it's not...
185 It's vapour done up like a new-born babe –

149 **the breathless fellow** a murderer who has taken sanctuary in the church.
170 **niece** perhaps a euphemism for mistress.
174 E. H. Gombrich 'Art and scholarship' *Meditations on a Hobby Horse* (1963) 115: 'We have no evidence that there ever was such a prior.'
185 The prior here is resorting to an iconographic device for depicting souls as babies that was current a hundred years before (in the Last Judgement, Campo Santo, Pisa, for instance). This tends to confirm Gombrich's doubts about the Prior.

(In that shape when you die it leaves your mouth)
It's...well, what matters talking, it's the soul!
Give us no more of body than shows soul!
Here's Giotto, with his Saint a-praising God,
190 That sets us praising, – why not stop with him?
Why put all thoughts of praise out of our head
With wonder at lines, colours, and what not?
Paint the soul, never mind the legs and arms!
Rub all out, try at it a second time.
195 Oh, that white smallish female with the breasts,
She's just my niece...Herodias, I would say, –
Who went and danced and got men's heads cut off!
Have it all out!' Now, is this sense, I ask?
A fine way to paint soul, by painting body
200 So ill, the eye can't stop there, must go further
And 'can't fare worse! Thus, yellow does for white
When what you put for yellow's simply black,
And any sort of meaning looks intense
When all beside itself means and looks nought.
205 Why can't a painter lift each foot in turn,
Left foot and right foot, go a double step,
Make his flesh liker and his soul more like,
Both in their order? Take the prettiest face,
The Prior's niece...patron-saint – is it so pretty
210 You can't discover if it means hope, fear,
Sorrow or joy? won't beauty go with these?
Suppose I've made her eyes all right and blue,
Can't I take breath and try to add life's flash,
And then add soul and heighten them threefold?
215 Or say there's beauty with no soul at all –
(I never saw it – put the case the same –)
If you get simple beauty and nought else,
You get about the best thing God invents:
That's somewhat: and you'll find the soul you have missed,
220 Within yourself, when you return him thanks.
'Rub all out!' Well, well, there's my life, in short,
And so the thing has gone on ever since.
I'm grown a man no doubt, I've broken bounds:
You should not take a fellow eight years old
225 And make him swear to never kiss the girls.

---

189 Giotto Giotto di Bondone (*ca.*1267–1337): the most important painter in
the transition of Italian art from Medieval to Renaissance.
196 B., in confusing Herodias with Salome (who actually did the dancing:
Matt. 14.3–11), may be following Vasari.

[69] Robert Browning

I'm my own master, paint now as I please –
Having a friend, you see, in the Corner-house!
Lord, it's fast holding by the rings in front –
Those great rings serve more purposes than just
230 To plant a flag in, or tie up a horse!
And yet the old schooling sticks, the old grave eyes
Are peeping o'er my shoulder as I work,
The heads shake still – 'It's art's decline, my son!
You're not of the true painters, great and old;
235 Brother Angelico's the man, you'll find;
Brother Lorenzo stands his single peer:
Fag on at flesh, you'll never make the third!'
Flower o' the pine,
You keep your mistr... manners, and I'll stick to mine!
240 I'm not the third, then: bless us, they must know!
Don't you think they're the likeliest to know,
They with their Latin? So, I swallow my rage,
Clench my teeth, suck my lips in tight, and paint
To please them – sometimes do and sometimes don't;
245 For, doing most, there's pretty sure to come
A turn, some warm eve finds me at my saints –
A laugh, a cry, the business of the world –
(*Flower o' the peach,*
Death for us all, and his own life for each!)
250 And my whole soul revolves, the cup runs over,
The world and life's too big to pass for a dream,
And I do these wild things in sheer despite,
And play the fooleries you catch me at,
In pure rage! The old mill-horse, out at grass
255 After hard years, throws up his stiff heels so,
Although the miller does not preach to him

227 Corner-house the Medici palace is on a corner.
235 Brother Angelico Fra Angelico (1387–1455). A Dominican friar, a conservative artist influenced by Giotto, but also forward-looking enough to have painted the first identifiable landscape. The largest collection of his work is in the Convent of San Marco, Florence, begun 1436.
236 Brother Lorenzo Lorenzo Monaco (*c*. 1370–1425). A Giottesque painter, whom Berenson (56) describes as Lippi's first master. Worked in the Camaldolese monastery. His early work, such as the *Coronation of the Virgin* (Uffizi 1413), is in a non-naturalistic style, with gold backgrounds and flat figures; but his *Adoration of the Magi* (Uffizi) is in a more naturalistic style.
237 Fag on toil away.
254–60 A play on words reminiscent of the B. of the letters to E. Barrett: **out at grass** means pensioned off, but Lippo also glances at *1 Peter* 1.24: 'all flesh is as grass...'

The only good of grass is to make chaff.
What would men have? Do they like grass or no –
May they or mayn't they? all I want's the thing
260 Settled for ever one way. As it is,
You tell too many lies and hurt yourself:
You don't like what you only like too much.
You do like what, if given you at your word,
You find abundantly detestable.
265 For me, I think I speak as I was taught;
I always see the garden and God there
A-making man's wife: and, my lesson learned,
The value and significance of flesh,
I can't unlearn ten minutes afterwards.
270 You understand me: I'm a beast, I know.
But see, now – why, I see as certainly
As that the morning-star's about to shine,
What will hap some day. We've a youngster here
Comes to our convent, studies what I do,
275 Slouches and stares and lets no atom drop:
His name is Guidi – he'll not mind the monks –
They call him Hulking Tom, he lets them talk –
He picks my practice up – he'll paint apace,
I hope so – though I never live so long,
280 I know what's sure to follow. You be judge!
You speak no Latin more than I, belike,
However, you're my man, you've seen the world
– The beauty and the wonder and the power,
The shapes of things, their colours, lights and shades,
285 Changes, surprises, – and God made it all!
– For what? Do you feel thankful, ay or no,
For this fair town's face, yonder river's line,
The mountain round it and the sky above,

276 Guidi Tommaso di Giovanni (1401–38), better known as Masaccio.
Although the facts were available in 1853, B. has his chronology wrong here.
See J. Parr *ELN* 3 (1966) 197–201. He wrote to Edward Dowden (13 Oct.
1866): '... I was wide awake when I made Fra Lippo the elder practitioner of
Art, if not, as I believe, the earlier born. I looked into the matter long ago,
and long before I thought of my own poem, from my interest in the
Brancacci frescoes...' (Hood *Letters* 104). In fact, Masaccio has a better
claim than Fra Lippo to be the important realist of the early Quattrocento.
His work in the Carmine (reproduced Borsook pls 46, 47, 48, 49, 50),
influenced Lippo. Vasari was quite clear that Masaccio was the senior artist:
'many said that the spirit of Masaccio had entered into Fra Filippo'. Fra
Lippo's son, Filippino Lippi (1457–1504), completed the Brancacci Chapel
frescoes.

Much more the figures of man, woman, child,
290 These are the frame to? What's it all about?
To be passed over, despised? or dwelt upon,
Wondered at? oh, this last of course! – you say.
But why not do as well as say, – paint these
Just as they are, careless what comes of it?
295 God's works – paint anyone, and count it crime
To let a truth slip. Don't object, 'His works
Are here already; nature is complete:
Suppose you reproduce her – (which you can't)
There's no advantage! you must beat her, then.'
300 For, don't you mark? we're made so that we love
First when we see them painted, things we have passed
Perhaps a hundred times nor cared to see;
And so they are better, painted – better to us,
Which is the same thing. Art was given for that;
305 God uses us to help each other so,
Lending our minds out. Have you noticed, now,
Your cullion's hanging face? A bit of chalk,
And trust me but you should, though! How much more,
If I drew higher things with the same truth!
310 That were to take the Prior's pulpit-place,
Interpret God to all of you! Oh, oh,
It makes me mad to see what men shall do
And we in our graves! This world's no blot for us,
Nor blank; it means intensely, and means good:
315 To find its meaning is my meat and drink.
'Ay, but you don't so instigate to prayer!'
Strikes in the Prior: 'when your meaning's plain
It does not say to folk – remember matins,
Or, mind you fast next Friday!' Why, for this
320 What need of art at all? A skull and bones,
Two bits of stick nailed crosswise, or, what's best,
A bell to chime the hour with, does as well.
I painted a Saint Laurence six months since
At Prato, splashed the fresco in fine style:
325 'How looks my painting, now the scaffold's down?'
I ask a brother: 'Hugely,' he returns –
'Already not one phiz of your three slaves
Who turn the Deacon off his toasted side,
But's scratched and prodded to our heart's content,

307 **cullion** rascal.
323 **Saint Laurence** Roasted on a gridiron (c. 258). Lippo was working at Prato from 1452 to 1454, on the life of St Stephen (Borsook pls 62–4). The reference is either B.'s mistake or an imaginary invention.

330   The pious people have so eased their own
      With coming to say prayers there in a rage:
      We get on fast to see the bricks beneath.
      Expect another job this time next year,
      For pity and religion grow i' the crowd –
335   Your painting serves its purpose!' Hang the fools!
      – That is – you'll not mistake an idle word
      Spoke in a huff by a poor monk, God wot,
      Tasting the air this spicy night which turns
      The unaccustomed head like Chianti wine!
340   Oh, the Church knows! don't misreport me, now!
      It's natural a poor monk out of bounds
      Should have his apt word to excuse himself:
      And hearken how I plot to make amends.
      I have bethought me: I shall paint a piece
345   ...There's for you! Give me six months, then go, see
      Something in Sant' Ambrogio's! Bless the nuns!
      They want a cast o' my office. I shall paint
      God in the midst, Madonna and her babe,
      Ringed by a bowery flowery angel-brood,
350   Lilies and vestments and white faces, sweet
      As puff on puff of grated orris-root
      When ladies crowd to Church at midsummer.
      And then i' the front, of course a saint or two –
      Saint John, because he saves the Florentines,
355   Saint Ambrose, who puts down in black and white
      The convent's friends and gives them a long day,
      And Job, I must have him there past mistake,
      The man of Uz and (Us without the z,
      Painters who need his patience.) Well, all these

334 Emended by Jack *1970* to 'piety'. B.'s 'pity' makes sense: the priest is ironically critical of the simple people, who in their rage mutilate the torturers, but Lippo has greater breadth of vision than the Prato priest: he sees that art can encourage passions as well as the tenderer sympathies – though some of the passions lead to the destruction of art.
346 Sant' Ambrogio's the *Coronation of the Virgin*, painted for the nunnery of Saint Ambrogio's nunnery in Florence. It remained as the altar-piece until the C18.
347 cast o' my office example of my work.
351 orris-root Ruskin queried B. about the root; B. replied (10 Dec. 1855) that it was 'a corruption of *iris*-root...of world-wide fame as a good savour' (DeLaura *BJRL* 54 (1972) 326).
354 Saint John John the Baptist – patron saint of Florence.
358 *Job* 1.1: 'There was a man in the land of Uz, whose name was Job.' Since 'of us' in Italian would be '*per noi*' the pun only works in English.

360 Secured at their devotion, up shall come
Out of a corner when you least expect,
As one by a dark stair into a great light,
Music and talking, who but Lippo! I! –
Mazed, motionless and moonstruck – I'm the man!
365 Back I shrink – what is this I see and hear?
I, caught up with my monk's things by mistake,
My old serge gown and rope that goes all round,
I, in this presence, this pure company!
Where's a hole, where's a corner for escape?
370 Then steps a sweet angelic slip of a thing
Forward, puts out a soft palm – 'Not so fast!'
– Addresses the celestial presence, 'nay –
He made you and devised you, after all,
Though, he's none of you! Could Saint John there draw –
375 His camel-hair make up a painting-brush?
We come to brother Lippo for all that,
Iste perfecit opus!' So, all smile –
I shuffle sideways with my blushing face
Under the cover of a hundred wings
380 Thrown like a spread of kirtles when you're gay
And play hot cockles, all the doors being shut,
Till, wholly unexpected, in there pops
The hothead husband! Thus I scuttle off
To some safe bench behind, not letting go
385 The palm of her, the little lily thing

375 The camel-hair shirt was an attribute of John the Baptist, and paint-brushes were made of camel hair.
377 The painting referred to is now in the Uffizi Florence (reprod. Pittaluga pls 27–34). Its subject is the *Coronation of the Virgin*. The inscription means 'This is the man who caused the work to be made'. It used to be thought that the 'work' was the painting, and the man was a self-portrait of Fra Lippo Lippi, but in the *Burlington Mag.* 21 (1912) 194–200, M. Carmichael showed that the man (who is dressed in the robes of a secular priest) was Francesco Maringhi – the benefactor of the whole foundation. He repro-duces the only known likeness of Fra Lippo – the bust on his tomb in Spoleto.
380 kirtles skirts.
381 hot cockles See Joseph Strutt *Sports and Pastimes* (1830) 393 and G. F. Northall *English Folk Rhymes* (1892) 153–6. A game in which one was either blindfolded or hid one's head in someone's lap, was beaten on the bottom and guessed who had struck. There is clearly a sense of manual arousing. For the sexual overtones of the sport see John Gay *The Shepherd's Week: Monday* lines 99–102: 'As at hot-cockles once I laid me down, | And felt the weighty hand of many a clown, | Buxoma gave a gentle tap, and I | Quick rose, and read soft mischief in her eye.'
385 B. took the idea of the interceding nun from Vasari.

That spoke the good word for me in the nick,
Like the Prior's niece...Saint Lucy, I would say.
And so all's saved for me, and for the church
A pretty picture gained. Go, six months hence!
390 Your hand, sir, and good-bye: no lights, no lights!
The street's hushed, and I know my own way back,
Don't fear me! There's the grey beginning. Zooks!

70 Andrea del Sarto
(called 'the faultless painter')

Date Composed some time between 23 Nov. 1852 and March 1853.
Theme Written after Elizabeth's cousin Kenyon requested a reproduction of
Andrea del Sarto and his wife in the Pitti Palace, Florence. See A. Crosse
'John Kenyon and his Friends' *Temple Bar* 88 (1890) 477–96. *Andrea* may
have been one of the poems on art which B. described himself as working
on in a letter to Milsand of 24 Feb. 1853 (Griffin and Minchin 189).
Elizabeth describes B. as 'fond of digging at Vasari' (letter to Mrs Martin 13
Apr. 1853, B. L. Add. MSS 42228–31), perhaps in search of information for
this and other poems on Italian artists.
   Andrea del Sarto lived from 1486 to 1531. B.'s main source is Vasari's
Lives: a copy was in B.'s father's library. B. also may have consulted
Baldinucci's *Notizie de' Professori del Disegno*...(1767–74). Two articles
suggest that an additional source might have been Alfred de Musset's play
on *Andrea del Sarto* (published 1833, acted in Paris Sept. 1851–Nov. 1852,
when B. was there): R. M. Bachem, *Revue de Littérature Comparée* 38
(1964) and B. Melchiori *VP* 4 (1966) 132–36. S. T. Freedberg *Andrea del
Sarto* (Cambridge, Mass. 1963) 1.98 confirms the main outlines of B.'s
portrait: 'the hand, the eye, and the mind, in the sense of what we have
defined as an aesthetic intelligence, are all of them of the highest order that
can be attained in art, but the dimension of the spirit that controls all these
is not'; but in 2.269 he qualifies Vasari's view of Lucrezia.
Discussion The poem has two centres of interest: the psychological and the
artistic. It is the study of a flawed marital relationship and of a second-rate
artistic talent in which the inferiority is defined not by technical incompetence but by the absence of a strong creative genius. E. Jones *Imago* 2
(1913) 468 psychoanalysed Andrea as 'an "unappeased" latent homosexual.'
B. Miller 187 sees a connection between B. impeded by his wife as an artist
and Andrea, but his view has not found acceptance. For other discussion
see De Vane 244–48, King 11–31, Crowell 162–175.
Publication *1855*.

   But do not let us quarrel any more,
   No, my Lucrezia; bear with me for once:
   Sit down and all shall happen as you wish.

Title 'the faultless painter' 'His figures are simple and pure, well conceived,
flawless and perfect in every particular' (Vasari *Lives* 2.303).
2 Lucrezia Andrea's wife, the widow of a cap-maker, Lucrezia de Baccio del
Fede. Her portrait in the Prado is reproduced in Freedberg pl. 52.

You turn your face, but does it bring your heart?
5   I'll work then for your friend's friend, never fear,
Treat his own subject after his own way,
Fix his own time, accept too his own price,
And shut the money into this small hand
When next it takes mine. Will it? tenderly?
10   Oh, I'll content him, – but to-morrow, Love!
I often am much wearier than you think,
This evening more than usual, and it seems
As if – forgive now – should you let me sit
Here by the window with your hand in mine
15   And look a half-hour forth on Fiesole,
Both of one mind, as married people use,
Quietly, quietly the evening through,
I might get up to-morrow to my work
Cheerful and fresh as ever. Let us try.
20   To-morrow, how you shall be glad for this!
Your soft hand is a woman of itself,
And mine the man's bared breast she curls inside.
Don't count the time lost, neither; you must serve
For each of the five pictures we require:
25   It saves a model. So! keep looking so –
My serpentining beauty, rounds on rounds!
– How could you ever prick those perfect ears,
Even to put the pearl there! oh, so sweet –
My face, my moon, my everybody's moon,
30   Which everybody looks on and calls his,
And, I suppose, is looked on by in turn,
While she looks – no one's: very dear, no less.
You smile? why, there's my picture ready made,
There's what we painters call our harmony!
35   A common greyness silvers everything, –
All in a twilight, you and I alike
– You, at the point of your first pride in me

15 Fiesole hillside town five miles from Florence.
26 serpentining beauty Andrea borrowed from the Mannerist style – characterized by many modern critics as an art of the curving line. See, for instance, Mario Praz, 'Harmony and the Serpentine Line' *Mnemosyne* (Princeton 1970) 79–105. Yet as Freedberg 93 shows he mainly clung to classical principles.
29 Cf. *One Word More* (p. 268 below) for B.'s use of the public and private faces of the moon.
35 A common greyness not all of Andrea's paintings are dull in colour, and those that are probably owe it to decay. In any case, colour was a feature of Venetian rather than Florentine art.

(That's gone you know), – but I, at every point;
My youth, my hope, my art, being all toned down
40   To yonder sober pleasant Fiesole.
There's the bell clinking from the chapel-top;
That length of convent-wall across the way
Holds the trees safer, huddled more inside;
The last monk leaves the garden; days decrease,
45   And autumn grows, autumn in everything.
Eh? the whole seems to fall into a shape
As if I saw alike my work and self
And all that I was born to be and do,
A twilight-piece. Love, we are in God's hand.
50   How strange now, looks the life he makes us lead;
So free we seem, so fettered fast we are!
I feel he laid the fetter: let it lie!
This chamber for example – turn your head –
All that's behind us! You don't understand
55   Nor care to understand about my art,
But you can hear at least when people speak:
And that cartoon, the second from the door
– It is the thing, Love! so such things should be –
Behold Madonna! – I am bold to say.
60   I can do with my pencil what I know,
What I see, what at bottom of my heart
I wish for, if I ever wish so deep –
Do easily, too – when I say, perfectly,
I do not boast, perhaps: yourself are judge,
65   Who listened to the Legate's talk last week,
And just as much they used to say in France.
At any rate 't is easy, all of it!
No sketches first, no studies, that's long past:
I do what many dream of, all their lives,
70   – Dream? strive to do, and agonize to do,
And fail in doing. I could count twenty such
On twice your fingers, and not leave this town,

---

57 cartoon a preliminary drawing that was transferred to the surface of the final work, usually by pricking pinholes along the lines of the design.

60–77 Facility of this kind was admired in the Renaissance more than in C19. B. took the Romantic view that evidences of effort and struggle in the work were more to be cherished. See Ruskin 'The Nature of Gothic' *The Stones of Venice* vol. 2 (1853) (*Works* 10.180–269) and 'Of the Real Nature of Greatness of Style' *Modern Painters* vol. 3 (1856) (Works 5.44–69) for the fullest representation of this aesthetic.

65 the Legate possibly a Papal Legate from Leo X. It is not clear which event B. has in mind here.

Who strive – you don't know how the others strive
To paint a little thing like that you smeared
75 Carelessly passing with your robes afloat, –
Yet do much less, so much less, Someone says,
(I know his name, no matter) – so much less!
Well, less is more, Lucrezia: I am judged.
There burns a truer light of God in them.
80 In their vexed beating stuffed and stopped-up brain,
Heart, or whate'er else, than goes on to prompt
This low-pulsed forthright craftsman's hand of mine.
Their works drop groundward, but themselves, I know,
Reach many a time a heaven that's shut to me,
85 Enter and take their place there sure enough,
Though they come back and cannot tell the world.
My works are nearer heaven, but I sit here.
The sudden blood of these men! at a word –
Praise them, it boils, or blame them, it boils too.
90 I, painting from myself and to myself,
Know what I do, am unmoved by men's blame
Or their praise either. Somebody remarks
Morello's outline there is wrongly traced,
His hue mistaken; what of that? or else,
95 Rightly traced and well ordered; what of that?
Speak as they please, what does the mountain care?
Ah, but a man's reach should exceed his grasp,
Or what's a heaven for? All is silver-grey
Placid and perfect with my art: the worse!
100 I know both what I want and what might gain,
And yet how profitless to know, to sigh
'Had I been two, another and myself,
Our head would have o'erlooked the world!' No doubt.
Yonder's a work now, of that famous youth
105 The Urbinate who died five years ago.

76 Someone Michaelangelo.
80 Cf. Vasari 2.303: '...a timidity of spirit and a yielding simple nature prevented him from exhibiting a burning ardour and dash that, joined to his other qualities, would have made him divine.'
89 B. is possibly glancing at himself in addition to Andrea's contemporaries: creation did not come easy to him, and he was tetchy about criticism.
93 Morello a mountain north of Florence. B. is making Andrea voice a concept that would be more familiar to post-1800 artists: that the quint-essential artist (as opposed to the mere craftsman) is as spontaneous as a force in nature. See M. H. Abrams 'Unconscious genius and organic growth' in *The Mirror and the Lamp* (1953) 184–225.
96 Not in *1855*.
105 The Urbinate Raphael d'Urbino (1483–1520). This enables us to date the episode in 1525.

('T is copied, George Vasari sent it me.)
Well, I can fancy how he did it all,
Pouring his soul, with kings and popes to see,
Reaching, that heaven might so replenish him,
110 Above and through his art – for it gives way;
That arm is wrongly put – and there again –
A fault to pardon in the drawing's lines,
Its body, so to speak: its soul is right,
He means right – that, a child may understand.
115 Still, what an arm! and I could alter it:
But all the play, the insight and the stretch –
Out of me, out of me! And wherefore out?
Had you enjoined them on me, given me soul,
We might have risen to Rafael, I and you!
120 Nay, Love, you did give all I asked, I think –
More than I merit, yes, by many times.
But had you – oh, with the same perfect brow,
And perfect eyes, and more than perfect mouth,
And the low voice my soul hears, as a bird
125 The fowler's pipe, and follows to the snare –
Had you, with these the same, but brought a mind!
Some women do so. Had the mouth there urged
'God and the glory! never care for gain.
The present by the future, what is that?
130 Live for fame, side by side with Agnolo!
Rafael is waiting: up to God, all three!'
I might have done it for you. So it seems:
Perhaps not. All is as God over-rules.
Beside, incentives come from the soul's self;
135 The rest avail not. Why do I need you?
What wife had Rafael, or has Agnolo?
In this world, who can do a thing, will not;
And who would do it, cannot, I perceive:
Yet the will's somewhat – somewhat, too, the power –
140 And thus we half-men struggle. At the end,
God, I conclude, compensates, punishes.
'T is safer for me, if the award be strict,

---

106 Vasari (1511–74) a pupil of Andrea. Although a painter (he executed frescoes in the Palazzo Vecchio, Florence) he is principally known for his *Lives*...(1550; 2nd ed. 1568).
122–7 Here too, B. glances obliquely at his own situation: in choosing a perfectly beautiful muse, Andrea has guaranteed a limitation in his art. B.'s muse Elizabeth was no beauty, but she had a formidable mind.
130 Agnolo Michelangelo (1475–1564). He was the artist Vasari thought the culminating genius in the progress of art.

That I am something underrated here,
Poor this long while, despised, to speak the truth.
145 I dared not, do you know, leave home all day,
For fear of chancing on the Paris lords.
The best is when they pass and look aside;
But they speak sometimes; I must bear it all.
Well may they speak! That Francis, that first time,
150 And that long festal year at Fontainebleau!
I surely then could sometimes leave the ground,
Put on the glory, Rafael's daily wear,
In that humane great monarch's golden look, –
One finger in his beard or twisted curl
155 Over his mouth's good mark that made the smile,
One arm about my shoulder, round my neck,
The jingle of his gold chain in my ear,
I painting proudly with his breath on me,
All his court round him, seeing with his eyes,
160 Such frank French eyes, and such a fire of souls
Profuse, my hand kept plying by those hearts, –
And, best of all, this, this, this face beyond,
This in the background, waiting on my work,
To crown the issue with a last reward!
165 A good time, was it not, my kingly days?
And had you not grown restless... but I know –
'T is done and past; 't was right, my instinct said;
Too live the life grew, golden and not grey,
And I'm the weak-eyed bat no sun should tempt
170 Out of the grange whose four walls make his world.
How could it end in any other way?
You called me, and I came home to your heart.
The triumph was – to reach and stay there; since
I reached it ere the triumph, what is lost?
175 Let my hands frame your face in your hair's gold,
You beautiful Lucrezia that are mine!
'Rafael did this, Andrea painted that;
The Roman's is the better when you pray,

146 the Paris lords in 1518 Francis I of France invited Andrea to come and paint for him. Vasari 2.313 relates that Lucrezia called him home; and on his return he spent the money the King had given him to buy works of art: 'Francis became so angry at his faithlessness that he for a long time looked askance at Florentine painters, and he swore that if Andrea ever fell into his hands he would have more pain than pleasure, in spite of his ability.'
154–5 For Francis I's appearance see Jean Clouet's portrait in the Louvre.
178 The Roman's Raphael's: he had been working in Rome since 1509, although his birthplace was Urbino.

But still the other's Virgin was his wife –'
180 Men will excuse me. I am glad to judge
Both pictures in your presence; clearer grows
My better fortune, I resolve to think.
For, do you know, Lucrezia, as God lives,
Said one day Agnolo, his very self,
185 To Rafael...I have known it all these years...
(When the young man was flaming out his thoughts
Upon a palace-wall for Rome to see,
Too lifted up in heart because of it)
'Friend, there's a certain sorry little scrub
190 Goes up and down our Florence, none cares how,
Who, were he set to plan and execute
As you are, pricked on by your popes and kings,
Would bring the sweat into that brow of yours!'
To Rafael's! – And indeed the arm is wrong.
195 I hardly dare...yet, only you to see,
Give the chalk here – quick, thus the line should go!
Ay, but the soul! he's Rafael! rub it out!
Still, all I care for, if he spoke the truth,
    (What he? why, who but Michel Agnolo?
200 Do you forget already words like those?)
If really there was such a chance, so lost, –
Is, whether you're – not grateful – but more pleased.
Well, let me think so. And you smile indeed!
This hour has been an hour! Another smile?
205 If you would sit thus by me every night
I should work better, do you comprehend?
I mean that I should earn more, give you more.
See, it is settled dusk now; there's a star;
Morello's gone, the watch-lights show the wall,
210 The cue-owls speak the name we call them by.
Come from the windows, love, – come in, at last,
Inside the melancholy little house
We built to be so gay with. God is just.
King Francis may forgive me: oft at nights
215 When I look up from painting, eyes tired out,
The walls become illumined, brick from brick
Distinct, instead of mortar, fierce bright gold,

179 Vasari 2.312: 'He never painted a woman without using [Lucrezia] as his model.'
187 Probably Raphael's decorations of the *Stanza della Segnatura* in the Vatican, Rome: begun 1509.
210 **cue-owls** scops owls (first occurrence in *OED*).

That gold of his I did cement them with!
Let us but love each other. Must you go?
220 That Cousin here again? he waits outside?
Must see you – you, and not with me? Those loans?
More gaming debts to pay? you smiled for that?
Well, let smiles buy me! have you more to spend?
While hand and eye and something of a heart
225 Are left me, work's my ware, and what's it worth?
I'll pay my fancy. Only let me sit
The grey remainder of the evening out,
Idle, you call it, and muse perfectly
How I could paint, were I but back in France,
230 One picture, just one more – the Virgin's face,
Not yours this time! I want you at my side
To hear them – that is, Michel Agnolo –
Judge all I do and tell you of its worth.
Will you? To-morrow, satisfy your friend.
235 I take the subjects for his corridor,
Finish the portrait out of hand – there, there,
And throw him in another thing or two
If he demurs; the whole should prove enough
To pay for this same Cousin's freak. Beside,
240 What's better and what's all I care about,
Get you the thirteen scudi for the ruff!
Love, does that please you? Ah, but what does he,
The Cousin! what does he to please you more?

    I am grown peaceful as old age to-night.
245 I regret little, I would change still less.
Since there my past life lies, why alter it?
The very wrong to Francis! – it is true
I took his coin, was tempted and complied,
And built this house and sinned, and all is said.
250 My father and my mother died of want.
Well, had I riches of my own? you see
How one gets rich! Let each one bear his lot.
They were born poor, lived poor, and poor they died:

---

218 Vasari 2.313: 'When the time for his return to France had passed, he found that in building and pleasures, without working, he had spent all his money and the king's also.'
220 Cousin euphemism for lover. In de Musset's play he was called Cordiani.
221–2 Gaming debts not in Vasari: they occur in de Musset.
241 scudi coins with shields stamped on them. Worth about four shillings.
253 Andrea's father was a tailor (*sarto* Italian): see Vasari 2.304.

And I have laboured somewhat in my time
255 And not been paid profusely. Some good son
Paint my two hundred pictures – let him try!
No doubt, there's something strikes a balance. Yes,
You loved me quite enough, it seems to-night.
This must suffice me here. What would one have?
260 In heaven, perhaps, new chances, one more chance –
Four great walls in the New Jerusalem,
Meted on each side by the angel's reed,
For Leonard, Rafael, Agnolo and me
To cover – the three first without a wife,
265 While I have mine! So – still they overcome
Because there's still Lucrezia, – as I choose.

Again the Cousin's whistle! Go, my Love.

261 New Jerusalem *Rev.* 21.10–21.
262 reed a biblical unit of measurement, equal to six cubits. See *Ezek.* 42.16:
'He measured the north side, five hundred reeds...'
263 Leonard Leonardo da Vinci (1452–1519).

71 A Toccata of Galuppi's

Date Possibly as early as 1847. De Vane 219 cites G. W. Cooke, quoting from G. W. Curtis: 'B. at the organ chased a fugue, or dreamed out upon the twilight keys a faint throbbing toccata of Galuppi' (*Browning Collections* 6). It is much more likely that it is one of the poems referred to in a letter to Milsand of 24 Feb. 1853: 'I am writing...lyrics with more music and painting than before' (Griffin and Minchin 189).
Subject Galuppi (1706–85) was, after Scarlatti, one of the finest C18 Italian keyboard composers. B. first encountered his music in Venice in 1838 (Miller 78) and transcribed a popular piece (De Vane and K. *New Letters* 17). B. wrote in 1887: 'As for Galuppi, I had once in my possession two huge manuscript volumes almost exclusively made up of his "Toccata-pieces" – apparently a slighter form of the Sonata to be "touched" lightly off' (H. E. Greene *PMLA* 62 (1947) 1099). F. Torrefranca, *Rivista Musicale Italiana* 19 (1912) 135, suggests an original, but it is more probable that the work is an imagined one: see C. van den Borren *Musical Times* 64 (1923) 314–16.
Discussion There has been protracted and inconclusive discussion as to whether B. is satirizing both the speaker and Galuppi; see De Vane 219–21 and Crowell 126–9.
Style The metre is the same as Tennyson's *Locksley Hall* (1842) (see above pp. 88–99). though T. has rhyming couplets.
Publication *1855; 1863* (*Dramatic Lyrics*).

[71] Robert Browning

1
Oh Galuppi, Baldassaro, this is very sad to find!
I can hardly misconceive you; it would prove me deaf and
blind;
But although I take your meaning, 'tis with such a heavy
mind!

2
Here you come with your old music, and here's all the good it
brings.
5   What, they lived once thus at Venice where the merchants were
the kings,
Where Saint Mark's is, where the Doges used to wed the sea
with rings?

3
Ay, because the sea's the street there; and 't is arched
by... what you call
... Shylock's bridge with houses on it, where they kept the
carnival:
I was never out of England – it's as if I saw it all.

4
10   Did young people take their pleasure when the sea was warm
in May?
Balls and masks begun at midnight, burning ever to mid-day,
When they made up fresh adventures for the morrow, do you
say?

5
Was a lady such a lady, cheeks so round and lips so red, –
On her neck the small face buoyant, like a bell-flower on its
bed,
15   O'er the breast's superb abundance where a man might base
his head?

6
Well, and it was graceful of them – they'd break talk off and
afford
– She, to bite her mask's black velvet – he, to finger on his
sword,
While you sat and played Toccatas, stately at the clavichord?

6 In an annual ceremony the Doges threw a ring into the sea, thereby
wedding the city to it.
8 **Shylock's bridge** the Rialto, mentioned in Shakespeare *Merch.* 1.3.105.
18 **clavichord** a keyboard instrument in which the strings are struck by
hammers (rather than plucked as they are in the more powerful and sonorous
harpsichord).

7

What? Those lesser thirds so plaintive, sixths diminished, sigh
   on sigh,
20   Told them something? Those suspensions, those solutions
   'Must we die?'
Those commiserating sevenths – 'Life might last! we can but
   try!'

8

'Were you happy?' – 'Yes.' – 'And are you still as happy? –
   'Yes, And you?'
– 'Then, more kisses!' – 'Did *I* stop them, when a million
   seemed so few?'
Hark, the dominant's persistence till it must be answered to!

9

25   So, an octave struck the answer. Oh, they praised you, I dare
   say!
'Brave Galuppi! that was music! good alike at grave and gay!
I can always leave off talking when I hear a master play!'

10

Then they left you for their pleasure: till in due time, one by
   one.
Some with lives that came to nothing, some with deeds as well
   undone,
30   Death stepped tacitly and took them where they never see the
   sun.

11

But when I sit down to reason, think to take my stand nor
   swerve,
While I triumph o'er a secret wrung from nature's close
   reserve,
In you come with your cold music till I creep through every
   nerve.

19 lesser thirds minor thirds.   **sixths diminished** precise meaning obscure; Crowell 127 suggests they possess a semitone less than minor sixths.
20 suspensions . . . die? in a suspension a note from a chord is retained in the chord that follows it. If it produces a discord it has to be resolved (the solution) by a change in the second chord. The dynamics of music reproduces the dynamics of life.
21 sevenths perhaps dominant sevenths, a discord often used immediately before a perfect cadence.
24 the dominant's persistence the fifth note of the scale of any key, symbolising thoughts of mortality (Crowell 128).
25 an octave after the uncertainties of the dominant, the octave provides the resolution and symbolizes death and finality.

12

Yes, you, like a ghostly cricket, creaking where a house was
 burned:
35 'Dust and ashes, dead and done with, Venice spent what Venice
 earned.
The soul, doubtless, is immortal – where a soul can be
 discerned.

13

'Yours for instance: you know physics, something of geology,
Mathematics are your pastime; souls shall rise in their degree;
Butterflies may dread extinction, – you'll not die, it cannot be!

14

40 'As for Venice and her people, merely born to bloom and drop,
Here on earth they bore their fruitage, mirth and folly were the
 crop:
What of soul was left, I wonder, when the kissing had to stop?

15

'Dust and ashes!' So you creak it, and I want the heart to
 scold.
Dear dead women, with such hair, too – what's become of all
 the gold
45 Used to hang and brush their bosoms? I feel chilly and grown
 old.

39 Ironical: the speaker is as transient as the butterfly, the butterfly is
traditionally an emblem of the soul.
40–3 The decline of Venice into a city of masques was a commonplace, but
B. may have been thinking of Ruskin's *The Stones of Venice* 3 (1853), which
was subtitled 'The Fall'.

72 How it Strikes a Contemporary

Date and theme De Vane 236–7 suggests that it was written Dec. 1851–Jan.
1852 in Paris (see headnote to *Childe Roland*), and that *Lear* 5.3.8–19
influenced him: 'And take upon's the mystery of things, | As if we were
God's spies...' etc. B. also had in mind the discussion of the nature of the
poet in his essay on Shelley, finished by Dec. 1851. B. in a letter to Ruskin
of 10 Dec. 1855 criticized the traditional view of the poet 'enchanting stocks
and stones...standing up and being worshipped, – all nonsense and
impossible dreaming. A poet's affair is with God, to whom he is accountable,
and of whom is his reward...,(Ruskin *Works* 36 p. xxxvi). Miller 31 shows that
B. worked on an abridgement of *Le Gil Blas de la Jeunesse*, with Charles le
Roy and A. Loradoux, in which there is a corregidor of Valladolid, and a
housekeeper called Jacinte.
Publication *1855*.

I only knew one poet in my life:
And this, or something like it, was his way.

You saw go up and down Valladolid,
A man of mark, to know next time you saw.
His very serviceable suit of black
Was courtly once and conscientious still,
And many might have worn it, though none did:
The cloak, that somewhat shone and showed the threads,
Had purpose, and the ruff, significance.
He walked and tapped the pavement with his cane,
Scenting the world, looking it full in face,
An old dog, bald and blindish, at his heels.
They turned up, now, the alley by the church,
That leads nowhither; now, they breathed themselves
On the main promenade just at the wrong time:
You'd come upon his scrutinizing hat,
Making a peaked shade blacker than itself
Against the single window spared some house
Intact yet with its mouldered Moorish work, –
Or else surprise the ferrel of his stick
Trying the mortar's temper 'tween the chinks
Of some new shop a-building, French and fine.
He stood and watched the cobbler at his trade,
The man who slices lemons into drink,
The coffee-roaster's brazier, and the boys
That volunteer to help him turn its winch.
He glanced o'er books on stalls with half an eye,
And fly-leaf ballads on the vendor's string,
And broad-edge bold-print posters by the wall.
He took such cognizance of men and things,
If any beat a horse, you felt he saw;
If any cursed a woman, he took note;
Yet stared at nobody, – you stared at him,
And found, less to your pleasure than surprise,
He seemed to know you and expect as much.
So, next time that a neighbour's tongue was loosed,
It marked the shameful and notorious fact,
We had among us, not so much a spy,
As a recording chief-inquisitor,
The town's true master if the town but knew!
We merely kept a governor for form,
While this man walked about and took account

---

40 Cf. Shelley 'Poets are the unacknowledged legislators of the world' (the closing words of *A Defence of Poetry*).

Of all thought, said and acted, then went home,
And wrote it fully to our Lord the King

45   Who has an itch to know things, he knows why,
And reads them in his bedroom of a night.
Oh, you might smile! there wanted not a touch,
A tang of... well, it was not wholly ease
As back into your mind the man's look came.

50   Stricken in years a little, – such a brow
His eyes had to live under! – clear as flint
On either side the formidable nose
Curved, cut and coloured like an eagle's claw.
Had he to do with A.'s surprising fate?

55   When altogether old B. disappeared
And young C. got his mistress, – was't our friend,
His letter to the King, that did it all?
What paid the bloodless man for so much pains?
Our Lord the King has favourites manifold,

60   And shifts his ministry some once a month;
Our city gets new governors at whiles, –
But never word or sign, that I could hear,
Notified to this man about the streets
The King's approval of those letters conned

65   The last thing duly at the dead of night.
Did the man love his office? Frowned our Lord,
Exhorting when none heard – 'Beseech me not!
Too far above my people, – beneath me!
I set the watch, – how should the people know?

70   Forget them, keep me all the more in mind!'
Was some such understanding 'twixt the two?

I found no truth in one report at least –
That if you tracked him to his home, down lanes
Beyond the Jewry; and as clean to pace,

75   You found he ate his supper in a room
Blazing with lights, four Titians on the wall,
And twenty naked girls to change his plate!
Poor man, he lived another kind of life
In that new stuccoed third house by the bridge,

80   Fresh-painted, rather smart than otherwise!

45 he] He *1855*. Other capitalizations in lines 46, 68 and 70; they tended to invite an allegorical reading and an identification with the Deity.
76 Titian Tiziano Vecelli (*c.* 1487–1576). An Italian artist much prized by collectors (such as Charles V of Spain) who were able to enjoy eroticism presented under the cover of improving allegory. B. was probably most familiar with the *Venus of Urbino* in this genre (Uffizi).

The whole street might o'erlook him as he sat,
Leg crossing leg, one foot on the dog's back,
Playing a decent cribbage with his maid
(Jacynth, you're sure her name was) o'er the cheese
85 And fruit, three red halves of starved winter-pears,
Or treat of radishes in April. Nine,
Ten, struck the church clock, straight to bed went he.

My father, like the man of sense he was,
Would point him out to me a dozen times;
90 ''St – 'St,' he'd whisper, 'the Corregidor!'
I had been used to think that personage
Was one with lacquered breeches, lustrous belt,
And feathers like a forest in his hat,
Who blew a trumpet and proclaimed the news,
95 Announced the bull-fights, gave each church its turn,
And memorized the miracle in vogue!
He had a great observance from us boys;
We were in error; that was not the man.

I'd like now, yet had haply been afraid,
100 To have just looked, when this man came to die,
And seen who lined the clean gay garret-sides
And stood about the neat low truckle-bed,
With the heavenly manner of relieving guard.
Here had been, mark, the general-in-chief,
105 Through a whole campaign of the world's life and death,
Doing the King's work all the dim day long,
In his old coat and up to knees in mud,
Smoked like a herring, dining on a crust, –
And, now the day was won, relieved at once!
110 Nor further show or need for that old coat,
You are sure, for one thing! Bless us, all the while
How sprucely we are dressed out, you and I!
A second, and the angels alter that.
Well, I could never write a verse, – could you?
115 Let's to the Prado and make the most of time.

90 ''St – 'St' Sh!   **Corregidor** chief magistrate in a Spanish town.
115 Prado fashionable parade, or perhaps the Art Gallery in Madrid.

73 Two in the Campagna

Date Probably written in May 1854, when the Brownings were in Rome.
The campagna is a vast area of wild countryside outside Rome, scattered with
tombs and monuments.
Publication *1855; 1863 (Dramatic Lyrics).*

[73] Robert Browning

1

I wonder do you feel to-day
    As I have felt since, hand in hand,
We sat down on the grass, to stray
    In spirit better through the land,
5   This morn of Rome and May?

2

For me, I touched a thought, I know,
    Has tantalized me many times,
(Like turns of thread the spiders throw
    Mocking across our path) for rhymes
10   To catch at and let go.

3

Help me to hold it! First it left
    The yellowing fennel, run to seed
There, branching from the brickwork's cleft,
    Some old tomb's ruin: yonder weed
15   Took up the floating weft,

4

Where one small orange cup amassed
    Five beetles, – blind and green they grope
Among the honey-meal: and last,
    Everywhere on the grassy slope
20   I traced it. Hold it fast!

5

The champaign with its endless fleece
    Of feathery grasses everywhere!
Silence and passion, joy and peace,
    An everlasting wash of air –
25   Rome's ghost since her decease.

6

Such life here, through such lengths of hours,
    Such miracles performed in play,
Such primal naked forms of flowers,
    Such letting nature have her way
30   While heaven looks from its towers!

3–4 Miller 192–3 cites an incident on a campagna excursion: 'On one…occasion…the guests suggested taking a walk together to some distant spot. Elizabeth was too languid to join them, and at once B. offered to remain behind to keep her company…' This helps to make sense of 'better' i.e. better than people who walk through the landscape. De Vane 269 and Irvine and Honan 319 are reluctant to accept close biographical identification.

7

How say you? Let us, O my dove,
Let us be unashamed of soul,
As earth lies bare to heaven above!
How is it under our control
35   To love or not to love?

8

I would that you were all to me,
You that are just so much, no more.
Nor yours nor mine, nor slave nor free!
Where does the fault lie? What the core
40   O' the wound, since wound must be?

9

I would I could adopt your will,
See with your eyes, and set my heart
Beating by yours, and drink my fill
At your soul's springs, – your part my part
45   In life, for good and ill.

10

No. I yearn upward, touch you close,
Then stand away. I kiss your cheek,
Catch your soul's warmth, – I pluck the rose
And love it more than tongue can speak –
50   Then the good minute goes.

11

Already how am I so far
Out of that minute? Must I go
Still like the thistle-ball, no bar,
Onward, whenever light winds blow,
55   Fixed by no friendly star?

12

Just when I seemed about to learn!
Where is the thread now? Off again!
The old trick! Only I discern –
Infinite passion, and the pain
60   Of finite hearts that yearn.

36–8 'I wish you were everything to me, you that are incompletely committed: that are neither free nor a slave to love.'
53 no bar with no opposition.

74 Misconceptions

Date Unknown.
This poem is included as an interesting example of a stressed poetry that ante-dates Hopkins's theory and practice of 'sprung-rhythm'. The first five lines of each stanza have three stresses, and the last two have four. There is a highly complex rhythmic pattern which is repeated without variation in both stanzas.
Publication *1855; 1863 (Dramatic Lyrics).*

I

    This is a spray the bird clung to,
      Making it blossom with pleasure,
    Ere the high tree-top she sprung to,
      Fit for her nest and her treasure.
5   Oh, what a hope beyond measure
Was the poor spray's, which the flying feet hung to, –
So to be singled out, built in, and sung to!

2

    This is a heart the Queen leant on,
      Thrilled in a minute erratic,
10   Ere the true bosom she bent on,
      Meet for love's regal dalmatic.
      Oh, what a fancy ecstatic
Was the poor heart's, ere the wanderer went on –
Love to be saved for it, proffered to, spent on!

9 Ambiguous: it is not clear whether the heart that is thrilled is the Queen's or her lover's.
11 dalmatic robe worn by monarchs at their coronation.

75 One Word More
To E.B.B.

Date and theme There is a holograph of the poem in the Pierpont Morgan Library dated 22 Sept. 1855. The Brownings arrived in London on 12 July 1855 to deliver *Men and Women* to the publisher. This poem was written in the Autumn – possibly at 13 Dorset Street – and served as an epilogue and dedication for *Men and Women*. The poem's theme is of the artist trying to be more himself in an unfamiliar medium, and the form (trochaic pentameter, unrhymed) is unique to this poem.
Discussion De Vane 275–8.
Publication *1855* (with 20 sections); *1863* (with 19 sections).

Title *A Last Word: to E.B.B.* in the manuscript, perhaps unfortunate in suggesting contention (cf. *A Woman's Last Word*). *One Word More* has a private relevance: Elizabeth Barrett to B. 31 Aug. 1845: 'Therefore we must leave this subject – and I must trust you to leave it without one word more...' (Kintner *Letters* 1. 179). The subject was B.'s love.

1

There they are, my fifty men and women
Naming me the fifty poems finished!
Take them, Love, the book and me together:
Where the heart lies, let the brain lie also.

2

5   Rafael made a century of sonnets,
Made and wrote them in a certain volume
Dinted with the silver-pointed pencil
Else he only used to draw Madonnas:
These, the world might view – but one, the volume.
10   Who that one, you ask? Your heart instructs you.
Did she live and love it all her life-time?
Did she drop, his lady of the sonnets,
Die, and let it drop beside her pillow
Where it lay in place of Rafael's glory,
15   Rafael's cheek so duteous and so loving –
Cheek, the world was wont to hail a painter's,
Rafael's cheek, her love had turned a poet's?

3

You and I would rather read that volume,
(Taken to his beating bosom by it)
20   Lean and list the bosom-beats of Rafael,
Would we not? than wonder at Madonnas –
Her, San Sisto names, and Her, Foligno,
Her, that visits Florence in a vision,
Her, that's left with lilies in the Louvre –
25   Seen by us and all the world in circle.

5 Baldinucci 4.26 says that Guido Reni (1575–1642) owned Raphael's sonnets.

7 silver-pointed pencil a favourite C15 and C16 technique. The drawing is made with silver wire on paper coated with Chinese white (or a tint). Raphael has rested his drawing paper on the volume of poetry, which takes the impression of the pencil.

20 list listen to and enumerate.

22–4 Raphael's mistress may be portrayed in *La Fornarina* (Rome); the **San Sisto** Virgin is in Dresden, the **Foligno** is in the Vatican; she **that visits Florence in a vision** is the *Madonna del Granduca* (Pitti, Florence) (Berenson pl. 316); she **in the Louvre** is *La Belle Jardinière* (Berenson pl. 318).

25 The discontent evinced by B. with the public aspect of an artist shown in produced work, and the preference for the private life which is assumed to be the authentic fount of creativity is in a Romantic tradition.

4

You and I will never read that volume.
Guido Reni, like his own eye's apple
Guarded long the treasure-book and loved it.
Guido Reni dying, all Bologna
30 Cried, and the world cried too, 'Ours, the treasure!'
Suddenly, as rare things will, it vanished.

5

Dante once prepared to paint an angel:
Whom to please? You whisper 'Beatrice.'
While he mused and traced it and retraced it,
35 (Peradventure with a pen corroded
Still by drops of that hot ink he dipped for,
When, his left-hand i' the hair o' the wicked,
Back he held the brow and pricked its stigma,
Bit into the live man's flesh for parchment,
40 Loosed him, laughed to see the writing rankle,
Let the wretch go festering through Florence) –
Dante, who loved well because he hated,
Hated wickedness that hinders loving,
Dante standing, studying his angel, –
45 In there broke the folk of his Inferno.
Says he – 'Certain people of importance'
(Such he gave his daily dreadful line to)
'Entered and would seize, forsooth, the poet.'
Says the poet – 'Then I stopped my painting.'

6

50 You and I would rather see that angel,
Painted by the tenderness of Dante,
Would we not? – than read a fresh Inferno.

---

32 See *La Vita Nuova* Ch. 35; 'On that day which fulfilled the year since my
lady had been made of the citizens of eternal life, remembering me of her as
I sat alone, I betook myself to draw the resemblance of an angel upon
certain tablets. And while I did thus, chancing to turn my head, I perceived
that some were standing beside me to whom I should have given courteous
welcome...' (tr. Rossetti). B. engages in poetic licence here: the *Divina
Commedia* was not begun until ten years later. Rossetti's painting of this
incident is in the Ashmolean Museum, Oxford.
37 See *Inferno* 32.97–104: '*Allor lo presi per la cuticagna...*' 'At that I
grasped the scruff behind his head...'
46 '**Certain people of importance**' The exact phrase in Italian is '*uomi a' quali
si convenia di fare onore*'. It provides the title for *Parleyings With Certain
People of Importance...* (1887).
48 There is no line that corresponds to this in *La Vita Nuova*.

7

You and I will never see that picture.
While he mused on love and Beatrice,
55 While he softened o'er his outlined angel,
In they broke, those 'people of importance:'
We and Bice bear the loss for ever.

8

What of Rafael's sonnets. Dante's picture?
This: no artist lives and loves, that longs not
60 Once, and only once, and for one only,
(Ah, the prize!) to find his love a language
Fit and fair and simple and sufficient –
Using nature that's an art to others,
Not, this one time, art that's turned his nature.
65 Ay, of all the artists living, loving,
None but would forego his proper dowry, –
Does he paint? he fain would write a poem, –
Does he write? he fain would paint a picture,
Put to proof art alien to the artist's,
70 Once, and only once, and for one only,
So to be the man and leave the artist,
Save the man's joy, miss the artist's sorrow.

9

Wherefore? Heaven's gift takes earth's abatement!
He who smites the rock and spreads the water,
75 Bidding drink and live a crowd beneath him,
Even he, the minute makes immortal,
Proves, perchance, but mortal in the minute,
Desecrates, belike, the deed in doing.
While he smites, how can he but remember,
80 So he smote before, in such a peril,
When they stood and mocked – "Shall smiting help us?'
When they drank and sneered – 'A stroke is easy!'
When they wiped their mouths and went their journey,
Throwing him for thanks – 'But drought was pleasant.'

57 Bice Beatrice.
63–4 Cf. Shakespeare *Sonnet* 111, which discusses the dominance of art over
personality. B. thought that an artistic technique in unskilled hands was
closer to 'nature'.
73 'the artist's inspiration is lessened by human responses to it'.
74–5 Cf. *Exod.* 17.1–7: '...thou shalt smite the rock, and there shall come
water out of it, that the people may drink. And Moses did so in the sight of
the elders of Israel.' Also *Num.* 20.1–13. B. uses Moses as a symbol of the
artist, with the Israelites as the sceptical audience.

85   Thus old memories mar the actual triumph;
        Thus the doing savours of disrelish;
        Thus achievement lacks a gracious somewhat;
        O'er-importuned brows becloud the mandate,
        Carelessness or consciousness – the gesture.
90   For he bears an ancient wrong about him,
        Sees and knows again those phalanxed faces,
        Hears, yet one time more, the 'customed prelude –
        'How shouldst thou, of all men, smite, and save us?'
        Guesses what is like to prove the sequel –
95   'Egypt's flesh-pots – nay, the drought was better.'

                              10
        Oh, the crowd must have emphatic warrant!
        Theirs, the Sinai-forehead's cloven brilliance,
        Right-arm's rod-sweep, tongue's imperial fiat.
        Never dares the man put off the prophet.

                              11
100   Did he love one face from out the thousands,
        (Were she Jethro's daughter, white and wifely,
        Were she but the Aethiopian bondslave,)
        He would envy yon dumb patient camel,
        Keeping a reserve of scanty water
105   Meant to save his own life in the desert;
        Ready in the desert to deliver
        (Kneeling down to let his breast be opened)
        Hoard and life together for his mistress.

                              12
        I shall never, in the years remaining,
110   Paint you pictures, no, nor carve you statues,
        Make you music that should all-express me;
        So it seems: I stand on my attainment.

88 when the artist-prophet performs his miracle it is with a sense of strain.
95 See *Exod.* 16.3: 'And the children of Israel said unto them, Would to God we had died by the hand of the Lord in the land of Egypt, when we sat by the flesh pots.'
96–99 Discussed W. H. French *MLN* 61 (1946) 188. See *Exod.* 33. 16–23; 34. 29–35: 'And the children of Israel saw the face of Moses, that the skin of Moses' face shone:...'
97 cloven brilliance the Vulgate has it that Moses' face was '*cormita*', from Hebraic 'shone', which derived from a figurative sense of 'horn'.
101 Jethro's daughter Zipporah, Moses' wife (*Exod.* 2.21; 3.1).
102 Aethiopian bondslave another of Moses' wives (*Num.* 12.1).

This of verse alone, one life allows me;
Verse and nothing else have I to give you.
115 Other heights in other lives, God willing:
All the gifts from all the heights, your own, Love!

13

Yet a semblance of resource avails us –
Shade so finely touched, love's sense must seize it.
Take these lines, look lovingly and nearly,
120 Lines I write the first time and the last time.
He who works in fresco, steals a hair-brush,
Curbs the liberal hand, subservient proudly,
Cramps his spirit, crowds its all in little,
Makes a strange art of an art familiar,
125 Fills his lady's missal-marge with flowerets.
He who blows through bronze, may breath through silver,
Fitly serenade a slumbrous princess.
He who writes, may write for once as I do.

14

Love, you saw me gather men and women,
130 Live or dead or fashioned by my fancy,
Enter each and all, and use their service,
Speak from every mouth, – the speech, a poem.
Hardly shall I tell my joys and sorrows,
Hopes and fears, belief and disbelieving:
135 I am mine and yours – the rest be all men's,
Karshish, Cleon, Norbert and the fifty.
Let me speak this once in my true person,
Not as Lippo, Roland or Andrea,
Though the fruit of speech be just this sentence:
140 Pray you, look on these my men and women,
Take and keep my fifty poems finished;
Where my heart lies, let my brain lie also!
Poor the speech; be how I speak, for all things.

15

Not but that you know me! Lo, the moon's self!
145 Here in London, yonder late in Florence,
Still we find her face, the thrice-transfigured.

136 Karshish] Karshook *1855*. B. had written *Ben Karshook's Wisdom* in
1854, published in *The Keepsake* for 1856. As B. explained in a letter to
Furnivall (Hood *Letters* 196), it was a mistake – though not corrected until
the Tauchnitz edn. (*1872*).   **Cleon, Norbert** other characters in *Men and
Women*.
146 thrice-transfigured going through the stages of being new, waxing and
waning.

[75] Robert Browning

Curving on a sky imbrued with colour,
Drifted over Fiesole by twilight,
Came she, our new crescent of a hair's-breadth.
150 Full she flared it, lamping Samminiato,
Rounder 'twixt the cypresses and rounder,
Perfect till the nightingales applauded.
Now, a piece of her old self, impoverished,
Hard to greet, she traverses the houseroofs,
155 Hurries with unhandsome thrift of silver,
Goes dispiritedly, glad to finish.

16

What, there's nothing in the moon noteworthy?
Nay: for if that moon could love a mortal,
Use, to charm him (so to fit a fancy),
160 All her magic ('t is the old sweet mythos)
She would turn a new side to her mortal,
Side unseen of herdsman, huntsman, steersman –
Blank to Zoroaster on his terrace,
Blind to Galileo on his turret,
165 Dumb to Homer, dumb to Keats – him, even!
Think, the wonder of the moonstruck mortal –
When she turns round, comes again in heaven,
Opens out anew for worse or better!
Proves she like some portent of an iceberg
170 Swimming full upon the ship it founders,
Hungry with huge teeth of splintered crystals?

150 Samminiato San Miniato al Monte – a church on a hill S.E. of Florence.
160 mythos the myth of Endymion, loved by the moon; cf. Keats *Endymion* (1818).
161 B. B. Trawick suggests *N & Q* 206 (1959) 448 that B. may have been influenced, in the symbolism of the unknown face of the moon, by Clough's *On Latmos*. Plutarch *De facie in orbe lunae* 29 discusses the parts of the moon turned toward heaven (the Elysian plain) and toward earth (the plain of Persephone Antichthon); 30 describes the passage of blest souls to 'second death' (*Moralia* (Loeb 1957) 12.205–21).
163 Zoroaster Persian founder of the Magian religion (*c*. C6 B.C.), regarded by the ancients as the originator of Chaldaean astronomy.
164 Galileo Fiesole was associated with the astronomer; cf. *Andrea del Sarto* (above p. 246) line 15, and *Paradise Lost* 1.287–90.
165 Homer B. probably knew of Homer's *Hymn to the Moon* through Shelley's translation.   **Keats – him, even**! because Keats's invocation to the Moon in *Endymion* 3.40–71, though sensitive, is distanced.

Proves she as the paved work of a sapphire
Seen by Moses when he climbed the mountain?
Moses, Aaron, Nadab and Abihu
175 Climbed and saw the very God, the Highest,
Stand upon the paved work of a sapphire.
Like the bodied heaven in his clearness
Shone the stone, the sapphire of that paved work,
When they ate and drank and saw God also!

17

180 What were seen? None knows, none ever shall know.
Only this is sure – the sight were other,
Not the moon's same side, born late in Florence,
Dying now impoverished here in London.
God be thanked, the meanest of his creatures
185 Boasts two soul-sides, one to face the world with,
One to show a woman when he loves her!

18

This I say of me, but think of you, Love!
This to you – yourself my moon of poets!
Ah, but that's the world's side, there's the wonder,
190 Thus they see you, praise you, think they know you!
There, in turn I stand with them and praise you –
Out of my own self, I dare to phrase it.
But the best is when I glide from out them,
Cross a step or two of dubious twilight,
195 Come out on the other side, the novel
Silent silver lights and darks undreamed of,
Where I hush and bless myself with silence.

19

Oh, their Rafael of the dear Madonnas,
Oh, their Dante of the dread Inferno,
200 Wrote one song – and in my brain I sing it,
Drew one angel – borne, see, on my bosom!

R.B.

172–9 See *Exod.* 24.9–11: 'Then went up Moses, and Aaron, Nadab, and Abihu, and seventy of the elders of Israel. And they saw the God of Israel: and there was under his feet as it were a paved work of sapphire stone, and as it were the body of heaven in his clearness. And upon the nobles of the children of Israel he laid not his hand: also, they saw God, and did eat and drink.'

183 impoverished echoes the financial imagery in line 155.

192 Out of my own self as a member of the public.

194 dubious twilight Cf. B.'s essay on Tasso *FQR* 29 (1842) 467, in which he calls the unknown tracts of Tasso's life 'dubious twilight'. He was probably led to the phrase by reading Chatterton's etymology of 'gloomed': '"Glummong," in the Saxon signifies twilight, a dark or dubious light' (474).

76 Caliban Upon Setebos; Or, Natural Theology in the Island

'Thou thoughtest that I was altogether such a one as thyself'

Date and context 1859–64; C. R. Tracy *SP* 35 (1938) 487–99 argues for 1859–60, when Darwin's *The Origin of Species* had just been published, and B. met the American Unitarian Theodore Parker, who was writing *A Bumblebee's Thoughts on the Plan and Purpose of the Universe.* However, possible background might be the Huxley–Wilberforce debate of 1860 on the missing link and man's place in the Universe.

Source Caliban is a primitive being, taken from Shakespeare's *The Tempest,* who wants to find a God: 2.2.121; 140–52; 5.1. 296. His mother Sycorax worshipped Setebos: 1.2.373. B.'s Caliban speculates on the nature of God in a crudely rational manner: this is in the spirit of Shakespeare's monster who has learnt man's language but not the finer graces of humanity.

Discussion The poem has proved one of the most elusive for both B.'s contemporaries and modern critics. *The Athenaeum* interpreted it as a satire on orthodox theology; E. Paxton Hood in *The Eclectic Review* n.s. 7 (1864) 385–9 as a satire on anthropormorphic theology, and others as an attack on Calvinism and Predestination. L. Perrine argues that it might be both a satire and a sympathetic presentation of a primitive mind, *VP* 2 (1964) 124–7.

B., writing to Furnivall (25 Apr. 1884), said: 'I don't see that, because a clown's conception of the laws of the Heavenly bodies is grotesque and impossible, that of Newton must be necessarily as absurd...' (Hood *Letters* 228). This suggests that B. did not consider Caliban's method of thought a type for all mankind: progress leads to better knowledge, so that man is able to see the connection between the justice and the love of God, between the abstract God and God in human form. But at the same time, Caliban has taken the necessary first step in seeking God.

Natural theology – the induction of God from nature – is the science of the sophisticated theologian. Butler's *Analogy* (1736), Paley's *Natural Theology* (1802) and the Bridgewater Treatises (1833–1840) attempted to provide rational proofs for the deity, bypassing intuition and revelation. B. is probably satirizing its methods. See M. Timko *Criticism* 7 (1965) 141–150. Drew 151–52 draws comparisons with Hume's *Natural History of Religion* (1757) and *Dialogues Concerning Natural Religion* (1779), which criticized men who conceived of God in their own limited images.

See also E. K. Brown *MLN* 66 (1951) 392–5; Park Honan *TSL* 9 (1964) 87–98; De Vane 299–302; Crowell 220–37.

Publication 1864 (*Dramatis Personae*).

['Will sprawl, now that the heat of day is best,
Flat on his belly in the pit's much mire,
With elbows wide, fists clenched to prop his chin.

Epigraph *Ps.* 50.21.

And, while he kicks both feet in the cool slush,
5   And feels about his spine small eft-things course,
Run in and out each arm, and make him laugh:
And while above his head a pompion-plant,
Coating the cave-top as a brow its eye,
Creeps down to touch and tickle hair and beard,
10   And now a flower drops with a bee inside,
And now a fruit to snap at, catch and crunch, –
He looks out o'er yon sea which sunbeams cross
And recross till they weave a spider-web
(Meshes of fire, some great fish breaks at times)
15   And talks to his own self, howe'er he please,
Touching that other, whom his dam called God.
Because to talk about Him, vexes – ha,
Could He but know! and time to vex is now,
When talk is safer than in winter-time.
20   Moreover Prosper and Miranda sleep
In confidence he drudges at their task,
And it is good to cheat the pair, and gibe,
Letting the rank tongue blossom into speech.]

Setebos, Setebos, and Setebos!
25   'Thinketh, He dwelleth i' the cold o' the moon.

'Thinketh He made it, with the sun to match,
But not the stars; the stars came otherwise;
Only made clouds, winds, meteors, such as that:
Also this isle, what lives and grows thereon,
30   And snaky sea which rounds and ends the same.

'Thinketh, it came of being ill at ease:
He hated that He cannot change His cold,
Nor cure its ache. 'Hath spied an icy fish
That longed to 'scape the rock-stream where she lived,
35   And thaw herself within the lukewarm brine
O' the lazy sea her stream thrusts far amid,
A crystal spike 'twixt two warm walls of wave;
Only, she ever sickened, found repulse
At the other kind of water, not her life,
40   (Green-dense and dim-delicious, bred o' the sun)
Flounced back from bliss she was not born to breathe,

7 pompion pumpkin.
16 his dam C.'s mother Sycorax: Shakespeare *Tempest* 1.2. 263–281. 1.2. 375
'my dam's god, Setebos.'
25–6 Shakespeare's Caliban knows the names from Prospero: 'teach me how |
To name the bigger light, and how the less' *Tempest* 1.2.336–7.

And in her old bounds buried her despair,
Hating and loving warmth alike: so He.

'Thinketh, He made thereat the sun, this isle,
45 Trees and the fowls here, beast and creeping thing.
Yon otter, sleek-wet, black, lithe as a leech;
Yon auk, one fire-eye in a ball of foam,
That floats and feeds; a certain badger brown
He hath watched hunt with that slant white-wedge eye
50 By moonlight; and the pie with the long tongue
That pricks deep into oakwarts for a worm,
And says a plain word when she finds her prize,
But will not eat the ants; the ants themselves
That build a wall of seeds and settled stalks
55 About their hole – He made all these and more,
Made all we see, and us, in spite: how else?
He could not, Himself, make a second self
To be His mate; as well have made Himself:
He would not make what he mislikes or slights,
60 An eyesore to Him, or not worth His pains:
But did, in envy, listlessness or sport,
Make what Himself would fain, in a manner, be, –
Weaker in most points, stronger in a few,
Worthy, and yet mere playthings all the while,
65 Things He admires and mocks too, – that is it.
Because, so brave, so better though they be,
It nothing skills if He begin to plague.
Look now, I melt a gourd-fruit into mash,
Add honeycomb and pods, I have perceived,
70 Which bite like finches when they bill and kiss, –
Then, when froth rises bladdery, drink up all,
Quick, quick, till maggots scamper through my brain;
Last, throw me on my back i' the seeded thyme,
And wanton, wishing I were born a bird.
75 Put case, unable to be what I wish,
I yet could make a live bird out of clay:
Would not I take clay, pinch my Caliban
Able to fly? – for, there, see, he hath wings,
And great comb like the hoopoe's to admire,

45–55 Shakespeare's Caliban knows the natural life of the island very closely:
ibid. 2.2.166–72.
47 **auk** northern sea-bird.
50 **pie** woodpie or woodpecker.
51 **oakwarts** oak gall, sometimes oak-apple.
76 C. here develops a Promethean analogue of creation from clay.
79 **hoopoe** of family *upupidae*, with a large erectile crest.

80 And there, a sting to do his foes offence,
  There, and I will that he begin to live,
  Fly to yon rock top, nip me off the horns
  Of grigs high up that make the merry din,
  Saucy through their veined wings, and mind me not.
85 In which feat, if his leg snapped, brittle clay,
  And he lay stupid-like, – why, I should laugh;
  And if he, spying me, should fall to weep,
  Beseech me to be good, repair his wrong,
  Bid his poor leg smart less or grow again, –
90 Well, as the chance were, this might take or else
  Not take my fancy: I might hear his cry,
  And give the mankin three sound legs for one,
  Or pluck the other off, leave him like an egg,
  And lessoned he was mine and merely clay,
95 Were this no pleasure, lying in the thyme,
  Drinking the mash, with brain become alive,
  Making and marring clay at will? So He.

  'Thinketh, such shows nor right nor wrong in Him,
  Nor kind, nor cruel: He is strong and Lord.
100 'Am strong myself compared to yonder crabs
  That march now from the mountain to the sea,
  'Let twenty pass, and stone the twenty-first,
  Loving not, hating not, just choosing so.
  'Say, the first straggler that boasts purple spots
105 Shall join the file, one pincer twisted off;
  'Say, this bruised fellow shall receive a worm,
  And two worms he whose nippers end in red;
  As it likes me each time, I do: so He.

  Well then, 'supposeth He is good i' the main,
110 Placable if His mind and ways were guessed,
  But rougher than His handiwork, be sure!
  Oh, He hath made things worthier than Himself,
  And envieth that, so helped, such things do more
  Than He who made them! What consoles but this?
115 That they, unless through Him, do nought at all,
  And must submit: what other use in things?
  'Hath cut a pipe of pithless elder-joint
  That, blown through, gives exact the scream o' the jay
  When from her wing you twitch the feathers blue:
120 Sound this, and little birds that hate the jay

83 grigs grasshoppers or crickets.
102–3 An argument resembling Calvinist doctrines of Election; incidental rather than the central key to the poem.

Flock within stone's throw, glad their foe is hurt:
Put case such pipe could prattle and boast forsooth
'I catch the birds, I am the crafty thing,
I make the cry my maker cannot make
125 With his great round mouth; he must blow through mine!'
Would not I smash it with my foot? So He.

But wherefore rough, why cold and ill at ease?
Aha, that is a question! Ask, for that,
What knows, – the something over Setebos
130 That made Him, or He, may be, found and fought,
Worsted, drove off and did to nothing, perchance.
There may be something quiet o'er His head,
Out of His reach, that feels nor joy nor grief,
Since both derive from weakness in some way.
135 I joy because the quails come; would not joy
Could I bring quails here when I have a mind:
This Quiet, all it hath a mind to, doth.
'Esteemeth stars the outposts of its couch,
But never spends much thought nor care that way.
140 It may look up, work up, – the worse for those
It works on! 'Careth but for Setebos
The many-handed as a cuttle-fish,
Who, making Himself feared through what He does,
Looks up, first, and perceives he cannot soar
145 To what is quiet and hath happy life;
Next looks down here, and out of very spite
Makes this a bauble-world to ape yon real,
These good things to match those as hips do grapes.
'T is solace making baubles, ay, and sport.
150 Himself peeped late, eyed Prosper at his books
Careless and lofty, lord now of the isle:
Vexed, 'stitched a book of broad leaves, arrow-shaped,
Wrote thereon, he knows what, prodigious words;
Has peeled a wand and called it by a name;
155 Weareth at whiles for an enchanter's robe
The eyed skin of a supple ocelot;
And hath an ounce sleeker than youngling mole,
A four-legged serpent he makes cower and couch,
Now snarl, now hold its breath and mind his eye,
160 And saith she is Miranda and my wife:

137 **This Quiet** an invention of B.'s of a power above and beyond Setebos
that is apprehended intuitively rather than inductively. The relationship
between C. and Prospero gives C. an image of that between Setebos and the
Quiet.
156 **ocelot** South American jaguar.

'Keeps for his Ariel a tall pouch-bill crane
He bids go wade for fish and straight disgorge;
Also a sea-beast, lumpish, which he snared,
Blinded the eyes of, and brought somewhat tame,
165 And split its toe-webs, and now pens the drudge
In a hole o' the rock and calls him Caliban;
A bitter heart that bides its time and bites.
'Plays thus at being Prosper in a way,
Taketh his mirth with make-believes: so He.

170 His dam held that the Quiet made all things
Which Setebos vexed only: 'holds not so.
Who made them weak, meant weakness He might vex.
Had He meant other, while His hand was in,
Why not make horny eyes no thorn could prick,
175 Or plate my scalp with bone against the snow,
Or overscale my flesh 'neath joint and joint,
Like an orc's armour? Ay, – so spoil His sport!
He is the One now: only He doth all.

'Saith, He may like, perchance, what profits Him.
180 Ay, himself loves what does him good; but why?
'Gets good no otherwise. This blinded beast
Loves whoso places flesh-meat on his nose,
But, had he eyes, would want no help, but hate
Or love, just as it liked him: He hath eyes.
185 Also it pleaseth Setebos to work,
Use all His hands, and exercise much craft,
By no means for the love of what is worked.
'Tasteth, himself, no finer good i' the world
When all goes right, in this safe summer-time,
190 And he wants little, hungers, aches not much,
Than trying what to do with wit and strength.
'Falls to make something: 'piled yon pile of turfs,
And squared and stuck there squares of soft white chalk,
And, with a fish-tooth, scratched a moon on each,
195 And set up endwise certain spikes of tree,
And crowned the whole with a sloth's skull a-top,
Found dead i' the woods, too hard for one to kill.
No use at all i' the work, for work's sole sake;
'Shall some day knock it down again: so He.

200 'Saith He is terrible: watch His feats in proof!
One hurricane will spoil six good months' hope.

177 orc sea-monster; cf. *The Ring and the Book* 9.965: 'the snorting orc'.
192–199 A primitive view that creation is only to be justified by subsequent destruction.

He hath a spite against me, that I know,
Just as He favours Prosper, who knows why?
So it is, all the same, as well I find.
205 'Wove wattles half the winter, fenced them firm
With stone and stake to stop she-tortoises
Crawling to lay their eggs here: well, one wave,
Feeling the foot of Him upon its neck,
Gaped as a snake does, lolled out its large tongue,
210 And licked the whole labour flat: so much for spite.
'Saw a ball flame down late (yonder it lies)
Where, half an hour before, I slept i' the shade:
Often they scatter sparkles: there is force!
'Dug up a newt He may have envied once
215 And turned to stone, shut up inside a stone.
Please Him and hinder this? – What Prosper does?
Aha, if He would tell me how! Not He!
There is the sport: discover how or die!
All need not die, for of the things o' the isle
220 Some flee afar, some dive, some run up trees;
Those at His mercy, – why, they please Him most
When...when...well, never try the same way twice!
Repeat what act has pleased, He may grow wroth.
You must not know His ways, and play Him off,
225 Sure of the issue. 'Doth the like himself:
'Spareth a squirrel that it nothing fears
But steals the nut from underneath my thumb,
And when I threat, bites stoutly in defence:
'Spareth an urchin that contrariwise,
230 Curls up into a ball, pretending death
For fright at my approach: the two ways please.
But what would move my choler more than this,
That either creature counted on its life
To-morrow and next day and all days to come,
235 Saying, forsooth, in the inmost of its heart,
Because he did so yesterday with me,
And otherwise with such another brute,
So must he do henceforth and always.' – Ay?
Would teach the reasoning couple what 'must' means!
240 'Doth as he likes, or wherefore Lord? So He.

'Conceiveth all things will continue thus,
And we shall have to live in fear of Him
So long as He lives, keeps His strength: no change,
If He have done His best, make no new world
245 To please Him more, so leave off watching this, –

229 urchin hedgehog.

If He surprise not even the Quiet's self
Some strange day, – or, suppose, grow into it
As grubs grow butterflies: else, here are we,
And there is He, and nowhere help at all.
250 'Believeth with the life, the pain shall stop.
His dam held different, that after death
He both plagued enemies and feasted friends:
Idly! He doth His worst in this our life,
Giving just respite lest we die through pain,
255 Saving last pain for worst, – with which, an end.
Meanwhile, the best way to escape His ire
Is, not to seem too happy. 'Sees, himself,
Yonder two flies, with purple films and pink,
Bask on the pompion-bell above: kills both.
260 'Sees two black painful beetles roll their ball
On head and tail as if to save their lives:
Moves them the stick away they strive to clear.

Even so, 'would have Him misconceive, suppose
This Caliban strives hard and ails no less,
265 And always, above all else, envies Him;
Wherefore he mainly dances on dark nights,
Moans in the sun, gets under holes to laugh,
And never speaks his mind save housed as now:
Outside, 'groans, curses. If He caught me here,
270 O'erheard this speech, and asked 'What chucklest at?'
'Would, to appease Him, cut a finger off,
Or of my three kid yearlings burn the best,
Or let the toothsome apples rot on tree,
Or push my tame beast for the orc to taste:
275 While myself lit a fire, and made a song
And sung it, '*What I hate, be consecrate*
To celebrate Thee and Thy state, no mate
For Thee; what see for envy in poor me?'
Hoping the while, since evils sometimes mend,
280 Warts rub away and sores are cured with slime,
That some strange day, will either the Quiet catch
And conquer Setebos, or likelier He
Decrepit may doze, doze, as good as die.

[What, what? A curtain o'er the world at once!
285 Crickets stop hissing; not a bird – or, yes,

247–8 Caliban's notion that God may progress is analogous to B.'s belief
that man's awareness of God progresses through the ages.

There scuds His raven that has told Him all!
It was fool's play, this prattling! Ha! The wind
Shoulders the pillared dust, death's house o' the move,
And fast invading fires begin! White blaze –
290 A tree's head snaps – and there, there, there, there, there,
His thunder follows! Fool to gibe at Him!
Lo! 'Lieth flat and loveth Setebos!
'Maketh his teeth meet through his upper lip,
Will let those quails fly, will not eat this month
295 One little mess of whelks, so he may 'scape!]

286 His raven the bird traditionally associated with messages to and from God, e.g. *Gen.* 8.6.

294–5 Caliban characteristically thinks that self-denial will appease a God whom his reasoning faculty has made out to be vindictive. An oblique ref. to the quails in *Exod.* 16.13 associated with the coming of the manna to the Israelites in the wilderness of Sin.

77 Asolando: Fancies and Facts: extracts

Date The manuscript, in the Morgan Library, New York, 6 Sept. 1889. B. wrote to Mrs. C. Skirrow 15 Oct. 1889: 'This morning, I despatched to Smith the MS. of my new volume, – some thirty poems long and short, – some few written here, all revised and copied' (De Vane and K. *Letters* 384). With the exception of *The Cardinal and the Dog* (1842), the 28 poems in *Asolando* were written during the last three years of B.'s life.

Location Asolo, thirty-two miles N.W. of Venice, was a key place for B. He visited it in June 1838, searching for material later used in *Pippa Passes* and *Sordello*. He returned in Sept. 1878 and Sept. and Oct. 1889 – when he stayed with Mrs A. Bronson, who recalls the visit in *Century Magazine* 59 (1900) 920–31. Henry James describes the Asolo house in *Italian Hours* (1909) 81–2: 'It contained again its own small treasures, all in the pleasant key of the homelier Venetian spirit. The plain beneath it stretched away like a purple sea from the lower cliffs of the hills, and the white *campanili* of the villages,... showed on the expanse like scattered sails of ships.' Asolo had been the site of the court of the deposed Queen of Cyprus, Catherine Cornaro, between 1489 and 1510 – when she died. Cardinal Bembo had been one of her courtiers; B. possessed his copy of *Gli Asolani*, and followed him in punning on the name, by forming a verb 'asolare' – 'to disport in the open air, amuse oneself at random.'

Publication *1889;* dedicated to Mrs A. Bronson.

PROLOGUE

'The poet's age is sad: for why?
    In youth, the natural world could show
No common object but his eye
    At once involved with alien glow –
5   His own soul's iris-bow.

'And now a flower is just a flower:
 Man, bird, beast are but beast, bird, man –
Simply themselves, uncinct by dower
 Of dyes which, when life's day began,
10 Round each in glory ran!'

Friend, did you need an optic glass,
 Which were your choice? a lens to drape
In ruby, emerald, chrysopras,
 Each object – or reveal its shape
15 Clear outlined, past escape,

The naked very thing? – so clear
 That, when you had the chance to gaze,
You found its inmost self appear
 Through outer seeming – truth ablaze,
20 Not falsehood's fancy-haze?

How many a year, my Asolo,
 Since – one step just from sea to land –
I found you, loved yet feared you so –
 For natural objects seemed to stand
25 Palpably fire-clothed! No –

No mastery of mine o'er these!
 Terror with beauty, like the Bush
Burning but unconsumed. Bend knees,
 Drop eyes to earthward! Language? Tush!
30 Silence 'tis awe decrees.

And now? The lambent flame is – where?
 Lost from the naked world: earth, sky,
Hill, vale, tree, flower, – Italia's rare
 O'er-running beauty crowds the eye –
35 But flame? The Bush is bare.

Hill, vale, tree, flower – they stand distinct,
 Nature to know and name. What then?

5 **iris-bow** rainbow. Cf. Wordsworth: 'There was a time when meadow, grove, and stream, | The earth, and every common sight, | To me did seem | Apparelled in celestial light' *Intimations* lines 1–5. Line 10 mentions 'the rainbow'.

8 **uncinct** unencircled (not in *OED*).
13 **chrysopras** green onyx.
27–8 Cf. *Exod.* 3.2: 'And the angel of the Lord appeared unto [Moses] in a flame of fire out of the midst of a bush: and he looked, and, behold, the bush burned with fire, and the bush was not consumed.'

A Voice spoke thence which straight unlinked
    Fancy from fact: see, all's in ken:
40   Has once my eyelid winked?

No, for the purged ear apprehends
    Earth's import, not the eye late dazed:
The Voice said 'Call my works thy friends!
    At Nature dost thou shrink amazed?
45   God is it who transcends.'

                  Asolo: 6 Sept. 1889.

38 A Voice Cf. *Exod.* 3.4: 'God called Moses out of the midst of the bush.'
B. believes that the non-miraculous bush has as significant a message to
deliver as the burning bush. There is a similarity, in B.'s attitude, to
Wordsworth's in *Intimations*.... But, unlike W., B. neither continues to seek
solace in the faint residue of youthful vision, nor to take comfort from the
'sober colouring from an eye | That hath kept watch o'er man's mortality.'
He wants a more factual vision.

EPILOGUE

At the midnight in the silence of the sleep-time,
    When you set your fancies free,
Will they pass to where – by death, fools think, imprisoned –
Low he lies who once so loved you, whom you loved so,
5   – Pity me?

Oh to love so, be so loved, yet so mistaken!
    What had I on earth to do
With the slothful, with the mawkish, the unmanly?
Like the aimless, helpless, hopeless, did I drivel
10   – Being – who?

One who never turned his back but marched breast forward,
    Never doubted clouds would break,
Never dreamed, though right were worsted, wrong would
    triumph,
Held we fall to rise, are baffled to fight better,
15   Sleep to wake.

No, at noonday in the bustle of man's worktime
    Greet the unseen with a cheer!
Bid him forward, breast and back as either should be,
'Strive and thrive!' cry 'Speed, – fight on, fare ever
20   There as here!'

6 De Vane 552 cites a letter to Isa Blagden of 19 Apr. 1863 (*Dearest Isa*...
ed. E. C. McAleer (1951) 159) in which B. admitted to mistakes of
judgement in his relationship with Elizabeth, but reaffirmed his love.
19–20 A conclusion very similar to *Childe Roland*'s (p. 233).

Emily Brontë

Extraordinarily, Emily Brontë (1818–1848) has no independent entry in *DNB:* her life is incorporated into Charlotte's, exhibiting the general tendency to treat the sisters as a composite creative entity. She is listed as a poet neither in *NCBEL* nor in Faverty.

The family into which she was born had some culture: her father Patrick was a minor versifier and pamphleteer, and was able to provide an encouraging environment for the development of one of the closest knit literary circles that has ever existed in this country. In the isolated town of Haworth on the Yorkshire moors, where Patrick Brontë became a perpetual curate in 1820, the sisters and the slightly mad brother Branwell pursued their intense lives. Their mother died in 1821. The children were sent to Cowan Bridge School (to some extent portrayed in *Jane Eyre*), where two of them contracted fatal fevers in 1825. The survivors were then educated at home. Self-education was the most prominent feature of their upbringing – typified by the large-scale imaginative work which dominated their early creative life: The Gondal Saga. It is fully explored by F. A. Ratchford in *The Brontës' Web of Childhood* (New York 1941) and *Gondal's Queen* (1955), and in W. D. Paden's *An Investigation of Gondal* (1958). In general, it prolongs the fantastic, fanciful, gothic elements of the Romantic Movement.

The moors had a magnetic hold over the sisters, especially Emily, who found absence from them caused intense home-sickness. All three sisters were condemned to lead the typically irksome lives of pedagogical women. Emily's teaching experience in Halifax in 1836 was disastrous. In 1842 Charlotte and Emily went to Brussels to acquire French in a school run by M. and Mme. Heger (it appears, thinly disguised, in *Villette*).

In the 1840s the brother's conduct became increasingly erratic and irresponsible, although Emily was more tolerant of him than Charlotte and Anne. Certainly living in close proximity to Branwell familiarized her with *outré* and extreme states. In 1846 the three sisters published their first work: *Poems by Currer, Ellis and Acton Bell* (1846). The significant literary impact was made in Aug. 1847 when *Jane Eyre* was published. Emily's *Wuthering Heights* (Dec. 1847), although now regarded as the most remarkable of the sisters' works, made less impression at the time.

Emily died in Dec. 1848; Anne died in May 1849. Charlotte published Emily's literary remains in 1850, but, as one sees in the selections below, with considerable rewriting of her own.

Emily's poetry has not received the same degree of attention as her novel, but critics now recognize that it is of considerable importance, both in its own right, and as a further attestation of her curious genius, which was poetic rather than novelistic.

Editions and criticism The standard edition is C. W. Hatfield ed. *The Complete Poems of E.J.B.* (New York 1941). There is a biography by W. Gérin (Oxford 1971), see also J. Hewish *E.B.: a critical and biographical study* (1969).

Abbreviations

1846	*Poems by Currer, Ellis and Acton Bell* (1846).
1850	*Wuthering Heights and Agnes Grey* (1850); with 18 previously unpublished poems. Charlotte Brontë ed.
1941	*The Complete Works...* (1941) C. W. Hatfield.

The manuscripts are surveyed by Hatfield. The principal ones referred to are:

MS.A	The Honresfeld Manuscript
MS.B	The British Library Manuscript
MS.E	The Howe Manuscripts (in New York Public Library).

78 'I'm happiest when most away'

Date Feb. 1838. A fragment in *MS. E.* An unplaced Gondal poem.
Publication *1941*.

> I'm happiest when most away
> I can bear my soul from its home of clay,
> On a windy night when the moon is bright
> And the eye can wander through world of light –
>
> 5   When I am not and none beside –
> Nor earth nor sea nor cloudless sky –
> But only spirit wandering wide
> Through infinite immensity.

79 'A little while, a little while'

Date 4 Dec. 1838. *MS. A.*
  The longing for the visionary country of the Yorkshire moors is similar to Cathy's in *Wuthering Heights*, when she longs to return to earth from heaven.
Publication *1850*.

> A little while, a little while,
>   The noisy crowd are barred away;
> And I can sing and I can smile
>   A little while I've holiday!

2 The weary task is put away *1850*.
4 A little] Alike, *1850*.

5   Where wilt thou go, my harassed heart?
      Full many a land invites thee now;
      And places near and far apart
      Have rest for thee, my weary brow.

      There is a spot 'mid barren hills
10   Where winter howls and driving rain,
      But if the dreary tempest chills
      There is a light that warms again.

      The house is old, the trees are bare
      And moonless bends the misty dome
15   But what on earth is half so dear,
      So longed for as the hearth of home?

      The mute bird sitting on the stone
      The dank moss dripping from the wall,
      The garden-walk with weeds o'ergrown,
20   I love them – how I love them all!

      Shall I go there or shall I seek
      Another clime, another sky,
      Where tongues familiar music speak
      In accents dear to memory?

25   Yes, as I mused, the naked room,
      The flickering firelight died away
      And from the midst of cheerless gloom
      I passed to bright, unclouded day –

      A little and a lone green lane
30   That opened on a common wide;
      A distant, dreamy, dim blue chain
      Of mountains circling every side;

      A heaven so clear, an earth so calm,
      So sweet, so soft, so hushed an air
35   And, deepening still the dream-like charm,
      Wild moor-sheep feeding everywhere –

6 What thought, what scene invites thee now? *1850*.
7 What spot, or near or far apart *1850*.
14 Moonless above bends twilight's dome *1850*.
21–4 Not in *1850*.
26 flickering] alien *1850*.
33–4 Cf. George Herbert *Virtue* lines 1–2: 'Sweet day, so cool, so calm, so
bright, | The bridal of the earth and sky.'

That was the scene; I knew it well,
    I knew the path-ways far and near
That winding o'er each billowy swell
40   Marked out the tracks of wandering deer.

Could I have lingered but an hour
    It well had paid a week of toil,
But truth has banished fancy's power;
    I hear my dungeon bars recoil –

45   Even as I stood with raptured eye
    Absorbed in bliss so deep and dear
My hour of rest had fleeted by
    And given me back to weary care.

43–4 For the pattern of truth banishing fancy and the temporary solace of fanciful dreaming see *To Imagination* (no. 80).
44 Restraint and heavy task recoil *1850*.
48 And back came labour, bondage, care. *1850*.

80 To Imagination

Date 3 Sept. 1844. *MS. A.*
    A poem deriving much of its power from the principles of the major Romantics, especially Coleridge, although the beneficial power of imagination is registered as personal rather than primarily artistic.
Publication *1846*.

When weary with the long day's care,
    And earthly change from pain to pain,
And lost, and ready to despair,
    Thy kind voice calls me back again –
5   O my true friend, I am not lone
While thou canst speak with such a tone!

So hopeless is the world without,
    The world within I doubly prize;
Thy world where guile and hate and doubt
10   And cold suspicion never rise;
Where thou and I and liberty
Have undisputed sovereignty.

11–12 A nice reconciliation, with the Romantic Jacobinism of liberty taking on the monarchical power with which the Brontës were familiar in their dream kingdoms of Gondal.

What matters it that all around
Danger and grief and darkness lie,
15 If but within our bosom's bound
We hold a bright unsullied sky,
Warm with ten thousand mingled rays
Of suns that know no winter days?

Reason indeed may oft complain
20 For nature's sad reality,
And tell the suffering heart how vain
Its cherished dreams must always be;
And truth may rudely trample down
The flowers of fancy newly blown.

25 But thou art ever there to bring
The hovering visions back and breathe
New glories o'er the blighted spring
And call a lovelier life from death,
And whisper with a voice divine
30 Of real worlds as bright as thine.

I trust not to thy phantom bliss,
Yet still in evening's quiet hour
With never-failing thankfulness
I welcome thee, benignant power,
35 Sure solacer of human cares
And brighter hope when hope despairs.

13–18 For the self-sufficiency of the imaginative mind see Wordsworth's
Tintern Abbey lines 139–46.
14 grief] guilt *1846*.
23 truth the truth that is allied to reason and an enemy to imagination. The
major Romantic poets, viewing imagination as 'reason in her most exalted
mood' and hence a repository of truth, would have been reluctant to make this
traditional division.
24 fancy used here in a way not unlike Coleridge's in *Biographia Literaria*
(Ch. 13), as a weak, distracting faculty.
31 phantom bliss here too, a weaker version of imagination is represented.
Cf. Keats *Ode to the Nightingale* line 74: fancy is a 'deceiving elf'.
36 brighter] sweeter *1846*.

81 R. Alcona to J. Brenzaida

Date 3 March 1845; *MS. B.* A Gondal poem. The situation of mourning a
buried lover is reproduced in *Wuthering Heights* when Heathcliff lies on
Catherine's coffin in the snow.
Publication *1846*.

[81] Emily Brontë

Cold in the earth, and the deep snow piled above thee!
Far, far removed, cold in the dreary grave!
Have I forgot, my only love, to love thee,
Severed at last by time's all-wearing wave?

5   Now, when alone, do my thoughts no longer hover
Over the mountains on Angora's shore;
Resting their wings where heath and fern-leaves cover
That noble heart for ever, ever more?

Cold in the earth, and fifteen wild Decembers
10   From those brown hills have melted into spring –
Faithful indeed is the spirit that remembers
After such years of change and suffering!

Sweet love of youth, forgive if I forget thee
While the world's tide is bearing me along:
15   Sterner desires and darker hopes beset me,
Hopes which obscure but cannot do thee wrong.

No other sun has lightened up my heaven;
No other star has ever shone for me:
All my life's bliss from thy dear life was given –
20   All my life's bliss is in the grave with thee.

But when the days of golden dreams had perished
And even despair was powerless to destroy,
Then did I learn how existence could be cherished,
Strengthened and fed without the aid of joy;

25   Then did I check the tears of useless passion,
Weaned my young soul from yearning after thine;
Sternly denied its burning wish to hasten
Down to that tomb already more than mine!

And even yet, I dare not let it languish,
30   Dare not indulge in memory's rapturous pain;
Once drinking deep of that divinest anguish,
How could I seek the empty world again?

Title *Remembrance 1846.*
4 all-wearing] all-severing *1846.*
6 Angora's] that northern *1846.* Angora one of the kingdoms of Gondal.
The name is probably taken from the ancient name for Ankara (Turkey).
15 Sterner...darker] Other desires and other *1846.*
17 No other sun] No later night *1846.*
18 No other star] No second morn *1846.*

82 'No Coward Soul is Mine'

Date 2 Jan. 1846. *MS. A.* According to Charlotte Brontë 'the last lines my sister Emily ever wrote', although there are two more poems in *MS. B.* **Publication** *1850.*

No coward soul is mine
   No trembler in the world's storm-troubled sphere
I see heaven's glories shine
   And faith shines equal arming me from fear.

5   O God within my breast
   Almighty ever-present Deity
Life, that in me hast rest
   As I undying life, have power in Thee.

Vain are the thousand creeds
10   That move men's hearts, unutterably vain
Worthless as withered weeds
   Or idlest froth amid the boundless main

To waken doubt in one
   Holding so fast by thy infinity,
15 So surely anchored on
   The steadfast rock of immortality.

With wide-embracing love
   Thy spirit animates eternal years
Pervades and broods above,
20   Changes, sustains, dissolves, creates and rears.

Though earth and moon were gone
   And suns and universes ceased to be
And thou wert left alone
   Every existence would exist in thee.

25 There is not room for death
   Nor atom that his might could render void
Since thou art being and breath
   And what thou art may never be destroyed.

Arthur Hugh Clough

Life and works Arthur Hugh Clough was born on 1 January 1819 in Liverpool. The Clough family had been for centuries landed gentry on the Welsh Marches, but Arthur's father, James Butler Clough, was an example of the late C18 upper middle class trying its hand at trade. He was a cotton merchant, and falling on hard times in the depression following the Napoleonic Wars emigrated to America, and carried on an export business from Charleston. C.'s mother was a cultivated religious woman, with stern ideas on duty. C. accompanied his father on a trip to England in 1825, and came back permanently in 1828, first to attend a school in Chester, then to go to Rugby. It is not surprising that so much sea travel (and he was to undertake more later in life) left its mark on him and his poetry. Biographers have stressed the shock to the young boy of being uprooted and deprived of a close-knit and independent family. The family did not resettle in England until 1836.

At Rugby C. came under the spell of Thomas Arnold. He made friends with his sons, Tom and Matthew. The school ethos made a significant impact on C. and his friends, especially the social and religious views propagated. Thomas Arnold stood for a Broad Church ideal in which moral earnestness, scrupulous self-probing, purity of mind and willingness to serve society and its institutions were cultivated under the aegis of Christ's example and traditional Christian principles. The religion tended to be pragmatical rather than mystical, although the standards urged by it often had an unworldly and impractical tinge – not that this prevented the disciples from devoting their lives to propagating them and putting them into practice. The ethos at Rugby was advocacy of sports and physical fitness, and C., however frail he may have been, followed the '*mens sana in corpore sano*' dictum throughout much of his life. Another aspect of the school was that it fostered not only the classics and the traditional disciplines, but mathematics, the new sciences, modern history and modern languages. In positive and negative ways Rugby contributed much to C. as a poet.

In 1837 he went up to Balliol College as a scholar. The university was still participating in the long drawn out drama of the Oxford Movement, which had begun in 1833. C. encountered religious views very different from the 'liberal' ones of his old headmaster: Newman, Pusey and the Tractarians were trying to advocate a concept of the mystical body of the Church, which was far from liberal – and yet had some attractions, for a youth inculcated in principles of service. Thomas Arnold, of course, disapproved of the Oxford Movement, and said so in an *Edinburgh Review* article: 'The Oxford Malignants' (April 1836). C. came under the spell of his mathematical tutor W. G. Ward, whose intellectual energy created a 'vortex of Philosophism and Discussion.' Ward – like Newman – was going in the direction of Rome, and his *The Ideal of a Christian Church* (1844) was so indistinguishable from Romanism that it was condemned by Convocation (1845). When Ward went over to the Roman Catholic Church, the emotional strain felt by C. was immense. The conflicting views that he experienced and witnessed led

Arthur Hugh Clough

not to a definite alliance with one of the camps but a third, private position of religious disbelief. His apostasy was not even of the relaxed and genial kind that some Victorians exhibited, but an agonised and guilt-ridden one, which caused an inner mode of existence glimpsed by virtually no one, probably not even his wife. The dilemma accounts for the cultivation of a reserved *social* manner (some of his friends thought he was outwardly the Puseyite) and a private Byronic personality, which emerges in his poetry – especially in *Amours de Voyage* and *Dipsychus* (the latter almost completely unknown in his life time and up to 1951). It is possible that the upheavals in his intellectual and emotional life led to his second class degree in 1841, and his failure to get a Balliol fellowship. However he was a respected scholar, and in 1842 became a fellow of the college primarily associated with the dramas of the Oxford Movement – Oriel. Here he stayed until 1848, resigning, in the end, on the principle that he could not continue to subscribe to the Thirty-nine Articles of the Church of England. In ages of waning faith thousands of M.A.s had salved their consciences, but it is typical of C.'s scrupulousness that he could not. He may also have found the don's life irksome, and was very unsure of what he wanted to be and what he wanted to do. He spent much of 1849 in Italy witnessing the country's struggles for independence, and composing *Amours de Voyage*. He was not rich enough to be self-supporting, so it was necessary to earn money somehow. It may at first seem surprising that he did not become a man of letters, making most of his income from books and essays, and publishing poetry from time to time, and there is no doubt that he could have succeeded admirably in time, but there would have been painful years of hack work. He did not think of himself primarily as a 'poet' (very few poets have, when one looks into it): he wrote poetry, but a certain amount of it was for his own satisfaction and self-exploration, and it was, on the whole, too uncompromising for a wide Victorian public; although unlike a lot of 'private poetry' of the time it was not inaccessible or obscure, and the small circles of readers who knew it were very impressed. He took its creation seriously, and in some sense he was most himself writing it, but there was somewhere a streak of indolence in his make-up, and a self-defeating deference. He was poor at finishing work, and bringing it to that final point where it goes into print. Much of the poetry that was published in his life time was forced out of him by more resolute people such as Charles Eliot Norton. His characteristic procedure was to bring a work to near completion, leave it for Horace's nine years, and then find he had more or less lost interest in it. Presumably Horace meant that one should keep a perfected piece for nine years, not a provisional one. C. knew himself well enough to know that he could not work to a strict regime, and in any case he wished to keep the products of the inner life away from the marketplace. The duties of a man of letters might have kept him up to the mark, but would not necessarily have made him happy or successful. He also knew that the circumstances needed for creating the poetry were perhaps few and far between, and he had not reached the habitual certainty of being a poet: to create he needed leisure, a degree of isolation (his best work was written abroad), and a sense of strain that was productive rather than demoralising. Married life, for instance, gave him a happiness and security that made poetry almost irrelevant. His case is like the ones Henry James treated in stories of artists destroyed by marriage.

Arthur Hugh Clough

But he was also destroyed, as an artist, by his career, first as Professor of English at University College, Principal of University Hall, London (from which he resigned because he got into trouble with the principles of the Dissenters), then as an examiner in the Education Office. In between these posts he spent time in New England, inspecting the Boston Brahmins, and hovering over the idea of setting up a private school. His marriage to Blanche Smith in 1854 involved him in supporting a domestic establishment, which in turn took him further away from the hazards attendant upon a literary career. He seems to have had a vague notion that he was meant for something better, but he was not quite sure what, and he died in Florence in 1861, aged only forty-two. In some ways, although the poetry is very different, the pattern of his career reminds us of Arnold's – except that in the end, Arnold did achieve fame as man-of-letters and prophet, an achievement that may have come into C.'s grasp had he lived long enough and lost some of the fastidiousness.

The last years are famous for an episode that points to the split in C.'s personality. A part of him was drawn to America, to the freedom, vigour and activity of the place. At Rugby he was known as 'Tom Yankee'. Arnold thought he detected an American, futuristic leaven in his make-up. England, on the other hand, was much more set and machine-like, and more prone to drive the sensitive inwards, or to the culture and the intellectual knowledge that was available as an alternative to the materialist steam age. C. wrote to Emerson (22 Aug. 1854): 'But I think you are better and more happily off in America, where the vastness of the machinery does not destroy the sense of an individual moral purpose – the ship here is really so big that one cannot see that it moves' (*Letters* 2. 489). Yet some good he meant to do, despite his own nature, and the nature of English political life, and he threw himself into it. He may also have been influenced by the Carlylean conceptions of heroism and political reform which were so prominent in the 1840s and 50s. He sacrificed his leisure and equanimity of mind to Blanche's cousin Florence Nightingale's campaign for better military hospitals. It was as if he wished to confirm for himself that action was not merely the prerogative of the worldly and rationalist figure who appears as a kind of Mephistopheles in *Dipsychus*. All this took him further from the muse of poetry.

Style and editions There are analogies between C. and Hopkins. Their poetic outputs are not very large (though it should be remembered that C. wrote as much poetry as Arnold); they both died in early middle age; they both expressed a certain impatience with stilted poetic diction, and hoped for a revivification of poetry from colloquial sources; they both experimented with a prosody that took more account of stress than syllable; and their work was so bound up with their inner lives that it tended to 'live' for a long time as a developing organism, and then to be abandoned rather than finished and worked up for publication. So enormous responsibility has fallen on editorial midwives, and the poetry is perhaps best regarded as having a sort of provisional existence. This even applies in C.'s case to poetry published in his lifetime – such as *Amours* and *The Bothie*. There is not space in this edition to print all the variants, and readers are referred to the 'standard' Clough, edited for O.U.P. by F. L. Mulhauser (1974). As with Hopkins, the earlier editors were inevitably more limited and conventional than the poet himself: this was true of his wife Blanche, of F. T. Palgrave, who wrote the introduction for *Poems* (1862), and even (though to a lesser extent) of J.

Arthur Hugh Clough

Addington Symonds who assisted in the production of *Poems and Prose Remains* (1869).

C. remained in print and easily available until just after the Great War: he was well read and respected, especially for his honesty and earnestness. He attracted readers, even though, in his own words, he did not go 'a whoring' after 'Scenes and Scenery.' His imagery is not at all rich, and he wrote in the unpopular hexameter. His reputation went into decline until the 1951 O.U.P. edition, but in the revival of Victorian interests in the last two decades he has assumed a key position as a sensitive and intelligent dissenting voice in the age without being regarded as a freakish outsider. One could cite the testimonial Jowett wrote for him in 1845 as an evaluation not only of his diurnal personality, but of his poetic character too: '...of all the persons I have met with, who can be said to be of a speculative cast of mind he is the most free from peculiarities, whether of opinion or manner, still retaining a strong practical interest in the realities of life.'

The standard edition is now *1974*, which prints a greater number of manuscript variants than have ever been available before.

Biographies and discussion Clough scholarship is now extensive: it is surveyed by M. Timko (Faverty 150–162). The recent biographies include K. Chorley *A.H.C.: the uncommitted mind* (Oxford U.P. 1962), P. Veyriras *A.H.C.* (Paris 1964), D. Williams *Too Quick Despairer: the life and work of A.H.C.* (1969) and R. K. Biswas *A.H.C.: towards a reconsideration* (Oxford U.P. 1972). E. B. Greenberger's *A.H.C.: the growth of a poet's mind* (Cambridge, Mass. 1970) is an intellectual biography. The best studies of the poetry are W. E. Houghton *The Poetry of C.* (New Haven 1963) and M. Timko *Innocent Victorian: The Satiric Poetry of C.* (Columbus, Ohio 1966).

Manuscripts Since so much of C.'s poetry was published posthumously it is necessary to use manuscripts, not only to gain insights into the process of creation but to establish the texts. Another means of establishing text – to use American editions – is described by P. G. Scott *Harvard Lib. Bull.* 20 (1972) 320–36. For a fuller record of MSS consult *1974*. The following are the principal ones cited below: *1839–1842 Notebooks; 1845 Notebook; 1847 Notebook; 1852 (Smith) Notebook; MS. A; MS. V* (1850 (Venice) Notebook).

Abbreviations

1848	*The Bothie of Toper-Na-Fuosich* (1848).
1849	*Ambarvalia* (in collaboration with Thomas Burbidge) (1849).
1862	*Poems* (1862).
1862 Boston	*Poems* (with a memoir by Charles Eliot Norton) (Boston 1862).
1863	*Poems* (1863).
1865	*Letters and Remains* (1865).
1869	*Poems and Prose Remains* (1869).
1951	*Poems* ed. H. F. Lowry, H. L. P. Norrington and F. L. Mulhauser (Oxford U.P. 1951).
1974	*Poems* ed. F. L. Mulhauser (Oxford U.P. 1974).
Correspondence	*The Correspondence of A.H.C.* ed. F. L. Mulhauser (Oxford U.P. 1957).

Lowry *Letters*   *The Letters of Matthew Arnold to A.H.C.* ed. H. F. Lowry (Oxford U.P. 1932).

Trawick   *Selected Prose Works of A.H.C.* ed. B. B. Trawick (University, Alabama 1964).

Biswas   R. K. Biswas *A.H.C.: towards a reconsideration* (Oxford U.P. 1972).

Chorley   K. Chorley *A.H.C.: the uncommitted mind* (Oxford U.P. 1962).

Houghton   W. E. Houghton *The Poetry of C.: an essay in revaluation* (New Haven 1963).

Critical Heritage   *C.: The Critical Heritage* (1972) ed. M. Thorpe.

83 'Look you, my simple friend, 'tis one of those'

Date ? 1840. No MS. known.

Without intending to, Clough (always allowing for changes in social circumstances and diction) has come closer here to reproducing the feel of Elizabethan and Jacobean drama than those Victorians who made a deliberate attempt.

Publication *1849;* omitted *1862.*

> Look you, my simple friend, 'tis one of those,
> (Alack, a common weed of our ill time),
> Who, do whate'er they may, go where they will,
> Must needs still carry about the looking-glass
> 5   Of vain philosophy. And if so be
> That some small natural gesture shall escape them,
> (Nature will out) straightway about they turn,
> And con it duly there, and note it down,
> With inward glee and much complacent chuckling,
> 10   Part in conceit of their superior science,
> Part in forevision of the attentive look
> And laughing glance that may one time reward them,
> When the fresh ore, this day dug up, at last
> Shall, thrice refined and purified, from the mint
> 15   Of conversation intellectual
> Into the golden currency of wit
> Issue – satirical or pointed sentence,
> Impromptu, epigram, or it may be sonnet,
> Heir undisputed to the pinkiest page
> 20   In the album of a literary lady.

18 Impromptu sb. improvization.
19 pinkiest not in *OED*.

And can it be, you ask me, that a man,
With the strong arm, the cunning faculties,
And keenest forethought gifted, and, within,
Longings unspeakable, the lingering echoes
25 Responsive to the still-still-calling voice
Of God Most High, – should disregard all these,
And half-employ all those for such an aim
As the light sympathy of successful wit,
Vain titillation of a moment's praise?
30 Why, so is good no longer good, but crime
Our truest, best advantage, since it lifts us
Out of the stifling gas of men's opinion
Into the vital atmosphere of Truth,
Where He again is visible, tho' in anger.

25 **still-still-calling voice** the still voice that continues to call. Cf. 1 *Kings* 19.
12.

84 'Duty – that's to say complying'

Date ? 1840. Draft in *1839–42 Nbks*.
The poem is in cynical apposition to Wordsworth's *Ode to Duty* (1807).
C.'s mother attached great importance to duty.
Publication *1849, 1862*.

Duty, – that's to say complying
    With whate'er's expected here;
On your unknown cousin's dying;
    Straight be ready with the tear;
5   Upon etiquette relying,
    Unto usage naught denying,
    Lend your waist to be embraced,
        Blush not even, never fear;
Claims of kith and kin connection,
10   Claims of manners honour still,
    Ready money of affection
        Pay, whoever drew the bill.
With the form conforming duly,
    Senseless what it meaneth truly,
15 Go to church – the world require you,
    To balls – the world require you too,
And marry – papa and mamma desire you,
    And your sisters and schoolfellows do.

Title *Duty 1869*.
7 omitted *1862, 1863*.

Duty – 'tis to take on trust
20 What things are good, and right, and just;
And whether indeed they be or be not,
Try not, test not, feel not, see not:
'Tis walk and dance, sit down and rise
By leading, opening ne'er your eyes;
25 Stunt sturdy limbs that nature gave,
And be drawn in a Bath chair along to the grave.
'Tis the stern and prompt suppressing,
As an obvious deadly sin,
All the questing and the guessing
30 Of the soul's own soul within:
'Tis the coward acquiescence
In a destiny's behest,
To a shade by terror made.
Sacrificing, aye, the essence
35 Of all that's truest, noblest, best:
'Tis the blind non-recognition
Either of goodness, truth, or beauty,
Except by precept and submission;
Moral blank, and moral void,
40 Life at very birth destroyed,
Atrophy, exinanition!
Duty! –
Yea, by duty's prime condition
Pure nonentity of duty!

24 And all along to shut your eyes MS.
26 Bath chair invalid chair.
29 Individual prompting, guessing MS.
37 Either] Or *1862* etc.
38 Except] Save *1862* etc.
39–44 Mental and moral inanition | Yea, in duty's true condition | 'Tis the ignorance of duty. MS.
41 exinanition exhaustion.

85 'Is it true, ye gods, who treat us'

Date ? 1842. No MS known.
Publication *1849, 1869.*

Is it true, ye gods, who treat us
As the gambling fool is treated,
O ye, who ever cheat us,
And let us feel we're cheated!

Title *Wen Gott Betrügt Ist Wohl Betrogen 1869* ('When God betrays he betrays with a vengeance').

5   Is it true that poetical power,
     The gift of heaven, the dower
     Of Apollo and the Nine,
     The inborn sense, 'the vision and the faculty divine,'
     All we glorify and bless
10   In our rapturous exaltation,
     All invention, and creation,
     Exuberance of fancy, and sublime imagination,
     All a poet's fame is built on,
     The fame of Shakespeare, Milton,
15   Of Wordsworth, Byron, Shelley,
     Is in reason's grave precision,
     Nothing more, nothing less,
     Than a peculiar conformation,
     Constitution, and condition
20   Of the brain and of the belly?
     Is it true, ye gods who cheat us?
     And that's the way ye treat us?
     Oh say it, all who think it,
     Look straight, and never blink it!
25   If it is so, let it be so,
     And we will all agree so;
     But the plot has counterplot,
     It may be, and yet be not.

7 the Nine the Muses.
8 'the vision and the faculty divine' Cf. Wordsworth *Excursion* 1.79.
27 counterplot C. implies that in an era of scepticism one cannot even be
sure of the truth of a cynical theory.

86 Qui laborat, orat

Date 1845, but Thomas Arnold gives 1847, *Nineteenth Century* 93 (1898)
108.
Publication *1849, 1862, 1863, 1869.*

    O only Source of all our light and life,
       Whom as our truth, our strength, we see and feel,
    But whom the hours of mortal moral strife
       Alone aright reveal!

Title Means 'He who works prays', a Carlylean notion. The Rugby School
motto is '*laborare est orare*'.

5   Mine inmost soul, before Thee inly brought,
      Thy presence owns ineffable, divine;
    Chastised each rebel self-encentered thought,
      My will adoreth Thine.

    With eye down-dropped, if then this earthly mind
10   Speechless remain, or speechless e'en depart,
    Nor seek to see (for what of earthly kind
      Can see Thee as Thou art?) –

    If sure assured 'tis but profanely bold
      In thought's abstractest forms to seem to see,
15   It dare not dare thee dread communion hold
      In ways unworthy Thee, –

    O not unowned, Thou shalt unnamed forgive,
      In worldly walks the prayerless heart prepare,
    And if in work its life it seem to live,
20   Shalt make that work be prayer.

    Nor times shall lack, when, while the work it plies,
      Unsummoned powers the blinding film shall part,
    And scarce by happy tears made dim, the eyes
      In recognition start.

25   As wills Thy will, or give or e'en forbear
      The beatific supersensual sight,
    So, with Thy blessing blest, that humbler prayer
      Approach Thee morn and night.

7 self-encentered first ex. in *OED* 1843; the commoner form, self-centred, 1783.

87 Natura Naturans

Date ? 1846; it occurs in *1847 Nbks;* in a revised form.
Interpretation This poem, with *Dipsychus*, was one of the principal poems that C.'s widow wished to suppress, and she succeeded in *1862, 1863,* and *1865.* She wrote to C. E. Norton: 'I do so dislike the *Natura Naturans*...the only thing I particularly desire is to leave out *Natura Naturans* which is abhorrent to me...I do know that, at least in this country, it is liable to great misconception.' The misconception she had in mind was as follows: it is possible that the poem refers to an actual incident and an actual relationship in C.'s life *before* he met Blanche Smith; so that she may have been jealous of the earlier liaison, and unwilling to allow the public to imagine that C.'s devotion to her was not single-minded. There is a chance that the poem is imagined, with the first person a persona: C. wrote (19 Jan. 1852): 'People who have got at all used to write as authors are so incapable of

writing or even speaking except "in character" and will run through a whole
list of dramatic personae...' (Biswas 434). The poem draws its material
from deterministic philosophy; line 43 links the human love of the poem with
'blind elections' of lower forms of life, and Mrs C. may have been reluctant
to accept that the 'election' which brought her and C. together (as the
correspondence attests) was so much associated with absence of freedom.
For the tyrannical power of 'election' see *A Sunday Morning Contemplation*
(Biswas 424–7).
Publication *1849, 1869.*

> Beside me, – in the car, – she sat,
>   She spake not, no, nor looked to me:
> From her to me, from me to her,
>   What passed so subtly stealthily?
> As rose to rose that by it blows
>   Its interchanged aroma flings;
> Or wake to sound of one sweet note
>   The virtues of disparted strings.
>
> Beside me, nought but this! – but this,
>   That influent as within me dwelt
> Her life, mine too within her breast,
>   Her brain, her every limb she felt:
> We sat; while o'er and in us, more
>   And more, a power unknown prevailed,
> Inhaling, and inhaled, – and still
>   'Twas one, inhaling or inhaled.
>
> Beside me, nought but this; – and passed;
>   I passed; and know not to this day
> If gold or jet her girlish hair,
>   If black, or brown, or lucid-grey
> Her eye's young glance: the fickle chance

Line numbers in left margin: 5 (line 5), 10 (line 10), 15 (line 15), 20 (line 20).

Title means 'nature naturing'. See Coleridge *Philosophical Lectures:* '...in
speaking of the world without us as distinguished from ourselves, the
aggregate of phenomena ponderable and imponderable, is called nature in
the passive sense, – in the language of the old schools, *natura naturata* –
while the sum or aggregate of the powers inferred as the sufficient causes of
the forms...is nature in the active sense, or *natura naturans.*'
1 car railway carriage.
8 separate strings on a musical instrument are roused to sympathetic
vibration when a note is sounded near them.
9–10 Beside...dwelt] Beside me! nought but this! that e'en | As influent in
my members dwelt MS.
21 fickle] subtle MS.

That joined us, yet may join again;
But I no face again could greet
As hers, whose life was in me then.

25 As unsuspecting mere a maid
As, fresh in maidhood's bloomiest bloom,
In casual second-class did e'er
By casual youth her seat assume;
Or vestal, say, of saintliest clay,
30 For once by balmiest airs betrayed
Unto emotions too too sweet
To be unlingeringly gainsaid:

Unowning then, confusing soon
With dreamier dreams that o'er the glass
35 Of shyly ripening woman-sense
Reflected, scarce reflected, pass
A wife may-be, a mother she
In Hymen's shrine recalls not now,
She first in hour, ah, not profane,
40 With me to Hymen learnt to bow.

Ah no! – Yet owned we, fused in one,
The Power which e'en in stones and earths
By blind elections felt, in forms
Organic breeds to myriad births;
45 By lichen small on granite wall
Approved, its faintest feeblest stir
Slow-spreading, strengthening long, at last
Vibrated full in me and her.

25 As mere, methinks, a farmer's maid MS.
30 A nymph by balmiest airs betrayed MS.
38 Hymen God of marriage.
40 A line that C.'s widow may have thought open to misconception: there is a secondary sense in which it could mean that sexual intercourse took place – though the circumstances described in the poem do not support this.
41 fused Cf. Dylan Thomas *The Force that through the green fuse drives the flower*.
42 The power ... earths Cf. Wordsworth *Three years she grew* (1800) and *A slumber did my spirit steal* (1800), but the mystical implications of those lines are undercut by what follows.
43 blind elections a combination of the mechanical and malevolent principles of scientific determinism with the more Romantic and benign doctrine of elective affinities outlined by Goethe in *Die Wahlverwandtschaften* (1809); attractions MS.
45 granite] rocky MS.

In me and her – sensation strange!
50   The lily grew to pendent head,
To vernal airs and mossy bank
     Its sheeny primrose spangles spread,
In roof o'er roof of shade sun-proof
     Did cedar strong itself outclimb,
55 And altitude of aloe proud
     Aspire in floreal crown sublime;

Flashed flickering forth fantastic flies,
     Big bees their burly bodies swung,
Rooks roused with civic din the elms,
60   And lark its wild reveillez rung;
In Libyan dell the light gazelle,
     The leopard lithe in Indian glade,
And dolphin, brightening tropic seas,
     In us were living, leapt and played:

65 Their shells did slow crustacea build,
     Their gilded skins did snakes renew,
While mightier spines for loftier kind
     Their types in amplest limbs outgrew;
Yea, close compressed in human breast,
70   What moss, and tree, and livelier thing,
What earth, sun, star of force possessed,
     Lay budding, burgeoning forth for Spring.

Such sweet preluding sense of old
     Led on in Eden's sinless place
75 The hour when bodies human first
     Combined the primal prime embrace,
Such genial heat the blissful seat
     In man and woman owned unblamed,
When, naked both, its garden paths
80   They walked unconscious, unashamed:

Ere, clouded yet in mistiest dawn,
     Above the horizon dusk and dun,
One mountain crest with light had tipped
     That Orb that is the Spirit's Sun;

54 cedar see note to no. 68 line 57 (p. 228 above).
55 aloe in the Bible a perfumed, exotic plant; e.g. *Ps.* 45.8.
58 burly in addition to the standard meaning, there is the possibility that C. had in mind *OED* 2b: thickly coated.
61 Libyan] Afric MS. Altered to provide alliteration and to avoid Miltonism.
68 types] bounds MS.

85   Ere dreamed young flowers in vernal showers
      Of fruit to rise the flower above,
    Or ever yet to young Desire
    Was told the mystic name of Love.

88 Epi-Strauss-ion

Date *1847 Nbk.* has a rough draft; there is a fair copy on a loose sheet in the Bodleian, the text followed in *1951* and here.

Interpretation The poem explores what remains of religious belief in the wake of D. F. Strauss's *Leben Jesu* (1835). Chorley 124–5 suggests that C. knew the work through George Eliot's translation *The Life of Jesus* (1846). See a letter to Anne Clough of May 1847: 'I do not think that doubts respecting the facts related in the Gospels need give us much trouble. Believing that in one way or other the thing is of God, we shall in the end know perhaps in what way and how far it was so. Trust in God's justice and love, and belief in His commands as written in our conscience, stand unshaken though Matthew, Mark, Luke, and John or even St. Paul, were to fall' (*Correspondence* 1.182). R. A. Forsyth *VP* 7 (1969) 17–30 compares G. Herbert's *Church Windows;* C. Castan *VP* 4 (1966) 54–6 suggests the influence of an image in Carlyle *Past and Present* Bk 2 Ch. 14: 'Thus does the conscience of man...like light through coloured glass paint strange pictures....One day, this "coloured glass"...may it not become at once translucent and *uncoloured?* Painting no pictures more for us, but only the everlasting azure itself? That will be a right glorious consummation!'

Publication *1869; 1951.*

    Matthew and Mark and Luke and holy John
    Evanished all and gone!
    Yea, he that erst, his dusky curtains quitting,
    Through eastern pictured panes his level beams transmitting,
5   With gorgeous portraits blent,
    On them his glories intercepted spent,
    Southwestering now, through windows plainly glassed,
    On the inside face his radiance keen hath cast,
    And in the lustre lost, invisible and gone,
10   Are, say you, Matthew, Mark and Luke and holy John?

Title *Epi-Strauss-ium 1869, 1951.* Houghton 52–3 suggests it resembles the word 'Epithalamium' in this form, and that C. had *Ps.* 19. 1–6 in mind: 'The heavens declare the glory of God...' *Epi-Strauss-ion* is the title in *1847 Nbk.*
6–7 Formerly the sun (Christ) was made rich and mysterious by the interposition of stained glass, but in the late afternoon of belief it shines through windows that have clear glass, illuminating the inside walls of the building of faith through no intervening medium.

Lost, is it? lost, to be recovered never?
However,
The place of worship the meantime with light
Is, if less richly, more sincerely bright,
15   And in blue skies the orb is manifest to sight.

14 sincerely] serenely *1847 Nbk.*

89 'Why should I say I see the things I see not'

Date Composition probably begun *c.* 1845: *1974* 578–9 prints 13 lines of what may be an early draft from the *1845 Notebook*. Complete by Dec. 1847, when Arnold wrote to C.: 'And as a metrical curiosity the one about 2 musics does not seem to be happy' (Lowry *Letters* 61).
    C., who had weak ankles and an antisocial disposition, did not like dancing, but he refers here to the mysticism of the dance celebrated in e.g. Sir John Davies *Orchestra* (1596).
Publication *1849; 1862; 1863; 1869.*

1

Why should I say I see the things I see not,
    Why be and be not?
Show love for that I love not, and fear for what I fear not?
And dance about to music that I hear not?
5   Who standeth still i' the street
        Shall be hustled and justled about;
And he that stops i' the dance shall be spurned by the
        dancers' feet, –
Shall be shoved and be twisted by all he shall meet,
    And shall raise up an outcry and rout;
10   And the partner, too, –
        What's the partner to do?
While all the while 'tis but, perchance, an humming in mine
        ear,
    That yet anon shall hear,
    And I anon, the music in my soul,
15   In a moment read the whole;
    The music in my heart,
    Joyously take my part,
And hand in hand, and heart with heart, with these retreat,
        advance;

Title *The Music of the World and of the Soul 1869.*
1–28 omitted *1862, 1863.*

       And borne on wings of wavy sound,
20   Whirl with these around, around,
Who here are living in the living dance!
      Why forfeit that fair chance?
      Till that arrive, till thou awake,
      Of these, my soul, thy music make,
25   And keep amid the throng,
And turn as they shall turn, and bound as they are bounding, –
Alas! alas! alas! and what if all along
      The music is not sounding?

              2
Are there not, then, two musics unto men? –
30   One loud and bold and coarse,
      And overpowering still perforce
      All tone and tune beside;
      Yet in despite its pride
Only of fumes of foolish fancy bred,
35   And sounding solely in the sounding head:
      The other, soft and low,
      Stealing whence we not know,
Painfully heard, and easily forgot,
With pauses oft and many a silence strange,
40   (And silent oft it seems, when silent it is not)
Revivals too of unexpected change:
Haply thou think'st 'twill never be begun,
Or that 't has come, and been, and passed away;
      Yet turn to other none, –
45   Turn not, oh, turn not thou!
But listen, listen, listen, – if haply be heard it may;
Listen, listen, listen, – is it not sounding now?

---

28 ∧ 29 Age on age succeeding fast | From a far heroic past | They went their
rounds | And beat the bounds | Of old Imperial Rome | The Ambarvalian
brothers* Nine with hymns and sacred song | That immemorial line along |
Of that august and holy home. ‖ Even so Poets now | With more than
priestly vow | Made separate from their birth | Walk the great world and
mete the measures of the Earth | And following on their feet | The acolytes
withal | Who catching notes that haply fall | From the great prophetic song |
Tell them out loudly to the listening throng. *1847 Nbk.*
***Ambarvalian brothers** Strabo *Geography* 5.3.2 mentions the *Arvales Fratres*
who led sacrificial victims round the fields. There were twelve not nine
priests; they carried on the cult of *Dea Dia* in the time of Augustus. Pater
describes the ceremony in *Marius the Epicurean* (1885) Ch. 1. These
cancelled lines fit the poem more explicitly into the collection titled
Ambarvalia.
34–5 Cf. Shakespeare *Merch.* 3.2.63–4. 'Tell me where is fancy bred...'
40 when silent] when silence *1863.*

3

Yea, and as thought of some departed friend
By death or distance parted will descend,
50 Severing, in crowded rooms ablaze with light,
As by a magic screen, the seer from the sight
(Palsying the nerves that intervene
The eye and central sense between);
So may the ear,
55 Hearing, not hear,
Though drums do roll, and pipes and cymbals ring;
So the bare conscience of the better thing
Unfelt, unseen, unimaged, all unknown,
May fix the entrancèd soul 'mid multitudes alone.

48 departed] beloved *Boston 1862;* departed *1863, 1869.*
57 conscience inward knowledge or consciousness; *OED* 1.

90 The Bothie of Tober-Na-Vuolich:
extracts

Date 1848. A chronology C. made of his life for Blanche Smith notes that composition began in Sept. (*Correspondence* 2.621), i.e. at the time he was preparing to resign his Oriel College Fellowship.

The occasion The poem celebrates the phenomenon of the long vacation reading party, which C. doubtless thought he should put on record before losing contact altogether. He dedicated it to his pupils asking them not to 'be displeased if in a fiction, purely fiction, they are here and there reminded of times we enjoyed together.' The story is Philip Hewson's courtship and marriage to a Highland lassie Elspie Mackaye, and their emigration to New Zealand. The antipodean adventure was experienced by Tom Arnold (one of the pupils), and C. entertained the plan of taking up a post in Australia. The poem is in the form of a light-hearted pastoral, and this may have led Arnold to commemorate C. in pastoral form in *Thyrsis* (no. 106).

The title gave C. trouble. In the 1848 edition it was *The Bothie of Toper-Na-Fuosich.* The meaning has been since disputed, but C. thought it obscene: 'It turns out, they tell me, to mean what Horace calls "*teterrima belli causa*" – O mercy! – It is too ludicrous not to tell some one, but too appallingly awkward to tell anyone on this side of the globe' (*Correspondence* 1.244: to Thomas Arnold). It meant, according to *The Literary Gazette* 66 (18 Aug. 1849) 606, 'the hut of the bearded well', and it was a real place. C. changed the title to the above for *1862,* 'improvised without enquiry' (*Correspondence* 2.514).

Discussion There seem to have been *roman à clef* elements, but contemporaries disagree on identities (Biswas 264). C. Kingsley placed it in a context of advanced social thinking in his *Fraser's* review (*Critical Heritage* 37–47). See also Biswas 263–86; Houghton 92–118; Chorley 146–69. R. B. Rutland provides useful Highlands background in *VP* 14 (1976) 126–33, and

[90] Arthur Hugh Clough

J. Goode explores 1848 and 'the strange disease of modern love' in *Literature and Politics in the Nineteenth Century* ed. J. Lucas (1971) 45–76. **Metre** hexameters, but admitted by C. to be irregular. **Publication** *1848, 1862* (with revisions), *1863* (further revisions). **Text** *1862*.

3

This is one of the most characteristic passages in *The Bothie*, summing up the athleticism and love of nature that was common amongst nineteenth-century undergraduates on reading parties.

But in the interval here the boiling, pent-up water
35   Frees itself by a final descent, attaining a basin,
Ten feet wide and eighteen long, with whiteness and fury
Occupied partly, but mostly pellucid, pure, a mirror;
Beautiful there for the colour derived from green rocks under;
Beautiful, most of all, where beads of foam uprising
40   Mingle their clouds of white with the delicate hue of the stillness.
Cliff over cliff for its sides, with rowan and pendent birch boughs,
Here it lies, unthought of above at the bridge and pathway,
Still more enclosed from below by wood and rocky projection.
You are shut in, left alone with yourself and perfection of water,
45   Hid on all sides, left alone with yourself and the goddess of bathing.
Here, the pride of the plunger, you stride the fall and clear it;
Here, the delight of the bather, you roll in beaded sparklings,
Here into pure green depth drop down from lofty ledges.
Hither, a month agone, they had come, and discovered it; hither
50   (Long a design, but long unaccountably left unaccomplished),
Leaving the well-known bridge and pathway above to the forest,
Turning below from the track of the carts over stone and shingle,
Piercing a wood, and skirting a narrow and natural causeway
Under the rocky wall that hedges the bed of the streamlet,
55   Rounded a craggy point, and saw on a sudden before them
Slabs of rock, and a tiny beach, and perfection of water,
Picture-like beauty, seclusion sublime, and the goddess of bathing.
There they bathed, of course, and Arthur, the glory of headers,
Leapt from the ledges with Hope, he twenty feet, he thirty;

41 rowan mountain ash.

60 There, overbold, great Hobbes from a ten-foot height
      descended,
   Prone, as a quadruped, prone with hands and feet protending;
   There in the sparkling champagne, ecstatic, they shrieked
      and shouted
   'Hobbes's gutter' the Piper entitles the spot, profanely,
   Hope 'the Glory' would have, after Arthur, the glory of
      headers:
65 But, for before they departed, in shy and fugitive reflex
   Here in the eddies and there did the splendour of Jupiter
      glimmer,
   Adam adjudged it the name of Hesperus, star of the evening.
   Hither, to Hesperus, now, the star of evening above them,
   Come in their lonelier walk the pupils twain and Tutor;
70 Turned from the track of the carts, and passing the stone
      and shingle,
   Piercing the wood, and skirting the stream by the natural
      causeway,
   Rounded the craggy point, and now at their ease looked up;
      and
   Lo, on the rocky ledge, regardant, the Glory of headers,
   Lo, on the beach, expecting the plunge, not cigarless, the
      Piper, –
75 And they looked, and wondered, incredulous, looking yet
      once more.
   Yes, it was he, on the ledge, bare-limbed, an Apollo,
      down-gazing,
   Eying one moment the beauty, the life, ere he flung himself
      in it,
   Eying through eddying green waters the green-tinting floor
      underneath them,
   Eying the bead on the surface, the bead, like a cloud, rising
      to it,
80 Drinking-in, deep in his soul, the beautiful hue and the
      clearness,
   Arthur, the shapely, the brave, the unboasting, the glory of
      headers;
   Yes, and with fragrant weed, by his knapsack, spectator and
      critic,
   Seated on slab by the margin, the Piper, the Cloud-compeller.

83 the Cloud-compeller the producer of cigar-smoke. A mock-heroic epithet, in a Homeric tradition: suitable for the spirit of the academic working holiday. Νεφεληγερέτα may be traced through Pope's *Iliad* 16.556, etc. and *The Dunciad Variorum* 1.77; 3.337. Christopher Smart uses it in the mock-heroic sense (*Fable* 16 (1752)), as does Carlyle, *Sartor Resartus* 1.3, to describe smokers.

5

One of the powerful examples in the poem of Philip Hewson's radical and original thinking. He himself does not know whether to take his observations 'in irony...or earnest'.

> List to a letter that came from Philip at Balloch to Adam.
> I am here, O my friend! – idle, but learning wisdom.
> 40   Doing penance, you think; content, if so, in my penance.
> Often I find myself saying, while watching in dance or on
>   horseback
> One that is here, in her freedom, and grace, and imperial
>   sweetness,
> Often I find myself saying, old faith and doctrine abjuring,
> Into the crucible casting philosophies, facts, convictions, –
> 45   Were it not well that the stem should be naked of leaf and of
>   tendril,
> Poverty-stricken, the barest, the dismallest stick of the garden;
> Flowerless, leafless, unlovely, for ninety-and-nine long summers,
> So in the hundredth, at last, were bloom for one day at the
>   summit,
> So but that fleeting flower were lovely as Lady Maria.
> 50   Often I find myself saying, and know not myself as I say it,
> What of the poor and the weary? their labour and pain is
>   needed.
> Perish the poor and the weary! what can they better than
>   perish,
> Perish in labour for her, who is worth the destruction of
>   empires?
> What! for a mite, or a mote, an impalpable odour of honour,
> 55   Armies shall bleed; cities burn; and the soldier red from
>   the storming
> Carry hot rancour and lust into chambers of mothers and
>   daughters:
> What! would ourselves for the cause of an hour encounter the
>   battle,
> Slay and be slain; lie rotting in hospital, hulk, and prison;
> Die as a dog dies; die mistaken perhaps, and dishonoured.

40 ∧ 1 You have conjectured a change must have come to my mind: I believe it! | You will believe it too; if I tell you the thoughts that haunt me! *1848.*
58 C. worked on hospital reform with Florence Nightingale a decade later.
59 **mistaken...dishonoured**] secure that to uttermost ages *1848.*
59 ∧ 60 Not one ray shall illumine our midnight of shame and dishonour, | Yea, till in silence the fingers stand still on the world's great dial | Fathers and mothers, the gentle and good of unborn generations, | Shall to their little ones point out our names for their loathing and horror? *1848.*

60   Yea, – and shall hodmen in beer-shops complain of a glory
            denied them,
       Which could not ever be theirs more than now it is theirs as
            spectators?
       Which could not be, in all earth, if it were not for labour of
            hodmen?
          And I find myself saying, and what I am saying, discern not,
       Dig in thy deep dark prison, O miner! and finding be thankful;
65   Though unpolished by thee, unto thee unseen in perfection,
       While thou art eating black bread in the poisonous air of thy
            cavern,
       Far away glitter the gem on the peerless neck of a Princess,
       Dig, and starve, and be thankful; it is so, and thou hast been
            aiding.

60 hodmen building labourers.
67 glitter] glitters *London 1862, 1863, 1951*.

                                    7

This is the scene in which, after hesitations, Philip and Elspie become firmly
committed to each other, and the narrative voice uses the image of the
mountain stream flowing into the sea that occurred in her dream.

       But on the morrow Elspie kept out of the way of Philip;
       And at the evening seat, when he took her hand by the alders,
       Drew it back, saying, almost peevishly, 'No, Mr. Philip,
100   I was quite right, last night, it is too soon, too sudden.
       What I told you before was foolish perhaps, was hasty.
       When I think it over, I am shocked and terrified at it.
       Not that at all I unsay it; that is, I know I said it,
       And when I said it, felt it. But oh, we must wait, Mr. Philip!
105   We mustn't pull ourselves at the great key-stone of the centre;

100–1 Cf. *Rom.* 2. 2.118 'It is too rash, too unadvised, too sudden.'
105–8 The arch was important in Victorian theory on morally good
architecture; see especially Ruskin *Stones of Venice* I Chs. 10 and 11 (*Works*
9.153–81), and 'Lectures on Architecture and Painting' (1854): 'Stonehenge is
strong enough, but it takes some trouble to build in the manner of
Stonehenge: and Stonehenge itself is not so strong as an arch of the
Colosseum' (*Works* 12.24). Cf. D. H. Lawrence *The Rainbow* for extended
treatment of the arch as symbol of harmonious love. Biswas 280 interprets
the key-stone as phallic. Elspie thinks of divine sanction of the love: for
Christ as the key-stone see *Eph.* 2.20. The image repeats one used by Elspie
in 7. 67–72, and Philip 7. 84.
C.'s corrected copy of *1848* is much less visualized at this point: he tended
to make his conceptions more vivid in revision: 'We mustn't hurry things,
and insist of ourselves to complete them | Someone else, up above us, must
come and finish it for us | We shall only do harm if we try, too soon to do
all things | Only do damage and spoil perhaps all [illegible].'

[90] Arthur Hugh Clough

Some one else up above must hold it, fit it, and fix it;
If we try ourselves, we shall only damage the archway,
Damage all our own work that we wrought, our painful
up-building.
When, you remember, you took my hand last evening, talking,
110 I was all over a tremble: and as you pressed the fingers
After, and afterwards kissed it, I could not speak. And then,
too,
As we went home, you kissed me for saying your name. It
was dreadful.
I have been kissed before', she added, blushing slightly,
'I have been kissed more than once by Donald my cousin, and
others;
115 It is the way of the lads, and I make up my mind not to mind
it;
But Mr. Philip, last night, and from you, it was different quite,
Sir.
When I think of all that, I am shocked and terrified at it.
Yes, it is dreadful to me.'
She paused, but quickly continued,
Smiling almost fiercely, continued, looking upward.
120 'You are too strong, you see, Mr. Philip! just like the sea there,
Which *will* come, through the straits and all between the
mountains,
Forcing its great strong tide into every nook and inlet,
Getting far in, up the quiet stream of sweet inland water,
Sucking it up, and stopping it, turning it, driving it backward,
125 Quite preventing its own quiet running: and then, soon after,
Back it goes off, leaving weeds on the shore, and wrack and
uncleanness:
And the poor burn in the glen tries again its peaceful running,
But it is brackish and tainted, and all its banks in disorder.
That was what I dreamt all last night. I was the burnie,
130 Trying to get along through the tyrannous brine, and could
not;
I was confined and squeezed in the coils of the great salt tide,
that
Would mix-in itself with me, and change me; I felt myself
changing;
And I struggled, and screamed, I believe, in my dream. It was
dreadful.

129 burnie streamlet.
131–3 The fear of change or loss of identity in the love relationship is
frequently expressed in C.'s love-letters.

You are too strong, Mr. Philip! I am but a poor slender
    burnie,
135 Used to the glens and the rocks, the rowan and birch of the
    woodies,
Quite unused to the great salt sea; quite afraid and unwilling.'
    Ere she had spoken two words, had Philip released her
    fingers:
As she went on, he recoiled, fell back, and shook, and
    shivered;
There he stood, looking pale and ghastly; when she had ended,
140 Answering in hollow voice,
                        'It is true; oh quite true, Elspie;
Oh, you are always right; oh, what, what have I been doing!
I will depart to-morrow. But oh, forget me not wholly,
Wholly, Elspie, nor hate me, no, do not hate me, my Elspie.'

But a revulsion passed through the brain and bosom of
    Elspie;
145 And she got up from her seat on the rock; putting by her
    knitting,
Went to him, where he stood, and answered:
                            'No, Mr. Philip,
No, you are good, Mr. Philip, and gentle; and I am the
    foolish;
No, Mr. Philip, forgive me.'
                    She stepped right to him, and boldly
Took up his hand, and placed it in hers; he daring no
    movement;
150 Took up the cold hanging hand, up-forcing the heavy elbow.
'I am afraid,' she said, 'but I will!' and kissed the fingers.
And he fell on his knees and kissed her own past counting.

But a revulsion wrought in the brain and bosom of Elspie;
And the passion she just had compared to the vehement ocean,
155 Urging in high spring-tide its masterful way through the
    mountains,
Forcing and flooding the silvery stream, as it runs from the
    inland;
That great power withdrawn, receding here and passive,
Felt she in myriad springs, her sources, far in the mountains,
Stirring, collecting, rising, upheaving, forth-outflowing,
160 Taking and joining, right welcome, that delicate rill in the
    valley,
Filling it, making it strong, and still descending, seeking,
With a blind forefeeling descending ever, and seeking,

157 power] water *1848.*

With a delicious forefeeling, the great still sea before it;
There deep into it, far, to carry, and lose in its bosom,
165 Waters that still from their sources exhaustless are fain to be
added.
As he was kissing her fingers, and knelt on the ground before
her,
Yielding backward she sank to her seat, and of what she was
doing
Ignorant, bewildered, in sweet multitudinous vague emotion,
Stooping, knowing not what, put her lips to the hair on his
forehead:
170 And Philip, raising himself, gently, for the first time, round her
Passing his arms, close, close, enfolded her, close to his bosom.
As they went home by the moon, 'Forgive me, Philip,'
she whispered;
'I have so many things to think of, all of a sudden;
I who had never once thought a thing, – in my ignorant
Highlands.'

169 hair] curl *1848.*

91 *Amours de Voyage*: extracts

Date Apr.–Oct. 1849, by which time the poem was complete enough to
show Shairp and Walrond.
Context Composed and set in Rome during the French invasion. C. was
present at the revolutionary birth-pangs of France and Italy, and was
addressed by Arnold as 'A Republican Friend'. The story is of the love of a
proto-Prufrockian man called Claude for a girl of the commercial middle
class – Mary Trevellyn – told in epistolary manner. It is one of the most
remarkable of the long Victorian poems dealing with love, especially in its
emphatic eschewing of sentimentality.
Versions *1974* prints a greater wealth of manuscript material than has ever
been available before. Indeed, the contrasts between the drafts and the
published versions makes for one of the most interesting revelations of the
poet at work of any century.
Discussion Chorley 187–211, Biswas 298–321, Houghton 119–155.
Publication *Atlantic Monthly* (Feb.–May 1858), *1862* (64 extra lines), *1863*,
1869.

Canto 1 Letter 4

CLAUDE TO EUSTACE

65 No, the Christian faith, as at any rate I understood it,
With its humiliations and exaltations combining,
Exaltations sublime, and yet diviner abasements,
Aspirations from something most shameful here upon earth
and

In our poor selves to something most perfect above in the
    heavens, –
70 No, the Christian faith, as I, at least, understood it,
    Is not here, O Rome, in any of these thy churches;
    Is not here, but in Freiburg, or Rheims, or Westminster Abbey.
    What in thy Dome I find, in all thy recenter efforts,
    Is a something, I think, more *rational* far, more earthly,
75 Actual, less ideal, devout not in scorn and refusal,
    But in a positive, calm, Stoic-Epicurean acceptance.
    This I begin to detect in St. Peter's and some of the churches,
    Mostly in all that I see of the sixteenth-century masters;
    Overlaid of course with infinite gauds and gewgaws,
80 Innocent, playful follies, the toys and trinkets of childhood,
    Forced on maturer years, as the serious one thing needful,
    By the barbarian will of the rigid and ignorant Spaniard.
    Curious work, meantime, re-entering society; how we
    Walk a livelong day, great Heaven, and watch our shadows!
85 What our shadows seem, forsooth, we will ourselves be.
    Do I look like that? you think me that: then I am that.

72 Gothic churches of the pious Middle Ages.
74–5 For C.'s appreciation of rational, classical Renaissance architecture, as
opposed to gothic romance, obscurity and gloom see no. 94.1 lines 204–229.
See also C.'s letter to T. Arnold (24 May 1849): 'The idea of St. Peter's has
been wholly killed out of it, partly by the horrid internal ornaments, but still
more completely by the change of the form from a Greek to a Latin cross,
the latter belonging to a Gothic which Michael Angelo rejects because he
asserts *totality*.' (*Correspondence* 1.256).
85 Cf. Donne *His Picture* lines 3–4: ''Tis like me now, but I dead, 'twill be
more | When we are shadows both, than 'twas before.'

Canto 2 Letter 2

30 *Dulce* it is, and *decorum*, no doubt, for the country to fall, – to
    Offer one's blood an oblation to Freedom, and die for the
        Cause; yet
    Still, individual culture is also something, and no man
    Finds quite distinct the assurance that he of all others
        is called on,
    Or would be justified, even, in taking away from the world
        that
35 Precious creature, himself. Nature sent him here to abide
        here;

30 '*Dulce et decorum est pro patria mori*' Horace *Odes* 3.2. 13. See Wilfred
Owen *Dulce et Decorum Est.*
32 individual culture a reference to the growing philosophy of individualism
(see K. W. Swart *JHI* 23 (1962) 77–90), but in a more particular sense to
Emersonian self-culture.

Else why sent him at all? Nature wants him still, it is likely.
On the whole, we are meant to look after ourselves; it is
   certain
Each has to eat for himself, digest for himself, and in
   general
Care for his own dear life, and see to his own preservation;

40   Nature's intentions, in most things uncertain, in this
   most plain are decisive;
These, on the whole, I conjecture the Romans will follow,
   and I shall.
  So we cling to our rocks like limpets; Ocean may bluster,
Over and under and round us; we open our shells to imbibe
   our
Nourishment, close them again, and are safe, fulfilling
   the purpose

45   Nature intended, – a wise one, of course, and a noble,
   we doubt not.
Sweet it may be and decorous, perhaps, for the country
   to die; but,
On the whole, we conclude the Romans won't do it,
   and I shan't.

Canto 2 Letters 10–12

10. CLAUDE TO EUSTACE

250   I am in love, meantime, you think; no doubt you would
   think so.
I am in love, you say; with those letters, of course, you
   would say so.
I am in love, you declare. I think not so; yet I grant you
It is a pleasure, indeed, to converse with this girl. Oh, rare gift,
Rare felicity, this! she can talk in a rational way, can

255   Speak upon subjects that really are matters of mind and of
   thinking,
Yet in perfection retain her simplicity; never, one moment,
Never, however you urge it, however you tempt her, consents
   to
Step from ideas and fancies and loving sensations to those vain
Conscious understandings that vex the minds of man-kind.

260   No, though she talk, it is music; her fingers desert not the
   keys; 'tis

259–60 Never, however you tempt here, however you urge it, consents to |
Unsex herself, and come out as a Lady Macbeth of letters | Fit henceforward,
alas, to bear male offspring only* | And, in the season of life, be admired of
Art's apostles. *MS. A* canc.
*Cf. Shakespeare *Mac.* 1.7.73–5 'Bring forth men-children only! | For thy
undaunted mettle should compose | Nothing but males.'

Song, though you hear in the song the articulate vocables
    sounded,
Syllabled singly and sweetly the words of melodious meaning.
I am in love, you say; I do not think so exactly.

11. CLAUDE TO EUSTACE

There are two different kinds, I believe, of human attraction:
265 One which simply disturbs, unsettles, and makes you uneasy,
And another that poises, retains, and fixes and holds you.
I have no doubt, for myself, in giving my voice for the latter.
I do not wish to be moved, but growing where I was growing,
There more truly to grow, to live where as yet I had languished.
270 I do not like being moved: for the will is excited; and action
Is a most dangerous thing; I tremble for something factitious,
Some malpractice of heart and illegitimate process;
We are so prone to these things with our terrible notions of
    duty.

12. CLAUDE TO EUSTACE

Ah, let me look, let me watch, let me wait, unhurried,
    unprompted!
275 Bid me not venture on aught that could alter or end what is
    present!
Say not, Time flies, and Occasion, that never returns, is
    departing!
Drive me not you, ye ill angels with fiery swords, from my
    Eden,
Waiting, and watching, and looking! Let love be its own
    inspiration!
Shall not a voice, if a voice there must be, from the airs that
    environ,
280 Yea, from the conscious heavens, without our knowledge or
    effort,
Break into audible words? and love be its own inspiration?

263–64 12 cancelled lines in *MS. A 1974*, 631.
264–7 7 cancelled lines in *MS. A 1974*, 632.
264–73 omitted in *Atlantic Monthly*.

92 'Say not the struggle nought availeth'

Date Oct. 1849; composed while C. was in Rome.
    Its immediate circumstance was probably the siege, though the struggle symbolizes more general battles. C. expresses, for him, an unusual degree of optimism. Winston Churchill conferred an extra guarantee of immortality on the poem by quoting it in one of his wartime speeches: 27 Apr. 1941 (*Complete Speeches* ed. R. R. James (1974) 6.6384).

[93] Arthur Hugh Clough

Publication *The Crayon* (Aug. 1855), *1862, 1863, 1869*.
Text There are six *MSS.*: 1974 prints *MS.*[6] in *1852* (*Smith*) *Nbk.* – the text
followed here. For discussion of the text see A. L. P. Norrington in
Essays...Presented to Sir Humphrey Milford (Oxford, 1948).

> Say not the struggle nought availeth,
>   The labour and the wounds are vain,
> The enemy faints not, nor faileth
>   And as things have been, things remain.
>
> 5   If hopes were dupes, fears may be liars;
>   It may be, in yon smoke concealed,
> Your comrades chase e'en now the fliers,
>   And, but for you, possess the field.
>
> For while the tired waves, vainly breaking,
> 10   Seem here no painful inch to gain,
> Far back through creeks and inlets making
>   Came, silent, flooding in, the main,
>
> And not by eastern windows only,
>   When daylight comes, comes in the light,
> 15   In front the sun climbs slow, how slowly,
>   But westward, look, the land is bright.

4 things remain] they remain *1862, 1863, 1869*.
8 E'en now possess the peaceful field. *MS.*[2], *MS.*[3].
10 painful] tedious *MS.*[2], *MS.*[3]
11–12 Cf. no. 90.7. 120–5 for the image of the sea flooding into an inlet.
16 But westward] Behind you, *MS.*[1]

---

93 'Each for himself is still the rule'

Date 1850? The *1852* (*Smith*) *Nbk.* contains a fair copy dated 6 Apr. 1852,
the text printed here; but it seems that C. had been intending to use the
poem for *Dipsychus V* (*1974* 698) as one of the Spirit's speeches. See C.'s
letter to Burbidge, June 1844: '...I do believe too that in the some way [*sic*]
or other the problem [of the labourer] now solved by universal competition
or the devil take the hindmost may receive a more satisfactory solution'
(*Correspondence* 1.126).
Publication *1863, 1869*.

> Each for himself is still the rule,
>   We learn it when we go to school –
>   The devil take the hindmost, o!

Title *In the Great Metropolis 1869*.

And when the schoolboys grow to men,
5   In life they learn it o'er again –
    The devil take the hindmost, o!

For in the church, and at the bar,
On 'Change, at court, where'er they are,
The devil takes the hindmost, o!

10   Husband for husband, wife for wife,
    Are careful that in married life
    The devil take the hindmost, o!

From youth to age, whate'er the game,
The unvarying practice is the same –
15   The devil take the hindmost, o!

And after death, we do not know,
But scarce can doubt, where'er we go,
The devil takes the hindmost, o!

Tol rol de rol, tol rol de ro,
20   The devil take the hindmost, o!

8 'Change abbreviation for Exchange, where merchants conduct business.
19 Tol...tol] Ti...ti *1863, 1869.*

94 Dipsychus: extracts

Date Composition began Autumn 1850. C. visited Venice and began writing whilst there, or soon after.

The theme A manuscript draft has survived (*1850*) in which the two speakers are Faustulus and Mephistopheles, but in later manuscripts the speakers were Dipsychus and the Spirit. Dipsychus is a dreamy romantic figure disturbed by a cynical spirit who urges rationality and action. One is reminded that the traditions of C18 scepticism were not remote from C.'s time. *Dipsychus* is one of the most remarkable examples of a study of the split personality. It was not published in C.'s lifetime, and C. wrote to his fiancée (when she stumbled on the MS by accident): 'Dear Blanche, please don't read Dipsychus yet – I wish particularly not. You shall see it sometime – but now, not, please – dear, I beg not, please...' (*Correspondence* 2.350). That she was shocked by its sexual impropriety and religious free-thinking is evidenced by the excisions she made in preparing it for publication.

The text The textual problems in preparing an edition of the complete poem are enormous: for which see *1974* 681–723.

Publication *1865, 1869.*

Scene 5

SPIRIT

130 As I sat at the café, I said to myself
They may talk as they please about what they call pelf,
They may sneer as they like about eating and drinking,
But help it I cannot, I cannot help thinking
How pleasant it is to have money, heigh ho!
135 How pleasant it is to have money.

I sit at my table *en grand seigneur*,
And when I have done, throw a crust to the poor;
Not only the pleasure, one's self, of good living,
But also the pleasure of now and then giving,
140 So pleasant it is to have money, heigh ho!
So pleasant it is to have money.

It was but last winter I came up to Town,
But already I'm getting a little renown;
I make new acquaintance where'er I appear;
145 I am not too shy, and have nothing to fear.
So pleasant it is to have money, heigh ho!
So pleasant it is to have money.

I drive through the streets, and I care not a d—mn;
The people they stare, and they ask who I am;
150 And if I should chance to run over a cad,
I can pay for the damage if ever so bad.
So pleasant it is to have money, heigh ho!
So pleasant it is to have money.

We stroll to our box and look down on the pit,
155 And if it weren't low should be tempted to spit;
We loll and we talk until people look up,
And when it's half over we go out and sup.
So pleasant it is to have money, heigh ho!
So pleasant it is to have money.

160 The best of the table and best of the fare –
And as for the others, the devil may care;
It isn't our fault if they dare not afford

Sc. 5 variants A notebook contains a fair copy of an alternative version of
lines 130–235 (excluding lines 204–229). This version was printed in *1862*,
1863 with the title *Spectator ab Extra*, and it exists as an earlier draft on
paper C. used in America entitled *Philosophia Metropolitana. Spectator ab
Extra* reprinted in *1974* 698–702.
150 cad vulgar citizen – in 1830s applied in Oxford to townspeople.

To sup like a prince and be drunk as a lord.
So pleasant it is to have money, heigh ho!
165   So pleasant it is to have money.

We sit at our tables and tipple champagne;
Ere one bottle goes, comes another again;
The waiters they skip and they scuttle about,
And the landlord attends us so civilly out.
170   So pleasant it is to have money, heigh ho!
So pleasant it is to have money.

It was but last winter I came up to Town,
But already I'm getting a little renown;
I get to good houses without much ado,
175   Am beginning to see the nobility too.
So pleasant it is to have money, heigh ho!
So pleasant it is to have money.

O dear! what a pity they ever should lose it!
For they are the gentry that know how to use it;
180   So grand and so graceful, such manners, such dinners,
But yet, after all, it is we are the winners.
So pleasant it is to have money, heigh ho!
So pleasant it is to have money.

Thus I sat at my table *en grand seigneur*,
185   And when I had done threw a crust to the poor;
Not only the pleasure, one's self, of good eating,
But also the pleasure of now and then treating.
So pleasant it is to have money, heigh ho!
So pleasant it is to have money.

190   They may talk as they please about what they call pelf,
And how one ought never to think of one's self,
And how pleasures of thought surpass eating and drinking –
My pleasure of thought is the pleasure of thinking
How pleasant it is to have money, heigh ho!
195   How pleasant it is to have money.

(Written in Venice, but for all parts true,
'Twas not a crust I gave him, but a sou.)

---

171 ∧ **2** That fine looking girl whom we saw in the play | Was so very glad
when we met t'other day; | They tell me for sure she is one of the richest |
But she knows all about it, as well as the rest. | So pleasant – *MS. V.*

A gondola here, and a gondola there,
'Tis the pleasantest fashion of taking the air
200 To right and to left; stop, turn, and go yonder,
And let us repeat, o'er the tide as we wander,
　How pleasant it is to have money, heigh ho!
　How pleasant it is to have money.

Come, leave your Gothic, worn-out story,
205 San Giorgio and the Redemptore;
I from no building, gay or solemn,
Can spare the shapely Grecian column.
'Tis not, these centuries four, for nought
Our European world of thought
210 Hath made familiar to its home
The classic mind of Greece and Rome;
In all new work that would look forth
To more than antiquarian worth,
Palladio's pediments and bases,
215 Or something such, will find their places:
Maturer optics don't delight
In childish dim religious light,
In evanescent vague effects
That shirk, not face, one's intellects;
220 They love not fancies fast betrayed,
And artful tricks of light and shade,
But pure form nakedly displayed,
And all things absolutely made.
The Doge's palace though, from hence,
225 In spite of Ruskin's d——d pretence,
The tide now level with the quay,
Is certainly a thing to see.
We'll turn to the Rialto soon;
One's told to see it by the moon.

204–23 Printed separately *1862, 1863*.
204–229 The passage is anti-Ruskinian. By March 1851 R. had published
The Seven Lamps of Architecture and Vol. 1 of *The Stones of Venice*. C. and
the Ruskins were both in Venice in Sept. 1851, but there is no record of
their having been acquainted. C. seems to be thinking primarily of Ch. 3 of
The Seven Lamps ('The Lamp of Power') in which the Doge's Palace is
praised, and the Gothic habit of drawing 'with darkness upon light' is
contrasted with the Greek of drawing 'with light upon darkness'. The Spirit
is attracted, as in his ethical tastes, to a rational and classical architectural
taste, to Andrea Palladio, whose San Giorgio Maggiore was completed
1566–90 and Redentore 1577–92.
216–17 Cf. Milton *Il Penseroso* lines 159–60: 'And storied windows richly
dight, | Casting a dim religious light.'
225 Ruskin's d[amne]d pretence] doctrinaire pretence *1865*.

230   A gondola here, and a gondola there,
      'Tis the pleasantest fashion of taking the air.
      To right and to left; stop, turn, and go yonder,
      And let us repeat, o'er the flood as we wander,
          How pleasant it is to have money, heigh ho!
235   How pleasant it is to have money.

Scene 6

SPIRIT

      I'm not a judge, I own; in short,
135   Religion may not be my forte.
      The Church of England I belong to,
      But think Dissenters not far wrong too;
      They're vulgar dogs; but for his *creed*
      I hold that no man will be d——d.
140   My Establishment I much respect,
      Her ordinances don't neglect;
      Attend at Church on Sunday once,
      And in the Prayer-book am no dunce;
      Baptise my babies; nay, my wife
145   Would be churched too once in her life
      She's taken, I regret to state,
      Rather a Puseyite turn of late.
      To set the thing quite right, I went
      At Easter to the Sacrament.
150   'Tis proper once a year or so
      To do the civil thing and show –
      But come and listen in your turn
      And you shall hear and mark and learn.

      'There is no God,' the wicked saith,
155   'And truly it's a blessing,
      For what he might have done with us
          It's better only guessing.'

      'There is no God,' a youngster thinks,
          'Or really, if there may be,
160   He surely didn't mean a man
          Always to be a baby.'

140–51 Not in *1865*.
145 churched Churching was a thanksgiving ceremony for the safe delivery of a child. It tended to be a High Church practice.
147 Puseyite after the defection of Newman to the Roman Church (1845) Edward Bouverie Pusey (1800–82) became the leader of the Oxford (or Tractarian) Movement.
154–85 Printed separately *1862, 1863*.

'There is no God, or if there is,'
The tradesman thinks, "twere funny
If he should take it ill in me
165   To make a little money.'

'Whether there be,' the rich man says,
'It matters very little,
For I and mine, thank somebody,
Are not in want of victual.'

170   Some others, also, to themselves
Who scarce so much as doubt it,
Think there is none, when they are well,
And do not think about it.

But country folks who live beneath
175   The shadow of the steeple;
The parson and the parson's wife,
And mostly married people;

Youths green and happy in first love,
So thankful for illusion;
180   And men caught out in what the world
Calls guilt, in first confusion;

And almost every one when age,
Disease, or sorrows strike him,
Inclines to think there is a God,
185   Or something very like Him.

But *eccoci!* with our *barchetta*,
Here at the Sant' Elisabetta.

DIPSYCHUS
Vineyards and maize, that's pleasant for sore eyes.

162–5 omitted *1862, 1863*.
165 ∧ 6 Philosophers decide there's none | Yet as the World's a baby | The better way of putting it | Is saying that there may be. ‖ The fervent preacher cries aloud; | On our great revolution | We'll put him down as an arist – —| Ocratic institution. *MS. V.* canc.
177 ∧ 8 Poor souls that slave for daily bread | And do not always find it, | Who never are before the world | But generally behind it; *MS. V.* canc.
186 barchetta small boat.

SPIRIT

And on the island's other side,
190　The place where Murray's faithful Guide
Informs us Byron used to ride.

DIPSYCHUS

These trellised vines! enchanting! Sandhills, ho!
The sea, at last the sea – the real broad sea –
Beautiful! and a glorious breeze upon it.

SPIRIT

195　Look back; one catches at this station
Lagoon and sea in combination.

DIPSYCHUS

On her still lake the city sits,
Where bark and boat about her flits,
Nor dreams, her soft siesta taking,
200　Of Adriatic billows breaking.
I do; and see and hear them. Come! to the sea!

SPIRIT

The wind I think is the *sirocco*.
Yonder, I take it, is Malmocco.
Thank you! it never was my passion
205　To skip o'er sand-hills in that fashion.

DIPSYCHUS

Oh, a grand surge! we'll bathe; quick, quick! undress!
Quick, quick! in, in!
We'll take the crested billows by their backs
And shake them. Quick! in, in!
210　And I will taste again the old joy
I gloried in so when a boy.

190–1 See John Murray *Handbook for Travellers in N. Italy* (3rd edn 1847)
366: 'The shore of this Littorale towards the Adriatic constitutes the Lido,
now associated with the name of Byron, as the spot where he used to take
his rides, and where he designed to have been buried.'
191 ʌ 2 And that poor Shelley I don't doubt it | Talks somewhere in his
verse about it. *MS.*[1] canc. Cf. Shelley 'the bare strand of hillocks' *Julian and
Maddalo* lines 3–4.
197–200 Printed separately as *The Lido* (part of *At Venice*) *1862, 1863*.
202–5 Omitted *1865*.
202 sirocco a hot, ennervating wind blowing from North Africa.
206–225 D.'s swim combines Romantic nature-worship (typified by Byron's
Childe Harold 4.174, which also has the joy/boy rhyme) with a Victorian
muscular Christianity; see also no. 90.1 lines 76–81. The Spirit undercuts it,
and suggests it is closer to 'animal spirits' than mysticism.

[94] Arthur Hugh Clough

SPIRIT
Well; but it's not so pleasant for the feet;
We should have brought some towels and a sheet.

DIPSYCHUS
In, in! I go. Ye great winds blow,
215 And break, thou curly waves, upon my breast.

SPIRIT
Hm! I'm undressing. Doubtless all is well –
I only wish these thistles were at hell.
By heaven, I'll stop before that bad yet worse is,
And take care of our watches – and our purses.

DIPSYCHUS
220 Aha! come, come – great waters, roll!
Accept me, take me, body and soul! –
    Aha!

SPIRIT
Come, no more of that stuff,
I'm sure you've stayed in long enough.

DIPSYCHUS
That's done me good. It grieves me though
225 I never came here long ago.

SPIRIT
Pleasant perhaps. However, no offence,
Animal spirits are not common sense.
You think perhaps I have outworn them –
Certainly I have learnt to scorn them;
230 They're good enough as an assistance,
But in themselves a poor existence.
But you – with this one bathe, no doubt,
Have solved all questions out and out.
'Tis Easter Day, and on the Lido
235 Lo, Christ the Lord is risen indeed, O!

212–13 Omitted *1865*.
222–3 Omitted *1865*.
228–9 Omitted *1865*.
234–5 Omitted *1865*.
235 Cf. *Easter Day* refrain: 'Christ is not risen.'

95 'Put forth thy leaf, thou lofty plane'

Date Unknown. MS a single sheet in *Norton MSS*. (Harvard).
C. mentions the poem in a letter to Norton (16 Mar. 1859): 'Put forth thy
leaf – which I am glad to hear you have. – I couldn't find it.'
Publication *1862, 1863, 1869.*

> Put forth thy leaf, thou lofty plane,
>   East wind and frost are safely gone;
> With zephyr mild and balmy rain
>   The summer comes serenely on;
> 5   Earth, air, and sun and skies combine
>   To promise all that's kind and fair: –
> But thou, O human heart of mine,
>   Be still, contain thyself, and bear.
>
> December days were brief and chill,
> 10   The winds of March were wild and drear,
> And, nearing and receding still,
>   Spring never would, we thought, be here.
> The leaves that burst, the suns that shine,
>   Had, not the less, their certain date: –
> 15   And thou, O human heart of mine,
>   Be still, refrain thyself, and wait.

Title *In A London Square 1869.* If the title carried any authority, it might
imply that the poem was associated with C.'s chafing at London life: either
between 1850 and 1852, or after 1853. The plane is pre-eminently a London
tree, and it comes into leaf tantalizingly late in the spring.

96 'To spend uncounted years of pain'

Date Begun in 1851. The draft contains two unfinished stanzas, published in
1974 731, which include an allusion to Carlyle's favourite text: 'the night
cometh, when no man can work' (*John* 9.2.).
Publication *Putnam's Magazine* (July 1853), *1863, 1869.*

> To spend uncounted years of pain,
> Again, again, and yet again,
> In working out in heart and brain
>   The problem of our being here;

Title *Perche Pensa? Pensando S'Invecchia 1869.* (Why think? thinking makes
one grow old).
1 uncounted] unsolaced MS.
4 problem] riddle MS.

5   To gather facts from far and near,
       Upon the mind to hold them clear,
       And, knowing more may yet appear,
       Unto one's latest breath to fear
       The premature result to draw –
10   Is this the object, end and law,
          And purpose of our being here?

97 'If to write, rewrite, and write again'

Date 1851? (draft in *1851 Nbk.*).
Publication *1951*.

       If to write, rewrite, and write again,
       Bite now the lip and now the pen,
       Gnash in a fury the teeth, and tear
       Innocent paper or it may be hair,
5   In endless chases to pursue
       That swift escaping word that would do,
       Inside and out turn a phrase, o'er and o'er,
       Till all the little sense goes, it had before, –
       If it be these things make one a poet,
10   I am one – Come and all the world may know it.

       If to look over old poems and detest
       What one once hugged as a child to one's breast,
       Find the things nothing that once had been so much,
       The old noble forms gone into dust at a touch:
15   If to see oneself of one's fancied plumage stripped,
       If by one's faults as by furies to be whipped;
       If to become cool and, casting for good away
       All the old implements, take 'em up the next day;
       If to be sane to-night and insane again to-morrow,
20   And salve up past pains with the cause of future sorrow, –
       If to do these things make a man a poet,
       I am one – Come and all the world may know it.

       If nevertheless no other peace of mind,
       No inward unity ever to find,

2 Cf. Sidney *Astrophil and Stella* (1591) 1.13: 'Biting my tongue and pen, beating myself for spite' (this is not the text of *A & S* usually printed today. W. A. Ringler *The Poems of Sir Philip Sidney* (Oxford U.P. 1962) 453 regards it as descending from a manuscript 'with a considerable number of corruptions').
12 The mature poet not only rejects childish poetic products, but the matter of them.

25 No calm, well-being, sureness or rest
    Save when by that strange temper possessed,
    Out of whose kind sources in pure rhythm-flow
    The easy melodious verse-currents go;
    If so sit still while the world goes by,
30 Find old friends dull and new friends dry,
    Dinners a bore and dancing worse,
    Compared to the tagging of verse onto verse, –
    If it be these things make one a poet,
    I am [one] – Come [and] all the world [may] know [it].

34 [ ] indicate *lacunae* filled by F. L. Mulhauser (*1974*).

98 'The syringe cloud of aspiration'

Date Unknown. Written on upper half of the MS sheet preceding the following poem.
   This scientific image used to describe a state of mind establishes something of a kinship between Clough and the Metaphysical poets.
Publication *1951* 576.

    The syringe cloud of aspiration
    Wh[ich] travelling o'er the ocean of our soul
    Suddenly drops and sucks its waters up
    [Can't?] do it surely, cannot, must not do
5   Merely as the idle schoolboy with a quill
    Just for the fun of letting them fall again.

99 The Latest Decalogue

Date Unknown. The poem has two manuscripts, one in *Norton MSS.* (Harvard), in a folder with corrections for *Amours de Voyage* (so the poem is at least later than 1849 in this version); the other in B.L. (the version printed here and in *1951*). P. G. Scott *N & Q* 212 (1967) 378 argues that the *Norton MSS.* version may be later than the one printed here. See *1974* 676 for the *Norton MSS.* version.
Publication *1862* (variants between *London* and *Boston*), *1863*, *1869*.

    Thou shalt have one God only; who
    Would be at the expense of two?
    No graven images may be
    Worshipped, except the currency:
5   Swear not at all; for for thy curse
    Thine enemy is none the worse:

> At church on Sunday to attend
> Will serve to keep the world thy friend:
> Honour thy parents; that is, all
> 10 From whom advancement may befall:
> Thou shalt not kill; but needst not strive
> Officiously to keep alive:
> Do not adultery commit;
> Advantage rarely comes of it:
> 15 Thou shalt not steal; an empty feat,
> When it's so lucrative to cheat:
> Bear not false witness; let the lie
> Have time on its own wings to fly:
> Thou shalt not covet; but tradition
> 20 Approves all forms of competition.
>
> The sum of all is, thou shalt love,
> If any body, God above:
> At any rate shall never labour
> *More* than thyself to love thy neighbour.

11–12 Scott suggests an echo of Byron: 'Revenge in person's certainly no virtue, | But then 'tis not *my* fault if *others* hurt you' *Don Juan* 1.30.239–40.
11–16 Cf. C. 'The Militia' *The Balance* 6 Feb. 1846: 'the definitive "Thou shalt not do murder," and "Thou shalt not steal," may pass into a very dubious "Thou shalt do no murder, *without great provocation*," and "Thou shalt not steal, *except now and then.*"' (Trawick 214).
21–4 not in *Norton MSS.*, *1862*, *1863*, *1869*. Scott suggests an echo of Isaac Watts's versified summary of the Ten Commandments in *Divine Songs* (1715): 'With all thy Soul love God above, | And as thy self thy Neighbour love.'

100 'That there are powers above us I admit'

Date Unknown: MS. in Bodleian an undated loose sheet in pencil with changes in ink in an unknown hand. These changes are revealing (see notes below) since they indicate the conventionality of C.'s editors, by comparison with him.
Publication *1869* (in bowdlerized form); first printed thus *1974*.

> That there are powers above us I admit;
> It may be true too
> That while we walk the troublous tossing sea,
> That when we see the o'ertopping waves advance,

Title *O Thou of Little Faith 1869*.
1 Omitted *1869*.
2 too omitted *1869*.

5   And when [we] feel our feet beneath us sink,
There are who walk beside us; and the cry
That rises so spontaneous to the lips,
The 'Help us or we perish', is not nought,
An evanescent spectrum of disease.
10   It may be that in deed and not in fancy,
A hand that is not ours upstays our steps,
A voice that is not ours commands the waves,
Commands the waves, and whispers in our ear,
O thou of little faith, why didst thou doubt?
15   At any rate –
That there are beings above us, I suppose
(Hypothesis the soul of science is),
And when we lift up holy hands of prayer,
I will not say they will not give us aid.

16 suppose] may think MS. originally; both crossed out and 'believe' substituted, the reading for *1869, 1951.*
17 Cancelled in MS.; omitted *1869, 1951.*

Matthew Arnold

Life and works Matthew Arnold was the eldest son of Thomas Arnold. He was born in 1822. In 1828 the family moved to Rugby, where his father became one of the most famous public school headmasters of all time (see Headnote to Clough and no. 108). The years 1837–41 were spent at Rugby, where A. was already showing signs of being a poet with *Alaric at Rome.* He followed Clough to Balliol College, Oxford; like Clough he did not fare well in examinations, but became a Fellow of Oriel (1845). The relationship with Clough was a key element in A.'s life – as a human being and as a poet (see nos. 104 and 106). A. taught at Rugby, then became private secretary to the Marquis of Lansdowne (1847), who procured for him an inspectorship of schools (1851). His career established, he was able to marry Frances Wightman in the same year.

Many elements entered into his early make-up. Outwardly he was a dandy and a genial entertainer: his Gallic tastes lightened his character and ultimately gave him broader perspectives than most of his contemporaries possessed. Yet the urbane, even cosmopolitan, element was countered by a love of nature in the true Romantic style, reinforced by the completion of the family home at Fox How (near Ambleside, in the Lake District). In addition, he had a deep love and understanding of the classics, which helped to mould his poetic identity, and to develop an inner stability and melancholy at odds with the spirit of his age. But in contrast, he shared his father's interests in contemporary affairs and problems.

Matthew Arnold

In 1849 his first collection of poems appeared: *The Strayed Reveller*. His close friends and family were surprised at the spirit of earnestness and inquiry in the volume. As in Clough's case it has been recognized that the most central truths of A.'s character were embodied in his poetry rather than anywhere else. Like Clough, he felt the strain of the questioning atmosphere of the 1840s, the non-poetic and the anti-poetic quality of it all. He thought that poetry could operate as an opposing force by becoming the 'adequate' formative element in life that it had been in Sophoclean Greece. But during the 1850s he became more aware of the intractable nature of the modern dilemma; hence his regret in the preface to *1853* that 'the calm, the cheerfulness, the disinterested objectivity have disappeared: the dialogue of the mind with itself has commenced; modern problems have presented themselves'. He continued: 'We hear already the doubts, we witness the discouragement, of Hamlet and of Faust.' He managed to produce beautiful elaborately fabricated poetry – such as *Sohrab and Rustum* – but when he was honest with himself was unable to exclude the self-indulgent nostalgia, the ennui, the perplexity, the complaint, the dreariness that were so prevalent in modern life, especially for people like himself and Clough who had to earn their wages in mundane tasks. In his own terms this melancholy and disturbed poetry was hardly 'adequate'; but it was honest and symptomatic, it has survived best, and it takes priority in the present selection. He produced a sizeable body of poetic work up to the mid 1860s, although the bulk of his output was completed by 1853. Since he did not regard himself primarily as a poet, it is no surprise that eventually his critical spirit, his honesty, and his lack of 'motives' killed off poetic production. He continued to believe in poetry as a regenerative force in modern society, but not the poetry he was writing. As critic, Professor of Poetry at Oxford, journalist and prophet he urged the English Philistine to consider the claims of poetry and the life of the mind. His campaign was conducted in prose: sad proof that strong commitment, action and profound belief were more effectively fostered by the prose medium. He was more able to adapt himself to the journalistic world than Clough, and the dandyish bonhomie of his youth was eventually alchemized into the well-polished air of the professional entertainer. He continued to be known as 'Merry Matt', and the *DNB* (Richard Garnett) regretted that his Oxford lectures 'were disfigured by inexcusable flippancies at the expense of persons entitled to the highest respect'. The bulk of his critical work far outweighs that of the poetry. It covers an impressive range: classical, European, English and American literature; politics; religion; ethics; education; Celtic studies; and a wide variety of contemporary affairs. Yet he never entirely forgot the true inner sources of psychic health, associated with his youth and Clough, and persisting in the 'buried life' theme, both in the correspondence and in the poetry. *The Buried Life* (no. 103) is a well-known example, but as late as 1869 he published the following five lines in the *Cornhill Magazine*, which may have been composed that year.

> Below the surface-stream, shallow and light,
> Of what we *say* we feel – below the stream,
> As light, of what we *think* we feel – there flows
> With noiseless current strong, obscure and deep,
> The central stream of what we feel indeed.

Matthew Arnold

In 1883 he retired from the Civil Service when Gladstone conferred a pension on him. With his newfound leisure he was able to make two lecture tours of America, in 1883/4 and 1886. These helped him to become established as a respected and influential figure in American intellectual life. He died suddenly from heart disease on 15 April 1888.

A. as poet A. has never dropped out of circulation as a poet, though there has been a shift of emphasis away from his highly wrought poetry in the classical mode towards that probing and questioning poetry of which he was less than proud. The poetry takes some time to make its appeal, since it avoids the extremes that attract immediately enthusiastic readers: it is not richly coloured and exotic, it is not rare and ingenious, it is not colloquial and immediate and it is not notably musical. In fact, we tend to define it by negatives. However, poetry is not to be defined but read, and those who persist with A conclude by finding his work satisfying. It is very easy to approach A.'s poetic theory by way of his fascinating correspondence with Clough, his *1853* Preface and his critical work. What these tell us is that he was reluctant for his poetry to get enmeshed in the language and pre-occupations of the modern age. He wanted poetry to be beautiful and finished; he wrote to Clough on 24 Feb. 1848: 'A growing sense of the deficiency of the *beautiful* in your poems, and of this alone being properly *poetical* as distinguished from rhetorical, devotional or metaphysical, made me speak as I did.' He was worried by Clough's lack of propriety of form and by his tendency towards colloquial awkwardness – not seeing that in fact there was something appropriate in the rough form. A. as a 'maker' may be seen when he writes to his sister Jane in 1849: 'More and more I feel bent against the modern English habit (too much encouraged by Wordsworth) of using poetry as a channel for thinking aloud, instead of making anything...' A. had to steer a careful course, since another of his poetic bug-bears was the exuberance of the Elizabethans and the Romantics. Here too his correspondence with Clough provides a direct statement: 'Keats and Shelley were on a false track when they set themselves to reproduce the exuberance of expression, the charm, the richness of images, and the felicity, of the Elizabethan poets... modern poetry can only subsist by its *contents:* by becoming a complete magister vitae as the poetry of the ancients did: by including, as theirs did, religion with poetry, instead of existing as poetry only, and leaving religious wants to be supplied by the Christian religion, as a power existing independent of the poetical power. But the language, style and general proceedings of poetry which has such an immense task to perform, must be very plain direct and severe...' (28 Oct. 1852).

The sum total of A.'s prescriptions for himself and others was difficult to satisfy. A. ultimately had to regard himself as unequal to the task. He probably summed up his own place in the poetic tradition better than anyone else, in a letter to his mother of 5 June 1869: 'My poems represent, on the whole, the main movement of mind of the last quarter of a century and then they will probably have their day as people become conscious to themselves of what that movement of mind is, and inter-ested in the literary productions which reflect it. It might be fairly urged that I have less poetical sentiment than Tennyson, and less intellectual vigour and abundance than Browning; yet, because I have perhaps more of a fusion of the two than either of them, and have more regularly applied

Matthew Arnold

that fusion to the main line of modern development, I am likely enough to have my turn, as they have had theirs' (*Letters* 2.9).

Biographies There is still no first-rate biography of A. The two available are Louis Bonnerot *M.A.: Poète: Essai de biographie psychologique* (Paris 1947) and E. K. Chambers *M.A., a study* (1947).

Discussion and criticism Faverty 164–226 surveys Arnold scholarship. A.'s reputation as a poet has remained steadily high, but because he was an important social critic, the habit of studying his poetry as a purveyor of philosophy persisted in Arnold criticism longer than it did for his contemporaries. One of the most important studies of A. as a figure of moral and cultural significance is L. Trilling *Matthew Arnold* (1939). The approach represented by a work like H. C. Duffin *Arnold the Poet* (1962) came comparatively late. A.'s reputation as a poet is high, but the faint tinge of hostility in the criticism of Eliot and Leavis has never been entirely dispelled. Inevitably critics speculate on why A. abandoned the writing of poetry. W. D. Anderson, in *M. A. and the Classical Tradition* (1965), suggests that one element explaining this is A.'s attitude to classicism: for him it was as much a mode of thought as a hunting ground for sources, and was ultimately inimical to poetry.

The most significant recent contributions to the study of A. as a poet are: A. D. Culler *Imaginative Reason: The Poetry of M.A.* (New Haven 1966), G. R. Stange *M.A.: The Poet as Humanist* (Princeton 1967), W. A. Madden *M.A., a Study of the Aesthetic Temperament in Victorian England* (1967), R. H. Super *The Time-Spirit of M.A.* (Michigan U.P. 1970), H. Fulweiler *Letters from the Darkling Plain* (1972) and K. Allott *M.A.* (1975). K. Allott's annotated edition (Longman Annotated Poets 1965) is indispensable.

The standard text of the poetry is the Library edition of 1885.

Abbreviations

1849	*The Strayed Reveller, and Other Poems* (1849).
1852	*Empedocles on Etna, and Other Poems* (1852).
1853	*Poems.* A new edition (1853).
1854	*Poems.* Second edition (1854).
1855	*Poems.* Second series (1855).
1857	*Poems.* Third edition (1857).
1867	*New Poems* (1867).
1869	*Poems.* First collected edition (1869).
1877	*Poems.* Collected edition (1877).
1881	*Poems.* Collected edition (1881).
1965	*The Poems of M.A.* (1965) K. Allott ed.
Works	*The Complete Prose Works of M.A.* (Ann Arbor, Michigan 1960–1977) R. H. Super ed.
Letters	*Letters of M.A.* (1895) G. W. E. Russell ed.
Lowry *Letters*	*The Letters of M.A. to Arthur Hugh Clough* (1932) H. F. Lowry ed.
Baum	P. F. Baum *Ten Studies in the Poetry of M.A.* (Durham, N.C. 1958).
Culler	A. D. Culler *Imaginative Reason: The Poetry of M.A.* (New Haven 1966).

Roper	Alan Roper *A.'s Poetic Landscapes* (Baltimore 1969).
Stange	G. R. Stange *M.A.: The Poet as Humanist* (Princeton 1967).
Taunt	H. W. Taunt *The Oxford Poems of M.A.* (Oxford 1910).
Tinker and Lowry	C. B. Tinker and H. F. Lowry *The Poetry of M.A.: a commentary* (1940).

101 Switzerland

Text The poems are presented here in the *1857* order, with *The Terrace at Berne* added. *Destiny* may have been a Marguerite poem: in *1852* it appeared between *Absence* and *To Marguerite*, but I have not included it. The texts are of each poem as first published, except that indentation is standardized, not all capitalization has been retained, and punctuation has been emended slightly. The sequence has not been printed in this manner before.

Date and setting In Sept. 1848, whilst on holiday in Switzerland, A. fell in love with a French girl, who may have been called Marguerite (last name unknown). They were both at the Hotel Bellevue in Thun, but it is not known whether Marguerite was an employee or a guest. It seems certain that she existed, since A. wrote to Clough: 'Tomorrow I repass the Gemmi and get to Thun: linger one day at the Hotel Bellevue for the sake of the blue eyes of one of its inmates: and then proceed by slow stages...to...England' (Lowry *Letters* 91, 29 Sept. 1848). Exactly a year later he revisited Switzerland with Wyndham Slade, calling at Thun on his way to the Tyrol, and returning there after some days in the mountains. He wrote to Clough, on 23 Sept. 1849: 'I have never yet succeeded on any one great occasion in consciously mastering myself'. Marguerite gave him an opportunity to try. But he was probably helped in his renunciation by an awareness of the absence of anything durable on which to build a relationship. This, as well as the sense of responsibility, prevented him from hoisting 'the mainsail', and being driven before the wind. However, the experience stayed with him for the rest of his life, and ten years after (see no. 101.9) he had still not forgotten her, and she remained part of his buried life. A. had 'Switzerland' sequences in his collections of poems, but was cautious about presenting them as a unified group with a thread of narrative – if only to avoid betraying too much of himself and embarrassing his wife.

Discussion in Tinker and Lowry 151–9, Baum 58–84, Culler 117–37, Stange 213–48, Roper 140–7.

101.1 To my Friends, who ridiculed a tender Leave-taking

Date Written between Oct. 1848 and Jan. 1849.
Publication *1849; 1853–1869*, as 'Switzerland' 1; *1877*, as an 'Early Poem'.

Title *A Memory Picture 1869* etc.

Laugh, my friends, and without blame
Lightly quit what lightly came:
Rich to-morrow as to-day,
Spend as madly as you may.
5   I, with little land to stir,
Am the exacter labourer.
    Ere the parting kiss be dry,
    Quick, thy tablets, Memory!

But my youth reminds me – 'Thou
10   Hast lived light as these live now:
As these are, thou too wert such:
Much hast had, hast squandered much.'
Fortune's now less frequent heir,
Ah! I husband what's grown rare.
15   Ere the parting kiss be dry,
    Quick, thy tablets, Memory!

Young, I said: 'A face is gone
If too hotly mused upon:
And our best impressions
20   Those that do themselves repair.'
Many a face I then let by,
Ah! is faded utterly.
    Ere the parting kiss be dry,
    Quick, thy tablets, Memory!

25   Marguerite says: 'As last year went,
So the coming year'll be spent:
Some day next year, I shall be,
Entering heedless, kissed by thee.'
Ah! I hope – yet, once away,
30   What may chain us, who can say?
    Ere the parting kiss be dry,
    Quick, thy tablets, Memory!

1–8 Omitted *1869;* restored *1877* etc.
7 (and first line of refrain in each stanza) **kiss be dry**] hour go by *1857* etc.
8 tablets notebook for writing memoranda. Cf. Shakespeare *Ham.* 1.5.98:
'the table of my memory'.
9–16 Omitted *1869* etc.
17 Young,] Long *1877;* Once *1881* etc.
21 Many a face I so let flee *1869* etc.
30 Meaning either 'what will bind us together' or 'what will bind us to our
own duties and interests (and hence separate us)'.

Paint that lilac kerchief, bound
Her soft face, her hair around:
35   Tied under the archest chin
Mockery ever ambushed in.
Let the fluttering fringes streak
All her pale, sweet-rounded cheek.
    Ere the parting kiss be dry,
40   Quick, thy tablets, Memory!

Paint that figure's pliant grace
As she towards me leaned her face,
Half refused and half resigned   `
Murmuring, 'Art thou still unkind?'
45   Many a broken promise then
Was new made – to break again.
    Ere the parting kiss be dry,
        Quick, thy tablets, Memory!

Paint those eyes, so blue, so kind,
50   Eager tell-tales of her mind:
Paint, with their impetuous stress
Of inquiring tenderness,
Those frank eyes, where deep doth lie
An angelic gravity.
55   Ere the parting kiss be dry,
        Quick, thy tablets, Memory!

What, my friends, these feeble lines
Show, you say, my love declines?
To paint ill as I have done,
60   Proves forgetfulness begun?
Time's gay minions, pleased you see,
Time, your master, governs me;
    Pleased, you mock the fruitless cry:
    'Quick, thy tablets, Memory!'

65   Ah! too true. Time's current strong
Leaves us true to nothing long.
Yet, if little stays with man,
Ah! retain we all we can!

---

33 lilac kerchief Cf. 2.7. 'enkerchiefed hair.'
35–36 The tradition of evoking a mistress in pictorial terms has both
classical and English precedents, e.g. Marvell's *The Gallery*.
49 eyes, so blue Cf. 2.8. 'those sweet eyes of blue.'
53 deep . . . lie] deep doth be *1877–8;* deep will be *1880;* deep I see *1881.*
66 us true] us firm *1869;* us true *1877, 1878;* us joined *1881;* us fixed MS.
alteration in *1881.*

70
If the clear impression dies,
Ah! the dim remembrance prize!
Ere the parting kiss be dry,
Quick, thy tablets, Memory!

101.2 The Lake

Date Probably written Sept. 1849, one year after the first meeting with Marguerite, when A. went to Switzerland with Wyndham Slade. See letter to Clough of 23 Sept. 1849: 'Yes, I come, [to the mountains and torrents mentioned in *Parting*] but in three or four days I shall be back here, and then I must try how soon I can ferociously turn towards England' (Lowry *Letters* 111).
Publication *1852*, etc. As 'Switzerland' 2 *1853–1869;* 1 *1877* etc.

Again I see my bliss at hand;
The town, the lake are here;
My Marguerite smiles upon the strand,
Unaltered with the year.

5
I know that graceful figure fair,
That cheek of languid hue;
I know that soft, enkerchiefed hair,
And those sweet eyes of blue.

Again I spring to make my choice;
10
Again in tones of ire
I hear a God's tremendous voice:
'Be counselled, and retire!'

Ye guiding Powers, who join and part,
What would ye have with me?
15
Ah, warn some more ambitious heart,
And let the peaceful be!

Title *The Lake 1852–1857; Meeting 1869* etc.
11 Cf. 7.22: 'A God, a God their severance ruled' (p. 343 below).

101.3 A Dream

Date Written 1849–53.
Martin may be Wyndham Slade. The geography of the visionary landscape is in accord with A.'s symbolic thinking (see Culler 122–4).
Publication *1853, 1854, 1857.* Omitted *1869, 1877.* As 'Switzerland' 3 *1853–1857;* as an 'Early Poem' *1881.*

Was it a dream? We sailed, I thought we sailed,
Martin and I, down a green Alpine stream,
Under o'erhanging pines, the morning sun,
On the wet umbrage of their glossy tops,
5   On the red pinings of their forest-floor,
Drew a warm scent abroad; behind the pines
The mountain-skirts, with all their sylvan change
Of bright-leafed chestnuts and mossed walnut-trees,
And the frail scarlet-berried ash, began.
10 Swiss chalets glittered on the dewy slopes,
And from some swarded shelf high up, there came
Notes of wild pastoral music: over all
Ranged, diamond-bright, the eternal wall of snow.
Upon the mossy rocks at the stream's edge,
15 Backed by the pines, a plank-built cottage stood,
Bright in the sun; the climbing gourd-plant's leaves
Muffled its walls, and on the stone-strewn roof
Lay the warm golden gourds; golden, within,
Under the eaves, peered rows of Indian corn.
20 We shot beneath the cottage with the stream.
On the brown, rude-carved balcony, two forms
Came forth – Olivia's, Marguerite! and thine.
Clad were they both in white, flowers in their breasts;
Straw hats bedecked their heads, with ribbons blue
25 Which waved, and on their shoulders fluttering played.
They saw us, they conferred; their bosoms heaved,
And more than mortal impulse filled their eyes.
Their lips moved; their white arms, waved eagerly,
Flashed once, like falling streams; we rose, we gazed: –
30 One moment, on the rapid's top, our boat
Hung poised – and then the darting river of Life
Loud thundering, bore us by: swift, swift it foamed;
Black under cliffs it raced, round headlands shone.
Soon the planked cottage 'mid the sun-warmed pines
35 Faded – the moss – the rocks; us burning plains,
Bristled with cities, us the sea received.

1,23–6 Cf. Spenser *Amoretti* 77: 'Was it a dream, or did I see it plain,' a poem about the breasts of the beloved.
3 Under o'erhanging pines] Bordered, each bank, with pines *1881*.
5 pinings dead pine-needles (not in *OED*).
9 scarlet-berried ash the description of the rowan trees, the gourds and the Indian corn (lines 17–19) indicates early autumn.
31 ∧ 32 (Such now, methought, it was), the river of Life, *1881*.
34 'mid the sun-warmed] by the sun-warmed MS. alteration in *1881*.

101.4 Parting

Date *c.* 23 Sept. 1849: lines 25–34 quoted, with minor variants, in a letter to Clough (Lowry *Letters* 110).
Publication *1852* etc. As 'Switzerland' 4 *1853–1857;* 3 *1869;* 2 *1877* etc.

<blockquote>

Ye storm-winds of Autumn
Who rush by, who shake
The window, and ruffle
The gleam-lighted lake;
5   Who cross to the hill-side
Thin-sprinkled with farms,
Where the high woods strip sadly
Their yellowing arms –
Ye are bound for the mountains –
10 Ah, with you let me go
Where the cold distant barrier,
The vast range of snow,
Through the loose clouds lifts dimly
Its white peaks in air –
15 How deep is their stillness!
Ah! would I were there!

But on the stairs what voice is this I hear,
Buoyant as morning, and as morning clear?
Say, has some wet bird-haunted English lawn
20 Lent it the music of its trees at dawn?
Or was it from some sun-flecked mountain-brook
That the sweet voice its upland clearness took?
    Ah! it comes nearer –
    Sweet notes, this way!

25 Hark! fast by the window
The rushing winds go,
To the ice-cumbered gorges,
The vast seas of snow!
There the torrents drive upward
30 Their rock-strangled hum;
There the avalanche thunders
The hoarse torrent dumb.
  – I come, O ye mountains!
  Ye torrents, I come!

</blockquote>

11–16 A free imitation of Goethe's *Sehnsucht* (1802) lines 5–8: '*Wie dort sich die Wolken* | *Um Felsen verziehn!* | *Da mocht ich hinuber,* | *Da mocht ich wohl hin!*' (How the clouds there | Drift away past rocks. | Oh, were I but yonder, | It is there I should like to go.)

35   But who is this, by the half-opened door,
Whose figure casts a shadow on the floor?
The sweet blue eyes – the soft, ash-coloured hair –
The cheeks that still their gentle paleness wear –
The lovely lips, with their arch smile that tells
40   The unconquered joy in which her spirit dwells –
    Ah! they bend nearer –
    Sweet lips, this way!

Hark! the wind rushes past us!
Ah! with that let me go
45   To the clear waning hill-side,
Unspotted by snow,
There to watch, o'er the sunk vale,
The frore mountain-wall,
Where the niched snow-bed sprays down
50   Its powdery fall.
There its dusky blue clusters
The aconite spreads;
There the pines slope, the cloud-strips
Hung soft in their heads.
55   No life, but, at moments,
The mountain-bees' hum.
– I come, O ye mountains!
Ye pine-woods, I come!

Forgive me! forgive me!
60   Ah, Marguerite, fain
Would these arms reach to clasp thee!
But see! 'tis in vain.

In the void air, towards thee,
My strained arms are cast;
65   But a sea rolls between us –
Our different past!

To the lips, ah! of others
Those lips have been pressed,
And others, ere I was,
70   Were clasped to that breast;

48 frore frosty, a poeticism since Milton: 'The parching air burns frore'
(*Paradise Lost* 2.595).
52 aconite the Alpine aconite that flowers in the Autumn is *Aconitum Napellus* (Wolf's-bane), not the *Erantis hyemalis*, which is a yellow flower.
64 strained] stretched *1877*, etc.
70 clasped] strained *1877*, etc.

> Far, far from each other
>   Our spirits have grown;
> And what heart knows another?
>   Ah! who knows his own?
>
> 75 Blow, ye winds! lift me with you!
>   I come to the wild.
> Fold closely, O Nature!
>   Thine arms round thy child.
>
> To thee only God granted
> 80   A heart ever new –
> To all always open,
>   To all always true.
>
> Ah, calm me! restore me!
>   And dry up my tears
> 85 On thy high mountain-platforms,
>   Where morn first appears;
>
> Where the white mists, for ever,
>   Are spread and upfurled –
> In the stir of the forces
> 90   Whence issued the world.

75–8 Characteristic of the Romantic Movement. See Shelley *Ode to the West Wind* line 53: 'Oh, lift me as a wave, a leaf, a cloud!' Such intimate contact with nature is ridiculed by Clough's Spirit in *Dipsychus* lines 202–35 (see above pp. 321–2).

101.5 A Farewell

Date Probably written early Oct. 1849.
Publication *1852, 1854, 1857, 1869,* etc. As 'Switzerland' 5 *1854–1857;* 4 *1869;* 3 *1877,* etc.

> My horse's feet beside the lake,
>   Where sweet the unbroken moonbeams lay,
> Sent echoes through the night to wake
>   Each glistening strand, each heath-fringed bay.
>
> 5 The poplar avenue was passed,
>   And the roofed bridge that spans the stream;
> Up the steep street I hurried fast,
>   Lit by thy taper's starlike beam.

8 Lit] Led *1854,* etc.

I came! I saw thee rise! – the blood
10   Came flooding to thy languid cheek.
Locked in each other's arms we stood,
    In tears, with hearts too full to speak.

Days flew; ah! soon I could discern
    A trouble in thine altered air!
15 Thy hand lay languidly in mine,
    Thy cheek was grave, thy speech grew rare.

I blame thee not! – this heart, I know,
    To be long loved was never framed;
For something in its depth doth glow
20   Too strange, too restless, too untamed.

And women – things that live and move
    Mined by the fever of the soul –
They seek to find in those they love
    Stern strength, and promise of control

25 They ask not kindness, gentle ways –
    These they themselves have tried and known;
They ask a soul that never sways
    With the blind gusts which shake their own.

I too have felt the load I bore
30   In a too strong emotion's sway;
I too have wished, no woman more,
    This starting, feverish heart away.

I too have longed for trenchant force,
    And will like a dividing spear;
35 Have praised the keen, unscrupulous course,
    Which knows no doubt, which feels no fear.

But in the world I learnt, what there
    Thou too wilt surely one day prove,
That will, that energy, though rare,
40   Are yet far, far less rare than love.

Go, then! – till time and fate impress
    This truth on thee, be mine no more!
They will! – for thou, I feel, no less
    Than I, wert destined to this lore.

---

10 Came flooding] Came flushing *1854–1857;* Poured flushing *1869*, etc.
23–5 Cf. Clough *Amours de Voyage* 2. 293–5: 'For the woman, they tell you,
| Ever prefers the audacious, the wilful, the vehement hero; | She has no
heart for the timid, the sensitive soul'.

45   We school our manners, act our parts –
       But He, who sees us through and through,
    Knows that the bent of both our hearts
       Was to be gentle, tranquil, true.

    And though we wear out life, alas!
50   Distracted as a homeless wind,
    In beating where we must not pass,
       In seeking what we shall not find;

    Yet we shall one day gain, life past,
       Clear prospect o'er our being's whole;
55   Shall see ourselves, and learn at last
       Our true affinities of soul.

    We shall not then deny a course
       To every thought the mass ignore;
    We shall not then call hardness force,
60   Nor lightness wisdom any more.

    Then, in the eternal Father's smile
       Our soothed, encouraged souls will dare
    To seem as free from pride and guile,
       As good, as generous, as they are.

65   Then we shall know our friends! – though much
       Will have been lost – the help in strife;
    The thousand sweet, still joys of such
       As hand in hand face earthly life –

    Though these be lost, there will be yet
70   A sympathy august and pure;
    Ennobled by a vast regret,
       And by contrition sealed thrice sure.

    And we, whose ways were unlike here,
       May then more neighbouring courses ply;
75   May to each other be brought near,
       And greet across infinity.

56 affinities possibly alluding to Goethe's *Die Wahlverwandtschaften* (1809), which treats of 'elective affinities' (mysterious, pre-ordained bonds of love). *OED* cites 1868 for the first usage. A. also implies *OED* 9: the tendency of certain elements to unite and form new compounds.
67 Cf. *Paradise Lost* 8.601: 'Those thousand decencies that daily flow | From all her words and actions, mixed with love.'

> How sweet, unreached by earthly jars,
>   My sister! to behold with thee
> The hush among the shining stars,
> 80   The calm upon the moonlit sea!
>
> How sweet to feel, on the boon air,
>   All our unquiet pulses cease!
> To feel that nothing can impair
>   The gentleness, the thirst for peace –
>
> 85 The gentleness too rudely hurled
>   On this wild earth of hate and fear;
> The thirst for peace a raving world
>   Would never let us satiate here.

78 behold] maintain *1877*, etc.
81 boon gracious, benign.

101.6 To Marguerite

Date Probably written Sept. or Oct. 1849. Obviously a poem to precede 101.7, but not published in *1852* or *1854*, perhaps to save his newly wed wife embarrassment.
Publication *1857, 1869*, etc. As 'Switzerland' 6 *1857–1869;* 4 *1877*, etc.

> We were apart; yet, day by day,
>   I bade my heart more constant be;
> I bade it keep the world away,
>   And grow a home for only thee;
> 5 Nor feared but thy love likewise grew,
>   Like mine, each day, more tried, more true.
>
> The fault was grave! I might have known,
>   What far too soon, alas! I learned –
> The heart can bind itself alone,
> 10   And faith is often unreturned.
> Self-swayed our feelings ebb and swell –
> Thou lov'st no more; – Farewell! Farewell!
>
> Farewell! – and thou, thou lonely heart,
>   Which never yet without remorse
> 15 Even for a moment didst depart

Title *Isolation. To Marguerite 1869*, etc.
1 We were apart between Sept. 1848 and Sept. 1849.
10 faith is often] faith may well be *1877;* faith may oft be *1881*.
13 thou lonely heart A. addresses his own heart.

From thy remote and sphered course
To haunt the place where passions reign –
Back to thy solitude again!

Back! with the conscious thrill of shame
20   Which Luna felt, that summer-night,
Flash through her pure immortal frame,
    When she forsook the starry height
To hang over Endymion's sleep
Upon the pine-grown Latmian steep.

25   Yet she, chaste queen, had never proved
    How vain a thing is mortal love,
Wandering in Heaven, far removed.
    But thou has long had place to prove
This truth – to prove, and make thine own:
30   'Thou hast been, shalt be, art, alone.'

Or, if not quite alone, yet they
    Which touch thee are unmating things –
Ocean, and clouds, and night, and day;
    Lorn autumns and triumphant springs;
35   And life, and others' joy and pain,
And love, if love, of happier men.

Of happier men – for they, at least,
    Have *dreamed* two human hearts might blend
In one, and were through faith released
40   From isolation without end
Prolonged; nor knew, although not less
Alone than thou, their loneliness.

20 Luna the goddess of the moon.

101.7 To Marguerite, in Returning a Volume of the Letters of Ortis

Date Probably written Sept. or Oct. 1849.
    J. D. Coleridge *Christian Remembrancer* 3 April 1854 saw an indebtedness to S. T. Coleridge's *Christabel*, lines 418–23. Literary parallels are discussed by K. Tillotson, *RES* n.s. 3 (1952) 346–64. Ortis was an Italianate Werther in Foscolo's *Ultime Lettere di Jacopo Ortis* (1802),
Publication *1852, 1853, 1857, 1869* etc. As 'Switzerland' 5 *1853;* 6 *1854;* 7 *1857–1869;* 5 *1877,* etc.

Title *To Marguerite 1853, 1854; Isolation 1857; To Marguerite – Continued 1869,* etc.

Yes: in the sea of life enisled,
  With echoing straits between us thrown,
Dotting the shoreless watery wild,
  We mortal millions live *alone*.
5 The islands feel the enclasping flow,
  And then their endless bounds they know.

But when the moon their hollows lights,
  And they are swept by balms of spring,
And in their glens, on starry nights,
10   The nightingales divinely sing,
And lovely notes, from shore to shore,
  Across the sounds and channels pour;

Oh then a longing like despair
  Is to their farthest caverns sent;
15 For surely once, they feel, we were
  Parts of a single continent.
Now round us spreads the watery plain –
  Oh might our marges meet again!

Who ordered, that their longing's fire
20   Should be, as soon as kindled, cooled?
Who renders vain their deep desire?
  A God, a God their severance ruled;
And bade betwixt their shores to be
The unplumbed, salt, estranging sea.

15–16 Cf. *Empedocles on Etna* 2.372 and *The Buried Life* lines 30–98 (pp. 351, 354–5 below).
22–4 A combination of two phrases from Horace: *Epodes* 14.6, '*deus, deus, nam me vetat*' (God, God then forbade me), and *Odes* 1.3.21–3: '*nequiquam deus abscidit prudens Oceano dissociabili terras*' (vain was the purpose of the god in severing the lands by the estranging ocean).

101.8 Absence

Date Probably written between Oct. 1849 and early 1850.
Publication *1852, 1853, 1854, 1857, 1869*, etc. As 'Switzerland' 6 *1853;* 7 *1854;* 8 *1857;* 5 *1869,* 6 *1877,* etc.

In this fair stranger's eyes of grey
  Thine eyes, my love, I see.
I shudder: for the passing day
  Had borne me far from thee.

1 fair stranger almost certainly Frances Lucy Wightman, whom A. married June 1851.
3 shudder] shiver *1877*, etc.

[101] Matthew Arnold

5   This is the curse of life: that not
      A nobler calmer train
    Of wiser thoughts and feeling blot
      Our passions from our brain;

    But each day brings its petty dust
10   Our soon-choked souls to fill,
    And we forget because we must
      And not because we will.

    I struggle towards the light; and ye,
      Once longed-for storms of love!
15   If with the light ye cannot be,
      I bear that ye remove.

    I struggle towards the light; but oh,
      While yet the night is chill,
    Upon time's barren, stormy flow,
20   Stay with me, Marguerite, still!

20 Cf. Tennyson *In Memoriam* 50.1 (see above p. 113) 'Be near me when my light is low.' *In Memoriam* 50 also echoes line 9: 'And time, a maniac scattering dust.'

101.9 The Terrace at Berne

Date Written 26 Apr.–14 June 1863: A.'s unpublished diary. The poem was conceived 29–30 June 1859 when A. visited Berne, and in *1869*, etc. it was printed with the heading 'Composed Ten Years after the Preceding'.
Publication *1867, 1868, 1869*, etc. As 'Switzerland' 8 *1869;* 7 *1877*, etc.

    Ten years – and to my waking eye
      Once more the roofs of Berne appear;
    The rocky banks, the terrace high,
      The stream – and do I linger here?

5   The clouds are on the Oberland,
      The Jungfrau snows look faint and far;
    But bright are those green fields at hand,
      And through those fields comes down the Aar,

Title *The Terrace at Berne (Composed Ten Years after the Preceding) 1869*, etc.
1–8 Berne is fifteen miles N.W. of Thun, hence on the way back to England, and associated in 1849 with a poignant departure. The Aar, in 1849 and 1859, is the thread connecting A.'s memory to Thun; the mountains, which in Thun seem near, seem remote, viewed from Berne. W. Holman Hunt painted the view from the terrace (reproduced opposite 2.352 in *Pre-Raphaelitism and the Pre-Raphaelite Brotherhood* (1905)).

344

And from the blue twin lakes it comes,
10   Flows by the town, the church-yard fair;
And 'neath the garden-walk it hums,
    The house – and is my Marguerite there?

Ah, shall I see thee, while a flush
    Of startled pleasure floods thy brow,
15 Quick through the oleanders brush,
    And clap thy hands, and cry: "Tis thou!'

Or hast thou long since wandered back,
    Daughter of France! to France, thy home;
And flitted down the flowery track
20 Where feet like thine too lightly come?

Doth riotous laughter now replace
    Thy smile; and rouge, with stony glare,
Thy cheek's soft hue; and fluttering lace
    The kerchief that enwound thy hair?

25 Or is it over? – art thou dead?
    Dead! – and no warning shiver ran
Across my heart, to say thy thread
    Of life was cut, and closed thy span!

Could from earth's ways that figure slight
30 Be lost, and I not feel 'twas so?
Of that fresh voice the gay delight
    Fail from earth's air, and I not know?

Or shall I find thee still, but changed,
    But not the Marguerite of thy prime?
35 With all thy being re-arranged,
    Passed through the crucible of time;

With spirit vanished, beauty waned,
    And hardly yet a glance, a tone,
A gesture – anything – retained
40 Of all that was my Marguerite's own?

I will not know! For wherefore try,
    To things by mortal course that live,
A shadowy durability,
    For which they were not meant, to give?

9 twin-lakes Lakes Thun and Brienz.
31 Cf. *Parting* lines 17–18 (p. 336 above): 'But on the stairs what voice is this I hear, | Bouyant as morning, and as morning clear?'

45   Like driftwood spars, which meet and pass
      Upon the boundless ocean-plain,
      So on the sea of life, alas!
      Man nears man, meets, and leaves again.

      I knew it when my life was young;
50   I feel it still, now youth is o'er.
      The mists are on the mountains hung,
      And Marguerite I shall see no more.

48 Man meets man – meets, and quits again. *1877*, etc.
51 mountains] mountain *1877*, etc.

102 Empedocles on Etna: extract

Date Written 1849–52. See J. C. Shairp to Clough 30 June 1849: '[Arnold] was working at an "Empedocles" which seemed to be not much about the man who leapt into the crater – but his name and outward circumstances are used for the drapery of his own thoughts' (*Clough Correspondence* 1.270).

Empedocles was a by-product of A.'s intention to write a tragedy on Lucretius (cf. Tennyson's *Lucretius*, above no. 53 pp. 176–85). A.'s source material was in S. Karsten *Philosophorum Graecorum Veterum* (1838) 2.3–78. See Tinker and Lowry 289–90. *1965* 148 reproduces the notes in the Yale MS.

Discussion W. E. Houghton *VS* 1 (1958) 311–36; K. Allott *N & Q* 207 (1962) 300–3; Culler 153–77; F. Kermode *The Romantic Image* (1957).

Publication *1852* but dropped from *1853*, for reasons stated in the Preface: (*1965* 591): '[Empedocles]...survived his fellows, living on into a time when the habits of Greek thought and feeling had begun fast to change, character to dwindle, the influence of the Sophists to prevail...; the calm, the cheerfulness, the disinterested objectivity [of early Greek genius] have disappeared: the dialogue of the mind with itself has commenced;...we hear already the doubts, we witness the discouragement, of Hamlet and of Faust.' Published in *1867* at the request of Browning.

Act 2

(*Scene: Summit of Etna: Empedocles has left Pausanias and Callicles below, and meditates on the edge of the volcanic crater*)

      And lie thou there,
      My laurel bough!
      Scornful Apollo's ensign, lie thou there!
      Though thou hast been my shade in the world's heat –
195   Though I have loved thee, lived in honouring thee –
      Yet lie there,
      My laurel bough!

192 laurel the plant sacred to poets.

I am weary of thee.
I am weary of the solitude
200 Where he who bears thee must abide –
Of the rocks of Parnassus,
Of the gorge of Delphi,
Of the moonlit peaks, and the caves.
Thou guardest them, Apollo!
205 Over the grave of the slain Pytho,
Though young, intolerably severe!
Thou keepest aloof the profane,
But the solitude oppresses thy votary!
The jars of men reach him not in thy valley –
210 But can life reach him?
Thou fencest him from the multitude –
Who will fence him from himself?
He hears nothing but the cry of the torrents,
And the beating of his own heart.
215 The air is thin, the veins swell,
The temples tighten and throb there –
Air! air!

Take thy bough, set me free from my solitude;
I have been enough alone!

220 Where shall thy votary fly then? back to men?
But they will gladly welcome him once more,
And help him to unbend his too tense thought,
And rid him of the presence of himself,
And keep their friendly chatter at his ear,
225 And haunt him, till the absence from himself,
That other torment, grow unbearable;
And he will fly to solitude again,
And he will find its air too keen for him,
And so change back; and many thousand times
230 Be miserably bandied to and fro
Like a sea-wave, betwixt the world and thee,
Thou young, implacable God! and only death
Can cut his oscillations short, and so
Bring him to poise. There is no other way.

235 And yet what days were those, Parmenides!
When we were young, when we could number friends

202 Delphi near Parnassus: the centre of the prophetic Delphic oracle.
205 Pytho the dragon which guarded Delphi; slain by Apollo.
232–4 only death ... to poise contradicted by lines 345–72.
235 Parmenides said to have been a pupil of Empedocles, was at the centre
of the School of Elea, and associated with the 'Doctrine of Rest'.

In all the Italian cities like ourselves,
When with elated hearts we joined your train,
Ye sun-born virgins! on the road to truth.
240 Then we could still enjoy, then neither thought
Nor outward things were closed and dead to us;
But we received the shock of mighty thoughts
On simple minds with a pure natural joy;
And if the sacred load oppressed our brain,
245 We had the power to feel the pressure eased,
The brow unbound, the thoughts flow free again,
In the delightful commerce of the world.
We had not lost our balance then, now grown
Thought's slaves, and dead to every natural joy.
250 The smallest thing could give us pleasure then –
The sports of the country-people,
A flute-note from the woods,
Sunset over the sea;
Seed-time and harvest,
255 The reapers in the corn,
The vinedresser in his vineyard,
The village-girl at her wheel.

Fullness of life and power of feeling, ye
Are for the happy, for the souls at ease,
260 Who dwell on a firm basis of content!
But he, who has outlived his prosperous days –
But he, whose youth fell on a different world
From that on which his exiled age is thrown –
Whose mind was fed on other food, was trained
265 By other rules than are in vogue to-day –
Whose habit of thought is fixed, who will not change,
But, in a world he loves not, must subsist
In ceaseless opposition, be the guard
Of his own breast, fettered to what he guards,
270 That the world win no mastery over him –
Who has no friend, no fellow left, not one;
Who has no minute's breathing space allowed
To nurse his dwindling faculty of joy –
Joy and the outward world must die to him,
275 As they are dead to me.

238–9 Cf. *Fragments of Parmenides:* 'The maidens of the sun, leaving the halls of night, led the way to the light' (cited by A. in *1867*).
268 Cf. Cowper *The Task* 1.367: 'By ceaseless action, all that is subsists.'; Wordsworth *The Excursion* 4. 1146–7: 'And central peace, subsisting at the heart | Of endless agitation.'
273–4 Cf. Coleridge *Dejection: An Ode* for joy as dejection's antithesis: esp. lines 67–8: 'Joy, Lady! is the spirit and the power, | Which wedding nature to us gives in dower.'

A long pause, during which Empedocles remains motionless, plunged in thought. The night deepens. He moves forward and gazes round him, and proceeds:

276   And you, ye stars,
        Who slowly begin to marshal,
        As of old, in the fields of heaven,
        Your distant, melancholy lines!
280   Have you, too, survived yourselves?
        Are you, too, what I fear to become?
        You, too, once lived;
        You, too, moved joyfully
        Among august companions,
285   In an older world, peopled by Gods,
        In a mightier order,
        The radiant, rejoicing, intelligent Sons of Heaven.
        But now, ye kindle
        Your lonely, cold-shining lights,
290   Unwilling lingerers
        In the heavenly wilderness,
        For a younger, ignoble world;
        And renew, by necessity,
        Night after night your courses,
295   In echoing, unneared silence,
        Above a race you know not –
        Uncaring and undelighted,
        Without friend and without home;
        Weary like us, though not
300   Weary with our weariness.

        No, no, ye stars! there is no death with you,
        No languor, no decay! languor and death,
        They are with me, not you! ye are alive –
        Ye, and the pure dark ether where ye ride
305   Brilliant above me! And thou, fiery world,
        That sapp'st the vitals of this terrible mount
        Upon whose charred and quaking crust I stand –
        Thou, too, brimmest with life! – the sea of cloud,
        That heaves its white and billowy vapours up
310   To moat this isle of ashes from the world,
        Lives; and that other fainter sea, far down,
        O'er whose lit floor a road of moonbeams leads

276–300 Printed separately as *The Philosopher and the Stars* 1855.
295 unneared distant (the only ex. in *OED*).
300–322 Cf. Shelley *Stanzas Written in Dejection Near Naples* for a similar mood of self-pity in one excluded from the life and beauty of nature.

To Etna's Liparean sister-fires
And the long dusky line of Italy –
315 That mild and luminous floor of waters lives,
With held-in joy swelling its heart; I only,
Whose spring of hope is dried, whose spirit has failed,
I, who have not, like these, in solitude
Maintained courage and force, and in myself
320 Nursed an immortal vigour – I alone
Am dead to life and joy, therefore I read
In all things my own deadness.

A long silence. He continues:

Oh, that I could glow like this mountain!
Oh, that my heart bounded with the swell of the sea!
325 Oh, that my soul were full of light as the stars!
Oh, that it brooded over the world like the air!

But no, this heart will glow no more; thou art
A living man no more, Empedocles!
Nothing but a devouring flame of thought –
330 But a naked, eternally restless mind!

After a pause:

To the elements it came from
Everything will return –
Our bodies to earth,
Our blood to water,
335 Heat to fire,
Breath to air;
They were well born, they will be well entombed –
But mind?...

And we might gladly share the fruitful stir
340 Down in our mother earth's miraculous womb;
Well would it be
With what rolled of us in the stormy main;
We might have joy, blent with the all-bathing air,
Or with the nimble, radiant life of fire.

313 The Lipari Islands north-east of Sicily. Stromboli is one of the volcanoes there.
331–7 Empedoclean philosophy; see esp. Fragment 17: 'as [the elements] course along | Through one another, now this, now that is born – | And so forever down eternity' (transl. W. E. Leonard).
344 nimble] active *1852*.

345 But mind, but thought –
If these have been the master part of us –
Where will *they* find their parent element?
What will receive *them*, who will call *them* home?
But we shall still be in them, and they in us,
350 And we shall be the strangers of the world,
And they will be our lords, as they are now;
And keep us prisoners of our consciousness,
And never let us clasp and feel the All
But through their forms, and modes, and stifling veils.
355 And we shall be unsatisfied as now;
And we shall feel the agony of thirst,
The ineffable longing for the life of life
Baffled for ever; and still thought and mind
Will hurry us with them on their homeless march,
360 Over the unallied unopening earth,
Over the unrecognising sea; while air
Will blow us fiercely back to sea and earth,
And fire repel us from its living waves.
And then we shall unwillingly return
365 Back to this meadow of calamity,
This uncongenial place, this human life;
And in our individual human state
Go through the sad probation all again,
To see if we will poise our life at last
370 To see if we will now at last be true
To our own only true, deep-buried selves,
Being one with which we are one with the whole world;
Or whether we will once more fall away
Into some bondage of the flesh or mind,
375 Some slough of sense, or some fantastic maze
Forged by the imperious lonely thinking-power.
And each succeeding age in which we are born
Will have more peril for us than the last;
Will goad our senses with a sharper spur,
380 Will fret our minds to an intenser play,
Will make ourselves harder to be discerned.
And we shall struggle awhile, gasp and rebel –
And we shall fly for refuge to past times,
Their soul of unworn youth, their breath of greatness;

364–90 Empedocles was interested in reincarnation. *1865* cites Karsten
2.508–9.
370–1 For the buried self see *The Buried Life* (No. 103).

385 And the reality will pluck us back
Knead us in its hot hand, and change our nature;
And we shall feel our powers of effort flag,
And rally them for one last fight – and fail;
And we shall sink in the impossible strife,
390 And be astray for ever.
                  Slave of sense
I have in no wise been; but slave of thought?...
And who can say: I have been always free,
Lived ever in the light of my own soul? –
I cannot; I have lived in wrath and gloom,
395 Fierce, disputatious, ever at war with man,
Far from my own soul, far from warmth and light.
But I have not grown easy in these bonds –
But I have not denied what bonds these were.
Yea, I take myself to witness,
400 That I have loved no darkness,
Sophisticated no truth,
Nursed no delusion,
Allowed no fear!

    And therefore, O ye elements! I know –
405 Ye know it too – it hath been granted me
Not to die wholly, not to be all enslaved.
I feel it in this hour. The numbing cloud
Mounts off my soul; I feel it, I breathe free
Is it but for a moment?
410 – Ah, boil up, ye vapours!
Leap and roar, thou sea of fire!
My soul glows to meet you.
Ere it flag, ere the mists
Of despondency and gloom
415 Rush over it again,
Receive me, save me!

           [*He plunges into the crater.*

390–91 Empedocles is distinguished from Lucretius, who was a slave of sense. See Tennyson *Lucretius* (p. 177 above).
401 Sophisticated falsified by misstatement or unauthorized alteration (*OED* 4).
416 A.'s explanation of Empedocles' death reads: 'Before he becomes the victim of depression and overtension of mind, to the utter deadness to joy, grandeur, spirit, and animated life, he desires to die; to be reunited with the universe, before by exaggerating his human side he has become utterly estranged from it.' (*Yale MS.*).

103 The Buried Life

Date Unknown, but *Commentary* 195 suggests that the material closely resembles that in the Marguerite poems. See general introduction to A. (p. 328 above) for an 1869 poem on the same theme. A. speaks of the secret inner life in a letter to his mother of 24 Dec. 1863: '...I can feel, I rejoice to say, an inward spring which seems more and more to gain strength, and to promise to resist outward shocks, if they must come, however rough. But of this inward spring, one must not talk, for it does not like being talked about, and threatens to depart if one will not leave it in mystery' (*Letters* 1.213).
Publication *1852; 1855; 1869*, etc.

Light flows our war of mocking words, and yet,
Behold, with tears mine eyes are wet!
I feel a nameless sadness o'er me roll.
Yes, yes, we know that we can jest,
5   We know, we know that we can smile!
But there's a something in this breast,
To which thy light words bring no rest,
And thy gay smiles no anodyne.
Give me thy hand, and hush awhile,
10   And turn those limpid eyes on mine,
And let me read there, love! thy inmost soul.
Alas! is even love too weak
To unlock the heart, and let it speak?
Are even lovers powerless to reveal
15   To one another what indeed they feel?
I knew the mass of men concealed
Their thoughts, for fear that if revealed
They would by other men be met
With blank indifference, or with blame reproved;
20   I knew they lived and moved
Tricked in disguises, alien to the rest
Of men, and alien to themselves – and yet
The same heart beats in every human breast!

But we, my love! – doth a like spell benumb
25   Our hearts, our voices? must we too be dumb?

Ah! well for us, if even we,
Even for a moment, can get free
Our heart, and have our lips unchained;
For that which seals them hath been deep-ordained!

21–2 Cf. *Parting* lines 73–4 (p. 338) above, 'And what heart knows another? | Ah! who knows his own?'
29 Cf. *To Marguerite...* line 22 (p. 343) above, 'A God, a God their severance ruled'.

30   Fate, which foresaw
     How frivolous a baby man would be –
     By what distractions he would be possessed,
     How he would pour himself in every strife,
     And well-nigh change his own identity –
35   That it might keep from his capricious play
     His genuine self, and force him to obey
     Even in his own despite his being's law,
     Bade through the deep recesses of our breast
     The unregarded river of our life
40   Pursue with indiscernible flow its way;
     And that we should not see
     The buried stream, and seem to be
     Eddying at large in blind uncertainty,
     Though driving on with it eternally.

45   But often, in the world's most crowded streets,
     But often, in the din of strife,
     There rises an unspeakable desire
     After the knowledge of our buried life;
     A thirst to spend our fire and restless force
50   In tracking out our true, original course;
     A longing to inquire
     Into the mystery of this heart which beats
     So wild, so deep in us – to know
     Whence our lives come and where they go.
55   And many a man in his own breast then delves,
     But deep enough, alas! none ever mines.
     And we have been on many thousand lines,
     And we have shown, on each, spirit and power;
     But hardly have we, for one little hour,
60   Been on our own line, have we been ourselves –
     Hardly had skill to utter one of all
     The nameless feelings that course through our breast,
     But they course on for ever unexpressed.
     And long we try in vain to speak and act
65   Our hidden self, and what we say and do
     Is eloquent, is well – but 'tis not true!
     And then we will no more be racked
     With inward striving, and demand

42–4 Cf. 'Below the surface stream' (p. 328) above.
43 Eddying cf. *Rugby Chapel* line 60 (p. 382) below.
60 Cf. *Empedocles* 2.371 (p. 351) above, 'our own only true, deep-buried selves.'
67 'And then we wish no more to be racked.'

Of all the thousand nothings of the hour
70   Their stupefying power;
Ah yes, and they benumb us at our call!
Yet still, from time to time, vague and forlorn,
From the soul's subterranean depth upborne
As from an infinitely distant land,
75   Come airs, and floating echoes, and convey
A melancholy into all our day.
Only – but this is rare –
When a belovéd hand is laid in ours,
When, jaded with the rush and glare
80   Of the interminable hours,
Our eyes can in another's eyes read clear,
When our world-deafened ear
Is by the tones of a loved voice caressed –
A bolt is shot back somewhere in our breast,
85   And a lost pulse of feeling stirs again.
The eye sinks inward, and the heart lies plain,
And what we mean, we say, and what we would, we know.
A man becomes aware of his life's flow,
And hears its winding murmur; and he sees
90   The meadows where it glides, the sun, the breeze.

And there arrives a lull in the hot race
Wherein he doth for ever chase
That flying and elusive shadow, rest.
An air of coolness plays upon his face,
95   And an unwonted calm pervades his breast.
And then he thinks he knows
The hills where his life rose,
And the sea where it goes.

104 The Scholar Gipsy

Date Composed some time in 1852–3, but conceived in broad terms perhaps as early as 1848.
Source The story is from Joseph Glanvill's *The Vanity of Dogmatizing* (1661) which A. bought in 1844. Glanvill (1636–1680) was, in some ways, a C17 equivalent of Arnold. He was a Fellow of the Royal Society and a votary of the new sciences. He disliked scholastic philosophy, and his approval of the new critical spirit of the age has affinities with A.'s, the progressive and the rational. But at the same time he disapproved of the materialism of Hobbes, was sympathetic to the Cambridge platonists, and hoped to find empirical grounds for belief in the supernatural. In Ch. 20 he tells the story of the scholar gipsy:
'There was very lately a lad in the University of Oxford, who being of very pregnant and ready parts, and yet wanting the encouragement of

preferment, was by his poverty forced to leave his studies there, and to cast himself upon the wide world for a livelihood...he was at last forced to join himself to a company of vagabond gipsies...he quickly got so much of their love and esteem as that they discovered to him their mystery, in the practice of which, by the pregnancy of his wit and parts, he soon grew so good a proficient as to be able to out-do his instructors. After he had been a pretty while well exercised in the trade, there chanced to ride by a couple of scholars, who had formerly been of his acquaintance. The scholars had quickly spied out their old friend among the gipsies; and their amazement to see him among such society, had well-nigh discovered him; but by a sign he prevented their owning him before that crew, and taking one of them aside privately, desired him with his friend to go to an Inn, not far distant thence, promising there to come to them....The Scholar-Gipsy having given them an account of the necessity which drove him to that kind of life told them that the people he went with were not such impostors as they were taken for, but that they had a traditional kind of learning among them, and could do wonders by the power of imagination, and that himself had learnt much of their art, and improved it further than themselves could. And to evince the truth of what he told them, he said he'd remove into another room, leaving them to discourse together and upon his return tell them the sum of what they had talked of; which accordingly he performed....The scholars being amazed at so unexpected a discovery, earnestly desired him to unriddle the mystery. In which he gave them satisfaction, by telling them that what he did was by the power of imagination, his fancy binding theirs; and that himself had dictated to them the discourse they held together while he was from them; that there were unwarrantable ways of heightening the imagination to that pitch, as to bind another's, and that when he had compassed the whole secret...he intended to leave their company and give the world an account of what he had learned' (195–8). A. provided his own paraphrase of this, leaving out the specific references to mind-control, thereby making the fugitive scholar an imaginative figure in the Romantic Movement sense of the word, and suppressing the mesmeric aspect which had been in his mind when composition began on the poem. See J. P. Curgenven *Litera* 2 (1955) 41–58 and 3 (1956) 1–13.

Just as *Thyrsis* is not entirely about Clough, so *The Scholar Gipsy* is not entirely about the C17 scholar, but about A.'s idyllic Oxford days, when the myth was woven in the lives of his circle: 'the freest and most delightful part, perhaps, of my life, when with you [Tom Arnold] and Clough and Walrond I shook off all the bonds and formalities of the place, and enjoyed the spring of life and that unforgotten Oxfordshire and Berkshire country' (Mrs H. Ward *A Writer's Recollections* (1918) 54). The impulse to reach back to instinctive knowledge and the past as a mode of escape from the impress of the present is described in *Empedocles* 2. 383–4: 'And we shall fly for refuge to past times, | Their soul of unworn youth, their breath of greatness' (above p. 351).

Style and discussion Like *Thyrsis*, the poem is elegiac, and the stanza consists of a sestet followed by the first half of the octet of a Petrarchan sonnet, with line 6 containing three stresses. It has similarities to the ten line stanza of Keats's *Ode of a Nightingale* – where line 8 is the three stress line. A. was reading Keats in June and August 1853 (*Note-books* 553–4). See M. R. Ridley *Keats' Craftsmanship* (1933) 208–9. G. Wilson Knight, *RES* n.s. 6

(1955) 53–62, suggests, somewhat fancifully, that the gipsies opposed Oxford's Apollonian power with their Dionysian power, but A. E. Dyson *RES* n.s. 8 (1957) 257–65, is sceptical. See also Roper 209–24.

For photographs of the locales see Taunt.

Publication *1853*.

    Go, for they call you, shepherd, from the hill;
      Go, shepherd, and untie the wattled cotes!
        No longer leave they wistful flock unfed,
        Nor let thy bawling fellows rack their throats,
5   Nor the cropped herbage shoot another head;
          But when the fields are still,
        And the tired men and dogs all gone to rest,
        And only the white sheep are sometimes seen
        Cross and recross the strips of moon-blanched green,
10   Come, shepherd, and again begin the quest!

    Here, where the reaper was at work of late –
      In this high field's dark corner, where he leaves
        His coat, his basket, and his earthern cruse,
        And in the sun all morning binds the sheaves,
15   Then here, at noon, comes back his stores to use –
          Here will I sit and wait,
        While to my ear from uplands far away
        The bleating of the folded flocks is borne,
        With distant cries of reapers in the corn –
20   All the live murmur of a summer's day.

    Screened is this nook o'er the high, half-reaped field,
      And here till sun-down, shepherd! will I be.
        Through the thick corn the scarlet poppies peep,
        And round green roots and yellowing stalks I see
25   Pale pink convolvulus in tendrils creep;
          And air-swept lindens yield
        Their scent, and rustle down their perfumed showers
        Of bloom on the bent grass where I am laid,
        And bower me from the August sun with shade;
30   And the eye travels down to Oxford's towers.

1 shepherd Clough.
2 wattled cotes stall of woven twigs.
5 herbage] grasses *1853–1881*.
10 begin the quest] renew the quest *1853–1857, 1877–1881;* 'begin the quest' first used in *1869*.
13 cruse drinking vessel.
25 pink] blue *1853–1881*.

And near me on the grass lies Glanvil's book –
Come, let me read the oft-read tale again!
The story of the Oxford scholar poor,
Of pregnant parts and quick inventive brain,
35   Who, tired of knocking at preferment's door,
One summer-morn forsook
His friends, and went to learn the gipsy-lore,
And roamed the world with that wild brotherhood,
And came, as most men deemed, to little good,
40   But came to Oxford and his friends no more.

But once, years after, in the country-lanes,
Two scholars, whom at college erst he knew,
Met him, and of his way of life enquired;
Whereat he answered, that the gipsy-crew,
45   His mates, had arts to rule as they desired
The workings of men's brains,
And they can bind them to what thoughts they will.
'And I,' he said, 'the secret of their art,
When fully learned, will to the world impart;
50   But it needs heaven-sent moments for this skill.'

This said, he left them, and returned no more.
But rumours hung about the country-side,
That the lost Scholar long was seen to stray,
Seen by rare glimpses, pensive and tongue-tied,
55   In hat of antique shape, and cloak of grey,
The same the gipsies wore.
Shepherds had met him on the Hurst in spring;
At some lone alehouse in the Berkshire moors,
On the warm ingle-bench, the smock-frocked boors
60   Had found him seated at their entering,

But, 'mid their drink and clatter, he would fly.
And I myself seem half to know thy looks,
And put the shepherds, wanderer! on thy trace;
And boys who in lone wheatfields scare the rooks

---

34 pregnant parts shining parts *1869–1878, 1881*
45–50 It is clear in Glanvill (see headnote) that the 'arts' are those of hypnotism, but A. omitted this in his own extract from Glanvill, and in the poem itself, in order for the powers to bear a closer implied relationship to the poetic art and imagination.
50 heaven-sent happy *1853*.
57 the Hurst Cumnor Hurst, a hill top between Cumnor and Boar's Hill, about two and a half miles S.W. of Oxford. Also mentioned in *Thyrsis* lines 216–17 (pp. 378 below).

65   I ask if thou hast passed their quiet place;
            Or in my boat I lie
      Moored to the cool bank in the summer-heats,
         'Mid wide grass meadows which the sunshine fills,
         And watch the warm, green-muffled Cumner hills,
70   And wonder if thou haunt'st their shy retreats.

      For most, I know, thou lov'st retiréd ground!
         Thee at the ferry Oxford riders blithe,
            Returning home on summer-nights, have met
         Crossing the stripling Thames at Bab-lock-hithe,
75   Trailing in the cool stream thy fingers wet,
            As the punt's rope chops round;
      And leaning backward in a pensive dream,
         And fostering in thy lap a heap of flowers
         Plucked in shy fields and distant Wychwood bowers,
80   And thine eyes resting on the moonlit stream.

      And then they land, and thou art seen no more!
         Maidens, who from the distant hamlets come
            To dance around the Fyfield elm in May,
         Oft through the darkening fields have seen thee roam,
85   Or cross a stile into the public way.
            Oft thou hast given them store
      Of flowers – the frail-leafed, white anemone,
         Dark bluebells drenched with dews of summer eves,
         And purple orchises with spotted leaves –
90   But none hath words she can report of thee.

      And, above Godstow Bridge, when hay-time's here
         In June, and many a scythe in sunshine flames,
            Men who through those wide fields of breezy grass
         Where black-winged swallows haunt the glittering Thames,
95   To bathe in the abandoned lasher pass,
            Have often passed thee near
      Sitting upon the river bank o'ergrown;
         Marked thine outlandish garb, thy figure spare,
         Thy dark vague eyes, and soft abstracted air –
100   But, when they came from bathing, thou wast gone!

74 Bab-lock-hithe Five miles upstream from Oxford, on the Upper Thames.
76 punt's rope chops] slow punt swings *1853–7*.   **chops** changes
91 above Godstow Bridge the same location described in *Thyrsis* line 123 as
'Wytham flats' (below p. 375).
95 lasher the pool below a weir.

At some lone homestead in the Cumner hills,
Where at her open door the housewife darns,
Thou hast been seen, or hanging on a gate
To watch the threshers in the mossy barns.
105   Children, who early range these slopes and late
For cresses from the rills,
Have known thee eying, all an April-day,
The springing pastures and the feeding kine;
And marked thee, when the stars come out and shine,
110   Thtough the long dewy grass move slow away.

In autumn, on the skirts of Bagley Wood –
Where most the gipsies by the turf-edged way
Pitch their smoked tents, and every bush you see
With scarlet patches tagged and shreds of grey,
115   Above the forest-ground called Thessaly –
The blackbird, picking food,
Sees thee, nor stops his meal, nor fears at all;
So often has he known thee past him stray,
Rapt, twirling in thy hand a withered spray,
120   And waiting for the spark from heaven to fall.

And once, in winter, on the causeway chill
Where home through flooded fields foot-travellers go,
Have I not passed thee on the wooden bridge,
Wrapped in thy cloak and battling with the snow,
125   Thy face tow'rd Hinksey and its wintry ridge?
And thou hast climbed the hill,
And gained the white brow of the Cumner range;
Turned once to watch, while thick the snowflakes fall,
The line of festal light in Christ-Church hall –
130   Then sought thy straw in some sequestered grange.

But what – I dream! Two hundred years are flown
Since first thy story ran through Oxford halls,
And the grave Glanvil did the tale inscribe
That thou wert wandered from the studious walls
135   To learn strange arts, and join a gipsy-tribe;
And thou from earth art gone
Long since, and in some quiet churchyard laid –
Some country-nook, where o'er thy unknown grave
Tall grasses and white flowering nettles wave,
140   Under a dark, red-fruited yew-tree's shade.

107 eying] watching *1853–1857;* haunting *1869.*
121 the causeway connecting Oxford to North Hinksey.
129 Christ-Church one of the most magnificent of the Oxford colleges (its chapel is the cathedral of the Oxford diocese).

– No, no, thou hast not felt the lapse of hours!
   For what wears out the life of mortal men?
      'Tis that from change to change their being rolls;
      'Tis that repeated shocks, again, again,
145   Exhaust the energy of strongest souls
        And numb the elastic powers.
   Till having used our nerves with bliss and teen,
      And tired upon a thousand schemes our wit,
      To the just-pausing Genius we remit
150   Our worn-out life, and are – what we have been.

Thou hast not lived, why should'st thou perish, so?
   Thou hadst *one* aim, *one* business, *one* desire;
      Else wert thou long since numbered with the dead!
      Else hadst thou spent, like other men, thy fire!
155   The generations of thy peers are fled,
        And we ourselves shall go;
   But thou possessest an immortal lot,
      And we imagine thee exempt from age
      And living as thou liv'st on Glanvil's page,
160   Because thou hadst – what we, alas! have not.

For early didst thou leave the world, with powers
   Fresh, undiverted to the world without,
      Firm to their mark, not spent on other things;
      Free from the sick fatigue, the languid doubt,
165   Which much to have tried, in much been baffled, brings
        O life unlike to ours!
   Who fluctuate idly without term or scope,
      Of whom each strives, nor knows for what he strives,
      And each half-lives a hundred different lives;
170   Who wait like thee, but not, like thee, in hope.

Thou waitest for the spark from heaven! and we,
   Light half-believers of our casual creeds,
      Who never deeply felt, nor clearly willed,
      Whose insight never has borne fruit in deeds,
175   Whose vague resolves never have been fulfilled;
        For whom each year we see
   Breeds new beginnings, disappointments new;

146 elastic buoyant, not easily depressed.
147 teen archaism for 'grief' or 'woe'.
149 Genius the tutelary spirit that presides over a man's life; the good
Agdistes Spenser describes in the Garden of Adonis, *Faerie Queene* 3.6.31–3.
173 Who never deeply felt Cf. A.'s note in the Yale MS: 'The misery of the
present age is…in [men's] incapacity to suffer, enjoy, feel at all, wholly and
profoundly.'

Who hesitate and falter life away,
And lose to-morrow the ground won to-day –
180   Ah! do not we, wanderer! await it too?

Yes, we await it! – but it still delays,
And then we suffer! and amongst us one,
Who most has suffered, takes dejectedly
His seat upon the intellectual throne;
185   And all his store of sad experience he
Lays bare of wretched days;
Tells us his misery's birth and growth and signs,
And how the dying spark of hope was fed,
And how the breast was soothed, and how the head,
190   And all his hourly varied anodynes.

This for our wisest! and we others pine,
And wish the long unhappy dream would end,
And waive all claim to bliss, and try to bear;
With close-lipped patience for our only friend,
195   Sad patience, too near neighbour to despair –
But none has hope like thine!
Thou through the fields and through the woods dost stray,
Roaming the country-side, a truant boy,
Nursing thy project in unclouded joy,
200   And every doubt long blown by time away.

O born in days when wits were fresh and clear,
And life ran gaily as the sparkling Thames;
Before this strange disease of modern life,
With its sick hurry, its divided aims,
205   Its heads o'ertaxed, its palsied hearts, was rife –
Fly hence, our contact fear!
Still fly, plunge deeper in the bowering wood!
Averse, as Dido did with gesture stern
From her false friend's approach in Hades turn,
210   Wave us away, and keep thy solitude!

182–90 For A.'s identification of the 'one' as Goethe see C. H. Leonard *MLN* 46 (1931) 119. Tinker and Lowry 209–11 argue the case for Tennyson. The suffering could refer to the record of grief in *In Memoriam*. 'Intellectual throne' is taken from *The Palace of Art* line 216 (see above p. 65).
190 anodynes assuagers of pain.
207–9 See Virgil *Aen.* 6. 469–73. Dido committed suicide when Aeneas left her (*Aen.* 4. 641–705) and would not speak to him when he visited the underworld.

Still nursing the unconquerable hope,
  Still clutching the inviolable shade,
    With a free, onward impulse brushing through,
  By night, the silvered branches of the glade –
215   Far on the forest-skirts, where none pursue,
      On some mild pastoral slope
  Emerge, and resting on the moonlit pales
  Freshen thy flowers as in former years
    With dew, or listen with enchanted ears,
220 From the dark dingles, to the nightingales!

But fly our paths, our feverish contact fly!
  For strong the infection of our mental strife,
    Which, though it gives no bliss, yet spoils for rest;
  And we should win thee from thy own fair life,
225   Like us distracted, and like us unblest.
      Soon, soon thy cheer would die,
  Thy hopes grow timorous, and unfixed thy powers,
  And thy clear aims be cross and shifting made;
    And then thy glad perennial youth would fade,
230 Fade, and grow old at last, and die like ours.

Then fly our greetings, fly our speech and smiles!
  – As some grave Tyrian trader, from the sea,
    Descried at sunrise an emerging prow
  Lifting the cool-haired creepers stealthily,
235   The fringes of a southward-facing brow
      Among the Aegean isles;
  And saw the merry Grecian coaster come,
  Freighted with amber grapes, and Chian wine,
    Green, bursting figs, and tunnies steeped in brine –
240 And knew the intruders on his ancient home,

The young light-hearted masters of the waves –
  And snatched his rudder, and shook out more sail;
    And day and night held on indignantly

217 **pales** the stakes of a fence.
220 **dingles** wooded dells.
232 **Tyrian** inhabitant of Tyre, in Asia Minor.
232–50 Doubts have been expressed concerning the total appropriateness of the simile, and certainly the merry Greeks do not resemble the C19 men with their palsied hearts. In a more general sense, however, they do resemble the noisy groups of people in C17 and C19 who disturb the meditation of the Gipsy. *Stanzas from the Grande Chartreuse* also closes with a contrast between the contemplative world and the boisterous extrovert one. Discussion by D. Douglas *RES* n.s. 25 (1974) 422–36 and D. Carroll *MLR* 64 (1969) 27–33.

O'er the blue Midland waters with the gale,
245 Betwixt the Syrtes and soft Sicily,
   To where the Atlantic raves
  Outside the western straits; and unbent sails
   There, where down cloudy cliffs, through sheets of foam,
   Shy traffickers, the dark Iberians come;
250 And on the beach undid his corded bales.

245 Syrtes Gulf of Sidra on the North coast of Africa.
246–50 For method of Iberian trade, *1965* cites Herodotus *History* 4. 196.
249 Iberians inhabitants of the peninsula comprising present day Spain and Portugal.

105 Stanzas from the Grande Chartreuse

Date Written between 7 Sept. 1851 (the date of A.'s visit to the abbey) and Apr. 1855. The stanzaic form also occurs in *To Marguerite* (No. 101.6), and *Morality*. The abbey near Grenoble was a favourite tourist venue: Gray went there in 1739 and Wordsworth in 1790, as he recalls in Book 6 of *The Prelude*. A. visited it on his honeymoon; he slept within the precincts, and his wife without. For a fuller discussion of the circumstances see J. Broderick *MP* 66 (1968) 157–62. Other discussion Tinker and Lowry 248–53, Culler 26–28.
Publication *Fraser's Magazine* (Apr. 1855), *1867*, *1869*, etc.

Through Alpine meadows soft-suffused
  With rain, where thick the crocus blows,
 Past the dark forges long disused,
  The mule-track from Saint Laurent goes.
5   The bridge is crossed, and slow we ride,
   Through forest, up the mountain-side.

The autumnal evening darkens round,
  The wind is up, and drives the rain;
 While, hark! far down, with strangled sound
10 Doth the Dead Guier's stream complain,
   Where that wet smoke, among the woods,
   Over his boiling cauldron broods.

Swift rush the spectral vapours white
  Past limestone scars with ragged pines,
15 Showing – then blotting from our sight! –

10 Dead Guier translates the river's French name *Le Guiers Mort*.
13 Swift] Fast *Fraser's*.

Halt – through the cloud-drift something shines!
   High in the valley, wet and drear,
   The huts of Courrerie appear.

   'Strike leftward!' cries our guide; and higher
20   Mounts up the stony forest-way.
At last the encircling trees retire;
   Look! through the showery twilight grey
    What pointed roofs are these advance? –
    A palace of the Kings of France?

25   Approach, for what we seek is here!
   Alight, and sparely sup, and wait
For rest in this outbuilding near;
   Then cross the sward and reach that gate.
    Knock; pass the wicket! Thou art come
30   To the Carthusians' world-famed home.

The silent courts, where night and day
   Into their stone-carved basins cold
The splashing icy fountains play –
   The humid corridors behold!
35   Where, ghostlike in the deepening night,
    Cowled forms brush by in gleaming white.

The chapel, where no organ's peal
   Invests the stern and naked prayer –
With penitential cries they kneel
40   And wrestle; rising then, with bare
    And white uplifted faces stand,
    Passing the Host from hand to hand;

Each takes, and then his visage wan
   Is buried in his cowl once more.
45   The cells! – the suffering Son of Man
    Upon the wall – the knee-worn floor –
    And where they sleep, that wooden bed,
    Which shall their coffin be, when dead!

18–24 For the significance, in moral and psychological terms, of the approach to the monastery, see *Culler* 26–8 who sees A. reascending to his childhood through the gorge in which his faith has died.
30 the Carthusians founded by St Bruno (1033–1101). A strict and ascetic order.
40–2, 46–7 *1965* indicates errors in A.'s account of Carthusian practices; the Host is not passed from hand to hand. A. was probably confused by the circulation of the tablet of the Pax.

The library, where tract and tome
50   Not to feed priestly pride are there,
To hymn the conquering march of Rome,
    Nor yet to amuse, as ours are!
      They paint of souls the inner strife,
      Their drops of blood, their death in life.

55 The garden, overgrown – yet mild,
    See, fragrant herbs are flowering there!
Strong children of the Alpine wild
    Whose culture is the brethren's care;
      Of human tasks their only one,
60   And cheerful works beneath the sun.

Those halls, too, destined to contain
    Each its own pilgrim-host of old,
From England, Germany, or Spain –
    All are before me! I behold
65   The House, the Brotherhood austere!
      – And what am I, that I am here?

For rigorous teachers seized my youth,
    And purged its faith, and trimmed its fire,
Showed me the high, white star of Truth,
70   There bade me gaze, and there aspire.
      Even now their whispers pierce the gloom:
      'What dost thou in this living tomb?'

Forgive me, masters of the mind!
    At whose behest I long ago
70 So much unlearnt, so much resigned –
    I come not here to be your foe!
      I seek these anchorites, not in ruth,
      To curse and to deny your truth;

Not as their friend, or child, I speak!
80   But as, on some far northern strand,
Thinking of his own Gods, a Greek
    In pity and mournful awe might stand
      Before some fallen Runic stone –
      For both were faiths, and both are gone.

67 rigorous teachers various suggestions have been made as to who these may be; amongst them Carlyle, Goethe, Senancour and Spinoza. It is less likely that they are figures from Rugby School.
68 And pruned its faith and quenched its fire, *Fraser's*.
69 high white] pale cold *Fraser's*.
83 Runic stone a sacred tablet engraved with mystical hieroglyphs; associated with Germanic cultures.

85   Wandering between two worlds, one dead,
        The other powerless to be born,
    With nowhere yet to rest my head,
        Like these, on earth I wait forlorn.
        Their faith, my tears, the world deride –
90   I come to shed them at their side.

    Oh, hide me in your gloom profound,
        Ye solemn seats of holy pain!
    Take me, cowled forms, and fence me round,
        Till I possess my soul again;
95   Till free my thoughts before me roll,
        Not chafed by hourly false control!

    For the world cries your faith is now
        But a dead time's exploded dream;
    My melancholy, sciolists say,
100   Is a passed mode, an outworn theme–
        As if the world had ever had
        A faith, or sciolists been sad!

    Ah, if it *be* passed, take away,
        At least, the restlessness, the pain;
105   Be man henceforth no more a prey
        To these out-dated stings again!
        The nobleness of grief is gone –
        Ah, leave us not the fret alone!

    But – if you cannot give us ease –
110   Last of the race of them who grieve
    Here leave us to die out with these
        Last of the people who believe!
        Silent, while years engrave the brow;
        Silent – the best are silent now.

85–8 Cf. Carlyle 'Characteristics' (1831), *Crit. and Misc. Essays*, in *Works* (1899), 28.29–32: 'Belief, Faith has well nigh vanished from the world.... For Contemplation and love of Wisdom, no Cloister now opens its religious shades; the Thinker must, in all sense, wander homeless.... The doom of the Old has long been pronounced, and irrevocable; the Old has passed away: but alas, the New appears not in its stead; the Time is still in pangs of travail with the New.' See also Chateaubriand's *Mémoires d'outre tombe* (1849–50), which A. records reading in his 1851 Diary: '*entre les souvenirs de deux sociétés, entre un monde éteint et un monde prêt a s'éteindre.*'
93 Invest me, steep me, fold me round, *Fraser's.*
99 sciolists superficial pretenders to knowledge.
108 fret] pang *Fraser's.*

115 Achilles ponders in his tent,
     The kings of modern thought are dumb;
   Silent they are, though not content,
     And wait to see the future come.
       They have the grief men had of yore,
120   But they contend and cry no more.

   Our fathers watered with their tears
     This sea of time whereon we sail,
   Their voices were in all men's ears
     Who passed within their puissant hail.
125   Still the same same ocean round us raves,
       But we stand mute, and watch the waves.

   For what availed it, all the noise
     And outcry of the former men? –
   Say, have their sons achieved more joys,
130   Say, is life lighter now than then?
       The sufferers died, they left their pain –
       The pangs which tortured them remain.

   What helps it now, that Byron bore,
     With haughty scorn which mocked the smart,
135 Through Europe to the Aetolian shore
     The pageant of his bleeding heart?
       That thousands counted every groan,
       And Europe made his woe her own?

   What boots it, Shelley! that the breeze
140   Carried thy lovely wail away,
   Musical through Italian trees
     Which fringe thy soft blue Spezzian bay?
       Inheritors of thy distress
       Have restless hearts one throb the less?

145 Or are we easier, to have read,
     O Obermann! the sad, stern page,

115 Achilles refused to take part in the Trojan war until after the death of Patroclus; he withdrew when Agamemnon made him surrender Briseis (*Iliad* 1.320–56).
116 kings of modern thought Cf. Shelley's *Adonais* lines 430–1: 'the kings of thought | Who waged contention with their time's decay.'
133–42 Cf. Carlyle's 'Characteristics' *Works* 28. 31: 'Behold a Byron, in melodious tones, "cursing his day"...Hear a Shelley filling the earth with inarticulate wail; like the infinite, inarticulate grief of foresaken infants.'
146 Obermann A fictional C18 letter-writer created by Etienne Pivert de Senancour (1770–1848). A. thought the creation was of 'profound inwardness' and 'austere sincerity'. For Senancour's importance for A. see Tinker and Lowry 253–74 and *Stanzas in Memory of the Author of 'Obermann'*.

Which tells us how thou hidd'st thy head
From the fierce tempest of thine age
In the lone brakes of Fontainebleau,
150 Or chalets near the Alpine snow?

Ye slumber in your silent grave! –
The world, which for an idle day
Grace to your mood of sadness gave,
Long since hath flung her weeds away.
155 The eternal trifler breaks your spell;
But we – we learnt your lore too well!

Years hence, perhaps, may dawn an age,
More fortunate, alas! than we,
Which without hardness will be sage,
160 And gay without frivolity.
Sons of the world, oh, speed those years;
But, while we wait, allow our tears!

Allow them! We admire with awe
The exulting thunder of your race;
165 You give the universe your law,
You triumph over time and space!
Your pride of life, your tireless powers,
We laud them, but they are not ours.

We are like children reared in shade
170 Beneath some old-world abbey wall,
Forgotten in a forest-glade,
And secret from the eyes of all.
Deep, deep the greenwood round them waves,
Their abbey, and its close of graves!

175 But, where the road runs near the stream,
Oft through the trees they catch a glance
Of passing troops in the sun's beam –
Pennon, and plume, and flashing lance!
Forth to the world those soldiers fare,
180 To life, to cities, and to war!

And through the wood, another way,
Faint bugle-notes from far are borne,
Where hunters gather, staghounds bay,

168 We laud them] They awe us *Fraser's:* We mark them *1867–1869;* We praise them *1877–1881.*
181–192 Perhaps influenced by Wordsworth's *Descriptive Sketches* (1793) lines 59–60 in which Chartreuse is woken from its deathlike sleep: 'The voice of blasphemy the fane alarms. | The cloister startles at the gleam of arms.'

185 Round some fair forest-lodge at morn.
  Gay dames are there, in sylvan green;
  Laughter and cries – those notes between!

The banners flashing through the trees.
 Make their blood dance and chain their eyes;
The bugle-music on the breeze
190 Arrests them with a charmed surprise.
  Banner by turns and bugle woo:
  'Ye shy recluses, follow too!'

O children, what do ye reply? –
 'Action and pleasure, will ye roam
195 Through these secluded dells to cry
 And call us? – but too late ye come!
  Too late for us your call ye blow,
  Whose bent was taken long ago.

'Long since we pace this shadowed nave;
200 We watch those yellow tapers shine,
Emblems of hope over the grave,
 In the high altar's depth divine;
  The organ carries to our ear
  Its accents of another sphere.

205 'Fenced early in this cloistral round
 Of reverie, of shade, of prayer,
How should we grow in other ground?
 How can we flower in foreign air?
  – Pass, banners, pass, and bugles, cease;
210 And leave our desert to its peace!'

210 desert] forest *Fraser's*.

106 Thyrsis

Date Conceived 1862–3, probably written 1864–5 and finished late Jan. 1866. Clough died 13 Nov. 1861; on 22 Jan. 1862 A. wrote to C.'s widow: 'I shall take them [verses by C.] with me to Oxford, where I shall go alone after Easter; – and there, among the Cumner Hills where we have so often rambled, I shall be able to think him over as I could wish' (Lowry *Letters* 160). A. was in Oxford in late March or early May 1862, and again in April 1863, but on the latter occasion the circumstances were inauspicious, as A. explained to his mother: 'The weather was fine but with a detestable cold wind, so that a new poem about the Cumner hillside, and C., in connexion with it...I could not begin. I have been accumulating stores for it however' (*Letters* 1. 221-2). Composition may have begun in late November 1863 — the 'winter-eve' of line 16 – and have continued in June 1864, see R. L. Brooks, *RES* n.s. 14 (1963) 173–4. At that time A. was staying at Woodford, Essex, and he told his mother that lines 51–80 were reminiscent of that place (*Letters* 1. 325).

Associations Like *the Scholar Gipsy*, with which it is intimately linked, *Thyrsis* is a celebration of the lost youth and half-forgotten springs of inspiration associated with the Oxford countryside. It is in the tradition of pastoral elegy of Milton's *Lycidas* (which was also called a 'monody'), and of Virgil and Theocritus before him. A. is closer to the classical mode than Milton, since he confines himself to the poetic and rural identity of himself and the mourned one (at least, as the subject that is endorsed and treated in a mythopoeic manner), whereas Milton drew in the priestly sense of pastoral care. For a fuller treatment of the pastoral elegy see J. H. Hanford *PMLA* 25 (1910) 403–47, T. P. Harrison, Jr *The Pastoral Elegy* (Austin, Texas 1939) and S. Elledge *Milton's 'Lycidas'* (New York 1966). Thyrsis is found in Theocritus, *Idylls* 1, and Virgil *Eclogues* 7 – where he is in rivalry with Corydon. A. said that he had been 'much reading' Theocritus 'during the two years this poem has been forming itself' (*Letters* 1.325). A. also read Moschus – to whom *The Lament for Bion* was then attributed.

A. realized the shortcomings of *Thyrsis* as a statement about Clough: 'One has the feeling, if one reads the poem as a memorial poem, that not enough is said about Clough in it.... Still Clough *had* this idyllic side, too; to deal with this suited my desire to deal again with that Cumner country; anyway, only so could I treat the matter this time' (*Letters* 1.327). But it should be read in the elegiac tradition established by Milton's *Lycidas* and Shelley's *Adonais*.

Discussion E. D. H. Johnson *The Alien Vision of Victorian Poetry* (Princeton 1952) 202–4; Roper 224–9. For the topography see Sir Francis Wylie (Tinker and Lowry 351–73); E. K. Chambers *A Sheaf of Studies* (1942) 1–19; and Taunt.

Publication *Every Saturday* (U.S.A.) (10 March 1866); *Macmillan's Mag.* (April 1866); *1867, 1868, 1869*, etc.

A MONODY,
to commemorate the author's friend,
ARTHUR HUGH CLOUGH,
who died at Florence, 1861

How changed is here each spot man makes or fills!
In the two Hinkseys nothing keeps the same;
  The village street its haunted mansion lacks,
  And from the sign is gone Sibylla's name,

Heading followed by four lines from A.'s unpublished *Lucretius 1867–8:* 'Thus yesterday, to-day, to-morrow come, | They hustle one another and they pass; | But all our hustling morrows only make | The smooth to-day of God. **2–4 two Hinkseys** North and South Hinksey, two miles W. of Oxford. Sybella Curr was landlady of the Cross Keys in S. Hinksey. She died in 1860. **3 haunted mansion** in N. Hinksey. Its last tenant was Mark Scragg or Scroggs, who sold his soul to the devil, in C17. He imprisoned witches in a nearby elm which stood until circa 1900.

5   And from the roofs the twisted chimney-stacks –
        Are ye too changed, ye hills?
     See, 'tis no foot of unfamiliar men
       To-night from Oxford up your pathway strays!
     Here came I often, often, in old days –
10   Thyrsis and I; we still had Thyrsis then.

   Runs it not here, the track by Childsworth Farm,
      Past the high wood, to where the elm-tree crowns
     The hill behind whose ridge the sunset flames?
    The signal-elm, that looks on Ilsley Downs,
15   The Vale, the three lone weirs, the youthful Thames?
      This winter-eve is warm,
   Humid the air! leafless, yet soft as spring,
     The tender purple spray on copse and briers!
    And that sweet city with her dreaming spires,
20   She needs not June for beauty's heightening,

   Lovely all times she lies, lovely to-night –
     Only, methinks, some loss of habit's power
      Befalls me wandering through this upland dim.
    Once passed I blindfold here, at any hour;
25   Now seldom come I, since I came with him.
      That single elm-tree bright
   Against the west – I miss it! is it gone?
     We prized it dearly; while it stood, we said,
     Our friend, the Gipsy-Scholar, was not dead;
30   While the tree lived, he in these fields lived on.

   Too rare, too rare, grow now my visits here,
     But once I knew each field, each flower, each stick;
     And with the country-folk acquaintance made
    By barn in threshing time, by new-built rick.

11 Childsworth Farm more commonly called Chilswell Farm.
14 The signal-elm the subject of much controversy: Wylie has a lengthy discussion; see also E. K. Chambers *A Sheaf of Studies* (1942). For a photograph of A.'s tree see Taunt *The Oxford Poems of M.A.* It was however not an elm but an oak, with no view of Ilsley Downs (Berks.). Two other trees have been proposed, and the confused route taken by A. It may be that his memory played him false with the topography.
19–21 Cf. A.'s Preface to *Essays in Criticism* 1 (1865) *Works* 3.290: 'Beautiful city! so venerable, so lovely, so unravaged by the fierce intellectual life of our century, so serene!...Adorable dreamer, whose heart has been so romantic!' This is the moonlit view of Oxford, which A. tended to adopt when distanced from it by time or space.

35   Here, too, our shepherd-pipes we first assayed.
    Ah me! this many a year
My pipe is lost, my shepherd's holiday!
Needs must I lose them, needs with heavy heart
Into the world and wave of men depart;
40   But Thyrsis of his own will went away.

It irked him to be here, he could not rest.
He loved each simple joy the country yields,
    He loved his mates; but yet he could not keep,
For that a shadow loured on the fields,
45   Here with the shepherds and the silly sheep.
    Some life of men unblest
He knew, which made him droop, and filled his head.
He went; his piping took a troubled sound
Of storms that rage outside our happy ground;
50   He could not wait their passing, he is dead.

So, some tempestuous morn in early June,
When the year's primal burst of bloom is o'er,
    Before the roses and the longest day –
When garden-walks and all the grassy floor
55   With blossoms red and white of fallen May
    And chestnut-flowers are strewn –
So have I heard the cuckoo's parting cry,
From the wet field, through the vexed garden-trees,
Come with the volleying rain and tossing breeze:
60   'The bloom is gone, and with the bloom go I!'

Too quick despairer, wherefore wilt thou go?
Soon will the high Midsummer pomps come on,
    Soon will the musk carnations break and swell,
Soon shall we have gold-dusted snapdragon,
65   Sweet-William with his homely cottage-smell,
    And stocks in fragrant blow;
Roses that down the alleys shine afar,
And open, jasmine-muffled lattices,
And groups under the dreaming garden-trees,
70   And the full moon, and the white evening-star.

35–7 shepherd-pipes poetic song in the pastoral convention. Cf. Spenser *Shepherd's Calendar.*
40–50 Probably a reference to Clough's resignation of his Oriel fellowship in Oct. 1848. For the resignation see Chorley *A. H. Clough* 94–104 and above p. 289. It was occasioned by his dissatisfaction with Subscription to the Thirty-nine Articles rather than by a positive attraction to 'each simple joy the country yields'. His poetry did not become particularly troubled after he left.
64–8 Flower-catalogues were common in the pastoral elegy.

He hearkens not! light comer, he is flown!
What matters it? next year he will return,
    And we shall have him in the sweet spring-days,
With whitening hedges, and uncrumpling fern,
75   And blue-bells trembling by the forest-ways,
        And scent of hay new-mown.
But Thyrsis never more we swains shall see;
    See him come back, and cut a smoother reed,
    And blow a strain the world at last shall heed –
80 For Time, not Corydon, hath conquered thee!

Alack, for Corydon no rival now!
    But when Sicilian shepherds lost a mate,
        Some good survivor with his flute would go,
    Piping a ditty sad for Bion's fate;
85   And cross the unpermitted ferry's flow,
        And relax Pluto's brow,
    And make leap up with joy the beauteous head
        Of Proserpine, among whose crownéd hair
        Are flowers first opened on Sicilian air,
90 And flute his friend, like Orpheus, from the dead.

O easy access to the hearer's grace
    When Dorian shepherds sang to Proserpine!
        For she herself had trod Sicilian fields,
    She knew the Dorian water's gush divine,
95   She knew each lily white which Enna yields,
        Each rose with blushing face;
    She loved the Dorian pipe, the Dorian strain.
        But ah, of our poor Thames she never heard!
        Her foot the Cumner cowslips never stirred;
100 And we should tease her with our plaint in vain!

71–77 The cyclic nature of the seasons contrasted to the temporal life of man is typical of the pastoral elegy. See *Lament for Bion* lines 99–104.

78 smoother reed shepherd's pipe, and hence a metonymy for poetic styles. A. thought that Clough's poetry could be harsh and excessively colloquial. See his letter of 24 Feb. 1848 accusing C. of 'deficiency of the *beautiful*'. (Lowry *Letters* 66).

80 Corydon Corydon conquers Thyrsis in the singing-match in Virgil *Eclogues* 7.

82–100 Cf. *Lament for Bion* lines 115–26. The poet mourning Bion wished to imitate Orpheus' example by attempting to charm the rulers of the underworld with his song.

88–9 See Ovid *Met.* 5. 391–2, 395 and *Paradise Lost* 4. 268–71.

97 the Dorian strain the stately and simple style of ancient Greece; = Doric, i.e. in contrast to soft Lydian modes.

Well! wind-dispersed and vain the words will be,
   Yet, Thyrsis, let me give my grief its hour
     In the old haunt, and find our tree-topped hill!
   Who, if not I, for questing here hath power?
105   I know the wood which hides the daffodil,
      I know the Fyfield tree,
    I know what white, what purple fritillaries
     The grassy harvest of the river-fields,
     Above by Ensham, down by Sandford, yields,
110   And what sedged brooks are Thames's tributaries;

I know these slopes; who knows them if not I?
   But many a dingle on the loved hill-side,
     With thorns once studded, old, white-blossomed trees,
   Where thick the cowslips grew, and far descried
115   High towered the spikes of purple orchises,
      Hath since our day put by
    The coronals of that forgotten time;
     Down each green bank hath gone the ploughboy's team,
     And only in the hidden brookside gleam
120   Primroses, orphans of the flowery prime.

Where is the girl, who by the boatman's door,
   Above the locks, above the boating throng,
     Unmoored our skiff when through the Wytham flats,
   Red loosestrife and blond meadow-sweet among
125   And darting swallows and light water-gnats,
      We tracked the shy Thames shore?
    Where are the mowers, who, as the tiny swell
     Of our boat passing heaved the river-grass,
     Stood with suspended scythe to see us pass?
130   They all are gone, and thou art gone as well!

Yes, thou art gone! and round me too the night
   In ever-nearing circle weaves her shade.
     I see her veil draw soft across the day,
   I feel her slowly chilling breath invade
135   The cheek grown thin, the brown hair sprent with grey;
      I feel her finger light
    Laid pausefully upon life's headlong train;

---

106 the Fyfield tree Cf. *The Scholar Gipsy* lines 82–3 (p. 359 above).
109 Ensham Eynsham, about six miles N.W. of Oxford.
123 Wytham flats Cf. *The Scholar Gipsy* lines 91–6 (p. 359 above).
129 suspended scythe at once a literal detail and a discreet emblem of suspended time.

The foot less prompt to meet the morning dew,
The heart less bounding at emotion new,
140 And hope, once crushed, less quick to spring again.

And long the way appears, which seemed so short
To the less practised eye of sanguine youth;
And high the mountain-tops, in cloudy air,
The mountain-tops where is the throne of Truth,
145 Tops in life's morning-sun so bright and bare!
Unbreachable the fort
Of the long-battered world uplifts its wall;
And strange and vain the earthly turmoil grows,
And near and real the charm of thy repose,
150 And night as welcome as a friend would fall,

But hush! the upland hath a sudden loss
Of quiet! – Look, adown the dusk hill-side,
A troop of Oxford hunters going home,
As in old days, jovial and talking, ride!
155 From hunting with the Berkshire hounds they come.
Quick! let me fly, and cross
Into yon farther field! – 'Tis done; and see,
Backed by the sunset, which doth glorify
The orange and pale violet evening-sky,
160 Bare on its lonely ridge, the Tree! the Tree!

I take the omen! Eve lets down her veil,
The white fog creeps from bush to bush about,
The west unflushes, the high stars grow bright,
And in the scattered farms the lights come out.
165 I cannot reach the signal-tree to-night,
Yet, happy omen, hail!
Hear it from thy broad lucent Arno-vale
(For there thine earth-forgetting eyelids keep
The morningless and unawakening sleep
170 Under the flowery oleanders pale),

Hear it, O Thyrsis, still our tree is there!
Ah, vain! These English fields, this upland dim,
These brambles pale with mist engarlanded,
That lone, sky-pointing tree, are not for him;

141–5 Cf. Donne *Satire* 3. 79–84.
153–5 Cf. *The Scholar Gipsy* lines 72–3. (p. 359 above).
156–7 The poet flees as the Scholar Gipsy did from worldly contact. Cf. *The Scholar Gipsy* lines 221, 231 (p. 363 above).
167 Arno Vale Clough died in Florence and is buried there.

175   To a boon southern country he is fled,
And now in happier air,
Wandering with the great Mother's train divine
(And purer or more subtle soul than thee,
I trow, the mighty Mother doth not see)
180   Within a folding of the Apennine,

Thou hearest the immortal chants of old!
Putting his sickle to the perilous grain
In the hot cornfield of the Phrygian king,
For thee the Lityerses-song again
185   Young Daphnis with his silver voice doth sing;
Sings his Sicilian fold,
His sheep, his hapless love, his blinded eyes –
And how a call celestial round him rang,
And heavenward from the fountain-brink he sprang,
190   And all the marvel of the golden skies.

There thou art gone, and me thou leavest here
Sole in these fields! yet will I not despair.
Despair I will not, while I yet descry
'Neath the mild canopy of English air
195   That lonely tree against the western sky.
Still, still these slopes, 'tis clear,
Our Gipsy-Scholar haunts, outliving thee!
Fields where soft sheep from cages pull the hay,
Woods with anemones in flower till May,
200   Know him a wanderer still; then why not me?

177 great Mother Demeter, the mother of Persephone (Proserpine).
182–90 'Daphnis, the ideal Sicilian shepherd of Greek pastoral poetry, was said to have followed in Phrygia his mistress Piplea, who had been carried off by robbers, and to have found her in the power of the king of Phrygia, Lityerses. Lityerses used to make strangers try a contest with him in reaping corn, and to put them to death if he overcame them. Hercules arrived in time to save Daphnis, took upon himself the reaping-contest with Lityerses, overcame him, and slew him. The Lityerses-song connected with this tradition was, like the Linus-song, one of the early plaintive strains of Greek popular poetry, and used to be sung by corn-reapers. Other traditions presented Daphnis as beloved by a nymph who exacted from him an oath to love no one else. He fell in love with a princess, and was struck blind by the jealous nymph. Mercury, who was his father, raised him to Heaven, and made a fountain spring up in the place from which he ascended. At this fountain the Sicilians offered yearly sacrifices' (A.'s note; first added *1869*). See Servius, *Comment. in Virgil. Bucol.* 5.20 and 8.68.

A fugitive and gracious light he seeks,
Shy to illumine; and I seek it too.
This does not come with houses or with gold,
With place, with honour, and a flattering crew;
205 'Tis not in the world's market bought and sold –
But the smooth-slipping weeks
Drop by, and leave its seeker still untired;
Out of the heed of mortals he is gone,
He wends unfollowed, he must house alone;
210 Yet on he fares, by his own heart inspired.

Thou too, O Thyrsis, on like quest wast bound;
Thou wanderedst with me for a little hour!
Men gave thee nothing; but this happy quest,
If men esteemed thee feeble, gave thee power,
215 If men procured thee trouble, gave thee rest.
And this rude Cumner ground,
Its fir-topped Hurst, its farms, its quiet fields,
Here cam'st thou in thy jocund youthful time,
Here was thine height of strength, thy golden prime!
220 And still the haunt beloved a virtue yields.

What though the music of thy rustic flute
Kept not for long its happy, country tone;
Lost it too soon, and learnt a stormy note
Of men contention-tossed, of men who groan,
225 Which tasked thy pipe too sore, and tired thy throat
It failed, and thou wast mute!
Yet hadst thou alway visions of our light,
And long with men of care thou couldst not stay,
And soon thy foot resumed its wandering way,
230 Left human haunt, and on alone till night.

211–40 D. J. DeLaura *VP* 7 (1969) 191–202 argues that the last three stanzas are influenced by A.'s reading of Clough's *Letters and Remains* (1865).
221–6 Many critics have observed that these are unfair and inaccurate lines as a judgment on Clough's poetry. C.'s satirical verse did not put strains on his poetic muse. A. admitted, writing to J. C. Shairp 12 Apr. 1866, that he had misrepresented C.: 'there is much in Clough (the whole *prophet* side, in fact) which one cannot deal with in this way' (*Letters* 1. 327).
230 It would not be true to say that Clough avoided human haunts whilst still alive, since he was a sociable being; but it may be that A. refers to C.'s continued search for truth *after* death.

Too rare, too rare, grow now my visits here!
  'Mid city-noise, not, as with thee of yore,
    Thyrsis! in reach of sheep-bells is my home.
  – Then through the great town's harsh, heart-wearying roar,
235   Let in thy voice a whisper often come,
      To chase fatigue and fear:
  'Why faintest thou? I wandered till I died.
    Roam on! The light we sought is shining still.
    Dost thou ask proof? Our tree yet crowns the hill,
240   Our Scholar travels yet the loved hill-side.'

107 Dover Beach

Date *1965* 239 suggests June 1851, when A. and his wife visited Dover.
    It should be compared with *Stanzas from the Grande Chartreuse* (no. 105) as a statement of the loss of orthodox religious faith.
Discussion U. C. Knoepflmacher, *VP* 1 (1963) 17–26, and R. Pitman, *EC* 23 (1973) 109–36, relate the poem to Wordsworth's *'It is a beauteous evening...'* and *September, 1802, Near Dover*, showing that W. posits a faith in the Invisible and the harmonization of the 'still sad music of humanity' in a way impossible for A. Dover is an important point of arrival and departure, with symbolic appeal especially to poets: one thinks of W. H. Auden's *Dover 1937*. See also Baum 95–6; Culler 39–41; Tinker and Lowry 73–8 (reproducing a MS draft); R. M. Gollin *English Studies* 48 (1967) 493–511.
Publication *1867; 1869*, etc.

    The sea is calm to-night.
    The tide is full, the moon lies fair
    Upon the straits; on the French coast the light
    Gleams and is gone; the cliffs of England stand,
5   Glimmering and vast, out in the tranquil bay.
    Come to the window, sweet is the night-air!
    Only, from the long line of spray
    Where the sea meets the moon-blanched land,
    Listen! you hear the grating roar
10   Of pebbles which the waves draw back, and fling,
    At their return, up the high strand,
    Begin, and cease, and then again begin,
    With tremulous cadence slow, and bring
    The eternal note of sadness in.

9 Cf. Wordsworth, *'It is a beauteous evening...'* line 6: 'Listen! the mighty Being is awake'.

15   Sophocles long ago
       Heard it on the Aegaean, and it brought
       Into his mind the turbid ebb and flow
       Of human misery; we
       Find also in the sound a thought,
20   Hearing it by this distant northern sea.

       The Sea of Faith
       Was once, too, at the full, and round earth's shore
       Lay like the folds of a bright girdle furled.
       But now I only hear
25   Its melancholy, long, withdrawing roar,
       Retreating, to the breath
       Of the night-wind, down the vast edges drear
       And naked shingles of the world.

       Ah, love, let us be true
30   To one another! for the world, which seems
       To lie before us like a land of dreams,
       So various, so beautiful, so new,
       Hath really neither joy, nor love, nor light,
       Nor certitude, nor peace, nor help for pain;
35   And we are here as on a darkling plain
       Swept with confused alarms of struggle and flight,
       Where ignorant armies clash by night.

15–18 Sophocles was A.'s favourite Greek dramatist. In 'On the Modern Element in Literature' (1857) he wrote: '...the peculiar characteristic of the poetry of Sophocles is its consummate, its unrivalled *adequacy*,...it represents the highly developed human nature of that age...in its completest and most harmonious development....And therefore I have ventured to say of Sophocles, that he "saw life steadily, and saw it whole"' (*Works* 1.28). The closest parallel is in the *Trachiniae* lines 112 ff.: 'For as the tireless South or Northern blast | Billow on billow rolls o'er ocean wide, | So on the son of Cadmus follows fast | Sea upon sea of trouble...' (Loeb transl.).

20 Cf. *Stanzas from the Grande Chartreuse* lines 80–2 (p. 366 above).

23 girdle] garment MS.

35–7 The source is Thucydides' *History of the Peloponnesian War* Ch. 44, where the moonlit battle of Epipolae is described. A.'s father translated Thucydides (1830–5). S. Feshback *VP* 4 (1966) 273–4 suggests the influence of Empedocles *Fragment* 121: 'A joyless land, | Where slaughter and grudge, and troops of dooms besides, etc.' (W. E. Leonard transl.).

108 Rugby Chapel November, 1857

Date of composition unknown; A. visited Rugby in Nov. 1855 and 1856. His thoughts may have been turned to Rugby in 1857 by reading Tom Hughes's *Tom Brown's Schooldays*, a novel idolizing A.'s father Dr Thomas Arnold (1795–1842). A. was also perhaps prompted by Fitzjames Stephen's statement in the *Edinburgh Review* Jan. 1858 that Dr Arnold was 'a narrow bustling fanatic' (Lowry *Letters* 164). A. wrote to his mother 27 Feb. 1855: 'But this is just what makes him great – that he was not only a good man saving his soul by righteousness, but that he carried so many others along with him in his hand, and saved them...along with himself' (*Letters* 1. 42). A. may have chosen November as the quintessential Rugby time; he visited it in Nov. 1849 after parting with Marguerite (suggesting a rejection of uncertain pleasure and an encounter with images of duty and responsibility). In a letter to his brother Tom of Dec. 1886 he refers to the 'November dimness over everything' when he thinks of Rugby (see W. T. Arnold, 'Thomas Arnold the Younger', *Century Magazine* 1 (1903) 118). The dusk setting is reminiscent, as W. S. Peterson *ELN* 3 (1966) 204–6 observes, of the final chapter of *Tom Brown's Schooldays*, although the 'town boys playing cricket' presumably sets the time outside November. The elegy is a tribute to values in life transcending selfish individualism. For a similar view see *Culture and Anarchy* (1869), *Works* 5.94: 'The individual is required, under pain of being stunted and enfeebled in his own development if he disobeys, to carry others along with him in his march towards perfection...'
Discussion For a discussion of the metrics of the poem see J. Ranta *VP* 10 (1972) 333–49.
Publication *1867*.

    Coldly, sadly descends
    The autumn-evening. The field
    Strewn with its dank yellow drifts
    Of withered leaves, and the elms,
5   Fade into dimness apace,
    Silent; hardly a shout
    From a few boys late at their play!
    The lights come out in the street,
    In the school-room windows; but cold,
10   Solemn, unlighted, austere,
    Through the gathering darkness, arise
    The chapel-walls, in whose bound
    Thou, my father! art laid.

    There thou dost lie, in the gloom
15   Of the autumn evening. But ah!
    That word, *gloom*, to my mind
    Brings thee back, in the light
    Of thy radiant vigour, again;

12–13 Dr. Arnold died in 1842, at Rugby, but the last post he occupied was Professor of Modern History at Oxford.

In the gloom of November we passed
20   Days not dark at thy side;
Seasons impaired not the ray
Of thy buoyant cheerfulness clear.
Such thou wast! and I stand
In the autumn evening, and think
25   Of bygone autumns with thee.

Fifteen years have gone round
Since thou arosest to tread,
In the summer-morning, the road
Of death, at a call unforeseen,
30   Sudden. For fifteen years,
We who till then in thy shade
Rested as under the boughs
Of a mighty oak, have endured
Sunshine and rain as we might,
35   Bare, unshaded, alone,
Lacking the shelter of thee.

O strong soul, by what shore
Tarriest thou now? For that force,
Surely, has not been left vain!
40   Somewhere, surely, afar,
In the sounding labour-house vast
Of being, is practised that strength,
Zealous, beneficent, firm!

Yes, in some far-shining sphere,
45   Conscious or not of the past,
Still thou performest the word
Of the Spirit in whom thou dost live –
Prompt, unwearied, as here!
Still thou upraisest with zeal
50   The humble good from the ground,
Sternly repressest the bad!
Still, like a trumpet, dost rouse
Those who with half-open eyes
Tread the border-land dim
55   'Twixt vice and virtue; reviv'st
Succourest! – this was thy work,
This was thy life upon earth.

What is the course of the life
Of mortal men on the earth? –
60   Most men eddy about
Here and there – eat and drink,
Chatter and love and hate,

Gather and squander, are raised
Aloft, are hurled in the dust,
65   Striving blindly, achieving
Nothing; and then they die –
Perish; – and no one asks
Who or what they have been,
More than he asks what waves,
70   In the moonlit solitudes mild
Of the midmost Ocean, have swelled
Foamed for a moment, and gone.

And there are some, whom a thirst
Ardent, unquenchable, fires,
75   Not with the crowd to be spent,
Not without aim to go round
In an eddy of purposeless dust,
Effort unmeaning and vain.
Ah yes! some of us strive
80   Not without action to die
Fruitless, but something to snatch
From dull oblivion, nor all
Glut the devouring grave!
We, we have chosen our path –
85   Path to a clear-purposed goal,
Path of advance! – but it leads
A long, steep journey, through sunk
Gorges, o'er mountains in snow.
Cheerful, with friends, we set forth –
90   Then, on the height, comes the storm.
Thunder crashes from rock
To rock, the cataracts reply,
Lightnings dazzle our eyes.
Roaring torrents have breached
95   The track, the stream-bed descends
In the place where the wayfarer once
Planted his footstep – the spray
Boils o'er its borders! aloft
The unseen snow-beds dislodge
100   Their hanging ruin; alas,
Havoc is made in our train!
Friends, who set forth at our side,
Falter, are lost in the storm
We, we only are left!

85–123 The journey in this poem is largely figurative, but *Resignation* describes the literal journey through the mountains in which Dr Arnold took the part of the succouring leader. See Culler 274–77, Roper 131–7.

105 With frowning foreheads, with lips
Sternly compressed, we strain on,
On – and at nightfall at last
Come to the end of our way,
To the lonely inn 'mid the rocks;
110 Where the gaunt and taciturn host
Stands on the threshold, the wind
Shaking his thin white hairs –
Holds his lantern to scan
Our storm-beat figures, and asks:
115 Whom in our party we bring?
Whom we have left in the snow?

Sadly we answer: We bring
Only ourselves! we lost
Sight of the rest in the storm.
120 Hardly ourselves we fought through,
Stripped, without friends, as we are.
Friends, companions, and train,
The avalanche swept from our side.

But thou would'st not *alone*
125 Be saved, my father! *alone*
Conquer and come to thy goal,
Leaving the rest in the wild.
We were weary, and we
Fearful, and we in our march
130 Fain to drop down and to die.
Still thou turnedst, and still
Beckonedst the trembler, and still
Gavest the weary thy hand.

If, in the paths of the world,
135 Stones might have wounded thy feet,
Toil or dejection have tried,
Thy spirit, of that we saw
Nothing – to us thou wast still
Cheerful, and helpful, and firm!
140 Therefore to thee it was given
Many to save with thyself;
And, at the end of thy day,
O faithful shepherd! to come,
Bringing thy sheep in thy hand.

145 And through thee I believe
In the noble and great who are gone;
Pure souls honoured and blest

124–7 See headnote.

By former ages, who else –
Such, so soulless, so poor,
150 Is the race of men whom I see –
Seemed but a dream of the heart,
Seemed but a cry of desire.
Yes! I believe that there lived
Others like thee in the past,
155 Not like the men of the crowd
Who all round me to-day
Bluster or cringe, and make life
Hideous, and arid, and vile;
But souls tempered with fire,
160 Fervent, heroic, and good,
Helpers and friends of mankind.

Servants of God! – or sons
Shall I not call you? because
Not as servants ye knew
165 Your Father's innermost mind,
His, who unwillingly sees
One of his little ones lost –
Yours is the praise, if mankind
Hath not as yet in its march
170 Fainted, and fallen, and died!

See! In the rocks of the world
Marches the host of mankind,
A feeble, wavering line.
Where are they tending? – A God
175 Marshalled them, gave them their goal.
Ah, but the way is so long!
Years they have been in the wild!
Sore thirst plagues them, the rocks
Rising all round, overawe;
180 Factions divide them, their host
Threatens to break, to dissolve.
– Ah, keep, keep them combined!
Else, of the myriads who fill
That army, not one shall arrive;
185 Sole they shall stray; in the rocks
Stagger for ever in vain,
Die one by one in the waste.

Then, in such hour of need
Of your fainting, dispirited race,

173 Cf. *Resignation* line 61: 'Our wavering, many-coloured line.'
186 **Stagger**] Labour *MS., 1867–1869;* Batter *1877–1881.*

190 Ye, like angels, appear,
   Radiant with ardour divine!
   Beacons of hope, ye appear!
   Languor is not in your heart,
   Weakness is not in your word,
195 Weariness not on your brow.
   Ye alight in our van! at your voice,
   Panic, despair, flee away.
   Ye move through the ranks, recall
   The stragglers, refresh the outworn,
200 Praise, re-inspire the brave!
   Order, courage, return.
   Eyes rekindling, and prayers,
   Follow your steps as ye go.
   Ye fill up the gaps in our files,
205 Strengthen the wavering line,
   Stablish, continue our march,
   On, the bound of the waste,
   On, to the City of God.

206 Stablish make secure, reinforce *OED* 7.
208 City of God a secular and humanitarian equivalent of St Augustine's City of God.

109 Growing Old

Date Probably composed 1864–7.
 Similar in tone and point of view to several late poems. It is possibly a riposte to Browning's *Rabbi Ben Ezra* (1864), with the title alluding to: 'Grow old along with me | The best is yet to be, | The last of life, for which the first was made.' There are also oblique references to Wordsworth *The Excursion* 9. 50–69. A. invented the stanza.
Publication *1867, 1869,* etc.

   What is it to grow old?
   Is it to lose the glory of the form,
   The lustre of the eye?
   Is it for beauty to forgo her wreath?
5 – Yes, but not this alone.

   Is it to feel our strength –
   Not our bloom only, but our strength – decay?
   Is it to feel each limb
   Grow stiffer, every function less exact,
10 Each nerve more loosely strung?

10 loosely strung] weakly strung *1867–1877.*

Yes, this, and more; but not
Ah, 'tis not what in youth we dreamed 'twould be!
'Tis not to have our life
Mellowed and softened as with sunset-glow,
15 A golden day's decline.

'Tis not to see the world
As from a height, with rapt prophetic eyes,
And heart profoundly stirred;
And weep, and feel the fullness of the past,
20 The years that are no more.

It is to spend long days
And not once feel that we were ever young;
It is to add, immured
In the hot prison of the present, month
25 To month with weary pain.

It is to suffer this,
And feel but half, and feebly, what we feel.
Deep in our hidden heart
Festers the dull remembrance of a change,
30 But no emotion – none.

It is – last stage of all –
When we are frozen up within, and quite
The phantom of ourselves,
To hear the world applaud the hollow ghost
35 Which blamed the living man.

31 last stage of all cf. Shakespeare *A.Y.L.I.* 2.7.163–6: 'Last scene of all, |
That ends this strange eventful history, | Is second childishness and mere
oblivion.'

Coventry Patmore

Life and works Coventry Kersey Dighton Patmore (b. 1823) was the son of
Peter George Patmore, a minor man of letters and friend of Hazlitt and
Lamb. His father was a Freethinker, but Patmore inclined to Anglican
orthodoxy. In 1844 his first volume of poetry was published, containing *The
River, The Woodman's Daughter, Lilian* and *Sir Hubert*. In 1845 Patmore
senior lost a good deal of money in railway speculation, and Coventry was
forced to earn a living as a man of letters and an assistant in the British

Coventry Patmore

Museum. In 1847 he married Emily Augusta Andrews, the daughter of a Congregational minister and the inspiration for *The Angel in the House*. Patmore was on the fringes of the Pre-Raphaelite Brotherhood (contributing to *The Germ*), and was responsible for bringing Ruskin's attention to the merits of the group's paintings. In 1853 *Tamerton Church Tower* was published, and in 1854 (anonymously) *The Betrothal* – the first part of *The Angel in the House*. Part II (*The Espousals*) followed in 1856. In 1862 *The Victories of Love* appeared, the same year as the death of his first wife. In 1864 he married Marianne Caroline Byles, who was a Catholic, and he himself became a Catholic. He retired from the British Museum, living first at Heron's Ghyll in Sussex, then at The Mansion, Hastings. In 1868 he printed (for private circulation) nine odes: these were added to and printed in 1877 as *The Unknown Eros and Other Odes*. He wrote a prose piece on the Virgin entitled *Sponsa Dei*, but destroyed it. Like Hopkins (with whom he corresponded) Patmore's relationships with the Catholic priesthood were not always harmonious. In 1880 his second wife died; and in 1881 he married Miss Harriet Robson. His 1886 *Collected Works* were preceded by an appendix on metrical principles, and before his death in 1895 he had produced a sizeable body of critical and religious writing, and some remarkable prose/poetry.

Biographies and criticism Most of the biographical information on Patmore is to be found in Basil Champneys *Memoirs and Correspondence* (1900), but it has been supplemented and updated by Derek Patmore's *The Life and Times of Coventry Patmore* (1949). The poetry was reviewed (after a period of eclipse) by Osbert Burdett in *The Idea of Coventry Patmore* (1921) and F. Page *Patmore: A Study in Poetry* (1933). There is an important essay by Herbert Read in *The Great Victorians* (1932). Mario Praz appends a study of Patmore as domestic artist to *The Hero in Eclipse* (translated by Angus Davidson, 1956). Recent works are E. J. Oliver *Coventry Patmore* (1956) and J. G. Reid *The Mind and Art of Coventry Patmore* (1957). Criticism of Patmore has long recognized that his poetry has a well-manipulated intellectual and spiritual content. In some senses he is an heir to the poise and discipline of C17 poetry. As J. Holloway indicates in *The Charted Mirror* (1960), Browning is not the only significant Victorian follower of Donne.

That P. is not currently in print is an indication of his present unpopularity. J. G. Reid provides an excellent survey of the fluctuations in his readership. In the present age of liberated women his traditional view of the woman as the angel in the house has not worn well – even though, on more detailed inspection, his women are found to have fresh and independent minds. His poetic language also has a tendency to be dated. P.'s character is summed up by Richard Garnett in *DNB:* 'Haughty, imperious, combative, sardonic, he was at the same time sensitive, susceptible, and capable of deep tenderness. He was at once magnanimous and rancorous; egotistic and capriciously generous; acute and credulous; nobly veracious and prone to the wildest exaggerations.' P. wrote at length, but short selections do less injustice to him than to some other poets; since, as Garnett says, some of the 'descriptions of exquisite charm' are 'easily detached from their context and remembered for their own sakes'.

The standard text is F. Page's Oxford Edition (1949).

Abbreviations

1853	*Tamerton Church-Tower and Other Poems* (1853).
1856	*The Angel in the House* (1856).
1868	*Odes* (1868).
1877	*The Unknown Eros and Other Odes* (1877).
1878	*The Unknown Eros* (1878).
1878(2)	*Amelia, Tamerton Church-Tower etc.* (1878).
1880	*The Unknown Eros* (1880).
Connolly	Connolly, T. L., S.J. *Mystical Poems of Nuptial Love* (Boston, 1938).

110 A London Fête

Public executions took place in England until 1868. The poem may be compared with Thackeray's 'Going to See a Man Hanged' (*Fraser's Magazine* Aug. 1840), written on the occasion of Courvoisier's execution at Newgate, and Dickens's letters to *The Times* of Nov. 1849 protesting at the public execution of the Mannings. P.'s poem has, in scrupulous attention to unsavoury detail, a Pre-Raphaelite air about it. P. writes: 'I understand that these verses, which were first printed some years ago, have been regarded as indirectly advocating the abolition of punishment by death. I had no such intention in composing them.'
Publication *1853*.

  All night fell hammers, shock on shock;
  With echoes Newgate's granite clanged:
  The scaffold built, at eight o'clock
  They brought the man out to be hanged.
5 Then came from all the people there
  A single cry, that shook the air;
  Mothers held up their babes to see,
  Who spread their hands, and crowed for glee;
  Here a girl from her vesture tore
10 A rag to wave with, and joined the roar;

Title *A Sketch in the Manner of Hogarth 1853;* it is significant that the London club of the Pre-Raphaelites was later called the Hogarth Club, in honour of the artist of aggressive realism.
1 An 8-line introduction *1853*.
6–7 A single cry, that turned to storm | Of yells and noises multiform, | Where each, with mad gesticulations, | Rivalled the rest in execrations: *1853*.
10–11 In shrieks, and singing, and savage jests, | Tossing about her naked breasts; *1853*.

There a man, with yelling tired,
Stopped, and the culprit's crime inquired;
A sot, below the doomed man dumb,
Bawled his health in the world to come;
15   These blasphemed and fought for places;
Those, half-crushed, cast frantic faces,
To windows, where, in freedom sweet,
Others enjoyed the wicked treat.
At last, the show's black crisis pended;
20   Struggles for better standings ended;
The rabble's lips no longer cursed,
But stood agape with horrid thirst;
Thousands of breasts beat horrid hope;
Thousands of eyeballs, lit with hell,
25   Burnt one way all, to see the rope
Unslacken as the platform fell.
The rope flew tight; and then the roar
Burst forth afresh; less loud, but more
Confused and affrighting than before.
30   A few harsh tongues for ever led
The common din, the chaos of noises,
But ear could not catch what they said.
As when the realm of the damned rejoices
At winning a soul to its will,
35   That clatter and clangour of hateful voices
Sickened and stunned the air, until
The dangling corpse hung straight and still.
The show complete, the pleasure past,
The solid masses loosened fast:
40   A thief slunk off, with ample spoil,
To ply elsewhere his daily toil;
A baby strung its doll to a stick;
A mother praised the pretty trick;
Two children caught and hanged a cat;
45   Two friends walked on, in lively chat;
And two, who had disputed places,
Went forth to fight, with murderous faces.

19 pended a slightly macabre play on *OED* v³ 2 'was imminent' and 2b,
literally 'hung up'.
37 hung] was *1853*.
46 And two] Two foes, *1853*.
47– These, heavy-paced and heavy-hearted, | Whose dinners were to earn,
departed, | Jealous of those who had pence to stay | At gin-shops by, and
make it a day. *1853*.

111 The Angel in the House: extract

Love's Perversity

A good example of the continuity in P.'s poetry of a C17 spirit. In rhyme scheme and metre it is very similar to Marvell's *Definition of Love*, and indeed very few words are post 1650, an exception being 'propriety' of line 7 (first used thus in 1782). The arch use of whimsical images and the skilled modulation of hyperbole is also very reminiscent of Donne, Herrick and Marvell.
Publication *1856:* Bk. 2 Canto VI.1.

> How strange a thing a lover seems
>   To animals that do not love!
> Lo, where he walks and talks in dreams,
>   And flouts us with his Lady's glove;
> 5 How foreign is the garb he wears;
>   And how his great devotion mocks
> Our poor propriety, and scares
>   The undevout with paradox!
> His soul, through scorn of worldly care,
> 10 And great extremes of sweet and gall,
> And musing much on all that's fair,
>   Grows witty and fantastical;
> He sobs his joy and sings his grief,
>   And evermore finds such delight
> 15 In simply picturing his relief,
>   That 'plaining seems to cure his plight;
> He makes his sorrow, when there's none;
>   His fancy blows both cold and hot;
> Next to the wish that she'll be won,
> 20 His first hope is that she may not;
> He sues, yet deprecates consent;
>   Would she be captured she must fly;
> She looks too happy and content,
>   For whose least pleasure he would die.
> 25 Oh, cruelty, she cannot care
>   For one to whom she's always kind!
> He says he's nought, but, oh, despair,
>   If he's not Jove to her fond mind!
> He's jealous if she pets a dove,
> 30 She must be his with all her soul;

12 fantastical = *OED* 4 fantastic: capricious, imaginative, extravagant: much in vogue in C17.
16 'plaining complaining.

Yet 'tis a postulate in love
That part is greater than the whole;
And all his apprehension's stress,
When he's with her, regards her hair,
35   Her hand, a ribbon of her dress,
As if his life were only there;
Because she's constant, he will change,
And kindest glances coldly meet,
And, all the time he seems so strange,
40   His soul is fawning at her feet;
Of smiles and simple heaven grown tired,
He wickedly provokes her tears,
And when she weeps, as he desired,
Falls slain with ecstasies of fears;
45   He blames her, though she has no fault,
Except the folly to be his;
He worships her, the more to exalt
The profanation of a kiss;
Health's his disease; he's never well
50   But when his paleness shames her rose;
His faith's a rock-built citadel,
Its sign a flag that each way blows;
His o'erfed fancy frets and fumes;
And Love, in him, is fierce, like Hate,
55   And ruffles his ambrosial plumes
Against the bars of time and fate.

31 postulate *OED* 2 a proposition demanded or claimed to be granted.
48 profanation Lat. *profanus*, literally 'outside the temple', so that kissing is
not a rite for the most sacred exercises of love: more Platonic behaviour is
required. The kiss hence becomes exciting and illicit if achieved.
55 ambrosial plumes the winged spirit of love angrily flutters his feathers
against the oppositions of time and fate.

112 The Unknown Eros : extracts

112.1 Tired Memory

This represents P.'s struggle to reconcile his love for his second wife with
fidelity to the memory of his first, who was anxious that he should marry
again if she died before him.
Discussed Connolly 174–7.
Publication *1868* (no. 3); *1877; 1878* (no. 24); *1880* (Bk. 1.11 of *The Unknown
Eros*).

The stony rock of death's insensibility
Welled yet awhile with honey of thy love
And then was dry;
Nor could thy picture, nor thine empty glove,

5 Nor all thy kind, long letters, nor the band
  Which really spanned
  Thy body chaste and warm,
  Thenceforward move
  Upon the stony rock their wearied charm.
10 At last, then, thou wast dead.
  Yet would I not despair,
  But wrought my daily task, and daily said
  Many and many a fond unfeeling prayer,
  To keep my vows of faith to thee from harm.
15 In vain.
  'For 'tis,' I said, 'all one,
  The wilful faith, which has no joy or pain,
  As if 'twere none.'
  Then looked I miserably round
20 If aught of duteous love were left undone,
  And nothing found.
  But, kneeling in a Church, one Easter-Day,
  It came to me to say;
  'Though there is no intelligible rest,
25 In Earth or Heaven,
  For me, but on her breast,
  I yield her up, again to have her given,
  Or not, as, Lord, Thou wilt, and that for aye.'
  And the same night, in slumber lying,
30 I, who had dreamed of thee as sad and sick and dying,
  And only so, nightly for all one year,
  Did thee, my own most Dear,
  Possess,
  In gay, celestial beauty nothing coy,
35 And felt thy soft caress
  With heretofore unknown reality of joy.
  But, in our mortal air,
  None thrives for long upon the happiest dream,
  And fresh despair
40 Bade me seek round afresh for some extreme
  Of unconceived, interior sacrifice
  Whereof the smoke might rise
  To God, and 'mind him that one prayed below.
  And so,
45 In agony, I cried:
  'My Lord, if thy strange will be this,
  That I should crucify my heart,
  Because my love has also been my pride,
  I do submit, if I saw how, to bliss
50 Wherein She has no part.'

And I was heard,
And taken at my own remorseless word.
O, my most Dear,
Was't treason, as I fear?
55 'Twere that, and worse, to plead thy veiled mind,
Kissing thy babes, and murmuring in mine ear,
'Thou canst not be
Faithful to God, and faithless unto me!'
Ah, prophet kind!
60 I heard, all dumb and blind
With tears of protest; and I cannot see
But faith was broken. Yet, as I have said,
My heart was dead,
Dead of devotion and tired memory,
65 When a strange grace of thee
In a fair stranger, as I take it, bred
To her some tender heed,
Most innocent
Of purpose therewith blent,
70 And pure of faith, I think, to thee; yet such
That the pale reflex of an alien love,
So vaguely, sadly shown,
Did her heart touch
Above
75 All that, till then, had wooed her for its own.
And so the fear, which is love's chilly dawn,
Flushed faintly upon lids that drooped like thine,
And made me weak,
By thy delusive likeness doubly drawn,
80 And Nature's long suspended breath of flame
Persuading soft, and whispering Duty's name,
Awhile to smile and speak
With this thy Sister sweet, and therefore mine;
Thy Sister sweet,
85 Who bade the wheels to stir
Of sensitive delight in the poor brain,
Dead of devotion and tired memory,
So that I lived again,
And, strange to aver,
90 With no relapse into the void inane,
For thee;
But (treason was't?) for thee and also her.

53–4 O, my most Dear, | Another wears thy ring upon her hand. *1868.*
55 thy veiled mind,] 'twas thy command, *1868.*
57 'Thou canst not be] 'It is thy duty and thou canst not be *1868.*
68–70 Unmeant by me; | Unmeant by me, yet such *1868.*
92 Followed in *1868* by 23 more lines.

112.2 To the body

One of the clearest statements of the great importance P. attached to the body as the temple of God (see also his essay 'Christianity an Experimental Science').
Discussion Connolly 237–43.
Publication *1878* (no. 40); *1880* (Bk 2.7 of *The Unknown Eros*).

Creation's and Creator's crowning good;
Wall of infinitude;
Foundation of the sky,
In heaven forecast
5   And longed for from eternity,
Though laid the last;
Reverberating dome,
Of music cunningly built home
Against the void and indolent disgrace
10   Of unresponsive space;
Little, sequestered pleasure-house
For God and for His spouse;
Elaborately, yea, past conceiving, fair,
Since, from the graced decorum of the hair,
15   Ev'n to the tingling, sweet
Soles of the simple, earth-confiding feet,
And from the inmost heart
Outward unto the thin
Silk curtains of the skin,
20   Every least part
Astonished hears
And sweet replies to some like region of the spheres;
Formed for a dignity prophets but darkly name,
Lest shameless men cry 'Shame!'
25   So rich with wealth concealed
That Heaven and Hell fight chiefly for this field;
Clinging to everything that pleases thee
With indefectible fidelity;
Alas, so true
30   To all thy friendships that no grace
Thee from thy sin can wholly disembrace;
Which thus 'bides with thee as the Jebusite,

8 Cf. Donne: 'I am a little world made cunningly'. P. is writing in the Marian hymn tradition of chains of figurative phrases for the body.
28 indefectible not liable to fail.
32 the Jebusite a tribe of Canaanites, dispossessed of Jerusalem by David; signifying the abiding effects of original sin anagogically; see *Joshua* 15.63. Not to be confused with the meaning assigned by Dryden: Roman Catholics.

That, maugre all God's promises could do,
The chosen people never conquered quite,
35   Who therefore lived with them,
And that by formal truce and as of right,
In metropolitan Jerusalem.
For which false fealty
Thou needs must, for a season, lie
40   In the grave's arms, foul and unshriven,
Albeit, in Heaven,
Thy crimson-throbbing glow
Into its old abode aye pants to go,
And does with envy see
45   Enoch, Elijah, and the Lady, she
Who left the lilies in her body's lieu.
O, if the pleasures I have known in thee
But my poor faith's poor first-fruits be,
What quintessential, keen, ethereal bliss
50   Then shall be his
Who has thy birth-time's consecrating dew
For death's sweet chrism retained,
Quick, tender, virginal, and unprofaned!

37 **metropolitan Jerusalem** the city within the jurisdiction of the theocratic government.
45 **Enoch, Elijah** O.T. prophets translated to Heaven: Enoch *Heb.* 11.5; Elijah *2 Kings* 2.11.
46 The Blessed Virgin left flowers in her tomb.
51 **consecrating dew** holy water of baptism.
52 **death's sweet chrism** extreme unction.

113 The Girl of All Periods: An Idyll

A well-observed fragment of modern life, a glimpse of the liberated girl who is yet, at bottom, the conventional woman.
Publication *1878(2).*

'And even our women,' lastly grumbles Ben,
'Leaving their nature, dress and talk like men!'
A damsel, as our train stops at Five Ashes,
Down to the station in a dog-cart dashes.
5   A footman buys her ticket, 'Third class, parly;'
And, in huge-buttoned coat and 'Champagne Charley'

6 **'Champagne Charley'** would seem to be some article of clothing; but *OED* provides no examples. There was a song called *Champagne Charley* (1868); Charley Prescot, was rhyming slang for waistcoat – a possible meaning.

And such scant manhood else as use allows her,
Her two shy knees bound in a single trouser,
With, 'twixt her shapely lips, a violet
10   Perched as a proxy for a cigarette,
She takes her window in our smoking carriage,
And scans us, calmly scorning men and marriage.
Ben frowns in silence; older, I know better
Than to read ladies 'haviour in the letter.
15   This aping man is crafty Love's devising
To make the woman's difference more surprising;
And, as for feeling wroth at such rebelling,
Who'd scold the child for now and then repelling
Lures with 'I won't!' or for a moment's straying
20   In its sure growth towards more full obeying?
'Yes' she had read the "Legend of the Ages,"
'And George Sand too, skipping the wicked pages.'
And, whilst we talked, her protest firm and perky
Against mankind, I thought, grew lax and jerky;
25   And, at a compliment, her mouth's compressure
Nipped in its birth a little laugh of pleasure;
And smiles, forbidden her lips, as weakness horrid,
Broke, in grave lights, from eyes and chin and forehead;
And, as I pushed kind 'vantage 'gainst the scorner,
30   The two shy knees pressed shier to the corner;
And Ben began to talk with her, the rather
Because he found out that he knew her father,
Sir Francis Applegarth, of Fenny Compton,
And danced once with her sister Maude at Brompton;
35   And then he stared until he quite confused her,
More pleased with her than I, who but excused her;
And, when she got out, he, with sheepish glances,
Said he'd stop too, and call on old Sir Francis.

21 "Legend of the Ages" Victor Hugo, *La Légende des Siècles* (1859–77).
22 George Sand a liberated and *risqué* author.
23 perky a comparatively new word, perhaps first used in *Maud* I. 10.1.

Dante Gabriel Rossetti

Dante Gabriel Rossetti, the eldest son of the exiled Italian patriot Gabriele Rossetti and the half-Italian Frances *née* Polidori, was born in Charlotte Street London on 12 May 1828. He had two sisters, Maria and Christina, and a brother, William Michael.

Dante Gabriel Rossetti

R. began writing at an early age. The divided artistic aim, described perhaps in *Lost on Both Sides* (no. 119.5), manifested itself early, since the young R. started drawing at school, and in 1842–6 attended F. S. Cary's drawing academy. The conservative traditions of such institutions are well evoked in Thackeray's *The Newcomes*. The influences on R.'s artistic style were extremely varied: Retsch, academic 'High Art', Madox Brown, and the bold and satirical Gavarni. He was admitted to the Royal Academy School in 1846, but was unenthusiastic about the studies there, and in March 1848 applied to Madox Brown for instruction. Brown put him to routine work developing oil-painting technique with still life studies. R. found this irksome, and sought help from Holman Hunt, who already knew Millais. In 1848 the Pre-Raphaelite Brotherhood was founded, with seven members. The story of the Brotherhood belongs more to art history than literary history. There is now a vast literature on it, outlined by William E. Fredeman in *Pre-Raphaelitism: a bibliocritical study* (1965) and his chapter on the Pre-Raphaelites in Faverty.

The make-up of Pre-Raphaelitism was complicated from the outset, if only because of the divergence of its adherents and the tendencies in the arts that inspired it. Most of the aims of the Brotherhood are outlined in its brief-lived periodical *The Germ* (1850). The artists strove for realism and truth, and thought that since bad habits fostered by academies had grown in strength since Raphael (1483–1520; though a genius himself he had had an unfortunate influence) a purification would necessarily take place under the aegis of artists who lived before him. Since few trecento and quattrocento works were available in England at the time, the Brotherhood was largely inspired by Lasinio's poorish engravings of the frescoes in the Campo Santo, Pisa. Holman Hunt later admitted that had he known the work of Tintoretto he might have gone to him for influence. Generally, the Pre-Raphaelites did not wish to return to the inadequacies and inaccuracies of the Italian primitives; they were anxious to put into practice the strenuous recommendations that Ruskin was making in *Modern Painters* (Vol. 1 1843). Hunt said that Pre-Raphaelitism should not be confused with Pre-Raphaelism. However, the cult of quaintness and pseudo-medievalism was part of the spectrum of influence, filtering via Brown and the German Nazarenes. R. was more drawn to this side of the tradition than to that represented by Holman Hunt and Millais, if only because imitations of primitives were easier for an amateur such as R. to master, and the literary element in his make-up responded more readily to the mystical and medieval traditions. From the first, R.'s paintings were out of line with those of Hunt and Millais, and when the public got hold of the meaning of the secret initials P.R.B. the label proved an embarrassment to the realist side of the movement – especially since R. and the second-wave of pre-Raphaelitism, dominated by Burne-Jones and William Morris, worked in a pseudo-archaic vein. Ruskin's pamphleteering on behalf of the Hunt and Millais tradition in the 1850s made considerable impact on the public however.

The Rossetti contribution to the Brotherhood was of immense value. He, more than the others, realized the importance of subjective experience, and of perception that is not only visual but psychic. Without the influence of R. the efforts of the group might have dwindled into the naturalism of the photograph. He gave to the movement an invaluable sense of poetry. One of the enduring contributions of his poetry is to our sense of Pre-Raphaelite painting. R. continued painting for the rest of his life; but it is significant that he was not able to finish the modern subject *Found* (Delaware Art Museum), and that he took the way of least resistance by painting scores of female portraits that all look more or less the same. He discovered and propagated a new type of feminine beauty.

It is difficult to make comparative evaluations in different arts but it is probably true to say that R. was a more significant painter than poet. His poetry is often used as an adjunct to studying the painting. He was impressed by the mysticism and romance of Dante and Malory, and liked the sort of dreamy medievalism that percolated into the modern age by way of Keats. But he was not exclusively a swooning romantic: his letters are usually very racy, and he had a zestful Bohemian taste for modern life. He had more success tackling 'the modern subject' in poetry than painting. Cruelty and sensuality are often encountered in R.'s poetry, and although they are usually softened in their impact by the elliptical devices of art (the dramatic monologue for instance) their presence reminds us that he did not wish to step aside when he encountered the unpleasant facts of life.

More than any other Victorian poet R. deals with love. When Lizzie Siddal died in 1862 he was haunted by her, and yearned for a mystical relationship that was almost Dantesque. After her death his most significant liaison was with Jane Morris.

R. published his own poetry late – in 1870. His paintings were rarely exhibited in public. And yet he exerted an enormous influence over the developing aesthetic movement. The last years of his life were marred by 'The Fleshly School of Poetry' controversy, by persecution mania and a dependence on chloral. Nevertheless he continued to produce. *Ballads and Sonnets* (1881) was the last work printed in his lifetime. He died near Margate on 10 April 1881.

Inevitably the question arises of the applicability of the label 'Pre-Raphaelite' to poetry. L. Stevenson's *The Pre-Raphaelite Poets* (1972) surveys the field. R. himself was more eclectic than some in the school: he was an early collector of oriental china, for instance, and was partly responsible for creating the vogue for the Queen Anne style. He was prepared to recognize and respond to beauty wherever he found it. If influence on others is to be a way of measuring artistic greatness then it is impossible to regard R. as a minor figure.

Biographies and discussion The standard edition is *Works* ed. W. M. Rossetti (1911); the standard biography is O. Doughty *A Victorian Romantic: D.G.R.* (2nd edn. 1960). G. H. Fleming *R. and the Pre-Raphaelite Brotherhood* (1967) studies the links with Millais and Holman Hunt. R. M. Cooper *Lost on Both Sides: D.G.R.: critic and poet* (Athens, Ohio 1970) assesses the dispersal of energies by an artist attempting to work in more than one medium. Lady Mander *Portrait of Rossetti* (1964) is a general survey; D. Sonstroem *R. and the Fair Lady* (Middleton, Conn. 1970) deals with the manifestations of woman in his poetry and painting as sinful woman, *femme fatale*, victimized woman and Heavenly Lady. R. R. Howard *The Dark Glass: vision and technique in the poetry of D.G.R.* (Athens, Ohio 1972) is one of the fullest studies of the poetry and its enigmas. J. Nicholl *Rossetti* (Oxford 1975) concentrates on the visual work. The standard study of the art is V. Surtees *The Paintings and Drawings of D.G.R.* (Oxford 1971). R.'s letters to Jane Morris have been edited by J. Bryson (Oxford 1976).

Abbreviations

1869[1]	*Poems* (1st trial edition) (1869).
1869[2]	*Poems* (2nd trial edition) (1869).
1870	*Poems* (1870).
1872	*Poems* (Tauchnitz edition) (1872).
1873	*Poems* (1873).
1881	*Poems.* A New Edition (1881).
1895	*D.G.R.: His Family Letters* ed. W. M. Rossetti (1895).
Letters	*The Letters of D.G.R.* ed. O. Doughty and J. R. Wahl (Oxford 1965–7).
Caine	T. Hall Caine *Recollections of D.G.R.* (1882).

114 London to Folkestone
(Half-past one to half-past five)

Date 27 Sept. 1849.

R. travelled to France and Belgium with Holman Hunt and Thomas Woolner. The trip prompted several poems, startling for their direct response to immediate experience. They were in accord with the realistic Pre-Raphaelite ethic. This poem is among the earliest to register the novel experience of rapid train travel. R. sent it in a letter to W. M. Rossetti, who was at that time writing a poem, *Mrs Holmes Grey*, according to 'the same principle of strict actuality and probability of detail'.

Publication *1895.*

A constant keeping past of shaken trees,
And a bewildered glitter of loose road;
Banks of bright growth, with single blades atop
Against white sky; and wires – a constant chain –
5   That seem to draw the clouds along with them
(Things which one stoops against the light to see
Through the low window: shaking by at rest,
Or fierce like water as the swiftness grows);
And, seen through fences or a bridge far off,
10   Trees that in moving keep their intervals
Still one 'twixt bar and bar; and then at times
Long reaches of green level, where one cow,
Feeding among her fellows that feed on,
Lifts her slow neck, and gazes for the sound.

15   There are six of us: I that write away;
Hunt reads Dumas, hard-lipped, with heavy jowl
And brows hung low, and the long ends of hair

2 loose gravelled.

Standing out limp. A grazier at one end
(Thank luck not my end!) has blocked out the air,
20   And sits in heavy consciousness of guilt.
The poor young muff who's face to face with me,
Is pitiful in loose collar and black tie,
His latchet-button shaking as we go.
There are flowers by me, half upon my knees,
25   Owned by a dame who's fair in soul, no doubt:
The wind that beats among us carries off
Their scent, but still I have them for my eye.
Fields mown in ridges; and close garden-crops
Of the earth's increase; and a constant sky
30   Still with clear trees that let you see the wind;
And snatches of the engine-smoke, by fits
Tossed to the wind against the landscape, where
Rooks stooping heave their wings upon the day.
Brick walls we pass between, passed so at once
35   That for the suddenness I cannot know
Or what, or where begun, or where at end.
Sometimes a station in grey quiet; whence,
With a short gathered champing of pent sound,
We are let out upon the air again.
40   Now merely darkness; knees and arms and sides
Feel the least touch, and close about the face
A wind of noise that is along like God.
Pauses of water soon, at intervals,
That has the sky in it; – the reflexes
45   O' the trees move towards the bank as we go by,
Leaving the water's surface plain. I now
Lie back and close my eyes a space; for they
Smart from the open forwardness of thought
Fronting the wind. –
                – I did not scribble more,
50   Be certain, after this; but yawned, and read,
And nearly dozed a little, I believe;
Till, stretching up against the carriage-back,
I was roused altogether, and looked out
To where, upon the desolate verge of light,
55   Yearned, pale and vast, the iron-coloured sea.

21 muff awkward, stupid man.
23 latchet shoe thong.
44 reflexes reflections.
55 Cf. *The Portrait* lines 89–90: 'Upon the desolate verge of light | Yearned
loud the iron-bosomed sea.'

115 The Sea-Limits

Date First two stanzas in letter to W. M. Rossetti (20 Sept. 1849) as *At Boulogne. Upon the Clifffs: Noon* (*Letters* 1.61–2). With minor variations this was the text of *The Germ* version.
Publication *The Germ* (March, 1850) as *From the Cliffs: Noon; 1870* (as Song 11 in *The House of Life*).

Consider the sea's listless chime:
   Time's self it is, made audible, –
   The murmur of the earth's own shell.
Secret continuance sublime
5   Is the sea's end: our sight may pass
   No furlong further. Since time was,
This sound hath told the lapse of time.

No quiet, which is death's, – it hath
   The mournfulness of ancient life,
10   Enduring always at dull strife.
As the world's heart of rest and wrath,
   Its painful pulse is in the sands.
   Last utterly, the whole sky stands,
Grey and not known, along its path.

15   Listen alone beside the sea,
   Listen alone among the woods;
   Those voices of twin solitudes
Shall have one sound alike to thee:
   Hark where the murmurs of thronged men
20   Surge and sink back and surge again, –
Still the one voice of wave and tree.

Gather a shell from the strown beach
   And listen at its lips; they sigh
   The same desire and mystery,
25   The echo of the whole sea's speech.
   And all mankind is thus at heart
   Not anything but what thou art:
And earth, sea, man, are all in each.

1–6 The sea is in its listless chime, | Like time's lapse rendered audible; | The murmur of the earth's large shell. | In a sad blueness beyond rhyme | It ends; sense, without thought, can pass | No stadium* further. Since time was, (letter to W.M.R.).
*stadium one-eighth of a roman mile.
8–11 No stagnance that death wins, – it hath | The mournfulness of ancient life, | Always enduring at dull strife. | Like the world's heart, in calm and wrath, (letter to W.M.R.).
12 sands the beaches measure time as sand in hour-glasses.

116 The Blessed Damozel

Date About 1846–7: R. to Hall Caine refers to the poem 'which I wrote (and have altered little since) when I was eighteen.'
Versions A Pierpont Morgan MS. purports to represent the pre-publication version; K. L. Knickerbocker *SP* 29 (1932) 485–504 and P. Baum in his edition (1937) accept it as such, but J. A. Sanford *SP* 35 (1938) 471–86 argues that it is a memorial reconstruction influenced by later redactions, written 'to substantiate the legend of his own precocity.' The true placing of the MS. is probably that made by W. Fredeman in *English Studies Today* 5 (1973) 239–69: between *The Germ* and second publication in 1856. R. wrote to his mother, 20 May 1873, asking for an early version: 'I remember that for the family *Hotch-potch*, long and long ago, I wrote *The Blessed Damozel*....Have you these ancient documents?' She had not. R. continued to be occupied with the poem in the 1870s, when he painted a picture based on it (Lady Lever Gallery, Port Sunlight).
Only stanza 18 remained unchanged throughout the frequent revisions. 144 lines, dividing neatly into three 48-line units, with pauses and changes of direction at lines 48 and 96.
Theme R. told Hall Caine that the poem originated out of E. A. Poe's *The Raven:* '"I saw," he said, "that Poe had done the utmost it was possible to do with the grief of the lover on earth, and so I determined to reverse the conditions, and give utterance to the yearning of the loved one in heaven"' (Caine 284). R. drew widely from other material: A. D. Walker *MLR* 26 (1931) 129–41 demonstrates the influence of Dante's *Vita Nuova* and A. D. McKillop *MLN* 34 (1919) 93–7 that of P. J. Bailey's spasmodic poem *Festus*. The atmosphere is R.'s own: a poignant awareness of the division between flesh and spirit, made especially tantalizing and poignant by the very narrowness of the separation.
Form Stanzas consist of alternate four- and three-stress lines, rhyming *abcbdb*, a form used by Wordsworth in *The Primrose of the Rock*. Megroz in the 1911 edn. of D.G.R.'s works thought it derived from his translation of Ciullo d'Alcamo's *Dialogue between a Lover and his Lady*, with the final couplet dropped. The form was also used by R. in *The Card-Dealer*.
The poem is a key work in the Pre-Raphaelite movement: its first four publications were in journals associated with Pre-Raphaelitism, and it captured the spirit that was to dominate the 'mystical Pre-Raphaelites' for the last four decades of the century. For the relationship to R.'s own painting see W. S. Johnson *VP* 3 (1965) 14–18.
Publication *The Germ* (Jan. 1850); *The Oxford and Cambridge Mag.* (1856); *The Crayon* (May 1858); *The New Path* (Dec. 1863); *1869; 1870*.

> The blessed damozel leaned out
>   From the gold bar of Heaven;
> Her eyes were deeper than the depth

1 damozel . . . out] damsel leaned against *MS.*
2 gold] silver *MS.*
3–4 Her blue grave eyes were deeper much | Than a deep water, even. *The Germ*; Her eyes knew more of rest and shade | Than waters stilled at even; *1856;* Her eyes knew more of rest and shade. Than a deep water, even. *MS*

Of waters stilled at even;
5   She had three lilies in her hand,
And the stars in her hair were seven.

Her robe, ungirt from clasp to hem,
No wrought flowers did adorn,
But a white rose of Mary's gift,
10   For service meetly worn;
Her hair that lay along her back
Was yellow like ripe corn.

Herseemed she scarce had been a day
One of God's choristers;
15   The wonder was not yet quite gone
From that still look of hers;
Albeit, to them she left, her day
Had counted as ten years.

(To one, it is ten years of years.
20   ... Yet now, and in this place,
Surely she leaned o'er me – her hair
Fell all about my face...
Nothing: the autumn fall of leaves.
The whole year sets apace.)

25   It was the rampart of God's house
That she was standing on;
By God built over the sheer depth
The which is Space begun;
So high, that looking downward thence
30   She scarce could see the sun.

It lies in Heaven, across the flood
Of ether, as a bridge.
Beneath, the tides of day and night
With flame and darkness ridge
35   The void, as low as where this earth
Spins like a fretful midge.

9 rose] robe *MS*. The white rose was perhaps a symbol of purity?
10 On the neck meetly worn *Germ*.
11 And her hair lying down her back *Germ–1869²*.
25 rampart] terrace *Germ*.
30 scarce could] could scarce *Germ*.
31–6 Not in *MS*.
32 ether an element filling space between the stars and planets.
34 darkness] blackness *Germ*, *1856*.
36 ∧ 7 But in those tracts, with her, it was | The peace of utter light | And silence. For no breeze may stir | Along the steady flight | Of Seraphim; no echo there, | Beyond all depth or height. *Germ*.

Around her, lovers, newly met
'Mid deathless love's acclaims,
Spoke evermore among themselves
40   Their heart-remembered names;
And the souls mounting up to God
Went by her like thin flames.

And still she bowed herself and stooped
Out of the circling charm;
45   Until her bosom must have made
The bar she leaned on warm,
And the lilies lay as if asleep
Along her bended arm.

From the fixed place of Heaven she saw
50   Time like a pulse shake fierce
Through all the worlds. Her gaze still strove
Within the gulf to pierce
Its path; and now she spoke as when
The stars sang in their spheres.

55   The sun was gone now; the curled moon
Was like a little feather
Fluttering far down the gulf; and now
She spoke through the still weather.
Her voice was like the voice the stars
60   Had when they sang together.

(Ah sweet! Even now, in that bird's song,
Strove not her accents there,
Fain to be hearkened? When those bells
Possessed the mid-day air,
65   Strove not her steps to reach my side
Down all the echoing stair?)

38 Playing at holy games, *Germ, 1856, MS.;* Amid their loving games *1869¹–*
1870; In joy no sorrow claims *1872.*
40 heart-remembered] virginal chaste *Germ–1870;* rapturous new *1872, 1873.*
41-2 Souls mount up like the purest of the elements – fire.
45 Until...bosom] Till her bosom's pressure *Germ, MS.*
49 place] lull *Germ, MS.*
53 Its path] The swarm *Germ, MS.*
54 Cf. *Job* 38.7: 'When the morning stars sang together.'
55–60 Not in *Germ, MS.*
61–66 Not in *Germ;* after line 96 *1856–1870, MS.* This stanza was curiously
prophetic of an incident in R.'s life at Penkill in 1869; see W. Bell Scott
Autobiographical Notes... (1892) 2.113–4, and C. Franklin *EC* 14 (1964)
331–5.
66 Down all the trembling stair?) *1856–1870* proof copy; Upon a silver stair?)
MS.

  'I wish that he were come to me,
   For he will come.' she said.
  'Have I not prayed in Heaven? – on earth,
70 Lord, Lord, has he not prayed?
  Are not two prayers a perfect strength?
   And shall I feel afraid?

  'When round his head the aureole clings,
   And he is clothed in white,
75 I'll take his hand and go with him
   To the deep wells of light;
  As unto a stream we will step down,
   And bathe there in God's sight.

  'We two will stand beside that shrine,
80 Occult, withheld, untrod,
  Whose lamps are stirred continually
   With prayer sent up to God;
  And see our old prayers, granted, melt
   Each like a little cloud.

85 'We two will lie i' the shadow of
   That living mystic tree
  Within whose secret growth the Dove
   Is sometimes felt to be,
  While every leaf that His plumes touch
90 Saith His Name audibly.

  'And I myself will teach to him,
   I myself, lying so,
  The songs I sing here; which his voice
   Shall pause in, hushed and slow,
95 And find some knowledge at each pause,
   Or some new thing to know.'

69 in Heaven? – on earth] in solemn heaven? *Germ.*
70 Lord, Lord,] On earth, *Germ.*
76–8 Cf. *Rev.* 22.1: 'And he shewed me a pure river of water of life, clear as crystal, proceeding out of the throne of God.'
81 are stirred] tremble *Germ.*
83 old] own *MS.*
83–4 And where each need, revealed, expects | Its patient period. *Germ.* Cf. *Rev.* 5.8: 'golden vials full of odours, which are the prayers of saints.'
86 mystic tree *Rev.* 22.2: 'on either side of the river was there the tree of life.'
93 voice] mouth *Germ.*

(Alas! We two, we two, thou say'st!
   Yea, one wast thou with me
That once of old. But shall God lift
100   To endless unity
The soul whose likeness with thy soul
   Was but its love for thee?)

'We two,' she said, 'will seek the groves
   Where the lady Mary is,
105 With her five handmaidens, whose names
   Are five sweet symphonies,
Cecily, Gertrude, Magdalen,
   Margaret and Rosalys.

'Circlewise sit they, with bound locks
110   And foreheads garlanded;
Into the fine cloth white like flame
   Weaving the golden thread,
To fashion the birth-robes for them
   Who are just born, being dead.

115 'He shall fear, haply, and be dumb:
   Then will I lay my cheek
To his, and tell about our love,
   Not once abashed or weak:
And the dear Mother will approve
120   My pride, and let me speak.

'Herself shall bring us, hand in hand,
   To Him round whom all souls
Kneel, the clear-ranged unnumbered heads

97–102 Omitted *1856–1870* proof copy; they had 61–66 at this point instead; (Alas! to *her* wise simple mind | These things were all but known | Before: they trembled on her sense, – | Her voice had caught their tone. | Alas for lonely Heaven! Alas | For life wrung out alone! | Alas, and though the end were reached?   Was *thy* part understood | Of borne in trust? And for her sake | Shall this too be found good? – | May the close lips that knew not prayer | Praise ever, though they would?) *Germ.*

105–8 The Virgin Mary's attendants are apposite numerically (cf. *The Wreck of the 'Deutschland'* lines 169–76 (below p. 502). They are all well-known saints, with the exception of Rosalys.

109–10 Circle-wise sit they, with bound locks | And bosoms covered; *Germ;* They sit in circle, with bound locks | And brows engarlanded; *MS.*

115–20 Not in *MS.*

123 the ... heads] the unnumbered solemn heads *Germ;* the unnumbered ransomed heads *1856, MS.*

Bowed with their aureoles:
125 And angels meeting us shall sing
To their citherns and citoles.

'There will I ask of Christ the Lord
Thus much for him and me: –
Only to live as once on earth
130 With Love, – only to be,
As when awhile, for ever now
Together, I and he.'

She gazed and listened and then said,
Less sad of speech than mild, –
135 'All this is when he comes.' She ceased.
The light thrilled towards her, filled
With angels in strong level flight.
Her eyes prayed, and she smiled.

(I saw her smile.) But soon their path
140 Was vague in distant spheres:
And then she cast her arms along
The golden barriers,
And laid her face betwen her hands,
And wept. (I heard her tears.)

126 citoles C13–15 stringed instruments.
131–2 As then we were, – being as then | At peace. Yea, verily. *Germ.*
132 ∧ 3 'Yea, verily; when he is come | We will do thus and thus: | Till this my vigil seem quite strange | And almost fabulous; | We two will live at once, one life; | And peace shall be with us.' *Germ.*
136 towards] past *Germ, 1856, MS.*
137 flight]lapse *Germ, 1856, MS.*
139 path] flight *Germ, 1856, MS.*
140 in distant] 'mid the poised *Germ.*
141 cast] laid *1856, MS.*
142 golden] shining *MS.*

117 My Sister's Sleep

Date 1847–8.
  In Sept. 1848 R. wrote to W. Holman Hunt: 'I quite agree with you in what you say of the "hotness" of my verses, if you mean (as I suppose) a certain want of repose and straining after original modes of expression. Of these aspects I am endeavouring to rid myself, and hoped in some degree to have cast them off in *My Sister's Sleep*, which is one of the last things I have written, and which, I confess seems to me simpler and more like nature than those I have shown you' (*Letters* 1.45). When in 1869 H. Buxton Forman praised the poem in *Tinsley's Magazine* R. wrote to Jane Morris: 'I

had left it out of my present reprint, but may now perhaps be obliged to include it; as any attention gradually attracted to it might otherwise lead to its ultimately getting into print without the necessary corrections.' The stanzaic form is the same as that of *In Memoriam*, which it preceded by two years.

Publication *The New Monthly Belle Assemblée* 29 (Sept. 1848), reprinted by D. M. R. Bentley *VP* 12 (1974) 321–34; *The Germ* (Jan. 1850) as *Songs of One Household, No. 1;* 1870.

> She fell asleep on Christmas Eve:
>   At length the long-ungranted shade
>   Of weary eyelids overweighed
> The pain nought else might yet relieve.

5   Our mother, who had leaned all day
>   Over the bed from chime to chime,
>   Then raised herself for the first time,
> And as she sat her down, did pray.

> Her little work-table was spread
10   With work to finish. For the glare
>   Made by her candle, she had care
> To work some distance from the bed.

> Without, there was a cold moon up,
>   Of winter radiance sheer and thin;
15   The hollow halo it was in
> Was like an icy crystal cup.

> Through the small room, with subtle sound
>   Of flame, by vents the fireshine drove
>   And reddened. In its dim alcove
20   The mirror shed a clearness round.

2–4 Upon her eyes' most patient calms | The lids were shut; her uplaid arms | Covered her bosom, I believe. *Belle A.; Germ.*

13 cold] good *Belle A.; Germ.*

14 Whose trailing shadow fell within *Belle A.;* Which left its shadows far within; *Germ.*

15 The depth of clouds that it was in *Belle A.;* The depth of light that it was in *Germ.*

16 Seemed hollow like an altar-cup. *Belle A.; Germ.*

17–20 I watched it through the lattice-work; | We had some plants of ever green | Standing upon the sill: just then | It passed behind, and made them dark. *Belle A.*

18 fireshine not in *OED.*

I had been sitting up some nights,
    And my tired mind felt weak and blank;
    Like a sharp strengthening wine it drank
The stillness and the broken lights.

25 Twelve struck. That sound, by dwindling years
    Heard in each hour, crept off; and then
    The ruffled silence spread again,
Like water that a pebble stirs.

Our mother rose from where she sat:
30   Her needles, as she laid them down,
    Met lightly, and her silken gown
Settled: no other noise than that.

'Glory unto the Newly Born!'
    So, as said angels, she did say;
35   Because we were in Christmas Day,
Though it would still be long till morn.

Just then in the room over us
    There was a pushing back of chairs,
    As some who had sat unawares
40 So late, now heard the hour, and rose.

With anxious softly-stepping haste
    Our mother went where Margaret lay,
    Fearing the sounds o'erheard – should they
Have broken her long watched-for rest!

45 She stopped an instant, calm, and turned;
    But suddenly turned back again;
    And all her features seemed in pain
With woe, and her eyes gazed and yearned.

For my part, I but hid my face,
50   And held my breath, and spoke no word:
    There was none spoken; but I heard
The silence for a little space.

24 broken lights a painterly term; the synaesthetic experience typical of
aestheticism.
24 ∧ 5 Silence was speaking at my side | With an exceedingly clear voice: | I
knew the calm as of a choice | Made in God for me, to abide. | I said, 'Full
knowledge does not grieve: | This which upon my spirit dwells | Perhaps
would have been sorrow else: | But I am glad 'tis Christmas Eve.' *Germ.*
25 by dwindling] which all the *Germ.*
31 lightly] harshly *Belle A.*
32 Settled] Rustled *Belle A.*

Our mother bowed herself and wept:
And both my arms fell, and I said,
55   'God knows I knew that she was dead.'
And there, all white, my sister slept.

Then kneeling, upon Christmas morn
A little after twelve o'clock
We said, ere the first quarter struck,
60   'Christ's blessing on the newly born!'

59 ere . . . struck] as when the last chime struck *Belle A.*
60 Christ's blessing on those newly born into this life and into the after-life –
as the dead sister has been. Cf. *The Blessed Damozel* line 114 (p. 407).

118 Jenny

Date P. F. Baum *MP* 39 (1941) 48–52 prints the Bancroft MS., purporting
to date from 1847–8 (130 lines); 'mostly written' 1858–69 according to W.
M. Rossetti. In 1860 R. offered it to *The Cornhill;* on 29 Nov. he described
it to Allingham as 'the most serious thing I have written' (*Letters* 1.384).
The theme of the fallen woman had had a long fascination for R.: the major
modern subject he attempted in oil-painting was of a prostitute discovered
by a former lover (*Found*). In its original form it was not in dramatic
monologue and Jenny was not asleep ('under the lids thine eyes' wild glee |
Looketh kindly and laughs to me', lines 119–20). The speaker did not leave.
Before publication R. showed the proofs to Swinburne, who implored him
not to let the poem 'go forth from your cabinet maimed and lacerated' like
de Sade's Justine: 'I entreat you not to think of cancelling those two
passages – poetically perfect, and practically requisite to explain how the
man (without being a Laureate or Prince Consort in Wardour Street
armour) sits on in reverie till morning' (22 Dec. 1869: *Letters* ed. Lang 2.73).
Publication *1870.*

'Vengeance of Jenny's case! Fie on her! Never name her, child!' – (Mrs
Quickly)

Lazy laughing languid Jenny,
Fond of a kiss and fond of a guinea,
Whose head upon my knee to-night
Rests for a while, as if grown light
5   With all our dances and the sound
To which the wild tunes spun you round:
Fair Jenny mine, the thoughtless queen
Of kisses which the blush between

Epigraph Shakespeare *Wives* 4.1.53–4. It is unlikely that R. failed to be
aware of the indecent play on the meaning of 'case'.

Could hardly make much daintier;
10 Whose eyes are as blue skies, whose hair
Is countless gold incomparable:
Fresh flower, scarce touched with signs that tell
Of Love's exuberant hotbed: – Nay,
Poor flower left torn since yesterday
15 Until to-morrow leave you bare;
Poor handful of bright spring-water
Flung in the whirlpool's shrieking face;
Poor shameful Jenny, full of grace
Thus with your head upon my knee; –
20 Whose person or whose purse may be
The lodestar of your reverie?

This room of yours, my Jenny, looks
A change from mine so full of books,
Whose serried ranks hold fast, forsooth,
25 So many captive hours of youth, –
The hours they thieve from day and night
To make one's cherished work come right,
And leave it wrong for all their theft,
Even as to-night my work was left:
30 Until I vowed that since my brain
And eyes of dancing seemed so fain,
My feet should have some dancing too: –
And thus it was I met with you.
Well, I suppose 'twas hard to part,
35 For here I am. And now, sweetheart,
You seem too tired to get to bed

It was a careless life I led
When rooms like this were scarce so strange
Not long ago. What breeds the change, –
40 The many aims or the few years?
Because to-night it all appears
Something I do not know again.

The cloud's not danced out of my brain, –
The cloud that made it turn and swim
45 While hour by hour the books grew dim.
Why, Jenny, as I watch you there, –
For all your wealth of loosened hair,

---

18 Parody of the 'Hail Mary'; an undercurrent of ironical association with
the Virgin continues, e.g. the 'lily' (her flower) line 97, the 'roses' line 114.
21 'The object of your dreams.'
37–9 'I was once more familiar with the haunts of prostitutes.'

Your silk ungirdled and unlaced
And warm sweets open to the waist,
50 All golden in the lamplight's gleam, –
You know not what a book you seem,
Half-read by lightning in a dream!
How should you know, my Jenny? Nay,
And I should be ashamed to say: –
55 Poor beauty, so well worth a kiss!
But while my thought runs on like this
With wasteful whims more than enough,
I wonder what you're thinking of.

If of myself you think at all,
60 What is the thought? – conjectural
On sorry matters best unsolved? –
Or inly is each grace resolved
To fit me with a lure? – or (sad
To think!) perhaps you're merely glad
65 That I'm not drunk or ruffianly
And let you rest upon my knee.

For sometimes, were the truth confessed,
You're thankful for a little rest, –
Glad from the crush to rest within,
70 From the heart-sickness and the din
Where envy's voice at virtue's pitch
Mocks you because your gown is rich;
And from the pale girl's dumb rebuke,
Whose ill-clad grace and toil-worn look
75 Proclaim the strength that keeps her weak
And other nights than yours bespeak;
And from the wise unchildish elf
To schoolmate lesser than himself
Pointing you out, what thing you are: –
80 Yes, from the daily jeer and jar,
From shame and shame's outbraving too,
Is rest not sometimes sweet to you? –
But most from the hatefulness of man
Who spares not to end what he began,
85 Whose acts are ill and his speech ill,
Who, having used you at his will,

48–9 When the boddice, being loosened therewith, | Tells the beautiful secret underneath: – | When thy worm, that dieth not, slumbereth. MS.
52 Possibly a reminiscence of Coleridge *Table Talk* (1835) 27 Apr. 1823: 'To see [Kean] act, is like reading Shakespeare by flashes of lightning.'
62–3 'Are you trying to present your charms to captivate me?'

Thrusts you aside, as when I dine
I serve the dishes and the wine.

Well, handsome Jenny mine, sit up,
90   I've filled our glasses, let us sup,
And do not let me think of you,
Lest shame of yours suffice for two.
What, still so tired? Well, well then, keep
Your head there, so you do not sleep;
95   But that the weariness may pass
And leave you merry, take this glass.
Ah! lazy lily hand, more blessed
If ne'er in rings it had been dressed
Nor ever by a glove concealed!

100   Behold the lilies of the field,
They toil not neither do they spin;
(So doth the ancient text begin, –
Not of such rest as one of these
Can share.) Another rest and ease
105   Along each summer-sated path
From its new lord the garden hath,
Than that whose spring in blessings ran
Which praised the bounteous husbandman,
Ere yet, in days of hankering breath,
110   The lilies sickened unto death.

What, Jenny, are your lilies dead?
Aye, and the snow-white leaves are spread
Like winter on the garden-bed.
But you had roses left in May, –
115   They were not gone too. Jenny, nay,
But must your roses die, and those
Their purfled buds that should unclose?
Even so; the leaves are curled apart,
Still red as from the broken heart,
120   And here's the naked stem of thorns.

Nay, nay, mere words. Here nothing warns
As yet of winter. Sickness here
Or want alone could waken fear, –
Nothing but passion wrings a tear.

88 serve push aside, deal with (*OED* sense 47).
100 Cf. *Matt.* 6.28; *Luke* 12.27.
117 purfled embroidered; primarily poetic diction by the C19.
120 A passing allusion to the crucifixion, and to Mary Magdalen's crown of thorns.

125 Except when there may rise unsought
Haply at times a passing thought
Of the old days which seem to be
Much older than any history
That is written in any book;
130 When she would lie in fields and look
Along the ground through the blown grass,
And wonder where the city was,
Far out of sight, whose broil and bale
They told her then for a child's tale.

135 Jenny, you know the city now.
A child can tell the tale there, how
Some things which are not yet enrolled
In market-lists are bought and sold
Even till the early Sunday light,
140 When Saturday night is market-night
Everywhere, be it dry or wet,
And market-night in the Haymarket.
Our learned London children know,
Poor Jenny, all your pride and woe;
145 Have seen your lifted silken skirt
Advertise dainties through the dirt;
Have seen your coach-wheels splash rebuke
On virtue; and have learned your look
When, wealth and health slipped past, you stare
150 Along the streets alone, and there,
Round the long park, across the bridge,
The cold lamps at the pavement's edge
Wind on together and apart,
A fiery serpent for your heart.

155 Let the thoughts pass, an empty cloud!
Suppose I were to think aloud, –
What if to her all this were said?
Why, as a volume seldom read
Being opened halfway shuts again,
160 So might the pages of her brain
Be parted at such words, and thence
Close back upon the dusty sense.
For is there hue or shape defined
In Jenny's desecrated mind,
165 Where all contagious currents meet,

133 **bale** torment, pain; modelled on alliterative phrases such as 'bliss and bale'.
142 **Haymarket** one of the haunts of London prostitutes.

A Lethe of the middle street?
Nay, it reflects not any face,
Nor sound is in its sluggish pace,
But as they coil those eddies clot,
170 And night and day remember not.

Why, Jenny, you're asleep at last! –
Asleep, poor Jenny, hard and fast, –
So young and soft and tired; so fair,
With chin thus nestled in your hair,
175 Mouth quiet, eyelids almost blue
As if some sky of dreams shone through!

Just as another woman sleeps!
Enough to throw one's thoughts in heaps
Of doubt and horror, – what to say
180 Or think, – this awful secret sway,
The potter's power over the clay!
Of the same lump (it has been said)
For honour the dishonour made,
Two sister vessels. Here is one.

185 My cousin Nell is fond of fun,
And fond of dress, and change, and praise,
So mere a woman in her ways:
And if her sweet eyes rich in youth
Are like her lips that tell the truth,
190 My cousin Nell is fond of love.
And she's the girl I'm proudest of.
Who does not prize her, guard her well?
The love of change, in cousin Nell,
Shall find the best and hold it dear:
195 The unconquered mirth turn quieter
Not through her own, through others' woe:
The conscious pride of beauty glow
Beside another's pride in her,
One little part of all they share.
200 For Love himself shall ripen these
In a kind soil to just increase
Through years of fertilizing peace.

166 The waters of forgetfulness are in the gutter that flows down the middle
of the street.
180–84 Cf. *The Rubáiyát of Omar Khayyám* (no. 59) 145–152; 325–360. It is
possible that R. was influenced by FitzGerald here, although the source
behind both is biblical: e.g. *Jer.* 18.6: 'Behold, as the clay *is* in the potter's
hand, so *are* ye in mine hand, O house of Israel.'

Of the same lump (as it is said)
For honour and dishonour made,
205 Two sister vessels. Here is one.

It makes a goblin of the sun.

So pure, – so fall'n! How dare to think
Of the first common kindred link?
Yet, Jenny, till the world shall burn
210 It seems that all things take their turn;
And who shall say but this fair tree
May need, in changes that may be,
Your children's children's charity?
Scorned then, no doubt, as you are scorned!
215 Shall no man hold his pride forewarned
Till in the end, the Day of Days,
At Judgement, one of his own race,
As frail and lost as you, shall rise, –
His daughter, with his mother's eyes?

220 How Jenny's clock ticks on the shelf!
Might not the dial scorn itself
That has such hours to register?
Yet as to me, even so to her
Are golden sun and silver moon,
225 In daily largesse of earth's boon,
Counted for life-coins to one tune.
And if, as blindfold fates are tossed,
Through some one man this life be lost,
Shall soul not somehow pay for soul?

230 Fair shines the gilded aureole
In which our highest painters place
Some living woman's simple face.
And the stilled features thus descried
As Jenny's long throat droops aside, –
235 The shadows where the cheeks are thin,
And pure wide curve from ear to chin, –
With Raffael's or Da Vinci's hand
To show them to men's souls, might stand,
Whole ages long, the whole world through,
240 For preachings of what God can do.
What has man done here? How atone,
Great God, for this which man has done?

220–9 Cf. no. 119.1 for the characteristic Rossetti association of time, money
and life. It is possible that Jenny's clock has a sun and moon on the dial.

And for the body and soul which by
Man's pitiless doom must now comply
245   With lifelong hell, what lullaby
Of sweet forgetful second birth
Remains? All dark. No sign on earth
What measure of God's rest endows
The many mansions of his house.

250   If but a woman's heart might see
Such erring heart unerringly
For once! But that can never be.

Like a rose shut in a book
In which pure women may not look,
255   For its base pages claim control
To crush the flower within the soul;
Where through each dead rose-leaf that clings,
Pale as transparent psyche-wings,
To the vile text, are traced such things
260   As might make lady's cheek indeed
More than a living rose to read;
So nought save foolish foulness may
Watch with hard eyes the sure decay;
And so the life-blood of this rose,
265   Puddled with shameful knowledge, flows
Through leaves no chaste hand may unclose:
Yet still it keeps such faded show
Of when 'twas gathered long ago,
That the crushed petals' lovely grain,
270   The sweetness of the sanguine stain,
Seen of a woman's eyes, must make
Her pitiful heart, so prone to ache,
Love roses better for its sake: –
Only that this can never be: –
275   Even so unto her sex is she.

Yet, Jenny, looking long at you,
The woman almost fades from view.
A cipher of man's changeless sum

249 Cf. *John* 14.2: 'In my Father's house are many mansions.'
258 psyche-wings butterfly wings and wings of the soul, since Eros was often
portrayed with butterfly wings.
265 puddled dirtied.
269 grain dye.
276–97 For a study of the appeal of this kind of sinister feminine beauty see
M. Praz *The Romantic Agony* (1951) 25–50; 189–286.

Of lust, past, present, and to come,
280 Is left. A riddle that one shrinks
To challenge from the scornful sphinx.

Like a toad within a stone
Seated while time crumbles on;
Which sits there since the earth was cursed
285 For man's transgression at the first;
Which, living through all centuries,
Not once has seen the sun arise;
Whose life, to its cold circle charmed,
The earth's whole summers have not warmed;
290 Which always – whitherso the stone
Be flung – sits there, deaf, blind, alone; –
Aye, and shall not be driven out
Till that which shuts him round about
Break at the very Master's stroke,
295 And the dust thereof vanish as smoke,
And the seed of man vanish as dust: –
Even so within this world is Lust.

Come, come, what use in thoughts like this?
Poor little Jenny, good to kiss, –
300 You'd not believe by what strange roads
Thought travels, when your beauty goads
A man to-night to think of toads!
Jenny, wake up... Why, there's the dawn!

And there's an early waggon drawn
305 To market, and some sheep that jog
Bleating before a barking dog;
And the old streets come peering through
Another night that London knew;
And all as ghostlike as the lamps.

310 So on the wings of day decamps
My last night's frolic. Glooms begin
To shiver off as lights creep in
Past the gauze curtains half drawn-to,
And the lamp's doubled shade grows blue, –
315 Your lamp, my Jenny, kept alight,

282–97 Cf. Tennyson *The Kraken* (above p. 57) for a malevolent being hidden from the light until the Last Judgement. See Tervarent 1. 135 for the motif of the toad and its association with the dead.
304–9 In R.'s painting *Found* a tethered calf on a waggon acts in a similar way as an emblem of the main action.

Like a wise virgin's, all one night!
And in the alcove coolly spread
Glimmers with dawn your empty bed;
And yonder your face I see
320   Reflected lying on my knee,
Where teems with first foreshadowings
Your pier-glass scrawled with diamond rings.

And now without, as if some word
Had called upon them that they heard,
325   The London sparrows far and nigh
Clamour together suddenly;
And Jenny's cage-bird grown awake
Here in their song his part must take,
Because here too the day doth break.

330   And somehow in myself the dawn
Among stirred clouds and veils withdrawn
Strikes greyly on her. Let her sleep.
But will it wake her if I heap
These cushions thus beneath her head
335   Where my knee was? No, – there's your bed,
My Jenny, while you dream. And there
I lay among your golden hair
Perhaps the subject of your dreams,
These golden coins.
                For still one deems
340   That Jenny's flattering sleep confers
New magic on the magic purse, –
Grim web, how clogged with shrivelled flies!
Between the threads fine fumes arise
And shape their pictures in the brain.
345   There roll no streets in glare and rain,

---

316 Cf. *Matt.* 25. 2–13: the parable of the five wise and the five foolish virgins. The speaker, rather than Jenny, has watched: 'for ye know neither the day nor the hour wherein the Son of man cometh.'
322 Jenny's customers have signed her mirror, so that the engraved lines cross the reflected image of her face, adumbrating the wrinkles to come.
323–6 Cf. *Matt.* 10.29: 'Are not two sparrows sold for a farthing? and one of them shall not fall on the ground without your Father.' The preceding verse may have significance for the poem as a whole: 'fear him which is able to destroy both soul and body in hell.'
327 cage-bird a common emblem of the imprisoned soul: cf. Hopkins *The Caged Skylark.*
341–2 Jenny's hair is at once a purse and a trap; it is possible that she is wearing some sort of decorative hair net.

Nor flagrant man-swine whets his tusk;
But delicately sighs in musk
The homage of the dim boudoir;
Or like a palpitating star
350 Thrilled into song, the opera-night
Breathes faint in the quick pulse of light;
Or at the carriage-window shine
Rich wares for choice; or, free to dine,
Whirls through its hour of health (divine
355 For her) the concourse of the Park.
And though in the discounted dark
Her functions there and here are one,
Beneath the lamps and in the sun
There reigns at least the acknowledged belle
360 Apparelled beyond parallel.
Ah Jenny, yes, we know your dreams.

For even the Paphian Venus seems
A goddess o'er the realms of love,
When silver-shrined in shadowy grove:
365 Aye, or let offerings nicely placed
But hide Priapus to the waist,
And whoso looks on him shall see
An eligible deity.

Why, Jenny, waking here alone
370 May help you to remember one,
Though all the memory's long outworn
Of many a double-pillowed morn.
I think I see you when you wake,
And rub your eyes for me, and shake
375 My gold, in rising, from your hair,
A Danaë for a moment there.

356 **discounted dark** Jenny's dreams of the illuminated world of the *demi-mondaine* take no account of the night-time activity, which will follow the same pattern of prostitution; 'discounted' also establishes a financial motif, whereby Jenny is seen as borrowing, and will have to pay by future night-work.
362 **Paphian Venus** The goddess of love in one of her most licentious manifestations. Like 'Cyprian', 'Paphian' had long been synonymous with prostitution.
366 **Priapus** God of fertility, whose phallic statues were important in ceremonies of procreation. In the ancient world the statues were not regarded as indecent.
376 **Danaë** Jupiter appeared to her in a shower of gold. Mythologising of everyday life is also a characteristic procedure in R.'s paintings.

> Jenny, my love rang true! for still
> Love at first sight is vague, until
> That tinkling makes him audible.

> 380 And must I mock you to the last,
> Ashamed of my own shame, – aghast
> Because some thoughts not born amiss
> Rose at a poor fair face like this?
> Well, of such thoughts so much I know:
> 385 In my life, as in hers, they show,
> By far gleam which I may near,
> A dark path I can strive to clear.

> Only one kiss. Good-bye, my dear.

119 The House of Life: extracts

Date The earliest sonnets date from 1847; the introductory sonnet is 1880.
Fifty were published in 1870; by Aug. 1871 thirty more had been written. F.
M. Tidsel *MP* 15 (1917) 257–76 suggests dates for a large proportion of the
101 sonnets finally forming the cycle. It is in the tradition of the non-
narrative Elizabethan sonnet cycles. W. M. Rossetti writes: 'When a good
number had been written, they came to form, if considered collectively, a
sort of record of his feelings and experiences...he certainly never professed,
nor do I consider that he ever wished his readers to assume, that all items
had been primarily planned to form one connected and indivisible whole'
(*D.G.R. as Designer and Writer* (1888) 181–2). The predominant theme in the
poems is love: presented in a guise so abstract that it is impossible to
distinguish between works arising from his love for Elizabeth Siddal and
Jane Morris – even though we now know that both are present in the cycle,
and other women real and imaginary. R. C. Wallerstein *PMLA* 42 (1927)
492–504 overstressed the importance of Lizzie, and was not aware of the
intense love of R. for Jane Morris that is expressed in some of the poems of
the 1870s. W. Fredeman *BJRL* 47 (1965) 298–341 questions the 'accepta-
bility of using the poem to substantiate biographical speculation'.
Publication (in complete form) *1881*.

119.1 The Sonnet

Date 1880, Caine 120–1.
Publication 1881 (prefatory poem).

> A sonnet is a moment's monument, –
>   Memorial from the soul's eternity
>   To one dead deathless hour. Look that it be,
> Whether for lustral rite or dire portent,

4 lustral purifying.

5   Of its own arduous fullness reverent:
      Carve it in ivory or in ebony,
      As day or night may rule; and let time see
    Its flowering crest impearled and orient.

    A sonnet is a coin: its face reveals
10   The soul, – its converse, to what power 'tis due; –
    Whether for tribute to the august appeals
      Of life, or dower in love's high retinue,
    It serve; or, 'mid the dark wharf's cavernous breath,
    In Charon's palm it pay the toll to death.

9–10 R. perhaps has in mind the public and private aspects of poetic meaning – rather as in *One Word More* (above p. 268) Browning considers the light and dark sides of the moon. D. Stauffer *The Nature of Poetry* (1946) 237 suggests that the sonnet's division at the octet represents the two sides of the coin.
14 Charon the boatman who ferried souls of the dead across the Styx to the underworld when given a coin.

119.2 Nuptial Sleep

Date Possibly 1868 according to W.M.R. Possibly based on the experience of marriage with Elizabeth Siddal (d. 1862).
    This was one of the poems singled out for attack by Robert Buchanan – 'so sickening a desire to reproduce the sensual mood, so careful choice of epithet to convey mere animal sensations, that we merely shudder at the shameless nakedness.'
Publication *1870;* omitted *1881,* etc. Restored *1911.* Usually numbered 6a. See W. Fredeman *BJRL* 47 (1965) 299.

    At length their long kiss severed, with sweet smart:
      And as the last slow sudden drops are shed
      From sparkling eaves when all the storm has fled,
    So singly flagged the pulses of each heart.
5   Their bosoms sundered, with the opening start
      Of married flowers to either side outspread
      From the knit stem; yet still their mouths, burnt red,
    Fawned on each other where they lay apart.

    Sleep sank them lower than the tide of dreams,
10   And their dreams watched them sink, and slid away.
    Slowly their souls swam up again, through gleams
      Of watered light and dull drowned waifs of day;
    Till from some wonder of new woods and streams
      He woke, and wondered more: for there she lay.

9–12 The association of love with the subaqueous world was a favourite Pre-Raphaelite motif: see the Burne-Jones painting *The Depths of the Sea* (1886).

[119] Dante Gabriel Rossetti

119.3 Silent Noon

Date Tidsel 75 suggests it is associated with R.'s reawakened interest in nature when he stayed at Kelmscott in July and Aug. 1871 with Jane Morris (her husband was in Iceland). **Publication** *1881* (no. 19).

Your hands lie open in the long fresh grass, –
  The finger-points look through like rosy blooms:
  Your eyes smile peace. The pasture gleams and glooms
'Neath billowing skies that scatter and amass.
5 All round our nest, far as the eye can pass,
  Are golden kingcup-fields with silver edge
  Where cow-parsley skirts the hawthorn-hedge.
'Tis visible silence, still as the hour-glass.

Deep in the sun-searched growths the dragon-fly
10 Hangs like a blue thread loosened from the sky: –
  So this winged hour is dropped to us from above.
Oh! clasp we to our hearts, for deathless dower
  This close-companioned inarticulate hour
  When twofold silence was the song of love.

6 kingcup buttercup.

119.4 Lost Days

Date 1858, Caine 237.
Publication *Fortnightly Review* (March 1869) as no. 12 in *Of Life, Love, and Death; 1870; 1881* (no. 86).

The lost days of my life until to-day,
  What were they, could I see them on the street
  Lie as they fell? Would they be ears of wheat
Sown once for food but trodden into clay?
5 Or golden coins squandered and still to pay?
  Or drops of blood dabbling the guilty feet?
  Of such spilt water as in dreams must cheat
The undying throats of Hell, athirst alway?

I do not see them here; but after death
10 God knows I know the faces I shall see,
Each one a murdered self, with low last breath.
  'I am thyself, – what hast thou done to me?'
  'And I – and I – thyself,' (lo! each one saith,)
  'And thou thyself to all eternity!'

8 The throats of men in Hell, who thirst alway? *Fortnightly Review, 1870.*

119.5 Lost on Both Sides

Date 21 July 1854 (*Letters* 1.206–7). W.M.R. thought it expressed R.'s rival ambitions in poetry and painting. There seems no reason to restrict the sonnet to that interpretation.

Publication *Fortnightly Review* (March 1869) as no. 6 in *Of Life, Love, and Death; 1870; 1881* (no. 91).

As when two men have loved a woman well,
   Each hating each, through love's and death's deceit;
   Since not for either this stark marriage-sheet
And the long pauses of this wedding-bell;
5   Yet o'er her grave the night and day dispel
   At last their feud forlorn, with cold and heat;
   Nor other than dear friends to death may fleet
The two lives left that most of her can tell: –

So separate hopes, which in a soul had wooed
10   The one same peace, strove with each other long,
   And peace before their faces perished since:
So through that soul, in restless brotherhood,
   They roam together now, and wind among
   Its bye-streets, knocking at the dusty inns.

3 stark] strait *Fortnightly Rev.*   **marriage-sheet** shroud: the bride is marrying death.
4 wedding-bell funeral knell: for the marriage with death.
12 restless] mindful *Letters.*
13–14 (When silence may not be) sometimes they throng | Through high-streets and at many dusty inns. *Letters.*

119.6 The Woodspurge

Date ?
Publication *1870* (as Song 8 in *The House of Life*).

The wind flapped loose, the wind was still,
Shaken out dead from tree and hill:
I had walked on at the wind's will. –
I sat now, for the wind was still.

5   Between my knees my forehead was, –
My lips, drawn in, said not Alas!
My hair was over in the grass,
My naked ears heard the day pass.

George Meredith

My eyes, wide open, had the run
10   Of some ten weeds to fix upon;
Among those few, out of the sun,
The woodspurge flowered, three cups in one.

From perfect grief there need not be
Wisdom or even memory:
15   One thing then learnt remains to me, –
The woodspurge has a cup of three.

12 woodspurge genus *Euphorbia;* the flower is formed of three petals.

George Meredith

Meredith's early story is remarkably like Dickens's: both were born in Portsmouth (M. in 1828, sixteen years after Dickens); both were virtually orphans as children; both found their way into journalism before winning fame; both wooed the genius of comedy – albeit in distinctly divergent manifestations of that lady.

It may be that M.'s novels are his most remarkable literary achievement, since he deals so courageously and inventively with so many intractable problems at the meeting point of the novel and poetry. But he often seems more at home in the poems proper, which, curiously, are less dominated by the tendency to go a-whoring after the novelistic than Browning's. *Love in a Valley* is delightfully and naturally conceived as a poem, and even *Modern Love*, despite its novelistic tendencies, is presented in poetic terms. It was based on first-hand experience: M. knew the pains of modern love when his highly-strung wife (the daughter of Thomas Love Peacock) ran away with the Pre-Raphaelite painter Henry Wallis in 1858. The other sense in which M. is fundamentally a poet is in his taste for system-building (novelists proper are usually more fascinated by the gratuitous and the contingent than poets). He developed a philosophy of 'Earth' in which man merged with the life-force and liberated from egoism will discover love and eternal significance. The gist of the message resembles D. H. Lawrence's – although the jocular cynicism he could not resist adopting alongside effusive mysticism is totally unlike anything in Lawrence.

In 1864 M. married Marie Vulliamy. He settled down at Box Hill as one of the national institutions to which literary pilgrimages were made. The combination of deafness and stubbornness made him an even more insulated figure than Swinburne, and although he was for some part of his life ahead of his time, he was not so far ahead as to seem more than nominally living in the twentieth-century when he died in 1909. It will not be the ideas of M. that will make his poetry survive, but the capacity for sharp observation and for producing the distinctive and fine-sounding line on occasions. M. is in the tradition of Victorian prophetic poets who were unable to assume the effortless faith in transcendental order available to the Romantics, yet like their predecessors were able to feel and express the regenerative and suggestive power of Nature.

The standard text is the Memorial Edition (1909–12).

Biographies and discussion There are biographies by S. M. Ellis (1919), L. Stevenson (1953) and J. Lindsay (1956). For general studies of the poetry: see G. O. Trevelyan *The Poetry and Philosophy of M.* (1906) and N. Kelvin *A Troubled Eden: nature and society in the works of M.* (1961); also J. Lucas 'M. as Poet' in I. Fletcher ed. *Meredith Now* (1971).

Abbreviations

1851	*Poems* (1851).
1862	*Modern Love and Poems of the English Roadside* (1862).
1883	*Poems and Lyrics of the Joy of Earth* (1883).
1912	*The Poetical Works of G.M.* (1912) G. O. Trevelyan ed.
Cline *Letters*	*The Letters of G.M.* (1970) C. L. Cline ed.
Critical Heritage	*M: The Critical Heritage* (1971) I. Williams ed.

120 Love in the Valley

Date 1850 when M. lived in Surrey.

V. A. Paterson, *VN* no. 15 (1959) 28–9, thinks this a development of these lines in Tennyson's *The Princess* (1847): 'Come down, O maid, from yonder mountain height: | What pleasure lives in height... | For love is of the valley...' (7.177–185).

Metre: trochaic, but with much variation in short syllables according to stress of the accent.

Publication *1851* (10 stanzas); *Macmillan's Magazine* (Oct. 1878) (in revised form); *1883*.

1

Under yonder beech-tree single on the green-sward,
    Couched with her arms behind her golden head,
Knees and tresses folded to slip and ripple idly,
    Lies my young love sleeping in the shade.
5   Had I the heart to slide an arm beneath her,
    Press her parting lips as her waist I gather slow,
Waking in amazement she could not but embrace me:
    Then would she hold me and never let me go?

1 single] standing *1851*.
2 golden] little *1851*.
3 Her knees folded up, and her tresses on her bosom, *1851*.
6 parting] dreaming *1851*.   **gather**] folded *1851*.

2

Shy as the squirrel and wayward as the swallow,
10   Swift as the swallow along the river's light
Circleting the surface to meet his mirrored winglets,
     Fleeter she seems in her stay than in her flight.
Shy as the squirrel that leaps among the pine-tops,
     Wayward as the swallow overhead at set of sun,
15   She whom I love is hard to catch and conquer,
     Hard, but O the glory of the winning were she won!

3

When her mother tends her before the laughing mirror,
     Tying up her laces, looping up her hair,
Often she thinks, were this wild thing wedded,
20   More love should I have, and much less care.
When her mother tends her before the lighted mirror,
     Loosening her laces, combing down her curls,
Often she thinks, were this wild thing wedded,
     I should miss but one for many boys and girls.

4

25   Heartless she is as the shadow in the meadows
     Flying to the hills on a blue and breezy noon.
No, she is athirst and drinking up her wonder:
     Earth to her is young as the slip of the new moon.
Deals she an unkindness, 'tis but her rapid measure,
30   Even as in a dance; and her smile can heal no less:
Like the swinging May-cloud that pelts the flowers with
     hailstones
     Off a sunny border, she was made to bruise and
     bless.

5

Lovely are the curves of the white owl sweeping
     Wavy in the dusk lit by one large star.
35   Lone on the fir-branch, his rattle-note unvaried,
     Brooding o'er the gloom, spins the brown eve-jar.

10 along...light] when athwart the western flood *1851*.
12 Is that dear one in her maiden bud. *1851*.
13 that leaps] whose nest *1851*.
14–16 Gentle – ah! that she were jealous as the dove! | Full of all the
wildness of the woodland creatures, | Happy in herself is the maiden that I
love! *1851*.
16 ∧ 17 *1851* has an extra stanza here.
21 lighted] bashful *1851*.
25–208 Not in *1851;* instead 7 stanzas, totally different.
36 eve-jar night jar or goatsucker (bird).

Darker grows the valley, more and more forgetting:
    So were it with me if forgetting could be willed.
Tell the grassy hollow that holds the bubbling well-
    spring,
40   Tell it to forget the source that keeps it filled.

6

Stepping down the hill with her fair companions,
    Arm in arm, all against the raying west,
Boldly she sings, to the merry tune she marches,
    Brave in her shape, and sweeter unpossessed.
45   Sweeter, for she is what my heart first awaking
    Whispered the world was; morning light is she.
Love that so desires would fain keep her changeless;
    Fain would fling the net, and fain have her free.

7

Happy happy time, when the white star hovers
50   Low over dim fields fresh with bloomy dew,
Near the face of dawn, that draws athwart the darkness,
    Threading it with colour, like yewberries the yew.
Thicker crowd the shades as the grave east deepens
    Glowing, and with crimson a long cloud swells.
55   Maiden still the morn is; and strange she is, and secret;
    Strange her eyes; her cheeks are cold as cold sea-shells.

8

Sunrays, leaning on our southern hills and lighting
    Wild cloud-mountains that drag the hills along,
Oft ends the day of your shifting brilliant laughter
60   Chill as a dull face frowning on a song.
Ay, but shows the south-west a ripple-feathered bosom
    Blown to silver while the clouds are shaken and ascend
Scaling the mid-heavens as they stream, there comes a sunset
    Rich, deep like love in beauty without end.

9

65   When at dawn she sighs, and like an infant to the window
    Turns grave eyes craving light, released from dreams,
Beautiful she looks, like a white water-lily
    Bursting out of bud in havens of the streams.
When from bed she rises clothed from neck to ankle
70   In her long nightgown sweet as boughs of May,
Beautiful she looks, like a tall garden lily
    Pure from the night, and splendid for the day.

10

Mother of the dews, dark eye-lashed twilight,
　　Low-lidded twilight, o'er the valley's brim,
75　Rounding on thy breast sings the dew-delighted skylark,
　　Clear as though the dewdrops had their voice in him.
　　Hidden where the rose-flush drinks the rayless planet,
　　　Fountain-full he pours the spraying fountain-showers.
　　Let me hear her laughter. I would have her ever
80　　Cool as dew in twilight, the lark above the flowers.

11

All the girls are out with their baskets for the primrose;
　　Up lanes, woods through, they troop in joyful bands.
　　My sweet leads: she knows not why, but now she
　　　loiters,
　　　Eyes the bent anemones, and hangs her hands.
85　Such a look will tell that the violets are peeping,
　　Coming the rose: and unaware a cry
　　Springs in her bosom for odours and for colour,
　　　Covert and the nightingale; she knows not why.

12

Kerchiefed head and chin she darts between her tulips,
90　　Streaming like a willow grey in arrowy rain:
　　Some bend beaten cheek to gravel, and their angel
　　　She will be; she lifts them, and on she speeds again.
　　Black the driving raincloud breasts the iron gateway:
　　　She is forth to cheer a neighbour lacking mirth.
95　So when sky and grass met rolling dumb for thunder
　　Saw I once a white dove, sole light of earth.

13

Prim little scholars are the flowers of her garden,
　　Trained to stand in rows, and asking if they please.
　　I might love them well but for loving more the wild
　　　ones:
100　　O my wild ones! they tell me more than these.
　　You, my wild one, you tell of honied field-rose,
　　　Violet, blushing eglantine in life; and even as they,
　　They by the wayside are earnest of your goodness,
　　　You are of life's, on the banks that line the way.

14

105　Peering at her chamber the white crowns the red rose,
　　Jasmine winds the porch with stars two and three.
　　Parted is the window; she sleeps; the starry jasmine
　　　Breathes a falling breath that carries thoughts of me.
　　Sweeter unpossessed, have I said of her my sweetest?

110   Not while she sleeps: while she sleeps the jasmine
      breathes,
    Luring her to love; she sleeps; the starry jasmine
    Bears me to her pillow under white rose-wreaths.

15

Yellow with birdfoot-trefoil are the grass-glades;
    Yellow with cinquefoil of the dew-grey leaf;
115 Yellow with stonecrop; the moss-mounds are yellow;
    Blue-necked the wheat sways yellowing to the sheaf.
Green-yellow bursts from the copse the laughing yaffle;
    Sharp as a sickle is the edge of shade and shine:
Earth in her heart laughs looking at the heavens,
120   Thinking of the harvest: I look and think of mine.

16

This I may know: her dressing and undressing
    Such a change of light shows as when the skies in sport
Shift from cloud to moonlight; or edging over thunder
    Slips a ray of sun; or sweeping into port
125 White sails furl; or on the ocean borders
    While sails lean along the waves leaping green.
Visions of her shower before me, but from eyesight
    Guarded she would be like the sun were she seen.

17

Front door and back of the mossed old farmhouse
130   Open with the morn, and in a breezy link
Freshly sparkles garden to stripe-shadowed orchard,
    Green across a rill where on sand the minnows wink.
Busy in the grass the early sun of summer
    Swarms, and the blackbird's mellow fluting notes
135 Call my darling up with round and roguish challenge:
    Quaintest, richest carol of all the singing throats!

18

Cool was the woodside; cool as her white dairy
    Keeping sweet the cream-pan; and there the boys from
      school,
Cricketing below, rushed brown and red with sunshine;
140   O the dark translucence of the deep-eyed cool!
Spying from the farm, herself she fetched a pitcher
    Full of milk, and tilted for each in turn the beak.
Then a little fellow, mouth up and on tiptoe,
    Said, 'I will kiss you': she laughed and leaned her
      cheek.

117 yaffle green woodpecker.

19

145 Doves of the fir-wood walling high our red roof
    Through the long noon coo, crooning through the coo.
Loose droop the leaves, and down the sleepy roadway
    Sometimes pipes a chaffinch; loose droops the blue.
Cows flap a slow tail knee-deep in the river,
150   Breathless, given up to sun and gnat and fly.
Nowhere is she seen; and if I see her nowhere,
    Lightning may come, straight rains and tiger sky.

20

O the golden sheaf, the rustling treasure-armful!
    O the nutbrown tresses nodding interlaced!
155 O the treasure-tresses one another over
    Nodding! O the girdle slack about the waist!
Slain are the poppies that shot their random scarlet
    Quick amid the wheatears: wound about the waist,
Gathered, see these brides of Earth one blush of ripeness!
160   O the nutbrown tresses nodding interlaced!

21

Large and smoky red the sun's cold disk drops,
    Clipped by naked hills, on violet shaded snow:
Eastward large and still lights up a bower of moonrise,
    Whence at her leisure steps the moon aglow.
165 Nightlong on black print-branches our beech-tree
    Gazes in this whiteness: nightlong could I.
Here may life on death or death on life be painted.
    Let me clasp her soul to know she cannot die!

22

Gossips count her faults; they scour a narrow chamber
170   Where there is no window, read not heaven or her.
'When she was a tiny,' one aged woman quavers,
    Plucks at my heart and leads me by the ear.
Faults she had once as she learnt to run and tumbled:
    Faults of feature some see, beauty not complete.
175 Yet, good gossips, beauty that makes holy
    Earth and air, may have faults from head to feet.

23

Hither she comes; she comes to me; she lingers,
    Deepens her brown eyebrows, while in new surprise
High rise the lashes in wonder of a stranger;
180   Yet am I the light and living of her eyes.

---

162 Clipped embraced, also trimmed at the edges, like a coin.

Something friends have told her fills her heart to
   brimming,
Nets her in her blushes, and wounds her, and
   tames. –
Sure of her haven, O like a dove alighting,
Arms up, she dropped: our souls were in our names.

24

185 Soon will she lie like a white-frost sunrise.
Yellow oats and brown wheat, barley pale as rye,
Long since your sheaves have yielded to the thresher,
   Felt the girdle loosened, seen the tresses fly.
Soon will she lie like a blood-red sunset.
190 Swift with the to-morrow, green-winged spring!
Sing from the south-west, bring her back the truants,
   Nightingale and swallow, song and dipping wing.

25

Soft new beech-leaves, up to beamy April
   Spreading bough on bough a primrose mountain, you,
195 Lucid in the moon, raise lilies to the skyfields,
   Youngest green transfused in silver shining through:
Fairer than the lily, than the wild white cherry:
   Fair as in image my seraph love appears
Borne to me by dreams when dawn is at my eyelids:
200 Fair as in the flesh she swims to me on tears.

26

Could I find a place to be alone with heaven,
   I would speak my heart out: heaven is my need.
Every woodland tree is flushing like the dogwood,
   Flashing like the whitebeam, swaying like the reed.
205 Flushing like the dogwood crimson in October;
   Streaming like the flag-reed south-west blown;
Flashing as in gusts the sudden-lighted whitebeam:
   All seem to know what is for heaven alone.

204 Flashing like the whitebeam Cf. Hopkins *The Starlight Night* (no. 143)
line 6 'Wind-beat whitebeam'.

121 Modern Love: extracts

Date From *c.* 1858, when M.'s wife eloped with Henry Wallis, to 1861, when
she died. Composition first mentioned in letter to Mrs J. Ross 19 Nov. 1861
(Cline *Letters* 1.125). Cline thinks *A Love Match* was M.'s tentative title.
Proofs ready Jan. 1862.
   P. Bartlett, *Yale Univ. Lib. Gazette* 40 (1966) 185–7, describes the Beinecke
MS., which has 36 sonnets. The cycle is a fictional interpretation of M.'s

experience of marriage, with four principal actors: the husband and wife and their illicit partners. We see the dissolution of the marriage, the doubtful pleasures with 'My Lady', an attempt at reconciliation, and the suicide of the wife. The modernity of the love is both in the situations and the probing scepticism of the narrative voice. In conservative quarters it was harshly received, as were all deviant views of the sanctity of marriage. Notices in the *Spectator* (R. H. Hutton) and the *Saturday Review* (*Critical Heritage* 92–5; 106–7), provide typical reactions. It is clear from the MS that the relationship with 'My Lady' was not platonic.

There are 50 sixteen-line sonnets in the work. It draws on both the narrative and reflective traditions of the great Elizabethan sonnet cycles. The time-span of the narrative is from the spring of one year to the summer of the next. Discussion E. C. Wright *VN* no. 13 (1958) 1–9; N. Friedman *MLQ* 18 (1957) 9–26.

Publication *1862*.

1

By this he knew she wept with waking eyes:
   That, at his hand's light quiver by her head,
   The strange low sobs that shook their common bed,
Were called into her with a sharp surprise,
5   And strangled mute, like little gaping snakes,
   Dreadfully venomous to him. She lay
   Stone-still, and the long darkness flowed away
With muffled pulses. Then, as midnight makes
   Her giant heart of memory and tears
10   Drink the pale drug of silence, and so beat
   Sleep's heavy measure, they from head to feet
Were moveless, looking through their dead black years,
   By vain regret scrawled over the blank wall.
   Like sculptured effigies they might be seen
15   Upon their marriage-tomb, the sword between;
Each wishing for the sword that severs all.

2

It ended, and the morrow brought the task.
   Her eyes were guilty gates, that let him in
   By shutting all too zealous for their sin:
Each sucked a secret, and each wore a mask.
5   But, oh, the bitter taste her beauty had!
   He sickened as at breath of poison-flowers:
   A languid humour stole among the hours,
And if their smiles encountered, he went mad.
And raged deep inward, till the light was brown

1.15 Tristan and Isolde slept thus to enforce chastity: here the imaginary sword represents a psychic separation.
2 The pain and wickedness of physical love without spiritual.

10   Before his vision, and the world, forgot,
      Looked wicked as some old dull murder-spot.
      A star with lurid beams, she seemed to crown
      The pit of infamy: and then again
      He fainted on his vengefulness, and strove
15   To ape the magnanimity of love,
      And smote himself, a shuddering heap of pain.

3

      This was the woman; what now of the man?
      But pass him. If he comes beneath a heel,
      He shall be crushed until he cannot feel,
      Or, being callous, haply till he can.
5   But he is nothing: – nothing? Only mark
      The rich light striking out from her on him!
      Ha! what a sense it is when her eyes swim
      Across the man she singles, leaving dark
      All else! Lord God, who mad'st the thing so fair,
10   See that I am drawn to her even now!
      It cannot be such harm on her cool brow
      To put a kiss? Yet if I meet him there!
      But she is mine! Ah, no! I know too well
      I claim a star whose light is overcast:
15   I claim a phantom-woman in the past
      The hour has struck, though I heard not the bell!

4

      All other joys of life he strove to warm,
      And magnify, and catch them to his lip:
      But they had suffered shipwreck with the ship,
      And gazed upon him sallow from the storm.
5   Or if delusion came, 'twas but to show
      The coming minute mock the one that went.
      Cold as a mountain in its star-pitched tent,
      Stood high philosophy, less friend than foe:
      Whom self-caged passion, from its prison-bars,
10   Is always watching with a wondering hate.
      Not till the fire is dying in the grate,
      Look we for any kinship with the stars.
      Oh, wisdom never comes when it is gold,

3.1 **the man** the wife's adulterous lover.
3.8 **singles** singles out.
3.15 **phantom-woman** the image of the woman he once loved.
4.7–10 A situation similar to *Lucifer in Starlight* (no. 122 below): impotent passion encountering reason in an abstract space.

And the great price we pay for it full worth:
15   We have it only when we are half earth.
Little avails that coinage to the old!

5

A message from her set his brain aflame.
  A world of household matters filled her mind,
    Wherein he saw hypocrisy designed:
She treated him as something that is tame,
5   And but at other provocation bites.
  Familiar was her shoulder in the glass,
    Through that dark rain: yet it may come to pass
That a changed eye finds such familiar sights
More keenly tempting than new loveliness.
10   The 'What has been' a moment seemed his own:
  The splendours, mysteries, dearer because known,
Nor less divine: Love's inmost sacredness,
Called to him, 'Come!' – In his restraining start,
  Eyes nurtured to be looked at scarce could see
15   A wave of the great waves of destiny
Convulsed at a checked impulse of the heart.

6

It chanced his lips did meet her forehead cool.
  She had no blush, but slanted down her eye.
    Shamed nature, then, confesses love can die:
And most she punishes the tender fool
5   Who will believe what honours her the most!
  Dead! is it dead? She has a pulse, and flow
    Of tears, the price of blood-drops, as I know,
For whom the midnight sobs around Love's ghost,
Since then I heard her, and so will sob on.
10   The love is here; it has but changed its aim.
  O bitter barren women! what's the name?
The name, the name, the new name thou hast won?
Behold me striking the world's coward stroke!
  That will I not do, though the sting is dire.
15   Beneath the surface this, while by the fire
They sat, she laughing at a quiet joke.

4.15 half earth nearly dead.
6.13 the world's coward stroke the aggression society resorts to in calling the adulterous woman 'whore'.
6.16 They his wife and her lover: his anger is contained.

7

She issues radiant from her dressing-room,
　Like one prepared to scale an upper sphere:
　– By stirring up a lower, much I fear!
How deftly that oiled barber lays his bloom!
5　That long-shanked dapper cupid with frisked curls
　Can make known women torturingly fair;
　The gold-eyed serpent dwelling in rich hair
Awakes beneath his magic whisks and twirls.
His art can take the eyes from out my head,
10　Until I see with eye of other men;
　While deeper knowledge crouches in its den,
And sends a spark up: – is it true we are wed?
Yea! filthiness of body is most vile,
　But faithlessness of heart I do hold worse.
15　The former, it were not so great a curse
To read on the steel-mirror of her smile.

8

Yet it was plain she struggled, and that salt
　Of righteous feeling made her pitiful.
　Poor twisting worm, so queenly beautiful!
Where came the cleft between us? whose the fault?
5　My tears are on thee, that have rarely dropped
　As balm for any bitter wound of mine:
　My breast will open for thee at a sign!
But, no: we are two reed-pipes, coarsely stopped:
　The God once filled them with his mellow breath;
10　And they were music till he flung them down,
　Used! used! Hear now the discord-loving clown
Puff his gross spirit in them, worse than death!
I do not know myself without thee more:
　In this unholy battle I grow base:
15　If the same soul be under the same face,
Speak, and a taste of that old time restore!

9

He felt the wild beast in him betweenwhiles
　So masterfully rude, that he would grieve
　To see the helpless delicate thing receive
His guardianship through certain dark defiles.

7.16 the steel-mirror cf. Gascoigne *The Steel Glass* (1576): a satirical poem.
8.1–2 The wife's adulterous guilt made her an object of pity.
8.3 Poor twisting worm,] O abject worm, *1862*.
8.8 coarsely stopped with the rough musical divisions of a rustic instrument.
9 The last poem until no. 49 spoken by the omniscient narrator.

5   Had he not teeth to rend, and hunger too?
         But still he spared her. Once 'Have you no fear?'
       He said: 'twas dusk; she in his grasp; none near.
       She laughed: 'No, surely; am I not with you?'
       And uttering that soft starry 'you,' she leaned
10   Her gentle body near him, looking up;
         And from her eyes, as from a poison-cup,
       He drank until the flittering eyelids screened.
       Devilish malignant witch! and oh, young beam
         Of heaven's circle-glory! Here thy shape
15   To squeeze like an intoxicating grape –
       I might, and yet thou goest safe, supreme.

                         *

                        16
       In our old shipwrecked days there was an hour
         When in the firelight steadily aglow,
         Joined slackly, we beheld the red chasm grow
       Among the clicking coals. Our library-bower
5   That eve was left us: and hushed we sat
         As lovers to whom time is whispering.
       From sudden-opened doors we heard them sing:
       The nodding elders mixed good wine with chat.
       Well knew we that life's greatest treasure lay
10   With us, and of it was our talk. 'Ah, yes!
         Love dies!' I said: I never thought it less
       She yearned to me that sentence to unsay.
       Then when the fire domed blackening, I found
         Her cheek was salt against my kiss, and swift
15   Up the sharp scale of sobs her breast did lift: –
       Now am I haunted by that taste! that sound!

                        17
       At dinner, she is hostess, I am host.
         Went the feast ever cheerfuller? She keeps
         The topic over intellectual deeps
       In buoyancy afloat. They see no ghost.
5   With sparkling surface-eyes we ply the ball:
         It is in truth a most contagious game:
         'Hiding the skeleton' shall be its name.
       Such play as this, the devils might appal!

16 For a similar treatment of lovers' discords by firelight see *Tess of the
d'Urbervilles* Ch. 34.
16.8 M.'s father-in-law Thomas Love Peacock was a *bon viveur* and
conversationalist.
16.15 Cf. the musical analogy in 8.8.

But here's the greater wonder; in that we,
10   Enamoured of an acting nought can tire,
Each other, like true hypocrites admire;
Warm-lighted looks, love's ephemeridae,
Shoot gaily o'er the dishes and the wine.
We waken envy of our happy lot.
15   Fast, sweet, and golden, shows the marriage-knot.
Dear guests, you now have seen love's corpse-light shine.

18

Here Jack and Tom are paired with Moll and Meg.
Curved open to the river-reach is seen
A country merry-making on the green.
Fair space for signal shakings of the leg.
5   That little screwy fiddler from his booth,
When flows one nut-brown stream, commands the joints
Of all who caper here at various points.
I have known rustic revels in my youth:
The May-fly pleasures of a mind at ease.
10   An early goddess was a country lass:
A charmed Amphion-oak she tripped the grass.
What life was that I lived? The life of these?
Heaven keep them happy! Nature they seem near.
They must, I think, be wiser than I am;
15   They have the secret of the bull and lamb.
'Tis true that when we trace its source, 'tis beer.

*

25

You like not that French novel? Tell me why.
You think it quite unnatural. Let us see.
The actors are, it seems, the usual three:
Husband, and wife, and lover. She – but fie!
5   In England we'll not hear of it. Edmond,
The lover, her devout chagrin doth share;
Blanc-mange and absinthe are his penitent fare,
Till his pale aspect makes her over-fond:

17.10–11 Enamoured of our acting and our wits, | Admire each other like true hypocrites *1862*.
17.12 ephemeridae] ephemerae *1862;* insects with short lives.
17.16 corpse-light *ignis fatuus* seen in church-yards and portending a funeral.
18.6 nut-brown stream ale.
18.11 Amphion charmed stones and trees with music, to build civilization.
18.13 seem] are *1862*.
18.15 The rustics are in contact with the primitive sexual and mystical rhythms of the earth.

So, to preclude fresh sin, he tries rosbif.
10   Meantime the husband is no more abused:
Auguste forgives her ere the tear is used.
Then hangeth all on one tremendous 'If': –
If she will choose between them. She does choose;
And takes her husband, like a proper wife.
15   Unnatural? My dear, these things are life:
And life, some think, is worthy of the muse.

*

29

Am I failing? For no longer can I cast
A glory round about this head of gold.
Glory she wears, but springing from the mould;
Not like the consecration of the past!
5   Is my soul beggared? Something more than earth
I cry for still: I cannot be at peace
In having love upon a mortal lease.
I cannot take the woman at her worth!
Where is the ancient wealth wherewith I clothed
10   Our human nakedness, and could endow
With spiritual splendour a white brow
What else had grinned at me the fact I loathed?
A kiss is but a kiss now! and no wave
Of a great flood that whirls me to the sea.
15   But, as you will! we'll sit contentedly,
And eat our pot of honey on the grave.

*

43

Mark where the pressing wind shoots javelin-like
Its skeleton shadow on the broad-backed wave!
Here is a fitting spot to dig love's grave;
Here where the ponderous breakers plunge and strike,
5   And dart their hissing tongues high up the sand:
In hearing of the ocean, and in sight
Of those ribbed wind-streaks running into white.
If I the death of love had deeply planned,
I never could have made it half so sure,
10   As by the unblest kisses which upbraid

25.9 rosbif French for roast beef.
25.16 some think] they say *1862*.
29.2 head of gold on the mistress.
29.3 the mould human form.
29.9–14 Cf. Coleridge *Dejection*... for a presentation of the inner incapacity to transform outer reality.

George Meredith [121]

The full-waked sense; or failing that, degrade!
'Tis morning: but no morning can restore
What we have forfeited. I see no sin:
The wrong is mixed. In tragic life, God wot,
15   No villain need be! Passions spin the plot:
We are betrayed by what is false within.

*

49

He found her by the ocean's moaning verge,
Nor any wicked change in her discerned;
And she believed his old love had returned,
Which was her exultation and her scourge.
5   She took his hand, and walked with him, and seemed
The wife he sought, though shadow-like and dry.
She had one terror, lest her heart should sigh,
And tell her loudly she no longer dreamed.
She dared not say, 'This is my breast; look in.'
10   But there's a strength to help the desperate weak.
That night he learned how silence best can speak
The awful things when pity pleads for sin.
About the middle of the night her call
Was heard, and he came wondering to the bed.
15   'Now kiss me, dear! it may be, now!' she said.
Lethe had passed those lips, and he knew all.

50

Thus piteously love closed what he begat:
The union of this ever-diverse pair!
These two were rapid falcons in a snare,
Condemned to do the flitting of the bat.
5   Lovers beneath the singing sky of May,
They wandered once; clear as the dew on flowers:
But they fed not on the advancing hours:
Their hearts held cravings for the buried day.
Then each applied to each that fatal knife,
10   Deep questioning, which probes to endless dole.
Ah, what a dusty answer gets the soul
When hot for certainties in this our life! –
In tragic hints here see what evermore
Moves dark as yonder midnight ocean's force,
15   Thundering like ramping hosts of warrior horse,
To throw that faint thin line upon the shore!

49.13–16 The wife kills herself, and at the moment of death seems to forget the estrangement. M. told Trevelyan that her death was suicide (*1912* 584).
50.14–16 The waves come out of the darkness with violence, but the highest point they reach leaves only a line in the sand.

William Morris

122 Lucifer in Starlight

Date ? For discussion of a possible connection with M.'s revision of Ch. 23 of *The Ordeal of Richard Feverel* in 1878 see J. W. Morris *VP* 1 (1963) 76–86. There may also be a relation to *Modern Love* 4 (see above p. 435). **Publication** *1883*.

> On a starred night Prince Lucifer uprose.
> Tired of his dark dominion swung the fiend
> Above the rolling ball in cloud part screened,
> Where sinners hugged their spectre of repose.
> 5 Poor prey to his hot fit of pride were those.
> And now upon his western wing he leaned,
> Now his huge bulk o'er Afric's sands careened,
> Now the black planet shadowed Arctic snows.
> Soaring through wider zones that pricked his scars
> 10 With memory of the old revolt from awe,
> He reached a middle height, and at the stars,
> Which are the brain of heaven, he looked, and sank.
> Around the ancient track marched, rank on rank,
> The army of unalterable law.

7 o'er Afric's sands] o'er Africa *1883*.
14 See T. S. Eliot *Cousin Nancy* line 13, for a reminiscence of this.

William Morris

William Morris was born in 1834 into a prosperous landowning Essex family of Evangelical persuasion. As a precocious child he developed a taste for Walter Scott, Gothic architecture, and 'sad lowland country'. In 1848 he went to Marlborough College, then dominated by a High Anglican spirit, and from there, after private tuition, to Exeter College, Oxford in Jan. 1853. He and his exact contemporary Edward Burne-Jones became the centre of a group of undergraduates who cultivated Pre-Raphaelitism, medievalism, and a wide range of cultural and even social interests. Overlaying the artistic enthusiasm was a religious enthusiasm which led to a plan for a sort of art-producing monastery. Ruskin was a dominant influence. In 1856 M. articled himself to George Edmund Street, one of the foremost neo-gothic architects. A colleague was Philip Webb, the principal figure in English domestic architecture from the 1870s onwards. In 1857 M. and Burne-Jones took up painting as disciples of Rossetti.

Meanwhile, M. was also dabbling in literature, and was one of the originators of the *Oxford and Cambridge Magazine* (for his contributions

William Morris

and its character see *The Wellesley Index of Victorian Periodicals* (1972) 2.723–31).

The year 1857 was important in M.'s life: he decorated the roof and one of the bays of the Oxford Union, as a member of the group (sometimes called 'the Oxford Pre-Raphaelites') led by Rossetti. It was while he was in Oxford that he met his future wife Jane Burden, whom he married in April 1859. His first volume of poems was *The Defence of Guenevere* (1858).

M. lived in a house at Upton in Kent designed for him by Webb. Called 'The Red House' it was of seminal importance in the C19 revival of sturdy vernacular traditions of domestic building in brick, and exhibited a kind of solidity and unpretentiousness that was characteristic of all M.'s creations, poetic included. The construction and furnishing of the house led to the formation of the manufacturing firm Morris, Marshall and Faulkner in 1861. From 1866 onwards M. was engaged in composing poems for *The Earthly Paradise*. It occupied a key place in the history of aestheticism, since Pater's review 'Aesthetic Poetry', *Westminster Review* 90 (1868) 300–12, was one of the earliest important formulations of the art for art's sake ethic.

In addition to his literary production, M. was passionately interested in the appearance of his books, in their typography, design and binding. Here too he produced a highly individual fusion of traditional and personal styles that had a large influence on late C19 book design. In the 1870s he became interested in Icelandic sagas, translated the Volsunga saga, and visited Iceland in 1871.

In that same year, he discovered Kelmscott Manor, on the banks of the upper Thames: it appears at the climax of *News from Nowhere* as the achieved dream of perfection. And yet there was a discordant note in the real house, since it was the setting for Jane's adulterous liaison with D. G. Rossetti.

In 1874 'the Firm' broke up. M. continued translating; he published in 1875 a translation of *The Aeneid*, and in 1876 *Sigurd the Volsung and the Fall of the Niblungs*, a stark Northern work, eschewing quaintness and lightness of touch. This was virtually his last imaginative work for the next thirteen years, during which time he was writing instructive and polemical literature. In 1877 he was amongst the founders of the Society for the Protection of Ancient Buildings ('Anti-Scrape'). He was engaged in a host of practical affairs, becoming more involved with the politics of emerging socialism as in the early 1880s he grew discontent with liberalism and adopted a more radical stance. In 1883 he joined the Democratic Federation. It split in 1884, the Socialist League faction being led by M. His political beliefs are expressed directly in pamphlets and in the romance *A Dream of John Ball* (1888). From the late 1880s onwards M. published a sequence of prose romances. He came to see that there was not going to be a rapid changeover of power, and that the long-term future for the working man lay in an extended programme of education. He withdrew from the Socialist League in 1890, when it was becoming too radical for his tastes. In 1890 he founded the Kelmscott Press, a bold and experimental venture into archaic styles of book production. He died in 1896.

Although poetry represents a comparatively small part of his output, M. is the Pre-Raphaelite poet *par excellence*, and up to 1870, when Rossetti published his first volume of poetry, he was the main literary exponent of the school in the public's eye. In a lecture delivered in Birmingham in 1891 he asserted that 'naturalism, a complete fidelity to nature' was one of the principal aspects of Pre-Raphaelitism. However, his poetry followed more consistently the other two aspects he identified: 'the conscientious present-ment of incident' and the adoption of 'definite, harmonious, conscious beauty'. Paradoxically, M.'s poetry is more escapist than any other of the period, even though it was based closely on experience that was vivid and direct for him.

The standard edition of M.'s poetry is in *The Collected Works* (1910–15) edited by his daughter May.

Biography and discussion The standard biography is by J. M. Mackail (1899).

Recent studies The best are by E. P. Thompson (1955), P. Henderson (1967), P. Thompson (1967), R. Watkinson (1967) and J. Lindsay (1975). The classic essay on M. as a poet is Yeats's 'The Happiest of Poets' in *Ideas of Good and Evil* (1903). Ch. 5 of L. Stevenson *The Pre-Raphaelite Poets* (Chapel Hill, N.C. 1972) is devoted to M.

Abbreviations

1858   *The Defence of Guenevere and Other Poems* (1858).
1868–70   *The Earthly Paradise* (1868–70).

123 Riding Together

Date Written at Oxford early in 1855 as *The Midnight Tilt*.
Publication *1858*.

> For many, many days together
>   The wind blew steady from the east;
> For many days hot grew the weather,
>   About the time of our Lady's Feast.
>
> 5   For many days we rode together,
>   Yet met we neither friend nor foe;
> Hotter and clearer grew the weather,
>   Steadily did the east wind blow.
>
> We saw the trees in the hot, bright weather,
> 10   Clear-cut, with shadows very black
> As freely we rode on together
>   With helms unlaced and bridles slack.
>
> And often as we rode together,
>   We, looking down the green-banked stream,
> 15   Saw flowers in the sunny weather,
>   And saw the bubble-making bream.

4 Lady's Feast March 25, the Feast of the Annunciation.
16 bubble-making bream fish blowing bubbles.

And in the night lay down together,
And hung above our heads the rood,
Or watched night-long in the dewy weather.
20   The while the moon did watch the wood.

Our spears stood bright and thick together,
Straight out the banners streamed behind,
As we galloped on in the sunny weather,
With faces turned towards the wind.

25   Down sank our threescore spears together,
As thick we saw the pagans ride;
His eager face in the clear fresh weather,
Shone out that last time by my side.

Up the sweep of the bridge we dashed together,
30   It rocked to the crash of the meeting spears,
Down rained the buds of the dear spring weather,
The elm-tree flowers fell like tears.

There, as we rolled and writhed together,
I threw my arms above my head,
35   For close by my side, in the lovely weather
I saw him reel and fall back dead.

I and the slayer met together,
He waited the death-stroke there in his place,
With thoughts of death, in the lovely weather,
40   Gapingly mazed at my maddened face.

Madly I fought as we fought together;
In vain: the little Christian band
The pagans drowned, as in stormy weather,
The river drowns low-lying land.

45   They bound my blood-stained hands together,
They bound his corpse to nod by my side:
Then on we rode, in the bright March weather,
With clash of cymbals did we ride.

We ride no more, no more together;
50   My prison-bars are thick and strong.
I take no heed of any weather,
The sweet Saints grant I live not long.

18 rood cross.

124 The Tune of Seven Towers

Date 1857–8. The poem is a reverie over (not a description of) Rossetti's
painting of the same name (Surtees pl. 130).
Publication *1858*.

No one goes there now:
   For what is left to fetch away
From the desolate battlements all arow,
   And the lead roof heavy and grey?
5 *'Therefore,' said fair Yoland of the flowers,*
   'This is the tune of Seven Towers.'

No one walks there now;
   Except in the white moonlight
The white ghosts walk in a row;
10   If one could see it, an awful sight, –
 'Listen!' said fair Yoland of the flowers,
   'This is the tune of Seven Towers.'

But none can see them now,
   Though they sit by the side of the moat,
15 Feet half in the water, there in a row,
   Long hair in the wind afloat.
 'Therefore,' said fair Yoland of the flowers,
   'This is the tune of Seven Towers.'

If any will go to it now,
20   He must go to it all alone,
Its gates will not open to any row
   Of glittering spears – will *you* go alone?
 'Listen!' said fair Yoland of the flowers,
   'This is the tune of Seven Towers.'

25 By my love go there now,
   To fetch me my coif away,
My coif and my kirtle, with pearls arow,
   Oliver, go today!
 'Therefore,' said fair Yoland of the flowers,
30 *'This is the tune of Seven Towers.'*

I am unhappy now,
   I cannot tell you why;
If you go, the priests and I in a row
   Will pray that you may not die.
35 *'Listen!' said fair Yoland of the flowers,*
   'This is the tune of Seven Towers.'

26 coif a close fitting cap.

If you will go for me now,
   I will kiss your mouth at last;
   [*She sayeth inwardly.*]
40   (*The graves stand grey in a row*),
   Oliver, hold me fast!
'*Therefore,' said fair Yoland of the flowers,*
'*This is the tune of Seven Towers.*'

125 The Haystack in the Floods

Date *c.* 1857. M. and Rossetti were both interested, at about this time, in Froissart: R. told C. E. Norton: 'These chivalric, Froissartian themes are quite a passion of mine.'
   The *Chronicles* describe a degenerate and brutal C14 France, in total contrast to the dreamlike and distanced world of Malory. See J. M. Patrick *N & Q* 203 (1958) 425–7 and D. Staines *SP* 70 (1973) 439–64 on M.'s free treatment of medieval sources.
Publication *1858.*

   Had she come all the way for this,
   To part at last without a kiss?
   Yea, had she borne the dirt and rain
   That her own eyes might see him slain
5   Beside the haystack in the floods?

   Along the dripping leafless woods,
   The stirrup touching either shoe,
   She rode astride as troopers do;
   With kirtle kilted to her knee,
10   To which the mud splashed wretchedly;
   And the wet dripped from every tree
   Upon her head and heavy hair,
   And on her eyelids broad and fair;
   The tears and rain ran down her face.
15   By fits and starts they rode apace,
   And very often was his place
   Far off from her; he had to ride
   Ahead, to see what might betide
   When the roads crossed; and sometimes, when
20   There rose a murmuring from his men,
   Had to turn back with promises;
   Ah me! she had but little ease;
   And often for pure doubt and dread
   She sobbed, made giddy in the head

9 kilted gathered up.

25   By the swift riding; while, for cold,
      Her slender fingers scarce could hold
      The wet reins; yea, and scarcely, too,
      She felt the foot within her shoe
      Against the stirrup: all for this,
30   To part at last without a kiss
      Beside the haystack in the floods.

      For when they neared that old soaked hay,
      They saw across the only way
      That Judas, Godmar, and the three
35   Red running lions dismally
      Grinned from his pennon, under which
      In one straight line along the ditch,
      They counted thirty heads.
                   So then,
      While Robert turned round to his men
40   She saw at once the wretched end,
      And, stooping down, tried hard to rend
      Her coif the wrong way from her head,
      And hid her eyes; while Robert said:
      'Nay, love, 'tis scarcely two to one,
45   At Poictiers where we made them run
      So fast – why, sweet my love, good cheer,
      The Gascon frontier is so near,
      Nought after this.'
                But, 'O!' she said,
      'My God! my God! I have to tread
50   The long way back without you; then
      The court at Paris; those six men;
      The gratings of the Chatelet;
      The swift Seine on some rainy day
      Like this, and people standing by
55   And laughing, while my weak hands try
      To recollect how strong men swim.

41–3 'She tried to twist the long trailing part of her cap to the front to shield her eyes from Robert's death.'
45 Poictiers the scene of an English victory over the French in 1356.
47 Gascon Gascony in C14 was ruled by men loyal to England.
51 those six men judges.
52 Chatelet a Paris prison.
56 M. believed that an accused witch underwent a trial by water in which she was judged innocent if she drowned and guilty if she survived. Not historically accurate, but related to the argument (see J. Hollow *VP* 7 (1969) 353–5).

All this, or else a life with him,
For which I should be damned at last.
Would God that this next hour were past!'

60 He answered not, but cried his cry,
'St. George for Marny!' cheerily;
And laid his hand upon her rein.
Alas! no man of all his train
Gave back that cheery cry again;
65 And, while for rage his thumb beat fast
Upon his sword-hilt, some one cast
About his neck a kerchief long,
And bound him.
                    Then they went along
To Godmar; who said: 'Now, Jehane,
70 Your lover's life is on the wane
So fast, that, if this very hour
You yield not as my paramour,
He will not see the rain leave off –
Nay, keep your tongue from gibe and scoff,
75 Sir Robert, or I slay you now.'

She laid her hand upon her brow,
Then gazed upon the palm, as though
She thought her forehead bled, and – 'No!'
She said, and turned her head away,
80 As there were nothing else to say,
And everything were settled: red
Grew Godmar's face from chin to head:
'Jehane, on yonder hill there stands
My castle, guarding well my lands:
85 What hinders me from taking you,
And doing that I list to do
To your fair wilful body, while
Your knight lies dead?'
                    A wicked smile
Wrinkled her face, her lips grew thin,
90 A long way out she thrust her chin:
'You know that I should strangle you
While you were sleeping; or bite through
Your throat, by God's help – ah!' she said,
'Lord Jesu, pity your poor maid!
95 For in such wise they hem me in,
I cannot choose but sin and sin,
Whatever happens: yet I think

57 **him** Godmar.

They could not make me eat or drink,
And so should I just reach my rest.'
100 'Nay, if you do not my behest,
O Jehane! though I love you well,'
Said Godmar, 'would I fail to tell
All that I know?' 'Foul lies.' she said.
'Eh? lies, my Jehane? by God's head,
105 At Paris folks would deem them true!
Do you know, Jehane, they cry for you:
"Jehane the brown! Jehane the brown!
Give us Jehane to burn or drown!" –
Eh – gag me Robert! – sweet my friend,
110 This were indeed a piteous end
For those long fingers, and long feet,
And long neck, and smooth shoulders sweet;
An end that few men would forget
That saw it – So, an hour yet:
115 Consider, Jehane, which to take
Of life or death!'
                              So, scarce awake,
Dismounting, did she leave that place,
And totter some yards: With her face
Turned upward to the sky she lay,
120 Her head on a wet heap of hay,
And fell asleep: and while she slept,
And did not dream, the minutes crept
Round to the twelve again; but she,
Being waked at last, sighed quietly,
125 And strangely childlike came, and said:
'I will not.' Straightway Godmar's head,
As though it hung on strong wires, turned
Most sharply round, and his face burned.

For Robert – both his eyes were dry,
130 He could not weep, but gloomily
He seemed to watch the rain; yea, too,
His lips were firm; he tried once more
To touch her lips; she reached out, sore
And vain desire so tortured them,
135 The poor grey lips, and now the hem
Of his sleeve brushed them,
                              With a start
Up Godmar rose, thrust them apart;
From Robert's throat he loosed the bands
Of silk and mail; with empty hands
140 Held out, she stood and gazed, and saw

450

The long bright blade without a flaw
Glide out from Godmar's sheath, his hand
In Robert's hair; she saw him bend
Back Robert's head; she saw him send
145   The thin steel down; the blow told well,
Right backward the knight Robert fell,
And moaned as dogs do, being half dead,
Unwitting, as I deem: so then
Godmar turned grinning to his men,
150   Who ran, some five or six, and beat
His head to pieces at their feet.

Then Godmar turned again and said:
'So, Jehane, the first fitte is read!
Take note, my lady, that your way
155   Lies backward to the Chatelet!'
She shook her head and gazed awhile
At her cold hands with a rueful smile,
As though this thing had made her mad.

This was the parting that they had
160   Beside the haystack in the floods.

153 fitte section of a poem.

126 The Earthly Paradise: extracts

Date Composition began 1865.
   M. planned to have the poem illustrated by Burne–Jones with 500 wood-cuts; but this plan was not realized. The complete work, running to 42,000 lines, is a collection of 24 tales (two for each month of the year) told by the survivors of a group of Norsemen who fled from a plague in their native land in search of an earthly paradise, and by the dwellers of a city in which the Norsemen settle. The stories are retellings of classical, medieval and Norse myths and legends. M. composed rapidly and easily: he is supposed to have written 700 lines of *Jason* in one day.
Publication *1868–1870.*

AN APOLOGY

Of Heaven or Hell I have no power to sing,
   I cannot ease the burden of your fears,
Or make quick-coming death a little thing,
   Or bring again the pleasure of past years,
5   Nor for my words shall ye forget your tears,
   Or hope again for aught that I can say,
   The idle singer of an empty day.

An Apology is a medieval form (rhyme royal).

But rather, when aweary of your mirth,
From full hearts still unsatisfied ye sigh,
10 And, feeling kindly unto all the earth,
Grudge every minute as it passes by,
Made the more mindful that the sweet days die –
Remember me a little then I pray,
The idle singer of an empty day.

15 The heavy trouble, the bewildering care
That weighs us down who live and earn our bread,
These idle verses have no power to bear;
So let me sing of names remembered,
Because they, living not, can ne'er be dead,
20 Or long time take their memory quite away
From us poor singers of an empty day.

Dreamer of dreams, born out of my due time,
Why should I strive to set the crooked straight?
Let it suffice me that my murmuring rhyme
25 Beats with light wing against the ivory gate,
Telling a tale not too importunate
To those who in the sleepy region stay,
Lulled by the singer of an empty day.

Folk say, a wizard to a northern king
30 At Christmas-tide such wondrous things did show,
That through one window men beheld the spring.
And through another saw the summer glow,
And through a third the fruited vines a-row,
While still, unheard, but in its wonted way,
35 Piped the drear wind of that December day.

So with this Earthly Paradise it is,
If ye will read aright, and pardon me,
Who strive to build a shadowy isle of bliss
Midmost the beating of the steely sea,
40 Where tossed about all hearts of men must be;
Whose ravening monsters mighty men shall slay,
Not the poor singer of an empty day.

INTRODUCTION

Forget six counties overhung with smoke,
Forget the snorting steam and piston stroke,
Forget the spreading of the hideous town;

Apol. 25 ivory gate the cave of sleep had an ivory gate which released false
dreams (true dreams came through the gate of horn): see Hom. *Od.* 19. 562–
7 and Virgil *Aen.* 6.893–6.
Intro. 1 six counties London's 'home counties'.

Think rather of the pack-horse on the down,
5   And dream of London, small and white and clean,
The clear Thames bordered by its gardens green;
Think, that below bridge the green lapping waves
Smite some few keels that bear Levantine staves,
Cut from the yew wood on the burnt-up hill,
10   And pointed jars that Greek hands toiled to fill,
And treasured scanty spice from some far sea,
Florence gold cloth, and Ypres napery,
And cloth of Bruges, and hogsheads of Guienne;
While nigh the thronged wharf Geoffrey Chaucer's pen
15   Moves over bills of lading – mid such times
Shall dwell the hollow puppets of my rhymes.

OCTOBER

O love, turn from the unchanging sea and gaze
    Down these grey slopes upon the year grown old,
A-dying mid the autumn-scented haze,
    That hangeth o'er the hollow in the wold,
5   Where the wind-bitten ancient elms enfold
Grey church, long barn, orchard, and red-roofed stead,
Wrought in dead days for men a long while dead.

Come down, O love; may not our hands still meet,
    Since still we live to-day, forgetting June,
10   Forgetting May, deeming October sweet –
    O hearken, hearken! through the afternoon,
        The grey tower sings a strange old tinkling tune!
Sweet, sweet, and sad, the toiling year's last breath,
Too satiate of life to strive with death.

15   And we too – will it not be soft and kind,
    That rest from life, from patience and from pain,
That rest from bliss we know not when we find,
    That rest from Love which ne'er the end can gain? –
        Hark, how the tune swells, that erewhile did wane!
20   Look up, love! – ah, cling close and never move!
How can I have enough of life and love?

NOVEMBER

Are thine eyes weary? is thy heart too sick
    To struggle any more with doubt and thought,
Whose formless veil draws darkening now and thick

Intro. 5–6 See M.'s *News from Nowhere* (1891) for a fully realized vision of a utopian London.
Intro. 12 Ypres napery Flemish linen.
Intro. 14 Geoffrey Chaucer's pen Chaucer was for a time a customs official.

James Thomson (B.V.)

Across thee, e'en as smoke-tinged mist-wreaths brought
5   Down a fair dale to make it blind and nought?
Art thou so weary that no world there seems
Beyond these four walls, hung with pain and dreams?

Look out upon the real world, where the moon,
    Half-way 'twixt root and crown of these high trees,
10 Turns the dread midnight into dreamy noon,
    Silent and full of wonders, for the breeze
    Died at the sunset, and no images,
No hopes of day, are left in sky or earth –
Is it not fair, and of most wondrous worth?

15 Yea, I have looked, and seen November there;
    The changeless seal of change it seemed to be,
Fair death of things that, living once, were fair;
    Bright sign of loneliness too great for me,
    Strange image of the dread eternity,
20 In whose void patience how can these have part,
These outstretched feverish hands, this restless heart?

James Thomson (B.V.)

James Thomson was born at Port-Glasgow in 1834. His father was a
merchant sailor, who was disabled by a paralytic stroke which led to mental
deficiency and dipsomania. The family came to London in 1842, but by 1853
both parents were dead. T. became a schoolmaster in the army, teaching in
Chelsea and Ballincollig, Ireland. He fell in love with Matilda Weller, and
the profoundest experience of his whole life was her sudden death in 1853.
T. began publishing in *Tait's Edinburgh Magazine* in 1858. The same year he
adopted the pseudonym 'Bysshe Vanolis', which combined one of Shelley's
names with an anagram of the mystic German poet Novalis. Subsequently
the name was shortened to its initials: B.V. Shelley was T.'s favourite poet;
he wrote an essay on him for the *National Reformer* in 1860.

In 1862 T. was court-martialled for swimming in a pool where bathing was
prohibited. He then became a clerk, and in 1872 the secretary of a mining
company. This gave him the opportunity to travel to Colorado. The
following year, as a reporter for the *New York World*, he visited Spain to
witness the struggle between the Republicans and the Carlists.

The poem that brought him fame, and by which he is principally known, is
The City of Dreadful Night (1874). His first volume of poetry was published
in 1880. To his contemporaries he was as well known a journalist as a poet.
The only other volume of poetry to be published in his life-time was *Vane's*

Story,... and other poems (1881). The last years of his life were marked by serious alcoholism. He died in June 1882.

The first biography of T. was H. S. Salt's (1889). There are studies by B. Dobell (1910), I. B. Walker (Cornell U.P. 1950) and W. D. Schaefer (1965).

Abbreviations

1880   *The City of Dreadful Night and Other Poems* (1880).

1963   *Poems and Some Letters* (1963) A. Ridler ed.

127 Sunday at Hampstead: extract

(An idle idyll by a very humble member of the great and noble London mob)

Date On MS. in British Library: 1863–5.

This poem, and *Sunday up the River*, are charming attempts to deal with a city more familiar and homely than *The City of Dreadful Night*, although even in these works one catches a glimpse of the macabre and oppressive metropolis. Hampstead, N. London, was one of the principal 'breathing spaces' of the city-dweller.

Publication *National Reformer* (15 and 22 July 1866); *1880*.

1

This is the Heath of Hampstead,
   There is the dome of Saint Paul's;
Beneath, on the serried house-tops,
   A chequered lustre falls:

5 And the mighty city of London,
   Under the clouds and the light,
Seems a low wet beach, half shingle,
   With a few sharp rocks upright.

Here will we sit, my darling,
10   And dream an hour away:
The donkeys are hurried and worried,
   But we are not donkeys to-day:

Through all the weary week, dear,
   We toil in the murk down there,
15 Tied to a desk and a counter,
   A patient stupid pair!

But on Sunday we slip our tether,
   And away from the smoke and the smirch;
Too grateful to God for His Sabbath
20   To shut its hours in a church.

Away to the green, green country,
    Under the open sky;
Where the earth's sweet breath is incense
    And the lark sings psalms on high.

25 On Sunday we're lord and lady,
    With ten times the love and glee
Of those pale and languid rich ones
    Who are always and never free.

They drawl and stare and simper,
30   So fine and cold and staid,
Like exquisite waxwork figures
    That must be kept in the shade:

We can laugh out loud when merry,
    We can romp at kiss-in-the-ring,
35 We can take our beer at a public,
    We can loll on the grass and sing...

Would you grieve very much, my darling,
    If all yon low wet shore
Were drowned by a mighty flood-tide,
40   And we never toiled there more?

Wicked? – there is no sin, dear,
    In an idle dreamer's head;
He turns the world topsy-turvy
    To prove that his soul's not dead.

45 I am sinking, sinking, sinking;
    It is hard to sit upright!
Your lap is the softest pillow!
    Good night, my love, good night!

2

How your eyes dazzle down into my soul!
50   I drink and drink of their deep violet wine,
And ever thirst the more, although my whole
    Dazed being whirls in.drunkenness divine.

Pout down your lips from that bewildering smile,
    And kiss me for the interruption, sweet!
55 I had escaped you: floating for awhile
    In that far cloud ablaze with living heat:

I floated with it through the solemn skies,
    I melted with it up the crystal sea
Into the Heaven of Heavens; and shut my eyes
60   To feel eternal rest enfolding me...

Well, I prefer one tyrannous girl down here,
   You jealous violet-eyed bewitcher, you!
To being lord in Mohammed's seventh sphere
   Of meekest houris threescore ten and two!

3

65 Was it hundreds of years ago, my love,
       Was it thousands of miles away,
    That two poor creatures we know, my love,
       Were toiling day by day;
          Were toiling weary, weary,
70   With many myriads more,
       In a city dark and dreary
          On a sullen river's shore?

    Was it truly a fact or a dream, my love?
       I think my brain still reels,
75 And my ears still throbbing seem, my love,
       With the rush and the clang of wheels;
          Of a vast machinery roaring
          For ever in skyless gloom;
       Where the poor slaves peace imploring,
80   Found peace alone in the tomb.

    Was it hundreds of years ago, my love,
       Was it thousands of miles away?
    Or was it a dream to show, my love,
       The rapture of to-day?
85   This day of holy splendour,
          This Sabbath of rich rest,
       Wherein to God we render
          All praise by being blest.

64 72 was the number of the houris: see E. C. Brewer *Dictionary of Phrase and Fable* (1970) 550.
65–80 This section is closer in spirit to *The City of Dreadful Night*. There are nine more sections in the poem.

128 The City of Dreadful Night: extracts

Date 1870–74; sections 19 and 21 June–Oct. 1873.
The theme of the gloomy city had appealed to T. as early as 1857 in *The Doom of a City* (Part 3 section 2 first published in the *National Reformer* 18 Aug. 1867). In Jan. 1870 T. was 35, the mid-point of life at which Dante experienced his visionary pilgrimage. T. set out to express the urban nightmare hell experienced by the isolated individual. W. D. Schaefer *PMLA* 77 (1962) 609–16 demonstrates that in the course of composition the theme

[128] James Thomson (B.V.)

became more universal. Doubtless modern cities, such as London, influenced him, but one's predominant impression is that the city is of the mind, with a host of literary precedents; of *The Voyage* T. writes: 'a penny steam boat will not carry one to a city where the people are all petrified', and this is generally applicable to his visions.

Sources The Tale of Zobeide in *The Arabian Nights* is a source . Flavour is lent to the poem by sources as varied in tone as Leopardi (translated by T. for the *National Reformer* 1867), Dante, Aeschylus, Marston, the Book of Job, *Titus Andronicus* and Shelley's *The Triumph of Life*. The apocalyptic strain may have been influenced by Edward Irving (1792–1834). Some of the pessimism in the poem is serious and bleak; some of it lugubriously self-indulgent. Herman Melville was responding to only a part of its effect when he called it 'the modern book of Job'.

MSS There are MSS. in the British Library and the Pierpont Morgan Library. The MS. variants below are from the latter: Section 21 not in British Library MS.

Publication *The National Reformer* (22 March, 12 and 26 Apr., 17 May 1874); *1880*.

19

> The mighty river flowing dark and deep,
>   With ebb and flood from the remote sea-tides
> Vague-sounding through the City's sleepless sleep,
>   Is named the River of the Suicides;
> 5 For night by night some lorn wretch overweary,
> And shuddering from the future yet more dreary,
>   With its cold secure oblivion hides.
>
> One plunges from a bridge's parapet,
>   As by some blind and sudden frenzy hurled;
> 10 Another wades in slow with purpose set
>   Until the waters are above him furled;
> Another in a boat with dreamlike motion
> Glides drifting down into the desert ocean,
>   To starve or sink from out the desert world.
>
> 15 They perish from their suffering surely thus,
>   For none beholding them attempts to save,
> The while each thinks how soon, solicitous,
>   He may seek refuge in the self-same wave;
> Some hour when tired of ever-vain endurance
> 20 Impatience will forerun the sweet assurance
>   Of perfect peace eventual in the grave.
>
> When this poor tragic-farce has palled us long,
>   Why actors and spectators do we stay? –
> To fill our so-short roles out right or wrong;

21 eventual] to follow MS.

458

25   To see what shifts are yet in the dull play
       For our illusion; to refrain from grieving
       Dear foolish friends by our untimely leaving:
         But those asleep at home, how blest are they!

       Yet it is but for one night after all:
30   What matters one brief night of dreary pain?
       When after it the weary eyelids fall
       Upon the weary eyes and wasted brain;
       And all sad scenes and thoughts and feelings vanish
       In that sweet sleep now power can ever banish,
35   That one best sleep which never wakes again.

35 best] good MS.

21

    Anear the centre of that northern crest
       Stands out a level upland bleak and bare,
       From which the city east and south and west
         Sinks gently in long waves; and thronèd there
5   An Image sits, stupendous, superhuman,
       The bronze colossus of a wingèd Woman,
         Upon a graded granite base foursquare.

    Low-seated she leans forward massively,
       With cheek on clenched left hand, the forearm's might
10   Erect, its elbow on her rounded knee;
       Across a clasped book in her lap the right
       Upholds a pair of compasses; she gazes
       With full set eyes, but wandering in thick mazes
         Of sombre thought beholds no outward sight.

15   Words cannot picture her; but all men know
       That solemn sketch the pure sad artist wrought
       Three centuries and threescore years ago,
         With phantasies of his peculiar thought:

2 bleak] stern MS.
4 sinks] falls MS.
5 stupendous] Titanic MS.
14 beholds] regards MS.
16 that solemn sketch Dürer's *Melencolia I* (1514). For a discussion of the symbolism see E. Panofsky *Albrecht Dürer* (Princeton U.P. 1943) 1.156–71, R. Klibansky *et al. Saturn and Melancholy* (1964) and W. Waetzoldt *Dürer* (1955) 76–83. T. possessed a copy of the engraving by Johan Wiricx (1602). *1963* 66–7 prints a T. poem of the 1860s, *The 'Melencolia' of Albrecht Dürer*, modelled on Shelley's *On the Medusa of Leonardo*. The titanic mother figure first appears in the prose *Our Lady of Sorrow* 1862–4.

The instruments of carpentry and science
20 Scattered about her feet, in strange alliance
With the keen wolf-hound sleeping undistraught;

Scales, hour-glass, bell, and magic-square above;
The grave and solid infant perched beside,
With open winglets that might bear a dove,
25 Intent upon its tablets, heavy-eyed;
Her folded wings as of a mighty eagle,
But all too impotent to lift the regal
Robustness of her earth-born strength and pride;

And with those wings, and that light wreath which seems
30 To mock her grand head and the knotted frown
Of forehead charged with baleful thoughts and dreams,
The household bunch of keys, the housewife's gown
Voluminous, indented, and yet rigid
As if a shell of burnished metal frigid,
35 The feet thick shod to tread all weakness down;

The comet hanging o'er the waste dark seas,
The massy rainbow curved in front of it,
Beyond the village with the masts and trees;
The snaky imp, dog-headed, from the Pit,
40 Bearing upon its batlike leathern pinions
Her name unfolded in the sun's dominions,
The 'MELENCOLIA' that transcends all wit.

Thus has the artist copied her, and thus
Surrounded to expound her form sublime,
45 Her fate heroic and calamitous;
Fronting the dreadful mysteries of Time,
Unvanquished in defeat and desolation,
Undaunted in the hopeless conflagration
Of the day setting on her baffled prime.

50 Baffled and beaten back she works on still,
Weary and sick of soul she works the more,
Sustained by her indomitable will:
The hands shall fashion and the brain shall pore
And all her sorrow shall be turned to labour,
55 Till death the friend-foe piercing with his sabre
That mighty heart of hearts ends bitter war.

21 With the prone creature for dissection brought. MS. T. had to change the
line after reading in Ruskin's *Modern Painters* 5 (*Works* 7.314) that the
animal was a sleeping wolf-hound rather than a dead sheep, but thought the
revision 'a villainous makeshift' (letter to W. M. Rossetti, 30 Jan. 1874).
55 piercing] cleaving MS.

But as if blacker night could dawn on night,
   With tenfold gloom on moonless night unstarred,
A sense more tragic than defeat and blight,
60   More desperate than strife with hope debarred,
More fatal than the adamantine Never
Encompassing her passionate endeavour,
   Dawns glooming in her tenebrous regard:

The sense that every struggle brings defeat
65   Because Fate holds no prize to crown success;
That all the oracles are dumb or cheat
   Because they have no secret to express;
That none can pierce the vast black veil uncertain
Because there is no light beyond the curtain;
70   That all is vanity and nothingness.

Titanic from her high throne in the north,
   That City's sombre Patroness and Queen,
In bronze sublimity she gazes forth
   Over her Capital of teen and threne,
75   Over the river with its isles and bridges,
The marsh and moorland, to the stern rock-ridges,
   Confronting them with a coeval mien.

The moving moon and stars from east to west
   Circle before her in the sea of air;
80   Shadows and gleams glide round her solemn rest.
   Her subjects often gaze up to her there:
The strong to drink new strength of iron endurance,
The weak new terrors; all, renewed assurance
   And confirmation of the old despair.

65 **Fate**] life MS.
68 **black**] dark MS.
71 **Titanic**] Gigantic MS.
73 **sublimity**] austerity MS.
74 **Capital...threne**] dark metropolis of threne MS.   **threne** song of lamentation, threnody.
75 The river with its islands and its bridges MS.
82 **iron endurance**] stern defiance MS.
83–4 The weak new terror sapping self-reliance | And all new confirmation of Despair. MS.

Algernon C. Swinburne

Algernon Charles Swinburne was born in the year of Queen Victoria's accession. He died in 1909. In terms of both poetic subject-matter and technique he often strikes one as being Shelley's heir: the poetic line is impetuous and musical and the image of the poet he projected has affinities with Shelley's, especially in the aristocratic disdain of the bourgeoisie, the fastidious classical tastes, the political radicalism, the emotional excitability. Like Shelley, he felt the need to develop a vivid poetic persona, and between about 1860 and 1880 he was the dominant poetic figure in the public's imagination. Like Hopkins, S. was a son of Balliol, but in the 1850s it was a college with an ethos different from that of a decade later, dominated as it was by the 'Old Mortality' club, whose attitudes Hopkins' 'Hexameron' set out to attack. From Rossetti, whom S. met at the time of the decoration of the Oxford Union (1857), came much of the excitement of aestheticism; but the disciple outstripped the master in the panache of his excesses. S. is a difficult figure for us to apprehend, especially when we know him only by the standard poetry of the anthologies. It is easy to miss his sense of humour if one only reads the poetry (some of his prose makes one laugh aloud); it is easy to forget his modernity (he looked with much more fiery enthusiasm than Arnold to the modern literature of other countries). At this distance he seems precious and limited; and we are prone to accept the reservations of Hopkins (*Dixon Correspondence* 156–7) and T. S. Eliot ('Swinburne as poet') as the last word not only on the poems but the whole career.

Something like premature death set in in 1879 when Theodore Watts-Dunton became a custodian of the national monument at the Pines, Putney.

Editions The standard edition of S. is the 'incomplete and shockingly corrupt' (Hyder) 'Bonchurch' (1925–7) The standard edition of the letters is by C. Y. Lang (6 vols, 1959–62).

Biographies and criticism There are biographies by G. Lafourcade (1932) and J. O. Fuller (1968). T. E. Connolly *S.'s Theory of Poetry* (1964), R. L. Peters *The Crown of Apollo* (Detroit 1965) and M. B. Raymond *S.'s Poetics: Theory and Practice* (1970) study the poetic theory. S. is discussed in L. Stevenson *The Pre-Raphaelite Poets* (Chapel Hill 1972) 184–252. I. Fletcher's pamphlet in the *Writers and their Work* series (1973) is an excellent introduction. C. K. Hyder surveys the field of S. studies in Faverty 228–50.

Abbreviations

1865	*Atalanta in Calydon*
1866	*Poems and Ballads.*
Chew	S. C. Chew *Swinburne* (1931).
McGann	J. J. McGann *S. An Experiment in Criticism* (1972).

129 Atalanta in Calydon: extract

Date The drama composed between summer 1863 and Feb. 1864.

The first chorus, beginning at line 65, celebrates the return of spring as an equivocal blessing. S. enters into the tragic spirit of the Dionysian festivals of spring, in which Artemis hunts winter. The movement of the complete play is adumbrated in miniature. S. began composition of *Atalanta* here. He dedicated it to Landor, who died six months before its publication.

S.'s source probably Ovid *Met.* 10.560–739.

MSS Since S. gave manuscripts of the choruses to his friends, they are now as scattered as the bones of Osiris: see C. Y. Lang '*Atalanta* in Manuscript' *Yale Univ. Lib. Gaz.* 37 (1963) 19–24. The *B.L. MS.* lacks the first two strophes. C. Y. Lang *Yale Univ. Lib. Gaz.* 27 (1953) 119–122 prints 24 lines of a very early draft of the chorus (*Neufeld MS.*).

Discussion Chew 57–65; McGann 95–107.

Publication *1865*.

CHORUS

1

65 When the hounds of spring are on winter's traces,
   The mother of months in meadow or plain
  Fills the shadows and windy places
   With lisp of leaves and ripple of rain;
  And the brown bright nightingale amorous
70 Is half assuaged for Itylus,
  For the Thracian ships and the foreign faces,
   The tongueless vigil, and all the pain.

2

  Come with bows bent and with emptying of quivers,
   Maiden most perfect, lady of light,
75 With a noise of winds and many rivers,
   With a clamour of waters, and with might;
  Bind on thy sandals, O thou most fleet,
  Over the splendour and speed of thy feet,
  For the faint east quickens, the wan west shivers,
80 Round the feet of the day and the feet of the night.

66 The mother of months Diana or Artemis.

70 Itylus the son of Tereus, King of Thrace, killed by his mother Procne in revenge for the rape of her sister Philomela by Tereus.

72 The tongueless vigil Philomela's tongue was torn out: later she was changed into a nightingale.

73–77 With a noise of all the winds and all the rivers, | With a clamour of great waters, and with might, | With bows bending, and with emptying of quivers, | Rise, put on thy beauty, gird thyself with light (*Neufeld MS.* st. 4).

[129] Algernon C. Swinburne

3

Where shall we find her, how shall we sing to her,
 Fold our hands round her knees, and ´cling?
O that man's heart were as fire and could spring to her,
 Fire, or the strength of the streams that spring!
85 For the stars and the winds are unto her
 As raiment, as songs of the harp-player;
For the risen stars and the fallen cling to her,
 And the southwest-wind and the west-wind sing.

4

For winter's rains and ruins are over,
90 And all the season of snows and sins;
The days dividing lover and lover,
 The light that loses, the night that wins;
And time remembered is grief forgotten,
And frosts are slain and flowers begotten,
95 And in green underwood and cover
 Blossom by blossom the spring begins.

5

The full streams feed on flower of rushes,
 Ripe grasses trammel a travelling foot,
The faint fresh flame of the young year flushes
100 From leaf to flower and flower to fruit;
And fruit and leaf are as gold and fire,
And the oat is heard above the lyre,
And the hoofed heel of a satyr crushes
 The chestnut-husk at the chestnut-root.

6

105 And Pan by noon and Bacchus by night,
 Fleeter of foot than the fleet-foot kid,
Follows with dancing and fills with delight
 The Maenad and the Bassarid;
And soft as lips that laugh and hide
110 The laughing leaves of the trees divide,
And screen from seeing and leave in sight
 The god pursuing, the maiden hid.

82–7 Her who is more than love or than spring? | Wine shall we shed for her, wreathes shall we bring to her, | Life shall we give her, and fire shall we bring? | For her feet are fair in the wet sweet ways, | From the sea-bank to the sea-bays, | And the risen stars and the fallen cling to her, (*B.L. MS.*).
102 the oat the straw pipe of the shepherd, signifying a ruder music than the Apollonian lyre.
108 Maenad and the Bassarid female followers of Bacchus.

7

The ivy falls with the Bacchanal's hair
Over her eyebrows hiding her eyes;
115 The wild vine slipping down leaves bare
Her bright breast shortening into sighs;
The wild vine slips with the weight of its leaves,
But the berried ivy catches and cleaves
To the limbs that glitter, the feet that scare
120 The wolf that follows, the fawn that flies.

130 Hymn to Proserpine
(After the Proclamation in Rome of the Christian Faith)

Date of composition unknown.

In 311 the Emperor Galerius made the edict of toleration of the Christian faith; in 313 the Emperor Constantine's Edict of Milan proclaimed official toleration; and in 379–85 Christianity was established as the religion of the Empire by Theodosius the Great. S. described the poem as 'the deathsong of spiritual decadence'. Writing to Lady Trevelyan (10 Dec. 1865) S. said he had been 'advised to omit [poems such as the *Hymn to Proserpine* and the *Last Pagan*] as likely to hurt the feeling of a religious public' (Lang *Letters* 1.141). Ruskin had misgivings about the morality of S., but wrote: 'I've got the original MS of the Hymn to Proserpine, and wouldn't part with it for much more than leaf gold' (Lang *Letters* 1. 184).

Publication *1866*. R. Peters *PMLA* 83 (1968) 1400–06 studies the work-sheets (Huntington Library), but makes several mistakes in transcription.

Vicisti, Galilaee

I have lived long enough, having seen one thing, that love hath
an end;
Goddess and maiden and queen, be near me now and befriend.
Thou art more than the day or the morrow, the seasons that
laugh or that weep;
For these give joy and sorrow; but thou, Proserpine, sleep.
5 Sweet is the treading of wine, and sweet the feet of the dove;
But a goodlier gift is thine than foam of the grapes or love.
Yea, is not even Apollo, with hair and harpstring of gold,
A bitter God to follow, a beautiful God to behold?

Epigraph Thou hast conquered, Galilean. Lat. trans. of Theodoret *Hist. Eccles.* 3.20: the dying words of the Emperor Julian (361–3). Ch. 23 of Gibbon's *The Decline and Fall of the Roman Empire* describes the hopeless attempts of Julian to restore the vanished spirit of paganism.

4 Proserpine Queen of the Underworld.

8 A bitter God witness the flaying of Marsyas.

[130] Algernon C. Swinburne

I am sick of singing: the bays burn deep and chafe: I am fain
10   To rest a little from praise and grievous pleasure and pain.
For the Gods we know not of, who give us our daily breath,
We know they are cruel as love or life, and lovely as death.
O Gods dethroned and deceased, cast forth, wiped out in a
day!
From your wrath is the world released, redeemed from your
chains, men say.
15   New Gods are crowned in the city; their flowers have broken
your rods;
They are merciful, clothed with pity, the young compassionate
Gods.
But for me their new device is barren, the days are bare;
Things long past over suffice, and men forgotten that were.
Time and the Gods are at strife; ye dwell in the midst thereof,
20   Draining a little life from the barren breasts of love.
I say to you, cease, take rest; yea, I say to you all, be at peace,
Till the bitter milk of her breast and the barren bosom shall
cease.
Wilt thou yet take all, Galilean? but these thou shalt not
take,
The laurel, the palms and the paean, the breast of the nymphs
in the brake;
25   Breasts more soft than a dove's that tremble with tenderer
breath;
And all the wings of the loves, and all the joy before death;
All the feet of the hours that sound as a single lyre,
Dropped and deep in the flowers, with strings that flicker
like fire,
More than these wilt thou give, things fairer than all these
things?
30   Nay, for a little we live, and life hath mutable wings.
A little while and we die; shall life not thrive as it may?
For no man under the sky lives twice, outliving his day.
And grief is a grievous thing, and a man hath enough of
his tears:
Why should he labour, and bring fresh grief to blacken his
years?
35   Thou hast conquered, O pale Galilean; the world has grown
grey from thy breath;
We have drunken of things Lethean, and fed on the fulness
of death.

9 **bays** laurel leaves of the poet's wreath.
15 Christ and his saints.
26 **loves** amoretti, Cupids *OED* 5b.

466

Laurel is green for a season, and love is sweet for a day;
But love grows bitter with treason, and laurel outlives
    not May.
Sleep, shall we sleep after all? for the world is not sweet
    in the end;
For the old faiths loosen and fall, the new years ruin
    and rend.
40   Fate is a sea without shore, and the soul is a rock
    that abides;
But her ears are vexed with the roar and her face with the
    foam of the tides.
O lips that the live blood faints in, the leavings of racks
    and rods!
O ghastly glories of saints, dead limbs of gibbeted Gods!
45   Though all men abase them before you in spirit, and all
    knees bend,
I kneel not neither adore you, but standing, look to the end.
All delicate days and pleasant, all spirits and sorrows are cast
Far out with the foam of the present that sweeps to the surf of
    the past:
Where beyond the extreme sea-wall, and between the remote
    sea-gates,
50   Waste water washes, and tall ships founder, and deep death
    waits:
Where, mighty with deepening sides, clad about with the seas
    as with wings,
And impelled of invisible tides, and fulfilled of unspeakable
    things,
White-eyed and poisonous-finned, shark-toothed and
    serpentine-curled,
Rolls, under the whitening wind of the future, the wave of
    of the world.
55   The depths stand naked in sunder behind it, the storms flee
    away;
In the hollow before it the thunder is taken and snared as a
    prey;
In its sides is the north-wind bound; and its salt is of all men's
    tears;

47–71 *H.MS.* draft.   **cast]** whirled *H.MS.* canc.
48 sweeps] swells MS. canc.
49 between...gates] (*a*) beyond the reach and the reef, (*b*) the black bare
fangs of the reef, earlier *H.MS.* canc. versions.
53 poisonous] murderous *H.MS.* canc.
56 prey] bird *H.MS.* canc.
57 salt] foam *H.MS.* canc.

With light of ruin, and sound of changes, and pulse of years:
With travail of day after day, and with trouble of hour upon
    hour;
60 And bitter as blood is the spray; and the crests are as fangs
    that devour:
And its vapour and storm of its stream as the sighing of spirits
    to be;
And its noise as the noise in a dream; and its depth as the
    roots of the sea:
And the height of its heads as the height of the utmost stars of
    the air:
And the ends of the earth at the might thereof tremble and
    time is made bare.
65 Will ye bridle the deep sea with reins, will ye chasten the high
    sea with rods?
Will ye take her to chain her with chains, who is older than
    all ye Gods?
All ye as a wind shall go by, as a fire shall ye pass and be
    past;
Ye are Gods, and behold, ye shall die, and the waves be upon
    you at last.
In the darkness of time, in the deeps of the years, in the
    changes of things,
70 Ye shall sleep as a slain man sleeps, and the world shall
    forget you for kings.
Though the feet of thine high priests tread where thy lords and
    our forefathers trod,
Though these that were Gods are dead, and thou being dead
    art a God,
Though before thee the throned Cytherean be fallen, and
    hidden her head,
Yet thy kingdom shall pass, Galilean, thy dead shall go down
    to thee dead.

58 changes] earthquake *H.MS.* canc.
61 its vapour] (*a*) the smoke (*b*) the foam earlier *H.M.S.* canc. versions.
65 deep sea] rivers *H.MS.* canc.
65–6 Cf. *Job* 38.11- 'Hitherto shalt thou come, but no further: and here shall
thy proud waves be stayed.'
68 and the waves...last] (*a*) and one shall endure at the last. (*b*) and the
waves shall devour you at last, earlier *H.MS.* canc. versions.
    There is a paradox here that the Gods are not immortal.
69 years] sea *H.MS.* canc.
71 And thy kingdom shall pass Galilean, thy dead shall go down to thee
dead. *H.MS.*
73 the throned Cytherean Venus – who was born in the sea and came to
shore on Cytherea.

75   Of the maiden thy mother men sing as a goddess with grace
      clad around;
     Thou art throned where another was king; where another
      was queen she is crowned.
     Yea, once we had sight of another: but now she is queen,
      say these.
     Not as thine, not as thine was our mother, a blossom of
      flowering seas,
     Clothed round with the world's desire as with raiment, and
      fair as the foam,
80   And fleeter than kindled fire, and a goddess, and mother of
      Rome.
     For thine came pale and a maiden, and sister to sorrow; but
      ours,
     Her deep hair heavily laden with odour and colour of flowers,
     White rose of the rose-white water, a silver splendour, a
      flame,
     Bent down unto us that besought her, and earth grew sweet
      with her name.
85   For thine came weeping, a slave among slaves, and rejected;
      but she
     Came flushed from the full-flushed wave, and imperial, her
      foot on the sea.
     And the wonderful waters knew her, the winds and the viewless
      ways,
     And the roses grew rosier, and bluer the sea-blue stream
      of the bays.
     Ye are fallen, our lords, by what token? we wist that ye
      should not fall.
90   Ye were all so fair that are broken; and one more fair than
      ye all.
     But I turn to her still, having seen she shall surely abide
      in the end;
     Goddess and maiden and queen, be near me now and
      befriend.
     O daughter of earth, of my mother, her crown and blossom
      of birth,
     I am also, I also, thy brother; I go as I came unto earth.
95   In the night where thine eyes are as moons are in heaven, the
      night where thou art,
     Where the silence is more than all tunes, where sleep overflows
      from the heart.

76 Christ's mother became Queen of Heaven.
80 mother of Rome Venus Genetrix – mother of Aeneas.
85 slave among slaves the Jews were a subject race, but Mary was not a slave.

Where the poppies are sweet as the rose in our world, and the
    red rose is white,
And the wind falls faint as it blows with the fume of the
    flowers of the night.
And the murmur of spirits that sleep in the shadow of
    Gods from afar
100 Grows dim in thine ears and deep as the deep dim soul of a
    star,
In the sweet low light of thy face, under heavens untrod by
    the sun,
Let my soul with their souls find place, and forget what is
    done and undone.
Thou art more than the Gods who number the days of our
    temporal breath;
For these give labour and slumber; but thou, Proserpina,
    death.
105 Therefore now at thy feet I abide for a reason in silence. I
    know
I shall die as my fathers died, and sleep as they sleep; even so.
For the glass of the years is brittle wherein we gaze for a span;
A little soul for a little bears up this corpse which is man.
So long I endure, no longer; and laugh not again, neither
    weep.
110 For there is no God found stronger than death; and death is a
    sleep.

97 poppies associated with Proserpine.
108 Cf. Epictetus *Morals* 63: 'For we ought to look upon that is done to the
body as things by the bye, and the improvement of the soul as that which
challenges our time.'

131 Nephelidia

Date ? One of S.'s parodies of contemporary poets in *Heptalogia, or The
Seven Against Sense* (the title itself is a parody of *Seven Against Thebes*). See
no. 57 (above pp. 192–3) for the Tennyson parody. This poem is a self parody,
both of his rhythms, diction, alliteration and shadowy eroticism.
Publication *1880*.

From the depth of the dreamy decline of the dawn through a
    notable nimbus of nebulous noonshine,
    Pallid and pink as the palm of the flag-flower that flickers
      with fear of the flies as they float,
Are they looks of our lovers that lustrously lean from a marvel
    of mystic miraculous moonshine,

These that we feel in the blood of our blushes that thicken
and threaten with throbs through the throat?
5   Thicken and thrill as a theatre thronged at appeal of an actor's
appalled agitation,
Fainter with fear of the fires of the future than pale with the
promise of pride in the past;
Flushed with the famishing fullness of fever that reddens with
radiance of rathe recreation,
Gaunt as the ghastliest of glimpses that gleam through the
gloom of the gloaming when ghosts go aghast?
Nay, for the nick of the tick of the time is a tremulous touch
on the temples of terror,
10   Strained as the sinews yet strenuous with strife of the dead
who is dumb as the dust-heaps of death:
Surely no soul is it, sweet as the spasm of erotic emotional
exquisite error,
Bathed in the balms of beatified bliss, beatific itself by
beatitude's breath.
Surely no spirit or sense of a soul that was soft to the spirit
and soul of our senses
Sweetens the stress of suspiring suspicion that sobs in the
semblance and sound of a sigh;
15   Only this oracle opens Olympian, in mystical moods and
triangular tenses –
"Life is the lust of a lamp for the light that is dark till the
dawn of the day when we die."
Mild is the mirk and monotonous music of memory,
melodiously mute as it may be,
While the hope in the heart of a hero is bruised by the
breach of men's rapiers, resigned to the rod;
Made meek as a mother whose bosom-beats bound with the
bliss-bringing bulk of a balm-breathing baby,
20   As they grope through the grave-yard of creeds, under skies
growing green at a groan for the grimness of God.
Blank is the book of his bounty beholden of old, and its
binding is blacker than bluer:
Out of blue into black is the scheme of the skies, and their
dews are the wine of the bloodshed of things;
Till the darkling desire of delight shall be free as a fawn
that is freed from the fangs that pursue her,
Till the heart-beats of hell shall be hushed by a hymn from
the hunt that has harried the kennel of kings.

5 Cf. *Stage Love* (1866) for a serious treatment of the theatrical metaphor.
7 rathe prompt, eager, earnest.
15 triangular tenses S. gives a triad of times.
23 For the motif of the pursued fawn cf. no. 129 line 120.

Thomas Hardy

Thomas Hardy was born in 1840. He began the career of an architect in the 1860s but by the end of the decade he was turning to writing – both poetry and novels. His first novel, *Desperate Remedies* (discounting the lost *The Poor Man and the Lady*), was published in 1871, but his first volume of poetry, *Wessex Poems*, was 1898. None of the poems he submitted to magazines in 1866 was printed. H. then is another anomaly in this collection, since his published work is after the terminal date; however, the poems selected here were written before 1890, even though they may have been revised for publication.

Criticism of the novels continues to demonstrate that there are close connections between H.'s life and work. This is even more true of the poetry: H. said in a letter of 1919, 'Speaking generally, there is more autobiography in a hundred lines of Mr. Hardy's poetry than in all the novels' (*Life* 392); and again, in 1923, he wrote, 'you will gather [from the poems] more personal particulars than I could give you in an interview, circumstances not being veiled in the verse as in the novels' (Bailey 4). Bailey writes: 'It seems that Hardy felt some compulsion to express himself in poetry about matters he did not wish known' (p. 5). Nevertheless, poetry at the best of times is treacherous ground on which to base firm biographical speculation, and it is dangerous in H.'s case to assume that the 'I' of the poems is always the historical H. He said in the Preface to *1898* that 'the pieces are in a large degree dramatic or personative in conception'.

Many of the circumstances of H.'s early life are still shrouded in mystery. We know that he fell in love with Emma Lavinia Gifford in Aug. 1872 and married her in Sept. 1874. She was the subject of much of his best poetry – some of the finest written after her death in Nov. 1912. But a regiment of other women troops through his poetic and fictional work: his roving fancy was one of the dominant elements in his creative imagination, and there is no knowing how much is based on actual liaisons. The exact nature and even the precise dates of his relationship with his cousin Tryphena Sparks are unknown: at one extreme, biographical inventiveness has fathered H.'s illegitimate child on her (L. Deacon and T. Coleman *Providence and Mr Hardy* (1966)). A more balanced assessment is found in Gittings. Longing, regret, nostalgia – these are the characteristic notes of H.'s poetry, and the intensity of these states is often heightened by the very impalpability of experience from which they develop. Like Emily Brontë, H. was pre-eminently a poet rather than a novelist. He stopped writing fiction 33 years before his death. Most of the best parts of the novels grow from perceptions that are poetic, and the handling of the language is poetic. H. seems not to have thought of diction being split up into compartments available for varying uses, but as totally available for the writer: this disregard of associations stood him in better stead as a poet than a novelist. His rhythm and verse forms are extremely varied: not perhaps because he was an experimenter, but because he searched spontaneously for forms that served his immediate expressive purposes. H. straddles two ages. It is not always easy to say which he belonged to: his earnest and even angry stoicism reminds us of the great Victorian free-thinkers; his deep sensitivity to the natural world seems closer to the C19 poetic traditions than ours, and yet his blunt directness and strained colloquiality seem to have more affinities with the C20. The literary influences on H. are too wide and varied to be of much immediate significance. He had a great fondness for Shelley. Of his contemporaries he seems to have been most impressed by Browning and Swinburne: he appreciated their skill to capture vivid dramatic moments. He continued the Tennysonian tradition of investing poetry with the spirit of scientific inquiry – especially its dark and melancholy manifestations. Philosophically, H. was a pessimistic thinker, touched by the gloom of Schopenhauer and Von Hartmann, yet not so as to be unable to find room for wry irony and an appreciative interest in ordinary human activity. At times it might seem that H. is trying to rival or answer Browning as a 'thinker', but his poetry, in his own words, records 'impressions, not convictions'. His is the unusual case of an artist who continues to develop and produce high-class work in old age. In his eighties he was still writing fine things, and adding to an *oeuvre* that ultimately reached almost 1,000 poems. What he was trying to do in his poetry is summed up in a Journal entry of Oct. 1896: 'Perhaps I can express more fully in verse ideas and emotions which run counter to the inert crystallized opinion – hard as a rock – which the vast body of men have vested interests in supporting' (*Life* 284).

Reputation The fame of Hardy the novelist has so far eclipsed Hardy the poet, but there are signs that this is changing. There have been half a dozen books exclusively on his poetry since the war. He is now seen not as a minor Victorian poet whose work petered out in Georgianism, but as a major poet who has been a dominant influence on a line of English poets that includes Sassoon, Graves, Pound, Dylan Thomas, Auden and Larkin.

Editions The standard edition of H.'s poetry is *The Complete Poems of T.H.* ed. J. Gibson (1976).

Biographies and criticism *The Life of T.H. 1840–1928* (1962) is actually H.'s autobiography. The best recent biographical study is R. Gittings *Young T.H.* (1975) and *The Older Hardy* (1978). The best critical studies are J. G. Southworth *The Poetry of T.H.* (New York 1947), S. Hynes *The Pattern of H.'s Poetry* (Chapel Hill 1961), K. Marsden *The Poems of T.H.: A Critical Introduction* (1969), D. Davie *T.H. and British Poetry* (1972), P. Zietlow *Moments of Vision: The Poetry of T.H.* (Cambridge, Mass. 1974) and T. Paulin *T.H.: The Poetry of Perception* (1975).

Abbreviations

1898	*Wessex Poems* (1898).
1912	*Poems* (the Wessex Edition) (1912).
Bailey	J. O. Bailey *The Poetry of T.H.* (Chapel Hill 1970).
Deacon and Coleman	L. Deacon and T. Coleman *Providence and Mr. Hardy* (1966).
Life	*The Life of T.H. 1840–1928* (1962) ed. F. E. Hardy.
Pinion	F. B. Pinion *A Commentary on the Poems of T.H.* (1976).
G.M.	*Gentleman's Magazine.*

132 The Bride-Night Fire

(A Wessex Tradition)

Date Written 1866; it was influenced by William Barnes (*Life* 302). Frederick Harrison took the poem seriously; H. recalled the misunderstanding in a conversation with Robert Graves: 'the man must have been thick-witted not to see that' (*Goodbye to All That* (1929) 376–7). Pinion 26 suggests an influence of the story, which H. may have known for many years, and which also appears in *Desperate Remedies* (1871). The glossary first appeared in *1912*.
Publication *The Gentleman's Magazine* (Nov. 1875); *1898; 1912.*

They had long met o' Zundays – her true love and she –
And at junketings, maypoles, and flings;
But she bode wi' a thirtover uncle, and he
Swore by noon and by night that her goodman should be
5   Naibour Sweatley – a wight often weak at the knee
From taking o' sommat more cheerful than tea –
Who tranted, and moved people's things.

She cried, 'O pray pity me!' Nought would be hear;
Then with wild rainy eyes she obeyed.
10   She chid when her love was for clinking off wi' her:
The pa'son was told, as the season drew near,
To throw over pu'pit the names of the pair
As fitting one flesh to be made.

The wedding-day dawned and the morning drew on;
15   The couple stood bridegroom and bride;
The evening was passed, and when midnight had gone
The feasters horned, 'God save the King', and anon
The pair took their homealong ride.

Title *The Fire at Tranter Sweatley's. A Wessex Ballad G.M.,* 1898.
1 Zundays] Sundays *G.M.*
3 bode] dwelt *G.M.*   **thirtover** crabbed *G.M.;* cross (H.'s note).
4 goodman] husband *G.M.*
5 wight] man *G.M.;* gaffer *1898.*
7 tranted traded as carrier (H.'s note).
10 clinking] vanishing *1912.*
12 pair] peäir *1898.*
17 horned] horned out *G.M.; 1898;* sang loudly (H.'s note).
18 The . . . ride] To their home the pair gloomily hied *G.M.;* The two homealong gloomily hied *1898;* The twain took their home-along ride *1912.*   **homealong** homeward (H.'s note).

The lover Tim Tankens mourned heart-sick and leer
20   To be thus of his darling deprived:
He roamed in the dark ath'art field, mound, and mere,
And, a'most without knowing it, found himself near
The house of the tranter, and now of his dear,
Where the lantern-light showed 'em arrived.

25   The bride sought her chamber so calm and so pale
That a northern had thought her resigned;
But to eyes that had seen her in tidetimes of weal,
Like the white cloud o' smoke, the red battlefield's vail,
That look spak' of havoc behind.

30   The bridegroom yet laitered a breaker to drain,
Then reeled to the linhay for more,
When the candle-snoff kindled some chaff from his grain –
Flames spread, and red vlankers wi' might and wi' main
Around beams, thatch, and chimley-tun roar.

35   Young Tim away yond, rafted up by the light,
Through brimbles and underwood tears,
Till he comes to the orchet, when crooping from sight
In the lewth of a codlin-tree, bivering wi' fright,
Wi' on'y her night-rail to cover her plight,
40   His lonesome young Barbree appears.

19 Tim] Sim *G.M.*   **leer**] drear *G.M.; 1898;* lear *1912;* empty-stomached (H.'s note).
21 ath'art] around *G.M.*
24 lantern-light] moving lights *G.M.*   **'em**] they'd *G.M.*
25 chamber] chimmer *G.M.*
27 tidetimes] seasons *G.M.*   **tidetimes** holidays (H.'s note).
28 vail] veil *G.M.*
29 spak'] told *G.M.*
30 laitered] loitered *G.M.* & *1912.*
31 linhay lean-to building (H.'s note).
32 some] the *G.M.*
33 Flames ... vlankers] Flames sprout and rush upwards *G.M.*   **red vlankers** fire-flakes (H.'s note).
34 chimley-tun chimney-stack (H.'s note).
35 away yond] in the distance *G.M.;* aroused *G.M.*   **rafted** roused (H.'s note).
37 when ... sight] where slap in his sight *G.M.;* when crooping thereright *1898.*
38 In the lewth of a] Beneath a bowed *G.M.*   **lewth** shelter (H.'s note).   **bivering**] trimbling *G.M.*   **bivering** with chattering teeth (H.'s note).
39 Wi' ... plight] In an old coat she'd found on a scarecrow bedight *G.M.;* to screen her from sight *1898.*   **night-rail** night-dress.
40 lonesome] gentle *G.M.*   **Barbree**] Barbara *G.M.*

[132] Thomas Hardy

Her cwold little figure half-naked he views
Played about by the frolicsome breeze,
Her light-tropping totties, her ten little tooes,
All bare and besprinkled wi' Fall's chilly dews,
45 While her great gallied eyes through her hair hanging loose
Shone as stars through a tardle o' trees.

She eyed him; and, as when a weir-hatch is drawn,
Her tears, penned by terror afore,
With a rushing of sobs in a shower were strawn,
50 Till her power to pour 'em seemed wasted and gone
From the heft o' misfortune she bore.

'O Tim, my *own* Tim I must call 'ee – I will!
All the world has turned round on me so!
Can you help her who loved 'ee, though acting so ill?
55 Can you pity her misery – feel for her still?
When worse than her body so quivering and chill
Is her heart in its winter o' woe!

'I think I mid almost ha' borne it,' she said,
'Had my griefs one by one come to hand;
60 But O, to be slave to thik husbird, for bread,
And then, upon top o' that, driven to wed,
And then, upon top o' that, burnt out o' bed,
Is more than my nater can stand!'

Like a lion 'ithin en Tim's spirit outsprung –
65 (Tim had a great soul when his feelings were wrung) –
'Feel for 'ee, dear Barbree?' he cried;

41 Her...naked] Her form in these cold mildewed tatters *1875*.
43 totties feet (H.'s note).
44 Fall autumn (H.'s note).
45 gallied] frightened *G.M.*; frightened (H.'s note). Cf. *Lear* 3.2.44: 'Gallow the very wanderers of the dark'.　　**hair]** ringlets *G.M.*
46 Shone as] Shone like *G.M.*; Sheened as *1898*.　　**tardle of]** tangle of *G.M.*; entanglement (H.'s note).
47 him] en *1898*.
48 afore] before *G.M.*
49 With] Wi' *G.M.*　　**shower]** torrent *G.M.*
51 heft weight (H.'s note).
53 has] hev *G.M.*; ha' *1898*.
58 ha'] hev *G.M.*　　**mid]** could *G.M.*
60 thik husbird] an uncle *G.M.*; that rascal (H.'s note).
64 Like...spirit] Sim's soul like a lion within him *G.M.*; Tim's soul like a lion 'ithin en *1898*.
66 Barbree] Barbie *G.M.*

476

And his warm working-jacket then straightway he flung
Round about her, and horsed her by jerks, till she clung
Like a chiel on a gipsy, her figure uphung
70   By the sleeves that he tightly had tied.

Over piggeries, and mixens, and apples, and hay,
They lumpered straight into the night;
And finding ere long where a halter-path lay,
Sighted Tim's house by dawn, on'y seen on their way
75   By a naibour or two who were up wi' the day,
But who gathered no clue to the sight.

Then tender Tim Tankens he searched here and there
For some garment to clothe her fair skin;
But though he had breeches and waistcoats to spare,
80   He had nothing quite seemly for Barbree to wear,
Who, half shrammed to death, stood and cried on a chair
At the caddle she found herself in.

There was one thing to do, and that one thing he did,
He lent her some clothes of his own,
85   And she took 'em perforce; and while swiftly she slid
Them upon her Tim turned to the winder, as bid,
Thinking, 'O that the picter my duty keeps hid
To the sight o' my eyes mid be shown!'

---

67 then straightway] about her *G.M., 1898.*
68 Round . . . clung] Made a back, horsed her up, till behind him she clung *G.M., 1898.*
69 her figure uphung] her round figure hung *G.M.*
70 By . . . tied] As the two sleeves before him he tied *G.M.;* By the sleeves that around her he tied *1898.*
71 mixens manure-heaps (H.'s note).
72 lumpered] stumbled *G.M.;* stumbled (H.'s note).
73 ere long] at length *G.M.;* by long *1898.*   **halter-path**] bridle-path *G.M.;* bridle-path (H.'s note).
74 Sighted Tim's house] At dawn reached Tim's house *1898.*
74–91 Shortened and bowdlerized in *G.M.,* completely altering the story, and providing an illustration of the principles of Grundyism that so afflicted his career as a novelist.
76 But who] But they *1898.*
81 shrammed numbed (H.'s note).
82 caddle quandary (H.'s note).
84 clothes] clouts *1898.*
85 swiftly she slid] in 'em she slid *1898.*
86 Tim turned to the winder, as modestly bid, *1898.*

In the tallet he stowed her; there huddied she lay,
90   Shortening sleeves, legs, and tails to her limbs;
But most o' the time in a mortal bad way,
Well knowing that there'd be the divel to pay
If 'twere found that, instead o' the elements' prey,
She was living in lodgings at Tim's.

95   'Where's the tranter?' said men and boys; 'where can he be?'
'Where's the tranter?' said Barbree alone.
'Where on e'th is the tranter?' said everybod-y:
They sifted the dust of his perished roof-tree,
And all they could find was a bone.

100   Then the uncle cried, 'Lord, pray have mercy on me!'
And in terror began to repent.
But before 'twas complete, and till sure she was free,
Barbree drew up her loft-ladder, tight turned her key –
Tim bringing up breakfast and dinner and tea –
105   Till the news of her hiding got vent,

Then followed the custom-kept rout, shout, and flare
Of a skimmity-ride through the naibourhood, ere
Folk had proof o' wold Sweatley's decay.

---

89 tallet loft (H.'s note).   **huddied** hidden (H.'s note).
90 The incident of Barbree hiding in Tim's house, and changing into his clothes is a comic version of the similar episode in *Jude the Obscure* Part 3 Ch. 3.
91 mortal bad] terrible *G.M.*
92 the divel] the piper *G.M.*
93 If 'twere] When 'twas *G.M.*
95 he] er *1898*.
97 e'th] earth *G.M.*
104 Tim bringing up] Sim handing in *G.M.*
105 Till the news of her hiding got vent] Till the crabbed man gied his consent *G.M.*
106 Then ... ere] There was skimmity riding with rout, shout, and flare, | In Weatherbury, Stokeham, and Windleton, ere *G.M. G.M.* places the event in a way that the later texts do not: Weatherbury is Puddletown, Stokeham is Milborne Stileham (?), Windleton is Tincleton. Skimmity riding is a mocking procession to draw attention to shrewish or unfaithful wives. The word perhaps derives from skimming ladle, with which wives beat their husbands. The classic description of such a ride is in *The Mayor of Casterbridge*, Ch. 39. The year before the poem was written, 'A Gossip About Lyme Regis' says, 'The "skymmington" is still used for henpecked husbands and shrewish wives'. *St. James's Magazine* 511.
108 Folk ... wold] They had proof of old *G.M.;* old (H.'s note).

Whereupon decent people all stood in a stare,
110 Saying Tim and his lodger should risk it, and pair:
So he took her to church. An' some laughing lads there
Cried to Tim, 'After Sweatley!' She said, 'I declare
I stand as a maiden to-day!'

109–13 The Mellstock and Yalbury folk stood in a stare │ (The tranter owned houses and garden-ground there), │ But little did Sim or his Barbara care, │ For he took her to church the next day. *G.M.*

133 Hap

Date 1866 (H.'s date).
 A key statement of one of H.'s intellectual positions: that the forces governing man are indifferent to him (the other belief, that there is a willed malevolence in fate, he maintained less vigorously). H. realized that his philosophy would shock the orthodox: 'To cry out in a passionate poem that the Supreme Mover or Movers, the Prime Force or Forces, must be either limited in power, unknowing, or cruel...will cause [the vast body of men] merely a shake of the head...' In *Life* 48 H. writes: 'The world does not despise us; it only neglects us.'
Publication *1898.*

If but some vengeful god would call to me
    From up the sky, and laugh: 'Thou suffering thing,
Know that thy sorrow is my ecstasy,
    That thy love's loss is my hate's profiting!'

5 Then would I bear it, clench myself, and die,
    Steeled by the sense of ire unmerited;
Half-eased in that a Powerfuller than I
    Had willed and meted me the tears I shed.

But not so. How arrives it joy lies slain,
10   And why unblooms the best hope ever sown?
– Crass Casualty obstructs the sun and rain,
    And dicing Time for gladness casts a moan...
These purblind Doomsters had as readily strown
Blisses about my pilgrimage as pain.

Title *Chance* MS.
5 Then would I bear, and clench myself, and die, *1898.*
7 Half-eased in] Half-eased, too, *1898.*
10 unblooms fails to bloom; not in *OED.*
11 Casualty Chance (as a state of things) *OED* 1.
12 Cf. the lurid dicing scene in *The Return of the Native* Bk 3 Ch. 8.

134 Neutral Tones

Date 1867 (H.'s date); but Deacon and Coleman 81–2 suggest it could be later (1871), from the time H. and Tryphena Sparks went through the crisis of separation.

The pond may be Rushy Pond, near Puddletown. For a novelistic presentation of a visually intense memory associated with a pond see *Far from the Madding Crowd* Ch. 5. The poem is in the *In Memoriam* stanza. **Publication** *1898*.

> We stood by a pond that winter day,
>   And the sun was white, as though chidden of God,
>   And a few leaves lay on the starving sod;
>   – They had fallen from an ash, and were gray.
>
> 5   Your eyes on me were as eyes that rove
>   Over tedious riddles of years ago;
>   And some words played between us to and fro
> On which lost the more by our love.
>
> The smile on your mouth was the deadest thing
> 10   Alive enough to have strength to die;
>   And a grin of bitterness swept thereby
> Like an ominous bird a-wing...
>
> Since then, keen lessons that love deceives,
>   And wrings with wrong, have shaped to me
> 15   Your face, and the God-curst sun, and a tree,
>   And a pond edged with grayish leaves.

Title suggests a scene without colour, but the emotion of the poem (*pace* Pinion 7: 'It is as if the poet were trying to present a non-subjective impression') is, by contrast, very strong.

1–2 Cf. *The Woodlanders* Ch. 4: 'The bleared white visage of a sunless winter day emerged like a dead-born child.'

3 starving perhaps both perished with cold and withered from lack of nutriment.

6 Over tedious riddles solved long ago; *1898*.

135 Her Dilemma: (In———Church)

Date 1866 (H.'s date). L. Deacon *The Moules and Thomas Hardy* (1968) 130 suggests 1872/3, since she is convinced the poem is about the love-affair between Horace Moule and Tryphena Sparks. Gittings however, *Young Thomas Hardy* 243, thinks it very unlikely that Moule ever knew her.

1898 was accompanied by the drawing (see opposite) of Fordington St George church, of which Moule's father was the Vicar. L. Deacon 131–2 also cites a church scene between Aeneas Manston and Cytherea Graye

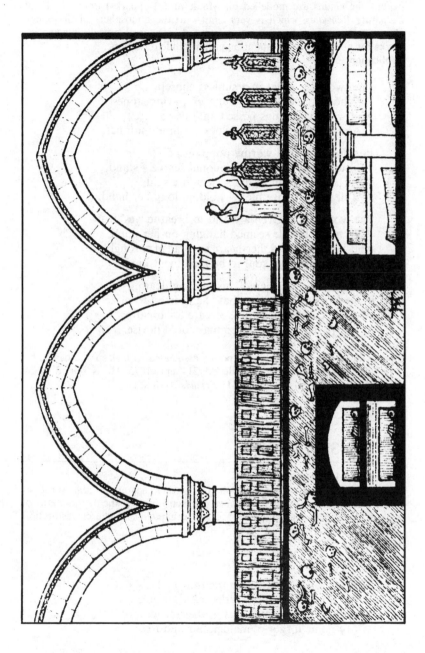

(whom she claims are modelled on Moule and T. Sparks) from Ch. 12 of
Desperate Remedies, which is very similar to the atmosphere of the poem.
However, too many details are unconfirmed by sources outside imaginative
works for us to be certain about biographical identifications.
Publication *1898*.

> The two were silent in a sunless church,
>   Whose mildewed walls, uneven paving-stones.
> And wasted carvings passed antique research;
>   And nothing broke the clock's dull monotones.
>
> 5 Leaning against a wormy poppy-head,
>   So wan and worn that he could scarcely stand,
>   – For he was soon to die, – he softly said,
>   'Tell me you love me!' – holding long her hand.
>
> She would have given a world to breathe 'yes' truly,
> 10 So much his life seemed hanging on her mind,
> And hence she lied, her heart persuaded throughly
>   'Twas worth her soul to be a moment kind.
>
> But the sad need thereof, his nearing death, ˙
>   So mocked humanity that she shamed to prize
> 15 A world conditioned thus, or care for breath
>   Where Nature such dilemmas could devise.

5 poppy-head carved pew-end; the poppy associated with sleep and death.
7 Horace Moule committed suicide on 21 Sept. 1873. He is buried in St
George's Fordington (see '*Before My Friends Arrived*').
8 long] hard *1898*.

136 She, To Him

Date 1866 (H.'s date).
  This sequence of poems shows H. getting nearer to the spirit of
Shakespeare than any other C19 poet. The sensitivity to the depradations of
time is Shakespearean, heightened for H., perhaps, by his church restoration
work.
Publication *1898*.

1

> When you shall see me in the toils of Time,
>   My lauded beauties carried off from me,
> My eyes no longer stars as in their prime,
>   My name forgot of maiden fair and free;

1 When you shall see me lined by tool of Time, *1898*.

5   When, in your being, heart concedes to mind,
       And judgement, though you scarce its process know,
    Recalls the excellencies I once enshrined,
       And you are irked that they have withered so:

    Remembering mine the loss is, not the blame,
10   That Sportsman Time but rears his brood to kill,
    Knowing me in my soul the very same –
       One who would die to spare you touch of ill! –
    Will you not grant to old affection's claim
       The hand of friendship down life's sunless hill?

9 Remembering that with me lies not the blame, *1898.*
10 Cf. *The Puzzled Game-Birds* and *Tess* Ch. 41, where pheasants are associated with the victimization of Fate. Pinion 170–1 discusses 'the insignificance of the individual in time and space' as an important theme.

2

Perhaps, long hence, when I have passed away,
    Some other's feature, accent, thought like mine,
Will carry you back to what I used to say,
    And bring some memory of your love's decline.
5   Then you may pause awhile and think, 'Poor jade!'
    And yield a sigh to me – as ample due,
Not as the tittle of a debt unpaid
    To one who could resign her all to you –

And thus reflecting, you will never see
10   That your thin thought, in two small words conveyed,
Was no such fleeting phantom-thought to me,
    But the whole life wherein my part was played;
And you amid its fitful masquerade
A thought – as I in your life seem to be!

1–4 This theme, of the identity of the loved object partly visible in others, is what makes specific biographical identifications in H. so treacherous. MS. adds, referring to Ch. 6, 'Prosed in *Desperate Remedies*'.
5 Cf. *Desperate Remedies* 13.4: 'And they will pause for just an instant, and give a sigh to me, and think, "Poor Girl!"'
6 as ample due] as gift benign *1898.* H.'s revision makes the sense more Shakepearean.
8 resign her all to you –] to you her all resign – *1898.*
14 your life seem to be!] yours but seem to be. *1898.*

                                        3
    I will be faithful to thee; aye, I will!
    And Death shall choose me with a wondering eye
    That he did not discern and domicile
       One his by right ever since that last good-bye!

5   I have no care for friends, or kin, or prime
       Of manhood who deal gently with me here;
    Amid the happy people of my time
       Who work their love's fulfilment, I appear

    Numb as a vane that cankers on its point,
10   True to the wind that kissed ere canker came:
    Despised by souls of now, who would disjoint
       The mind from memory, making life all aim,
    My old dexterities in witchery gone,
       And nothing left for love to look upon.

1 Cf. Shakespeare *Sonnets* 123 line 14: 'I will be true, despite thy scythe and thee.'
9–10 The speaker will rust on the spot, pointing in the direction of the wind (the love) she is faithful to.
13 dexterities in witchery] dexterities of hue quite *1898*.

                                        4
    This love puts all humanity from me;
       I can but maledict her, pray her dead,
    For giving love and getting love of thee –
       Feeding a heart that else mine own had fed!

5   How much I love I know not, life not known,
       Save as one unit I would add love by;
    But this I know, my being is but thine own –
       Fused from its separateness by ecstasy.

    And thus I grasp thy amplitudes, of her
10   Ungrasped, though helped by nigh-regarding eyes;
    Canst thou then hate me as an envier
       Who see unrecked what I so dearly prize?
    Believe me, lost one, love is lovelier
       The more it shapes its moan in selfish-wise.

2 maledict curse; *OED*'s first ex. 1780.

137 In a Wood

(from *The Woodlanders*)

Date 1887: 1896 (H.'s date).
A poetic version of the harshly realistic view of nature in Ch. 7 of *The Woodlanders* (1887). In marked contrast to the Wordsworthian view of a wood as an image of harmonious society.
Publication *1898*.

 Pale beech and pine so blue,
  Set in one clay
 Bough to bough cannot you
  Live out your day?
5 When the rains skim and skip,
 Why mar sweet comradeship,
 Blighting with poison-drip
  Neighbourly spray?

 Heart-halt and spirit lame,
10 City-oppressed,
 Unto this wood I came
  As to a nest;
 Dreaming that sylvan peace
 Offered the harrowed ease –
15 Nature a soft release
  From men's unrest.

 But, having entered in,
  Great growths and small
 Show them to men akin –
20 Combatants all.
 Sycamore shoulders oak,
 Bines the slim sapling yoke,
 Ivy-spun halters choke
  Elms stout and tall.

25 Touches from ash, O wych,
  Sting you like scorn!
 You, too, brave hollies twitch
  Sidelong from thorn.
 Even the rank poplars bear
30 Lothly a rival's air,

4 Live] Bide *1898*.
17–32 Cf. Spenser *Faerie Queene* 1.1.7–10, where the moral wood contains all but four of H.'s trees.
30 Lothly] Illy *1898*.

Cankering in black despair
If overborne.
Since, then, no grace I find
Taught me of trees,
35   Turn I back to my kind,
Worthy as these.
There at least smiles abound,
There discourse trills around,
There, now and then, are found
Life-loyalties.

138 Postponement

Date 1866 (H.'s date). Whatever personal allegory this may have had for H.
is now irrecoverable.
Publication *1898*.

Snow-bound in woodland, a mournful word,
Dropped now and then from the bill of a bird,
Reached me on wind-wafts; and thus I heard,
  Wearily waiting: –

5   'I planned her nest in a leafless tree,
But the passers eyed and twitted me,
And said: "How reckless a bird is her,
  Cheerily mating!"

'Fear-filled, I stayed me till summer-tide,
10   In lewth of leaves to throne her bride;
But alas! her love for me waned and died,
  Wearily waiting.

'Ah, had I been like some I see,
Born to an evergreen nesting-tree,
15   None had eyed and twitted me,
  Cheerily mating!'

10 lewth shelter (dial.).
13–16 H. in a conversation with V. H. Collins (27 Dec. 1920): H.: 'You see,
earlier in the poem the young man is described as not being able to marry
for want of money; and the woman as not waiting, but marrying someone
else.' C.: 'I understand that. The "being born to an evergreen tree" means,
then, simply and solely having money?' H.: 'Yes.' (*Talks with Thomas
Hardy*..., New York 1928, 23).

139 Nature's Questioning

Date 1880s ? H.'s '*1867*' *Nbk.* entry 182 quotes from an 1886 translation of Zola's *Abbé Mouret's Transgressions*: 'If you live all alone you get to see things queerly... The trees are no longer trees, the earth puts on the ways of a living being, the stones seem to tell you tales.' The poem may be related to the quotation.

H.'s drawing for *1898* was of a broken ornamental key, symbolic of the insoluble question, and perhaps also representing (Pinion 23) misfortune – associated with this device in *Far from the Madding Crowd* Ch. 33. In Ch. 24 of *The Woodlanders* H. describes 'that aspect of mesmeric passivity which the quietude of day-break lends to [objects]'.
Publication *1898.*

When I look forth at dawning, pool,
    Field, flock, and lonely tree,
    All seem to gaze at me
Like chastened children sitting silent in a school;

5   Their faces dulled, constrained, and worn,
    As though the master's ways
    Through the long teaching days
Had cowed them till their early zest was over-borne.

    Upon thems stirs in lippings mere
10   (As if once clear in call,
    But now scarce breathed at all) –
'We wonder, ever wonder, why we find us here!

    'Has some vast imbecility,
    Mighty to build and blend,
15   But impotent to tend,
Framed us in jest, and left us now to hazardry?

    'Or come we of an automaton
    Unconscious of our pains?
    Or are we live remains
20   Of Godhead dying downwards, brain and eye now gone?

    'Or is it that some high plan betides
    As yet not understood,
    Of evil stormed by good,
We the forlorn hope over which achievement strides?'

8 Their first terrestrial zest had chilled and overborne. *1898.*
9 **lippings** whisperings (a sense not recorded exactly or represented by quotation in *OED* or *EDD*); cf. Barnes (no. 33 p. 36 above), who uses 'lippèns' in the same sense.

25   Thus things around, No answerer I...
       Meanwhile the winds, and rains,
       And earth's old glooms and pains
    Are still the same, and life and death are neighbours nigh.

28 and ... nigh] and gladdest death neighbours nigh. *1898*.

140 In a Eweleaze Near Weatherbury

Date 1890 (H.'s date).

Bailey 105–6 identifies the spot as 2 miles from Higher Bockhampton. H.'s drawing accompanied the poem in *1898*. Deacon and Coleman 113 associate it with H.'s affair with Tryphena Sparks (d. 17 Mar. 1890), and another recollection of the same place in '*My Spirit Will not Haunt the Mound*'. Weatherbury is Puddletown. Novel parallels: *Two on a Tower* Ch. 2; *The Woodlanders* Ch. 4.

Hardy's drawing *1898*. It is curious that the spectacle lenses do not distort the landscape. There may be a symbolic significance in this: H.'s ageing has not distorted memory.

Publication *1898*.

    The years have gathered grayly
      Since I danced upon this leaze
    With one who kindled gaily
      Love's fitful ecstasies!

2 leaze grazing for ewes and lambs.

5   But despite the term as teacher,
      I remain what I was then
      In each essential feature
      Of the fantasies of men.

      Yet I note the little chisel
10   Of never-napping Time
      Defacing wan and grizzel
      The blazon of my prime.
      When at night he thinks me sleeping
      I feel him boring sly
15   Within my bones, and heaping
      Quaintest pains for by-and-by.

      Still, I'd go the world with beauty,
      I would laugh with her and sing,
      I would shun divinest duty
20   To resume her worshipping.
      But she'd scorn my brave endeavour,
      She would not balm the breeze
      By murmuring 'Thine for ever!'
      As she did upon this leaze.

5–8 Cf. '*I Look Into My Glass*' (1898) for H.'s notion of continuity of youthful feelings in an ageing body.
10 never-napping] ever-napping *1898*. H. discarded the original reading perhaps because it was obscure: v³1 *OED* to steal or snatch, with a suggestion of v³2 to cheat at dice – appropriate in view of H.'s interest in time as a gambler, e.g. in *Hap* (no. 133).
11 wan] ghast *1898*.   **grizzel** *OED* quotes this as only ex. of adv. 'horribly', but H. could intend the adj.: 'grey'.
12 blazon cf. Shakespeare *Sonnet* 106: 'the blazon of sweet beauty's best'.   **prime** also a favourite of Shakespeare: cf. *Sonnets* 3, 12, 70, 97.

Gerard Manley Hopkins

Gerard Manley Hopkins was born on 28 July 1844 at Stratford, Essex. He was the eldest of nine children. His father, a minor poet (though by profession the head of a firm of average adjusters), wrote *The Philosopher's Stone* (1843), and *Spicilegium Poeticum* (1892). The involvement in settling insurance for trading vessels and dealing with claims after shipwrecks may be traced in two of H.'s poems: *The Wreck of the Deutschland* and *The Loss of the Eurydice*. Two of his brothers (Arthur and Everard) became professional artists, and from an early age he himself took a great interest in

Gerard Manley Hopkins

draughtsmanship, producing landscapes in which the Pre-Raphaelite tradition of rendering the particularity of the scene is pursued to an extreme analogous to that of his verbal descriptions of nature. The family background was highly congenial to the budding creative artist.

He attended Highgate School in North London, where he won the Poetry Prize with *The Escorial* (1860). In October 1863 he went up to Balliol College, Oxford, as an Exhibitioner, to read classics. He was under the spell of a great many conflicting influences, ranging from the proto-aestheticism of Rossetti and Pater (his tutor for a time) on the one hand, to the mystical asceticism of the fag end of the Oxford Movement, represented by such figures as Pusey and Liddon, on the other. Somewhere in between was a Ruskinian element, which encouraged the close observation and recording of nature. A part of this activity led in the direction of dangerous aestheticism: the diaries show that H. gave up looking at the sky for Lent as an undergraduate. But another part led to a greater awareness of the immanence of God in the created world. And running alongside these interests were H.'s literary studies – official and unofficial – in which he saw adumbrations of his view of the world, not only at a theoretical level, but in the mode of existence of languages themselves. Contradictory and even irreconcilable as the various influences were, when H. made the decisive step of entering the Roman Catholic Church (October 1866), he was received by a renegade of an earlier Oxford generation, Dr Newman. Nevertheless he did not renounce his previous interests altogether, but modified and adapted them to his new mode of life in such a way that the 'taste' of himself became more distinctive and original than almost any English poet. One of the most striking things about H., both as man and as poet, is his particular quality, his originality, his uniqueness verging on downright oddity. The striking aspects are of mind. We have his very full diaries up to 1875. But they do not contain much about activities or friends; they are mainly concerned with the life of perception, and there is no doubt that in a comparatively uneventful life the important events were mental ones.

To join the Roman Church was a big step. It estranged him from his family (see no. 152), and it estranged him from whole sections of English Establishment life. To gain an impression of what an 'issue' it was in the Victorian period, one merely has to turn to *Jackson's Oxford Journal* for 27 March 1875 (the year of *The Wreck of the Deutschland*) to see the published list of converts to Rome – 'perverts' they are called in the article. Although the Catholics had been emancipated since 1828 they were still treated with suspicion, and were very much a minority church. The priests were often Irish and Italian, and the congregations working-class. H. moved from a situation in which he could easily have become deeply involved in the social machinery of orthodox English life to one where he was virtually an alien. A letter written soon after his conversion registers this: 'The masters' table appears to be the dregs of Great Britain...I am fallen among Radicals.' Even the forms of worship and conditions must have seemed abhorrent, and he wrote to his father that the last reason why anyone should join the Roman Church was the aesthetic one.

This feeling of alienation never left him, and it dominates many poems. But in his outcast situation, H. reached for a deeper kind of patriotic identification with England and Wales, based not on social and political allegiances, but spiritual and geographic. His awareness of the essential and vulnerable nature of the countryside, and of the more enduring and resilient nature of the people, is more acute than that of almost any other English poet. This act of identification doubtless struck deep and life-giving roots. The exile who returned to Oxford in 1879 sought out not his old human acquaintances (with the exception of Pater) but the Binsey Poplars and the Thames. His Journal for 8 April 1873 reads: 'The ash tree growing in the corner of the garden was felled. It was lopped first: I heard the sound and looking out and seeing it maimed there came at that moment a great pang and I wished to die and not to see the inscapes of the world destroyed any more.'

In 1868 H. entered the Society of Jesus, and began training for the priesthood. He attempted to destroy all his early poetry, but a certain amount has survived. All that had been published by this time was *Winter with the Gulf Stream* (1863) and *Barnfloor and Winepress* (1865). He 'resolved to write no more as not belonging to my profession, unless it were by the wish of my superiors'. There followed a seven-year silence, with the exception of *Ad Mariam* and *Rosa Mystica*, broken by *The Wreck of the Deutschland*, which was a remarkable extension of his earlier experimental practices. One may regret that an artist, whose genius needed to be fed in an atmosphere of openness and freedom, should have been fettered by external controls on his inner and outer life, and if it is true that a great poet is partly defined by bulk of output, then the qualified status of H. is largely to be attributed to his membership of the Society of Jesus. At the same time, however, the sense of strain, of bursting against barriers, of tautness, which is so much the hall-mark of all that is best and most characteristic of H., could only have been achieved when he was forced to sail against the wind. A characteristic tactic of H. was that whereas St Thomas Aquinas was the official theologian of the Jesuit order, H. found his views of individuality or *haecceitas* better catered for by Duns Scotus: a characteristic tactic was to extend his philosophy into the realms of poetic creation. The old aestheticism was not completely dormant, and he wrote: 'Poetry is in fact speech only employed to carry the inscape of speech for the inscape's sake – and therefore the inscape must be dwelt on.' 'Inscape' and the related term 'instress' are H.'s coinings to describe, respectively, the essential attributes of things, and the energy holding them in place. Another source of philosophic tension was Loyola's *The Spiritual Exercises* (1548), which taught at once strict principles of service and the necessity of employing the senses in contemplative exercises. He must have needed all the strength that self-abnegation could muster, since *The Month* refused to publish both his shipwreck poems, not for doctrinal reasons but because the Catholic organs were no less conservative in their views of the techniques of poetry than the rest of the British press.

H.'s theological studies had been pursued at St Bueno's College in North Wales, amongst the gently rolling hills of the Clwyd Valley. Here were the added side-attractions of learning Welsh and the skills of classical Welsh poetry, and of course beautiful scenery. As a parish priest, however, H. was to experience the horrors and depressions of Victorian urban life, and two poems in my selection grow from this (nos. 148 and 159). A lifeline to the literary and poetic world was the correspondence he maintained with a variety of poets and scholars, the most famous being Coventry Patmore, Robert Bridges and Richard Watson Dixon.

Gerard Manley Hopkins

In 1884 he was made Professor of Greek Literature at University College, Dublin. Although some aspects of the employment must have been pleasant for him, he felt the force of exile strongly, especially since he had little sympathy with Catholic supporters of Irish Nationalism, and found many of the administrative duties irksome. It is from this period that the so-called 'Terrible Sonnets' (nos. 151–156) date. His originality of mind continued to the last. In 1885 he studied musical composition, and in a very short space of time managed to make radical divergences from received views on the subject, in an entirely characteristic fashion. H. died on 8 June 1889 of typhoid fever, and was buried in Glasnevin cemetery, Dublin. He was only 45 years old.

Reputation and influence When H. died he was virtually unknown as a poet except to a very few people. Since the time when it has been usual for a poet to achieve his fame through the printed word there are probably only three poets whose fame as *major* poets has been entirely posthumous: Thomas Traherne, Robert Herrick and H. H. did not publish his major poems in his lifetime, because the Order did not wish it, and he anticipated that the publishers would find the works too revolutionary in technique. One hesitates to say that they were too revolutionary in vision, since although it is true that H.'s vision was completely out of key with that of the average Victorian reader, other poets of alienated vision managed to slip into circulation. H.'s rhythmical experiments and his views on diction may in theory have been different in degree rather than in kind from those of Clough, say, or Browning, but pushed to the degree found in H. his practice really amounts to a difference in kind. He rejected the techniques of syllabic verse for those of stressed verse (dominated by what he called 'Sprung Rhythm') and the fashion of poetic diction for a diction that although not closely resembling everyday speech once it got into his poetry, clearly had its origins there rather than in a Parnassian tradition. Robert Bridges thought H.'s poems odd, and one may follow his bewilderment in the correspondence, but he also recognized that they were remarkable. From the 1890s onwards he began to filter them into the public consciousness, publishing some in Miles's *Poets of the Century*, and some in *The Spirit of Man*. The first edition approaching completeness was Bridges's of 1918, which included H.'s preface.

This posthumous reputation has led to a curious situation in which it makes as much sense to see H.'s poetry as a twentieth-century phenomenon as a nineteenth. He seems to be a part of a movement that includes Dylan Thomas, James Joyce and E. E. Cummings, not merely because he may have influenced them, but because he appeals to the taste that has thrived on these poets. And on a broader view, when one thinks of the tough uncompromising poetry of Eliot and Auden, it is clear that they owe something, indirectly, to H., and that their work establishes a climate of opinion in which H. is more accessible than he would have been to a public nurtured on Patmore, Rossetti and Tennyson. Even so, there are many important senses in which H. *is* a great Victorian. It is better, ultimately, to see him as a poet fitting into this period rather than as a Rip van Winkle with a difference, waking up after a long sleep and finding the poetic world even more familiar than he remembered it.

The standard edition is now the 'fourth edition' of *1918* edited by W. H. Gardner and N. H. MacKenzie.

Gerard Manley Hopkins

The Main Manuscripts For a fuller survey of the mss see D. A. Bischoff 'The Manuscripts of G.M.H.' *Thought* 26 (1951) 551–80.
Biographies There is still no first rate biography in English, but Jean-Georges Ritz's *Le poète G.M.H., S.J. 1844–1889: Le Homme et l'oeuvre* (1963) may be consulted. G. F. Lahey's *G.M.H.* (1930) is too short for adequacy; the best material is still in the letters and journals. Specific aspects of H.'s life have been treated at fuller length in D. A. Downes *Victorian Portraits: Hopkins and Pater* (1965), A. Sulloway *G.M.H. and the Victorian Temper* (New York 1972), and A. Thomas *Hopkins the Jesuit* (1969).
Criticism The criticism of H. is colossal; the main works are listed in the abbreviations. There are two bibliographies: E. H. Cohen *Works and Criticism of G.M.H.: A Comprehensive Bibliography* (Washington: D.C. 1969) and T. Dunne *G.M.H.: A Comprehensive Bibliography* (Oxford 1976). J. Pick surveys the scholarship in Faverty 318–51. It would be risky to identify any one dominant trend in current criticism: suffice it to say that there is a tendency now for critics to concentrate on the Victorian aspects of Hopkins – perhaps as a reaction to the earlier vogues that regarded him as 'timeless'.

Abbreviations

Miles	A. H. Miles *The Poets and the Poetry of the Century* (1893).
1918	*Poems*. First edition, ed. R. Bridges (1918).
1930	*Poems*. Second edn, ed. C. Williams (1930).
1948	*Poems*. Third edn, ed. W. H. Gardner (1948).
1970	*Poems*. Fourth edn, ed. W. H. Gardner and N. H. MacKenzie (1970; first published 1967, rprtd. with corrections).
Journals	*The Journals and Papers of G.M.H.* ed. H. House and G. Storey (1959).
Sermons	*The Sermons and Devotional Writings of G.M.H.* ed. C. Devlin S.J. (1959).
Bridges Letters	*The Letters of G.M.H. to Robert Bridges* ed. C. C. Abbott (1935).
Dixon Corresp.	*The Correspondence of G.M.H. and Richard Watson Dixon* ed. C. C. Abbott (1935).
Further Letters	*Further Letters of G.M.H.* ed. C. C. Abbott (2nd edn 1956).
Gardner	W. H. Gardner *G.M.H. 1844–1889: A Study of Poetic Idiosyncrasy in Relation to Poetic Tradition* (2nd edn. 1948).
Keating	J. E. Keating *'The Wreck of the Deutschland': An Essay and Commentary* (Kent, Ohio 1963).
McChesney	D. McChesney *A Hopkins Commentary: An Explanatory Commentary on the Main Poems, 1876–89* (1968).
Mariani	P. L. Mariani *A Commentary on the Complete Poems of G.M.H.* (Ithaca, New York 1970).

Schneider	E. W. Schneider *The Dragon in the Gate: Studies in the Poetry of G.M.H.* (Berkeley and Los Angeles 1968).
Weyand	*Immortal Diamond: Studies in G.M.H.* ed. N. Weyand (New York 1949).

Manuscripts

A (Owned by Lord Bridges) Holographs and copies of poems.
B (Bodleian) Copied by R. Bridges from *A* up to 1883, but with emendations by H. and new poems up to 1887.
D (Owned by Lord Bridges) Holographs in *Dixon Letters*.
H (Bodleian) Miscellaneous drafts and some late poems and fragments.

141 The Wreck of the 'Deutschland'

Date 1875–6. The *Deutschland* was a German ship wrecked on 6–7 Dec. 1875 off the Kentish coast in the mouth of the Thames. The *Times* report reads: 'After 3 a.m. on Tuesday morning [7 Dec.] a scene of horror was witnessed. Some passengers clustered for safety within or upon the wheel-house, and on the top of other slight structures on deck. Most of the crew and many of the emigrants went into the rigging, where they were safe enough as long as they could maintain their hold. But the intense cold and long exposure told a tale.... Women and children and men were one by one swept away from their shelters on the deck. Five German nuns, whose bodies are now in the dead-house here, clasped hands and were drowned together, the chief sister, a gaunt woman of 6 ft. high, calling out loudly and often "O Christ, come quickly!" till the end came. The shrieks and sobbing of women and children are described by the survivors as agonizing' (11 Dec. 1875). Fuller quotation in Weyand 353–74 and *Further Letters* 440–3. The nuns referred to, who had been exiled from Germany by the Falck Laws, caught H.'s imagination. On 5 Oct. 1878 he writes: 'I was affected by the account and happening to say so to my rector he said that he wished some one would write a poem on the subject' (*Dixon Corresp.* 14). To his mother on 26 June 1876 he writes: 'I have asked Fr. Coleridge the editor [of *The Month*]...to take it, but I had to tell him that I felt sure he would personally dislike it very much, only that he was to consider not his tastes but those of the *Month*'s readers (*Further Letters* 138). His understanding was that the poem was to appear in the August number, but in a letter to his father of 6 Aug. 1876 he writes: 'my poem is not in the August *Month* and whether it will be in the September number or in any I cannot find out: altogether it has cost a good deal of trouble' (*Further Letters* 139). It was not published in H.'s own lifetime. He interpreted this as a rejection of his poetic abilities by his order. The poem gave difficulties to Bridges, who called it 'presumptious jugglery'; but H. tried to defend it in a letter of 21 May 1878 (*Bridges Letters* 50–1). Bridges obviously continued to find it difficult, not only because of its metrical experiments, but its 'full-blooded

Roman theology' and in *1918* he described the poem as 'a great dragon folded in the gate to forbid all entrance'. For C20 reactions to the poem see Gardner 1.38–70; Mariani 47–73; McChesney 33–50; P. Milward *A Commentary on G.M.H.'s 'The Wreck of the Deutschland'* (Tokyo 1968); J. E. Keating *'The Wreck of the Deutschland': an essay and commentary* (Kent, Ohio (1963).

Though originally written by H. in two parts, the content of the poem in fact falls into three main sections: Part the First: lines 1–80, meditation on God's power; and Part the Second: lines 81–168, the wreck and the poet's interpretation of its significance; and 169–280, general reflection on God's purposes and request for the nun to intercede for the conversion of Britain to Roman Catholicism.

It seems that H. interpreted the event as a possible miracle that would convert his countrymen to the true Church. He envisaged the possibility of such a conversion in 1881 – the 300th anniversary of the martyrdoms of Sherwin, Bryant and Campion: 'from which I expect of heaven some, I cannot guess what, great conversion or other blessing to the Church of England.' He thought that Christ had actually appeared to the nun on the *Deutschland*. This is H.'s most comprehensive poem, embracing as it does a study of the paradoxical nature of God, the similarly paradoxical character of the natural world, and the experience of the individual in the presence of these.

Rhythm and syntax Possibly the most striking feature of the poem is its rhythm. H. writes at length on rhythm in 'Rhythm and the other structural parts of rhetoric-verse' (*Journals* 267–89), in his Author's Preface (*1970* 45–9), and in a note on rhythm and scansion (*1970* 255–6). For detailed understanding these should be consulted. He writes: 'I had long had haunting my ear the echo of a new rhythm which now I realized on paper. To speak shortly, it consists in scanning by accents or stresses alone, without any account of the number of syllables, so that a foot may be one strong syllable or it may be many light and one strong. I do not say the idea is altogether new; there are hints of it in music, in nursery rhymes and jingles, in the poets themselves...' (*Dixon Corresp.* 14). On 25 Feb. 1878 he writes that he employs sprung rhythm 'because it is the nearest to the...natural rhythm of speech, the least forced, the most rhetorical and emphatic of all possible rhythms' (*Bridges Letters* 46). Schneider has experienced difficulty in scanning the poem, and remains sceptical about much of H.'s theorizing, but usually the stress falls on the first (or the only) syllable in each metrical foot, with the following number of stresses in the lines of each stanza: 2, 3, 4, 3, 5, 5, 4, 6. In Part 2 (from stanza 11) the first line of each stanza has 3 stresses. These stresses fall, and this applies to much of H.'s poetry, without regard to the number of syllables in each line. H. said that there were no 'outrides' in *The Wreck of the Deutschland*.

Diction and syntax·are as original as the rhythm. However much H. believed that his poetic language had its roots in everyday speech, the final impression is of a *made* language as individual (or 'selved' as H. called it) as any invented by other poets.

Publication *1918*, but stanza 1 in *The Spirit of Man* no. 53 (1916) (the original *A* version).

[141] Gerard Manley Hopkins

To the happy memory of five Franciscan nuns, exiles by the Falck Laws, drowned between midnight and morning of
Dec. 7th, 1875

PART THE FIRST

1

Thou mastering me
God! giver of breath and bread;
World's strand, sway of the sea;
Lord of living and dead;
5   Thou hast bound bones and veins in me, fastened me flesh,
And after it almost unmade, what with dread,
Thy doing: and dost thou touch me afresh?
Over again I feel thy finger and find thee.

2

I did say yes
10   O at lightning and lashed rod;
Thou heardest me truer than tongue confess
Thy terror, O Christ, O God;
Thou knowest the walls, altar and hour and night:
The swoon of a heart that the sweep and the hurl of thee
      trod
15   Hard down with a horror of height:
And the midriff astrain with leaning of, laced with fire of
stress.

3

The frown of his face
Before me, the hurtle of hell
Behind, where, where was a, where was a place?
20   I whirled out wings that spell

1–2 'God mastering me; | Giver of breath and bread;' *A* and *B*.
5 Cf. no. 154 line 11. See *Job* 10.8–11.
6 'And after at times almost unmade me with dread,' earlier draft in *A* and *B*.
10 H. notes (*Bridges Letters* 46): 'If it is forcible in prose to say "lashed: rod", am I obliged to weaken this in verse, which ought to be stronger, not weaker, into "láshed birch-ród" or something?'
20 spell Gardner and Peters suggest 'time', with 'that' as a demonstrative adj. The rhythm does not support this reading. Sister Mary Adorita makes the unlikely suggestion that H. means speel or spel (vb): to climb or ascend (*MLR* 70 (1955) 345–7). Boyle suggests (Weyand 335) the bird's wings spell out a cross. I believe spell is *OED* vb. 1 from O.E. *spellian* to discourse or preach. Elements of vb. 4 'to charm' may be present. This is a good illustration of the problem Bridges wrote about in his *SPE* tract 'Homophones' (1919). See *Sermons* 305.

And fled with a fling of the heart to the heart of
    the Host.
My heart, but you were dovewinged, I can tell,
    Carrer-witted, I am bold to boast,
To flash from the flame to the flame then, tower from
    the grace to the grace.

4

25   I am soft sift
       In an hourglass-at the wall
    Fast, but mined with a motion, a drift,
       And it crowds and it combs to the fall;
   I steady as a water in a well, to a poise, to a pane,
30   But roped with, always, all the way down from the tall
       Fells or flanks of the voel, a vein
Of the gospel proffer, a pressure, a principle, Christ's gift.

5

       I kiss my hand
       To the stars, lovely-asunder
35   Starlight, wafting him out of it; and
       Glow, glory in thunder;
Kiss my hand to the dappled-with-damson west:
Since, though he is under the world's splendour and wonder,
    His mystery must be instréssed, stressed;
40   For I greet him the days I meet him, and bless when I
    understand.

6

       Not out of his bliss
       Springs the stress felt
    Nor first from heaven (and few know this)

23 Carrier-witted with the homing instincts of a carrier pigeon. See *Ps.* 55: 'Oh that I had wings like a dove!'
24 'to leap, in imagination, from the inner flame to the fire of God, and from the revealed grace to the source of grace.'
27 Fast steady – the sand at the edge of an hourglass is still.
28 combs falls in ridges (a sense not quite recorded in *OED*). Close to 'combs' in line 107.
29 to a ... pane in a state of equilibrium and glasslike steadiness.
30 roped formed into viscous threads (*OED* vb. 1). The appearance given by streams running down steep hills, *Journals* 230.
31 voel bare hill or mountain.
32 proffer the act of offering.
34 lovely-asunder beautiful even though it emanates from a multiplicity of sources.
39 instress a H. coinage. For the importance of the concept of stress to H. see above p. 491.

Swings the stroke dealt –
45   Stroke and a stress that stars and storms deliver,
That guilt is hushed by, hearts are flushed by and melt –
But it rides time like riding a river
(And here the faithful waver, the faithless fable and miss).

7

It dates from day
50   Of his going in Galilee;
Warm-laid grave of a womb-life grey;
Manger, maiden's knee;
The dense and the driven Passion, and frightful sweat:
Thence the discharge of it, there its swelling to be,
55   Though felt before, though in high flood yet –
What none would have known of it, only the heart, being hard
at bay,

8

Is out with it! Oh,
We lash with the best or worst
Word last! How a lush-kept plush-capped sloe
60   Will, mouthed to flesh-burst,
Gush! – flush the man, the being with it, sour or sweet,
Brim, in a flash, full! – Hither then, last or first,
To hero of Calvary, Christ's feet –
Never ask if meaning it, wanting it, warned of it – men go.

9

65   Be adored among men,
God, three-numberèd form;
Wring thy rebel, dogged in den,
Man's malice, with wrecking and storm.
Beyond saying sweet, past telling of tongue,
70   Thou art lightning and love, I found it, a winter and warm;
Father and fondler of heart thou hast wrung:
Hast thy dark descending and most art merciful then.

---

48 fable *OED* vb. 4: To say or talk about fictitiously; to relate as in a fable, fiction, or myth; to fabricate, invent (as incident, a personage, story, etc.).
56 The heart of man in a state of suffering is best able to understand Christ's passion.
58–9 the best or worst word yes and no.
59–62 Awareness of the rich paradoxes of nature should shoot through man with the instantaneous picquancy of a sloe berry.

10

With an anvil-ding
And with fire in him forge thy will
75   Or rather, rather then, stealing as Spring
Through him, melt him but master him still:
Whether at once, as once at a crash Paul,
Or as Austin, a lingering-out swéet skíll,
Make mercy in all of us, out of us all
80 Mastery, but be adored, but be adored King.

PART THE SECOND

11

'Some find me a sword; some
The flange and the rail; flame,
Fang, or flood' goes Death on drum,
And storms bugle his fame.
85   But wé dream we are rooted in earth – Dust!
Flesh falls within sight of us, we, though our flower
the same,
Wave with the meadow, forget that there must
The sour scythe cringe, and the blear share come.

12

On Saturday sailed from Bremen,
90   American-outward-bound,
Take settler and seamen, tell men with women,
Two hundred souls in the round –
O Father, not under thy feathers nor even as guessing
The goal was a shoal, of a fourth the doom to be drowned;
95   Yet did the dark side of the bay of thy blessing
Not vault them, the million of rounds of thy mercy not reeve
even them in?

77 Paul Saul of Tarsus, the persecutor of Christians, was converted to the Apostle Paul. See *Acts* 9.1–30.
78 Austin St Augustine of Hippo (354–430). In *Confessions* he writes: '"Let me be for a little while" stretched out for a long time' (Bk 8 Ch. 6; J. K. Ryan trans. (N.Y. 1960) 190).
82 flange synechdoche for 'wheel of a railway train'.
88 cringe the line seems to demand a transitive sense – to make or cause to cower – but this is not supported by *OED*. Possibly an analogy with Shakespeare *Sonnet* 126: 'bending sickle'. The scythe of death bends in a motion that resembles man's cringing from death.
95 bay the space between two columns (*OED* sb³ 1); this interpretation might be required by the architectural context introduced by the 'vault' of line 96, but the sense is probably not far removed from *OED* sb²: 'an indentation of the sea into the land'.
96 reeve gather.

13

Into the snows she sweeps,
Hurling the haven behind,
The Deutschland, on Sunday; and so the sky keeps,
100   For the infinite air is unkind,
And the sea flint-flake, black-backed in the regular blow,
Sitting Eastnortheast, in cursed quarter, the wind;
Wiry and white-fiery and whirlwind-swivellèd snow
Spins to the widow-making unchilding unfathering deeps.

14

105   She drove in the dark to leeward,
She struck – not a reef or a rock
But the combs of a smother of sand: night drew her
Dead to the Kentish Knock;
And she beat the bank down with her bows and the ride
of her keel;
110   The breakers rolled on her beam with ruinous shock;
And canvas and compass, the whorl and the wheel
Idle for ever to waft her or wind her with, these she endured.

15

Hope had grown grey hairs,
Hope had mourning on,
115   Trenched with tears, carved with cares,
Hope was twelve hours gone;
And frightful a nightfall folded rueful a day
Nor rescue, only rocket and lightship, shone,
And lives at last were washing away:
120   To the shrouds they took, – they shook in the hurling and
horrible airs.

16

One stirred from the rigging to save
The wild woman-kind below,
With a rope's end round the man, handy and brave –

107 combs ridges of sand.   **drew her | D** run-over required if this is to
rhyme with 'leeward' line 105. See also lines 246–7, 247–8, and 273–4 for
other uses of the device. Discussed *Bridges Letters* 180.
11 whorl propeller. It broke when the engines were turned full speed astern
immediately after the ship went aground.
118 lightship the Knock Edge Light.
121–8 a portrait of a H. folk-hero, who places his services in the hands of
humanity. 'One brave sailor, who was safe in the rigging, went down to try
and save a child or woman who was drowning on deck. He was secured by
a rope to the rigging, but a wave dashed him against the bulwark, and when
daylight dawned his headless body, detained by the rope, was seen swaying
to and fro with the waves' (*The Times* 11 Dec. 1875).

He was pitched to his death at a blow,
125 For all his dreadnought breast and braids of thew:
They could tell him for hours, dandled the to and fro
 Through the cobbled foam-fleece. What could he do
With the burl of the fountains of air, buck and the flood of the
 wave?

<h3 style="text-align:center">17</h3>

They fought with God's cold –
130 And they could not and fell to the deck
(Crushed them) or water (and drowned them) or
 rolled
With the sea-romp over the wreck.
Night roared, with the heart-break hearing a heart-broke
 rabble,
The woman's wailing, the crying of child without check –
135 Till a lioness arose breasting the babble,
A prophetess towered in the tumult, a virginal tongue told.

<h3 style="text-align:center">18</h3>

Ah, touched in your bower of bone,
Are you! turned for an exquisite smart,
Have you! make words break from me here all alone,
140 Do you! – mother of being in me, heart.
O unteachably after evil, but uttering truth,
Why, tears! is it? tears; such a melting, a madrigal start!
Never-eldering revel and river of youth,
What can it be, this glee? the good you have there of your
 own?

<h3 style="text-align:center">19</h3>

145 Sister, a sister calling
A master, her master and mine! –
And the inboard seas run swirling and hawling;
The rash smart sloggering brine
Blinds her; but she that weather sees one thing, one;
150 Has one fetch in her: she rears herself to divine
Ears, and the call of the tall nun
To the men in the tops and the tackle rode over the storm's
 brawling.

126 tell take account of (a sense not recorded in *OED*).
128 burl disturbance, confused noise – related to 'hurly-burly' (obs. *OED*).
137 bower of bone H.'s version of O.E. *ban hus*.
141 after evil striving to achieve evil.
147 hawling not in *OED*: related to hail 2 – to rain down blows, or to haul 2?
148 sloggering assailing violently (a C19 word).
150 fetch expedient. Schneider 30 suggests it could mean 'spirit'.

20
She was first of a five and came
Of a coifèd sisterhood.
155   (O Deutschland, double a desperate name!
O world wide of its good!
But Gertrude, lily, and Luther, are two of a town,
Christ's lily and beast of the waste wood:
From life's dawn it is drawn down,
160   Abel is Cain's brother and breasts they have sucked the same.)

21
Loathed for a love men knew in them,
Banned by the land of their birth,
Rhine refused them, Thames would ruin them;
Surf, snow, river and earth
165   Gnashed: but thou art above, thou Orion of light;
Thy unchancelling poising palms were weighing the worth,
Thou martyr-master: in thy sight
Storm flakes were scroll-leaved flowers, lily showers – sweet
heaven was astrew in them.

22
Five! the finding and sake
170   And cipher of suffering Christ.
Mark, the mark is of man's make
And the word of it Sacrificed.
But he scores it in scarlet himself on his own bespoken,
Before-time-taken, dearest prizèd and priced –
175   Stigma, signal, cinquefoil token
For lettering of the lamb's fleece, ruddying of the rose-flake.

157 Gertrude (c. 156–c. 1302) lived in Eisleben, Saxony: Luther's birthplace.
165 Orion Christ hovers over the wreck like the giant hunter of classical myth. The constellation Orion is prominent in the night sky in November and December.
166 unchancelling removing from the protection of the chancel: i.e. ultimately God himself is responsible for the exile.
169 finding emblem.   **sake** 'It is the *sake* of "for the sake of", *forsake, namesake, keepsake.* I mean by it the being a thing has outside itself, as a voice by its echo, a face by its reflection, a body by its shadow, a man by his name, fame, or memory, *and also* that in the thing by virtue of which especially it has this being abroad, and that is something distinctive, marked, specifically or individually speaking, as for a voice and echo clearness;...' (*Bridges Letters* 83).
170 cipher Christ's five wounds.
176 rose-flake the red rose is the Christian emblem of martyrdom.

23

Joy fall to thee, father Francis,
Drawn to the Life that died;
With the gnarls of the nails in thee, niche of the lance,
his
180   Lovescape crucified
And seal of his seraph-arrival! and these thy daughters
And five-livèd and leavèd favour and pride,
Are sisterly sealed in wild waters,
To bathe in his fall-gold mercies, to breathe in his all-fire
glances.

24

185   Away in the loveable west,
On a pastoral forehead of Wales,
I was under a roof here, I was at rest,
And they the prey of the gales;
She to the black-about air, to the breaker, the thickly
190   Falling flakes, to the throng that catches and quails
Was calling 'O Christ, Christ, come quickly':
The cross to her she calls Christ to her, christens her wildworst
Best.

25

The majesty! what did she mean?
Breathe, arch and original Breath.
195   Is it love in her of the being as her lover had been?
Breathe, body of lovely Death.
They were else-minded then, altogether, the men
Woke thee with a *We are perishing* in the weather of
Gennesareth.
Or is it that she cried for the crown then,
200   The keener to come at the comfort for feeling the combating
keen?

177 father Francis Francis of Assisi (*c.* 1182–1226), the founder of the Order
to which the nuns belonged.
180 Lovescape the pattern of Christ's wounds, reproduced in St. Francis's
stigmata (*Little Flowers of St. Francis* trans. James Rhoades 1925, 111).
186 H. was at St Bueno's College, at the time of the wreck, on a hill
overlooking the Vale of Clwyd.
191 'the chief sister, a gaunt woman 6 ft. high calling out loudly and often
"O Christ, come quickly!" till the end came' (*The Times* 11 Dec. 1875).
194 arch and original see *John* 1.1: 'In the beginning was the Word.'
195 her lover the nuns regarded themselves as spouses of Christ.
198 Gennesareth the sea where Christ walked on the waters (*Matt.* 14.22–
23).
199 the crown of martyrdom.

[141] Gerard Manley Hopkins

26

For how to the heart's cheering
The down-dugged ground-hugged grey
Hovers off, the jay-blue heavens appearing
Of pied and peeled May!
205   Blue-beating and hoary-glow height; or night, still higher,
With belled fire and the moth-soft Milky Way,
What by your measure is the heaven of desire,
The treasure never eyesight got, nor was ever guessed what for
the hearing?

27

No, but it was not these.
210   The jading and jar of the cart,
Time's tasking, it is fathers that asking for ease
Of the sodden-with-its-sorrowing heart,
Not danger, electrical horror; then further it finds
The appealing of the Passion is tenderer in prayer apart:
215   Other, I gather, in measure her mind's
Burden, in wind's burly and beat of endragonèd seas.

28

But how shall I... make me room there:
Reach me a... Fancy, come faster –
Strike you the sight of it? look at it loom there,
220   Thing that she... There then! the Master,
Ipse, the only one, Christ, King, Head:
He was to cure the extremity where he had cast her;
Do, deal, lord it with living and dead;
Let him ride, her pride, in his triumph, despatch and have done
with his doom there.

202 down-dugged clouds dug or pushed down into the ground. Many critics plausibly suggest that 'down' is not an adverb but a noun, and 'dugged' means 'uddered'. Etymologically it is impossible to hold *both* these readings simultaneously, as it would have been for G.M.H., since he only allowed multiple meanings to operate within the scope of *actual* connections between homophones.
211–2 It is the impositions placed by time on the grief-stricken heart that encourage the request for peace.
216 burly bluster.   **endragoned** H. coining: seas as wild as dragons.
221 Ipse Christ's very self: meaning that the nun did not have a hallucination.

29

225   Ah! there was a heart right!
           There was single eye!
           Read the unshapeable shock night
           And knew the who and the why;
           Wording it how but by him that present and past,
230   Heaven and earth are word of, worded by? –
           The Simon Peter of a soul! to the blast
        Tarpeïan-fast, but a blown beacon of light.

30

           Jesu, heart's light,
           Jesu, maid's son,
235   What was the feast followed the night
           Thou hadst glory of this nun? –
           Feast of the one woman without stain.
           For so conceivèd, so to conceive thee is done;
           But here was heart-throe, birth of a brain,
240   Word, that heard and kept thee and uttered thee outright.

31

           Well, she has thee for the pain, for the
           Patience; but pity of the rest of them!
           Heart, go and bleed at a bitterer vein for the
           Comfortless unconfessed of them –
245   No not uncomforted: lovely-felicitous Providence
           Finger of a tender of, O of a feathery delicacy, the breast of the
           Maiden could obey so, be a bell to, ring of it, and
           Startle the poor sheep back! is the shipwrack then a harvest,
           does tempest carry the grain for thee?

32

           I admire thee, master of the tides,
250   Of the Yore-flood, of the year's fall;

226 single eye fixed on God. Cf. *Luke* 11.34: 'therefore when thine eye is single, thy whole body also is full of light.'
231 Simon Peter the founder of the Church. Christ himself made a play of his name as the foundation rock (*petra*) of the Church (*Matt.* 16.18).
232 Tarpeïan-fast as firm as the Tarpeian rock on the Capitoline Hill in Rome; from it the condemned were hurled.   blown beacon 'which suggests a very human reaction to the winds of adversity' *1970* 261–2. But it also suggests the light which shines 'before the world' (*Matt.* 5.16).
237 The Feast of the Immaculate Conception 8 Dec., following the night of the wreck.
250 Yore-flood both Noah's flood, and the primordial waters which covered the face of the earth before Creation.

[141] Gerard Manley Hopkins

<blockquote>

The recurb and the recovery of the gulf's sides,
    The girth of it and the wharf of it and the wall;
Stanching, quenching ocean of a motionable mind;
Ground of being, and granite of it: past all

255   Grasp God, throned behind
Death with a sovereignty that heeds but hides, bodes but
    abides;

33

With a mercy that outrides
    The all of water, an ark
For the listener; for the lingerer with a love glides

260   Lower than death and the dark;
A vein for the visiting of the past-prayer, pent in prison,
The-last-breath penitent spirits – the uttermost mark
    Our passion-plungèd giant risen,
The Christ of the Father compassionate, fetched in the storm
    of his strides.

34

265   Now burn, new born to the world,
    Double-naturèd name,
The heaven-flung, heart-fleshed, maiden-furled
    Miracle-in-Mary-of-flame,
Mid-numberèd he in three of the thunder-throne!

270 Not a dooms-day dazzle in his coming nor dark as he
    came;
    Kind, but royally reclaiming his own;
A released shower, let flash to the shire, not a lightning of fire
    hard-hurled.

</blockquote>

251 'The ebb and flow of the tides, and the advancings and retreats of the shore-line.'
253 motionable H. coining: motile.
255–6 'God hides behind death: caring for man, but inscrutable and not directly showing his compassion.'
260 Lower than death Purgatory.
262–4 'Those at the end of their lives recognise God, overthrown by the crucifixion, but now risen, summoned in the storm, striding on the waves.' Thus Schneider *PMLA* 81 (1966) 119, but Keating 105–6 and *1970* 262 take 'fetched' as 'reached' with its subject 'giant', and its object a rel. pronoun omitted after the noun 'mark'.
266 Double-naturèd] Doubled-natured in *B; 1918–1948.*
269 Mid-numberèd he in the sequence Father, Son and Holy Ghost, Christ is central.
272 shire] *G* has 'shore', but Bridges notes (*1918*) that '*shire* is doubtless right; it is the special favoured landscape visited by the shower.'

35

Dame, at our door
Drowned, and among our shoals,
275   Remember us in the roads, the heaven-haven of the
         reward:
     Our King back, Oh, upon English souls!
Let him easter in us, be a dayspring to the dimness of us,
     be a crimson-cresseted east,
     More brightening her, rare-dear Britain, as his reign rolls,
     Pride, rose, prince, hero of us, high-priest,
280 Our hearts' charity's hearth's fire, our thoughts' chivalry's
     throng's Lord.

275 roads water near the shore (*OED* 3).
277 easter as a vb. H.'s coinage.

142 Moonrise

Date 19 June 1876. Unfinished: in *H*.
Publication *1918*.

I awoke in the Midsummer not-to-call night, / in the white
    and the walk of the morning:
The moon, dwindled and thinned to the fringe / of a fingernail
    held to the candle,
Or paring of paradisaical fruit, / lovely in waning but
    lustreless,
Stepped from the stool, drew back from the barrow, / of dark
    Maenefa the mountain;
5   A cusp still clasped him, a fluke yet fanged him, / entangled
    him, not quit utterly.
This was the prized, the desirable sight, / unsought, presented
    so easily,
Parted me leaf and leaf, divided me, / eyelid and eyelid of
    slumber.

4 Maenefa near St Bueno's. H.'s bardic name was Brân Maenefa.
5 cusp sharp point of the moon.   **fluke** barbed point.   **fanged** gripped
(dial.).
6 For the notion of a beautiful spectacle as a prize cf. no. 143.
7 Possibly meaning that H. was divided from sleep by the intensity of the
experience.

143 The Starlight Night

Date 24 Feb. 1877. Autographs in *A* and *B*. H. sent a copy to his mother in March 1877 (*Further Letters* 145 and facs. pl. 8).

H.'s friend Dixon sent this poem to Hall Caine 'not of course for publication without your consent: but for inspection to gratify him' (*Dixon Corresp.* 46). H. also sent three to Caine (*ibid.* 47). This was probably the closest H. came to publishing his mature work in a context that might have commanded wide circulation.

Publication The version in *A* was first published in Miles, then in *The Oxford Book of Victorian Verse* (1912) ed. A. Quiller-Couch.

> Look at the stars! look, look up at the skies!
> O look at all the fire-folk sitting in the air!
> The bright boroughs, the circle-citadels there!
> Down in dim woods the diamond delves! the elves' eyes!
> 5   The grey lawns cold where gold, where quickgold lies!
> Wind-beat whitebeam! airy abeles set on a flare!
> Flake-doves sent floating forth at a farmyard scare! –
> Ah well! it is all a purchase, all is a prize.
>
> Buy then! bid then! – What? – Prayer, patience, alms, vows.
> 10   Look, look: a May-mess, like on orchard boughs!
> Look! March-bloom, like on mealed-with-yellow sallows!
> These are indeed the barn; withindoors house
> The shocks. This piece-bright paling shuts the spouse
> Christ home, Christ and his mother and all his hallows.

3 circle-citadels] glimmering citadels *Further Letters*; quivering citadels *A*.
4 Look, the elf-rings! look at the out-round earnest eyes! *Further Letters;* The dim woods quick with diamond wells; the elf-eyes! *A*.
5 where gold, where quickgold lies!] where quaking gold-dew lies! *Further Letters* and *A*.
6 whitebeam . . . abeles trees whose leaves have whitish undersides which show in a wind.
8 Cf. George Herbert: 'Take stars for money; stars not to be told | By any art, but to be purchased' (*The Church Porch* st. 29).
9 What? i.e. at what price, to which the answer is prayer etc.
11 sallows a species of willow: the catkins look yellow and mealy in Spring.
12 the barn the profitable part of outward experience (as opposed to the tares). See *Matt.* 13.30.
13 shocks stooks.   **piece-bright** paling a fence as shiny as coins. Cf. the fragment: 'The stars were packed so close that night | They seemed to press and stare | And gather in like hurdles bright | The liberties of air' (*1970* 139).
14 hallows saints.

144 In the Valley of the Elwy

Date 23 May 1877. In addition to the two manuscript versions of the poem, Lady Christabel Pooley discovered one in 1964, which provides the exact date.

This is a poem that grows from Hopkins' happy Welsh experience (the Elwy is a tributary of the Clwyd that joins it below St Asaph), but in a letter of 8 Apr. 1879, H. writes: 'The kind people of the sonnet were the Watsons of Shooter's Hill, nothing to do with the Elwy. The facts were as stated. You misunderstand the thought, which is very far fetched. The frame of the sonnet is a rule of three sum *wrong*, thus: As the sweet smell to those kind people so the Welsh landscape is NOT to the Welsh; and then the author and the principle of all four terms is asked to bring the sum right' (*Bridges Letters* 76–7).

Publication Bridges *The Spirit of Man* (1916) no. 358; *1918*.

I remember a house where all were good
　To me, God knows, deserving no such thing:
　Comforting smell breathed at very entering,
Fetched fresh, as I suppose, off some sweet wood.

5　The cordial air made those kind people a hood
　All over, as a bevy of eggs the mothering wing
　Will, or mild nights the new morsels of Spring:
Why, it seemed of course; seemed of right it should.

Lovely the woods, waters, meadows, combes, vales,
10　All the air things wear that build this world of Wales;
　Only the inmate does not correspond:

God, lover of souls, swaying considerate scales,
Complete thy creature dear O where it fails,
　Being mighty a master, being a father and fond.

5 cordial both adj. (*OED* 2) and noun.
12 considerate both *OED* 1 'deliberate' and *OED* 4 'thoughtful for others'.

145 The Windhover: To Christ our Lord

Date Two autographs in *A;* corrected in *B* 30 May 1877; and an amended copy 22 June 1879: 'I shall shortly send you an amended copy of *The Windhover:* the amendment only touches a single line, I think, but as that is the best thing I ever wrote I should like you to have it in its best form' (*Bridges Letters* 85).

There are many antecedents for the bird as the Spirit of God: one possible is paragraphs 65–6 of Ruskin's *The Queen of the Air* (1869). The poem may be approached by way of a letter of 3 Feb. 1883, in which H. studies *Phil.* 2.5–11: '[Christ] thought it ... no snatching-matter for him to

[145] Gerard Manley Hopkins

be equal with God, but annihilated himself, taking the form of servant;...It is this holding of himself back, and not snatching at the truest and highest good...which seems to me the root of all his holiness and the imitation of this the root of all moral good in other men' (*Bridges Letters* 175). The Windhover is a small hawk, though it is the spiralling nature of its flight and its extraordinary ability to lean motionlessly on the air before its drop that caught H.'s attention rather than its predatory habits. B. Wallis, ignoring the specificity of the bird, relates it to the eagle – seen by St Gregory as a symbol of resurrection.

Criticism Gardner 1. 97–100, 180–4; Mariani 110–3; McChesney 66–9; F. X. Shea, S.J. *VP* 2 (1964) 219–39.

Publication *1918*.

> I caught this morning morning's minion, king-
> > dom of daylight's dauphin, dapple-dawn-drawn Falcon, in
> > > his riding
> Of the rolling level underneath him steady air, and striding
> High there, how he rung upon the rein of a wimpling wing
5 > In his ecstasy! then off, off forth on swing,
> > As a skate's heel sweeps smooth on a bow-bend: the hurl and
> > > gliding
> > Rebuffed the big wind. My heart in hiding
> Stirred for a bird, – the achieve of, the mastery of the thing!
>
> Brute beauty and valour and act, oh, air, pride, plume, here
10 > Buckle, AND the fire that breaks from thee then, a billion
> Times told lovelier, more dangerous, O my chevalier!

2 Cf. Shakespeare *H.5* 3.7.11 (the Dauphin's praise of his horse): 'When I bestride him I soar, I am a hawk: he trots the air.' A strain of chivalric imagery runs through the poem, evoking a knightly crusade against evil.

4 rung to 'ring on the rein' a horse-training term: the horse circles at the end of a rein. The bird seems to be subject to a similar control by the wind. **wimpling** curved and rippling.

7–8 either 'My heart longed to understand the full nature of the bird, its achievement, its supreme nature' or 'My heart longed to enter into the body of the bird so that it could share in its self-control and its command of the elements.'

10 buckle vb., either imperative or indicative, for which a multiplicity of meanings have been offered, including fasten, buck, grapple, submit, bend, crumple. They are not all etymologically connected, and since H. liked to restrict his meanings to senses that had some claim to inter-relation one has to eliminate some of them. My interpretation is: 'In the moment of transitory revelation of essential beauty, power and significance, we need to witness the elements under strain, but Christ's revelation of his beauty (especially on the cross) was much more beautiful than the falcon's, though also similar to it, as a tense control of the surrounding elements of history.'

No wonder of it: shéer plód makes plough down sillion
Shine, and blue-bleak embers, ah my dear,
Fall, gall themselves, and gash gold-vermilion.

12–13 sheer . . . shine either 'hard work makes the soil of the plough-down shine' or 'hard work makes the ploughshare shine as it moves down the furrow'. The latter is more likely if one regards the lines as an echo of Virgil's *'sulco attritus splendescere vomer'* ('the share glistens when rubbed by the furrow') *Georg.* 1.146.
13–14 blue-bleak . . . gold vermilion 'seemingly dead coals fall and reveal that they are glowing and alight within': perhaps suggesting the crucifixion. See *Sermons* 37: 'Poor was his station, laborious his life, bitter his ending: through poverty, through labour, through crucifixion his majesty of nature more shines.'

146 Pied Beauty

Date Summer 1877. Autograph in *A* and *B*.
A. has a note by H. on scansion: 'when the last syllable of a word has an *l* or *n* preceded in punctuation by a dull pass-vowel (as *dappled, bitten*) this last syllable is not so much a syllable by itself as strengthens the one before it, so that the true scansion is – "dappled: things" etc. But when a vowel begins the next word the syllable counts.' For H.'s interest in things dappled see also no. 149. H. may have been influenced by Ruskin's *Aratra Pentilici* (1872), which describes the Greek love for the speckled and mottled.
Publication *1918*.

Glory be to God for dappled things –
    For skies of couple-colour as a brinded cow;
        For rose-moles all in stipple upon trout that swim;
Fresh-firecoal chestnut-falls; finches' wings;
5   Landscape plotted and pieced – fold, fallow and plough;
        And áll trádes, their gear and tackle and trim.

All things counter, original, spare, strange;
    Whatever is fickle, freckled (who knows how?)
        With swift, slow; sweet, sour; adazzle, dim;
10   He fathers-forth whose beauty is past change: Praise him.

4 Fresh-firecoal chestnut falls when the nuts fall from the tree and burst from their husks they are as bright as coal. It is uncertain whether the coal is alight, though a Journal entry for 17 Sept. 1868 suggests it may be: 'Chestnuts as bright as coals or spots of vermilion.'
6 plotted divided into fields.
8 counter presenting an unusual contrary appearance.
10 The paradox is that a stable God creates variable things.

147 Binsey Poplars
felled 1879

Date 13 Mar. 1879. H. spent nine months in 1878–9 as a parish priest at St Aloysius' Oxford. In a long letter begun in Feb. H. wrote: 'I...need not go far to have before my eyes "the little-headed willows two and two" and that landscape charm of Oxford, green shouldering grey, which is already abridged and soured and perhaps will soon be put out altogether' (*Dixon Corresp.* 20). On Mar. 13 he wrote: 'I have been up to Godstow this afternoon. I am sorry to say that the aspens that lined the river are everyone felled' (*ibid.* 26). For further notes on this landscape see notes to nos. 104 and 106. Binsey poplars (which were replaced with others now full grown) were on the west bank of the Thames south of Godstow.
Publication *1918*.

> My aspens dear, whose airy cages quelled,
> Quelled or quenched in leaves the leaping sun,
> All felled, felled, are all felled;
>   Of a fresh and following folded rank
> 5   Not spared, not one
>   That dandled a sandalled
>   Shadow that swam or sank
> On meadow and river and wind-wandering weed-winding bank.
>
> O if we but knew what we do
> 10   When we delve or hew –
> Hack and rack the growing green!
>   Since country is so tender
>   To touch, her being só slender,
>   That, like this sleek and seeing ball
> 15 But a prick will make no eye at all,
>   Where we, even where we mean
>   To mend her we end her,
>   When we hew or delve:
> After-comers cannot guess the beauty been.
> 20   Ten or twelve, only ten or twelve
>   Strokes of havoc únselve
>   The sweet especial scene,
>   Rural scene, a rural scene,
>   Sweet especial rural scene.

4 folded rank the view down a 'foreshortened row, each trunk protruding from behind its predecessor' (Gardner 2.272).
8 weed-winding] weed-wounden in manuscript draft.
21 únselve to remove the identity and individuality. A belief in the individual and unrepeatable nature of each scene is central to H.'s view of nature. Another Oxford poem of the same month, *Duns Scotus's Oxford*, also celebrates the vulnerability of the *haeccitas* of a place.

148 Felix Randal

Date 28 Apr. 1880. Autograph in *A* and *B*.
For the circumstances see Alfred Thomas, *TLS* 19 Mar. 1971. In Oct.
1879 H. went to St Joseph's, Leigh, Lancs. as parish priest, and in Dec. as
junior curate to St Francis Xavier's, Liverpool. He was fond of the working-
class people of the North: 'I felt as if [I] had been born to deal with them.
Religion, you know, enters very deep.... Now these Lancashire people of
low degree or not of high degree are those who most seemed to me to
welcome me and make much of me' (*Further Letters* 245). On 21 Apr. one
of H.'s parishioners, Felix Spencer, died. Thomas suggests that H. got the
name 'Randal' from the great Provincial, and founder of St Bueno's, Randal
Lythgoe, and that the poem is not only about a specific blacksmith, but the
whole process of the dutiful life described in *Ecclesiasticus* 28.30–31: '[The
smith] batters his ear with the din of the hammer, his eyes are fixed on the
pattern; he sets his heart on completing his work and stays up late putting
the finishing touches.'
Publication *1918*.

Felix Randal the farrier, O is he dead then? my duty all ended,
    Who have watched his mould of man, big-boned and hardy-
        handsome
    Pining, pining, till time when reason rambled in it and some
    Fatal four disorders, fleshed there, all contended?

5   Sickness broke him. Impatient, he cursed at first, but mended
    Being anointed and all; though a heavenlier heart began some
    Months earlier, since I had our sweet reprieve and ransom
    Tendered to him. Ah well, God rest him all road ever he
        offended!

This seeing the sick endears them to us, us too it endears.
10   My tongue had taught thee comfort, touch had quenched thy
        tears,
    Thy tears that touched my heart, child, Felix, poor Felix
        Randal;

How far from then forethought of, all thy more boisterous
        years,
    When thou at the random grim forge, powerful amidst peers,
    Didst fettle for the great grey drayhorse his bright and
        battering sandal!

7 sweet reprieve Holy Communion, preceded by confession and absolution.
8 tendered word play, with senses of 'offer' and 'show tenderness'. (The two
senses are etymologically connected).   **all road ever** in whatever way he
may have (dial.).
13 random built with stones of irregular size and shape.
14 fettle prepare, with implied sense that smith and horse are both 'in fine
fettle'.

149 Inversnaid

Date 28 Sept. 1881. Autograph in *H*.
  H. was beginning to compose a poem 'on the decline of wild nature', with lines very similar to these, in Feb. 1879 (*Bridges Letters* 73–4). They may have been based on a visit to Inveraray in 1871, or on a more long-standing love of wild places in England and Wales. The particular inspiration was a brief holiday in Scotland before taking up parish work in Glasgow. Inversnaid empties into the east side of Loch Lomond.
Publication Miles, without stress marks; *1918*.

This darksome burn, horseback brown,
His rollrock highroad roaring down,
In coop and in comb the fleece of his foam
Flutes and low to the lake falls home.

5   A windpuff-bonnet of fáwn-fróth
Turns and twindles over the broth
Of a pool so pitchblack, féll-frówning,
It rounds and rounds Despair to drowning.

Degged with dew, dappled with dew
10   Are the groins of the braes that the brook treads through,
Wiry heathpacks, flitches of fern,
And the beadbonny ash that sits over the burn.

What would the world be, once bereft
Of wet and of wildness? Let them be left,
15   O let them be left, wildness and wet;
Long live the weeds and the wilderness yet.

3 coop hollow or enclosed place.   **comb** crest or ridge, see note to no. 141 line 107; possibly also water combing through obstacles.
4 flutes vb. forms into channels; perhaps also the musical sense.
5 fáwn-fróth peaty water churned up.
6 twindles portmanteau coinage of 'twists', 'twitches', and 'dwindles'. See *Journal* 223: 'the foam dwindling and twitched into long chains of suds' (10 Aug. 1872). *1970* suggests obs. vb. 'twindle' – to describe a whirlpool split (twinned).
9 degged (Lancashire dial.) sprinkled.
11 heathpacks heather.   **flitches** tufts or clumps.
12 burn stream.

150 Spelt from Sibyl's Leaves

Date Composition began in Oct. 1884 and continued over the next few months, when H. went through a dark night of the soul; see letter of 11 Dec. 1886: 'I mean to enclose my long sonnet, the longest, I still say, ever made; longest by its own proper length, namely by the length of its lines, for anything can be made long by eking, by tacking, by trains, tails, and flounces.... Of this long sonnet above all remember what applies to all my verse, that it is, as living art should be, made for performance and that its performance is not reading with the eye but loud, leisurely, poetical (not rhetorical) recitation' (*Bridges Letters* 246).

Each line has 8 stresses. For the title and argument see *Dies irae:* 'As David and the Sibyl testify...what terror shall affright the soul when the Judge comes'. The Cumaean Sibyl appears in Virgil *Aen.* 6. For the connection between Pagan and Christian uses of the sibyl see Edgar Wind 'Michaelangelo's Prophets and Sibyls' *PBA* 51 (1965) 46–84.

The poem celebrates the horror of a world in which the varied identities of objects have been reduced to harsh warring simplicities in the stark light of evening, after the benign daylight has gone.

Publication *1918.*

> Earnest, earthless, equal, attuneable, / vaulty, voluminous,
> ...stupendous
> Evening strains to be tíme's vást, / womb-of-all, home-of-all,
> hearse-of-all night.
> Her fond yellow hornlight wound to the west, / her wild
> hollow hoarlight hung to the height
> Waste; her earliest stars, earlstars, / stárs principal, overbend
> us,
> 5 Fíre-féaturing heaven. For earth / her being has unbound; her
> dapple is at end, as-
> tray or aswarm, all throughther, in throngs; / self ín self
> steepèd and páshed – qúite
> Disremembering, dísmémbering / áll now. Heart, you round
> me right
> With: Óur évening is over us; óur night / whélms, whélms,
> ánd will end us.
> Only the beakleaved boughs dragonish / damask the tool-
> smooth bleak light; black,
> 10 Ever so black on it. Óur tale, O óur oracle! / Lét life, wáned,
> ah lét life wind

1 attuneable susceptible and conducive to harmony.
3 hornlight either the light of setting sun (lanterns, i.e. lanthorns, give out dim light through panes of horn), or of the crescent (horned) moon. If the latter is possible H. may have meant both senses of hornlight to be applicable to the moon. Cf. opening of *Kingis Quair.*
4 earlstars noble stars; earl and early not etymologically related. **overbend** look over.
6 throughther dialect form of through-other, mixed-up.   **pashed** beaten. Cf. Tennyson *Lucretius* (no. 53 lines 36–43, above).
7 disremembering forgetting.   **round** whisper to.
8 With with the fact that something is troubling the heart.
9 damask vb. to ornament with patterns like those on swords (originally Damascus).

[151] Gerard Manley Hopkins

Off hér once skéined stained véined varíety / upon, áll on twó
  spools; párt, pen, páck
Now her áll in twó flocks, twó folds – black, white; / right,
  wrong; reckon but, reck but, mind
But thése two; wáre of a wórld where bút these / twó tell, each
  off the óther; of a rack
Where, selfwrung, selfstrung, sheathe-and shelterless, / thóughts
  agaínst thoughts ín groans grínd.

11 **párt, pen, páck** sort out.
12 **twó flocks** perhaps a ref. to the separation of the sheep and goats for
judgement, *Matt.* 25.31–33.
13 **ware** beware of.
14 **sheathe-** sheathless, i.e. without protection. For the idea of thoughts as
torturers see no. 155.

151 Carrion Comfort

Date 1885.
This is the first of the six so-called 'sonnets of desolation', or 'terrible
sonnets'; the other 5 follow immediately, and are all in *H*. Their arrangement as a group is discussed in *1970* xlvii–xlviii. In a letter of 17 May
1885 H. wrote: 'I have after long silence written two sonnets, which I am
touching: if ever anything was written in blood one of these was' (*Bridges
Letters* 219). It is not certain to which poems he refers, but they are almost
certainly to be found among those included here.
Publication *1918*.

Not, I'll not, carrion comfort, Despair, not feast on thee;
  Not untwist – slack they may be – these last strands
    of man
  In me ór, most weary, cry 'I can no more.' I can;
Can something, hope, wish day come, not choose not to be.

5   But ah, but O thou terrible, why wouldst thou rude on me
       Thy wring-world right foot rock? lay a lionlimb
         against me? scan

1 **carrion comfort, Despair** Despair may seem comforting, since it provides
the sufferer with release through expression, but it is as life-giving as feeding
on a putrefying corpse.
2 **strands of man** Cf. Donne *The Ecstasy* line 64: 'That subtle knot, which
makes us man.'
5 **rude on me** rudely.
6 **lionlimb** Cf. *Job* 10. 16: 'Thou huntest me as a fierce lion.'   **rock** verb
governing foot.

With darksome devouring eyes my bruisèd bones? and fan,
O in turns of tempest, me heaped there; me frantic to
    avoid thee and flee?
Why? That my chaff might fly; my grain lie, sheer and
    clear.
10   Nay in all that toil, that coil, since (seems)
    I kissed the rod,
Hand rather, my heart lo! lapped strength, stole joy,
    would laugh, chéer.
Cheer whom though? The hero whose heaven-handling
    flung me, fóot tród
Me? or me that fought him? O which one? is it each
    one? That night, that year
Of now done darkness I wretch lay wrestling with
    (my God!) my God.

7–9 H. is adapting 2 *Kings* 6.27 to describe God in judgement as winnower:
'And he said, "If the Lord do not help thee, whence shall I help thee? out of
the barnfloor, or out of the winepress?"'
9 **sheer** bright.
11 **Hand rather** unlike the rod, which is exclusively punitive, the hand may
be at once punitive and able to offer gifts.
12 **The hero** Christ.
14 **(my God!)** colloquial ejaculation.

152 'No worst, there is none'

For date and circumstances of composition see headnote to *Carrion
Comfort*.

No worst, there is none. Pitched past pitch of grief,
    More pangs will, schooled at forepangs, wilder wring.
    Comforter, where, where is your comforting?
    Mary, mother of us, where is your relief?
5   My cries heave, herds-long; huddle in a main, a chief-

1 **Pitched past pitch** thrown beyond the limits of grief.
2 **schooled at forepangs** trained by previous suffering.
3 **Comforter** Holy Spirit.
5 **herds-long** as large as flocks of animals.   **main** adj.

> woe, world-sorrow; on an age-old anvil wince and sing
> > Then lull, then leave off. Fury had shrieked 'No ling-
> ering! Let me be fell: force I must be brief'.
> O the mind, mind has mountains; cliffs of fall

10   Frightful, sheer, no-man-fathomed. Hold them cheap
> May who ne'er hung there. Nor does long our small
> > Durance deal with that steep or deep. Here! creep,
> Wretch, under a comfort serves in a whirlwind: all
> Life death does end and each day dies with sleep.

6 wince to kick restlessly from impatience or pain (*OED* 1). H. either knew the word as a dialect word, or from Chaucer: 'Wynsynge she was as is a ioly colt' (Miller's T.).
8 fell savage.   **force** because by necessity.
10 Frightful, sheer down, not fathomed. MS. draft.
11 May they may.
12 Durance strength to endure.
13 comfort serves comfort that serves.

153 'To seem the stranger'

For date and circumstances of composition see headnote to *Carrion Comfort*.
Publication First printed in Miles, with unimportant variants in spelling and punctuation; *1918*.

> To seem the stranger lies my lot, my life
> > Amongst strangers. Father and mother dear,
> Brothers and sisters are in Christ not near
> > And he my peace / my parting, sword and strife.

5   England, whose honour O all my heart woos, wife
> > To my creating thought, would neither hear
> Me, were I pleading, plead nor do I: I wear-
> > y of idle a being but by where wars are rife.

2–3 H.'s family, not Roman Catholics, disapproved of his conversion.
4 Cf. *Matt.* 10.34–5: 'Think not that I am come to send peace on earth: I came not to send peace, but a sword. For I am come to set a man at variance against his father.'
5 Cf. H.'s *What shall I do for the land that bred me*.
5–6 For the sexual metaphor for artistic creation (ultimately from Shakespeare) cf. no. 160.
8 where wars are rife the Irish movement for independence.

I am in Ireland now; now I am at a third
10   Remove. Not but in all removes I can
Kind love both give and get. Only what word

Wisest my heart breeds dark heaven's baffling ban
Bars or hell's spell thwarts. This to hoard unheard,
Heard unheeded, leaves me a lonely began.

9 H. went to Dublin in 1884.
10 all removes perhaps including the most important 'remove' of all – the absence of mortal man from direct experience of the love of God.
12 dark both adv. (qualifying 'breeds') and adj. (qualifying 'heaven's ban').
14 began either 'leaves me a lonely one who only began' or 'leaves me a lonely beginner'.

154 'I wake and feel the fell of dark'

For date and circumstances of composition see headnote to *Carrion Comfort*.

I wake and feel the fell of dark, not day.
What hours, O what black hoürs we have spent
This night! what sights you, heart, saw; ways you went!
And more must, in yet longer light's delay.

5   With witness I speak this. But where I say
Hours I mean years, mean life. And my lament
Is cries countless, cries like dead letters sent
To dearest him that lives alas! away.

I am gall, I am heartburn. God's most deep decree
10   Bitter would have me taste: my taste was me;
Bones built in me, flesh filled, blood brimmed the curse.

Selfyeast of spirit a dull dough sours. I see
The lost are like this, and their scourge to be
As I am mine, their sweating selves; but worse.

1 fell hairy skin; cf. Shakespeare *Macb.* 5.5.11: 'My fell of hair'.
4 'And you, heart, must see yet more sights and go yet more ways whilst waiting for the delayed coming of light.'
11 Cf. No. 141 line 5: 'Thou hast bound bones and veins in me, fastened me flesh.'
12 Judging by the drafts it is probable that 'selfyeast' is the subject of 'sours': 'this curse – | Self stuff, and by selfyeast so soured.'
14 but worse at once 'the damned in Hell are in an even worse plight than me,' and 'I share the fate of the self-tormented in Hell'.

155 'Patience, hard thing!'

For circumstances of composition see headnote to *Carrion Comfort.*

Patience, hard thing! the hard thing but to pray,
But bid for, Patience is! Patience who asks
Wants war, wants wounds; weary his times, his tasks;
To do without, take tosses, and obey.

5   Rare patience roots in these, and, these away,
Nowhere. Natural heart's ivy, Patience masks
Our ruins of wrecked past purpose. There she basks
Purple eyes and seas of liquid leaves all day.

We hear our hearts grate on themselves: it kills
10   To bruise them dearer. Yet the rebellious wills
Of us we do bid God bend to him even so.

And where is he who more and more distills
Delicious kindness? – He is patient. Patience fills
His crisp combs, and that comes those ways we know.

3 wants lacks.
4 take tosses take falls and disappointments.
7 basks generously exhibits (a transitive sense not recorded in *OED*).
8 Purple eyes perhaps the ivy-berries.
10 dearer more seriously, related to *OED* adj.[2]; cf. Shakespeare *Jul. Caes.* 3.1.196: 'shall it not grieve thee dearer than thy death.'
12 distills lets fall (*OED* 2).
13 patient suffering (*OED* 1).   **Patience** bearing the faults of others with tolerance (*OED* 1b).
14 combs honeycombs. Cf. *Judges* 14.14: 'out of the strong came forth sweetness.'

156 'My own heart let me more have pity on'

For date and circumstances of composition see headnote to *Carrion Comfort.*

My own heart let me more have pity on; let
Me live to my sad self hereafter kind,
Charitable; not live this tormented mind
With this tormented mind tormenting yet.

5   I cast for comfort I can no more get
    By groping round my comfortless, than blind
    Eyes in their dark can day or thirst can find
    Thirst's all-in-all in all a world of wet.

    Soul, self; come, poor Jackself, I do advise
10 You, jaded, let be; call off thoughts awhile
    Elsewhere; leave comfort root-room; let joy size

    At God knows when to God knows what; whose smile
    's not wrung, see you; unforeseen times rather – as skies
    Betweenpie mountains – lights a lovely mile.

6 comfortless comfortless world.
8 all-in-all complete satisfaction *OED* 8d.
9 Jackself the diurnal self (cf. no. 158 line 23).
10–11 'be a little more casual, relax for health's sake' and 'be reconciled to having your pleasure whenever and however God wills it' (Gardner 2.116).
11–12 size At correspond with (not in *OED*).
14 betweenpie a H. coining: intervariegates, i.e. skies seen between mountains create a dappled effect of sky alternating with mountain.

157 Harry Ploughman

Date Sept. 1887.
   Sonnet with 'burden lines'. One of the poems in which H. responds to the dignity and grace of the working man. H. was interested in ploughing: 'I talked to Br. Duffy ploughing: he told me the names of the cross, side-plate, muzzle, regulator, and short chain' (*Journal* 237, 8 Sept. 1873). But in addition P. L. Mariani *The Month* n.s. 40 (1968) 37–45 argues that Frederick Walker's *The Plough* (Tate, *c*. 1870) may have inspired him. H. writes of his brilliant, masculine genius (*Dixon Corresp.* 133–4, 30 June 1886). Three letters contain references to the poem: in one he writes: 'The rhythm of this sonnet, which is altogether for recital, not for perusal (as by nature verse should be), is very highly studied. From much considering it I can no longer gather any impression of it: perhaps it will strike you as intolerably violent and artificial' (*Bridges Letters* 263, 11 Oct. 1887). H. also wrote: 'let me know if there is anything like it in Walt Whitman, as perhaps there may be, and I should be sorry for that' (*ibid.* 262, 28 Sept. 1887). He would have regretted resemblance to Whitman for two reasons: (i) that it would make his theme less original and (ii) that he did not wish to exhibit an overtly homosexual appreciation in W.'s characteristic manner.
Publication *1918*.

[157] Gerard Manley Hopkins

Hard as hurdle arms, with a broth of goldish flue
Breathed round; the rack of ribs; the scooped flank; lank
Rope-over thigh; knee-nave; and barrelled shank –
　　Head and foot, shoulder and shank –
5　By a grey eye's heed steered well, one crew, fall to;
Stand at stress. Each limb's barrowy brawn, his thew
That onewhere curded, onewhere sucked or sank –
　　Soared ór sánk –,
Though as a beechbole firm, finds his, as at a rollcall, rank
10　And features, in flesh, what deed he each must do –
　　His sinew-service where do.

He leans to it, Harry bends, look. Back, elbow, and liquid
　　waist
In him, all quail to the wallowing o' the plough. 'S cheek
　　crimsons; curls
Wag or crossbridle, in a wind lifted, windlaced
　　See his wind- lilylocks -laced;
15　Churlsgrace too, child of Amansstrength, how it hangs or
　　hurls
Them – broad in bluff hide his frowning feet lashed! raced
With, along them, cragiron under and cold furls –
　　With-a-fountain's shining-shot furls.

1 hurdle portable wooden fence.　　**flue** downy hair.
3 Rope-over thigh muscular thigh.　　**knee-nave** knee-cap.
6 barrowy brawn] barrowy-brawned MS. variant.
7 curded bunched, became knotted.
10 features vb.
13 quail yield to: the senses of being daunted or dejected are probably not
present here.　　**'S** his.
14 crossbridle not in *OED;* hair blown across the face like a bridle.
Throughout H. emphasises visual correspondences between horse and
man.　　**in a wind lifted, windlaced]** windloft or windlaced MS. variant,
windlaced (not in *OED*) probably laced with or by the wind; perhaps related
to windlass v.[2] = to hoist or haul (windlace is an archaic spelling).
14 wind- lilylocks -laced probably the compound divided by a clause of
which H. wrote: 'I do not feel that it was an unquestionable success'
(*Bridges Letters* 265, 6 Nov. 1887).
15 churlsgrace the grace of a churl or peasant, but without the adverse
connotations of churl since C16.　　**Amansstrength** possibly a portmanteau
word, combining 'a man's strength' with 'Ammon's (Jove's) strength'.
16 frowning feet the creases in the boots seem to frown.
17 cragiron under the ploughshare under the earth.　　**cold furls** flame-furls
MS. variant.
18 Other MS. variants: 'With -a-wét-sheen-shot furls. and With-a-wét-fire-
flushed furls. Cf. no. 145 lines 12–14 for a similar treatment of the
transformation of plodding work to brilliant activity.

158 That Nature is a Heraclitean Fire and of the comfort of the Resurrection

Date 26 July 1888. Autograph in *A*.
Sonnet with three coda lines. H. writes (25 Sept. 1888): 'Lately I sent you a sonnet, on the Heraclitean Fire, in which a great deal of early Greek philosophical thought was distilled; but the liquor of the distillation did not taste very Greek, did it?' (*Bridges Letters* 291). The Greek philosopher Heraclitus (*c*. 535–*c*. 475 B.C.) taught that nature is in a state of flux, and that matter is merely a differentiation of the principal element of fire. The poem also refers to the Empedoclean theory of the metamorphic cycle of elements. H. provides a Christian counterstatement to the philosophies of dissolution.

H.'s knowledge of Heraclitus would have been partly gleaned from Pater. For the conception that nature's bonfire has a finite amount of fuel see *Plato and Platonism* (1893) 13: 'He reflects; and his reflexion has the characteristic melancholy of youth when it is forced suddenly to bethink itself, and for a moment feels already old, feels the temperature of the world about it sensibly colder.' The Hellenic opponent to Heraclitus was Parmenides, who speaks of the 'ethery flame of fire. comforting the heart' (*Journal* 127–30). The final lines, in which human existence is asserted, owe something to Plato's *Cratylus*, where man is seen as 'the measure of all things'. H. offers a Christian fortification of Plato, whereby the 'god in man' becomes that measure. There was a new Heracliteanism in the Victorian age, as Pater indicates: 'The entire modern theory of "development", in all its various phases, proved or unprovable – what is it but old Heracliteanism awake once more in a new world, and grown to full proportion?' (*loc. cit.* 19). The argument of the poem may also have close connections with 'The Law of Help' in Ruskin's *Modern Painters* 5 (1860). R. writes of the war of the elements that produces both slime and higher matter: 'In next order the soot sets to work; it cannot make itself white at first, but instead of being discouraged, tries harder and harder, and comes out clear at last, and the hardest thing in the world; and for the blackness that it had, obtains in exchange the power of reflecting all the rays of the sun at once in the vividest blaze that any solid thing can shoot. We call it then a diamond' (*Works* 7.208).
Commentaries include Gardner 1.161–4, *1970* 293–5, Mariani 280–90, Lahey 104–5, McChesney 172–5.
Publication *1918*.

> Cloud-puff ball, torn tufts, tossed pillows / flaunt forth, then
>   chevy on an air-
> built thoroughfare: heaven-roisterers, in gay-gangs / they
>   throng; they glitter in marches.
> Down roughcast, down dazzling whitewash, / wherever an elm
>   arches,

1 chevy to race or scamper.
2 marches boundaries, or perhaps military marches.

[158] Gerard Manley Hopkins

Shivelights and shadowtackle in long / lashes lace, lance,
and pair.
5 Delightfully the bright wind boisterous / ropes, wrestles, beats
earth bare
Of yestertempest's creases; / in pool and rutpeel parches
Squandering ooze to squeezed / dough, crust, dust; stanches,
starches
Squadroned masks and manmarks / treadmire toil there
Footfretted in it. Million-fuelèd, / nature's bonfire burns on.
10 But quench her bonniest, dearest / to her, her clearest-selvèd
spark
Man, how fast his firedint, / his mark on mind, is gone!
Both are in an unfathomable, all is in an enormous dark
Drowned. O pity and indig / nation! Manshape, that shone
Sheer off, disseveral, a star, / death blots black out; nor
mark
15 Is any of him at all so stark
But vastness blurs and time / beats level. Enough! the
Resurrection,
A heart's-clarion! Away grief's gasping, / joyless days,
dejection.
Across my foundering deck shone
A beacon, an eternal beam. / Flesh fade, and mortal trash
20 Fall to the residuary worm; / world's wildfire, leave but ash:
In a flash, at a trumpet crash,
I am all at once what Christ is, / since he was what I am, and
This Jack, joke, poor potsherd, / patch, matchwood, immortal
diamond,
Is immortal diamond.

4 shivelights splinters of light. Cf. Shakespeare *Tit.* 2.1.86–7: 'easy it is | of a
cut loaf to steal a shive.'   **lashes** possibly both whipcords and bindings.
6 rutpeel possibly the dried up surface in muddy ruts that curls like fruit
rind.   **parches** vb. (transitive).
7 stanches stops the flow.
9 Footfretted marked (and worried) by feet.
10 clearest-selvèd most distinct creation. Cf. *Sermons* 122: Human nature is
'more highly pitched, selved, and distinctive than anything in the world'.
11 fast both 'durable' and 'evanescent'?
14 disseveral portmanteau from 'dissever' and 'severalled,' (made into
several).
20 residuary worm implies both 'the worm that will inherit what remains'
and 'the worm that will remain when all else is gone'.
21 In a flash Cf. 'at a crash' no. 141 line 77.
23 Jack base person.   **potsherd** piece of broken pot. See *Job.* 10.9
'remember thou hast made me as the clay; and wilt thou bring me into dust
again?' See also *Isa.* 30.14.   **patch** possibly a piece of cloth or the 'portion

of any surface markedly different from what is around it', but more likely 'fool': from It. *pazzo.* H. may share with Shakespeare a mingling of the senses, as in Shakespeare *M.N.D.* 4.1.215: 'patch'd fool'.

23–4 immortal diamond in the first use of the phrase a deliberate cliché: the diamond is still a product of the corruptible and transitory world, but provides a spark of life before darkness closes in. Even in the first usage there is a sense that the diamond, like the human being, is able to withstand the forces of dissolution. In the second occurrence the metaphorical sense is uppermost: the diamond is the symbol of the eternal world.

159 Tom's Garland: Upon the Unemployed

Date Sept. 1887.

A sonnet with two codas, modelled on Milton's political satire *On the New Forcers of Conscience.* It grows from immediate political circumstances (the Third Reform Bill of 1884, and the march of the Unemployed on 'Bloody Sunday' 1886), as well as the more general concern of H. for the working classes. H. wrote that this poem was conceived at the same time as the following one, *Harry Ploughman,* and that '*Tom's Garland* approached bluster and will remind you of Mr. Podsnap with his back to the fire. They are meant for, and cannot properly be taken in without, emphatic recitation; which nevertheless is not an easy performance' (*Dixon Corresp.* 22 Dec. 1887). Dixon and Bridges found the poem difficult; the following extract from a letter to Bridges of 10 Feb. 1888 is printed complete, since it is one of the longest and most interesting comments by a poet of any period on his own work:

'It is plain I must go no farther on this road: if you and he cannot understand me who will? Yet, declaimed, the strange constructions would be dramatic and effective. Must I interpret it? It means then that, as St. Paul and Plato and Hobbes and everybody says, the commonwealth or well ordered human society is like one man; a body with many members and each its function; some higher, some lower, but all honourable, from the honour which belongs to the whole. The head is the sovereign, who has no superior but God and from heaven receives his or her authority: we must then imagine his head as bare (see St. Paul much on this) and covered, so to say, only with the sun and stars, of which the crown is a symbol, which is an ornament but not a covering; it has an enormous hat or skull cap, the vault of heaven. The foot is the daylabourer, and this is armed with hobnail boots, because it has to wear and be worn by the ground, which again is symbolical; for it is navvies or day-labourers who, on the great scale or in gangs and millions, mainly trench, tunnel, blast, and in other ways disfigure, "mammock" the earth and, on a small scale, singly, and superficially stamp it with their footprints. And the "garlands" of nails they wear are therefore the visible badge of the place they fill, the lowest in the commonwealth. But this place still shares the common honour, and if it wants one advantage, glory or public fame, makes up for it by another, ease of mind, absence of care; and these things are symbolized by the gold and the iron garlands. (O, once explained, how clear it all is!) Therefore the scene of the poem is laid at

[159] Gerard Manley Hopkins

evening, when they are giving over work and one after another pile their
picks, with which they earn their living, and swing off home, knocking
sparks out of mother earth not now by labour and of choice but by the
mere footing, being strongshod and making no hardship of hardness, taking
all easy. And so to supper and bed. Here comes a violent but effective
hyperbaton or suspension, in which the action of the mind mimics that of
the labourer – surveys his lot, low but free from care; then by a sudden
strong act throws it over the shoulder or tosses it away as a light matter.
The witnessing of which lightheartedness makes me indignant with the fools
of Radical Levellers. But presently I remember that this is all very well for
those who are in, however low in, the Commonwealth and share in any way
the Common weal; but that the curse of our times is that many do not
share it, that they are outcasts from it and have neither security nor
splendour; that they share care with the high and obscurity with the low,
but wealth or comfort with neither. And this state of things, I say, is the
origin of Loafers, Tramps, Cornerboys, Roughs, Socialists and other pests of
society. And I think that is a very pregnant sonnet and in point of execution
very highly wrought. Too much so, I am afraid.' (*Bridges Letters* 272–4).
Publication *1918*.

Tom – garlanded with squat and surly steel
Tom; then Tom's fallowbootfellow piles pick
By him and rips out rockfire homeforth – sturdy Dick;
Tom Heart-at-ease, Tom Navvy: he is all for his meal
5   Sure, 's bed now. Low be it: lustily he his low lot (feel
That ne'er need hunger, Tom; Tom seldom sick,
Seldomer heartsore; that treads through prickproof, thick
Thousands of thorns, thoughts) swings though. Commonweal
Little Í reck ho! lacklevel in, if all had bread:
10   What! Country is honour enough in all us – lordly head,
With heaven's lights high hung round, or, mother-ground

1 Tom for centuries the generic name for the common man. John Sutherland
VP 10 (1972) 113–4 suggests Tom Bakewell in Meredith's *The Ordeal of
Richard Feverel* (Ch. 7) as an immediate source: 'There lay Tom; hobnail
Tom! a bacon-munching, reckless, beer-swilling animal! and yet a man; a
dear brave human heart notwithstanding; capable of devotion and unselfishness. [Richard's] better spirit was touched, and it kindled his imagination to realize the abject figure of poor clodpole Tom, and surround it
with a halo of mournful light.' See also the Henry Wallis painting '*Thou
wert our conscript*' 1858 (Birmingham Museum) based on Carlyle *Sartor
Resartus* 3.4. C. refers to the labouring man 'fighting our battles' and H. also
has in mind the quasi-military nature of service (as in no. 157), and the post-
Napoleonic Wars connotation of Tom: Thomas Atkins, hence 'Tommy'
(familiar name for soldier, 1893).
2 fallowbootfellow Tom's fellow-worker after the day's work has ended.
8 Commonweal Sutherland suggests that H. refers both to the common good
and to William Morris's socialist journal *The Commonweal*.

That mammocks, mighty foot. But nó way sped,
Nor mind nor mainstrength; gold go garlanded
With, perilous, O nó; nor yet plod safe shod sound;
15   Undenizened beyond bound
Of earth's glory, earth's ease, all; no one, nowhere,
In wide the world's weal; rare gold, bold steel, bare
    In both; care, but share care –
This, by Despair, bred Hangdog dull; by Rage,
20   Manwolf, worse; and their packs infest the age.

12 mammocks tears. Cf. Shakespeare *Coriol.* 1.3.65 'how he mammocked it!'
H. also had the play in mind in the prose summary: for the body image of
the commonweal see *Coriol.* 1.1.
15 Undenizened not in *OED:* deprived of natural birthright.

160 To R.B.

Date This poem was sent to Bridges in H.'s last letter to him, 29 Apr. 1889.
He writes: 'But we greatly differ in feeling about copying one's verses out: I
find it repulsive, and let them lie months and years in rough copy
untransferred to my book. Still I hope to send you my accumulation. This
one is addressed to you' (*Bridges Letters* 304).
Publication Miles; *1918*, etc.

The fine delight that fathers thought; the strong
    Spur, live and lancing like the blowpipe flame,
    Breathes once and, quenchèd faster than it came,
Leaves yet the mind a mother of immortal song.

5   Nine months she then, nay years, nine years she long
    Within her wears, bears, cares and combs the same:
    The widow of an insight lost she lives, with aim
Now known and hand at work now never wrong.

1 For the notion of sexual activity in artistic creation see no. 152.
2 Spur implying at once the goading of the creative drive (cf. Milton *Lycidas*
line 70: 'Fame is the spur') and the curved shape of the flame.   **lancing** in
both senses: shooting out (*OED* vb. 1.1) and piercing (*OED* vb. 2.1).
5 H. plays with the biological period of generation, in months, and the
Horatian in years: see *Ars Poet.* 388–9: '*nonumque prematur in annum,* |
membranis intus positis' ('then put your parchment in the closet and keep it
back till the ninth year').
6 combs in double sense of unravels, and stores or matures, as in a
honeycomb. In Miles, Bridges substituted 'moulds' for 'combs' and thus
1918–1930.

Sweet fire, the sire of muse, my soul needs this;
10   I want the one rapture of an inspiration.
O then if in my lagging lines you miss

The roll, the rise, the carol, the creation,
My winter world, that scarcely breathes that bliss
Now, yields you, with some sighs, our explanation.

Francis Thompson

Francis Thompson was born in 1859 into a Catholic family. He went to London to follow his father's profession as a doctor, but soon became a down-and-out. The efforts of a prostitute and his first publishers, Wilfred and Alice Meynell, rescued him from total oblivion. His three volumes of poetry were *Poems* (1893), *Sister Songs* (1895) and *New Poems* (1897). Much of T.'s work is in the C19 Parnassian tradition, but in addition, he drew sustenance from C17 religious poetry, especially Crashaw and Cowley. Arthur Symons called T. 'a verbal intelligence', and Lionel Johnson (letter to K. Tynan) wrote: 'He has done more to harm the English language than the worst American newspapers.' T.'s work is one of the last important flourishings of poetic diction as a medium entirely separate from everyday speech. It is a period piece, but of some distinction.
The standard edition is the *Complete Poetical Works* ed. W. Meynell (1913).
Biographies The two most important are by J. C. Reid (1960) and P. van Kuykendall Thompson (1961).

Abbreviations

1893	*Poems* (1893).
Reid	J. C. Reid *Francis Thompson Man and Poet* (1959).

161 The Hound of Heaven

Date Written early in 1890 (Reid 60), when T. was living in Paddington.
The poem is an expression of a traditional idea (found in St Augustine *Confessions*, St John of the Cross, St Ignatius *Spiritual Exercises*, Silvio Pellico *Dio Amore*) of God the pursuer. The principal influence, stylistically and thematically, is Shelley's *Epipsychidion* (first noticed by E. H. W. Meyerstein *TLS* 17 March 1945). T. was writing an essay on Shelley in 1890. Discussion Reid 82–7. M. Turnell *Poetry and Crisis* (1938) 77–8 regards the diction as 'tired, effete, stale'.
Publication *Merry England* (July, 1890); *1893*.

I fled Him, down the nights and down the days;
I fled Him, down the arches of the years;
I fled Him, down the labyrinthine ways

1–3 **I fled Him** I fled from Him.

Of my own mind; and in the mist of tears
5   I hid from Him, and under running laughter.
Up vistaed hopes I sped;
And shot, precipitated,
Adown titanic glooms of chasmèd fears,
From those strong feet that followed, followed after.
10   But with unhurrying chase,
And unperturbèd pace,
Deliberate speed, majestic instancy,
They beat – and a voice beat
More instant than the feet –
15   'All things betray thée, who betrayest Me.'
I pleaded outlaw-wise,
By many a hearted casement, curtained red,
Trellised with intertwining charities;
(For, though I knew His love Who followèd,
20   Yet was I sore adread)
Lest, having Him, I must have naught beside).
But, if one little casement parted wide,
The gust of His approach would clash it to.
Fear wist not to evade, as Love wist to pursue.
25   Across the margent of the world I fled,
And troubled the gold gateways of the stars,
Smiting for shelter on their clangèd bars;
Fretted to dulcet jars
And silvern chatter the pale ports o' the moon.
30   I said to Dawn: Be sudden – to Eve: Be soon;
With thy young skyey blossoms heap me over
From this tremendous Lover –
Float thy vague veil about me, lest He see!
I tempted all His servitors, but to find
35   My own betrayal in their constancy,
In faith to Him their fickleness to me,
Their traitorous trueness, and their loyal deceit.
To all swift things for swiftness did I sue;
Clung to the whistling mane of every wind.
40   But whether they swept, smoothly fleet,
The long savannahs of the blue;

7–8 Cf. Hopkins *No worst, there is none* (no. 155 above) lines 9–10:
'O the mind, mind has mountains; cliffs of fall | Frightful'.
12 instancy insistency.
16–18 'I pleaded to human hearts that were enriched with generosity'.
25 margent margin.
28–9 'Wearing the pale gates of the moon until they made a sweet noise'.

Or whether, Thunder-driven,
They clanged His chariot 'thwart a heaven,
Plashy with flying lightnings round the spurn o' their feet: –
45 Fear wist not to evade as Love wist to pursue.
Still with unhurrying chase,
And unperturbèd pace,
Deliberate speed, majestic instancy,
Came on the following Feet,
50 And a Voice above their beat –
'Naught shelters thee, who wilt not shelter Me.'

I sought no more that after which I strayed
In face of man or maid;
But still within the little children's eyes
55 Seems something, something that replies,
They at least are for me, surely for me!
I turned me to them very wistfully;
But just as their young eyes grew sudden fair
With dawning answers there,
60 Their angel plucked them from me by the hair.
'Come then, ye other children, Nature's – share
With me' (said I) 'your delicate fellowship;
Let me greet you lip to lip,
Let me twine with you caresses,
65 Wantoning
With our Lady-Mother's vagrant tresses,
Banqueting
With her in her wind-walled palace,
Underneath her azured dais,
70 Quaffing, as your taintless way is,
From a chalice
Lucent-weeping out of the dayspring.'
So it was done:
I in their delicate fellowship was one –
75 Drew the bolt of nature's secrecies.
I knew all the swift importings
On the willful face of skies;
I knew how the clouds arise
Spumèd of the wild sea-snortings;
80 All that's born or dies
Rose and drooped with; made them shapers
Of mine own moods, or wailful or divine;

44 **Plashy** dashing or falling like water.
72 **Lucent-weeping** dripping luminous drops.
79 **Spumèd** like the spray cast by the waves.

With them joyed and was bereaven.
I was heavy with the even,
85   When she lit her glimmering tapers
Round the day's dead sanctities.
I laughed in the morning's eyes.
I triumphed and I saddened with all weather,
Heaven and I wept together,
90   And its sweet tears were salt with mortal mine;
Against the red throb of its sunset-heart
I laid my own to beat,
And share commingling heat;
But not by that, by that, was eased my human smart.
95   In vain my tears were wet on Heaven's grey cheek.
For ah! we know not what each other says,
These things and I; in sound *I* speak –
Their sound is but their stir, they speak by silences.
Nature, poor stepdame, cannot slake my drouth;
100   Let her, if she would owe me,
Drop yon blue bosom-veil of sky, and show me
The breasts o' her tenderness:
Never did any milk of hers once bless
My thirsting mouth.
105   Nigh and nigh draws the chase,
With unperturbèd pace,
Deliberate speed, majestic instancy;
And past those noisèd Feet
A Voice comes yet more fleet –
100   'Lo! naught contents thee, who content'st not Me.'

Naked I wait Thy love's uplifted stroke!
My harness piece by piece Thou hast hewn from me,
And smitten me to my knee;
I am defenseless utterly.
115   I slept, methinks, and woke,
And, slowly gazing, find me stripped in sleep.
In the rash lustihead of my young powers,
I shook the pillaring hours
And pulled my life upon me; grimed with smears,
120   I stand amid the dust o' the mounded years –
My mangled youth lies dead beneath the heap.
My days have crackled and gone up in smoke,
Have puffed and burst as sun-starts on a stream.

---

100 owe own.
118 pillaring hours like Samson pulling down the temple: *Judges* 16.23–30.
123 sun-starts bubbles.

Yea, faileth now even dream
125 The dreamer, and the lute the lutanist;
Even the linked fantasies, in whose blossomy twist
I swung the earth a trinket at my wrist,
Are yielding; cords of all too weak account
For earth with heavy griefs so overplussed.
130   Ah! is Thy love indeed
A weed, albeit an amaranthine weed,
Suffering no flowers except its own to mount?
Ah! must –
Designer infinite! –
Ah! must Thou char the wood ere Thou canst limn with it?
135 My freshness spent its wavering shower i' the dust;
And now my heart is as a broken fount,
Wherein tear-drippings stagnate, spilt down ever
From the dank thoughts that shiver
146 Upon the sighful branches of my mind.
Such is; what is to be?
The pulp so bitter, how shall taste the rind?
I dimly guess what Time in mists confounds;
Yet ever and anon a trumpet sounds
145 From the hid battlements of Eternity;
Those shaken mists a space unsettle, then
Round the half-glimpsèd turrets slowly wash again.
But not ere him who summoneth
I first have seen, enwound
150 With glooming robes purpureal, cypress-crowned;
His name I know, and what his trumpet saith.
Whether man's heart or life it be which yields
Thee harvest, must Thy harvest fields
Be dunged with rotten death?
155 Now of that long pursuit
Comes on at hand the bruit;
That Voice is round me like a bursting sea:
'And is thy earth so marred,
Shattered in shard on shard?

131 amaranthine immortal; a Miltonism, first used *Paradise Lost* 9.78.
135 limn draw (with charcoal in this case).
139–40 Cf. Keats *Ode to Psyche* lines 51–2: 'In some untrodden region of my mind, | Where branched thoughts, new grown with pleasant pain'.
150 cypress symbolising death.
152–4 Cf. Robert Southwell *St. Peter's Complaint* lines 109–12: 'Is this the harvest of his sowing toil? | Did Christ manure thy heart to breed him briars? | Or doth it need this unaccustomed soil, | With hellish dung to fertile heaven's desires?'
156 bruit noise.

160   Lo, all things fly thee, for thou fliest Me!
       Strange, piteous, futile thing!
   Wherefore should any set thee love apart?
     Seeing none but I makes much of naught'
        (He said),
   'And human love needs human meriting.
165   How hast thou merited –
   Of all man's clotted clay the dingiest clot?
     · Alack, thou knowest not
   How little worthy of any love thou art!
   Whom wilt thou find to love ignoble thee,
170   Save Me. save only Me?
   All which I took from thee I did but take,
       Not for thy harms,
   But just that thou might'st seek it in My arms.
      All which thy child's mistake
175   Fancies as lost, I have stored for thee at home:
     Rise, clasp My hand, and come!'

     Halts by me that footfall:
      Is my gloom, after all,
   Shade of His hand, outstretched caressingly?
180   'Ah, fondest, blindest, weakest,
     I am He Whom thou seekest!
   Thou dravest love from thee, who dravest Me.'

176 The rhythmical simplicity of this six-syllabled line following very varied lines, and representing the security of God, is reminiscent, both in character and placing, of the final line of Herbert's *The Collar:* 'And I replied, "My Lord".'
180–1 Cf. Shelley *Epipsychidion* lines 232–3: 'When a voice said: – "O thou of hearts the weakest, | The phantom is beside thee whom thou seekest."'

Index of Titles and First Lines

Index of Titles and First Lines

Index of Titles and First Lines

Index of Titles and First Lines

538

Index of Titles and First Lines

Index of Titles and First Lines

Index of Titles and First Lines

Index of Titles and First Lines

Index of Titles and First Lines